MICHAEL SPERANSKY
STATESMAN OF IMPERIAL RUSSIA
1772-1839

М. Сперанскій.

# MICHAEL SPERANSKY
## STATESMAN OF IMPERIAL RUSSIA
### 1772–1839

*by*

MARC RAEFF

MARTINUS NIJHOFF — THE HAGUE
1957

PRINTED IN THE NETHERLANDS

# INTRODUCTION

"An autocracy tempered by assassination", clever foreigners used to say about the Russian empire in the 18th and 19th centuries. With this *bon mot* the average curiosity about the Tsars' government was satisfied and there seemed to be no need to look further into the matter. There was, on the surface of things, some justification for such a definition: many rulers had suffered violent death and little did the autocracy abate between 1725 and 1905. The impression created by travelers, by historians and journalists, as well as by Russia's own discontented intelligentsia was that nothing really ever changed in Russia, that the autocracy was the same in 1905 as it had been at the death of Peter the Great in 1725. Not that the outside world had remained ignorant of the efforts at reform, the changes, and the modernization wrought in Russia since the day Peter I had "cut a window into Europe." But the prevailing opinion was that such changes as occurred were merely external and did not affect the fundamental structure of the government or of society.

Yet, inspite of its apparent immobility, Russia did change: literature and social thought developed and burst forth in an extraordinary flowering by the middle of the 19th century; society underwent a radical transformation following the emancipation of the serfs in 1861; economic developments in the late 19th century put Russia on the way of becoming an important industrial power; new administrative and judiciary institutions were gradually transforming the pattern of local life. Did none of these transformations bring some changes to the structure of the imperial government itself? And, in the absence of an overt revolution, were these changes themselves not the result of the actions of an allegedly static and inflexible autocracy? An answer to these questions is not readily available because, absorbed by the dramatic story of revolutionary and intellectual movements, historians have failed to study closely the institutional and political developments which took place in the administration in the course of the 18th and 19th centuries.

Peter the Great had provided the Russian administration with a modern, European framework. But it took almost a century for this skeleton to grow a body and to become conscious of its functions and problems. At the death of Catherine II in 1796 the task set by Peter I had been accomplished. But in the meantime Russia had become a great European power, a multinational empire extending from Scandinavia to Central Asia, its economy had developed, its upper classes had become Westernized and had received something of a corporate organization. New problems had to be faced now, and for this many parts in the administrative machinery had to be changed and the principles and methods of government had to be redefined. This the generation of the first quarter of the 19th century set out to do.

Coming after the capricious tyranny of Paul I, under the influence of the ideas of both the enlightenment and romanticism, the reign of Alexander I (1801—1825) was a critical period during which the principles and practice of the imperial government were subjected to examination, evaluation, and discussion. As a result of the critique, new ideas and approaches were advanced and plans of reform suggested. Emperor Alexander I himself seemed to lead the way as he searched for new principles on which to found his absolute rule, and to this end he sought out young, energetic, and talented advisors and assistants. Among these, the most outstanding proved to be the son of a village priest, Michael M. Speransky. Rising to positions of great trust and influence, Speransky left a profound mark on the attitudes and practices of the imperial administration and helped to create the framework within which the social, economic, and administrative changes of the 1860s were to take place.

The present volume aims at giving as comprehensive an account as possible of the administrative and political activities, ideas, and plans of Speransky and also hopes to interpret and assess their significance for the political evolution of Imperial Russia. As there is but scant knowledge of the workings of the Russian imperial administration, the account of Speransky's career and work will be accompanied by a description of the institutional and social setting. At one time or another Speransky was involved in almost every aspect of Russian administration and to each he brought fresh ideas, rational organization, and new goals. The legacy he left was great and important, less perhaps in terms of practical accomplishments as in terms of mental attitudes and methods. He helped to identify and analyse the most essential social, economic, and political problems that beset Russia and in so doing he prepared the way for their solution by "bureaucratic" means, within the framework of the autocracy. In this sense, he is one of the major figures in the domestic history of 19th century Russia.

In view of the significance of his ideas and career, it is surprising that Speransky has been a relatively neglected (and therefore often misunderstood) figure in Russian historiography. True enough, his name is always mentioned in the histories of the period, even the most general ones. But he is described only as the author of an allegedly liberal constitutional plan and as the codifier of Russian law. While the latter achievement is treated as the special concern of legal scholars, the former is pronounced an unfortunate failure, illustrating once more the basic inability of the autocracy to reform itself. But the bulk of Speransky's work and thought remains unknown to the general historian. By undertaking a full scale biography, the present writer hopes to give a fuller and more balanced picture, both of Speransky and of the imperial administration.

The history of Speransky's bibliography well reflects the evolution of the political climate in Russia. Soon after Speransky's death in 1839 there appeared several articles which contained valuable information. But being in the nature of eulogies or of reminiscences by his colleagues, they have to be approached very critically and cannot be considered historical studies in the true sense. The only attempt at a comprehensive biography appeared in two volumes in 1861. Though written by an official of unblemished loyalty, Baron Modest A. Korf, it is quite incomplete, as the author was not allowed to discuss Speransky's plans of reform and describe fully his fall from favor and exile in 1812. The main value of Baron Korf's compilation lies in the information it gives about Speransky's family life (Korf was in a position to interview surviving friends and associates) and the details of his official assignments and honors.

Reflecting perhaps the disillusionment of Russian society with the "Great Reforms" of the 1860s, there was little interest in Speransky in the 1870s and 1880s. The re-awakening of interest in the 1890s and 1900s brought forth a number of valuable studies (numerous articles and a few books) dealing with various phases of Speransky's career. But however informative and insightful, these studies were very limited in scope and none ever attempted a full assessment of Speransky's ideas and work. More important than these articles for an understanding of his career were the publications of numerous sources from the first half of the 19th century, particularly the papers of the leading administrative institutions (Council of State, Committee of Ministers, the Senate, etc.). At the same time a large body of memoir and epistolary material from the reigns of Alexander I and Nicholas I was accumulated, helping the historian to a good understanding of Speransky's time and associates. The only thing lacking for the raw materials of a Speransky biography to be complete was the publication of all his remaining public and private papers; (most of his projects had already been published). The first step towards such a publication was taken (a catalogue of the papers seized at his house in 1812 appeared in 1916), but the first World War and the Revolution put an end to the project. Except for a few short biographical essays, no life of Speransky had been written by 1917, although most of the raw material had been made available. The Soviets have evinced little interest in the subject, satisfied with repeating trite generalities about Speransky's lukewarm liberalism. Abroad also scholars have left the topic unexplored, merely restating the opinions found in older general histories. (The important articles by A. Fateev, published in Prague in the 1920s and 1930s, are based on material collected before the revolution; they are also quite fragmentary, serving as *Vorarbeiten* to a full biography which was not completed).

It seemed, therefore, desirable to fill the gap somewhat by a summary of all the evidence published until now and an evaluation of Speransky's career and accomplishments. Fortunately such an assessment is possible on the basis of material contained in the government records published in the last decades before the Revolution. Perhaps it will also contribute to a better understanding of the problems, traditions, and methods of the imperial government.

# ACKNOWLEDGMENTS

It is an author's pleasant obligation to acknowledge the help and advice received in the course of a research which occupied the better part of five years. In a sense, it is impossible to do so fully, as much is owed to passing remarks and casual conversations with friends, colleagues, and students. But I do wish to thank my teachers and colleagues who read the manuscript and gave me the benefit of their knowledge and judgment. Professors Michael Karpovich and Dwight E. Lee read the entire *opus* and their criticisms and suggestions helped greatly in eliminating obscurities and improving the exposition. My colleagues, Professors Morris H. Cohen, Sherman S. Hayden, H. Donaldson Jordan, and James A. Maxwell read some of the chapters and made valuable comments within their special areas of knowledge. They are, of course, in no way responsible for whatever defects and inaccuracies that remain. I am most grateful to Mr. James M. Miller for his able assistance in compiling the index under a grant from the Bland Fund of the History Department of Clark University. My sincere appreciation goes to the numerous staff members of Widener Library, the New York Public Library, the Library of Congress, the Hoover Library, and the National Archives who helped me in locating obscure and bulky publications. What I owe to my wife for her encouragement, prodding, advice, and patient help is not to be expressed here.

The publication of the book was made possible thanks to the generosity of the Humanities Fund Inc., the Joint Committee on Slavic Studies of the Social Science Research Council, and the Committee for the Promotion of Advanced Slavic Cultural Studies Inc.

I am grateful to the Board of Editors of the *American Slavic and East European Review* and of the *Slavonic and East European Review* for permission to make use of materials that first appeared in article form on the pages of the reviews.

February 1957

Clark University
Worchester, Massachusetts

All dates referring to events in Russia are given according to the Julian calendar (in force in Russia until 1918), which lags behind the Gregorian by twelve days in the 19th century and by eleven in the 18th.

Russian words, names, and titles have been transliterated on the basis of current spelling and according to the system in use at the Widener Library of Harvard University, with a few minor diacritical simplifications. Names commonly found in English publications have been spelled in the manner that tradition has imposed, unless they are part of a Russian title.

The following abbreviations occur commonly in the notes and bibliographies:

*Chteniia*        *Chteniia v Moskovskom obshchestve istorii i drevnostei rossiiskikh pri moskovskom universitete* (Moscow 1846—1918)

PSZ        *Polnoe Sobranie Zakonov Rossiiskoi Imperii,* 1st series (St. Petersburg 1830).

*Sbornik IRIO* *Sbornik Imperatorskogo russkogo istoricheskogo obshchestva* (St. Petersburg 1867—1916).

St. Pbg.      Saint-Petersburg.

# CONTENTS

# CHAPTER I

# THE BEGINNINGS

As so often happens with illustrious men who have risen from the lower classes, we know but little of the early years of the life of Michael Speransky. Even his contemporaries were unable to gather much information: the family records and papers perished in a fire in 1834, and Speransky himself was not very communicative. Whatever information we possess has been collected by Speransky's first biographer, the industrious baron Modest A. Korf. To fill the gap in the written documentation, Korf endeavored to interview, personally or by means of written questionnaires, all those who had had any contacts with Speransky. But memories about a remote period — Korf was inquiring about events that had taken place fifty years earlier — are likely to be quite dim and strongly influenced by the knowledge of subsequent happenings. Unfortunately too, Baron Korf was not always sufficiently critical of his sources, and we must be careful in using the evidence he has assembled. We must, perforce, be content with a few details and a bare outline of Speransky's formative years.

Michael Speransky was born on January 1, 1772, the son of the priest of Cherkutino village, the family estate of the Saltykovs, in the province of Vladimir.[1] At first the future State Secretary was known only as Michael, the son of Michael the priest of Cherkutino. Family names had been introduced legally shortly before Speransky's birth, but many peasants had not received any yet; and in this respect — as in so many others — the village priests were not much different from their flocks. Apparently, Speransky received his last name only upon entering the theological seminary of Vladimir, and following a tradition current among the clergy, the name was derived from the Latin. In Speransky's case, the choice proved to be both appropriate and prophetic.

[1] For a long time the date of his birth was in doubt, and only the patient investigations of Baron Korf have definitely established it. Records were not kept too carefully in those times, even by the clergy, and Speransky himself was not too sure whether he had been born in 1771 or 1772.

The boy's childhood passed quite uneventfully. The records that have been preserved, indicate that he was a healthy, normal and happy child. He spent his days playing with the peasant children of his native village, and together with them he received the first rudiments of education from his father. Tradition has it that Speransky showed a strong interest in books and learning at a very early age, withdrawing from the company of his playmates in order to read. Was this really so, or was it only one of those common pious fancies which transform future great men into precocious bookworms and *Einzelgänger?* — we do not know, although the latter explanation seems more likely. The only noteworthy event in Speransky's childhood was the visit to Cherkutino of the famous court chaplain A. A. Samborskii, who was a guest at the nearby estate of Count Saltykov. Samborskii noticed the bright, lively, and likeable boy and suggested that young Michael keep in touch with him when he was ready to start on his advanced education. Speransky remembered the offer and made good use of it when he went to St. Petersburg.

If little can be related about Speransky's boyhood, not much more can be said about his family. The father, a rather colorless and ineffectual man, died when Speransky was still a boy. The family was kept together and run by the mother, who was an exceptionally intelligent and energetic woman. Her physical and moral strength provided a psychological anchor for the entire family. She commanded everybody's devotion and obedience, and the love her children had for her was always mixed with the awe and respect usually shown the father. Speransky, in later years, regularly corresponded with his mother until the end of her long life (she died in 1824 when her son was Privy Councillor and a member of the Council of State). Characteristically, in his letters Speransky never allowed himself any familiarity or unrestrained show of feeling; and while he made allowance for his mother's lack of education and limited horizon, he addressed her only in the polite form ("vy") and never failed to ask humbly and respectfully for her blessings and prayers.

The most striking and unusual person in the family was Speransky's grandmother. In later years Speransky often recalled the awe and fear he experienced when, waking up in the middle of the night, he saw his grandmother's tall, gaunt and grey figure prostrated in fervent prayer before the icons, heaving mournful sighs as she bowed her head to the ground; thus she would spend the whole night. The waking hours too she spent in constant prayer. Every year, in spite of her advanced age, she undertook long and difficult pilgrimages to distant shrines. She led a rigorously ascetic life, ate only a little of the simplest and coarsest food, kept all fasts most strictly, wore a hair-shirt and was scantily clad and shod even in mid-winter. She had mystical experiences and visions, and the villagers thought of her as a semi-saint, a godly person (*bozhii chelovek*). Watching his grandmother, the boy could directly observe the mystical and emotional manifestations of religion, even before his initiation into the formalism of theology and ritual. And many years later the memory of his grandmother's mysticism guided Speransky towards a fuller and more satisfying religious experience.

At about the age of twelve, young Speransky left his native village to attend the seminary at Vladimir, the provincial capital. This separation, which was to be for life, did not, however, break his ties with the family and village. Even at the top of the official world of St. Petersburg, as an intimate adviser of the Emperor, Speransky neither forgot nor denied his lowly origins and relatives. He was always willing to contribute towards the improvement of the economic and social position of those members of his family who had stayed in the village. He provided for the education of his younger brother, Cosmas (Koz'ma) and of his nephew, placing them in the schools of the capital and paying for their tuition. [1] And on the rare visits to his home village he was unaffectedly friendly towards his former playmates and neighbors.

Today, when we take the easy and relatively pleasant acquisition of knowledge as a matter of course, we find it difficult to understand the problems which accompanied the process of education in the past. We often do not realize that the character both of the student body and the faculty, as well as available facilities, played a decisive role in shaping not only the form, but also the contents of the instruction. Inadequate buildings, lack of books and texts, a heterogeneous student body certainly were some of the factors which gave learning its "scholastic" form in the Middle Ages. The survival of "scholastic" teaching methods in 18th century Russia was, to a large measure, due to the physical and social environment in which the process of education took place.

---

[1] See Letter of Prince A. Kurakin to Prince F. N. Golitsyn (August 1798), *Russkii Arkhiv*, 1863, p. 810 in which the former requests Golitsyn to assist in the admission of Koz'ma Speransky (brother of Michael) to the University of Moscow. In a letter to his brother-in-law, M. F. Tretiakov, dated 13 June 1827, Speransky wrote that although a university education was expensive, he was willing to pay for it in the case of his nephew(?) Petrusha, after the latter had graduated from the seminary, *V Pamiat' grafa M. M. Speranskogo* (ed. by A. F. Bychkov), St. Pbg. 1872, p. 443 — this important collection of Speransky's papers and correspondence will be referred to hereafter as *Pamiati*.

In the second half of the 18th century the Russian clergy and nobility had not yet learned to like education for its own sake. In part, this was the result of the imposition of school attendance from above, as Peter the Great had made schooling obligatory for a reluctant nobility. Numerous contemporary reports describe the opposition and hatred this new form of service provoked. The ridiculous and comical incidents which often accompanied the implementation of Peter's rules cannot hide the personal tragedies that lay behind them. The young nobleman left for the "cypher schools" accompanied by the wail and tears of his parents and domestics. No wonder that the students hated and feared the school even before coming to it, and attempts at escape were numerous. The prospective student would take flight on the way to school, hide from the police with the connivance and help of his relatives. Peter the Great and his successors issued decree after decree ordering the "truants" back to school, and even used regular troops to go after the unwilling pupils in their own homes or bring back to school those that had taken flight. Not until the second half of the 18th century — and mollified by a relaxation of this school "service" — did the average nobleman realize the usefulness and pleasure of study and acquire a genuine thirst for knowledge.

Peter the Great's heavy hand had bent the clergy under a similar yoke. The clergy became a hereditary corporation, with the sons compelled to follow in the footsteps of their fathers — or else become ordinary peasants, a glum prospect indeed in those times. Like the nobleman's son, the prospective young clergyman, whether he felt the "call" or not, had to leave his home and go to the provincial seminary for training in the rudiments of his future profession. Little wonder that the priest's education was debased and made difficult and unpleasant from the very start. In addition, the system took no account of the individual capacities and interests of the students. The prescribed course had to be completed by the students, regardless of the time it might take them to do so. The less gifted and the lazy were left to repeat the forms year after year; in the same class were to be found ages ranging from 12 to about 20 years. Naturally, under these circumstances, the young and the weak were tyrannized, demoralized and corrupted by the older and more pernicious students in the school.

Most important of all, perhaps, the school system of the Russian clergy suffered from poverty. This poverty was twofold: the schools had a miserable budget, and the pupils themselves had no resources either. This was the result of the inferior status of the clergy in 18th century Russia and the neglect the Church was suffering at the hands of the government. Peter the Great's religious policy had made of the Church a handmaid of the state, the state department for religious affairs. [1] Peter wished to see the clergy's educational facilities used for the benefit of the state, hence his endeavors to attract the more able seminary students into government service, leaving the mediocre to care for the souls. Although the Reformer's successors were not as energetic and consistent in pursuing this policy, they were not overly enthusiastic about promoting the Church either, as they shared the anti-clerical scepticism of the Enlightenment. Finally, Catherine II deprived the Church of its last independent economic support by secularizing its land holdings. Under these conditions, the Church had great difficulty in maintaining adequate educational facilities for its future members.

The secularization of ecclesiastical property forced the state to take over the financial burden of the Church's activities, including the schools. The government set the budget for the Church schools every year. But that budget was ridiculously small, even allowing for the greater purchase value of money at the time. For instance, between 1764 and 1796 the total budget for *all* episcopal seminaries and other religious schools in Russia varied between 38,000 and 70,000 rubles a year. In 1797, thanks to the generosity of Paul I, the budget was fixed at 180,000 rubles. What this meant in terms of the resources of an individual school appears from the 1797 budget of the seminary of Vladimir, Speransky's school: with a student body of 1,200 students, the seminary received 8,000 rubles for all its expenses. [2] Little wonder that the physical facilities of the schools were deplorable, that the teachers received such low wages that the better ones preferred to go into private tutoring or government service. Descriptions of the provincial seminaries in the 18th century, and even down into the 19th if we are to judge by N. G. Pomialovskii's *Sketches of the Bursa,* read like the accounts of the Englisch poorhouses in Charles Dickens' times. The buildings, dirty and in disrepair, remained practically unheated throughout the long and harsh Russian winter months, and the poor students huddled around embering stoves, wrapped in all their miserable clothes, in a vain attempt at keeping one another warm. The food was

[1] On the other hand — and probably as a reaction to the subordinate role of the official Church — the second half of the 18th century witnessed a remarkable revival of religious life and thought, both monastic and secular. See: G. Florovski, *Puti russkogo bogosloviia;* V. V. Zen'kovskii, *Istoriia russkoi filosofii,* vol. I, (Parizh 1948), part I, ch. 2; G. P. Fedotov (ed.), *A Treasury of Russian Spirituality,* N. Y., 1948, chapters on St. Tychon and St. Seraphim (pp. 182—279).

[2] Titlinov, *Dukhovnye shkoly v XIX st.,* p. 14—15.

not only poor in quality, but also not sufficient in quantity; a gnawing state of "half-hunger" was the ever-present companion of the young seminarians (and even their teachers). Returning from the summer vacations spent in their home villages, many pupils brought with them some provisions (flour, potatoes), and the luckier ones might receive a few food parcels during the winter. But even this outside help was not enough, and the students tried to earn some money to buy food, for only in the rarest cases did they bring a few rubles from home. The older and abler students were at times engaged as tutors to the children of some local merchant or official. This type of employment was highly desirable not so much for the salary as for the opportunity it offered to spend a few hours in a warm house and to receive some crumbs from the table of the employer. Students who had less social grace and intellectual ability might become assistants to some ecclesiastic functionary. Those unsuitable for either position were reduced to petty stealing and begging to supplement the inadequate diet of the school refectory.

Even among these poverty-ridden students there were differences in status. Worst off were the children of very poor village priests who lived exclusively on what the government provided. They were always hungry and, in winter, cold. To survive they allowed themselves to be exploited by more prosperous fellow-pupils and became the most demoralized and demoralizing group of the school population. A higher social and economic status was enjoyed by those who received some assistance from home. They banded together to rent some cheap quarters on the outskirts of the town and shared the provisions they received from home. But they had to live far from school and spend much time and effort in scraping together the bare necessities of life. They had little to spare for the acquisition of knowledge. Finally, the "aristocracy" among the student body consisted of the few fortunate enough to have friends or relatives in the town itself where they could stay and where they could count on a full meal regularly.

Under the circumstances, we should not be surprised that the purely academic accomplishments at the school left much to be desired. The teachers were so poorly paid that they cared little for their duties. They tried to exploit the pupils for their own selfish ends — sending them out to do errands, using their labor — instead of imparting to them whatever knowledge they might possess. Drunkenness was the most common vice, and Speransky often had to replace one of his teachers who was almost constantly drunk. Not that the instructors had nothing to teach the students; quite a few were well read and educated for their times — but grinding poverty and social humiliation had demoralized them, had sapped their energy and ability at overcoming the laziness and apathy of their students. Serious learning and effective teaching were handicapped by the very heterogeneous composition of the student body. Half-wits and intelligent boys, old and young, the industrious and the lazy — all were thrown together into one class, in one room. Under these conditions, only a very few ideas and facts could at best penetrate into the reluctant minds of the students. To attain even a limited result, the only method known then was to rely exclusively on formal learning and memory. The essential aim of this pedagogy was to develop the ability to repeat accurately what was in the textbooks, to solve model problems by a mechanical application of a few formal rules. Unfortunately, too, the major fields of study — theology, philosophy, some smattering of mathematics, religious history, and apologetics — easily lent themselves to such a "scholastic" approach. The harshest discipline was imposed in an effort at securing a minimum of the students' attention and at producing some results. Fear of punishment was the only principle of control and incentive: motionless kneeling in the corner for long hours, deprivation of what little food and heat there was, cruel beatings. Such were the usual means by which a demoralized and ineffectual faculty endeavored to keep the seminarians in line and force something into their heads.

Only the hardiest, the ablest, and luckiest could survive the system and extract any benefits from it; it is not surprising, therefore, that many of the best "heads" in Russia at the end of the 18th century had come through the tough mill of the seminaries. Alone, these rare individuals succeeded in absorbing the positive features of the "scholastic" methods: the principles of clear factual exposition, of exact logical analysis, and of convincing argumentation. The successful seminary graduate also learned early, and to perfection, how to make the best of a most unfavorable environment; he learned how to be ingratiatingly obedient towards his superiors and to perform the assigned tasks to the satisfaction of an individual's idiosyncrasy; he learned how to make use of his less gifted fellow students; he knew how to recognize and assess the informal "power structures" and to operate carefully within their framework. In short, the theological seminaries inculcated habits of submissive obedience, a skillful use of tact and diplomacy, and a mastery of the formal techniques of intellectual work.

It was to such a school in Vladimir that the young Michael Speransky was sent when he was about twelve years old. Immediately he was singled out as an outstanding and one of the most hopeful students. From the very beginning he eagerly looked forward to the knowledge he would acquire at school, the advantages this knowledge would give him in his future life. In the second place, he did not belong to the most destitute and unhappy among seminarians; on the contrary, he could consider his material circumstances as most favorable. Indeed, Speransky's aunt, married to a priest in the city, lived in Vladimir, and she took care of him as if he were her own son. Unlike most of his friends, Speransky had a "home" to go to, somebody to look after his clothes, his health, and other wants. During the first years, this aunt helped the boy materially and provided a much needed moral and psychological support for the lonely youngster. Speransky retained an ever-grateful attachment to his aunt, an attachment even stronger than that to his own family at Cherkutino. With his physical wants taken good care of (during his last years at the seminary he actually lived at his aunt's house), psychologically strengthened by the cheer and warmth of a friendly family, Speransky easily coped with the crudity, harshness, and bitter struggle for physical and moral survival at the seminary. We might add that living in his aunt's house, he was shielded from the temptations of corrupting influences at school, such as drinking, gambling, and other vices (he himself confessed that he had acquired only the rather innocuous habit of snuffing tobacco). He adjusted himself well to the environment and was not unpopular with his fellow students. Naturally he was highly esteemed by his teachers and superiors who considered him the most promising student of the school. Freed from the worst difficulties and pains of school life, Speransky devoted all his time and energy to learning, and in this he succeeded remarkably well. [1]

To satisfy the crying need for better trained and educated hierarchs and priests, the government, in 1788, established, at first on an experimental basis, a central theological seminary for advanced training in the capital (on the model of the one at Kiev). Set up at the Alexandro-Nevskii Monastery on the outskirts of St. Petersburg, the seminary (promoted to the rank of a Theological Academy in 1797) was opened in 1790. Enjoying the favor and personal attention of the Metropolitan of the capital, the seminary's students could expect to receive desirable appointments and rapid promotion after their

---

[1] Speransky's early interest in the pursuit of knowledge for its own sake rather than for an ecclesiastical career appears clearly from a letter to A. Samborskii, dated 16 June 1788 from Vladimir, in *Russkii Arkhiv*, 1871, p. 1944. In the letter Speransky asks for Samborskii's help to go to the University of Moscow to study mathematics and French.

graduation. It is also to be noted that in spite of some shortcomings, the Alexandro-Nevskii Seminary was by far the best ecclesiastic school in Russia where students received a thorough and wellrounded education, and lived in quite tolerable circumstances. The student body of this selective superior school was drawn from all Russia, each diocesan seminary sending its two most promising graduates. When the administration of the seminary of Vladimir had to make their selection of candidates, their choice fell naturally on Speransky. In 1790, as member of its first class, Speransky entered the Alexandro-Nevskii Seminary in St. Petersburg.

Speransky distinguished himself rapidly among the highly select students of the Alexandro-Nevskii Seminary as he had earlier among the ordinary pupils of Vladimir. The practice sermons he preached in the presence of the Metropolitan himself, created a deep impression. Most of them were on strictly theological subjects, but we find also the first statement of his views on political problems in a sermon he delivered in 1794. This sermon will engage our attention later in connection with our analysis of the development of Speransky's political philosophy. His academic successes made him a beloved figure at the school, respected by masters and students alike. One of his classmates, the future littérateur and classical scholar, I. Martynov, noted later the pleasure and happiness he experienced after he had delivered his practice sermon and Speransky came up to congratulate him, for, "the praise of a respected fellow student is more valuable than that of a teacher one does not esteem".[1]

This same Martynov reports another incident which throws light on an interesting aspect of Speransky's personality. One day Martynov and Speransky, who were staying on at the Seminary as junior members of the staff, were saying farewell to some common friends who were returning to their home province after graduation. Using the opportunity offered by farewell confidences, Speransky told the friends who were leaving that he was very pained by Martynov's apparent dislike for him. This was particularly surprising and painful to him, Speransky explained, as he himself had the most friendly feelings and highest esteem for Martynov and would wish to see them returned. The recipients of this confidence repeated it right away to Martynov, as Speransky hoped they would. It was Martynov's turn to express surprise, for his regard for Speransky was such that he had hesitated to take the initiative, afraid of appearing too familiar in view of Speransky's apparent aloofness vis-à-vis most fellow students. As a result

[1] Martynov, "Zapiski," *Pamiatniki Novoi Russkoi Istorii,* II, 1872, p. 80.

of this exchange of confidences through third persons, a lasting friendship was established between Speransky and Martynov, a friendship which continued after both had abandoned a career in the clergy to take up government service. [1] This anecdote provides us with our first direct information on two basic traits in Speransky's psychological make-up. On the one hand, he showed a cold and disdainful aloofness, stressed his intellectual superiority, while, on the other hand, he craved for friendship, esteem, and wished to receive constant proof that he was loved and respected. Modern psychologists would characterize it as manifestations of a basic feeling of inadequacy and insecurity, a feeling that may perhaps be understood in terms of his own humble origin and the depressing atmosphere of his early training. Because of this feeling, Speransky avoided all relationships in which his inferiority — be it social, intellectual, or political — would come to light.

Speransky's academic successes at the Alexandro-Nevskii Seminary led to his rapid promotion and his superiors' decision to keep him at the school as a member of the teaching staff. On May 29, 1792, he was appointed teacher of mathematics, a field for which he had shown great aptitude and interest. In August of the same year, two courses, one in physics and another in rhetoric, were entrusted to him. The teaching and practice of rhetoric resulted in Speransky's writing a treatise on the subject, "Rules of the art of beautiful speech", in which he showed his own mastery of the Russian language. At the very same time, when Karamzin was helping to create a modern, clear, concise Russian prose, an obscure student and teacher at a theological school was writing in an equally elegant and modern style, quite unaware of the efforts of the future Historiographer. On April 8, 1795, Speransky was promoted to instructor of philosophy and "prefect", that is supervisor of the student body (a kind of "dean of men"). A brilliant academic career in the Seminary, should he wish to embrace it, was open to his talents. [2]

---

1 Martynov, "Zapiski," p. 86.
2 The following is a fellow student's description of Speransky's academic achievements at the Alexandro-Nevskii Seminary. We must make allowance for the excessive sentimentality as well as for the distorting effect of time, as these reminiscences go back 40 years; but the basic impression Speransky made on his fellow students is probably reported accurately: "Speransky surpassed all his comrades by his successes in pure mathematics, physics, and philosophy. He distinguished himself by the piety of his thoughts, words, and feeling. His heart even then, one may say, was fragrant with fresh, clean air. In 1792, as a student, Speransky delivered a sermon on the Last Judgment ... with such enthusiasm, that the signs of conviction visibly spread on the faces of his listeners ... Metropolitan Gabriel, who was present in the Church, asked the Rector to convince the young preacher to take monastic vows; and in this expectation, upon the completion of Speransky's

Speransky had made good use of the years he had spent at the Alexandro-Nevskii Seminary. He acquired a great deal of knowledge and, what was more important, widened his intellectual horizon immensely, so that he could easily take his place among the best educated men in Russia at the time. In addition to the traditional seminary subjects of metaphysics, theology, apologetics, religious literature, and history, Speransky became quite familiar with the secular writings of the period. He learned French (to write and speak as well as to read), and this opened up to him the works of the *philosophes.* Unfortunately no detailed record of his readings has been preserved, but his own writings of later years show that he had absorbed the major authors of the Enlightenment quite thoroughly. It may be noted in passing that this acquaintance with the writings of the *philosophes* was not obtained in secret or illicitly; the teachers themselves expounded the ideas of the "radical" authors of the age. One of the instructors, when not drunk, was always lecturing on Voltaire, Diderot, and others. Contemporaries and historians have noted that the intellectual atmosphere of the Seminary was saturated with the rationalism and "materialism" of 18th century thought. [1] Speransky's own interests, and the necessity of preparing lectures on philosophy, made him undertake a systematic study of the major philosophic systems. Not content with the textbook exposition of Baumeister and Winckler, he read and studied the works of Descartes, Locke, Leibniz, Kant, and Condillac. [2] Needless to add that, like most of his educated contemporaries, Speransky was very much at home among the classics, which he used as models and illustrations in his own treatise on rhetoric, and to which he turned for relaxation and inspiration.

Speransky shared his century's interest in the natural sciences, and as he also had to teach scientific subjects, he became more thoroughly

studies, he entrusted him (Speransky) with the teaching of rhetoric and physics." Letter of P. A. Slovtsov to I. Kalashnikov, dated 6 February 1840, quoted in Kalashnikov, "Zapiski irkutskogo zhitelia" *Russkaia Starina*, vol. 123, Aug. 1905, p. 399.

[1] A. Fateev, "M. M. Speranskii — vliianie sredy na sostavitelia Svoda Zakonov v 1-i period ego zhizni," *Iuridicheskii Vestnik*, X (1915), No. 11 p. 140.

[2] Speransky's classmate, Slovtsov reminisced many years later: "In 1794, I recall, I found Speransky reading Newton, in 1795 he was appointed instructor of philosophy and in addition to his teaching obligations, he engaged for two years in a critical study of philosophical systems, beginning with Descartes, Locke, Leibniz, etc. down to Condillac, very renowned at the time. Occasionally Mikhail Mikhailovich would read to me his critical observations." Quoted in Kalashnikov, "Zapiski irkutskogo zhitelia," *loc. cit.*, p. 399. For further details on Speransky's scientific interests and readings, see my article, "The Philosophical Views of Count M. M. Speransky," *Slavonic and East European Review*, XXXI, No. 77 (June 1953), pp. 439—440.

acquainted with this important area of learning than even the best
educated layman of his time. [1] The contents of the course on physics
which he gave at the Seminary, is known to us, thanks to the very
complete notes taken by one of his students and probably edited by
Speransky himself. The notes show that Speransky was familiar not
only with the classical founders of modern science, Newton, Leibniz,
Euler, etc., but that he also tried to keep informed of the latest
developments, for he made reference to the new discoveries of Franklin,
Priestley, and Lavoisier. [2] We shall have occasion to return to a more
detailed examination of the role played by science in the genesis of
his philosophical views.

Speransky not only acquired the factual and intellectual contents of
the literature, philosophy, and science of his age, but he also made
his own the form in which the Enlightenment clothed its learning and
thought. One of the characteristic traits of 18th century philosophy
and science was the presentation of even complex and abstruse ideas
in such a clear, simple and elegant form that they could be easily
understood by all the educated. No idea, no theory achieved recognition
unless it could be discussed in the salons. Fontenelle had shown how
this could be done without loss of scientific accuracy and philosophic
precision; though at the price of a shallowing out of the metaphysical
and epistemological implications. Voltaire had elevated this form of
presentation into a literary art. Well served by his natural stylistic
talent, Speransky mastered the canons of 18th century technical and
"philosophic" writing to perfection. Learning from the example set
by the French and English writers on philosophy, politics, and science,
he acquired a mastery for stating a difficult and involved problem in
a clear, coherent, and concise form. His writing had none of the

[1] The fact of Speransky's scientific education also favorably impressed his later
adviser and assistant on the Commission for Codification, professor L. H. Jacob
who noted: "Dabei war Speranski einer von den wenigen Reussen, welche eine
wissenschaftliche Bildung erhalten haben." L. H. Jacob, *Denkwürdigkeiten aus meinem
Leben für meine Familie und für vertraute Freunde aus den Jahren 1802 bis 1820*
(Manuscript copy, Library of Halle), p. 276. Hereafter, these memoirs will be
referred to as *Denkwürdigkeiten*. I wish to take this opportunity to express my
gratitude to professor D. I. Čiževsky for having called my attention to the existence
of this manuscript in Germany. The Halle Library kindly provided me with a
microfilm copy of the sections relating to Jacob's stay in Russia.

[2] See: "Fizika vybrannaia iz luchshikh avtorov, raspolozhennaia i dopolnennaia
Nevskoi Seminarii filosofii i fiziki uchitelem M. M. Speranskim 1797-go g. v Sankt
Peterburge," in *Chteniia*, 1871, bk. 3, section 2, pp. 1—56 and 1872, bk. 1, section 2,
pp. 57—248 *passim* (cf. in particular pp. 3, 76 ff, 83 ff, 168, 196, 209 ff). Martynov
in his memoirs says that several of the seminary students used to attend lectures
on biology and other natural sciences given at the Medical Institute of the capital.
He does not say whether Speransky was among these auditors. "Zapiski" *loc. cit.*,
p. 79.

prolixity, disorganization, redundance, and ponderousness of the ordinary government papers of the period. His clear and analytical mind grasped immediately the main fact and inner structure of the problem under consideration and pointed up the implications and relationships to other issues. These findings of his, Speransky then described in a lively, graphic, clear and pleasantly readable manner. The value of such a talent to a busy and exacting ruler, himself without serious technical preparation for the task of government, was indeed great. Much of Speransky's later success can be attributed directly to his ability in setting forth complicated and technical questions in a readable and engaging manner, a talent none of the other bureaucrats and high dignitaries possessed. [1] No doubt, this very quality contained some serious drawbacks, as it could — and often did — lead to a mechanistic and superficial approach to difficult and perplexing questions of national policy. But at first only the advantages of Speransky's manner were perceived. To use a modern American comparison, like the editor of the popularizing mass-appeal magazines, Speransky had a wonderful "knack" for simplifying and "digesting" complex issues, and of coming up with a "formula" prescription for their solution — how such a procedure can easily become a double-edged weapon, we know all too well. [2]

Men of Speransky's talents and promise were rare in Russia at the end of the 18th century, and it was a foregone conclusion that he would be the object of enticing offers. In the first place, his superiors at the Alexandro-Nevskii Seminary wanted to retain him as a permanent member of the faculty. Secondly, the ecclesiastic authorities — in particular the Metropolitan of St. Petersburg — would have liked to see Speransky join the ranks of the regular clergy where men

[1] The thesis that Speransky's administrative originality and creativity lay more in his style than in his thoughts has been developed at length, and, in this writer's judgment, overstated by A. Nol'de in an unpublished biography of Speransky. A. Nol'de, *Biografiia Speranskogo* (Manuscript, at present deposited at the Archive of Russian and East European History and Culture, Columbia University). I wish to take this opportunity to thank Mr. Emmanuel Nol'de of Paris who has kindly put the manuscript at my disposal. May I also express my gratitude to Professor M. Karpovich who called my attention to the existence of this biography.

[2] In this connection, the following words of Professor Jacob bear quotation, as they show the favorable impression Speransky's approach made — at the height of his career — on an intelligent foreign scholar: "Er fasste das, was man ihm sagte sehr leicht auf, und studierte sich schnell in des anderen Ideengang; er hörte sehr auf die Gründe anderer und gab seine Meinung auf, sobald sie gründlich widergelegt wurde. Er hatte seine Laufbahn als Lehrer begonnen und dabei gelernt seine Gedanken andern deutlich und ordentlich mitzuteilen ... Alles was er schrieb war logisch gerundet, bestimmt und deutlich gefasst und mit einer ungemeinen Eleganz ausgedrückt. Es konnte nicht fehlen, dass ein Mann von solchen Talenten und in solchen Posten sehr bald dem Kaiser bekannt wurde." Jacob, *Denkwürdigkeiten*, pp. 276—277.

with his abilities were all too rare. But in this case, he would have had to take monastic vows, and this he was as yet unwilling to do, and he therefore resisted firmly all the entreaties and cajoleries of the Metropolitan. In 1796 an unexpected event completely changed the direction of Speransky's life. The influential magnate, Prince Alexis Kurakin, needed a private secretary to take care of his personal correspondence. Some acquaintance told him that a suitable candidate could surely be found among the teachers or students of the Alexandro-Nevskii Seminary. Acting on this advice, Prince Kurakin sent his majordomo to the Rector of the Seminary to see whether some acceptable young man could be found. The Rector suggested Speransky as the best suited candidate. An anecdote, probably apocryphal but quite revealing of the mores of the time, relates that Prince Kurakin's majordomo had come to the Seminary in his master's coach; as Speransky was about to drive to the Prince's residence for an interview, his first movement was to stand on the footboard of the carriage. On second thought he overcame this impulse and, somewhat hesitatingly, took a seat next to the majordomo inside the coach. True or not, the anecdote graphically illustrates the social position of the future State Secretary: he was only a poor seminary teacher, treated almost like a servant, not quite fit to ride inside the carriage of his prospective employer.

Speransky made a good impression, and to test him, Prince Kurakin asked him to write a dozen letters, whose tenor he explained in very general terms. Speransky had until the next morning to prepare the drafts of these letters. But when he entered his study the next morning, Prince Kurakin was amazed to find on his desk all the letters ready, perfectly elegant in composition and so appropriately phrased that he needed only to sign them. Even the best and most experienced official secretary could not have done better. Speransky was hired on the spot, and a few days later he moved into Prince Kurakin's house. Here his position was not an exalted one; he was barely more than a "high-class" servant of the Prince. Speransky had a room in the servants' wing of the Prince's residence, and although he was invited to Kurakin's table, he prefered to take his meals with the domestics — he was too much embarrassed by the formality and glitter of the magnate's dining room. At first, Speransky was viewed with suspicion and animosity by the other secretaries and employees of the Prince, but he soon won their good graces by his modest, tactful and pleasant manner — the lessons of life learned in the Seminary of Vladimir were paying off. The only person at Prince Kurakin's with whom he established close relations was the tutor of the Prince's children, a German called Brueckner. Brueckner, a shy and meek but quite learned man, was probably the first to introduce him to the post-Kantian German idealism, which was to play an important part in Speransky's intellectual development.

Soon, luck served again the fortunes of the young seminary teacher and private secretary. Upon the death of Catherine II, not long after Speransky had entered his service, Prince Kurakin was appointed Procurator General of the Senate which, in Paul I's time, was almost equivalent to being prime minister. Naturally this imperial favor meant that the duties and functions of the Procurator General's private secretary, too, would become more numerous and important. Kurakin offered to obtain the admission of his talented young secretary into government service, and Speransky eagerly welcomed this opportunity of following a new career. His powerful employer and protector easily secured the reluctant consent of the ecclesiastic authorities to Speransky's release from their jurisdiction. Early in January 1797, the former seminarian formally entered into the ranks of government service. A new life was opening to him. The patronage of Prince Kurakin as well as his own outstanding talents contributed to his rapid rise in the bureaucratic hierarchy. Three months after he had entered government service, April 1797, he was given the eighth rank (*chin*), that of Collegiate Assessor (*kollezhskii assessor*), equivalent to a captaincy in the army, and which in those days conferred hereditary nobility on the bearer and his family. Barely a year later, on January 1, 1798, Speransky was appointed Court Councillor (*nadvornyi sovetnik*), and on November 18, 1798, Collegiate Councillor (*kollezhskii sovetnik*), the sixth rank of the hierarchy and equivalent to a colonelcy in the military branch.

At first, Speransky served in the chancery of the Procurator of the Senate, Prince Kurakin's office, which handled all the important administrative and judiciary problems of the Empire. As one of the responsible officials there, the young state servant was in a good position to become intimately acquainted with the entire mechanism of the state and to observe at close quarters its problems and defects. But there was little security in this position, for the jealous and capricious Paul I kept promoting and demoting the Procurators of the Senate without any rhyme or reason — in less than four years four different Procurators! But Speransky was an adaptable individual, and at the Seminary he had learned how to deal with people and how to please his superiors by playing on their idiosyncrasies and foibles. He not only maintained his position under all Procurators, but also gained their respect and favor. As an illustration of his ability to deal with difficult personalities, we may describe his first interview with the most dreaded, most ignorant, and crudest of all the Procurator Generals in Paul's reign, Obolianinov. Obolianinov's reputation of a worthy counterpart to his tyrannical and brutal imperial master had preceded him at the chancery of the Senate, and all subordinate officials were in mortal, cringing fear. Not so Speransky, who correctly figured that Obolianinov's brutal violence only served to hide his ignorance and incapacity; and that, therefore, he would welcome an able assistant whom he could trust and respect. Speransky behaved accordingly when he was first called before the new Procurator. When he entered Obolianinov's study to make his report, he found the Procurator seated at his desk, the back turned to the door, engrossed in the papers before him. Without lifting his head, Obolianinov gruffly asked Speransky to state his business. At the sound of the first words which Speransky spoke, in a clear, calm, and pleasant matter-of-fact tone, Obolianinov raised his head to look at the speaker. To his great surprise, instead of the servile and colorless figure of a frightened clerk in sloppy and tattered clothes, the Procurator beheld the pleasant countenance of a young man, soberly yet elegantly dressed, in a respectful but dignified posture, stating his business in a precise and self-assured manner. This expression of dignity and confidence impressed the bully. Obolianinov rose from his chair, politely forced Speransky to take a seat, and listened to his reports and comments with great interest and attention. From then on, Speransky became the right-hand man of the fearful Procurator of the Senate, and on occasion his work and advice helped to shield the dignitary from the Emperor's wrath.

Speransky owed his rapid rise along the hierarchic ladder not only to his tact in dealing with the difficult personalities of his superiors, but also to his remarkable power for work, his unusual analytic and stylistic talents, and the speed with which he could familiarize himself with a new problem. [1] Men of such abilities were especially sought after in the turbulent and irregular reign of Paul I, whose eccentricities and whims gave no rest to a harried bureaucracy. Among the numerous anecdotes concerning the reign and actions of Paul I, the following will perhaps illustrate the difficulties which the Emperor's caprices created for his ministers and which Speransky was adept at solving. One fine day, struck by some fancy, Paul I suddenly decided that Russia needed a commercial code. Such a need existed indeed, and to meet it would normally have required much preparation and study. But the

---

[1] N. S. Il'inskii, "Vospominaniia" *Russkii Arkhiv,* 1879, No. 12, p. 391.

impatient sovereign did not like to see the realization of his will postponed for long. So, Paul ordered to round up several prominent merchants of St. Petersburg, to lock them into a wing of the palace at Gatchina, and not to let them out until they had presented the draft of an acceptable commercial code. As the merchants might not be familiar with the technicalities and style of government papers, Speransky was assigned to help them. To make sure that the merchants did not become life-long prisoners at the palace, maintained at government expense without any benefit to the state, Paul set a time limit of two days at the expiration of which the merchants and Speransky must present the code, or else march off to Siberia. We can easily imagine the fright and despondency of the hapless merchants locked in the palace. But Speransky did not lose his head. The whole evening and part of the night he spent in talking to each merchant, asking specific questions on various aspects of their commercial activities. On the basis of this information, he drafted an outline for a commercial code by the following morning. The Emperor glanced at it, approved it; the merchants were released with gifts, and Speransky's reputation as a bureaucratic virtuoso soared sky-high. [1] Fortunately for Russian trade, Paul's interest in the code vanished as suddenly as it had arisen, so that Speransky's hasty improvisation was spared the test of application.

The growing reputation of the young official led to Speransky's appointment to the bureau of the Chief of Provisions for the Capital in 1799. Not only did this new function implement his modest income by 2,000 rubles a year for relatively little work; it also made his name known to the Chief of Provisions, Grand Duke Alexander, Paul's heir. The documents that have come down to us do not indicate that Speransky met Grand Duke Alexander personally at the time, but his written reports, no doubt, came to the attention of his chief, the future Emperor.

In the short span of not quite four years, the poor son of a village priest, the brilliant student of a theological seminary, and young private secretary to Prince Kurakin had attained a prominent and secure position in the central administration of the Empire. His career seemed to take very favorable shape and promised him a brilliant future. But in other ways, too, these years proved extremely rewarding and fruitful.

As he was rising in the ranks of the imperial bureaucracy, Speransky

[1] A. Fateev, "K istorii i teorii kodifikatsii," p. 5 and Grech, *Zapiski o moei zhizni*, pp. 64—65.

was also gradually becoming acquainted with the social and intellectual
life of the Capital. [1] When he came to the Alexandro-Nevskii Seminary
from the school at Vladimir, he had already one connection with St.
Petersburg society. We recall that as a boy in his village, he had been
befriended by the court chaplain, A. A. Samborskii. During his student
days at Vladimir, he had traveled to Moscow to visit Samborskii, and
when he came to the Capital, he naturally re-established contacts with
the court chaplain. Samborskii was an interesting figure, in many ways
quite unusual for a Russian priest of that time. He had been chaplain
of the Russian Embassy in London for many years, and there he had
met many important Russian dignitaries. Through these connections
he obtained an appointment of tutor in religion to the Grand Dukes
Alexander and Constantine, and thus found himself close to the Court.
In England, Samborskii had become well acquainted with the current
religious and spiritual revival as well as with the latest economic
doctrines, especially the physiocratic ideas on agriculture. After his
return to Russia, he actively propagandized both of these facets of
contemporary Western thought: spiritual betterment through a deeper
and more emotional religious experience and material improvement
of the people's life by means of modern agricultural techniques and
economic policies. More "worldly" and better educated than the
ordinary Russian priest, Samborskii was well received in society and
became himself an influential figure in the cultural and intellectual
life of the period.

The enthusiasm with which the Russian educated class had greeted
the outbreak of the French Revolution proved to be also the high
point of the "prépondérance française" in Russia. Catherine's and
Paul's "reactionary" policies after 1791, as well as the excesses of the
Jacobins, put an abrupt end to the gallomania of the Russian nobility
or drove its expression underground. Yet, it was not easy to discard
overnight all the ideological heritage of the Enlightenment, so that
the "discovery" of a more conservative and sensible application of the
political principles of the *philosophes* in England met with an
enthusiastic reception in Russian society. English ideas and English
ways seemed to satisfy also some of the basic intellectual, spiritual

1 The hypothesis has been expressed — but no decisive evidence found — that
Speransky was the author of a poem, signed "З", which was published in I.
Martynov's *Muza* 1796—1797. If this were true, it would indicate Speransky's early
and deep interest in belles-lettres as well as science, philosophy, religion, and
politics. See on this: D. F. Kobeko, "Neskol'ko psevdonimov v russkoi literature
XVIII v.," *Bibliograficheskie Zapiski*, 1861, No. 4, p. 115 (cited by M. Korf, *Zhizn'
grafa Speranskogo*, I, p. 34, note). The poem in question, "I moe schastie" is
reprinted by Kolbasin, "I. I. Martynov," *Sovremennik*, March 1856, p. 24.

needs of the educated classes in Russia, namely the craving for a deeper spiritual and religious life which neither the official Church nor French deism were able to provide. The spiritual revival in England, on the other hand, showed ways in which the extreme rationalism and scepticism of the French and the shallow dryness of official ecclesiastic policy could be overcome. The domination of French literature and thought had been primarily aesthetic, social and cultural. Under the influence of French Enlightenment, the educated Russian nobleman had become conscious politically and was searching for a model on which to pattern his conduct and political aspirations. The regime of terror having eliminated France as source of inspiration, where but in England could there be found "free" men governed by conservative and reasonable institutions which protected the rights, prosperity, and dignity of the citizens? Closer cultural and ideological rapprochement with England was facilitated by the development of economic ties: the export of Russian products (lumber, naval stores, and especially grain) was rapidly becoming the most important single element of the prosperity of the big landowners in Russia. England's contribution to the theory and practice of an active and modern economic system made an additional appeal to the Russian élite.

In this receptive atmosphere, Chaplain Samborskii acted as one of the chief agents in the spread of English ideas and habits among the high nobility of the Russian capital. His house became the meeting place for visiting Englishmen and for Russians interested in England. It was a wonderful anteroom to the circles of Russia's political and cultural élite, and Speransky had the good fortune of gaining access to it at the start of his career. Although Speransky did not have any social ambitions, in the ordinary and somewhat derogatory sense of the term, he still could not fail to take advantage of the opportunity offered to enter into the best society of the Capital. Soon another, more personal reason drew Speransky to the Chaplain's house. As the best known Anglo-Russian go-between, Samborskii received the visit of practically every Englishman who came to St. Petersburg. Quite naturally, therefore, when Mrs. Elizabeth Stephens, the widowed niece of the curator of the British Museum, Planta, arrived in Russia to take up a position as governess, she turned to Samborskii for guidance and help. Well recommended to Samborskii by her scholarly uncle and his literary acquaintances in England, Mrs. Stephens and her two daughters became frequent guests at the home of the Court Chaplain. It did not take long before the English ladies met the other regular visitors of Samborskii, and among them was Speransky, at the time

Director of the Chancery of the Procurator of the Senate. This is how Speransky later described his first meeting with Mrs. Stephens and one of her daughters: one evening, as Speransky was dining at Samborskii's, the seat across the table from his had remained empty as the guests sat down. Engrossed in some interesting conversation or busy with the food, Speransky did not take notice that somebody had eventually sat down in the empty chair. When a few minutes later he glanced to the opposite side, he was pleasantly surprised to see the pretty, modest, and pleasant figure of a young girl whose whole being appeared to radiate "spiritual purity". Speransky was delighted, and the sound of the girl's voice completely enchanted him. He had no rest until he had learned the name and identity of the young person. They were introduced to each other, and it was love at first sight for both. Frequently meeting at Samborskii's house, the two young people became better acquainted and after a brief courtship, announced their engagement. The courtship must have been somewhat unusual, for at first Speransky and his fiancée had no language in common: he knew no English, and Miss Elizabeth Stephens did not speak Russian; they communicated in an imperfect and stilted French. But love easily disregards linguistic barriers, and communication became easier as each tried to learn the other's mother tongue. We have a few of the letters Elizabeth Stephens wrote in Russian to her future husband, and while their spelling and grammar leave much to be desired, their meaning and sentiment are clear enough. Speransky learned languages rapidly and well, and soon he had a very good command of English, a rather unusual accomplishment even among the best educated men of his time and class; for all their anglomania, few Russians bothered to learn the language of the country they admired so much, and received their ideas about England through second-hand French reports and translations. [1]

Married in 1798, the Speransky couple settled in a modest apartment for a quiet and somewhat withdrawn life. Most of their friends were either Speransky's former fellow students from the Alexandro-Nevskii Seminary, who, like P. Slovtsov and I. Martynov, had also become government servants, or else young officials like V. N. Karazin. Through Samborskii and the English colony of St. Petersburg, the Speranskys were also close to some foreigners; among these their best friends were the English pastor Pitt, Dr. Weickardt (a nephew of Catherine's physician) and his wife, the daughter of the prominent banker

[1] For example, the *English Literary Journal* of Moscow was printed in English with a French translation on opposite pages.

Amburger. In other words, their circle could be described as that of the commercial and bureaucratic "tiers état".

After less than a year a daughter, also named Elizabeth, was born to the couple. But the happiness and promise of a quiet family life did not last long; Speransky's wife, a frail woman suffering from tuberculosis, did not survive the strain of childbirth, dying a few months later. Her death broke Speransky almost completely. The day after she had died he vanished from home; until the funeral he returned only for a few brief moments every day to approach the funeral bed, and then disappear again. Friends claimed to have seen him in outlying sections of the town, dishevelled, dirty and in such a state that they earnestly feared for his reason and life. Eventually Speransky pulled himself together and came to realize that his responsibility towards his infant daughter demanded his return to normal life. But the wound was never healed completely. [1]

Mrs. Stephens, his mother-in-law, moved into Speransky's home to take care of the little girl, with the help of devoted friends like Mrs. Weickardt. But Mrs. Stephens had a rather difficult personality; Speransky's financial circumstances were not particularly brilliant, and to increase his earnings, he accepted a heavy load of extra duties and assignments. As a result, he almost never experienced the repose and warmth of a happy family life and led a withdrawn, busy, and aloof existence. He steadfastly refused to marry again, even when, at the height of his career, he had the opportunity of making a brilliant and politically advantageous match. He scorned the proffered alliances with wealth, power, or high society and remained a lonely wolf in the "jungle" of the Court and government. For his scornful loneliness he was to pay dearly in 1812.

Deprived of the soothing joys of family life, Speransky threw himself, body and soul, into his work and became the most tireless and burdened "work horse" in the imperial administration. From that time, his biography consists almost exclusively of the events in his official career, of the plans of administrative reform which engaged all his energies and attention. The only thing outside his government duties that held Speransky's attention and filled his few hours of leisure, was the study of philosophy and religion. We shall have occasion to return to this often forgotten aspect of his life in greater detail; suffice here to say that this was no new interest of his, he had had it since his student days at the Seminary. But the tragic death of his wife, no doubt,

---

[1] Cf. letter to Karazin after the death of his wife, quoted in Longinov, "Graf Speranskii," *Russkii Vestnik*, XXIII, Oct. 1859, pp. 353—354.

reinforced the religious and mystical bent of his speculations. As a result, his personal life almost never intruded on his existence as a high government official and counselor to the Emperor. His private affairs, his philosophical and religious seekings occupied his full interest — and that of his biographer — only during the long years of lonely exile and enforced leisure. Until his fall from favor, seeking escape from an empty house and sorrow-laden memories, Speransky worked unceasingly, taking upon himself more than his share of tasks and assignments. He made himself indispensable by his truly astounding capacity for work; without any other time-absorbing interest, he was always willing and ready to perform any additional task that might be required. Whenever some project or law had to be worked out and composed quickly, whenever some problem demanded a great deal of preparation and study, Speransky was the person to take the assignment. This is why his name is associated with practically every aspect of Russian administration in the first decade of the reign of Alexander I. But before we turn to the description and analysis of his official activities, let us first try to give a brief sketch of his social life in that period. It will be helpful in understanding both his personality and his position in the government.

Scornfully avoiding the shallow and glittering world of high society, too busy to play the courtier, Speransky sought relaxation among people who were intellectually and socially his inferiors, or at most, equals. He wanted to be in a circle where he need not guard his every step and movement. As we have noted, he had to be reassured constantly that he was admired, respected and loved. That is why at the height of a successful career, his personal friends, his intimates were the same kind of people as those with whom he had associated when he was only an obscure small official. There were again former fellow students from the seminaries, the professional and business people from among the foreign colony of St. Petersburg, officials beginning their careers. [1] To some extent, certainly, one reason for these attachments was his loyalty to old friends and connections, but the selfish desire to be the superior individual in the group should not be discarded as a factor.

In the Chancery of the Senate and in the Commission of Provisions

1 Cf. the remarks of Alexander at a session of the Unofficial Committee (11 April 1802): "S. M. dit qu'on trouvait peu de séminaristes qui voulussent devenir prêtres. Sur quoi M. Novossiltsoff répondit que cela n'était pas étonnant, puisque depuis quelque temps beaucoup d'entre eux avaient pris la carrière civile où ils avaient fait de rapides progrès, ce qui engageait les autres à tâcher de sortir de la carrière ecclésiastique pour entrer dans la carrière civile..." Grand Duc Nicolas Mikhailovitch, Le Comte Paul Stroganov II (Paris 1905), p. 127.

for the Capital, Speransky formed two friendships which deserve to be mentioned, although they did not last very long. One of the members of the Commission of Provisions was A. Radishchev, author of the famous *Journey from St. Petersburg to Moscow,* who had been allowed to return from exile by Paul I. The evidence accessible to us does not tell how close Speransky and Radishchev were at the time. In any case, their acquaintance could not have lasted for long, as Radishchev took his own life in the fall of 1802. But recent research has shown that Speransky had a first-hand acquaintance with Radishchev's ideas and valued greatly his learning and knowledge. [1] Although Speransky's political ideology developed along somewhat different lines from that of Radishchev's, there can be no doubt that he benefited from the contact. [2]

In the Chancery of the Senate, Speransky made the acquaintance of V. N. Karazin, the visionary and enthusiastic correspondent and "friend" of Alexander I. Karazin fancied himself the Marquis Posa of Alexander I, but was not really up to this role. Later in life, Karazin played an active part in the successful establishment of the University of Kharkov and tried to make a political come-back by presenting an ingenious scheme for the improvement of the conditions of the serfs. The characteristic feature of Karazin's letters and projects and of his personal activity as curator (*popechitel'*) of the University of Kharkov and as big landowner in the Ukraine, was a high moral pathos. He did not approve of liberal social or political reforms, but he wanted to set a high standard for the moral leadership of the Emperor and the state. In all fairness to him it must be said that he applied this

[1] In his first plan for administrative reforms, Speransky recommended Radishchev as best qualified to write "a history of Russian law — a necessary work, and his (Radishchev's) talents and knowledge will shed much light on this unknown field." V. I. Semevskii, "Pervyi politicheskii traktat Speranskogo," *Russkoe Bogatstvo,* 1907, No. 1, p. 57.

[2] In 1801, upon the accession of Alexander I, Count A. Vorontsov submitted the proposal for a "Charter to the Russian people" by which the Emperor would guarantee certain basic rights to his subjects and set forth the guiding principles of his reign. The draft for this Charter was prepared by A. Radishchev, the final text is in Speransky's hand. On the evidence of this latter fact it was thought that Speransky was one of the authors of this Charter. Recent investigations, however, show that Speransky opposed the idea of the Charter and that, in any case, he did not participate in the drafting of the document. From all evidence, Speransky's participation was very small, limited to some stylistic improvements added after the Charter had been the subject of discussions in the Unofficial Committee. However, the fact remains that Speransky was familiar with the ideas contained in the Charter (the Charter itself was never promulgated). See: V. P. Semennikov, *Radishchev-ocherki i issledovaniia,* Moscow-Petrograd 1923, pp. 177, 430, 431, 433; Georg Sacke, *Graf A. Voroncov, A. N. Radiščev und der "Gnadenbrief für das russische Volk."* Emsdetten 1939 (?). On Radishchev's connections with young government officials see Vl. Orlov, *Russkie prosvetiteli 1790—1800kh gg.,* Moscow 1950 (in particular the Introduction and Chs. 1—3).

standard to himself in running his estates and in dealing with his serfs. Karazin's friendship with Speransky was at first very warm and intimate, as witness an anguished "cri du coeur" which Speransky addressed to Karazin on the death of his wife. But the closeness did not last long. The fault lay with Karazin who was anything but a steady and reliable individual, as even a superficial acquaintance with his biography will show. It is possible that Karazin, upon becoming Alexander I's "friend", drew the Emperor's attention to Speransky's talents. Furthermore, it is not impossible that Karazin helped Speransky to establish contact with the proponents of German idealistic philosophy (in particular Schelling's *Naturphilosophie*) who were teaching at the University of Kharkov. [1]

Radishchev and Karazin seem to have been the only acquaintances of Speransky who could have played an important and constructive role in the development of his political and philosophical ideas. As to the others, we do not know the exact dates when his friendships were formed, but we have some idea of the composition of his circle for the years 1808—1812, when Speransky was at the height of his influence in the government. The circle of "house friends" had not changed much over the years, and we meet still with the same names as at the beginning of his career. The closest friend of the Speransky family, almost a member, was Mrs. Weickardt whose help in bringing up Speransky's daughter was mentioned earlier. Through her husband, a court physician, Dr. Weickardt, Speransky was probably in touch with some of the important academic and scientific figures of the period, as for example, the early Russian Schellingian, Vellanskii (a member of the faculty of the Military Medical Academy). Through Mrs. Weickardt's father, the banker Amburger, Speransky was in touch with the *monde d'affaires,* prominent bankers and merchants of the Capital, like Kraemer, the Jewish tax farmer (*otkupshchik*) A. Perets, the Lazarev brothers, famous Armenian financiers and entrepreneurs, future founders of the Lazarev Institute for Oriental Languages, Masal'skii who became Speransky's faithful business agent. A few colleagues and assistants whom he had befriended completed the roster of familiar faces at the Speransky home. To the last named group belonged the devoted Tseier (Zeier) who became Speransky's official private secretary, Lubianovskii, and Magnitskii, whose sardonic wit and amusing social talents made him the favorite of Speransky's

---

1 On Karazin see: Shil'der, *Imperator Aleksandr Pervyi — ego zhizn' i tsarstvovanie,* vol. II (St. Pbg. 1904), pp. 33 ff, 327; V. Semevskii, *Krest'ianskii vopros v Rossii v XVIII i pervoi polovine XIX vekov,* I (St. Pbg. 1888), pp. 370—371.

young daughter. The only close friend who belonged to the higher classes and who was most nearly Speransky's "bureaucratic" equal, was Senator A. A. Stolypin, a wealthy landowner from the province of Penza and son-in-law of the well known and influential member of the Council of State, Admiral Count Mordvinov.

Only in this circle did Speransky feel quite at ease and relaxed. Leo Tolstoy, who did not think very highly of Speransky (as of any "great man") has given an exaggerated, caricatured, and unfriendly picture of Speransky's household in *War and Peace* (Vol. II, Part 3, Ch. XVIII). But Tolstoy's psychological intuition pointed out a very basic feature of Speransky's personality, even in this overdrawn characterization. Compared to the dignitaries and government personalities with whom Speransky came into contact in his official capacity, his personal friends make a poor impression indeed, both intellectually and socially, with the possible exception of A. Stolypin. One cannot escape the feeling that there is something a trifle unsavory in his relations to his intimate acquaintances. Many great men have found pleasure and relaxation in associating with people of much lower social, economic, and even intellectual status than they. Some prominent men who had risen to high eminence from the lowest classes of society often preferred the social contact of their former equals. In all these cases, however, the main reason for these "unequal" associations was that they provided a welcome sentiment of freedom and informality to men who were hemmed in by their high position. Peter the Great, Andrew Jackson and others liked the company of sailors, merchants, farmers, frontier-soldiers, because they could be free and uninhibited with these simple people, while they had to guard and disguise their thoughts and sentiments in their public life. In Speransky's case, however, his friends dit not perform this genuinely "liberating" function. In their midst Speransky felt not so much free and their equal as their superior, and could indulge his love for sarcasm at their expense. Perhaps he needed this kind of relief after spending his days with aristocratic high officials and dignitaries who were well above him in social status. But could he really feel exhilaratingly free amidst these intimate friends? Hardly, for how could he feel free in the midst of cringing and flattering individuals of much lower intellectual powers than he? Speransky's friends are overly servile, too humbly devoted to him, though no doubt sincerely so, and to see Speransky in their company makes an unpleasant impression on the observer; an impression which Tolstoy has masterfully conveyed in his description of Prince Andrei's visit to the State Secretary's home. And apparently conscious of the situation, Speransky treated his acquaintances almost like his flunkeys, or, in the case of Magnitsky, court buffoons. He was never impolite or rude; his kindness and softness of manners were quite exceptional among the bureaucrats of the time. Yet, beneath his ever-polite tone, one senses the underlying contempt and patronizing attitude towards his "friends". [1] In Speransky there always remained, in spite of all his polish, intellectual brilliance, politeness and tact, some of the hypocritical and unctuous manners of the young seminary student, pliant and submissive towards his betters, inwardly contemptuous of those inferior in status and intellect. Never secure in the high position he had attained, and justifiedly so, as the events of 1812 were to show, he apparently needed to surround himself at home with a few meek and flattering individuals to boost his own self-confidence.

We have dwelt so long on this aspect of Speransky's life and character, because it must be kept in mind for an understanding and appreciation of his position in Russia's political life. Speransky lived and worked alone; he was always cold and distant in dealing with people; [2] he had no personal friends neither among the high dignitaries nor among his equals in the official hierarchy of the government. Speransky, at least before his return from exile, was one of the few eminent individuals in the history of Imperial Russia, who did not even try to become part of the world of the court and high society to which they had gained access by virtue of their talents and services to the state. Even after he had become a trusted adviser to Alexander I and a most influential policy maker, he remained outside the "inner" circles of the Capital. It was no doubt very laudable of Speransky not to deny his lowly origins, to refuse to become part of the ruling caste at the price of renouncing his past; it was proof of his loyalty that he kept close to his family and his old friends of the seminaries. [3] This course was Speransky's own free choice, and in no sense was it due

1 This appears quite clearly from Speransky's letters to Masal'skii, Druzheskie pis'ma M. M. Speranskogo k G. P. Masal'skomu 1798—1819 St. Pbg. 1862, passim.

2 This is the impression Professor Jacob had after his first interview with Speransky: "Er nahm mich höflich auf, aber sein Äusseres behielt ein kaltes und zurückhaltendes Wesen," Jacob, Denkwürdigkeiten, p. 272.

3 Perhaps this idea of Speransky's loyalty to his friends should be qualified in the light of his response to the appeals of his classmate, Slovtsov. Slovtsov, suspected of harboring subversive ideas and sentiments, was exiled to his native Siberia. He asked Speransky to intervene for him, but the latter — instead of helping him — wrote him sanctimonious letters counselling submission and resignation. In extenuation it would be fair to add that Slovtsov was a stubborn and cantankerous individual, who seemed to take pleasure in provoking the authorities and worsening his position (until age and the hardships of Siberian isolation changed his personality). Cf. Ltrs of Speransky to Slovtsov, dated 22. VII. 1808, 15. I. 1809, 5. II. 1809 in Pamiati pp. 409—410; also Kalashnikov, "Zapiski irkutskogo zhitelia," loc. cit., passim.

to his being rejected by an arrogant ruling aristocracy. For the Russian nobility, whatever its many faults and its growing "class consciousness", was still not closed to newcomers from the lower classes (as witness even the case of Troshchinskii and Bezborodko in the late 18th century not to speak of "creations" of imperial caprice like Kutaisov). Speransky's education, intelligence, his tact and ingratiating personality, his ability to deal with the most difficult persons and situations, and the Emperor's trust and friendship would have made his acceptance by aristocratic society easy. But he did not care to become part of this society, and he remained in dangerous isolation amidst those whom he helped to govern. [1] Naturally, "society" resented being snubbed by an upstart and avenged itself with malicious cruelty.

There were, however, also other reasons for Speransky's isolation and unpopularity. In the first place, there was something unalterably "plebeian" about him. Beneath a veneer of erudition, good education, exquisitely polite manners, and his tact, people detected a sour and envious note. On the authority of contemporaries who were not all too friendly to Speransky, Tolstoy depicted him as hypocritical and as slippery as an eel. This was perhaps neither very fair nor quite correct, but it was an impression he made on many and with some justification, as his personal social life shows. Because he wanted to be esteemed and liked, he was excessively concerned about the opinion people might have of him. He was never quite at ease with his intellectual and social equals, let alone superiors. People noticed this insecurity and discomfort, and interpreted his expressions of consideration and politeness as mere hypocrisy and sham. On the other hand, if Speransky felt sure of having established his intellectual superiority, he grew over-confident, almost arrogant. He ignored, with contemptuous self-assurance, everyone, including his potential rivals or his willing allies. So it happened that after gaining the confidence and support of the Emperor, the only "friend" who really mattered, Speransky disdained the help and friendship of prominent officials and courtiers.

---

[1] Unlike a later reformer and statesman, Nicholas Miliutin, who also tended to withdraw from society to pursue his work, Speransky had no one to tell him the dangers such a course presented for his own aims. Grand Duchess Helen used to warn and remind Miliutin that an administrator and reformer had to live at peace with the society he belonged to: "Ce qu'elle lui reprochait depuis longtemps, c'était de trop s'absorber dans son service, de s'isoler, et, dans un pays où les relations personnelles sont toutes puissantes, de se tenir trop à l'écart de la société, du monde, de la cour. Le meilleur moyen, disait elle, de lutter contre les détracteurs, c'était de se faire voir, de montrer 'que le diable n'était pas aussi noir que sa réputation'." A. Leroy-Beaulieu, *Un homme d'état russe (Nicolas Milutine) d'après sa correspondance inédite — Etude sur la Russie et la Pologne pendant le règne d'Alexandre II (1855—1872)*, Paris 1884, pp. 29—30.

He appeared to proclaim to the world that the personal friendship and support of the Emperor were enough for him to carry out alone the program of reform that he felt was necessary to Russia's welfare. This boast was perhaps justified, but ministers, high officials, courtiers saw in it only the arrogance of a *parvenu*. In the final analysis, his apparent scorn and aloofness made him more enemies at court and among the nobility than his policies and reform measures.

In attempting to give a rounded picture of Speransky's private and social life during the period of his greatest activity and success (ca 1806—1812) we have exceeded the chronological limits of the "Beginnings". We must now retrace our steps and take up the story of his official activities from the end of the reign of Paul I. The accession of Alexander I in March 1801, found Speransky as chief of a department in the Chancery of the Procurator of the Senate and member of the Commission of Provisions for the Capital. A still wider field was opened to his talents when the young Emperor declared his desire to "transform the shapeless structure of the Empire" and inaugurated a decade of febrile political and administrative reorganization.

### SOURCES

For the basic facts of this period of Speransky's life see: baron M. A. Korf, *Zhizn' grafa Speranskogo*, vol. 1, St. Petersburg 1861.

For further details on the seminary days and the first steps in government office see: *Druzheskie pis'ma M. M. Speranskogo k P. G. Masal'skomu 1798—1819*, St. Pbg. 1862; A. N. Fateev, "M. M Speranskii — vliianie sredy na sostavitelia Svoda Zakonov v 1-i period ego zhizni", *Iuridicheskii Vestnik*, X (1915), No. 11, pp. 133—155; N. I. Grech, *Zapiski o moei zhizni*, St. Pbg. 1886; N. S. Il'inskii, "Vospominaniia", *Russkii Arkhiv*, 1879, No. 12, pp. 377—434; I. Kalashnikov, "Zapiski irkutskogo zhitelia," *Russkaia Starina*, vol. 123, July 1905, pp. 187—251, Aug. 1905, pp. 384—409, Sept. 1905, pp. 609—646; Kolbasin, "I. I. Martynov — perevodchik grecheskikh klassikov," *Sovremennik*, March-April 1859; M. N. Longinov, "Graf Speranskii," *Russkii Vestnik*, XXIII, Oct. 1859, pp. 337—378 and 527—576; P. M., "Iz proshlogo," *Russkii Vestnik*, vol. 74, Apr. 1868, pp. 438—513; I. I. Martynov, "Zapiski," *Pamiatniki Novoi Russkoi Istorii*, vol. II, 1872 pp. 68—182; D. P. Runich, "Iz zapisok D. P. Runicha" *Russkaia Starina*, vol. 105 (January—March 1901) pp. 47—77, 325—357, 597—633; P. A. Slovtsov, "Poslanie k Speranskomu," *Russkaia Starina*, V, 1872, pp. 469—470. The discussion and description of ecclesiastic seminaries is based on: F. N. Beliavskii, *O reforme dukhovnoi shkoly*, part I, St. Pbg. 1907; G. Florovskii, *Puti russkogo bogosloviia*, Parizh 1937 (Particularly Chapter IV, section 4); Dm. Protopopov, "Neskol'ko slov o Speranskom" (iz pis'ma k akademiku Ia. Grotu, 11. XII. 1861) *Russkii Arkhiv*, 1876, pp. 225—230; B. V. Titlinov, *Dukhovnye shkoly v XIX st.*, vyp. 1, Vil'na 1908; P. Znamenskii, *Dukhovnye shkoly v Rossii do reformy 1808 g*, Kazan' 1881.

# CHAPTER II

# THE "CONSTITUTIONALISM" OF EMPEROR ALEXANDER I

Rarely had an Emperor's death been greeted with more unabashed joy and happiness than the sudden end of Paul I on the night of March 11–12, 1801. While the Imperial family (in particular Paul's widow and his son, Alexander, the new Emperor) experienced a grief that was inextricably mixed with the pangs of a bad conscience, the capital celebrated exuberantly. The four years of Paul's reign had been well-nigh an uninterrupted nightmare for Russian "society" in general, and for the officers and officials in the capital in particular. The Emperor's odd caprices, manias, inconsistencies, and his outbursts of uncontrolled rage had kept the country trembling with fear. Getting ready for their tour of duty, officers always took extra money with them, for Paul's dissatisfaction or sudden impulse might turn into an order to march off to Siberia directly from the Parade Grounds. [1] The Monarch's suspiciousness in regard to his imperial and personal dignity (too long kept insecure by his mother, Catherine II), knew no bounds and manifested itself in the most obnoxious and silly ways. At his approach in the street, everybody was required to dismount or step off the carriage and curtsy; to underscore the distance between himself and other mortals, Paul forbade the inhabitants of St. Petersburg to harness more than two horses to their carriages. His hatred of the French Revolution led to a meticulous regulation of dress: round hats, long trousers, various feminine clothing accessories, reminiscent of French innovations in the domain of fashion, were banned under heavy penalties. To prevent the spread of harmful ideas from entering his realm, Paul closed the borders to all printed material, including musical scores, forbade the use of certain foreign words, and kept his subjects from traveling abroad. [2]

---

[1] See *Materialy dlia biografii imperatora Pavla I* pp. 29–33.
[2] A list of Paul's annoying and petty restrictions is given in *Mémoires de l'Amiral Tchitchagoff*, pp. 25–30.

These and other bothersome petty restrictions would have been only a superficial source of annoyance or grievance had Paul's regime satisfied the interests and needs of the various classes of the population, particularly the nobility. But the Emperor was so much taken up with the minutiae of military life (paradomania, Prince Adam Czartoryski called it) that he left the government at the mercy of ill-chosen and often changed favorites, like the brutal and grafting Obolianinov or the cruel and ignorant Kutaisov. Foreign policy was conducted with a cavalier disregard for what, in the reign of Catherine II, had been considered Russia's vital national interests, and diplomacy was subordinated to the romantic infatuations and caprices of the Emperor (as for instance, his championship of the Order of Malta). Paul's actions, especially in the first years of his reign, seemed to be dictated less by any purposeful conception of policy than by his intense personal craving to undo whatever his mother had done. This spirit of contradiction, raised to the status of "statesmanship" resulted in an even greater disorder in affairs than had been usual in Russia up to that time. It completely undermined the continuity, purposefulness, and stability of policy which Catherine II had finally succeeded in bringing about by a judicious use of "public opinion" and of the force of tradition. Oblivious and scornful of the feelings of his subjects, Paul I revoked the Charter of the Nobility, the Charter of the Towns, and inflicted serious damage to Russian trade by his break with England on account of Malta, which in truth was of no concern to Russia. Emperor Paul had at least one good intention, to set the maximum of the corvé at three days a week. However, incapable and unwilling to enforce this measure, he did not succeed in improving the wretched condition of the serfs, while at the same time he increased the nobility's anger and sulking opposition. It seemed that Paul had a talent for doing everything to displease and harm those who counted in the state. In fact, he distrusted a "free" nobility residing in its estates, away from his immediate supervision and running its own affairs without government direction and control. Paul wanted to return to an earlier tradition which saw in the nobleman exclusively a servant of the state. To the Emperor's mind, every able-bodied nobleman should serve in the army, and if physically disabled, in the civil government. He therefore forcibly impressed noblemen into service, in direct violation of the Charters of 1761 and 1785 which had "forever" freed the nobility from compulsory state service. Naturally, having once tasted the benefits of freedom from service, the nobility was unwilling to see the clock turned back half a century. The nobles would not easily let go their hard-won privileges and "corporate status".[1] Paul's disregard of the interests of the nobility, coupled with the superficial annoyances with which he beset his officers and courtiers, proved too much. By 1800 already, the violent end of the reign was a foreseeable conclusion.

The four years of imperial terror served as catalytic agent for the political maturation of the Russian nobility. The seeds of political consciousness, in a Western sense, had been planted in their minds by the policies of Catherine II and the penetration of French philosophic and literary works. It is, of course, quite true that Catherine's *engoûment* with the Enlightenment and liberalism *à la* Diderot and Voltaire had been mere window dressing and propaganda. Yet, her intention to give Russia a clear and orderly administration, consistent with the requirements of progress and civilization and the Empire's newly won position in Europe, had been genuine enough. In any case, both the propaganda and the practical efforts at "modern" legislation had greatly influenced the educated portions of the nobility. The glory and prosperity of her reign had enhanced the prestige of the tenets of the Enlightenment, and it established in many minds a direct connection between the country's progress and the implementation of Western ideologies in Russia. The excesses of the French Revolution turned many a Russian "liberal" aristocrat from the radical consequences of the *philosophes'* creed, but they could not, and did not, destroy the newly gained beliefs and social consciousness. Repelled by the extremism and brutality of the French course, the Russian nobility turned to the example provided by England. In England the "progressive" aristocracy of Russia found an impressive respect for a gentleman's liberty and dignity, and it could also observe how the "best" men participated in the administration of county and country.

At the time of Catherine's death in 1796, the educated nobleman who served and lived in St. Petersburg or Moscow was thoroughly conscious of his dignity and worth as an individual; he had come a long way from the timidity and cringiness of his forebears, the servants — *kholopy* — of the Tsars of Moscow. Now, he expected the government to treat him like a human being; he believed that he was entitled to feel secure in his life and property. But not alone as an individual had the educated Russian nobleman achieved self-respect and dignity, he also considered himself a member of the first "estate" (*soslovie*) of the realm — an estate that had earned a privileged position by its

[1] S. A. Korf, *Dvorianstvo i ego soslovnoe upravlenie za stoletie 1762—1855*, pp. 220—275 *passim*.

distinguished services to the crown. By the Charter of 1785 the nobility had received some degree of autonomy in the management of its "corporate" affairs, and the Statute on the Provinces of 1775 had assigned it an important role in local administration. Was this not telling proof of the monarch's recognition of the nobility's ability to take care of itself, to attend to the needs of its estate without harm to the interests of the state? And it does not really matter for our present purposes whether this privileged status had been wrung from the state by the nobility's own efforts or whether Catherine II had given it as a "sop" to insure the government's centralized and bureaucratic control of all really important matters of national policy.[1] Whatever its origin, the nobles interpreted their new status as evidence of their social and political maturity. Paul's regime presented a mortal danger to this newly gained social consiousness and individual self-esteem.

In the light of this situation, the almost indecent joy which greeted the news of Paul's violent demise becomes quite understandable. The exhilaration reached a higher pitch yet when Alexander's proclamation of accession promised a return to the principles of his grandmother, the great Catherine.[2] All shared the belief that Paul's course of arbitrariness and despotism was abandoned forever, and this belief found its strongest and most articulate expression among the upper ranks of the nobility. The old dignitaries of Catherine's time, supported by the aristocracy — the greatest and perhaps exclusive beneficiaries of the policy pursued by the Empress — wished to secure firmly the privileges of the first estate of the Empire. In their opinion, the principles of the Enlightenment — in their English form — should be put into practice for the benefit of the upper rungs of the nobility. The catchword which summarized and symbolized these aspirations was the term "constitution," or, in more careful mouths, "fundamental laws" and "fundamental institutions". The future for the realization of these aspirations looked very bright and hopeful indeed, for did not the young ruler, Alexander I, share these desires and did he not intend to give "fundamental laws" which would put Russia on an

1 The former interpretation is to be found most frequently in the general histories of Russia (cf. Stählin, Kornilov, Vernadsky). The latter explanation, which this writer favors, has been given most recently by P. Struve (in his article, "Istoricheskii smysl russkoi revoliutsii").

2 "We accept the obligation to rule the people entrusted to us by God according to the laws and spirit of Our August late grandmother, Empress Catherine the Great, whose memory will be eternally dear to us and the entire fatherland..." (quoted by Shil'der, *Imperator Aleksandr Pervyi — ego zhizn' i tsarstvovanie*, vol. II, p. 6); PSZ 19,779 (12. III. 1801), vol. 26, pp. 583—584.

equal footing with the civilized nations of Western Europe and prevent the recurrence of the despotism of a madman? In Russia where everything depended on the will and preference of the ruler, Alexander's alleged sympathy with these aims was a good omen. Strengthened by his "people's" enthusiastic love and loyalty, the young Emperor could lead his country to a new future in satisfying the aspirations and desires of his subjects.

Alexander's charm, youth, and sincere idealism held out the promise that the optimistic hopes of even the most ardent and enthusiastic advocates of fundamental reforms would not be disappointed. The approval he had apparently given to the removal, although not the murder, of his despotic father was viewed as a pledge of his loyalty to the interests of Russian society. The young sovereign's seeming liberalism did not come as a surprise, for Catherine had entrusted the education of her preferred grandchild to the liberal, enlightened, and virtuous Swiss republican, La Harpe. Young Alexander's confidences to La Harpe and to his friends, the Polish "hostage" Adam Czartoryski and Count Victor Kochubei, soon became known, at least in their general tenor. To Kochubei Grand Duke Alexander had confided that his only ambition was to give a constitution to Russia and then spend the remainder of his days in rustic retirement on the banks of the Rhine. [1] To the astonished Czartoryski the heir presumptive of the most autocratic state had declared his "hatred of despotism, wherever and by whatever manner it was exercised and that he loved liberty, that liberty was owed equally to all men." [2] At another time the Grand Duke surprised, and embarrassed, his Polish friend by asking him to write the draft of a proclamation of accession which would embody their liberal ideals. [3] One of Alexander's first acts when he acceded to the throne was to recall to his side his "liberal" friends whom Paul's suspicion and dislike had driven from St. Petersburg. With these friends the young

[1] Letter of 10 May 1796, quoted in Mel'gunov, *Dela i liudi aleksandrovskogo vremeni*, p. 39.

[2] "Il [i.e., Grand Duke Alexander] m'avoua qu'il détestait le despotisme partout et de quelque manière qu'il s'exerçât; qu'il aimait la liberté, qu'elle était due également à tous les hommes..." *Mémoires du Prince Adam Czartoryski et correspondance avec l'Empereur Alexandre Ier* (préface de Ch. de Mazade), vol. I (Paris 1887), p. 96. For a recent description of Czartoryski's relationship to Emperor Alexander, see Marian Kukiel, *Czartoryski and European Unity*, (Pinceton University, 1955).

[3] "Il me demanda enfin de lui laisser un projet de proclamation qui devait faire connaître ses résolutions au moment où le pouvoir souverain lui serait dévolu. J'eus beau m'en défendre, il ne me laissa ni paix ni repos avant que j'eusse formulé sur le papier les idées dont il était incessamment occupé. Il fallait pour le tranquilliser complaire à sa volonté de plus en plus inquiète et pressante. Je redigeai donc à la hâte, de mon mieux, ce projet de proclamation." Czartoryski, *op. cit.*, I, p. 150.

Emperor regularly consulted on the problems of government. Although they were not appointed to any official position, they formed an "Unofficial Committee" to consider, discuss, and work on a reorganization of the administration. [1] All this seemed to justify the country's hopeful optimism that Russia was about to enter a new era.

How sincere was Emperor Alexander about his constitutional plans? This question has been the subject of much debate and argument among historians. A definitive solution of the debate cannot be our purpose here. But for a proper understanding of the setting in which Speransky was to work, we must obtain some knowledge of the Emperor's attitude toward governmental reforms. Remembering the admonition, so often unheeded, of Fustel de Coulanges, "rien n'est plus nécessaire en histoire que de se faire une idée juste du sens des mots", we must first make sure that we have a proper understanding of the term "constitution" as it was used by Alexander and his friends. Did this key word have the same meaning for them as it did for the high dignitaries of Catherine's time, or for the Decembrists, or for the "progressive" and liberal scholars who wrote the history of this period? The most convenient way of determining Alexander's "definition" is to analyze his reaction to some of the plans of administrative reorganization and reform that were submitted to him in the first years of his reign.

No sooner had Paul I been laid to rest than many high officials and dignitaries from Catherine's times voiced their views on Russia's political organization. In spite of some variations of detail, these voices belonged to a rather homogeneous group composed of "elder statesmen" whose thinking revolved around a reform of the Senate. [2] For the sake of brevity we might call this the "senatorial party". The group commanded the young Emperor's attention and respect not only because its members were influential and experienced administrators,

---

[1] The members of the Unofficial Committee were: A. Czartoryski, Victor Kochubei, N. Novosiltsev, Paul Stroganov. Alexander's tutor, La Harpe, for a brief while back in Russia, was also consulted, but was not admitted to the deliberations of the Committee. Paul Stroganov kept detailed notes of the discussions, which have been published in the 2nd volume of Grand Duke Nicholas Mikhailovich's biography of Stroganov. See also Czartoryski's description of the informal character of the meetings in the *Mémoires du Prince Adam Czartoryski,* I pp. 266, 269–270. He concludes: "Et quoique ces réunions ne fussent pendant longtemps qu'un simple passe-temps et des discussions à perte de vue, sans aucun résultat pratique, il est vrai de dire qu'il n'a été question en Russie d'aucune amélioration intérieure, d'aucune réforme utile tentée ou accomplie pendant le règne d'Alexandre, qui n'ait pris naissance dans ces conciliabules." (p. 269)

[2] A good political characterization of the Senatorial party is to be found in G. G. Tel'berg, "Senat i 'pravo predstavleniia na vysochaishie ukazy'," *Zhurn. Min. Narodn. Prosv.* XXV (Jan. 1910), pp. 3–5.

but also because it had the support of the most active participants in
the palace revolution of March 11th, 1801.[1] The senatorial party
advocated the return to the traditions of Catherine II, as promised in
the Proclamation of Accession and enthusiastically welcomed by the
nobility. The senatorial group could, therefore, claim to speak with
the authority of a "public opinion" whose support the young ruler
needed and craved. Prodded by it, Alexander asked the Senate to
redefine its powers and functions and to present a plan for its
reorganization. The Senate complied readily, and several of its members
drafted proposals whose contents were eventually consolidated into
one paper, edited by Count Zavadovskii and submitted to the Emperor.
At the same time, several high dignitaries close to the Senate, in
particular the Counts Alexander and Simon Vorontsov, drafted a
charter to the Russian people which they intended to have promulgated
at the coronation of Alexander I.

In spite of some differences in detail, the members of the senatorial
party pursued the same aims. They proposed to give the dominant
role in the government to the higher nobility by re-establishing the
Senate (or in Count Panin's plan, an enlarged Council of State) as
the highest executive organ and by granting it a consultative voice
and limited power of initiative in the legislative process. In addition,
the Charter for the Russian People guaranteed to the Emperor's
subjects, and specifically to the nobility, legal safeguards which would
protect their life and property against the arbitrary caprices of the
monarch's bureaucracy. The Senators (or Councillors of State) were
to be selected among the high dignitaries of the realm; and, in addition,
perhaps — at a later stage — a few noblemen from each province might
be appointed by the government upon recommendation of the Governor.
The most important function assigned to the Senate was the supervision
of the administration and the execution of the decrees and edicts,
seeing to it that no bureaucrat violated the basic laws and privileges
of the nation. The actual task of legislation remained, as in the past,
in the hands of the Emperor and his immediate advisers, but the
Senate would have a "droit de remontrance". In this manner, without
specifically restricting the absolute power of the monarch, the Senate
would obtain effective means for safeguarding the "fundamental laws"
of the realm; that is, the rights and privileges of the various classes
of the Russian people, most particularly of course, those of the nobility.

---

[1] The personal link between the conspirators of March 1801 and the Senatorial
party was provided by Count P. Panin.

These proposals were quite clearly the basis for an aristocratic, oligarchic, "constitution". [1]

Although these projects did not abolish absolutism in Russia outright, they were frankly following the example of those Western European states where by securing a dominant political position, the nobility had been successful in checking the excesses of a monarchy's bureaucratic absolutism. The implicit reasoning of the Senatorial party was that the security and liberty of a *Rechtsstaat* could best be brought about in Russia by first securing intangible rights and privileges for one class of the nation. Eventually these rights and privileges — legally guaranteed and protected by the Senate — could be extended to other classes as well. The history of England, and perhaps Sweden, seemed to them a telling example of the benefits of such an evolution.

We should not dismiss these proposals as merely unabashed selfish "class" legislation. Undeniably, compared to the direction political thought and practice had taken in the West since 1789, the program of the Senatorial party does seem "reactionary", designed to protect a social class that appeared on its way out. But we should not forget that Russia was behind Western Europe in its political and social evolution. And at least we can recognize that the Senatorial party had "historical logic", if there be such a thing, on its side. The *Rechtsstaat* and representative institutions had originated in the West in a way that was not unlike that suggested by the Zavadovskiis and Vorontsovs; political and legal privileges had first been granted, or won, to one "estate", the nobility, and circumstances later forced their extension to other groups of society. In the meantime, the rights and privileges of one class kept monarchical absolutism and bureaucratic arbitrariness within bounds; the monarchy had been weakened in its ability to resist the extension of these rights and privileges; and an important segment of the population had had the experience of political responsibility. The classical illustration of such an evolution was of course England; but even France under the Ancien Régime had partaken of this trend, and so had Sweden and Prussia. All of this, naturally, does not mean to say that the program of the Senatorial group was the only or even the best approach to Russia's political and social problems. But inasmuch as Russia's most pressing need was the

---

1 The model for this kind of "constitution" is to be sought in the example of 18th century England which Count Vorontsov knew quite well from his long residence there. No doubt, the Senatorial party also drew inspiration from the so-called "Conditions" (*konditsii*) presented by the dignitaries to Empress Anne in 1730 (On the 1730 episode see: P. N. Miliukov, "Verkhovniki i shliakhetstvo," *Iz istorii russkoi intelligentsii*, St. Pbg. 1903).

establishment of a firm rule of law, this approach promised success in a country where only the upper nobility was prepared to participate actively in political life.

Emperor Alexander, however, either rejected the proposals out of hand (Count Panin's project, the Charter for the Russian people) or restricted their scope to such an extent that he rendered them practically meaningless (for example, the decree on the powers of the Senate, 1802). This reaction did not come as a result of the Emperor's realization of the true meaning and potential implications of the proposals. He had neither the necessary theoretical knowledge nor sufficient political experience for that. The projects of the Senatorial party were distasteful to Alexander for three main reasons. In the first place, imbued with the "esprit de système" of the 18th century, he had a fundamental dislike of anything that might give exceptional status to a group or a class. [1] For this reason he was unreceptive to any suggestion which was not derived from abstract general principles and which would not result in a clear, logical and neat system of organization. He was not to be impressed by appeals to historical traditions and precedents and hoped to base all his actions on grounds of natural reason alone. In this sense, and in spite of his later emotional and religious development, Alexander remained faithful to 18th century anti-historicist rationalism. In the second place, and subjectively this was a more weighty reason, he was naturally suspicious of an aristocracy which had just overthrown an Emperor and might do it again if given the power and opportunity. Lastly, and most important of all, despite his professed liberalism and republicanism, Alexander was very jealous of his autocratic power and prerogatives.

The Emperor's jealousy of his power took numerous and varied forms as Alexander was very quick to detect and react to anything that might be interpreted as a challenge to his position and will. As early as the times of the Unofficial Committee (1801—1803), the "honeymoon" of the young sovereign's liberalism, Count Stroganov noted that Alexander became very stubborn as soon as anyone disagreed with his preferences, so that it was best not to try to convince him by direct argument and open discussion, but rather bring up the subject later in an indirect way.[2] Every time a concrete plan for the reorganization

---

[1] "L'Empereur ajouta que c'était contre son gré qu'il avait remis en vigueur la Charte de la noblesse à cause des droits exclusifs qui lui repugnaient toujours" — Conférences avec l'Empereur, 1801, No. 112 (15 July 1801) — annexe IX, Grand Duke Nicolas Mikhailovitch, *Le Comte Paul Stroganov*, II, p. 38 (hereafter cited as *Comte Paul Stroganov*).

[2] *Comte Paul Stroganov*, II, p. 55 (Conférences avec l'Empereur, 1801, No. 118, 11. IX. 1801).

of the government along more "constitutional" lines was proposed, Alexander delayed his decision, refused to implement it, and eliminated everything that might even remotely constitute a restriction of his prerogatives. The incident with Count Severin Potocki in the Senate, was a very clear and dramatic illustration of Alexander's attitude to a consistent and literal implementation of the rights he himself had granted to the Senate in 1802. And later still, after he had given a constitution to the Kingdom of Poland in 1815, he refused to conform to it and constantly violated its provisions and principles (and in this respect, Nicholas I was a better "constitutional monarch" — at least as long as the Constitution remained in force). In 1816, when a group of high dignitaries and noblemen dared to request permission to coordinate their actions in liberating their serfs, under provisions of the law on Free Agriculturists (1803), the Emperor bluntly reminded them that he alone would decide if any coordinated action was to be taken and that he did not need anyone's advice on how to rule. Alexander's suspicion of anyone who might conceivably oppose his autocratic will was almost pathological. He had all dignitaries and even members of his own family shadowed by the police; to make sure of the police, his personal secret agents spied on the police. Anyone as concerned about the preservation of his power and prestige was not very likely to accept constitutional limitations on his will. And as a matter of record, he never did. [1]

And yet, all his life and throughout his reign, Alexander talked about giving a constitution to his peoples; he established commissions and committees to draft constitutional reforms, he asked his friends and his ministers to submit proposals of constitutions. If the projects of the Senatorial party were not due to the initiative of the Emperor, almost all others were. Besides discussing reforms with the Unofficial Committee, Alexander sought suggestions and advice from Jefferson and Bentham. [2] In 1814 he ordered the Baltic German Baron Rosen-kampf, newly arrived in St. Petersburg, to write a constitution —

---

[1] Alexander's jealous concern for his power is best described by S. Mel'gunov, "Sfinks na prestole (cherty dlia kharakteristiki Aleksandra I)," *Dela i liudi aleksandrovskogo vremeni,* pp. 35—83 passim.

[2] On Alexander's connections with Jefferson see: V. M. Kozlovskii, "Imperator Aleksandr I i Dzhefferson," *Russkaia Mysl',* (October 1910); N. Hans, "Tsar Alexander I and Jefferson: Unpublished correspondence," *Slavonic and East European Review,* XXXII-78 (December 1953), pp. 215—225; E. Hölzle, "Zar Alexander I und Thomas Jefferson," *Archiv für Kulturgeschichte,* 1952, No. 2; G. Vernadsky, "Reforms under Czar Alexander I. French and American Influences," *The Review of Politics* (Jan. 1947). On the relations between Alexander I and Bentham, see: A. Pypin, "Russkie otnosheniia Bentama," *Ocherki literatury i obshchestvennosti pri Aleksandre Im,* (Petrograd 1917), vol. III, pp. 1—109.

much to Rosenkampf's surprise and against his will and better judgment. A similar offer made to Freiherr vom Stein was rejected by the Prussian statesman; in 1809 came Speransky's plan. [1] This interest in constitutions did not disappear during the so-called "reactionary" period of Alexander's reign, i.e. after 1812 and the Congress of Vienna. At the opening of the Polish Sejm in 1818, the Emperor expressed his hope that he still would be able to give a constitution to his Russian lands too. And after General Balashev's experiment with a reform of the regional administration (1816) came the project of a Charter written by Novosiltsev (1820). [2] To the very end of his life, Alexander kept thinking about constitutional reforms and projects, as witness his words to Karamzin on the eve of his departure to Taganrog in August 1825. [3] This consistent interest which verges on obsession goes a long way to disprove the opinion held by some historians that his constitutionalism was only a youthful infatuation, a romantic pipe dream which evaporated soon after his accession. It further provides evidence that, contrary to the belief held by many in the 1820's, the Emperor had not turned away from his earlier intentions of reform under she influence of mysticism, the reactionary counsels of Metternich, or the brutal militarism of Arakcheev.

Was then Alexander's persistent toying with constitutional changes a hypocritical sham? Or perhaps was it only due to his meek yielding to the pressures of public opinion and the stronger wills of his advisers? Historians have now discredited the legend, which originated in his own lifetime, that Alexander was a weak person, easily influenced by his entourage. As a matter of fact, modern research and the publication of new documents at the beginning of this century, have clearly shown that some of the policies which had been attributed to outside influences, as for example, Arakcheev, Madame de Kruedener, Metternich, Queen Louise of Prussia, had been Alexander's own. More often than not, the Emperor pursued their implementation in the teeth of the most stubborn resistance and opposition of his family, ministers, and even

---

[1] For instance, in 1811 Alexander I declared to Count Armfelt (the Swedish-Finnish leader who had entered Russian service): "Je vous jure que ces formes (constitutionnelles) me plaisent bien davantage que cet exercice d'un libre arbitre, qui n'a pour base que ma volonté, et qui admet un principe de perfection chez le souverain qui n'est pas, hélas, dans l'humanité. Ici je ne peux me tromper que parceque je le veux bien; toutes les lumières me sont offertes; *là je ne suis entouré que d'incertitude et presque toujours d'habitudes qui ont suppléé aux lois*" (italics mine, MR), Shil'der, *Imperator Aleksandr Pervyi*, vol. III, p. 8.

[2] See G. Vernadsky, *La charte constitutionnelle de l'Empire russe de l'an 1820.*

[3] The conversation took place on August 28, 1825. Schiemann, *Geschichte Russlands unter Kaiser Nikolaus I,* vol. I, p. 498, also Shil'der, *Imperator Aleksander Pervyi,* vol. IV, p. 352.

favorite friends. [1] If Alexander was not an influenceable weakling, can we explain the apparent contradiction by pointing to his duplicity, his habit of "wearing" a different face for each one who approached him? At times it is asserted in the literature on the subject that the Emperor wore a mask of liberalism to conciliate "public opinion" and to gain popularity. But we have pointed out that too often he went against this opinion and that he did not fear loss of popularity. [2] To believe in Alexander's duplicity about constitutionalism is to read his entire reign in the light of the "reactionary" measures of the 1820's and to forget that even then he was still thinking of constitutional reform. [3] If we must speak of Alexander's duplicity, we should first get away from the dichotomy of liberal vs. reactionary. From his earliest days the Emperor had been put in a situation which required tactful diplomatic maneuvering, caught as he was between the demands of his grandmother and the duty he owed to his father. To hide his thoughts and to evade direct answers, became second nature to him; even as autocratic ruler, when he met with strong opposition to his plans, he rarely met the issue head on, but preferred to reach his ends in a roundabout way. This went well with his jealous concern for his power, his desire to appear friendly and well disposed to all. Rather than defend openly his position, rather than show his dislike or distrust of a person frankly, he resorted to back-stage intrigues and maneuvers. This evasiveness and indirectness coupled with suspicious distrust for his closest advisers, created the impression of vacillation,

[1] Reference to two instances may suffice here, as this is not a study of Alexander I. Alexander followed his own policy of "friendship" with Napoleon after Tilsit, in spite of the strong opposition of his own mother, most of his ministers, the Court, the nobility, and the people. In 1812 he refused to end the war and negotiate with Napoleon as long as the French were on Russian territory, and resisted all pleas for peace of his mother, his brother, and courtiers. And after 1815, Alexander I was alone responsible for the creation and operation of the military colonies. He insisted on their establishment and continuation even though Arakcheev advocated their abolition after the high cost and difficulties of the project had become apparent.

[2] "Il faut le dire, l'empereur Alexandre n'avait point alors (1803—1804) l'opinion russe pour lui, elle ne fut son partage que rarement pendant toute la durée de son règne." *Mémoires du prince Adam Czartoryski,* I, p. 335.

[3] This distortion of perspective, particularly common among the liberals of the 1820's and the Decembrists, which divided the reign of Alexander into two antithetical periods, is largely because most of the government's reform projects remained unknown to contemporaries. Of course, we are quite aware that for a proper and complete characterization of the period, we cannot dismiss the opinions of the contemporaries, however inaccurate and erroneous they might have been. The belief held by the generation of the 1820's that Alexander had betrayed the ideals and principles of his youth is a historical fact of great significance for the understanding of the origins and character of the Decembrist revolt. But this is not directly relevant here. We wish to determine what Alexander's constitutionalism was in fact and what the Emperor himself understood by that term; this is essential for an appreciation of Speransky's political role.

weakness. The Emperor seemed to pursue different, contradictory policies one after another. And while it is quite true that Alexander rarely had the patience and energy to apply his mind to the exacting task of implementing his plans completely and well, he did not waver as much in his basic principles as might appear from a superficial acquaintance with the facts of his reign. Behind the changeability and indirectness of means, there was a stubborn persistency of purpose. Duplicity and weakness are not the answer, and to discover the meaning the concept of constitution had for Alexander we must look in another direction.

The answer lies in the very contents the Emperor put into the term constitution. His idea of what "constitution" should imply was shared by many other personalities of the time — the four members of the Unofficial Committee, for one example — although they were at times willing to carry its implications further than was the monarch. As Alexander and his friends were neither experienced jurists nor learned in political philosophy, they did not state their definition of the term anywhere explicitly, unambiguously, or fully. However, the meaning they attached to the term can be inferred from scattered comments and the "twist" they gave their reform proposals. It will perhaps be easier to begin with what they did not mean by the term constitution. They did not have in mind that meaning of the term which gained currency after 1815, particularly in the 1820's, and which substantially is the meaning we still give it today. When about 1820 the future Decembrists, for instance, spoke of constitution, they referred to the concepts and traditions which had their origin in English parliamentarism and which found formal and extreme expression in the written constitutions of the American and French revolutions. Constitution then meant a written document clearly stating the sources and character of political sovereignty, guaranteeing the basic rights of all citizens, establishing the mechanism of a representative parliamentary government, and, most important, confining the executive to a position subordinate to that of the elected legislative power. Neither Alexander I nor the members of the Unofficial Committee subscribed to this definition of constitution.

What they called constitution should perhaps be termed "fundamental principles of administrative organization". The term constitution conveyed to them the idea of an orderly system of government and administration, free from the caprices and demoralizing tyranny of arbitrariness. To give Russia a constitution, therefore, implied bringing clarity and order to the administration and basing the relationship

between the government and the individual subject on the rule of
law.[1] The issues of popular sovereignty, "no taxation without
representation", the doctrine of separation and balance of powers were
of no direct concern to the Autocrat of All the Russias and his chosen
advisors. And while they spoke in terms of the concepts that had
gained popularity and currency in the latter part of the 18th century,
they applied them to a different situation and gave them a different
twist from that in Western Europe or America. The most striking
instance of this change was their use of the idea of separation of
powers. Montesquieu and other 18th century writers, following
Aristotle, and on the basis of their interpretation of the English
"constitution", had maintained that the executive, legislative and
judiciary had to be kept separate in terms of personnel, authority,
jurisdiction, so that none of them could monopolize all the political
power in the state. But while using the same terms, the Unofficial
Committee and Alexander meant only the mechanical division of
functions of government for the sake of more efficient and orderly
administration.

The primordial concern for order and clarity in the administrative
machinery becomes quite evident when we read Count Stroganov's
notes of the meetings of the Unofficial Committee and the various
proposals for reform discussed there. This excessive stress on clarity
and mechanistic harmony of the administration was far greater than
the objective situation of the Russian government demanded; after all,
the Senatorial party also aimed at improving the administration and

---

[1] The analysis of Alexander's "constitutionalism" has been arrived at on the
basis of the sum total of my readings of the sources and secondary studies of the
period — the most important of which are listed in the bibliography for this
chapter. Although some of the conclusions I arrive at have been formulated by
historians earlier, they have not — to my knowledge — been brought together in
quite the same way to characterize Alexander's political attitude. In all fairness to
Alexander and his advisers, it must be said that they were sincerely convinced
that orderly government, based on the rule of law, would contribute to a betterment
of the moral, social, and economic conditions of the Russian people. Freiherr vom
Stein, who in many respects shared a similar — though more liberal and "humanistic"
outlook — remarked quite correctly: "Der Hauptzug in seinem [Alexander's]
Charakter ist Gutmütigkeit, Freundlichkeit und ein Wunsch, die Menschen zu
beglücken und veredeln... Die ganze Geschäftsführung Alexanders beweist seinen
lebhaften Wunsch die Menschen zu beglücken. Er begann mit Unterrichtsanstalten,
Verbesserungen des Zustandes des Landmannes; er wollte Ordnung, Stätigkeit,
Weisheit in die Geschäftsbehandlungen bringen, sich gegen Überraschungen zu
schützen...," Freiherr vom Stein, Briefwechsel, Denkschriften und Aufzeichnungen
(bearbeitet von Erich Botzenhart, Berlin 1931—37), vol. IV (Tagebuchaufzeichnungen
14.VI.1812—23.IX.1812), pp. 108 (1.VII.1812), 112 (6.VII.1812). Czartoryski confirms
this impression: "Cependant, tout ce qui touchait à des idées pratiques, à la justice,
à l'émancipation des masses, à des reformes équitables à des institutions libérales, il
ne cessait d'y penser et de s'en occuper: c'était son délassement intime." Mémoires
du prince Adam Czartoryski, I, p. 266.

yet in their projects there was never so much emphasis on order and clarity. The reason for this stress on mechanical harmony is to be sought in the intellectual habits of the Emperor and his entourage. True to the *esprit de système* and the belief in mechanical laws of nature, no institutional structure appeared good to them unless it was composed of discreet, separate elements which functioned according to laws based on the dictates of logic and natural reason. Everything not essential to such a simple and orderly structure had to be eliminated, for it stifled the efficient working of the *machine* of government. In this respect Alexander and his friends were not so much the disciples of Montesquieu and Blackstone (as in a sense Catherine II had been) but of Bentham and the authors of the several French constitutions. In a sense too, this approach facilitated the development of an enlightened absolutism helped by a responsible and well controlled bureaucracy. In a word, the Unofficial Committee was the spiritual continuator of Joseph II, Frederick II and the First Consul.

In regard to the Emperor himself, an additional personality trait contributed to his insistence on orderliness, clarity and a well defined mechanical hierarchy of government institutions. Alexander I, as well as his younger brothers, had inherited his grandfather's and father's worship of the external trappings of army life, Czartoryski's "paradomania". Whatever the sincerity of Alexander's filial feelings, in one respect he was a convinced and admiring son of his father: the minutiae of army administration, daily drill, military ceremonial and parades, uniforms absorbed Alexander's interest as much as they had Paul's. Throughout his adult life Emperor Alexander preferred to devote his time to military details, even to the neglect of his other duties. He could spend hours on end drilling the regiments of the guard in preparation for a parade; in St. Petersburg he never missed the daily ceremony of the relief of the guard at the palace; often did a courier or minister wait with an urgent message or report until the Emperor had finished studying the details of a new uniform. Admittedly not all of this concern was vain and useless, Alexander did a great deal to modernize the army and make it into a more efficient fighting force. His mania for military regulations and detailed prescriptions found its most complete expression in the notorious Military Colonies which he established in the 1820's under the supervision of Count Arakcheev. No doubt, this predilection for detailed regimentation, order, and hierarchical organization also influenced his approach to the problems of government. Infatuated with the perfect discipline, mechanical simplicity, orderly hierarchy of military organization, he wanted to see the same traits prevail in the administration of his Empire.

The Emperor's understanding of the term constitution implied the rejection of all those features of a nation's life rooted in historical tradition and precedent, which did not develop in a very orderly or logical way and whose manifestations were not amenable to rigid bureaucratic control. In a sense, his mechanistic approach, directly derived from the precepts of Enlightened Absolutism, stood in direct contrast to the "organistic", historical approach of the Senatorial party, with its emphasis on the autonomous development of estates and institutions. Alexander and his friends were, therefore, receptive to borrowings from Napoleonic models and such imitation in turn served to reinforce the elements of enlightened bureaucratic absolutism contained in their plans. [1] The results of their labors illustrated this bureaucratic bent very clearly: they rejected the principle of collegiate rule, which under Russian conditions — as even Speransky admitted later — had a great deal to recommend itself, and they gave their preference to monocratic ministries (1802). It paved the way to a more intensive bureaucratization of the Russian government on the model of the army. The ministers, like staff officers of a commander, were responsible to their chief, the Emperor, only individually. On the provincial level, the governors, directly appointed by the Emperor were subordinated to the ministers, and became the local agents of execution of a highly centralized, para-military hierarchy. Quite naturally, throughout the reign of Alexander I, we witness an increasing monopolization of power and influence by governors and ministers, at the expense of the few institutions which could claim to represent the estates of the realm, as for example, the Senate, the marshals of the nobility, assemblies of the nobility, city assemblies and mayors. In turn, reliance on a centralized and hierarchical bureaucracy, led the Unofficial Committee to stress the need of preserving the autocratic power of the Emperor. Indeed, only the absolute power of a well-meaning, enlightened autocrat could bring about the necessary

---

1 Cf. the incisive judgment of Otto Hintze that Bonapartism is more an enlightened absolutism than a constitutional monarchical system; for France, Bonapartism (of Napoleon I, especially) has played the role enlightened absolutism had played in Prussia and Austria. O. Hintze, "Das monarchische Prinzip und die konstitutionelle Verfassung," *Staat und Verfassung (Gesammelte Abhandlungen zur allgemeinen Verfassungsgeschichte)*, (Leipzig 1941), pp. 349—379 (also in *Preussische Jahrbücher*, vol. 144, pp. 381—412). Tel'berg and Dovnar-Zapol'skii (*op. cit.*) have pointed out the bureaucratic and enlightened despotism features in the ideas of the Unofficial Committee members. Incidentally, we have in the text, preferred to use the phrase, "enlightened absolutism" which is more accurate than the contradictory "enlightened despotism" which has taken root in English historiography.

reforms in the face of a passive, or even unfriendly, nation. As Count Stroganov, the most "liberal" member of the Committee put it: "dans un pays despotique, ai-je lu quelque part, les changements sont bien plus faciles et bien moins dangereux, parce qu'il ne s'agit que de disposer de la volonté d'un seul. Tout le reste suit comme des moutons. Cette réflexion est bien juste et devrait rendre moins timide. Le tableau de notre noblesse ne doit pas paraître un parti bien dangereux." [1] The last sentence bespeaks the poor opinion the members of the Unofficial Committee had of the Russian nobility in general, and of the Senatorial party in particular.

The negative attitude towards the nobility as an "estate" gave further grounds for Alexander's belief in the leadership of a bureaucracy expressing the autocratic power and will of an enlightened sovereign. It points to a fundamental conception of political power, a conception which, as we shall have occasion to point out, runs as a guiding thread through the actions of the imperial government during the period of Speransky's activity. Novosiltsev hinted at it when he proposed to amend the Charter of the Nobility of 1785 in such a way as to "obliger la noblesse de sortir de l'ignorance dans laquelle elle croupit, en interdisant le droit de siéger dans les assemblées de la noblesse à ceux qui ne savent ni lire ni écrire et qui n'ont aucune idée des devoirs et des droits d'un gentilhomme." [2] Speaking for Alexander and the Unofficial Committee, Novosiltsev was here stating the pedagogical role of the government.

In passing, let us note two further characteristic traits of the Unofficial Committee's method, for we shall find them again when discussing the work of Speransky. First of all, the Committee laid down as an intangible rule and principle that all reforms were to be introduced in such a manner that there could be no doubt of their expressing only the will of the Emperor, and not that of any "party" or private interest. Secondly, the measures of reorganization were to be prepared in strict secrecy, without the participation of "society" and "public opinion" and issued all at once as the new and intangible law of the realm. [3] A far cry from the truly "liberal" and constitutional

---

1 *Comte Paul Stroganov*, II (annexe IX, Conférences avec l'Empereur 1801, No. 121, 18.XI.1801) pp. 62—63.

2 *Comte Paul Stroganov*, II (annexe IX, Conférences avec l'Empereur 1801, No. 112, 15.VII.1801) p. 37.

3 As Stroganov explained it: "Une loi dont le silence a couvert les préparatifs et qui sort de son sein sans avoir troublé le calme général par son attente, en offrant en même temps une obligation égale à tous, porte bien plus les caractères de cette grande loi de la nature, la necessité, contre laquelle les murmures, pour être infructueux, naissent et meurent presqu'en même temps, que celle qui ayant

approach in the West! It is interesting to observe also that in spite of their alleged partiality for things English, the Unofficial Committee found the best expression of their aims and the clearest statement of their purpose in the "constitution" of Prussia: an absolute monarchy ruling with the help of an efficient bureaucracy according to clearly defined laws which assured the security, life, property and freedom of economic action of the individual citizen.

The answer to our question, what was the meaning of Alexander's constitutionalism, is therefore quite clear. The Emperor and his close advisers in the Unofficial Committee defined constitution as the rule of law, and the clear, logical, hierarchical organization of the administration. Law, order, clear structure of the political machine were the contents they put into such words as constitution, fundamental laws, etc. At no time did they mean representative institutions, checks and balances, abolition of the autocracy — even though these might have been the long range dream, to come true for other generations; this conception and definition prevailed throughout the entire government career of Speransky.

True enough, such an approach might conceivably have brought about a true constitutional — in the modern sense — development. In this belief many "progressive" and truly liberal individuals in the 19th century in Russia spent all their energies in the service of an autocratic government. But today — with the superior benefit of hindsight — we can say that the hopes for such an evolution were doomed to failure as long as Russia's political transformation was directed by an all-powerful bureaucracy and at the mercy of the whim of an absolute ruler, with no social group or class strong enough to put a check on their despotism.

### SOURCES

On Paul I consult: M. V. Klochkov, *Ocherki pravitel'stvennoi deiatel'nosti vremeni Pavla I* (Petrograd 1916); S. Mel'gunov, "Istoricheskaia zagadka (Pavel I)," *Dela i liudi Aleksandrovskogo vremeni* (Berlin 1923), pp. 14–34; *Materialy dlia biografii imperatora Pavla I* (izd. E. Kasprovicha 1874 g.), reprinted Berlin n.d.; *Mémoires de l'Amiral Tchitchagoff 1767–1849* (Leipzig 1862).
The literature on Alexander I and his reign is immense; the

eu ses projets divulgués d'avance, aurait agité par l'incertitude inséparable d'une pareille imprudence et aurait eu à surmonter l'opposition que plus de discrétion simplement eut prévenue." *Comte Paul Stroganov*, II (annexe VIII, Principes de la réforme du gouvernement, No. 97: Plan général du travail avec l'Empereur pour la réforme, and No. 100: Essai sur le système à suivre dans la réformation de l'administration), p. 8.

following titles are of greatest value for our purposes: M. Bogdanovich, *Istoriia tsarstvovaniia imperatora Aleksandra I i Rossiia v ego vremia*, (6 vols. St. Pbg. 1869); I. A. Bychkov (ed.), "Aleksandr I i ego priblizhennye do epokhi Speranskogo," *Russkaia Starina*, 113 (Jan.-Feb. 1903) pp. 5—36, 211—234; M. V. Dovnar-Zapol'skii, *Obzor noveishei russkoi istorii*, vol. I (2d ed., Kiev 1914); Ar. Fatéev, "Le problème de l'individu et de l'homme d'état dans la personnalité historique d'Alexandre I, Empereur de toutes les Russies," *Zapiski nauchno-issledovatel'nogo ob'edineniia*, Russkii svobodnyi universitet v Prage, vols. III (1936), V (1937), XIV (1939); A. A. Kizevetter, "Aleksandr I," *Istoricheskie siluety, liudi i sobytiia* (Berlin 1931), pp. 124—145; S. Mel'gunov, "Imperator Aleksandr I," *Dela i liudi Aleksandrovskogo vremeni*, (Berlin 1923), pp. 35—114; A. E. Presniakov, *Aleksandr I*, (Petrograd 1924); Pierre Rain, *Un Tsar idéologue: Alexandre Ier (1777—1825)*, (Paris 1913); Th. Schiemann, *Geschichte Russlands unter Nikolaus I*, vol. I (*Kaiser Alexander I und die Ergebnisse seiner Lebensarbeit*), Berlin 1904; N. K. Shil'der, *Imperator Aleksandr Pervyi ego zhizn' i tsarstvovanie*, 4 vols. (2d ed. St. Pbg. 1904); M. I. Sukhomlinov, "Fridrikh-Tsezar' Lagarp," *Issledovaniia i stat'i*, vol. 2 (St. Pbg. 1889), pp. 35—205; Kenneth R. Whiting, *Aleksei Andreevich Arakcheev* (unpublished Ph. D. Thesis, Harvard University 1951 — used by kind permission of the author and the Chairman of the History Department, for which my thanks are rendered here.)

On Emperor Alexander's early reform projects and constitutionalism, see: M. V. Dovnar-Zapol'skii, "Zarozhdenie ministerstv v Rossii i ukaz o pravakh Senata 8. IX. 1802 g," *Iz istorii obshchestvennykh techenii v Rossii* (Kiev 1905), pp. 1—76; A. N. Fateev, "Bor'ba za ministerstva (epokha triumvirata)," *Sbornik statei posviashchennykh P. N. Miliukovu* (Praga 1929), pp. 405—433; A. N. Fateev, "Politicheskie napravleniia pervogo desiatiletiia XIX veka v bor'be za Senat," *Sbornik russkogo instituta v Prage*, I (1929), pp. 205—260; A. N. Filippov, "Istoricheskii ocherk obrazovaniia ministerstv v Rossii", *Zhurnal Ministerstva Iustitsii*, Sept. 1902, pp. 39—73 and Oct. 1902, pp. 1—26; S. A. Korf, *Dvorianstvo i ego soslovnoe upravlenie za stoletie 1762—1855 gg* (St. Pbg. 1906, especially Chs. V—VI); Nikolai Mikhailovich (velikii kniaz'), *Graf P. A. Stroganov 1774—1817 — istoricheskoe issledovanie epokhi imperatora Aleksandra I*, 3 vols. (St. Pbg. 1903 — I used the French edition: Grand Duc Nicolas Mikhailovitch, *Le Comte Paul Stroganov*, Paris 1905); B. E. Nol'de, "Sovet Ministrov", *Ocherki russkogo gosudarstvennogo prava* (St. Pbg. 1911), pp. 85—221; A. N. Pypin, *Obshchestvennoe dvizhenie v Rossii pri Aleksandre I* (St. Pbg. 1900); V. I. Semevskii, "Liberal'nye plany v pravitel'stvennykh sferakh v pervoi polovine tsarstvovaniia imperatora Aleksandra I", *Otechestvennaia voina i russkoe obshchestvo, vol. II* (Moscow 1912), pp. 152—194; V. I. Semevskii, "Vopros o preobrazovanii gosudarstvennogo stroia v Rossii v XVIII i v pervoi chetverti XIX veka," *Byloe* (1906), No. 3; S. M. Seredonin, *Istoricheskii obzor deiatel'nosti Komiteta Ministrov, tom I: Komitet Ministrov v tsarstvovanie imperatora Aleksandra I (1802, 8 sent. — 1825, noiabria 19)*, (St. Pbg. 1902); V. G. Shcheglov, *Gosudarstvennyi sovet v Rossii, v osobennosti v tsarstvovanie Aleksandra I*, vols. I—II (Iaroslavl', 1892—1896); V. M. Shtein, *Ocherki razvitiia russkoi obshchestvenno-ekonomicheskoi mysli XIX—XX vekov* (Leningrad 1948); P. B. Struve, "Istoricheskii smysl russkoi revoliutsii," *Sotsial'naia i ekonomicheskaia istoriia Rossii* (Paris 1952), pp. 310—316; S. Swatikow, *Die Entwürfe der Änderung der russischen Staatsverfassung*, (Heidelberg 1904); G. G. Tel'berg, "Proiskhozhdenie komiteta ministrov v Rossii", *Zhurnal Ministerstva Narodnogo Prosveshcheniia*, new series, part VIII (March 1907), pp. 38—62; G. G. Tel'berg, "Senat i 'pravo predstavleniia na vysochaishie ukazy' ", *Zhurnal Ministerstva Narodnogo Prosveshcheniia*, XXV (Jan. 1910), pp. 1—56; Georges Vernadsky, *La Charte Constitutionnelle de l'Empire russe de L'an 1820* (Paris 1933).

A. R. Vorontsov, "Primechanie o pravakh i preimushchestvakh Senata grafa A. R. Vorontsova," *Chteniia*, 48 (1864), Miscel. pp. 108—111; "Zapiska grafa A. R. Vorontsova o Rossii v nachale nyneshnego veka, predstavlennaia imperatoru Aleksandru Pavlovichu po vstuplenii v dolzhnost' Gosudarstvennogo Kantslera," *Arkhiv Vorontsovykh*, vol. 29 (1883), pp. 449—470; "Zapiska grafa S. R. Vorontsova o vnutrennem upravlenii v Rossii," *Arkhiv Vorontsovykh*, Vol. 15 (1880), pp. 441—452; P. V. Zavadovskii, "Mnenie o pravakh i preimushchestvakh Senata grafa Petra Vasil'evicha Zavadovskogo," *Chteniia*, 48 (1864), Miscel. pp. 100—107.

Further general information on the administration of the

Empire and the plans for its reorganization is to be found in
all the major treatises on Russian public law, as, for example: N. M. Korkunov,
*Russkoe gosudarstvennoe pravo*, 2 vols., St. Pbg. 1909; V. N. Latkin, *Uchebnik
istorii russkogo prava perioda imperii XVIII i XIX st.*, 2d ed., St. Pbg. 1909; N. I.
Lazarevskii, *Lektsii po russkomu gosudarstvennomu pravu*, — 2d ed., St. Pbg. 1910;
N. I. Lazarevskii, *Russkoe gosudarstvennoe pravo*, vol. I (Konstitusionnoe pravo), 3d
ed., St. Pbg. 1913; G. Vernadskii, *Ocherk istorii prava russkogo gosudarstva XVIII
i XIX vv.*, Praga 1924.

# CHAPTER III

# ADMINISTRATIVE ACTIVITIES 1802–1812

Whatever their differing views on the character of reform, everybody — from the Emperor down — agreed on one thing: the chaotic and cumbersome administrative structure of Russia had to be changed. For this difficult task, energetic and able functionaries were much needed, and Catherine's collaborators had the advantage of experience and eagerness to make a comeback after their eclipse under Paul I. Prominent among these old dignitaries was D. P. Troshchinskii, Procurator of the Senate under Catherine II, who was appointed Secretary of State and entrusted with the drafting of new decrees and legislation. Troshchinskii himself needed a capable and energetic younger assistant, and his choice fell on Speransky, who was the most gifted and promising junior functionary in the central administration.

A new period was beginning in Speransky's career, a period of intense and fruitful work for the improvement of Russia's central administration. During the first few years, from 1802 to 1807, Speransky was an important but still subordinate official; in that capacity he participated in the organization of the Ministry of the Interior, the reform of ecclesiastic education, and the formulation of the government's role in the country's economic development. In the following years, 1808 to 1812, he was the most intimate collaborator of Emperor Alexander I. In this capacity he devoted most of his creative energy to the working out of the basic schemes and plans for a thorough reorganization and transformation of Russia's central government institutions, the subject of later chapters. Besides this fundamental work of reform, however, Speransky was entrusted with a variety of other matters. They were of only peripheral and secondary concern to him, and his participation in them varied greatly; but they deserve some attention as they illustrate the wide range of his activities. The most significant areas of administration to which he made a contribution and which we propose to discuss briefly in the following pages, included such varied problems as the promotion of government officials, the establishment of a special school for noblemen, the drafting of a civil code, the organization of newly acquired Finland, and Russia's diplomacy and trade policy.

A decree dated 16 March 1801 transferred Speransky to the staff of Troshchinskii, and a few weeks later, on April 23, Speransky was put in charge of the Section for Civilian and Ecclesiastic Affairs of the newly reorganized Council of State. In this double capacity Speransky supervised the technical, bureaucratic aspects of a major portion of Russia's internal administration. His responsibility was to put the final touch to all state papers and reports submitted to the Emperor. Unfortunately our sources do not inform us about Speransky's personal contribution to the legislation and state papers in the first years of the new reign. Yet, his "editorial" role must have been great as can be gauged from the fact that Count S. Vorontsov's proposed draft of a Charter for the Russian people bears stylistic corrections in the hand of Speransky. [1]

The struggle between the "senatorial party" and the Emperor's younger friends in the Unofficial Committee was resolved by a compromise in the publication of two somewhat contradictory legislative acts in 1802. The first defined the privileges of the Senate, but it proved barren of any practical value when Count Severin Potocki put its provisions to a practical test. The second act, the manifesto of September 8, 1802, replaced the major colleges by ministries. Alexander's predilection for working with one individual at a time soon contributed to making the ministries the most important organs of the central administration. [2] The new ministers, too, needed competent assistants to give their institutions a good start. Count Kochubei, who had been appointed Minister of the Interior, immediately asked for the transfer of Speransky to his ministry as head of a department. Troshchinskii, whose role and influence were on the wane could not compete with Kochubei and had to consent — albeit reluctantly — to the loss of his

1 This has given rise to the legend that Speransky was the author of the Charter. Cf. V. P. Semennikov, *Radishchev: ocherki i issledovaniia*, (Petrograd 1923), pp. 177, 431, 433; G. Sacke, *Graf A. Voroncov, A. N. Radiščev und der 'Gnadenbrief für das russische Volk'*, Emsdetten 1939(?).

2 The appointment of members of the Unofficial Committee to the newly created ministries has led some historians to conclude that the origin and aim of the ministries had been to satisfy the ambitions of the members of the Unofficial Committee. Dovnar-Zapol'skii, "Zarozhdenie ministrov v Rossii...", *Iz istorii obshchestvennykh techenii v Rossii* (Kiev 1905), p. 18. This interpretation would bear out in Russia's case O. Hintze's conclusion that the ministries had their origin in the secret and private councils of the ruler, not in the regular feudal *Curia Regis* (or *Boiar Duma* in Moscow) — O. Hintze, "Die Entstehung der modernen Staatsministerien," *Staat und Verfassung* (Leipzig 1941) 265—310 (originally published in *Historische Zeitschrift*, vol. 100, pp. 53—111).

ablest assistant. Speransky was entrusted with the Second Department of the Ministry of the Interior which dealt with police functions and with the welfare of the realm. In other words, he became the chief of the central office dealing with all domestic affairs, a post he retained until 1807. In this capacity he participated in the drafting of some of the most important legislation in the first years of Alexander's reign. Unfortunately again we cannot always determine the extent of his personal participation and influence. All we know is that two important acts, the Law on the Free Agriculturists and the Statute on the Jews, were prepared in his department and received their final form under his direct supervision. [1] Furthermore, he was responsible for the internal organization of the Ministry. A firm believer in a clear and strict hierarchical "chain of command" for central government institutions he organized the Ministry along such lines (Statute of the Ministry of the Interior, July 1803, PSZ 20,852), which gave the various heads of departments and divisions full authority within their own spheres of competence and enabled them to act as expert advisers — staff officers — to the Minister. This organization served later as a model for the other ministries and as the basis for Speransky's general reorganization of the ministerial system in 1811. [2]

In the case of some measures, however, Speransky's initiative and role can be established with certainty. None of them can be counted among the most significant actions taken by the government at the time but they did initiate practices that survived for a long time. Moreover, they are quite characteristic of Speransky's thinking and methods. Although the periodical press had been introduced into Russia by Peter I, there was no official bulletin or newspaper through which the government could inform the country of its views and decisions. At a time when "public opinion" was becoming a factor to be taken into consideration, the periodical press was too good and effective a tool to be left unused. As a former teacher, Speransky clearly saw the

---

[1] S. M. Dubnow, *Die neueste Geschichte des jüdischen Volkes 1789/1914*, Bd. I, *Das Zeitalter der ersten Emanzipation 1789—1815* (Berlin 1920), Chapt. VI, § 47, pp. 293—300; S. M. Dubnow, *History of the Jews in Russia and Poland from the earliest times until the present day* (Transl. by I. Friedlaender), vol. I (From the Beginning until the death of Alexander I), (Philadelphia 1916), pp. 335—345; P. S. Usov, "Sluchai iz zhizni grafa M. Speranskogo", *Istoricheskii Vestnik*, X (1882) 721—722.

[2] Korkunov, *Gosudarstvennoe Pravo*, II, pp. 358—359; as Jacob characterized it: "Der grösste Theil der schönen Einrichtungen, welche dieses Ministerium [i.e. Ministry of the Interior under Kochubei] so rühmlich auszeichnete und die Aufmerksamkeit von ganz Europa auf dasselbe lenkte, war Speranskis Werk," *Denkwürdigkeiten*, 277. Cf. Storch, *Russland unter Alexander dem I*, vol. I, No. 3 (Nov.-Dec. 1803), pp. 393—410 and vol. II, No. 4, (1804), pp. 5—61, for the German version of the official notifications of these transformations.

immediate benefit and value the government could derive from an officially sponsored newspaper in the service of the new transformations and reforms. Consequently, he did much to establish the *Sankt Peter-burgskii Zhurnal* (St. Petersburg Journal), the first regular newspaper to be issued by the government. Besides reprinting official decrees and summaries of the most important public events, it also published articles — originals or translations — dealing with political and economic theory. [1] It was the first step in implementing the notion held by the enlightened despots and shared by Alexander I and his advisers, that the state should sponsor and guide the political and economic education of Russian "society" (*obshchestvo*).

Speransky also initiated the custom of presenting to the Emperor a yearly report of the activities and achievements of each ministry. His own Ministry of the Interior was the first to do so and, quite naturally, the report was written by Speransky himself, although under the supervision of Count Kochubei over whose signature it was submitted to Alexander I. The report, besides informing the monarch, served as a means for spreading new ideas among the members of the government. It can be viewed both as a summary of conditions and a blueprint for future action. Following a summary of the manifold activities of the Ministry, especially those which dealt with the preservation of law and order, the report presented some interesting considerations on Russia's economic progress and the role to be played in it by the government. Referring directly to the ideas of Adam Smith, Speransky wrote:

"There was a time when it was thought that the national economy could not prosper except under the direct supervision of the government, that the government must manage it, in one word maintain it in permanent tutelage. Most precise observation of the results of human labor and of the various methods for dividing and improving it has shown the error of this opinion and led to the establishment of another basis for the administration of the national economy. The rule is now accepted that need and private interests can direct human activity in industry and the economy better than all government measures. Therefore, the government should be only a spectator of private efforts in this field; it should have accurate information on these efforts and, without restricting them by any kind of direct control, remove

---

[1] Some important economic, statistical, and legal works appeared there. B. S. Osherovich, *Ocherki po istorii russkoi ugolovno-pravovoi mysli* (Moscow 1946), p. 15; V. M. Shtein, *Ocherki razvitiia russkoi obshchestvenno-ekonomicheskoi mysli XIX—XX vekov* (Leningrad 1948), p. 22; Storch, *op. cit.*, vol. II, No. 4, pp. 178—180. See also Orlov, *Russkie prosvetiteli 1790—1800kh godov*, pp. 448—449 (note 41).

from their path all obstacles which might stop them. Everything forces us to prefer this latter principle to the former: the experience of the states where all the areas of economic activity have been brought to perfection, allows no doubt as to its correctness. But in Russia, perhaps, some qualifications should be made to it [principle of free economic activity]. When the national industry, strengthened by time and conditions, will have reached, so to say, its full maturity, it can and must be allowed to proceed alone, its path being supervised only from afar. But in its early beginnings, when its weak forces do not allow the consolidation of its enterprises, when experience has not yet fully clarified its prospects; when many areas of the economy are yet unknown — the government has the obligation to guide it [the nation's industry], to show where its advantages lie, to promote it through encouragement and even — where there is lack of capital — to give it subsidies. Therefore, the three main principles which have guided me [Kochubei] in my report to Your Majesty on problems of national economy have been: to collect as much correct data as possible about all types of enterprises, to encourage those [industries] which have not reached their full strength, and, finally, to remove from their path everything that could hamper or stop them." [1]

This lengthy passage throws much interesting light on the thinking of Speransky (and other high officials) on the relationship between political power and economic activity. His ultimate aim is freedom for individual economic activity, the restriction of the state's role to that of "night watchman", at least in this particular area of national life. It was an ideal which he had taken from the more progressive thinkers of Western Europe whose efficacy he had found proven by the results achieved in those countries which had made the principle of free enterprise their own — England in particular. And yet, following the preconceptions of enlightened absolutism and bowing to Russian administrative tradition, doubtful of Russia's abilities of developing a high level of economic activity — largely because of many legal and social restrictions which Speransky was tactful enough to pass in silence — he felt that the state had to "educate" the country for economic freedom. It was up to the government to show the way and to support actively the nation's economic and industrial development

---

[1] "Doklad Ministra Vnutrennikh Del, 1803," *Zhurnaly Komiteta Ministrov*, I, Appendix 1, p. 61. The German text is in Storch, *op. cit.*, vol. VI No. 16, (Jan. 1805), pp. 1—148 (our quotation is on pp. 53—54). Some interesting details on the early penetration of A. Smith's ideas in Russia can be found in I. S. Bak, "Obshchestvennoekonomicheskie vozzreniia I. A. Tret'iakova," *Voprosy Istorii* (Sept. 1954), pp. 104—113.

through bureaucratic, paternalistic legislation. In so doing Speransky was at one with the bureaucratic prejudices of Alexander I and the Unofficial Committee. How individual initiative and free economic activity were to develop under the shadow of an omnipotent bureaucratic state, Speransky did not make clear in his report. Perhaps the young official was not aware of the inherent contradiction or, to say the least, lack of clarity in his position. We shall again meet this fundamental conflict between political means and economic ends in Speransky's thought and acts. An inconsistency which persisted in the thinking of most Russian political leaders throughout the 19th century and found its reflection in the legislation of the Imperial government.

As energetic and able an official as Speransky could not be contented with mere routine work. And the times, too, were such as to excite and spur on political talent; administrative reform was on everybody's lips and the ever-present preoccupation of all officials. Projects were drafted, and reform plans proposed not only by those whose official business it was, but also by many private individuals who thought they had something to contribute. Speransky could not remain a passive bystander; he was too close to this ferment of minds and too ambitious and eager to play a more significant role. Nor were his superiors averse to using his facile and elegant pen; they commissioned him to write projects which they later submitted to the Emperor. Speransky was always willing and ready to oblige. In 1802 he wrote an analysis and critique of conditions in the administration; in 1803, at the behest of a member of the Unofficial Committee (probably Count Kochubei), he formulated his own considerations on the state of Russia and his suggestions for reform. As far as we know, neither of these papers found any practical application, but they gave their author a chance to make a systematic exposition of his ideas on government and administration. As their interest and significance are mainly theoretical, we shall reserve their discussion for a later chapter.

The outstanding qualities of the young department chief at the Ministry of the Interior did not remain hidden from the Emperor. In 1807, Alexander had the opportunity of appreciating Speransky's talents in person, when Count Kochubei — confined to his home by illness — delegated Speransky to make the weekly oral report on the affairs of the Ministry. The Emperor was much impressed by Speransky's clear and elegant verbal exposition of intricate and dry matters and by the speed and efficiency of his paper work. He decided to keep the young official near his person, as his chief administrative secretary and assistant. In this new capacity, Speransky accompanied the Emperor to the meeting with Napoleon at Erfurt in 1808. Contemporary rumor had it that at Erfurt Speransky fell under the spell of Napoleon and French institutions. The story is told that soon after their arrival in Erfurt, Alexander asked his secretary what he thought of the French and Western European political systems; to this Speransky is alleged to have replied, "Their institutions are better, but we have the better people". Supposedly Alexander rejoined that this was his opinion too and that they would talk about it later ("nous en recauserons"). This incident, nowhere substantiated in contemporary documents, was probably fabricated in support of the belief that Speransky had fallen for the blandishments of the French. To anyone familiar with the attitudes of Alexander and Speransky, their alleged high opinion of the Russian bureaucratic personnel is, to say the least, highly implausible; and however much they might have been impressed by French institutions, they would hardly have compared them to the personnel of Russia. Moreover, Speransky was not at all ignorant of French institutions before he went to Erfurt; had he succumbed to their attraction at all, it would have been before the trip. Speransky's yielding to Napoleon's and Talleyrand's blandishments or bribery must be rejected as either legend or idle gossip. [1]

After their return from Erfurt, Speransky emerged as the most trusted and intimate collaborator of Alexander I on domestic political and administrative matters. As the Sardinian ambassador, Count Joseph de Maistre, described it, "le grand et tout puissant Speransky, Sécrétaire-Général de l'Empire, et dans le fait premier Ministre et peut-être même Ministre unique." [2] However, Speransky's official rank remained a modest one; he was relieved of his duties as chief of the Second Department of the Ministry of the Interior and appointed Assistant Minister of Justice in charge of codification and, later, State Secretary. But the range of his activities was almost universal and embraced nearly all aspects of Russia's administration and policy, the great exceptions being the military and, to some extent, diplomatic fields. There hardly was a significant administrative measure between 1808 and 1812 in the preparation of which Speransky did not participate. However, his participation was not significant enough in every case to detain us here. As this period of his most active

[1] Vandal's belief that Alexander took Speransky to Erfurt so that the latter could study the French governmental system is not supported by the evidence. Anyway, Vandal is not too reliable on the Russian domestic scene. Vandal, *Napoléon et Alexandre I*, vol. I, p. 408.
[2] Joseph de Maistre, *Oeuvres complètes — Correspondance*, vol. IV (Paris 1884—93), No. 304 (dated 2/21 April 1812), pp. 101—102.

participation in the government covered only a few years (1808—1812), we need not follow a strict chronological order in describing his work.

The reign of Alexander I looms as one of the significant periods in the history of Russian education. The burst of energy and enthusiasm in the first years of the reign resulted in a liberal statute for the universities, the founding of new schools of higher learning, and the opening of several institutions for secondary and technical education. [1] Speransky did not participate directly in these educational reforms which were the work of the most prominent and "progressive" friends of the Emperor, Count Stroganov and Prince Czartoryski. [2] Following upon the reorganization of the secular school system, the government turned its attention to the pitiful state of the schools for the clergy, the theological seminaries. Already Paul I had indicated his intention of improving the situation by increasing the budget for ecclesiastical affairs, but he had had no time to go further. The problem was particularly pressing, for it was in the schools run by the clergy that the majority of Russians received their rudiments of learning. We have already noted the fact that an ever-increasing number of the lower and middle bureaucracy was being recruited from among the students of theological seminaries. The government service's self interest required that these seminaries furnish adequate instruction and preparation for those who would be called to leadership, in the spiritual or bureaucratic fields. Finally, with the establishment of secular secondary and primary schools, the parish schools had become the lowest rung of the regular educational ladder.

In 1807, by the decree of November 29, Alexander I established a mixed commission of laymen and clergy and directed it to submit a plan for the complete overhauling of the ecclesiastical system of education. [3] It was a foregone conclusion that Speransky would be appointed to this commission, for what other prominent official possessed both a direct and intimate knowledge of the theological

1 For a brief summary in English of the reforms of education in the reign of Alexander I, see William H. E. Johnson, *Russia's Educational Heritage* (Carnegie Press, Pittsburgh, Pa., 1950), pp. 63—86.

2 Speransky's friends Martynov and Karazin were members of the Glavnoe Pravlenie Uchilishch and could, therefore, have given him first-hand accounts of this body's work and accomplishments. Cf. S. Rozhdestvenskii (ed.), *Istoricheskii obzor deiatel'nosti Ministerstva Narodnogo Prosveshcheniia 1802—1902* (St. Pbg. 1902), p. 37; M. Sukhomlinov, "Materialy dlia istorii obrazovanii v Rossii...", *Issledovaniia i stat'i po russkoi literature i prosveshcheniiu, I* (St. Pbg. 1889), p. 25.

3 The Commission consisted of: Metropolitan Ambrosius, Bishop Theophilactus, Speransky, Prince Golitsyn, Father Ioan Derzhavin, Krinitskii — PSZ 23,122. For details, including a list of subjects taught, see Storch, *op. cit.*, Vol. IX, No. 25 (Nov. 1806), pp. 83—85 ("Kurze Übersicht aller Bildungsanstalten für die Geistlichkeit").

schools and a thorough understanding of the government's aims and principles? The Commission went to work with great alacrity and by 1808 it had drafted a plan of reforms which was approved by the Emperor.

The condition of the theological seminaries had not improved since the time Speransky had been a student. They had been hampered in their development and progress mainly by two factors: lack of funds and a poor organization and geographic distribution. Not every diocese could boast of even one school at each level of the educational ladder. Some had no complete secondary theological seminaries, only the lower forms. Very few had advanced schools. Some districts even lacked elementary schools. There was no rhyme nor reason in the administrative organization and the hierarchical subordination of the various schools. Some depended on the local bishop, others on the archbishop in another province; and still others were directly under the Holy Synod. We have already had occasion to mention the inadequacy of funds. Since 1797 the yearly budget for 115 schools with about 29,000 students was 180,000 rubles, and though in 1807 Alexander raised it to 338,863 rubles, it was still far from adequate. With the accession of Alexander the clergy, too, was fired with the desire to do something about the situation and several reform projects were written. In 1804 Metropolitan Ambrosius received permission from the Emperor to submit an outline of the reforms he thought were necessary. In the course of the following years several other projects were submitted, the most important among them being that of Bishop Eugene. Bishop Eugene was the first to suggest the abolition of the old system under which the theological seminary included all levels of instruction for the clergy, with the exception of the very first rudiments of reading and writing which were imparted by priests in the villages. He proposed the establishment of three separate types of clerical schools to parallel the three major divisions of secular education: primary, secondary and higher. This principle was adopted by the Commission of 1808 and served as the basis for the new system.

The labors of the Commission on Ecclesiastical Schools resulted in a set of regulations issued by Imperial decree on June 26, 1808 (PSZ 23,122). The essence of this reorganization, which remained in force throughout the 19th century, was briefly as follows. The secular school system (as set up by PSZ 20,597) was paralled by the establishment of four academies for advanced theological studies (with a 4 year curriculum), one theological seminary in each diocese (4 year curriculum), equivalent to the secondary schools set up in each provincial capital, and, finally, district schools (2 year curriculum), varying in number from 10 to 30 per diocese, on the same level as primary schools. The student body, as formerly, was composed of the children of the clergy who were expected to follow their fathers' profession. A serious effort was made to give the prospective priests a good general academic education in addition to the specialized training of their future calling. For this purpose, the curriculum of the primary and secondary levels was expanded to include new subjects of general educational value (natural sciences, modern languages) and restricted so far as the narrowly theological and clerical subjects were concerned. The curriculum of the academies and of the upper classes of metropolitan seminaries was made frankly "professional", with courses in exegesis, apologetics, theology, church history, intensive study of Greek and Slavonic (as well as Latin). However, on all levels, there took place a modernization of method and contents, with greater emphasis given to modern languages, mathematics, and natural sciences, all of which were made compulsory.

Speransky's personal influence was clearly felt throughout all the labors of the Commission. He worked to secure a greater uniformity of ability and achievement among the student body by insisting that a student's promotion from one level to the other should depend on his performance at periodic examinations. The caliber of the teaching staff was improved by the setting of definite and uniform standards, and each candidate's qualifications were to be tested before he was allowed to teach. From the administrative point of view, order was brought about by subjecting the district and diocesan schools (i.e. primary and secondary levels) to the authority of the local bishop and by establishing separate school budgets for each diocese. The inner administration of each school was left in the hands of the regular teaching staff. The four academies were under the direct supervision of the Holy Synod and also allowed a large measure of internal administrative autonomy (on the model of the University statute of 1804).

These educational and administrative reforms would have remained a dead letter had not the ecclesiastic schools also been given a stronger economic foundation. The state had little to spare, it felt, from its own resources and was very reluctant to grant even an absolute minimum. Speransky realized that it was of the utmost importance that the reformed ecclesiastical schools have a regular and dependable source of revenue, unaffected by the fluctuations in the policy, personnel, and financial condition of the government. The solution he proposed was quite simple and proved to be very successful. [1] The idea was to restore to the Church its traditional monopoly of the sale of wax candles. This pivilege had lapsed some time in the 18th century, probably as a result of Peter the Great's fiscal needs. Speransky's scheme, approved by the Emperor and embodied in the decree of June 26, 1808, provided that part of the revenue from this monopoly be set aside and allowed to earn interest (by being "placed" with the government). At the conclusion of a six year period, the accumulated interest and the original capital were to form a reserve fund for expanding the Church's school system, while the regular yearly revenue from the monopoly was to be used for the current expenditures of operation. The new budget was estimated at 1.7 million rubles, a far cry from the 180,000 or 338,000 previously doled out by the state! The scheme worked very well, and soon the Church had a sizeable surplus for the needs of its schools and other institutions.

Not the least important aim of this reform was to provide the Church with a body of servants, priests, and hierarchs, capable of, and worthy of, ministering to the religious and spiritual needs of the people. As in so many other domains, the requirements of the country had outstripped the means of the institutions to satisfy them, and the Church was no exception to this. Especially pressing was the need for well trained and educated members of the upper ranks of the ecclesiastic hierarchy. [2] The establishment of four theological academies had been in response to this need, and as a former student of a higher theological school Speransky was asked to write the detailed statutes for the academies. Speransky consented to take on this task, but pointed out that regulations written *in abstracto* were of but little value if they could not be corrected and amended in the light of experience. He therefore advised — and his suggestion was accepted by both the Commission and the Emperor — that as a first step, a set of regulations be drafted for the Alexandro-Nevskii Academy only. After a short test period, the rules could be revised if necessary and extended to the other theological academies. This was a novel approach in the history of Russian administration, for until then, statutes had been issued for immediate execution, and any inconveniences revealed by experience were corrected — if at all — much too late, by new laws which

[1] The idea, it is true, had been suggested earlier by Anastas Bratanevskii in his comments on the reform project of Eugene, vicar to Metropolitan Ambrosius. However, Speransky was the first to formulate it clearly and implement it; and, therefore, deserves almost full credit for it. Titlinov, *Dukhovnye shkoly v XIXm stotelii*, p. 26.

[2] The ground had been prepared in PSZ 23,122 which provided for preferential treatment and promotion in the ecclesiastic hierarchy for holders of the degree of doctor of theology (PSZ, 23,122 — page 376 of vol. 30).

frequently conflicted with the original statutes. We may mention in passing, that Speransky had occasion to advocate a similar pragmatic and practical approach to legislation later, in connection with his more fundamental reform projects. His willingness to put to the test of practical life concepts and legislation based on considerations of theory and historical experience clearly shows that the usual characterization of Speransky as an abstract theoretican and *idéologue* must be strongly qualified.

Unfortunately for Russia, the Church was not alone in experiencing a lack of competent servants. The need was equally great in all branches of the state administration, especially in the lower and middle ranks of the bureaucracy. It was obvious that no reform or reorganization would bring the expected results unless a serious effort were made at educating better officials to implement them. This had been one of the important purposes of the reform of secular education in 1803—1804. But only institutions of higher learning had been reformed; and even these did not play the role destined them because of the woeful inadequacy of the secondary schools. For this reason, the suggestion of the Governor of New Russia, the Duke de Richelieu, to open a lycée on the French model received a warm welcome among Alexander's advisers. As Count Kochubei put it to Speransky — since 1809 a member of the Administration of Schools: "it is not universities, especially universities on the German model, that we need when there is no one to study at them; what we need are primary and secondary schools ... The system of the lycées is the best which can be adopted for Russia." [1]

The idea of a lycée found its expression in a creation which was to exert a great influence on the educational and cultural development of Russia: the Lycée at Tsarskoe Selo. For a long time there had been a desire to establish a special school to prepare young noblemen for careers in the civil and judicial administration, on the model of the Cadet Schools for the military and naval branches. Such a school became a pressing need at the end of the 18th century when a greater number of competent and educated noblemen was required to staff the administrative institutions created by Catherine II. An attempt at meeting this problem was made in 1804 by the creation of a law school connected with the Senate. But the experiment was not very successful, and the school was soon closed. The matter received new and serious consideration when Alexander I decided to give his younger brothers an education that would bring them into contact with young people

[1] Rozhdestvenskii, *Istoricheskii obzor Ministerstva Nar. Prosv.*, p. 76.

of their own age destined for careers in the government. The idea of a restricted school for future governors was also warmly welcomed by those who had fallen under the influence of Catholicism and who wished to see the Russian nobility educated in the great tradition of the Jesuit schools for the aristocracy. The Catholic party was quite strong at court and counted among its members some very influential dignitaries, e.g. the Minister of Education, Count A. K. Razumovskii, a close friend of Joseph de Maistre, and a patron of the Jesuits, who had been responsible for securing wide privileges for the Jesuit Academy in Polotsk.

Thus a variety of motives and considerations combined in support of the creation of a Lycée near the capital, under the direct supervision of the Emperor and the Court. The true authorship of the regulations and statute for the Lycée is still in doubt, but probably — as most legislation of that period — it was due to the combined efforts of several persons. The final draft of the regulations was written by I. Martynov, a former classmate's of Speransky at the Alexandro-Nevskii seminary, who was now a high official at the Ministry of Education. But most likely Martynov only gave literary and "bureaucratic" form to the ideas of all those who participated in the elaboration of the regulations. Officially, credit for the Lycée's organization was taken by the Minister of Education. However, later in a letter written to his friend and business agent from exile, Speransky maintained that he had been the real author of the statute for the *Tsarsko-Sel'skii Litsei*. [1] The Lycée's report for the year 1849—1850 reaffirmed Speransky's authorship, but modern investigators have so far failed to uncover the original draft of the statutes written by Speransky. [2]

Whatever the truth of the matter — and it cannot be established to our satisfaction at the moment — Speransky did exercise an appreciable influence on the pedagogical principles adopted for the Lycée. On December 11, 1808, he read to the Emperor a paper entitled "Preliminary rules for a *special* lycée." [3] Probably the paper was written

---

[1] Letter from Velikopol'e (Speransky's estate near Novgorod), dated 4 February 1815: "This school [the Tsarsko-Sel'skii lycée] was organized and its statute written by me, although others appropriated this work..." *Druzheskie pis'ma k P. G. Masal'skomu*, p. 65. A recent biographer of Alexandre Rennenkampf states that Rennenkampf talked to Speransky about his project of a special school for future officials; the conversation took place in 1810 upon Rennenkampf's return from study abroad. Jean Savant, *Alexandre de Rennenkampf et ses amis* (Paris 1946) p. 47.

[2] I. Ia. Seleznev, *Istoricheskii ocherk Imperatorskogo byvshego Tsarskosel'skogo nyne Aleksandrovskogo litseia za pervoe ego 50-i letie s 1811 po 1861 g.* (St. Pbg. 1861), p. 8.

[3] D. F. Kobeko, *Imperatorskii Tsarskosel'skii litsei* (St. Pbg. 1911), pp. 6—7.

in response to Alexander's desire to plan the education of his younger
brothers, grand-dukes Nicholas and Michael. In this paper, accessible
to us only through the summary in Kobeko's book, Speransky envisaged
the creation of a small school for about 15 students between the ages
of 10 and 12. He stressed very strongly a well-rounded general academic
education, with special attention paid to Russian language, rhetoric,
and physical sciences, more particularly mathematics. The school was
to do more than dispense factual knowledge and foster the pupils'
intellectual development; it was also to mold character. To this end,
all the daily activities of the students were to be supervised carefully
and constantly; their moral growth was to be fostered by close contacts
with the teachers. To facilitate these contacts, Speransky suggested
having one tutor for every four boys, in addition to the regular teaching
staff. In setting forth his pedagogical ideas, Speransky drew heavily on
the provisional regulations he had written for the Alexandro-Nevskii
Academy. It was wrong, Speransky suggested, to clutter up memory
with lengthy arguments learned by rote; on the contrary, the pupils
should be encouraged to express their own ideas. The task of the
teacher is not so much to impart fixed knowledge as to plant the seeds
for further intellectual growth, to develop the receptivity of the minds. [1]
Any educated and civilized human being should possess high qualities
of mind and character, but these were particularly important to the
future official in whose hands lay the happiness and fate of many
people. The prospective governor of men should have "une tête bien
faite plutôt que bien pleine", so as to be able to study further, to
reason independently, and to take the initiative, instead of relying on
a parrot-like imitation of poorly understood regulations and a blind
obedience to his superiors' orders. Such an education, moreover, was
essential for those who were to play the role of "public opinion" and
assist the absolute monarch with their information of local conditions
and advice. In other words, for Speransky, this *"special"* school was
another manifestation of the government's role of pedagogical and
moral leadership for the nation. Some of these views were incorporated,
albeit in a more limited and conservative form, in the rules for the
Lycée at Tsarskoe-Selo, even if Speransky himself did not participate
directly in the drafting of the final statute. His ideas were known to
the Emperor, and from all evidence, favorably received. In addition,

---

[1] However commonplace these ideas may sound today, we should not forget that
in Russia, Speransky was one of the first and systematic exponents of a modern
pedagogical approach which, no doubt, he had derived — at least in part — from
Rousseau, Pestalozzi, Monge, and the "progressive" educators of his day.

the main *rédacteur* of the statute was Martynov who often consulted Speransky for guidance and advice. [1]

However, these pedagogical principles — as carried out in the Lycée — were not readily accepted by everybody in St. Petersburg. In particular, the "liberal" and progressive features of the Lycée's curriculum found no sympathy with those who had wanted to introduce the educational philosophy of the Jesuits. These circles pursued the Lycée, its founders, staff, and pupils with unrelenting hatred. The point of their attacks was directed against Speransky, the reputed author of those features which even the influence of Count A. Razumovskii had proven incapable of eliminating (in particular the stress on the natural sciences). Denunciation of his pedagogical ideas and pernicious influence on Russian youth became a part of the campaign of calumny directed at Speransky in the following years. For instance, Joseph de Maistre, blaming enlightened and rational education for all the political evils of his day, expounded the view that Speransky had destined the Lycée for bringing up a generation that would subvert the traditional order of autocracy in Russia. [2] In this way way the foundation of the school, one of the centers of Russia's literary and cultural development in the 19th century, served to undermine the position of Speransky who, in any case, was but indirectly responsible for it. So deeply ingrained was the belief that Speransky was the creator of the Lycée and promoter of of its evil liberal, rationalistic, and sceptical spirit that Metternich, repeating de Maistre's argument, blamed the secret societies, discovered in the 1820's, on the Lycée and Speransky.[3]

Better schools for the future officials of the Empire were only one condition for a general reform and reorganization of the administration and its personnel. The most important stumbling block to any improvement lay in the very foundation of Russia's bureaucracy: the Table of Ranks of Peter the Great. True enough, the Table of Ranks

[1] Kolbasin, "I. I. Martynov — perevodchik grecheskikh klassikov", *Sovremennik*, (March—April 1859), p. 41.

[2] Joseph de Maistre, "Cinq lettres sur l'éducation publique en Russie, à Monsieur le comte Rasoumowski, ministre de l'instruction publique (Juin 1810)," *Oeuvres complètes*, VIII (Paris 1884), pp. 163—232; Ar. Fatéev, "La disgrâce d'un homme d'état. (à l'occasion du centenaire de la mort de Spéransky en 1839)", I, *Zapiski russkogo nauchno-issledovatel'skogo ob'edineniia v Prage* vol. X (old series vol. XV), Praha 1940, pp. 38—39. On Jesuit educational activities in Russia, see M. J. Rouet de Journel, *Un collège de Jésuites à Saint Petersbourg 1800—1816*, (Paris 1922).

[3] See the interesting dispatch of Metternich to the Austrian ambassador to St. Petersburg, Count Lebzeltern, dated 17 April 1826. Metternich writes, entre autres: "Je viens de réclamer de M. de Hauenschild [who had been director of the Lycée's boarding school] une histoire détaillée de l'établissement du Lycée de Zarskoie-Selo. Elle devra offrir beaucoup d'intérêt et fournir la clef du phénomène, que ce sont, pour ainsi dire, les propres enfants de l'infortuné Alexandre, qui avaient juré sa ruine et jusqu'à son assassinat." Kobeko, *op. cit.*, p. 260.

had performed a significant and useful function at the beginning of the 18th century in helping to destroy the *mestnichestvo* traditions and to instill a new outlook in the service nobility. But by the time of the first decade of the 19th century the situation had changed. The Table of Ranks had become a dead weight and handicap to good administration, for it put a premium on length of service rather than ability. Frequently it served to undermine the spirit of competition and pride in good performance, for certain ranks could be secured automatically, independently of accomplishments. Worst of all, the Table of Ranks killed all incentive for learning and self-improvement, as promotions and responsible assignments bore no relationship to the official's knowledge, only to his titular rank.

Himself a bureaucrat risen from the ranks, Speransky saw more clearly than anyone that an efficient bureaucracy depended upon the officials' knowledge and formal training. Education and learning must be encouraged among the bureaucracy; promotions should depend on knowledge and the quality of performance, not the lenghth of service. This program Speransky tried to put into practice, of course only gradually and cautiously, as many powerful interests were involved. True to his own bureaucratic pattern and bent of mind, he suggested that the first steps be taken within the existing framework of the Table of Ranks. Bolstered by the Emperor's support, he prepared two decrees which further contributed to rendering his name odious to the nobility. The first, dated April 3, 1809 (PSZ 23,559) required that all those who held the honorific title of Gentleman of the Chamber *(Kamerger)* either actually perform the duties appertaining to the title, or else transfer to some other active service — civilian or military — if they wished to retain their rank. Needless to say, this measure provoked the bitter anger of the courtiers. Not unjustifiably, Speransky was blamed for it, and numerous new enemies with powerful support at Court were added to the growing list of his ill-wishers. The second decree, August 6, 1809 (PSZ 23,771) went further still, although it harked back to the original intention of Peter the Great. It stipulated that before any official could be promoted to the rank equivalent to that of a staff officer — Collegiate Assessor, the 8th rank *(chin)* — or general officer — State Councillor, the 5th rank — he had to pass satisfactorily an examination which would test his general education and knowledge of essential subjects, for instance Russian, mathematics, Latin, modern languages. The shock and fearful indignation with which such an innovation was greeted by the nobility is easy to imagine. Particularly bitter were the officials from among the small nobility who had received but little education in their youth, had risen to their present rank by virtue of mere seniority, and now saw their hope of retiring with an esteemed rank and adequate pension suddenly imperiled by the policies of an upstart, a priest's son, a *popovich*. The two decrees, more than anything else, contributed to isolating Speransky and to putting him in a most exposed social and political position, while at the height of his influence with the Emperor. [1]

Even the best trained bureaucracy needs clear and precise rules and laws to administer effectively. This fundamental tenet had been well known to 18th century Western statesmanship, and it had been no accident that the bureaucratic enlightened absolutism of Frederick II and Joseph II sponsored the codification of laws, to guide their officials so that they would rule on the basis of law (*Rechtsstaat*). [2] Russia, however, possessed no up-to-date, complete, and easily accessible collection of laws and regulations to direct the functionaries in the performance of their duties, be they executive or judicial. The most recent code of Russian law dated back to 1649. But since that time Russia had undergone a profound transformation at the hands of Peter I and Catherine II, and the country was governed on the basis of decrees, laws and regulations issued after 1649. There was no reliable collection of the laws and decrees in force; the legislative acts were widely scattered among many offices, archives, and ministries. Conflicts and contradictions — the inevitable result of piecemeal legislation — had not been eliminated nor reconciled. Even the judges on the bench were often ignorant of very important legislation and not infrequently decided cases on the basis of obsolete and conflicting statutes. The senate, acting as highest court of review, was flooded with cases which could not be decided because of conflicting legal norms and lack of uniform procedure. It was imperative to bring some order into this chaos. Since Peter the Great, Russian monarchs had been keenly aware of the

[1] For instance, Count S. R. Vorontsov wrote to his son, M. S. Vorontsov, in 1812: "Le prince Koutousoff et le comte Rostopchine jouent des rôles brilliants et honorables de Pozharskii, quoiqu'ils ne savent pas plus de latin que leur modèle, en dépit de l'opinion de l'illustre Speranskoi, qui a décidé qu'un gentilhomme russe n'est bon à rien s'il ne sait pas le latin, et cela afin de remplacer la noblesse par des *popovichi* [sons of priests], des fils de *d'iachok* [sexton] et des *ponomar'* [lector] qui ont appris cette langue dans les séminaires. Ce Speransky et les pauvres ministres qui l'ont soutenu, ont fait l'impossible pour exaspérer cette noblesse vraiment noble." Letter dated Londres, 20 Novembre 1812, No. 134 — P. Bartenev (ed.) *Arkhiv Kniazia Vorontsova*, vol. 17, p. 255. Cf. also: D. P. Runich, "Iz zapisok D. P. Runicha," *Russkaia Starina*, vol. 105 (January—March 1901), p. 353; A. Ia. Bulgakov, "Vyderzhki iz zapisok Aleksandra Iakovlevicha Bulgakova 1811—1812," *Russkii Arkhiv*, 1867, pp. 1367—1368; A. Ia. Bulgakov, "Iz zapisok A. Ia. Bulgakova (o 1812m g.)," *Russkii Arkhiv*, (1900), pp. 14—17.

[2] P. Klassen, *Die Grundlagen des aufgeklärten Absolutismus* (List Studien — Untersuchungen zur Geschichte der Staatswissenschaften, Heft 4), Jena 1929, pp. 22, 115.

situation and had made many attemps to deal with it by establishing numerous commissions, committees, and conferences to codify the law of the Empire. [1] But not one of the codification commissions — there had been nine in the 18th century alone — had ever completed its assignment or even materially contributed to the improvement of the situation.

Determined to reform and reorganize the administration of the realm along clear, legal, bureaucratic lines, Alexander I felt that it was essential to order Russian law. In 1801 he decided on the establishment of a new Commission on Laws (the 10th) and explained his motives in a rescript to Count Zavadovskii, the President of the Commission, dated June 5, 1801:

> "Basing the foundation and source of the people's happiness in a *single law;* convinced that while other measures can bring happiness to the state, only the *law* can secure it for centuries, I felt the imperative need — from the very first days of my reign and my first study of the administration — to become acquainted with the true situation in this field. I have always known that from the publication of the *Ulozhenie* [Code of 1649] to our days, i.e. for about a century and a half, the laws which the legislative power had issued in various and frequently contradictory manner — and usually for specific cases and not on the basis of general considerations — had no connection with each other, no unity of purpose, no permanence in their effect.
>
> From this there has resulted a general confusion of the rights and obligations of everyone; a darkness which envelops judge and accused alike; an impotence in the execution of the laws; and a convenience in changing the laws at the first impulse of caprice or arbitrariness." [2]

The Commission was established and given its organization by the decree of August 25, 1801 (PSZ 19,989). In spite of the Emperor's active and interested support, its work did not proceed any more satisfactorily than that of its numerous predecessors. The first impulse of the Commission to collect and order all existing laws was abandoned as a

---

[1] A full bibliography on the history of Russian codification will be found in Chapter XI.

[2] Shil'der, *Imperator Aleksandr I,* vol. II, p. 22. The "rescript" is also quoted *in extenso* in P. M. Maikov, "Kommissiia sostavleniia zakonov pri imperatorakh Pavle I i Aleksandre I," *Zhurnal Ministerstva Iustitsii,* VII, (Sept. 1905), pp. 272—276. Compare Alexander's words to Turgot's a generation before: "Votre Majesté, tant qu'elle ne s'écartera pas de la justice, peut se regarder comme un législateur absolu... Vous êtes forcé de statuer sur tout, et le plus souvent par des volontés particulières, tandis que vous pourriez gouverner comme Dieu par des lois générales..." A. Turgot, "Mémoires sur les municipalités," in G. Schelle (ed.), *Turgot: Oeuvres et documents le concernant,* vol. 4 (Paris 1922), No. 188, p. 576.

result of Prince Lopukhin's suggestion (embodied in PSZ 21,187, February 28, 1804) to elaborate the *"principia juris,"* first. This led to an impasse as the government and the Commission could not formulate such principles. At this point the the chairmanship of the Commission passed to Novosiltsev who appointed the German Baltic Baron Rosenkampf as head of the working staff. Baron Rosenkampf, though he had received excellent training in jurisprudence in Germany, and was an able and learned man, was quite unsuited for the task, as he was not familiar with Russian law, Russian conditions, or even the Russian language. He was an ardent proponent of the historical and practical approach to codification. He believed in distilling the new code from the existing legislation, in determining the basic Russian concepts of law as they had been elaborated historically, and in preserving the peculiarities of local legal norms. Quite understandably, as a Balt, he wanted to prevent the absorption of local traditions in an uniform imperial code. The norms of law arrived at by the historico-empirical method would then be firmly established and secured permanently with the help of intangible *principia juris*. But these principles had either to be proclaimed by the government (as Lopukhin had suggested) or, as Rosenkampf felt, derived from Western, especially German, norms and concepts. However, the goverment was neither willing nor prepared to give Rosenkampf or the Commission any direction on what the *"principia juris"* should be. The Commission's time was idled away in useless researches and abstract definitions, without any concrete results emerging from all this labor. Finally, the Emperor decided to spur on the Commission's activity by appointing an efficient and energetic new chief. For this purpose Speransky was nominated Assistant Minister of Justice on December 20, 1808, with the specific mission of bringing the Commission's work to a satisfactory conclusion. True to Alexander's expectation with Speransky's appointment things got under way quickly. As one of the Commission's officials, Alexander Turgenev reported to his brother Nicholas in Goettingen, the pace and general atmosphere of the office changed almost overnight. [1]

It was the first time that Speransky had to deal with law in a technical sense — if we except, of course, the drafting of the Commercial Code for Paul I. Neither his education nor his previous experience, had prepared him for dealing with the complex problems

---

[1] The instructions to the Commission, written by Speransky, are in PSZ 23,525 (7 March 1809). See also the description of the change in atmosphere brought by Speransky to the Commission in the letters of Alexander I. Turgenev to his brother Nicholas dated 10 Sept. 1808, 10 March 1809, 1 May 1809, 31 May 1809 in *Arkhiv brat'ev Turgenevykh,* II, pp. 368—391 passim.

of jurisprudence. Furthermore he was far too busy with other matters to devote all his time and energy to jurisprudence and codification. However, Alexander I was very impatient and wanted the Code to be completed immediately. Eager to please his imperial master, Speransky organized the work of the Commission in such a way that it would bring immediate results, regardless of the quality or real value of these results, and in disregard of some opinions he had stated in 1802 (see chapter 5 *infra*). Speransky knew current laws only from the papers, reports, and cases that passed through the Senate and the Ministry of the Interior; and such an acquaintance could hardly have given him a high opinion of Russian law. Indeed, he referred disparagingly to the "barbarian laws" of the Empire. [1] So he turned away from Russian tradition to more enlightened and better models for inspiration. What model could be more attractive than the recently drafted *Code Civil* in France ("Code Napoléon") and — to a lesser degree — the codifications of Austria and Prussia? In them Speransky found both a clear and orderly framework and enlightened legal principles which allowed him to dispense with wearisome preparatory research and gathering of Russian laws. The Emperor could only welcome this approach, as it promised to bring rapid results in the form of lofty general principles which did not commit him to concrete action or a study of details. [2]

Speransky applied his high organizational and bureaucratic ability to devise an order of procedure which would yield the desired result quickly. This, incidentally, nicely illustrated how he could accomplish as much as he did. First he prepared the general outline and plan of the Code, in most respects copying the plan of the French *Code Civil*. Then each section of the outline was given to individual members of the Commission to be worked out in detail by a certain date. The Code Napoléon was used as framework, especially for the first part of the Code. The staff had to find Russian laws to which reference could be made for each paragraph taken from the French model. As one of the officials, Il'inskii, noted, frequently the relation between the text and the laws referred to was rather tenuous. [3] The sections of the Code were discussed by the Council of State once a week, on Monday. Every Monday morning, therefore, before the session of the Council, the chief *rédacteur* would bring to Speransky a draft of the section just completed

1 Legislation "barbares et indignes d'être etudiées" — quoted by A. N. Filippov, *Uchebnik istorii russkogo prava (posobie k lektsiiam)*, (5th ed., Iur'ev 1914), part I, p. 578.
2 A. Kizevetter, "Aleksandr I," *Istoricheskie siluety, liudi i sobytiia*, (Berlin 1931), p. 132.
3 N. Il'inskii, "Vospominaniia," *Russkii Arkhiv*, (1879), No. 12, pp. 431—434; Filippov, *Uchebnik istorii russkogo prava*, I, p. 580.

in the way described. As he read it, Speransky made the necessary textual corrections and changes, polished the style, while several clerks copied the final text as it issued from his pen. By noon the draft was completed and Speransky took it to the Council of State. Under such conditions the work progressed rapidly and by 1812 the first task — the Civil Code — had been completed and submitted to the Council of State. But the quality of the final product clearly reflected the speed and haste of its composition. The members of the Council of State, afraid of the Emperor's favorite and themselves not too well versed in law, accepted the Code without much discussion. But Speransky's enemies soon began to voice their dissatisfaction and indignation. They asserted that Speransky had foisted upon monarchical, autocratic, and orthodox Russia a code of laws copied from radical, revolutionary, atheistic France. In so doing, they said, the State Secretary had prepared the way for the enslavement of Russia by the usurper Napoléon Bonaparte. Speransky's ill wishers, in particular Karamzin, maintained that his civil code was nothing more than the exact translation — and a poor one at that — of the French *Code Civil*. This was certainly an exaggeration, but modern research has conclusively shown that Speransky drew very heavily on the *Code Napoléon*.[1] Speransky himself admitted some resemblance between his code and the French one, but he tried to defend himself by pointing out that the similarity was due to the common source of the two codes — Roman law.[2] It was a somewhat disingenuous plea; it can be excused only on the ground that Speransky felt unjustly branded as a French agent and was defending both his honor and patriotism. The truth remains, though, that in his Code he pretty much disregarded Russian legal tradition and history and tried to introduce *en bloc* a civil law worked out for completely different social and political conditions. The narrow-minded and formal bureaucrat had, in this instance, gotten the better of the able public servant and political adviser to the Emperor.[3]

[1] The full text of the code is to be found in *Arkhiv Gosudarstvennogo Soveta*, vol. IV, St. Pbg. 1874. See the literature on the history of Russian codification in Chapter XI. I am not convinced by the argument of Ar. Fateev ("K istorii i teorii kodifikatsii," *Russkii narodnyi universitet v Prage, Nauchnye trudy*, IV, (1931), p. 6) who shows that Speransky did not merely translate the Code Napoléon (something nobody, since Karamzin, has seriously contended); but Fateev offers no convincing evidence to disprove the fact that Speransky borrowed very heavily from French (and other European) models.

[2] Speranskii, "Pis'mo k Aleksandru I-u iz Permi," January 1813 in Shil'der, *Imperator Aleksandr I*, III, p. 520.

[3] Speransky admitted later the inapplicability of Roman law to Russian conditions. Cf. Speranskii, "Mysli grafa M. M. Speranskogo," *Arkhiv istor. i praktich. svedenii o Rossii* I-1 (1858—1859), pp. 4, 8; Speranskii, "O zakonakh rimskikh i razlichii ikh ot zakonov rossiiskikh," *Russkaia Starina*, XV, (1876), pp. 592—597.

It was probably fortunate for Russia that the Code was never put into effect. In the first place the remaining parts of the code had not been completed by the time of Speransky's fall from power, and after his exile the members of the Council of State became more critical and outspoken in their opinions. After 1815 Alexander cooled to the whole idea and did not push for completion, let alone insist on the first part being put into practice. Once he could consider his codification work objectively, without feeling the need to justify himself, Speransky readily recognized its inadequacy. He came to realize that before a definitive code of Russian law could be drawn up, all the legislation enacted since 1649 had first to be collected and ordered. Already in 1809—1812 he had had an inkling of the need of such a preparatory task, but had disregarded it. [1] In any case, the experience of his failure at codification stood him in good stead after 1826 when he again was set to the task of codifying Russian law.

In short, the ill-fated codification project had, on the one hand, given more ammunition to his enemies' claim that his policy was one of slavish imitation of alien and revolutionary French models, and, on the other hand, it had served as a valuable experience to Speransky and stimulated his interest in jurisprudence and law, leading him to more intensive study of the field.

Although Speransky devoted his attention primarily to domestic affairs, we should not forget that he was active during one of the most crucial periods in European diplomatic and military history. As a close and influential advisor to the Emperor, he could not fail to be drawn into matters relating to Russia's international position. His participation in problems of foreign relations began, naturally enough, in connection with the annexation of Finland following a successful war against Sweden.

The incorporation into the Russian Empire of the newly conquered Finnish territory had begun in 1808, even before the formal recognition of its transfer to Russian sovereignty by the treaty of Friederichsham (1809). The conquest and annexation of the Grand Duchy of Finland, an ancient possession of Sweden, had been facilitated by the intrigues and defection of an influential group of "Finnish" noblemen (actually of Swedish origin and language); for instance, Governor Sprengporten,

---

1 It had been Jacob's procedure in connection with his preparation of the Criminal section of the Code under Speransky's direction. Jacob, *Denkwürdigkeiten*, pp. 297, 303, 305. Speransky admitted to Jacob: "Ich muss gestehen, dass ich in diesem Fache nicht so bewandert bin, um Ihre Anfragen jetzt gehörig zu beantworten. Ich bin mit zu vielen heterogenen Sachen beschäftigt um mit Sorgfalt ein Fach, und insbesonderem dieses, studieren zu können." *Denkwürdigkeiten*, p. 302.

Count Armfelt, Bishop Tengström, Rehbinder, and many others. As a result, unlike most other Russian territorial conquests, Finland had a rather special — and not very clearly defined — status within the Empire. In some respects it was joined to Russia by bonds of a personal union, its grand duke being the same person as the Emperor; but in some other ways it was a real union, since the Grand Duchy had no independent existence of its own and — in the final analysis — received its basic laws and policies from St. Petersburg. However, Finland retained the autonomy of its legal system, its local administration and the traditional privileges of all its social classes. This novel and unusual relationship between the autocratic government of the Empire and the local authorities of the Grand Duchy had to be clearly defined and regulated by special legislation and the creation of appropriate institutional machinery. [1]

The task of working out these administrative and political relations fell to Speransky. Finland's inclusion in the Russian Empire — on an autonomous basis — was publicly sanctioned by the Finnish Diet; he put the final touch to the statutes which defined the rights and powers of Finland's autonomous local administration and its relation to the central government of the Empire. The system as worked out and ratified at Borgås remained basically unchanged (if we discount minor violations) until the first years of the 20th century, when, for a brief period, Nicholas II abolished the Grand Duchy's autonomy. Some years after the Diet of Borgås, in 1811—1812, Speransky recommended and helped to implement the reunion of Old Finland (Karelia and Vyborg) annexed by Russia in the reign of Peter the Great, with the newly acquired Grand Duchy of Finland (PSZ 24,907). [2] This measure which incensed Russian chauvinists (and future imperialists) was designed to conciliate the Finns and to remedy the distressing economic and administrative situation of Vyborg, arbitrarily separated from its natural hinterland for a century. The act of reunion illustrated Speransky's consideration for the ethnological and historical factors in a people's life. Such consideration naturally satisfied the national consciousness of the Finns, but could hardly have pleased the extreme nationalism of many Russians.

The legal and constitutional problems of the annexation of Finland and the status of Finnish social and individual rights cannot detain us here. The history of the Grand Duchy's political status concerns us

---

[1] A similar problem arose soon again and found an analogous solution— the Kingdom of Poland in 1815.
[2] The French text is in *La Constitution de la Finlande*, pp. 122—23.

only to the extent of Speransky's role in it. Helped by some Finnish dignitaries such as Rehbinder, Bishop Tengström and Count Armfelt, Speransky drew up the blueprint for Finland's administrative system. The Grand Duchy was to be governed in the name of the Emperor by a Governor, who, Speransky hoped, would be a real viceroy in full control of the executive; a hope which was foiled by the weakness of the first governor, Shteingel, and the energy and ability of the Finnish officials. A Governing Council, not unlike the Russian Senate, meeting under the chairmanship of the Governor, was to assist the executive and act as a high judiciary and a limited legislative body. The three estates of Finland were to send representatives to a Diet (*Seim*) which met at regular periods. The provision for a Diet has led many historians to believe that Speransky established a true constitutional regime in Finland, expecting it to serve as a model for a future Russian constitution. That he indeed had hopes of extending some of the features of the Finnish system to Russia is quite probable, as some of his later reform proposals tend to indicate. But it certainly would be misleading to call the regime established in Finland "constitutional", in the sense of the primacy of a representative legislature. The statute of the Diet made it quite clear that it had no legislative power whatever. The *Seim's* only function was to provide opinions and information on specific questions put to it by the Governor — and only matters brought up by the Governor could be put on the agenda of the Diet. [1]

The exact nature of the relationship which in 1809 bound Finland to the Russian Empire was not clearly defined (at least until 1909) and the question has given rise to much argument among historians and jurists of both nations. [2] The problem — as eventually defined — came down to this: had Finland voluntarily, through its Diet at Borgås, recognized the Emperor of Russia as its ruler while preserving its special institutions and organization without becoming part and parcel of the Russian Empire, or had the Grand Duchy been annexed to the Empire (by international treaty) and then been granted a special status and local autonomy by the sovereign will of the Grand-Duke-Emperor? The issue was vital indeed, for the autonomy of the Grand Duchy, and

---

[1] Borodkin, *Istoriia Finliandii*, I, p. 253. A French translation of excerpts of this statute is to be found in *La Constitution de la Finlande*, pp. 115–117.

[2] The works by Borodkin, Danielson, Erich, Ordin, Osten-Sacken, Schybergson cited in the bibliography of this chapter discuss the problem at some length. But see also the very suggestive analyses in: Korkunov, *Russkoe Gosudarstvennoe pravo*, II, 290 ff; N. I. Lazarevskii, *Russkoe gosudarstvennoe pravo*, I, p. 235; B. E. Nol'de, "Edinstvo i nerazdel'nost' Rossii," *Ocherki russkogo gosudarstvennogo prava* (St. Pbg. 1911), 475–554.

the rights enjoyed by its citizens were at stake. For Russian "public opinion" it was of concern too, as it was argued that the rights and institutions recognized by the Emperor in Finland should be extended to the Empire as a whole. It is neither within our task nor our ability to settle the thorny legal problem here. We can only mention the administrative form Speransky gave the relationship between Finland and Russia.[1] Speransky considered that "Finland is a state not a province" and its affairs had all the complexity of the business of an independent state. They could not be handled as a routine administrative matter by subordinate officials overburdened with other concerns.[2] Therefore the administration of the Grand Duchy in St. Petersburg became the responsibility of a special Commission for Finnish Affairs composed of Russian and Finnish dignitaries. The Commission was to receive and process the reports from the local authorities in Finland, and, having analyzed and summarized them, submit them to the Emperor. All legislation pertaining to Finland was to be drafted and — after approval by the Emperor — receive its final form in this Commission. In short, the Commission served as intermediary and transmission belt between the Emperor and his subjects in the Grand Duchy. Through its Finnish members, the Commission could bring directly to the Sovereign's attention the desiderata and needs of Finland, while the Grand Duke could be assured that his will and policy would be formulated in the manner best suited for the special conditions of Finland and thereby be implemented promptly and effectively. As far as Speransky was concerned, the principal merit of the system lay in the fact that it kept the monarch informed of the needs of the country through persons in direct touch with local conditions and yet not unaware of the point of view of the central administration. In a sense, it was a new version of the system that had prevailed in Finland under Swedish rule, before the latter part of the 18th century. While it clearly worked to the advantage of the Finnish nobility that had made common cause with Russia against Sweden, it also made for better contact between the governor and at least some of the governed.[3]

[1] See Borodkin, Schybergson, Ordin, and the shorter summary in Scheibert, *op. cit.*
[2] "Finland is a state and not a province, one cannot govern it on the side and amidst a multitude of current business." Speranskii, "Otchet v delakh 1810...," *Sbornik IRIO,* 21 (1877), p. 456.
[3] The Commission which prepared the new organization of Finland consisted of: Geiking, Teil'e, Emin, Friktsius, Rehbinder, Jegerhorn and its minutes were submitted to the Emperor through Speransky who was the chief *rapporteur* and *rédacteur.* The instructions to the Commission, dated October 18, 1809, can be found in *Sbornik istoricheskikh materialov izvlechennykh iz arkhiva S. E. I. V. Kantseliarii,* III, No. 362, pp. 267—269. The decree of instruction begins with the following words: "Desiring that the affairs concerning the administration of the

We note that the administrative arrangement worked out by Speransky respected the peculiarities and traditions of the newly annexed country. Clearly, he and the government had no intention of changing the way of life, customs, speech, religion, and culture of the Finns. The political organization and internal autonomy of the Grand Duchy guaranteed to the Finns all the privileges and rights they had enjoyed theretofore to which even the Russian nobility could not aspire. On the other hand, there is no denying that another principle underlay the new regime of Finland and tended in the opposite direction. In spite of the desire of the Finnish nobility and clergy, Alexander I and Speransky refused to introduce any truly constitutional and representative features which would go beyond the legal safeguards of life and property. Lip service was paid to the idea of a consultative representative assembly, but the Diet's competence and functions were so limited and its "representative" character so narrowly circumscribed that we cannot forbear feeling that at the bottom of their hearts neither Alexander nor Speransky cared to promote a real constitutional regime. [1] The "constitutional camouflage" was only designed to placate and attract the new subjects of the Empire. As a matter of fact, the organization and the limitations placed on the initiative and power of the Commission for Finnish Affairs in St. Petersburg strongly suggest that Speransky's ultimate aim was to bring about a structural identity between the Russian and Finnish administrations. It would have clearly been the case had his proposals for the reorganization of the Russian government been implemented in full. Such a result, then, would justify the view that the administrative system devised for Finland was only a first step in the "organic russification" of the Grand Duchy by giving it an administration identical to Russia's and by drawing the Finnish nobility into imperial government service. It would have been a familiar story, strongly reminiscent of the ways of the Grand Dukes of Moscow for bringing about the cultural, social, and political assimilation of newly acquired possessions. It would also have been very much in the tradition of Maria Theresa's policy of administrative and social centralization and *Gleichschaltung*.

If the foregoing interpretation be correct, we detect in the case of

newly acquired Finland which are submitted for My [i.e. Alexander I] decision be first examined and considered on those very principles and laws which are peculiar to that country and have been confirmed by Us..."

[1] As Speransky wrote to Governor Shteingel, May 19, 1811: "The Council has been established not on the basis of a constitutional right, but exclusively by a decision of the government." *Sbornik istoricheskikh materialov izvlechennykh iz arkhiva S.E.I.V. Kantseliarii*, III, No. 378, p. 307.

Finland an instance of Speransky's characteristically double pronged approach to the problem presented by the multinational make-up of the Russian Empire. He recognized, respected and safeguarded the traditions and customs of the non-Russian peoples, without forcing any special views, habits, or cultural patterns on them against their will. At the same time, however, he prepared the ground for an eventual, gradual, "organic," and voluntary russification by fostering those features which make for administrative and social uniformity. Eventually, he thought in typically bureaucratic and 18th century fashion, the political and social identity between the non-Russians and Russians would result in a *Kulturgemeinschaft,* the strongest foundation for an unitary, centralized Empire. This was the ultimate goal, but Speransky understood much better than some of his successors in the Russian government (and 18th century Western enlightened bureaucrats) that this aim was to be achieved gradually, while respecting local traditions and customs. Uniformity was the result of gradual displacement of primitive and historical patterns by a more modern, advanced cultural and political system. For once the romantic and historicist pattern of thought indicated the method for achieving an 18th century bureaucratic and uniformist aim. As we shall have occasion to observe, in most other instances Speransky promoted 19th century historicist and "conservative" goals by the methods of 18th century enlightened bureaucratic absolutism.

While the affairs of the Grand Duchy of Finland could be considered to have been primarily administrative in character, Russia's relationship to the events of the Napoleonic era was essentially diplomatic. Diplomacy, however, was the domain *par excellence* of Emperor Alexander, because of personal predilection and also because of his genuine outstanding diplomatic talents. Whoever the official head of the ministry of Foreign Affairs might be, the real foreign minister of Russia was its Emperor. Like Louis XV, but more successfully, Alexander I had his *cabinet noir,* his own agents and his own policy, which did not always coincide with the public policy of his Ministers. Alexander had shown his independence and secretiveness in his very first venture into the realm of international diplomacy, the Prussian alliance of 1802. Both the Chancellor of the Empire, Count Vorontsov, and the Assistant Minister of Foreign Affairs, the Emperor's close friend, Prince Adam Czartoryski, were left in the dark until the conclusion of the negotiations in Memel. Similar instances could be adduced for any period of his reign. But in order to pursue such a personal and secret course, Alexander had to have his own diplomatic agents, his own correspondents who kept him in touch with foreign governments without the knowledge of Russia's regularly accredited diplomatic representatives. Under these circumstances it could not come as a surprise that the Emperor's closest personal advisor would eventually be drawn into his diplomatic "game." Alexander made Speransky the recipient of the secret reports sent by his personal agents from abroad. In this manner, Speransky became involved in the Emperor's personal diplomacy, although formally he did not have any part in matters of foreign relations. Rumors about Speransky's knowledge of diplomatic secrets eventually seeped through to Court circles and bolstered the belief, held by many, that the State Secretary was an agent in the pay of Napoleon. His apparently frequent contacts and good relations with the French Ambassador, Caulaincourt, as well as his alleged slavish imitation of French administrative models, seemed further evidence for his "treason." [1] The documents made available since then, however, tell quite a different story.

Speransky early realized that sooner or later Russia and France would clash in a war whose outcome might spell either doom or triumph for the Russian Empire. In this he shared the conviction of Alexander I who had been preparing for the final struggle with Napoleon ever since Tilsit. To be able to face such a war with some chance of success, Russia's military establishment and administration had to be in good condition. Reorganization and reform of the government were, therefore, desirable for reasons of domestic policy and as a top priority requirement for the expected conflict with France. It was not enough for Russia to be strong at home and have a good military establishment; it was also of the utmost importance to know the enemy's circumstances and be able to foresee his moves. But vital information on the economic and political state of Napoleon's empire could not be gathered by Russia's official diplomatic agents. Firstly, it would be in flagrant violation of their status; secondly Alexander and Speransky did not think them capable of doing a good job of it — a sad commentary on the opinion in which the Russian government servant was held by his own sovereign. Speransky, therefore, suggested sending an unofficial or secret observer to Paris. [2] The suggestion was readily accepted by

---

[1] It is impossible to establish how frequent these contacts with Caulaincourt might have been. The only evidence available concerns the number of times both Speransky and Caulaincourt dined with the Emperor "en petit comité" (table set for about 15 to 20 persons). The *Kamerfur'erskii Zhurnal* reports 8 such dinners for the period between July 4, 1808 and June 20, 1809 inclusive.

[2] Speranskii, "O vidakh Frantsii po brachnomu soiuzu s Avstriei 1810," *Russkaia Starina*, vol. 104, (1900), pp. 429ff; *Lettres et papiers du chancelier comte de Nesselrode*, II, 69—70; III.

the Emperor who also wished to keep up the contact he had established with Talleyrand at Erfurt. Under the pretext of negotiating a financial agreement, Alexander sent to Paris the young Count Nesselrode, future Foreign Minister of Nicholas I. In order to avoid raising any suspicions and to leave in the dark the vice-chancellor Count Rumiantsev, whose francophilia was needed to keep up the pretense of cordial relations with France, Nesselrode was instructed to report in cypher directly to Speransky who in turn transmitted the reports to the Emperor in person.

This arrangement gave Speransky occasion to present his own views on Russia's diplomacy. Two of his papers on this subject have been preserved and published. His views, it is true, were not very original or interesting and do not seem to have played an important role in shaping Alexander's policy towards France. Even though Speransky recommended a course close to the one followed by the Emperor, it is by no means possible to establish a causal link. Yet, as Speransky's casual participation in diplomatic affairs has been so completely neglected by his biographers, we yield to the temptation of summarizing his views. [1] War with France, Speransky argued in 1810, is more than probable, but it is not an immediate prospect. Napoleon has his hands full in Spain, and his recently concluded alliance with Austria should contribute to his feeling of security. Napoleon's Austrian marriage, incidentally, may be a step towards a reconciliation with the Bourbons of Spain, for the Iberian peninsula can never be subdued unless South America were conquered too, which is certainly out of the question. The prospect of peace for the West does not diminish Napoleon's threat to Russia, especially in Poland. Even if France and England come to terms, it would be to France's advantage to have Russia embroiled in a lengthy and costly war with Turkey. Therefore, the present conflict with the Ottoman Empire should be ended as quickly as possible, but the steps towards peace should be taken in secret so that Napoleon can neither prevent nor influence the settlement. The most sensitive spot for Russia, and France's foremost permanent eastern ally, is Poland. To prevent French expansion (overt or secret) into Poland, Russia should prepare the ground for a potential defection of Poland from France. To this end, the Russian government should try to gain the help and friendship of the Polish nobility,

[1] Speranskii: "O vidakh frantsuzskogo pravitel'stva na Pol'shu" and "O vidakh Frantsii po brachnomu soiuzu s Avstriei," *Russkaia Starina* vol. 104, (1900), 429—436 — The former paper has been translated into German by Th. Schiemann and appears in his *Geschichte Russlands unter Kaiser Nikolaus I,* Bd. I (Berlin 1904) Anhang, pp. 519—526.

especially by supporting the Poles against the Lithuanians in the region of Vilna. [1] While this diplomacy is being pursued, Speransky continued his argument, the economic policy of the Empire must be adjusted to avoid the nation's bankruptcy. This means that Russia must continue to export her main staples — mostly to England. True, such a course would violate the Continental Blockade to which Alexander I had adhered, out of necessity, at Tilsit. Yet, lest Russia be ruined economically, the risk of displeasing Napoleon has to be taken, even if it brings war nearer. The best Russia can do to keep up the pretense of abiding by the Continental System is to prohibit imports from England. [2]

The first departure from a strict interpretation of Russia's obligations under the Continental Blockade came in connection with the lifting of the prohibition of grain exports from Odessa through the Black Sea. Originally the prohibition had been motivated by the existence of a state of war with Turkey and the fear that the vessels might fall into Turkish hands. But the closing of the Black Sea to Russian exporters was undermining the prosperity of the southern landowners and ruining the merchants of Odessa. The Governor of Odessa, Duke de Richelieu, therefore, petitioned the Emperor to allow free grain trade and, more specifically, to permit the export of this commodity through Odessa. Richelieu argued that while the embargo was ruining Russia, it did not harm the Turks in any way, for they could always be supplied by the British whose navy controlled the Mediterranean. Speransky and the Minister of Finance, Count Gur'ev, supported Richelieu's argument and bolstered it by some theoretical considerations — taken from Adam Smith — on the advantages of free trade. After some hesitation, Alexander approved Richelieu's request and even opened all Russian ports to free export of grain (PSZ 24,464, December 19, 1810). [3] This departure from the Continental System was followed by a more sweeping measure: the tariff of 1810. This tariff allowed almost complete freedom of export to Russian goods and permitted the import of some essential manufactured products, while keeping out luxury items. Almost overnight, after issuance of the tariff,

---

1 Speranskii, "O vidakh frantsuzskogo pravitel'stva na Pol'shu," loc. cit., p. 440.

2 It is quite true that the Russian government was under strong pressure from the nobility, whose economic interests were at stake, to keep open the trade with England. But that pressure alone would not have swayed Alexander I if he himself had not felt the wisdom of an active trade policy. Alexander, in spite of his apparent "softness," was quite capable of disregarding his nobility's clamors when he wished to, as he had proven during Tilsit, Erfurt, before Borodino, and also later, after 1815.

3 Seredonin, Istoricheskii obzor deitel'nosti Komiteta Ministrov, I, pp. 143—145, 149.

British ships — flying the flag of Téneriffe to preserve appearances and avoid seizure by the French — entered the harbor of St. Petersburg. Russian trade picked up, and the economic revival was soon felt by all classes. Quite correctly the tariff was interpreted as Russia's "first act of independence" from France. [1] Naturally, Napoleon was furious, and the measure contributed to exarcebating feelings, sharpening the disagreements between the two empires and bringing war nearer. Speransky's role in the "first act of independence from France" was not known, or conveniently forgotten, by his enemies. It did not spare him the insults and humiliations which accompanied his fall from power and exile in 1812. His views and contributions to Russia's foreign policy in 1810—1812 belie the frequently held conviction that he was an uncritical advocate of a pro-French orientation. [2] Today, reading the record carefully and dispassionately, we come out with the impression that Speransky advised the pursuance of a policy of "containment" to secure the most advantageous position in preparation for the inevitable struggle for the survival of Russia. As so often happens in times of great crisis, when the faith of a country has been seriously shaken by defeats, when public opinion is in a state of near-panic, level-headed counsels of caution are interpreted as capitulations to the enemy or even treason.

This brief account shows that Speransky's administrative activities in the years 1808 to 1812 were not only numerous but also varied. They all, however, exemplified a fundamental concern of his: to prepare and train a good bureaucracy and to guide its actions by clear, well defined laws, and an orderly administration. Speransky also displayed awareness of the relationships between domestic needs and imperial problems, as was manifested in his dealings with Finland and advice on foreign policy. He left the imprint of these considerations and approach on all the major aspects of Russian administration. But this was only a part — and perhaps the less significant part — of his work in those years. Most of his attention and energies were devoted to a fundamental reorganization of Russian political life, starting with its central administrative institutions. It is to this facet of his career that we must turn now.

---

[1] Vandal, *Napoléon et Alexandre I*, II, pp. 529—531.
[2] Referring to a dispatch of the Austrian ambassador, Schwartzenberg, from St. Petersburg, Vandal states that Speransky had also been influential in determining Russia's passive attitude during the Austro-French War (1809), contrary to the terms of the Franco-Russian Alliance. *Ibid.*

## SOURCES

General background: On Speransky, Korf: *Zhizn' grafa Speranskogo*, I; I. A. Bychkov (ed.), "Speranskii v 1808—1811 gg," *Russkaia Starina* 114—No. IV (1903) 29—40; A. Czartoryski, *Mémoires* (Paris 1887); F. M. Dmitriev, "Speranskii v ego gosudarstvennoi deiatel'nosti s obshchim ocherkom istorii vnutrennogo upravleniia v XVIII veke" *Russkii Arkhiv*, vol. VI (1868) No. 9, pp. 1527—1656; N. S. Il'inskii, "Vospominaniia," *Russkii Arkhiv*, (1879) No. 12, 377—434; M. N. Longinov, "Graf Speranskii," *Russkii Vestnik*, vol. XXIII (Oct. 1859), pp. 337—378 and 527—576; I. I. Martynov, "Zapiski" *Pamiatniki Novoi Russkoi Istorii*, vol. II, (1872), pp. 68—182; A. V. Romanovich-Slaviatinskii, "Gosudarstvennaia deiatel'nost' Speranskogo," *Otechestvennye Zapiski*, (1873), No. 4, 171—199; V. Semevskii, "M. M. Speranskii," *Entsiklopedicheskii Slovar' Brokgauza-Efron*, vol. XXXI (1900), 188—192; S. M. Seredonin, "Graf M. M. Speranskii," *Russkii Biograficheskii Slovar'* (St. Pbg. 1909); Al. I. Turgenev, "Pis'ma i dnevnik gettingenskogo perioda 1802—1804 i pis'ma ego k Kaisarovu i brat'iam v Gettingen 1805—1811," *Arkhiv brat'ev Turgenevykh*, vol. II (St. Pbg. 1911).

For information on Russia during the first years of Alexander's reign see Heinrich Storch, *Russland unter Alexander dem I*. 9 vols., St. Pbg.-Leipzig 1804—1808. On government policies 1807—1812, in addition to the general works on Alexander's reign cited in the previous chapter: "Doklad Ministra Vnutrennikh Del za 1803," *Zhurnaly Komiteta Ministrov*, vol. I, (1801—1810), Appendix I, pp. 54—79; M. V. Dovnar-Zapol'skii, *Obzor noveishei russkoi istorii*, vol. I (2d ed.) Kiev 1914; the same, "Zarozhdenie ministrov v Rossii i ukaz o pravakh Senata 8 sent. 1802 g.", *Iz istorii obshchestvennykh techenii v Rossii* (Kiev 1905), pp. 1—76; N. M. Korkunov, *Russkoe gosudarstvennoe pravo*, vol. II (6th ed.) St. Pbg. 1909; P. Maikov, "Baron Gustav Andreevich Rosenkampf," *Russkaia Starina*, vol. 120, (Oct. 1904), 140—185 and (Nov. 1904), 371—429.

For the reform of the ecclesiastical schools in addition to the literature cited in chapter I, see: PSZ, No. 23, 122, 26 June 1808 (vol. 30, pp. 368—395) "Ob obrazovanii, soderzhanii dukhovnykh uchilishch"; I. A. Chistovich, *Rukovodiashchie deiateli dukhovnogo prosveshcheniia v Rossii v XIX-m st.* St. Pbg. 1894; M. I. Sukhomlinov, "Materialy dlia istorii obrazovaniia v Rossii v tsarstvovanie imperatora Aleksandra I" *Issledovaniia i stat'i po russkoi literature i prosveshcheniiu*. I (St. Pbg. 1889) pp. 1—541.

On the annexation and administration of Finland, see: PSZ, Nos. 24, 301 and 24, 302 (1811, vol. 31, pp. 276 276 ff) "Uchrezhdenie osobennoi komisii finliandskikh del, vmesto naznachennoi ukazom 19. maia 1802 g i shtat onoi"; PSZ Nos. 24,907 (11 Dec. 1811) and 24,934 (31 Dec. 1811), vol. 31, "Ob imenovanii Staroi i Novoi Finlandii sovokupno Finlandieiu"; Speranskii, "O soedinenii Staroi i Novoi Finlandii pod odno naimenovanie i odin obraz pravleniia," *Arkhiv Gosudarstvennogo Soveta — Delo Gos. Soveta komiteta predsedatelei v 1810, 1811 — Zhurnal No. 35*, 1811 (St. Pbg. 1908); Speranskii, "Vsepodanneishaia zapiska M. M. Speranskogo 11 iunia 1811 po delam Finliandskim i Pol'skim," *Sbornik materialov 1go otdeleniia sobstvennoi E. I. V. kantseliarii, vol. II* (St. Pbg. 1876) 214—217; Speranskii, "Otchet v delakh 1810, predstavlennyi imperatoru Aleksandru I-u M. M. Speranskim, 11 fevralia 1811", *Sbornik IRIO*, vol. 21 (1877), 447—462; Some of the relevant documents are found in French or English in: *La Constitution du Grand Duché de Finlande*, Paris 1900; and Wolf, baron von der Osten Sacken, *The Legal Position of the Grand Duchy of Finland in the Russian Empire*, London 1912; N. Dubrovin (ed.) "Dokumenty otnosiashchiesia do voiny s Shvetsieiu i do prisoedineniia Finliandii 1809—1815," *Sbornik istoricheskikh materialov izvlechennykh iz arkhiva S. E. I. V. Kantseliarii* vyp. III (St. Pbg. 1890), Nos. 355—390, pp. 247—328; M. Borodkin, *Istoriia Finliandii — vremia imperatora Aleksandra I*, vol. I, St. Pbg. 1909; Joh. Richard Danielson, *Finlands Vereinigung mit dem Russichen Reiche* (Anlässlich der Arbeit von K. Ordin "Finlands Unterwerfung"), Helsingfors 1891; Rafael Erich, *Das Staatsrecht des Grossfürstentums Finland (Suomi)*, Tübingen 1912 (Bd. XVIII, Öffentliches Recht der Gegenwart); K. Ordin, *Pokorenie Finliandii (opyt opisaniia po neizdannym istochnikam)*, 2 vols., St. Pbg. 1882; Peter Scheibert, "Die Anfänge der finnischen Staatswerdung unter Alexander I," *Jahrbücher für Geschichte Osteuropas*, IV (1939), Heft 3/4, pp. 351—430; M. G. Schybergson, *Politische Geschichte Finnlands 1809—1919*, Gotha-Stuttgart, 1925.

On the diplomatic events of the period, see: N. Dubrovin (ed.), "Dve zapiski M. M. Speranskogo po politicheskim delam," *Russkaia Starina*, vol. 104, (1900), 429—436; *Ministerstvo Finansov 1802—1902*, vol. I, St. Pbg. 1902; Ministerstvo Finansov, *Istoricheskii ocherk oblozheniia torgovli i promyslov v Rossii*, St. Pbg. 1893; S. M. Seredonin, *Istoricheskii obzor deiatel'nosti Komiteta Ministrov*, vol. I (Komitet Ministrov v tsarstvovanie imperatora Aleksandra I-go), St. Pbg. 1902; A. de Nesselrode (ed.), *Lettres et papiers du chancelier comte de Nesselrode 1760—1856* (extraits de ses archives), vols. II and III (pp. 225—387 passim), Paris 1909 (?) — 1912; Grand Duc Nicolas Mikhailowitsch, *Les relations diplomatiques de la Russie et de la France d'après les rapports des ambassadeurs d'Alexandre et de Napoléon 1808—1812* (title also in Russian), 7 vols. St. Pbg. 1905—1914; A. Sorel, *L'Europe et la Révolution Française* (7e partie: *Le Blocus Continental — Le Grand Empire*), Paris 1903; A. Vandal, *Napoléon et Alexandre I (L'alliance russe sous le Premier Empire)*, 3 vols. Paris 1891—1893.

# CHAPTER IV

# REFORM OF RUSSIA'S FINANCES AND CENTRAL ADMINISTRATION

Speransky's main task was to bring order into the "chaotic structure" of the Empire and to give the imperial government a solid and modern foundation. Working in close contact with Emperor Alexander during the years 1808 to 1812, Speransky elaborated a series of concrete measures to take care of the immediate practcal needs of the administration and to prepare the ground for his long-range reform projects. Both the short-range acts and the general reform plans played a significant role in the history of Russian administration, and they must be considered in some detail. Reversing the order in which these measures are usually treated by historians, it seems more useful to describe and analyse first those reforms which were actually carried out. There is no full treatment of Speransky's plans and acts in English, and as they have been the object of much confusion and superficial interpretation in Russian historical literature, it seems desirable to support the analysis with detailed summaries of the legislation and projects concerned, even at the risk of incurring the reproach of undue length and tediousness. In the final analysis, Speransky's activity left an indelible mark on the methods and pattern of the imperial government throughout the 19th century, and for this reason alone it deserves as full a treatment as possible.

## 1. FINANCES

When Speransky became the Emperor's main secretary and advisor, Russia's financial situation stood first on the list of practical problems that had to be dealt with immediately. The seriousness of the monetary crisis cannot be blamed wholly on Alexander's foreign policy, even though the costly and unsuccessful wars against France had contributed a great deal to the deterioration of Russia's finances. The real origin

of the crisis dated back to the reign of Catherine II. In the second half
of the 18th century, the expenses of the government had risen very
sharply, while the revenues had failed to keep pace. As a matter of
fact, the revenues had fallen off — relatively speaking — as a result of
lower tax income due to Catherine's generous gifts to private individuals
of large tracts of state lands and a great number of state peasants. A
few figures will illustrate this trend: in 1784 the state had a revenue
of 40 millions rubles while its expenditures were 58 millions; in 1790
the expenses had increased to 73.5 millions, while the revenue had
remained more or less the same, 44.5 millions. [1] Under Paul I there
was no apparent decrease in this rising deficit, and it reached un-
controllable proportions in the first decade of the reign of Alexander I.
Thus in 1803 revenue was at 95.5 millions rubles, the expenses at 109.4
(the relative improvement was due to the brief period of peace for the
duration of Paul's alliance with France), in 1805 the revenue had increased to only 100 millions, while the expenses had reached 125.3
millions; in the next two years the deficit almost doubled and in 1807
the expenditures were 170 millions against 121 millions in receipts.
The disastrous war which ended with the Treaty of Tilsit resulted in
the following figures for the budget of 1809: 127.5 millions of revenue
and 278.5 millions of expenditures! [2]

The treasury had to be filled again, and the minds of all Russian
officials were busy seeking a method of solution. The first recourse
was the floating of a loan abroad. Catherine II had done this, and her
example was followed by her successors. In 1798 the Bureau of Court
Bankers was created for the express purpose of negotiating foreign
loans. The Bureau remained in existence until 1811 when the reorganized Ministry of Finance took over its function. As time went on,
however, it became increasingly more difficult to negotiate foreign
loans. Moreover, in the long run, it was proving to be quite an
expensive expedient, for the commission and conversion rates were

[1] Jean de Bloch, *Les Finances de la Russie au 19e s.* I (Paris 1899), p. 78 (figures
are in ruble-assignats).
[2] *Ibid.,* I, p. 113. Slightly different figures, based on a more detailed computation
in Khromov, *Ekonomicheskoe razvitie Rossii* (Moscow 1950), pp. 440—441 and 446—
447. From it we excerpt the following table:

| | ordinary receipts | extraord. rec's. (borrowings) | Expenditures |
|---|---|---|---|
| 1803 | 101,597 | 9,160 | 109,442 |
| 1805 | 107,180 | 29,606 | 125,449 |
| 1807 | 114,765 | 39,144 | 159,021 |
| 1808 | 122,633 | 39,229 | 248,213 |

(figures are in 1,000 rubles-assignats)

very high. As foreign loans proved inadequate as a source of extraordinary revenue, the government adopted another expedient, copied from Western Europe, and with equally unfortunate effects: the emission of paper money, assignats. In 1769 Catherine II approved the issuing of assignats as a short term measure. However, the temporary expedient became a regular policy. Such a course was the result of the naive conception concerning the assignats which prevailed at the time, and of the great demands made by the state on the treasury. Like most of their Western colleagues, the Russian financial "experts" of the time did not make a clear distinction between bank notes and paper money. They labored under the illusion that *money* could be created by government fiat. After a brief period of illusory success and prosperity, the harmful effect of the assignats came to light as the paper ruble began to fall sharply in relation to silver. Naturally enough, the lower value of the assignats in terms of silver contributed to increase the budgetary deficit. Claiming that paper money was "real money" and not merely a way of borrowing on the nation's wealth, the state kept printing more and more assignats. The obvious result did not fail to manifest itself soon. The amount of paper money in circulation reached enormous proportions; the value of the assignats kept falling and the government lost all control over the situation. [1]

Alexander I continued this disastrous policy, so that at the end of the first decade of his reign the paper ruble had dropped to almost ¼ of nominal value in silver. [2] The cost of Russia's wars agains Napoleon

| [1] | Year | Amount issued in the year | Amount in circulation on 31 Dec. of year | Value in silver of 1 ruble assignats |
|---|---|---|---|---|
| | 1769 | 2,169,975 | 2,169,975 | 99 |
| | 1770 | 3,757,700 | 6,378,675 | 99 |
| | 1774 | 2,207,075 | 20,051,800 | 100 |
| | 1778 | | 23,500,000 | 99 |
| | 1782 | 5,897,125 | 33,289,425 | 99 |
| | 1786 | 908,825 | 46,219,250 | 98 |
| | 1790 | 11,000,000 | 111,000,000 | 87 |
| | 1794 | 21,550,000 | 145,550,000 | 68.5 |
| | 1798 | 31,356,765 | 194,931,605 | 62.5 |
| | 1801 | 8,799,000 | 221,488,335 | $71^2/_3$* |
| | 1805 | 31,540,560 | 292,199,110 | 73 * |
| | 1809 | 55,832,720 | 533,201,300 | $43^1/_3$ |
| | 1810 | 46,172,580 | 579,373,880 | $25^2/_5$ |
| | 1811 | 2,020,520 | 581,394,400 | $26^2/_5$ |
| | 1812 | 64,500,000 | 645,894,400 | $25^1/_5$ |
| | 1814 | 48,791,500 | 798,125,900 | 20 |

M. Kashkarov, *Denezhnoe obrashchenie v Rossii*, vol. I, pp. 24, 25, 26.

* The appreciation in these years was due to the years of peace and the optimism generated by Alexander's accession.

2 de Bloch, *op. cit.*, I, pp. 110—111; Khromov, *op. cit.*, 121—122.

had been covered in part by English subsidies, and it was these subsidies that permitted Russia to resume the struggle in 1812. But while
the peace signed at Tilsit with France lasted, this extraordinary source
of revenue was closed to the Russian government. It was impossible to
float enough loans abroad anymore. Napoleon, Alexander's new
"ally," was of no help in this matter. On the contrary, he made things
worse by forcing Russia to join the Continental System which resulted
in serious loss of revenue from customs receipts and trade. If the
Russian state was to escape bankruptcy and if the country was to
avoid economic collapse, radical and well thought out measures had
to be taken.

Luckily, Russia was able to tackle this difficult task, for it was
prepared intellectually and had also the necessary personnel. In the
early years of Alexander's reign, political economy experienced an
extraordinary popularity. Anyone with intellectual pretensions or who
wanted to be considered as an educated person, read Adam Smith, J-B.
Say, and their many popularizers. We need only to mention *Eugene
Onegin* to remember that the fad for political economy affected even
the dandies and courtiers of St. Petersburg. The snobs and the *jeunesse
dorée* were not alone in their interest in economics. Officials, high
dignitaries, and scholars devoted much time and effort to the study
of problems of finance and economics. In 1803 a section for political
economy was founded at the Imperial Academy of Sciences; prizes were
offered for the best treatises on various economic questions, such as
the advantages of free labor, free competition, and the like. [1] Many
foreign scholars who resided and taught in Russia put their expert
knowledge of economics at the disposal of the imperial government.
Among these specialists, mostly Germans, by the way, were Storch,
Adelung, Hermann, Raupach, Jacob. To this list should be added the
names of two scholars, Western Slavs by nationality, but trained in
Germany: Balugianskii and Lodi. Foreign statesmen like vom Stein
and Kankrin helped introduce the government and the Court to the
principles of the new economic science. Finally, as time went on, the
government began to make use of young Russians who had been
trained at Goettingen, at the time the most important center for the
study of political economy. Among he German trained young generation,
the two brothers Turgenev, Alexander and Nicholas, are the best
known; but they were by no means the only ones.

[1] Cf. Shtein, Bliumin, Sviatlovskii cited in bibl. to chapter. See A. I. Khodnev,
*Istoriia Imperatorskogo Vol'nogo Ekonomicheskogo obshchestva s 1765 do 1865 gg*
(St. Pbg. 1865), pp. 38—46, 71 for the first statistical questionnaires sent out at
that time.

Nor did the experience of foreign countries go unnoticed in Russia, and Alexander's advisors on economic matters drew on this experience whenever possible. The financial history of foreign nations could provide much that was instructive, for Russia was not alone in being beset with the consequences of the uncontrolled emission of paper money. Some countries had failed to find a proper solution, with dire consequences to their political and economic stability. This was the case of the *Ancien Régime* in France, Austria, Denmark, and their fate served as a warning. Others, like England, Holland, Napoleon's France, had solved or were in the process of solving the problem; their methods might be very instructive for Russia. Finally, there was the far away, but nonetheless interesting and valuable experiment made by the young United States. In every instance, financial policy gave rise to lengthy and lively debates which in turn provided material for study and reflection. The Russians were well informed on all these developments, through the substantial accounts and translations published in the periodical press. Articles in the *St. Petersburzhskii Zhurnal,* the *Statisticheskii Vestnik* were supplemented by reports made to the Free Economic Society and the Academy of Sciences, as well as by personal contacts with Western statesmen and academic personalities. The information and experience from abroad found their way, more or less directly, into the proposals and projects submitted by Russian officials to their superiors.

Finding that the Ministry of Finance, under the inefficient direction of F. A. Golubtsov, had failed to initiate any meaningful financial reform-program, the Emperor ordered the establishment of a special Commission for Financial Affairs in 1806. The Commission was given the task of preparing a comprehensive plan for a healthier monetary policy. At first, the Commission did not justify the hopes put in it by Alexander, for it resorted to the traditional expedient of issuing more paper rubles. In 1809 the Emperor appointed Speransky to the Commission, and under the latter's energetic leadership, work progressed rapidly along new lines. Speransky secured the collaboration of several outstanding political economists, Professors Jacob, Balugianskii, and Lodi from the University of Kharkov. Their combined efforts resulted in an able and interesting report which provided the theoretical framework for Speransky's own Financial Plan in 1810. In his memoirs, Jacob claimed to have been the author of this important plan which Speransky only copied. But the claim of the learned professor is subject to doubt in view of Jacob's tendency to a naive exaggeration of his own importance. Soviet historians have contended that the most significant theoretical contributions belonged to the pen of Balugianskii and that Speransky merely translated the latter's work from the French, made some editorial changes, and then passed it off as his own. Unfortunately, Balugianskii's papers have not been published and it is impossible to form a definitive opinion on the basis of the few fragments quoted in secondary sources. It must be noted in this connection that at the time he wrote his analysis of Russian finances, Balugianskii was a newcomer to Russia and could hardly have been too familiar with the country's condition and administration. Nor was he in a position to obtain full and easy access to the information collected by the Ministry of Finance. [1] On the other hand, the Financial Plan of 1810 contains numerous remarks and references which testify to a profound and first-hand knowledge of Russian conditions. We must, perforce, conclude that while Balugianskii's theoretical considerations may have provided a framework for the reforms proposed, Speransky's creative participation cannot be denied. The latter alone made it possible to implement the Plan by legislation. Such a contribution certainly went beyond the limits of mere translation and editorial improvements. [2]

The way for a new approach to finance was cleared early in 1810 when Golubtsov was dismissed as Minister of Finances and replaced by a protégé of Speransky, Count A. D. Gur'ev, who had been associated with the Unofficial Committee and had been Treasurer of the Realm since 1808. Although formally Gur'ev was at the helm of Russian finances, it was Speransky who formulated the basic policies and who submitted the projects of reform to the Emperor. At the same time, early in 1810, the Commission for Financial Affairs was placed under the direct supervision of the Department for State Economy of the newly organized Council of State. The members of this department (Admiral Mordvinov, Baron Kampenhausen, Count Kochubei, Count Potocki, Councillor Balugianskii, Sablukov, Tutolmin, and Speransky) were well trained and experienced government officials who viewed with favor the economic theories then current in Western Europe. Speransky himself set to work on the financial problem with his customary energy and speed. Early in 1810 he was in a position to present his Plan for the consideration of the Department for State Economy of the Council of State. The Department and the Council adopted the basic principles of the Plan, and the Emperor gave his

---

[1] Jacob's memoirs mention the great difficulty he encountered in obtaining official information on the country's economic and financial state. *Denkwürdigkeiten*, pp. 273, 279. See also, Pogrebinskii, *Ocherki istorii finansov*, pp. 19—20.

[2] Even Jacob implies that much, *Denkwürdigkeiten*, pp. 279, 280, 289.

consent to its implementation. The first legislative measures based on Speransky's plan were issued in February 1810. The proposals and arguments for the reform of Russia's monetary and financial condition which Speransky presented marked a turning point in the history of Russian financial administration and thinking on economic matters and they deserve to be considered in some detail.

Appraising the situation created by several decades of financial disorder and of uncontrolled emission of paper money, Speransky points out in his Plan that all the burden falls on the Treasury of the Empire and on those who stand in direct obligation to it as creditors and tax payers. Obviously, the quickest and simplest method of solving the problem would be to buy back all the assignats; but this has now become impossible. Another suggestion has been made, namely to back the assignats with state lands. But this solution is equally unadvisable as the experience of the United States has shown, for fluid capital cannot be based on real estate. After all, it is not only a question of withdrawing from circulation the excessive amount of assignats over-night. The real problem consists in basing the financial system firmly upon the economic potential of the country. The foundation of a sound financial system, in Speransky's belief, consists in an easy availability of capital for the normal requirements of the national economy. "In every state," he writes in the Plan of 1810, "and in particular in a state which has more capital in goods than in money, the task of true economy demands a speeding up of the circulation of monetary capital, so that its smallest amount makes possible the fastest and largest turnover; i.e. true economy demands that metal species be represented by notes of credit. *The qualities of all notes of credit are proportional to the capital on which they are based.*" [1] Therefore, paper money based on silver must be issued in proportion to the availability of silver bullion, otherwise speculation will destroy its basic function. As for copper money, the other currency in use at the time, it should serve only as means of exchange for fractions of silver, and its value can be determined only on the basis of experience.

The capital needed by the state to support the instruments of credit and exchange is obtained through taxation. But what can serve as the basis of taxation, what can produce taxable wealth? "Any labor which brings in a net yearly income can be the object of taxation," answers Speransky. [2] But not all of this potential capital can be tapped by the

---

1 Speranskii, "Plan Finansov," *Sbornik IRIO,* XLV (1885), p. 31 (italics are Speransky's), cf. also pp. 32–33.
2 Plan Finansov, p. 36.

fisc. This is particularly true of a large country without excess capital and where many hidden treasures do not yield any revenue as they have not been touched by labor. How can these potential resources of revenue be exploited through the application of labor to them? By increasing the amount of capital which can be applied to such purposes, and this kind of capital must be obtained by borrowing, reasons Speransky. Sound private credit, well protected by law, contributes to the support of public credit. In Russia, however, this is not the case, for the capital borrowed by the state from the nation's wealth, i.e. the debt of the state, is not protected by laws and is therefore subject to constant fluctuation. [1] Indeed, the value of assignats is based on the people's faith in their redeemability, for by themselves the pieces of paper have no value. In saying this, Speransky is arguing against the theory current since the time of Catherine II that paper money actually "creates money," that it is money in the same sense as precious metals, and is capable of fulfilling the same functions. In fact, Speransky points out, assignats are only a disguised form of a state debt. [2] At the present time, this debt is covered in part by arbitrary taxation. But such taxation harms industry, its burden is very unequally distributed, for it works more hardship on the poor than on the rich. There are no positive gains to be derived from the existing system of assignats to make its defects more bearable. [3]

What should be done to remedy the situation? In his usual systematic manner, Speransky breaks up the problem into two courses of action: the ultimate goals and long range policies, and those measures which can, and must, be taken immediately to prepare the ground for the eventual solution of the crisis. He does not hide the fact that any nation's system of finance rests on a multiplicity of varied interests, passions, habits. Every change in the system is bound to bring forth sharp reactions from these interests and passions. A workable plan of financial reorganization must take this fact into account and provide means for overcoming temporary opposition and inconveniences for

[1] "Assignats are papers based on suppositions. Not having any intrinsic value, they are nothing else but hidden debts." Plan Finansov, p. 38.
[2] And that is why the emission of assignats is an undetermined taxation, imposed permanently, Plan Finansov, p. 39. The reasoning of the last two pages is very reminiscent of that of Richard Cantillon, who — according to Charles Rist — had the most correct insight into the problem of exchanges and credit of all the economists of the 18th century. Cantillon's ideas, not very widely known, had been summarized at length by Condillac; and from Slovtsov's statement (see note 2, p. 11) we know that Speransky had read and studied Condillac while still at the seminary. Cf. Charles Rist, *Histoire des doctrines relatives au crédit et à la monnaie — depuis John Law jusqu'à nos jours* (2e ed., Paris 1951), Chapter I, pp. 53—65 *passim*.
[3] Plan Finansov, pp. 39—41.

the sake of the long term benefits it will confer upon the country. To pretend that a fundamental reform of the financial structure can be accomplished without affecting some private vested interests, without reducing the ordinary expenses of the government, is to be dishonest and to fool the country into ruin. [1] Speransky is, therefore, well aware of the political difficulties facing him and he does not hide them from the Emperor. But he hopes that the government will make show of the necessary consistency of purpose and energy in overcoming the initial hurdles.

Speransky proposes to work for the realization of three limited and concrete goals: 1. absorption of the assignats currently in circulation, 2. establishment of a bank based on silver, 3. introduction of a sounder monetary system. Several steps will lead to this result. In the first place, the present level of credit should be maintained and faith in the economy of the nation restored. To this end, the government should make perfectly clear its intention of changing the financial system, its irrevocable resolution to stop the emission of new assignats, and its recognition of all paper money in circulation as a state debt on the security of the entire national wealth. The faith in this program will be strengthened if the government asks for the help and advice of representative leaders of the economy. For this latter purpose Speransky suggests inviting the merchants of the most important commercial cities, St. Petersburg, Moscow, and Riga, to elect one representative who will be appointed to the board of directors of the "Assignat Bank" to be created for the purpose of supervising the absorption of the assignats in circulation. [2] The absorption, or elimination, of the assignats in circulation is a matter of immediate concern, and the means for achieving it will be discussed later under the heading of short-range measures.

A second long-range reform consists in putting in order the system of direct taxation of non-agricultural incomes. The trouble with the system in force, asserts Speransky, is that the taxes are not always clearly stated and not based on definite rational principles. In Speransky's opinion, "all [state] revenues can be considered normal 1. when they do not dry up the sources of domestic wealth, 2. when they are distributed evenly, 3. when they do not affect the capital necessary for production but are deduced only from net benefits, 4. when the manner of their collection is cheap for the government and not burdensome to private individuals." [3] For an equitable assessment and re-

[1] Plan Finansov, pp. 2, 3.
[2] Plan Finansov, Sec. 38—39, p. 11.
[3] Plan Finansov, Sec. 101, p. 21.

partition of the taxes on the net profits of productive capital in proportion to the country's ability, it would be desirable to have complete and correct information on the flow of merchandise and on the exchanges in each province. Furthermore, as this tax primarily affects merchants and townspeople, it would be most efficient, just, and cheap to let the merchant groups take care of the repartition of the total tax assessment among themselves. [1] This participation of the merchants at some stage of the fiscal administration, however limited their role and independence, would greatly contribute to instilling confidence in the government's economic policies.

These measures — desirable as they are — are not sufficient, for they do not increase the treasury's receipts so as to cover the current expenditures and the cost of redeeming the assignats. New taxes, therefore, are unavoidable, the more so since the country has had the same taxes for the last quarter of a century. New sources of taxable revenue, however, cannot be found overnight, for they are only the consequence of expanding national income. In the promotion of new sources of national income, the government is hampered by its inadequate knowledge of the country's economy, actual and potential. It will be a long time before complete and adequate statistical data can be gathered, and much preparatory work will have to be done first. [2] But one source of new income for the state is immediately at hand: the sale of state domains to the peasants who live and work on them now. The advantages of such a measure are obvious. "The number of owners of land will increase, the land will be worked better, the treasury will receive regularly the payment of capital and interest, the ordinary quitrent revenues will, in due course of time, be replaced by a general land tax. These lands should be sold to entire villages with the right to re-sell them if other land is bought or found [by the peasants] for settlement." [3] In other words, Speransky wants to give the state peasants not only possession of the land, but full ownership, a most important idea in the history of the peasant question in Russia. In any case, he clearly favors the extension of independent peasant land holdings. It is also to be noted that he envisages the possibility of migration from areas where the land was becoming scarce or depleted and resettlement in other parts of the country.

The phrase, "replaced by a regular land tax," used by Speransky,

[1] Plan Finansov, Sec. 106, p. 22.
[2] Plan Finansov, Secs. 9, 10, p. 6. It may be noted that Speransky was the first Russian statesman to attempt basing the financial and economic policies of the state on statistical data and their analysis.
[3] Plan Finansov, Sec. 166, p. 62.

must be noted more particularly, as it is the very core of his proposal
for a new system of taxing the country's agricultural wealth. It marks
a new departure in the fiscal and economic thinking of the Russian
government. From that time on it will be included in all reform plans
and projects. The meaning and full import of the phrase is stated
clearly by Speransky in another part of the Financial Plan, and the
passage is worth quoting in its entirety:

> "The first source of new revenue is the *land tax*. The poll tax
> now in existence has no true foundation. The best proof for this
> is that the good common sense of landowners and state peasants
> does not recognize it in fact anywhere in the same sense as the
> government. Nowhere, in no village, is the tax repartitioned
> according to the number of 'revision souls' [i.e. taxable male souls
> as listed in the government census] of which many do not exist
> any more, while others have come to the village recently. On the
> contrary, everywhere the repartition is made on the basis of the
> amount of the *tiaglo* [i.e. a figure expressing the relation between
> the acreage tilled and the number of workers in a household].
> Therefore, this [poll tax] is in truth nothing else than an addition
> to the quitrent. Consequently, the poll tax even now exists only
> on paper and in the accounts of the government. In reality, it is
> a land tax, but a tax established on very inadequate and incorrect
> principles. Abolish this [poll] tax and introduce a land tax in its
> stead." [1]

Clearly, such a new land tax would relate the fiscal burden directly
to the productivity of the land and of agricultural labor.

The establishment of an orderly and effective system of taxation is
but half of the battle won. The goal will be achieved only with the
help of a proper financial administration. To this end, Speransky
proposes to introduce a standard schedule of the state's receipts and
expenditures which would serve as a basis for the yearly budget. To
insure budgetary uniformity and order, government accounting should
be done in terms of silver rubles instead of the fluctuating assignats
and multiple currencies. For the duration of the period when a stable
relationship between silver and paper will not have yet been achieved,
the yearly budget must also fix this relationship for the entire coming
fiscal year. Once established, the budget cannot be changed during the
fiscal year by the Minister of Finance. Any change — only for reasons
of absolute necessity — must be approved by the Emperor and its
implementation supervised by the Council of State. In no case should
new expenditures be incurred if no equivalent source of revenue has

1 Plan Finansov, Sec. 120—121, p. 26.

been found for them first. For, as Speransky has argued earlier, new expenditures of the state will benefit the country only if they are a consequence of the development of the country's industry and productivity. For extraordinary expenses the government should have at its disposal, instead of reserves of money, the means of obtaining additional revenue if and when needed. [1] Today such suggestions seem obvious, but never before had they been stated so clearly to a Russian Emperor. In so doing, Speransky was extending to the domain of public finance the principles of administrative and economic "rationality" prevailing in private enterprises.

The preceding summary of sections of the Financial Plan shows that Speransky is well aware of the truth of the dictum, "pauvre pays, pauvre roi." [2] An essential and organic part of his financial reforms is concerned with the fostering of economic activity and business enterprise in Russia. Speransky's Plan develops further some of the ideas stated in the Report of the Minister of the Interior for 1803 (cf. Chapter 3). Together with the opponents of mercantilism and state monopolies, Speransky does not believe that the government should have exclusive control over any aspect of economic activity or source of wealth. The state should not hamper the free play of individual enterprise and intitiative by its own unfair competition. Therefore, the Russian government should give up its monopoly of the salt trade. The Treasury's revenue will not suffer from it, for the monopoly can be more than adequately replaced by a production tax. Chances are that with free circulation of the commodity, the turnover will be greater, production will increase and the tax on it yield more. Similarly, the farming out of alcohol sales should be replaced by an excise tax. Nor should the state attempt to have its own factories, except those few which might be essential for military purposes. State factories are not advantageous to the government because of their inefficiency and low productivity. At the same time they create unfair competition for individual entrepreneurs who could do the job much better. [3] Furthermore, the government should not make any demands on the labor and time of its citizens, barring emergencies, of course. The Plan, therefore,

---

[1] Plan Finansov, Secs. 46, 51, 66, 70, 72, 78, 82, 94, pp. 13—19.

[2] Speranskii, "Ob uchrezhdeniiakh otnosiashchikhsia do ekonomii." *Arkhiv istoricheskikh i prakticheskikh svedenii*, (1859), No. 6, pp. 13—21 *passim*. After listing the sources of the power (*sily*) of the state (moral forces, intellectual forces, individual physical forces, natural forces [natural resources], labor forces) and of the government (justice and order, strength of government institutions, military forces, unmovable state property, fiscal resources), he concludes that the strength (power) of the government is based on the wealth of the state (pp. 13—14).

[3] Plan Finansov, Secs. 111, 112, 113, p. 24.

insists most energetically that dues in kind and services be replaced by taxes payable in money. This applies more particularly to local service obligations of road maintenance, the furnishing of horses for postal relays, the convoying of prisoners, etc. The government gains little from these services, Speransky argues, and for the population they are sources of hardship, innumerable abuse, and hence quite ruinous. The replacement of these services by monetary contributions would go a long way towards restricting the opportunities of abuse by local officials; this in turn would permit the government to collect the tax regularly in full. As to the services performed by the population, they would not suffer either. Instead of their being performed by reluctant and unskilled peasants, they could be conducted by a small efficient corps of specially trained employees, as in Western Europe. It should be noted that while this proposal concerning government dues in form of service was not adopted in 1810, Speransky was able to introduce it in Siberia in 1822. Its success there led to its eventual implementation in European Russia after Speransky's death. [1]

Reformed along the lines we have just noted, the financial structure of the Russian state would rest, Speransky maintains, on a monetary system working with controlled regularity. Such a system cannot be introduced overnight. But some things can be initiated, and they alone would take the country a long way in the right direction. First, stability and faith in the monetary structure must be secured. The people's natural propensity to speculate on the instability and fluctuation of the currency has to be checked, at least until the value of assignats and silver are brought into a stable relationship. There is only one perfect type of money: silver and notes of credit based on silver. These should be the standard of measure and accounting for all transactions, both private and public. [2] Speransky proposes to bring about such a state of affairs by the creation of private banks, based on silver. These banks will draw out the capital in silver available in Russia and which constitutes a most important source of credit. To regulate the flow of credit on the spot, the banks would have many local branches, and they would be allowed to purchase and sell silver and gold — but nothing else. As copper coins are a very common and important form of currency for small exchanges, these banks would also function as regulators of the value of copper. To do this, they should always be able and ready to buy silver in bullion and exchange it for copper currency, and vice versa. In this fashion the banks will limit

1 Plan Finansov, Sec. 108, p. 23.
2 Plan Finansov, p. 44.

and regulate speculation on copper, an activity which for a long time has been hampering trade and making smalle-scale commercial transactions a very risky affair. [1] True enough, so far the Treasury has benefited from the differential in the rate of silver and copper, but it is a very unhealthy and questionable advantage. In the long run it is bound to have detrimental effects on the country's economy. In abandoning this undesirable "profiteering" from the disorders of the monetary system,

> "the government will derive two advantages: 1. the circulation of credit notes of private banks will decrease the domestic need for silver, will shorten its [silver's] circuit, and, as a result, its larger mass will balance the burden of foreign credit; 2. the circulation of these credit notes will also diminish the need for small change and thereby increase the quantity of copper goods. The foregoing advantages are so notable that the establishment of private banks should be promoted by all means for the sake of good national economy." [2]

The long term measures just described should be implemented by a series of steps to be taken immediately. We recall that Speransky has argued that the assignats are only a hidden state debt. To end the chaos which results from the unregulated issuance of paper money and to prepare the way for a new and stable system, the government's first step should be a clear and emphatic declaration that it recognizes this debt and assumes the obligation to redeem it. Such a declaration, argues Speransky, will have primarily a psychological role in restoring confidence in the government's policies and thereby it will contribute to a rise in the value of the assignats. [3] After the country's faith has been restored, the next step of the programme can be taken: reduction of the quantity of assignats in circulation. This will be achieved by stopping further issues of paper money, by reducing expenditures, and by floating a domestic loan for a "caisse d'amortissement." [4]

It is easy to advocate cuts in government expenses, but in a period of unsettled political conditions, with the threat of war hanging over the country, it is not a simple operation to perform. Speransky was too close to the Emperor to ignore the state of affairs in the world and

---

[1] Plan Finansov, Sec. 176, p. 63 and pp. 47, 49.

[2] Plan Finansov, p. 51.

[3] This was also the reasoning of Thornton in 1802, incorporated in the English Bullion Report issued in early 1811, too late to have a direct influence on Speransky's plan, but whose preparatory stages might have been known to Speransky. On Thornton's ideas, cf. Rist op. cit., pp. 131–132, 152.

[4] Plan Finansov, Secs. 22–27, pp. 8–9.

to exclude from his calculations the possibility of a war with France (as noted in the previous chapter, he predicted such a conflict), and the need for emergency expenses. As if realising his, and the government's, helplessness in this respect, Speranky only repeats his entreaties that all assignats be considered a debt of the state, including even such new ones that might have to be issued in an emergency.[1] This is not much of a concrete proposal, but the only one Speransky felt he could reasonably make at this point. At any rate, cuts in the expenditures of the government should follow a reasonable system that would safeguard the economic welfare of the nation. For 1810, Speransky suggests that only the following be considered as useful expenditures: "those ... which are used for promoting and 'fertilizing' [sic] various branches of industry whose benefits are clearly proven; 2. those [expenditures] without which the various tasks of the administration could not be carried on ... 3. those expenditures whose delay ... can temporarily reduce the benefits of the government."[2] Admittedly, this is a somewhat broad and vague definition. But compared to the total picture of ordinary expenses, it limits expenditures to those which are shown to be clearly consonant with the welfare and interests of the state as a whole, and not merely of individuals and privileged institutions. But what about extraordinary expenditures, should they arise? In Speransky's view, the only real emergency expenditures would be for war. Should war break out, the military needs can be satisfied by levying a property tax (in form of a loan) and by increasing the sale of state lands. Barring war, there are only three kinds of extraordinary expenditures the government should permit: upkeep of the army, pensions, and rents (arendy) granted to officers and officials for meritorious service. Actually, payments on the last two items can be suspended for a year or two, and in case of urgent need, pensions can be replaced by "expectatives" or government promissory notes (apparently negotiable).[3]

It is not enough to limit the expenditures, it is the revenue of the state that must be increased by all means possible, argues Speransky. Such an increase can be obtained by a better distribution of the burden of taxation and by improving the state-enterprises (state lands, forests, mines, salt trade, etc.). As we have noted, he does not think that new sources of revenue can be found readily. But as capital for redeeming the assignats must be raised, he suggests that the following might yield some results: import duties, sale of copper bullion, sale of uninhabited

1 Plan Finansov, Sec. 40, p. 11.
2 Plan Finansov, Sec. 7, p. 6.
3 Plan Finansov, Sec. 34, p. 10.

state lands to private individuals (the sale of settled lands to the peasants working them was a long term project).[1]

Even after all the measures suggested so far have been taken, there still remains the task of tackling the most important problem of all: elimination of the tremendous quantity of assignats in circulation. To this end, Speransky proposes several measures to be initiated immediately and carried out with unflinching determination. The exchange of one issue of assignats for another, a common practice, must be forbidden completely. Such an exchange is, after all, not only a cumbersome operation, but a fictitious alleviation of the evil as well. Moreover, it falls most heavily on the poorer classes. The redemption of assignats has to proceed in orderly fashion under the supervision of a special bureau, a kind of "caisse d'amortissement." Its capital, as mentioned earlier, is to be raised by floating a domestic loan, bearing an interest paid at regular intervals. The interest on the loan must be paid at all costs, so as to bolster public confidence in the government's financial policy. Speransky proposes to float a 10-year loan of 25 millions rubles; the capital would be placed at interest and the interest earned would serve to build up a redemption fund. Should the first loan be unsuccessful, it can be complemented by state lotteries. But even in case of failure of the lotteries as well, the state should nonetheless start redeeming the assignats immediately. Of course, any additional source of revenue which the state might find, will be applied towards the redemption operation.[2]

For the administration of the loans and redemption fund, Speransky recommends the creation of a special state bank with a capital based on silver. Part of the bank's shares are to be held by the government, and a part is to be owned by private individuals who can purchase them by paying ¼ in silver and ¾ in assignats. One third of the shares will constitute the bank's active capital used for its regular banking operations: discounting of notes, safekeeping of jewels, payment of interest on short-term state loans. In avoidance of competition with the Nobility's Land Banks (established by Catherine II), this "redemption" bank would not be entitled to make loans upon the security of real estate. Nor would the bank be permitted to make transactions involving the sale and purchase of merchandise (except gold, silver, and copper bullion). The institution will be managed by the shareholders, proportionately to their participation in the bank's capital, the government being only one of the shareholders, albeit the most important one.[3]

[1] Plan Finansov, Secs. 117, 118, pp. 25—26.
[2] Plan Finansov, Secs. 143, 144, 147, 156, 159, 160, pp. 58—60.
[3] Plan Finansov, Secs. 178—185, pp. 64—65.

The models which inspired Speransky in suggesting this bank are, of course, not far to seek: the Bank of England, and more directly, the Banque de France established by Napoleon.

The operations of redemption and reorganization of the Empire's financial system are to be supervised by an efficient Ministry of Finance, renovated along functional lines. While the actual administration of Russia's finances remains the function of the Ministry, the Office of Accounts and the Treasury become autonomous institutions. Moreover, in order to check the overpowerful influence and possible arbitrary actions of the Minister of Finance, the overall policies are to be worked out by a Financial Council composed of the Minister, the Treasurer, the Chief Director of Accounts (*Glavnyi direktor upravleniia schetov*), and of the heads of those departments that have jurisdiction over the specific matter under discussion at a given time. For better coordination with the general administration of the Empire, other Ministers may be invited to participate in the deliberations of the Financial Council. [1]

The ideas and the approach Speransky presented in his Financial Plan of 1810 marked a new departure in the economic thinking of the imperial government. It was the first time that such an all-embracing program of fundamental reorganization had been proposed and developed on the basis of theoretical and practical considerations. In its programatic significance, in its effort at reorienting the thinking of the Russian administration, it could be compared only to Pososhkov's *O skudosti i bogatstve* which had provided a theoretical foundation for the economic policies of Peter the Great and his successors for almost a whole century. But Speransky was much more important as an administrator and organizer than Pososhkov had been. Only a specialist in the economics of currency and public finance — something the present writer is not — can give a thorough analysis and estimate of Speransky's views and proposals. But even the historian not initiated into the secrets of this most difficult field of economic analysis, cannot fail to note the character and significance of Speransky's approach. As has been pointed out earlier, without access to the archives it is impossible to establish satisfactorily the part played by Speransky's professional advisers, Professors Bulagianskii and Jacob in the formulation of the Plan's basic theoretical principles. Many general ideas on economics, as for instance those on free economic activity and non-participation of the state in business enterprises, were part and parcel of the period's general outlook shaped under the direct influence of Adam Smith. But as Charles Rist has suggested, the ideas of Adam

[1] Plan Finansov, Secs. 199—238, pp. 67—72.

Smith on money and credit were not distinguished by clarity and cogency. [1] In particular, Smith had held a somewhat confused notion about paper money, assignats, seeing them as a source of actual credit or money, and not as state obligations. Obviously, Speransky did not share Adam Smith's conception on this point. For his time and place, Speransky's emphatic assertion that, in the absence of expanding productivity or national income, assignats were a state debt, a hidden domestic loan that had to be repaid, was quite "revolutionary." The only important economic thinker of the 18th century who had had a similar understanding of the nature of assignats had been Richard Cantillon. Another significant aspect of Speransky's thinking, was an awareness of the importance of speeding up the circulation of money as a form of credit, especially in a country which was poor in capital and where it took a long time to create new capital. The idea of the function of money and notes of credit in the speed of the circulation of instruments of exchange had also been defended by Cantillon (against John Law). If Charles Rist's evaluation of Cantillon's theoretical position is correct, then Speransky shares with the latter the honor of defending a most sophisticated, modern, and accurate understanding of the principles which underlie the mechanism of credit and money circulation. It puts him above the popular economists of his time and brings him close to the important views expressed in England at about the same time by only a few specialists. Perhaps Speransky's knowledge of English and connections with English businessmen residing in St. Petersburg gave him direct access to the technical literature on the subject; whereas his colleagues had to be content with reading the French or Russian translations of the more general and popular works.

Speransky's notions about credit and money were only one aspect of his views on political economy. As must have become apparent from the summary of the Financial Plan, he had some very definite thoughts concerning the foundation of a country's economic prosperity. On this subject his views were rather syncretic, and he managed to blend the teachings of the Physiocrats with those of Adam Smith and his followers. He was also less of a precursor in this respect, for the theories of both Physiocrats and Adam Smith had been known in Russia before his time. Physiocratic notions were held by Catherine II — as one aspect of her enlightened absolutism — and they had been popularized among wide circles of the nobility by the Court Chaplain, A. A. Samborskii. The theories of Adam Smith became known as early as the 1770's through Russian students who had been sent to Glasgow and were

[1] Ch. Rist: *Histoire des doctrines relatives au crédit et à la monnaie* (Paris 1951).

taken up by the "liberal" publicists like A. Radishchev. Speransky's acquaintance and even close relations with both Samborskii and Radishchev would be sufficient reason, if proof were necessary, for his being well acquainted with the views of the Physiocrats and Classical economists. But Speransky's personal contribution from the Russian point of view was that he brought these ideas together, presented them in a systematic and comprehensive form, and — most important of all — drew the practical institutional lessons for his program of administrative reorganization. [1]

The foundation of a nation's prosperity, Speransky believed, resides in two elements: natural resources and labor. Russia has plenty of both, provided they are permitted to develop fully. Russia's natural resources consist in great quantities of fertile and arable land, in mineral wealth; they can be exploited more fully. The labor force of the country is, perhaps, not excessively large, but plentiful enough so far, and it is not inferior in quality to that of any other labor force in the world. Land, i.e. agriculture, is Russia's most important foundation of economic prosperity, and the government should not in any way stifle the freedom of action necessary for its development. Land — and the produce of agricultural labor — are not only the most valuable resource, they are also the principal source of revenue for the state. Therefore, a general tax on land must become the pillar of the state's fiscal policies and finances, and the arbitrary and economically indefensible poll tax must be abolished. The second foundation of the state's prosperity, and the Treasury's revenue, is industry (in the widest sense of the word). Here too the government should not only refrain from fettering industrial enterprise, but should encourage and foster the maximum of private activity. Under Russian conditions, however, the government must still take an active role in developing industry, at least for the time being. As will be seen subsequently, Speransky's belief in the unhampered development of all potentialities inherent in the country and the nation was closely related to his fundamental tenet of political philosophy. The task of the government is to help this maximum development of the nation's moral, spiritual, and economic possibilities. As long as the conditions for the full natural development of economic opportunities have not been achieved, the government can and should nurse it along by its fiscal, monetary, and tariff policies and by legal and institutional controls.

---

1 The following account of his ideas on economic problems is based on: "Ob uchrezhdeniiakh otnosiashchikhsia...," *loc. cit.*, pp. 17—19, 21. Also, cf. the "Doklad Ministra Vnutrennikh Del za 1803," cited in Chapter 3, and several letters written after his exile to Count Gur'ev (1817—1820, in *Pamiati* pp. 451—486 *passim*).

Speransky saw clearly and correctly Russia's financial problem and the desirable goal of her economic development. However, in suggesting concrete policies to deal with the situation, he proved inadequate. He had learned, and he fully understood, the best available theories of his time, theories which even in the West had not gained full acceptance. It would be unfair to criticize him, therefore, for having held certain conceptions that have been abandoned by economic science since. For instance, he failed to envisage the possibility that the raising of the country's economic potential would be a more effective means for absorbing the excess of assignats than their conversion into a fixed state debt. It might be added, however, that Speransky clearly saw that conversion was only a first step which must be followed and supported by a general raising of the nation's economy. But the greatest weakness of his Financial Plan was that he did not take into consideration the conditions under which he had to operate: Russia's economic and social backwardness, the critical political situation presented by the ever-renewed international conflicts. His was too much of a doctrinaire approach which disregarded the practical feasibility, within a reasonable time, and within the existing social and political framework, of his proposals for financial and economic reorganization and reform.

In the final analysis, Speransky's goal was that of the *laisser-faire,* free trade, individualistic theorists of the early 19th century. But he still shared with the enlightened absolutists and Physiocrats the belief that the state had to take positive action in guiding and educating the nation towards this goal. In other words, the road that led to freedom and individualism in economic life had to be travelled in conveyances provided and administered by the state. In taking this fundamentally bureaucratic approach, Speransky did not seem to realize that the means chosen might defeat the ends. This particular blind spot of his was inherited by successive ministers throughout the 19th century, down to the very end of the Imperial regime. [1]

As for the implementation of Speransky's Financial Plan, it was approved by the Emperor after it had received a favorable recommendation from the Department of State Economy of the Council of State. Speransky, then State Secretary and at the height of his influence, proceeded to implement the various measures he had proposed. The aims of the Plan were made public by the decree of February 2, 1810 (PSZ 24,116) which ordered the following steps: the assignats were recognized as a state debt and their eventual complete redemption

---

[1] Cf. Khromov, *op. cit.,* p. 131, note 2 (Bogolepov, *Gosudarstvennyi Dolg,* 1910, p. 405).

promised; in the meantime, further increase in their emission was strictly forbidden. In order to find the capital for the redemption of the debt (blamed on past wars) the expenditures were reduced by 20 millions rubles and various taxes increased. The introduction of a new stable monetary system was promised for the near future. A few months later, May 27, 1810 (PSZ 24,244), a public loan was floated to build up the capital needed for the redemption of assignats. In June and August of that same year, the relative values of silver and copper were set by law (PSZ 24,264, June 20) and state domains were put up for sale (PSZ 24,334, August 29). Finally, late in 1810 and early in 1811, the Ministry of Finances was reorganized along the lines proposed by Speransky in his Plan (the reorganization was completed by the decree of June 25, 1811, PSZ 24,688).

The reception of the concrete measures was mixed. It should be noted that the public could judge only on the basis of these separate legislative acts, for the Financial Plan itself was not published and remained largely unknown, except for possible indiscretions by members of the Council of State. Some observers, in particular the foreign residents, realizing for the first time the extent of Russia's financial disorders, approved of the decrees as first steps towards improvement. But they did not spare their criticism of the actual results immediately obtained. For instance, John Quincy Adams, at the time United States Minister to Russia, reported to the Secretary of State on June 25, 1810:

"I have the honor to enclose a copy in the French language of a Manifesto just published here, proposing a public loan to be received in the paper money of the country, and the sale of certain public domains for the redemption of this paper. — It will serve at once to show the disordered state of the finances of the Empire, and the laudable efforts of the present government to retrieve them [follows a history of the assignats in Russia] ... At the present, this loan upon terms extremely favorable to the lenders and proportionately burdensome to the government is proposed for the purpose of withdrawing from circulation some part of that excess which has occasioned the depreciated state of the bills [details of the loan and conversion rules] ... In the sale of the lands there are held out further advantages to the lenders, of no inconsiderable importance. The loan is to be opened on the 15th of July, but neither the manifesto nor the recent accounts of the splendid victories obtained over the Turks have yet raised the value of paper assignats in the market." [1]

1 National Archives, Foreign Relations Division, Department of State, Diplomatic Dispatches, Russia, vols. I and II, (Hereafter referred to as *Department of State — Russia*) John Quincy Adams to Secretary of State, dispatch No. 17, 25 June 1810. (Spelling modernized).

In his last sentence, John Quincy Adams correctly noted the difficulties that the government faced in its efforts at instilling greater public faith and confidence in its financial policies. A few weeks later, on August 11, J. Q. Adams wrote again to the Secretary of State concerning the financial reform:

> "Measures of a similar nature to this [i.e. fixing of the price and relation of copper coin to sheet copper] have been so often resorted to by all governments of Europe that this step has scarcely excited a sensation or a murmur. The new loan proposed to receive 2 rubles of assignation paper and to promise payment of the interest and principal of one for it in silver. But as the loan was altogether voluntary, it impaired none of the previous obligations of the government. It saved at least the appearances. The effect of this manifesto is well understood but as the diminution proposed in the coin falls short of the actual depreciation of the paper, the people do not appear at all affected by it. At Riga and the other Livonian ports, they have hitherto been accustomed to keep their accounts and transact all their commercial business in computation of German money. The object of this manifesto is to introduce an uniform system in this respect throughout the Empire." [1]

The last consideration noted by Adams was not formally stated in Speransky's proposals. But what we know of the government's policy of bringing greater consistency and uniformity into all aspects of public life, makes the American Minister's explanation quite plausible. Another keen observer, and an experienced and imaginative economist and statesman in his own right, Freiherr vom Stein, commented rather favorably on Speransky's efforts, although he was not a great admirer of the Russian statesman. In the course of a conversation vom Stein had in Freiburg in 1813 with Nicholas Turgenev (attached to his Chancelry for Liberated Territories), he remarked — as reported by Turgenev in his diary: "We talked about Speransky. Stein maintained that Speransky had done good: 1. he increased the revenue [of the state] (although he agreed with me that die Abgaben waren schlecht gewählt), and 2. that he stopped the issuance of assignats." [2]

Russian opinion was far less enthusiastic than these two foreign observers. The nation as a whole suffered a few new hardships, as Speransky had predicted it would temporarily, resulting from the increases in dues on passports, postal services, stamp paper, etc. We are, of course, in no position to gauge accurately the reaction of the general

[1] *Department of State — Russia*, I, John Quincy Adams to Secretary of State, Dispatch No. 20 (14 August 1810).

[2] N. I. Turgenev, "Dnevniki i pis'ma za 1811—1816 gg," *Arkhiv brat'ev Turgenevykh*, II, (St. Pbg. 1913), p. 232 (entry dated 21 Dec. 1813, Freiburg).

population. The peaants were surely not happy about the increase in the capitation (poll) tax which was ordered in 1811. Nor could the small village traders relish the yearly turn-over tax levied in proportion to the amount and nature of their trade. But the greatest outcry, and the one best known to us, came from the nobility. The landowners had been benefiting from the cheap money created by the assignats and their tax exempted status. Now the assignats threatened to rise in value, and in 1811 a temporary income tax was to be imposed on the landowners. This tax was not very burdensome, for not only was it a temporary emergency measure, it was also levied entirely on the basis of uncontrolled, voluntary, individual self-assessments. The government wanted to rely on the good faith and patriotism of the nobility. Nonetheless, the nobility considered this measure as an infringement of its privileges and as an effort on the part of an upstart minister to lower its social and political prestige.

As the author of these measures — which complemented and im- plemented the proposals contained in his Plan — Speransky became an object of hatred for all those whose interests had been hurt or privileges infringed. Speransky had expected this reaction, for, as he later wrote to Alexander I from exile, whoever introduces new taxes, however necessary they might be, is never very popular. Someone, though, had to do the job, and it fell to his lot to be the symbol of these unpopular measures. But Speransky indignantly rejected the accusation that the unpopularity of "his" fiscal decrees had under- mined the people's loyalty to the Emperor and given rise to rebellious feelings among the peasantry. [1] He was convinced that after a brief period of murmurs and dissatisfaction, the people would become aware of the advantages of the new policy. Unfortunately, the condi- tions were such as to prevent the beneficial effects from manifesting themselves rapidly. [2]

In spite of its solemn promise not to issue any more assignats, the government was forced to resort to this expedient again to meet the cost of its military preparations on the eve of the war with Napoleon. The maximum of 577 millions rubles of assignats in circulation, set by a decree in the summer of 1810, could not be maintained. The in- ternal loan on which Speransky had counted so much, met with but temporary and limited success, as John Quincy Adams had to note

---

[1] Speranskii, "Opravdatel'naia zapiska," *Russkii Arkhiv* (1892), pp. 67—68 and letter to Alexander I from Perm' (Jan. 1813), in Shil'der, *Imperator Aleksandr I*, III, p. 522.

[2] For what remained yet to be done, in Speransky's opinion, see his "Otchet v delakh 1810...", *Sbornik IRIO*, 21 (1877), pp. 452—455.

only a few weeks after it had been floated. By May 1811, when it was closed, the loan had produced 6.5 millions rubles, a good figure, but much less than had been hoped for. The sale of state lands went even less satisfactorily. The buyers were few, even after the terms of purchase had been liberalized in 1811. In any case, even if Speransky's measures had been more successful, it is quite doubtful that Russia's finances would have been put on a healthy basis, because no normal system could have proved adequate to the economic and financial burdens of the French invasion and the wars of 1812—1815. After some improvement — due to the psychological effects produced by Speransky's measures — the assignats sank to their lowest level during the campaign against Napoleon. The deficit reached such proportions that even the English subsidies could not make up for it. Lastly, the destructions wrought by the invasion undermined the very foundations of financial recovery and "saddled" the government with additional expenditures in the form of compensations for war damages.

In spite of the apparent failure of his Plan, Speransky's efforts did not remain entirely without beneficial effect on the country. Of more permanent significance than the temporary improvement in the value of assignats was the orderly organization of the financial administration: consolidation of the entire state debt under one authority, clear division of functions in the Ministry of Finance, the establishment of uniform methods of accounting and of a Chief Accounting Division, preparation of complete yearly budgets. Most important of all, however, was the fact that Speransky brought a fresh and modern outlook on the nation's economy and finances to the musty offices of the Imperial government. This new outlook — whatever its theoretical merit and immediate practical benefit — became an active element which influenced later projects, reform measures, and governmental policies towards agriculture and industry.

## 2.  THE CENTRAL ADMINISTRATION

The ambitious program of Russia's financial and economic rehabilitation needed, in Speransky's view, the guiding hand of an efficiently organized administration. An administration which possessed singleness of purpose and continuity of policy was something that Russia sadly lacked at the time. The executive branch of the government had neither purposefulness nor unity and clearly defined responsibility. The replacement by the Ministries of the chaotic and haphazard system of the central administration inherited from the 18th century had not materially improved the situation. As we recall, the creation of the Ministries had been the outcome of the struggle between the "Senatorial Party" and the reform-minded Unofficial Committee. Otto Hintze's "typological" analysis of the origin of ministries (in contrast to the English-type Cabinet) seems to apply to the present case quite well. The close personal advisers and favorites of the monarch, his private council, were given specific executive and administrative tasks. [1] Unwilling to create a real "cabinet" whose members would hold the same political views, Alexander let each minister secure approval for his proposals directly from him and did not encourage ministerial solidarity. The Ministers, therefore, became the executive tools of the absolute ruler, they were the "creatures" of the autocrat. They did not govern or administer in the name of the sovereign on the basis of a delegation of his authority; they were actually the "physical extension" of the monarch. Under these circumstances, the need for strictly defining the duties and areas of competence of individual ministers had at first not been felt strongly.

Unity of purpose and policy, whatever there was of it in the Russian government, resided in the person of the monarch. In the absence of the sovereign — and such absences became quite frequent in the reign of Alexander I — there was no organ or institution that could provide the necessary unity of action and *esprit de suite* in policy. Informally, the Ministers formed a Committee of Ministers that met irregularly under the chairmanship of the Emperor to discuss matters affecting several departments. But the Committee had no clearly defined rights or competence, its recommendations could be easily superseded by the personal appeal of an influential minister to the Emperor. Not only did the Committee meet very irregularly; there also was no political solidarity among its members. Personal considerations played the dominant role in the nomination of ministers, so that

[1] O. Hintze, "Die Entstehung der modernen Staatsministerien," *Staat und Verfassung*, pp. 287—306 *passim*. Hintze very aptly stresses the close connection between this approach to monocratic-ministerial government and the bent for philosophical systematization in the thought of the Enlightenment. A good illustration of this is found in the *Political Testament* of Frederick II of Prussia (1752): "Il faut qu'un gouvernement bien conduit ait un système aussi lié que peut l'être un système de philosophie... or, un système ne peut émaner que d'une tête; donc il faut qu'il parte de celle du souverain." *Die politischen Testamente Friedrich's des Grossen* (ed. by G. B. Volz), *Ergänzungsband, Politische Correspondenz Friedrich's des Grossen* (Berlin 1920) p. 38. Frederick's definition of the role of ministers was quite applicable to the conception held by Alexander I, in Hintze's words: "Für ihn [Frederick II] waren Minister nur unselbständige Werkzeuge des Monarchen; sie hatten ihn zu informieren, ohne dass er sich dabei auf sie allein verlassen hätte, und sie hatten die Ausführung seiner Befehle zu leiten und kontrollieren." (Hintze, *op. cit.*, p. 290); cf. Frederick's opinion on the nuisance of Councils, *Politische Testamente, loc. cit.*, p. 189 (the Testament of 1768).

frequently life-long enemies would belong to the same Committee. At times the Emperor purposefully appointed individuals with conflicting outlooks, so as to keep the balance of power in his own hands. Under no circumstance could Alexander's Committees adequately express or imprint unity of purpose and policy to the administration of the Empire. Speransky described this situation quite well when he wrote: "the reports of ministers were of two kinds: individual and general. Special days and hours were set for the individual reports. The general report was given at a general meeting of the ministers in the presence of the Emperor; this was called the Committee [of Ministers]. Consequently, the Committee was neither a [government] body, nor a special institution; it was only a manner of report." [1] The limited unity of purpose of the first Committee (1802) had been due to the fact that it was dominated by the members of the Unofficial Committee. And even then, a solidarity of outlook could not be obtained because adherents of the "Senatorial Party" had been appointed to several ministries. With the withdrawal from active participation and decline of influence of Alexander's erstwhile friends and advisers (ca 1805), even this shred of unity of outlook disappeared from the government. In 1809 Count Kochubei was the only member of the Unofficial Committee to occupy a position of importance, but his influence with the Emperor had declined a great deal.

With the passing of time, the undesirable effects of the lack of ministerial unity of action and purpose were becoming more and more apparent. The situation gave rise to frequent and bitter criticism, especially by those numerous officials and dignitaries who had never viewed the ministries with favor. A primary reason for introducing into Russia the monocratic, ministerial form of executive administration had been the feeling that the collegial principle of the 18th century made for slowness and confusion. The Ministries, however, it was felt, had not brought about unity and purposefulness either, nor had they eliminated the older collegial features. They were an inadequate compromise. Even in their internal organization they combined monocratic and collegial elements, except in the Ministry of the Interior where the monocratic principle had been carried through consistently by Speransky. In principle, Speransky was a staunch supporter of the ministries which he much preferred to the inchoate and abusive "system" — if it could be called such — prevailing at the end of the 18th century. But he was also keenly aware of the deficiencies of the

---

[1] *Zhurnal Komiteta Ministrov-tsarstvovanie imperatora Aleksandra I,* I, p. 14, also in *Arkhiv istoricheskikh i statisticheskikh svedenii,* III, (1859), 39ff.

ministries as they had been set up in 1802. These institutions, in Speransky's opinion, suffered from three major faults: insufficient responsibility of the individual ministers, lack of precision and proportion in the distribution of affairs among the ministries, inadequate rules of procedure. The first, lack of even individual responsibility of the ministers for their acts, was the most serious defect. An individual minister could take arbitrary action and then seek refuge in the fact that he was a "physical extension" of the autocratic Emperor. Under such circumstances, the success of any effort at correcting the abuse or bringing the official to account was very doubtful. [1]

The first step towards reform, taken at the behest of Speransky, consisted in an apportioning of the various areas of governmental concern among the existing ministries on the basis of some clear and logical scheme. This was done by the decree of July 25, 1810 (PSZ 24,307) on a preliminary basis, until such time as the statutes of all the ministries were completed. The wording of the decree clearly set forth the purpose and character of the reform: "The real significance of these additions [to the statute of the Ministries of 1802] consists in that they: introduce a better distribution of business, establish a higher degree of uniformity [of procedure], shorten and facilitate the processing of business, set precisely the limits of the power and obligations [of the ministries], and thereby enable the executive to carry out the laws more speedily and accurately." [2] The government's business was to be arranged logically and naturally under five main headings: 1. external relations, 2. the establishment for external security, 3. state economy, 4. organization of criminal and civil justice, 5. the establishment for internal security. The areas of competence of the major ministries and administrations were to be assigned along these same lines, with the result that the following list was drawn up: 1. Ministry of Foreign Affairs, 2. Ministries of War and Navy, 3. Ministries of the Interior,

---

1 It may be observed that Speransky's argumentation parallels fully that made by Freiherr vom Stein in his "Darstellung der fehlerhaften Organisation des Cabinets und der Nothwendigkeit der Bildung einer Ministerialen Conferenz" (Berlin, 26/27 April 1806): "Sie [Kabinettregierung] hat alle Gewalt, die endliche Entscheidung aller Angelegenheiten, die Besetzung aller Stellen, aber keine *Verantwortlichkeit*, da die Person des Königs ihre Handlungen sanctionirt." Freiherr vom Stein, *Briefwechsel, Denkschriften und Aufzeichnungen*, vol. II, p. 77. I have not been able to find any direct evidence that Speransky borrowed from or knew Stein's *Denkschrift*. But from the point of view of chronology, and considering the very close relations which existed between the courts of St. Petersburg and Berlin, it would have been quite possible for Speransky to know the contents of Stein's paper. Another possible source of information on Stein's reform proposals could have been provided by Prussian dignitaries and officials who took refuge in Russia after Jena and Tilsit (Stein himself came to Russia only in 1812).

2 PSZ, 24,307 (p. 278 of vol. 31).

Education, Finance, Treasury, Comptroller General, 4. Ministry of Justice, 5. Ministry of Police. [1] Some matters which transcended or did not accurately fit any of the divisions listed were handled by separate agencies, as for example the Holy Synod, the Main Administration for Transportation.

It is to be noted that not only was this division of the government based on the idea of functional organization of administration (*Ressort-trennung*); it went far beyond the traditional Russian concepts regarding the proper function of government. The traditional view had been that government existed only for the purpose of providing the financial and military means for the preservation of the security (and expansion) of the state. Hence, administration only meant the maintenance of military strength and the collection of taxes for that purpose. True enough, Peter the Great had held a broader view of the role of government; but his absorption in foreign affairs (in the widest sense of the term) forced him to treat all matters of internal administration mainly from the point of view of their usefulness as a source of revenue or military preparedness. Compared to this tradition, Speransky's views were an innovation in so far as they elevated the concern for the nation's economic and cultural prosperity, security, and progress to the status of a major governmental responsibility. [2] In Speransky's mind, the purpose of state economy was much more than giving a material foundation to the institutions devoted to the preservation of external security (army, navy, diplomacy). State economy meant that the state, through the agency of the Ministries of the Interior, Finance, Education, Treasury, the Administration of Transportation, actively helped to promote economic activity, and protected and stimulated the spiritual and cultural development of the people. And in a similar vein, internal security, in Speransky's view, was more than the prevention (and punishment) of acts detrimental to the state, as had been the traditional Russian concept. Internal security had a positive function, it guaranteed (through the Ministry of Police) the security of individual citizens in their life and property, it protected their peaceful and lawful economic and social pursuits against attacks from fellow citizens and bureaucratic arbitrary tyranny. The conception of the state as the watchman of the peace of Russian citizens, the idea of the police acting both as constable and teacher of the people — these were novelties in Russia. We should perhaps qualify the last statement by pointing out

[1] PSZ, 24,307 (p. 278), Sec. 3. Cf. also, PSZ 24,326 (17 August 1810).
[2] See Korkunov, *Russkoe gosudarstvennoe pravo*, II, p. 408.

that Peter the Great had had an inkling of such a role for the state, but he understood very little the humanitarian and enlightened administrative concerns this attitude implied. Catherine II had come closer in realizing Speransky's ideal. But her idea of security had been mainly external: the preservation of law and order. And to the extent that she thought of the government as an enlightened guide in developing the nation's potentialities, she limited its role to the upper classes, the nobility and big merchants. Speransky, on the other hand, extended this "pedagogical" concern of the government to all classes of society. In so doing, he acted in the spirit of enlightened absolutism, although he brought to it the humanitarian, religious, and moral preoccupations of late 18th century social theory. His contribution to Russian administrative practice consisted in that he was the first to give an institutional form to the pedagogical and "leadership" functions of modern government in respect to the nation's prosperity and progress. Whether under the conditions prevailing in Russia in his days the implementation of this conception could have been anything other than paternalistic and bureaucratic may well be doubted. The deplorably low level of the nobility's — let alone that of other classes — political and social consciousness certainly justifies such a doubt. The sad part of it, perhaps to be expected, was that the central administration and its local agents emphasized the protective, paternalistic, bureaucratic features rather than the pedagogical, enlightened, humanitarian ones. Speransky failed to provide adequate safeguards against such perversion of his aim, and thereby made possible an extension of the area in which the bureaucracy could exercise its vicious and corrupt practices. This failure, coming from a man who knew the low calibre of the bureaucracy all too well, must forever qualify a positive evaluation of his work. It might be added, that the conservative and traditionalist opponents of Speransky were aware of this danger, and condemned him for strengthening and extending the role of the bureaucracy.

In 1811, Speransky put the final touch to the reorganization of the central executive agencies of the Empire. On June 25, 1811, the Statute for the internal organization of the ministries, drawn up by Speransky, was made public (PSZ 24,686). This statute provided the basic form of organization for Russia's ministries until 1905. The general Statute was to be followed by separate special regulations for each individual ministry, but Speransky himself only drafted two of these (for the Ministries of Finance, PSZ 24,688, and Police, PSZ 24,687, both dated June 25, 1811) before his dismissal in 1812. The general

Statute defined clearly the jurisdiction of each ministry and set forth the pattern of internal organization along logical and efficient lines. The internal structure of the ministries was the most important and valuable contribution to Russian administrative practice of the period. The remnants of the collegial pattern were swept away; the minister became the sole effective master in his ministry. However, as an excellent and experienced administrator, Speransky knew that one individual could not do everything by himself, that the secret of administrative efficiency lay in the delegation of functions and responsibility. The minister's unquestionable right to formulate policy and to take responsibility for the entire ministry before the Emperor having been established, the Statute entrusted the technical preparation of legislation and the supervision of simple routine matters to subordinate officials. For this purpose, the ministries were subdivided into departments, each dealing with a specific function or concern of the ministry. The chiefs of the departments were, so to speak, the minister's staff officers; they prepared the material on which policy decisions and legislation were based; they saw to it that the minister's instructions were properly carried out; they conducted the mechanical routine affairs, which did not need special policy decisions, without referring to the minister. To advise the minister — who might be new to the business — a Council of the Ministry was established. The Council gave the minister the benefit of the experience of the permanent officials. It consisted of the Assistant Minister (a sort of "chief of staff"), the chiefs of the departments, as well as outside officials — other ministers or their assistants — when their help was needed on special or technical questions. The Council of the Ministry had no power of decision, nor were its recommendations binding on the minister. It could only advise and give the minister the benefit of the experience and technical knowledge of its members. Its value as a source of precise technical information and as the foundation for consistency and continuity of policy can be readily seen. [1]

Speransky went further yet. Better than anyone, he knew the distance which separated the government from the people, the inadequacy of the sources of information at the disposal of the ministers on matters concerning the interests and very lives of the subjects. To obviate this deficiency, the Statute provided that private individuals — who had no regular bureaucratic status or official position — could be invited to the Council of the Ministry on a consultative basis. The provision recalls to mind the institution of "public members" in contemporary

[1] PSZ, 24,686, *passim*.

American regulatory commissions, such as the NLRB. "In all ministries," reads the Statute, "at the discretion of the Minister and depending on the business at hand, there can be invited to the Council [of the Ministry] members from the outside, such as factory owners, for questions pertaining to manufacturing, prominent traders for commercial matters, etc." [1] Although the questions on which the consultation and counsel of private individuals were to be sought were limited to economic matters, this provision meant an increased participation of "public opinion" in the administration. It reflected the government's growing concern for the needs, desires, requirements, and interests of its subjects. Unfortunately, in practice the provision received less attention than it should or than Speransky had hoped for. It was not until 1828 that the Ministry of Finance got around to establishing a Manufactures' Council with "public members;" and a Commercial Council to which prominent merchants were invited was set up only in 1829. [2] Thereafter, these outside members played a significant part in influencing the economic policies of the government, especially in the development of the country's natural resources, by acting as intermediaries and informants for both the government and their fellow entrepreneurs.

The Statute of June 25, 1811 declared that the Ministries "are institutions by means of which the Supreme Executive Power [i.e. the Emperor] acts upon all parts of the administration." [3] In other words, the ministries were the direct executive organs of the Autocrat, for "the essence of power entrusted to the ministers belongs exclusively in the executive category. No new law, no new statute can be made, or any previous [law] revoked by authority of the Minister." [4] The minister's power only consisted in his right to compel the subordinate levels of the administration to execute the laws and statutes issued by the Emperor. In the performance of this function the minister was directly responsible to the Monarch. [5] Of course, the Ministers could recommend new legislation or request the withdrawal of current statutes, but the Emperor needed not, in any way, to follow these suggestions. The very limits of the functions assigned to the ministries immediately raised two important questions: What institution was to unify the administration and give it consistency of purpose? And where would the legislative function be vested? The legislation enacted at Speransky's behest

---

1 PSZ, 24,686, Sec. 30 (pp. 688—689).
2 Korkunov, op. cit., II, 395.
3 PSZ, 24,686, Sec. 206.
4 PSZ, 24,686, Sec. 208.
5 PSZ, 24,686, Sec. 210.

in 1811–1812, gave neither a full nor a satisfactory answer to these questions.

Speransky proposed the establishment of a Governing Senate whose function would be to give unity to the administration of the realm. But this proposal was never implemented and in the absence of any specific institution, the unifying function devolved on the Committee of Ministers. However, as in 1802, this body received neither legal status nor a formal definition of its powers, functions, and jurisdiction. It remained an *ad hoc* affair, growing out of Alexander's practice to consult with several ministers at a time on questions which transcended the competence of any one of them. True enough, the Committee's prestige and status rose in consequence of the Emperor's frequent absences from the capital (particularly after 1813) during which it was empowered to act on such matters as did not require specific imperial approval. But the Committee's "informal" and non-essential character became quite evident after 1815, especially in the 1820's, when all its functions were in fact taken over by Count Arakcheev. In short, the central administration was still not effectively unified as to policy and purpose.

Speransky gave an answer to the second question through the legislation he helped to enact. The sole and real source of legislative power in Russia was the Emperor. Of course, the Emperor could not take care of all legislative problems alone; he had to be advised and assisted by a special institution or group of men. In the great reform plan of 1809, to be discussed subsequently, the function of advising on new legislation was given to the State Duma and, in a limited way, to the Council of State. Of the two, only the Council of State ever came into existence and took over the role of legislative advisor to the Emperor. [1] In recommending a new Council of State, Speransky subjected to detailed and searching criticism all the existing institutions of the central government and pointed out that above all there lacked a body that would give coordination and unity to the legislative aspect of administration. But let Speransky state the case in his own words:

"Order and uniformity in government affairs require that there be one central place where they would be subjected to general consideration. In the present system of government in Russia there is no such institution. The Senate cannot fill its place, since

[1] It might be noted, that a Council of State had existed in Russia since the reign of Catherine II. But its functions were not very clearly defined and varied from reign to reign. The immediate predecessor of Speransky's creation had been the so-called *Nepremennyi Sovet* (the "constant" -sic- council) established in 1801 as a consultative body to young Alexander I (PSZ 19,806, dated March 30, 1801) — Cf. also Chapter 5 *infra*.

from its very inception the Senate has been the highest judiciary and executive and, therefore, cannot at the same time be the place for general deliberation on all government affairs. The most important acts of the reign of Catherine II... were never transmitted to the Senate for deliberation, but only for execution and enforcement in specific cases.

The Ministry was established to give the various parts of government more unity and strength. If the Senate, even in its renovated form [decree of 1802] did not become the body for legislative deliberation, then with the establishment of the ministries and the removal [from the Senate] of all excutive matters, it became even less suitable for the fulfillment of this function [of legislative deliberation]. The Council had been instituted at first to take care of temporary needs arising from conditions of war [Speransky is referring to Catherine's Council of 1768]. The Committee of Ministers is also an institution without any public [legal] status. In its very rationale, it was designed for dealing with executive matters only.

And thus the most important part of government, the planning of laws, statutes, and institutions has no permanent organization with us, and there is no place where government matters would be considered at all times and in uniform manner. How can there be harmony and direction when each [part] moves in its own direction and when these various directions are nowhere unified?

... all laws... with us seem based on arbitrariness and personal confidence, changing from case to case and from circumstance to circumstance. All [laws] possess as many different aspects as there have been persons who drew them up in turn.

Laws cannot have weight when they have been drafted on the basis of personal confidence, have been deliberated upon in secret and have been issued without any regard to publicity and uniformity."

No wonder, Speransky continued his observations, that the impression was created that any law could be replaced; that there were no permanent laws in Russia, as all or any one could be changed for individual needs in particular instances. Consequently, their execution was bound to leave much to be desired, for it was easier to replace a law by another, than to implement an existing statute in the face of difficulties.

"From all this," Speransky went on to say, "the following truths can be derived: 1. that in the present system of government there is no institution for the general deliberation of governmental affairs from the point of view of their legislative aspect; 2. the absence of such an institution leads to major disorders and confusion in all parts of the administration; 3. such an institution is essential for the sake of the strength and permanency of the law; 4. great states are governed by means of institutions; individuals change and die, but the spirit of an institution lives on for many centuries and protects its foundations." [1]

Moved by these considerations, Alexander I consented to the creation of a Council of State, whose first session he opened with great pomp on January 1, 1810. The Council was meant to be only a part of a larger plan of administrative reorganization, but it was the only one to come into existence. The decree of January 1, 1810 establishing the Council (PSZ 24,064) defined the role of the new body as follows:

"I. In the hierarchy of government institutions, the Council is the body (soslovie [2]) in which all aspects of the administration are considered in their relation to legislation, and from where they proceed to the Supreme Imperial Power. II. Therefore, the original drafts of all laws, statutes, institutions are proposed to and considered by the Council of State, and then, by act of the Sovereign Power, forwarded for implementation. III. No law, statute, or institution can be issued by the Council and none can obtain its full execution without approval of the Sovereign Power." [3]

The members of the Council were appointed by the Emperor, the Ministers were nominated ex officio; the President of the Council was the Sovereign himself. The Council was subdivided into five departments, one for each of the most important areas of government business: state economy, codification, military, justice, etc. under the chairmanship of a Councillor who was not a Minister. The individual departments and the Council in plenary session met regularly at specified times (in practice, about once a week). The Council was assisted by a special Chancelry under the direction of the State Secretary. The State Secretary was not merely a high ranking clerk; his was a most important role, for he organized and supervised the flow of business (drew up the agendas, drafted and kept the minutes), and coordinated the work of the various departments of the Council. The importance of this position can be readily gauged from the fact that none other than Speransky was appointed to it on January 1, 1810. The decree

---

[1] Speranskii, "O neobkhodimosti uchrezhdeniia Soveta," in Korkunov, Russkoe gosudarstvennoe pravo, II, pp. 70—72, passim.

[2] Speransky's term for "body" is soslovie. Contrary to the often expressed opinion, soslovie in Speransky's vocabulary did not mean "representative estate" (an embryonic Estates General or Parliament), it meant nothing more than a governmental institution or body, composed of a group of officials, for the discussion of administrative and legislative problems. In the same sense, he also used the term soslovie in his "Pervyi politicheskii traktat," pp. 66—67, and the "Zapiska 1803 g." (see ch. 5 infra). Cf. also Korkunov, Russkoe gosudarstvennoe pravo, II, pp. 75—83 passim.

[3] PSZ 24,064 (pp. 3—4 of vol. 31).

creating the Council also listed its immediate tasks: consideration of the Civil Code drafted by Speransky and the Commission on Laws, reorganization of the ministries, and discussion of Speransky's Financial Plan.

In the beginning, the Council worked well and rapidly. It considered and approved the Financial Plan and the statutes of the ministries. The discussion of the Civil Code took more time, but then the draft submitted was not very satisfactory, as we remember. The Department on State Economy, under the chairmanship of the able and enlightened Admiral Count Mordvinov, was particularly energetic, and with rewarding results. However, in addition to its consultative functions on new legislation, the Council took on also judicial cases, those on which the Senate could not come to an agreement or decision. This judicial role and the exclusively consultative participation in the drafting of new legislation became the main functions of the Council in later years and remained such throughout the 19th century. [1] This had not been Speransky's original intention, but it was the best that could come of an institution torn out of its original context and deprived of the support of those institutions with which it was supposed to have formed a harmonious, integrated, and organic unit.

Reporting on his accomplishments for the year 1810 in a report submitted to the Emperor, Speransky briefly outlined the ground covered so far and what, in his opinion, still remained to be done. At the time of his writing, the first perversions of his work and intentions were becoming apparent, and Speransky warned that the improvements would come to naught if this process were allowed to continue. He protested against the Council of State becoming a judicial body: "[the Council] has not been established for the solution of judicial problems, but to give a basic form, a framework of regularity, to the legislative function heretofore dispersed and variegated and to provide [the legislative] with permanency, solidity, and uniformity." [2] There was still a lack of adequate personnel for the Council of State, but this defect would certainly be obviated in the near future, Speransky wrote in answer to some criticisms that had been made of the new institution. In regard to the finances of the Empire, Speransky continued, the domestic loan had been floated and was proceeding successfully (which was an optimistic exaggeration, as we know), but the establishment of a solid system of credit was not in sight yet and the budget

1 Korkunov, *Russkoe gosudarstvennoe pravo*, II, p. 83.
2 Speranskii, "Otchet v delakh 1810," *Sbornik IRIO*, XXI, p. 449 (note).

remained unbalanced. Much had been accomplished in recent years, but it was only a beginning; nothing was fully completed. Speransky explained why so many things had been started and none brought to a satisfactory conclusion by pointing out that all the work had been concentrated in the hands of a single individual, Speransky himself. [1] In order to bring to a conclusion the most important and basic reforms and to give less of a hold to his enemies' criticism, Speransky requested to be relieved of his secondary and temporary duties. Let the new institutions develop normally, organically, as they should, within the context of a reformed state structure, Speransky pleaded, and there would be no need for his taking care of so many different things. [2] But Alexander did not listen to the State Secretary's reasonable plea.

In any case, Speransky felt that the first steps, the most important ones, had been taken and that the foundation had been laid for the new structure of government. In a letter to the Emperor written from exile in self justification, he quite correctly characterized his works in the last years:

"Toute l'année 1809 avait été employée à combiner les idées éparses sur les réformes et d'en faire un plan général. Ce n'est autre chose que le développement raisonné de tout ce qui a été conçu, médité, et, en partie, exécuté par l'Empereur dès l'année 1801. Il n'était basé que sur la même idée principale, de *régulariser les pouvoirs par les lois et d'assurer l'administration par les règlements et institutions.*" [3]

Thus, the reorganization of the ministries, the establishment of the Council of State, the renovation of Russia's financial policy, as well as his various other secondary administrative activities, were only parts and fragments of a larger design. The successful legislative implementation of Speransky's thinking depended on the adoption of his plan for a general reform of the Russian body politic. But this overall reform remained in the project-state, for when Speransky's career was abruptly interrupted in 1812, "his body was exiled to Nizhnii-Novgorod, while his spiritual children were exiled to the Archives" (Herzen).

[1] The partial list of the official papers seized at his home in March 1812, on the night of his exile, gives a good idea of Speransky's extraordinarily multiple and various duties. N. V. Golitsyn (ed.) *Opis' bumag M. M. Speranskogo 1812 goda,* Akademiia Nauk: Trudy Kommissii po izdaniiu sochinenii, bumag i pisem grafa M. M. Speranskogo, fascicle 1 (Petrograd 1916). Unfortunately, the planned edition of Speransky's writings never materialized, nor was the list of his papers and library followed up.

[2] "Otchet v delakh," *loc. cit.,* pp. 458, 460, 461.

[3] Speranskii, "Opravdatel'naia zapiska," *Russkii Arkhiv,* XXX (1892) No. 1, p. 66 (the original text is in French, the italics are Speransky's).

## SOURCES

### 1. On Russia's finances and Speransky's financial activities see:

Speranskii: "Plan Finansov M. M. Speranskogo 1809-go g.," in *Sbornik IRIO*, vol. XLV (St. Pbg. 1885) pp. 1—73; "Istoriia assignatsii," *Sbornik IRIO*, vol. XXX (St. Pbg. 1881), pp. 466—471; "O skorosti monetnogo dvizheniia — zamechaniia M. M. Speranskogo ot 4-go noiabria 1811," *Arkhiv grafov Mordvinovykh*. vol. IX, pp. 588—590; "Ob uchrezhdeniiakh, otnosiashchikhsia do ekonomii gosudarstvannoi i pravitel'stvennoi," *Arkhiv istoricheskikh i prakticheskikh svedenii*, 1859, No. 6, pp. 13—21.

*Ministerstvo Finansov 1802—1902*, part I, St. Pbg. 1902; P. Baranov, *Mikhail Andreevich Balugianskii, stats-sekretar', senator, tainyi sovetnik 1769—1847* (St. Pbg. 1882); I. G. Bliumin, *Ocherki ekonomicheskoi mysli v Rossii v pervoi polovine XIX v.* (Moscow-Leningrad 1940); I. Bliokh, *Finansy Rossii v XIX v.* (St. Pbg. 1882), I used the French translation, Jean de Bloch, *Les Finances de la Russie au XIXe siècle — historique et statistique*, (2 vols, Paris 1899); N. Kaidanov, *Kratkii khronologicheskii obzor deistvii departamentov vneshnei torgovli i tamozhennykh sborov po chasti torgovli Rossii s inostrannymi gosudarstvami 1811—1865* (St. Pbg. 1890); Kalachev, "O zaslugakh gr. Speranskogo v finansovom otnoshenii," *Iuridicheskii Vestnik*, pp. 3—16 (date and vol. unknown to me); undated offprint at Hoover Library used); M. Kashkarov, *Denezhnoe obrashchenie v Rossii*, (2 vols., St. Pbg. 1898); I. I. Kaufman, *Iz istorii bumazhnykh deneg v Rossii* (St. Pbg. 1909); P. A. Khromov, *Ekonomicheskoe razvitie Rossii v XIX—XX vekakh* (Moscow 1950); P. I. Liashchenko, *Istoriia narodnogo khoziaistva SSSR*, vol. I, (Moscow 1947); A. P. Pogrebinskii, *Ocherki istorii finansov dorevoliutsionnoi Rossii* (Moscow 1954); G. Sacke, "L. H. von Jakob und die russische Finanzkrise am Anfang des 19. Jahrhunderts," *Jahrbücher für Geschichte Osteuropas*, 3 (1938), pp. 601—619. V. M. Shtein, *Ocherki razvitiia russkoi obshchestvenno-ekonomicheskoi mysli XIX—XX vekov*, (Leningrad 1948); V. V. Sviatlovskii, *Istoriia ekonomicheskikh idei v Rossii* (Petrograd 1923); E. I. Tarasov, *Dekabrist N. I. Turgenev v Aleksandrovskuiu epokhu (ocherk po istorii liberal'nogo dvizheniia v Rossii)*, (Samara 1923).

### 2. On the reforms of the central administration see:

Speranskii: "O gosudarstvennykh ustanovleniiakh," *Plan Gosudarstvennogo preobrazovaniia grafa M. M. Speranskogo* (Moscow 1905), pp. 230—297 — also in *Arkhiv istoricheskikh i prakticheskikh svedenii*, 1859—III pp. 15—49; "O neobkhodimosti uchrezhdeniia soveta" (1809), in Korkunov, *Russkoe gosudarstvennoe pravo*, II (St. Pbg. 1909), pp. 70—72; "Opravdatel'naia zapiska," *Russkii Arkhiv*, XXX, No. 1 (1892), pp. 65—72, (Russ. transl. from original French pp. 72—78), also in Shil'der, *Imperator Aleksandr I*, vol. III, Appendix, pp. 527—532; "Otchet v delakh 1810, predstavlennyi imperatoru Aleksandru I-u M. M. Speranskim, 11 fevralia 1811," *Sbornik IRIO*, vol. XXI (St. Pbg. 1877), 447—462.

"Bumagi komiteta uchrezhdennogo vysochaishim respkriptom 6go dekabria 1826-go goda," *Sbornik IRIO*, vol. XC (St. Pbg. 1894); *Gosudarstvennyi Sovet 1801—1901*, St. Pbg. 1901; *Zhurnaly Komiteta Ministrov — tsarstvovanie imperatora Aleksandra I vols. I* (1802—1810) and II (1810—1812), St. Pbg. 1888—1891; Danevskii, *Istoriia obrazovaniia Gosudarstvennogo Soveta v Rossii* (St. Pbg. 1859); F. M. Dmitriev, "Speranskii v ego gosudarstvennoi deiatel'nosti s obshchim ocherkom istorii vnutrennogo upravleniia v XVIII v.," *Russkii Arkhiv* VI (1868—1869), pp. 1527—1656; N. M. Korkunov, *Russkoe gosudarstvennoe pravo* vol. II (6th ed., St. Pbg. 1909); S. M. Seredonin, *Istoricheskii obzor deiatel'nosti Komiteta Ministrov, tom I: Komitet Ministrov v tsarstvovanie imperatora Aleksandra I-go (1802g. sent. 8—1825, noiabria 19)*, St. Pbg. 1902; V. G. Shcheglov, *Gosudarstvennyi Sovet v Rossii, v osobennosti tsarstvovanie Aleksandra I*, vol. II (Iaroslavl' 1892—1896); F. M. Umanets, *Aleksandr i Speranskii* (St. Pbg. 1910).

The histories of Russian public law referred to in the bibliography of Chapter 2, contain discussions of the establishment of the Council of State, the reorganization of ministries.

# CHAPTER V

# PLANS OF REFORM

In reaction to the stifling regime of Paul I, the first years of the reign of Alexander saw a spirit of reform seize almost all those who were close to the government and administration. As a member of the bureaucracy and with many friends among the influential new officials of the government, Speransky was naturally caught up in this spirit. Everybody talked and wrote about what was wrong with Russia and what could be done to improve the situation, and so also did Speransky.

The first paper in which he set forth some of his general ideas on Russia's government was written in the year 1801—1802 and bears the imprint of the influence of his friend and colleague, the well known enlightened publicist, Alexander Radishchev. Unfortunately, the text of this paper, which was found in the archives of Nicholas Turgenev under the French title, *"Mémoire sur la législation fondamentale en général (une espèce d'introduction aux projets suivants),"* has never been published in full. It was, however, summarized at some length by V. Semevskii. Unfortunately, his epitome is not fully satisfactory for an understanding of all the implications of Speransky's words, the more so as Semevskii's dogmatic classification of Speransky as a "liberal constitutionalist" distorts the summary and makes a correct evaluation of the excerpts more difficult.

Speransky was mainly concerned in exploring the ways and means by which Russia could be given stable and fundamental laws so as to put an end to a disorderly and arbitrary system of administration. There was great need in Russia for a class of laws which no administrative agency could infringe or by-pass. In his opinion this was a novel requirement, for originally, when the relations between rulers and ruled were based on moral principles and patriarchal relations, there had been no need for such fundamental laws. But,

> when rulers ceased to be the fathers of their peoples, when the peoples realized that their rulers separated their own interests from those of the welfare of their peoples ... and often turned the

power entrusted to them against their peoples ... then, the peoples found it necessary to add specific rules and to determine more clearly what they wanted. These rules are called the *fundamental laws of the state,* and their collection is a general statute or constitution. [1]

From this, however, let us not conclude too rashly, as many historians have done, that Speransky advocated a constitution similar to the American or French ones. Examining his language more closely, we realize that the word constitution had for him the connotation of a body of traditions, principles, rights, and privileges not necessarily set down in a written document. Yet, he was quite vague and somewhat inconsistent on this point. On the one hand he maintained that fundamental laws, the permanent rules which determine the relationships between rulers and people, were not to be found in written documents and parchments. On the other hand, he spoke of setting up a distribution of "forces" in such a way that no single force could become prevalent. Referring specifically to Blackstone and Filangieri, Speransky noted that had the government of England no other limitation than the "visible," i.e. written, separation of powers, it still would be a tyranny, in spite of the existence of parliament and parliamentary debates — as had been so clearly shown by the reign of Henry VIII. [2] And if further proof were needed, despite the pompous privileges and rights of some Russian groups or institutions, Russia was ruled without clear, permanent, fundamental laws. With the fate of the decree on the rights of the Senate in mind, Speransky added: "those are making a great mistake who think that rights granted to various classes or privileges given to various judicial and legislative institutions can render the laws solid or establish a system of administration. It is only an edifice built on sand." [3] Laws that are not based solidly on the true relationships prevailing in a nation and which do not reflect the pattern of the people's life can, at the very best, serve only an educational function: "The only benefit that laws can derive from their formal characteristics is to acquaint the people with the concepts of rights. And if the laws remain inviolate over a span of many years, and find support in the rulers' moral qualities, they can become so engrained in the minds of the people that it will be more difficult and also more dangerous to abolish them subsequently. But it is evident

---

1 V. I. Semevskii, "Pervyi politicheskii traktat Speranskogo", *Russkoe Bogatstvo* (1907), No. 1, pp. 62—63 — hereafter cited as "Pervyi politicheskii traktat."
2 "Pervyi politicheskii traktat," pp. 64—65.
3 *ibid.,* pp. 66—67.

that such a benefit is quite accidental and, one may say, personal [i.e. dependent on the ruler's personality]." [1] From where then, if not from a written document, do the fundamental laws derive their strength and stability? In a paper he was to write a year later in 1803, Speransky — quoting Hume — noted approvingly that the strength and solidity of the English constitution rest on the spirit and way of life of the English people. In this first paper he also states — less precisely perhaps — that fundamental laws must rest on the true (moral?) "forces" available in the nation, as the people always have in themselves sufficient forces to counterbalance or limit the power of the government. [2] However, this is not quite clear, the more so as Speransky does not specify whom he means by "people" — the entire nation or a selected group within it? The available excerpts do not enlighten us on this and we can only note the looseness of the argumentation.

In any case, to strengthen the idea of law and to limit the realm of arbitrariness, "the state's first step, without doubt, should consist in preventing the waste of its strength in conflicts between classes..." [3] He, therefore, opposes any division of the nation along lines of private and class interests, for such a division helps arbitrariness and despotism to maintain themselves by playing off one interest against another. "There is nothing more stupid and deadly for freedom," he writes, "than the rule by which the estates are divided according to the occupation and special rights of each. Such a rule can be called the *fundamental law of despotism.*" [4] Yet, there is one type of a "classless" social structure which will not be conducive to the preservation of fundamental laws either. That is when all social groups are "equal" because they are all without rights, i.e. in the case of the equality of slavery. Unfortunately, this is Russia's case.

"I would like," Speransky pleads rhetorically, "someone to show the difference between the peasant's subservience to the landlords and the nobility's subservience to the Monarch. I wish someone would point out that the authority the sovereign wields over the landlord is in no way different from the power the landlord has over his peasants. And thus, instead of the pompous division of the free Russian people into the most free classes of the nobility, merchants, etc., I find in Russia only two estates: the slaves of the sovereign and the slaves of the landlord. The former are called free in relation to the latter; but in fact there are no free men

1 *ibid.*, p. 67.
2 *ibid.*, p. 65 (note), 68.
3 *ibid.*, p. 69. By state here, Speranskii meant the nation.
4 *ibid.*, p. 68.

in Russia, except beggars and philosophers ... And that all the
forces of the nation are deadened completely by the relations which
bind these two types of slaves to each other: the interest of the
nobility is to keep the peasants under their unlimited authority,
whereas the interest of the peasants lies in the nobility being
subjected in similar fashion to the Crown." [1]

Under these circumstances, some devices can bring no solution. For
instance, nothing is gained by giving an education to slaves, for it
would only make them more fully aware of their degradation and of
the difference between their spiritual and intellectual development and
their legal and social status. Education must follow the social and
political liberation of the nation, not precede it. This sentiment, which
to a modern liberal may seem paradoxical and perhaps even
"reactionary," was shared by all enlightened Russians of Speransky's
time, for they had all too frequently the opportunity of observing the
horrible situation of a serf with good education or special skill
relegated to the rank of a common "slave" [2]

The task, therefore, was not to educate serfs, but to form a class
whose members would be personally free, and still part and parcel
of the people. The function of such a class would be to "mediate"
between the common people and the sovereign power. Such mediators
were necessary, as sovereign power could not be exercised by many,
Speransky held, and had to rest in the hands of a single person,
obviously the autocratic Tsar. [3] To make sure that the Tsar is well
aware of the nation's needs, to help him to remain in close touch with
his people, there ought to be a class of intermediaries, "mediators,"
whose very existence will prevent the degeneration of political sovereignty into despotism and arbitrariness. As Speransky put it: "It is
not to be imagined that the entire people can occupy itself with
safeguarding the boundaries [of power] between the government and
itself. It is therefore necessary that there be a special class that will
stand between the throne and the people; a class of men sufficiently
enlightened to know exactly the limits of power, sufficiently independent not to fear the sovereign power, and through its own interests tied
to the interests of the people in such a way that it will never be to
its advantage to betray them. It will be a living guard which the people

1 *ibid.*, pp. 74—75. This is strongly reminiscent of 18th century complaints, in
particular those of Radishchev.
2 Cf. *Istoriia Moskvy*, vol. III (Moscow 1954), pp. 71—74 and the notes to the
interesting memoirs of S. P. Zhikharev, *Zapiski sovremennika*, 2 vols. (Moscow—
Leningrad 1934).
3 "Pervyi politicheskii traktat", pp. 62, 70—71.

will put in its own stead at the limits of government power." [1]

Concretely, what role did Speransky assign to these mediators who, at first glance, seem to imply very strong "constitutional" limits on the absolute government of the Tsar? In the first place — on the basis of the excerpts available to us — we must note that Speransky nowhere indicates how or by what means the class of "intermediaries" will exercise its implied function of checking the arbitrary actions of the government. The "optimates" or mediators advise and inform the sovereign of the people's needs, but they cannot in any way restrain the government. Speransky, it is true, did assume the existence of a general will. [2] But belief in a general will can be used to bolster the power of a God-appointed leader or monarch as well as to justify the vesting of power in the people as a whole. [3] Speransky's failure to specify any institutional forms for the manifestation of this general will leaves — under Russian conditions of the time — only the Tsar as the carrier and expression of this will. The young official appears to have distrusted formal institutional and written safeguards much more than he feared the possibility of the autocratic Emperor's betrayal of the "general will." This is the meaning which is suggested by the somewhat enigmatic and yet perhaps fearful question: "If, scorning the outcries of the people and any sentiment of fear, the government will dare to resort to all extremities ... what means does this institution [of mediators] present against such horrors? To this the answer is easy: what could human forces oppose to Tamerlanes and similar monsters and what laws could maintain themselves when empires crumbled?" Under such extraordinary circumstances a revolt would be like a storm that clears the atmosphere. [4]

It is particularly important to know how the class of mediators is to be recruited. Its members, Speransky argued, cannot be elected by the people. Unfortunately, our fragmentary source does not give his reason for this opinion. But neither can they be nominated by the government, for that would deprive them of their independence. The traditional recourse of calling in the old-type nobility is not satisfactory

---

[1] *ibid.*, p. 69 and also p. 71 for a restatement of the last quoted idea. It may be of interest to note the similarity Speransky's reasoning bears to the ideas and arguments of the slavophile publicist A. I. Koshelev (cf. my article, "Russia after the Emancipation — views of a gentleman-farmer," *Slavonic & East European Review*, XXIX, No. 73 [June 1951], pp. 470—485).

[2] "Pervyi politicheskii traktat," p. 67.

[3] J. L. Talmon, *The Origins of Totalitarian Democracy* (London 1952), pp. 43—49 *passim*.

[4] "Pervyi politicheskii traktat," pp. 73—74. One seems to hear an echo of medieval theories on rightful kingship and of Joseph de Maistre's evaluation of the French Revolution.

either, as even in the past it had been resorted to only for want of anything better. Eventually the solution Speransky suggests comes somewhat as a surprise from a bureaucrat of lowly origin, although it is organically related to the arguments we have just summarized. In fact, he proposes the creation of a squirearchy on the English model. Such a squirearchy, or gentry, would be organically tied to the interests of the people as its junior children revert to the ranks of commoners, and for the gentry "to oppress the people would mean to oppress its own children." [1] By securing the free and unrestricted right to private property, the class of squires — mediators — would be constantly replenished from below by those who have been successful in their economic endeavors. At first, however, only the nobility would be allowed to own settled and tilled land. For the preservation of the fundamental rights of private property, all cases involving property, i.e. civil cases, are to be dealt with in jury courts, the members of the jury being representatives of property owners. Drawing further on his English model, Speransky distinguishes among the class of "optimates" an upper group consisting of a few individuals, selected by the Tsar, who transmit their special status only to their oldest male children. Their property, however, can be divided among all children. [2] The idea of a special group within the "gentry," came almost as an afterthought and Speransky does not seem to have relished the idea very much, as is evident from his arguments in its favor. Speransky himself recognized that his "mediators" were nothing but another form of nobility when he quoted with approval Montesquieu's dictum *"pas de monarchie sans noblesse."* [3] The upper rank of this new-type nobility was to be created to meet the objections of those aristocratic old families which might resent being put on a par with upstarts from the bureaucracy. [4] The subdivision of the "gentry" would be more easily accepted as there was a precedent for it in the Muscovite distinction between *boiars* and *boiar children* (or later, *dvorianins*). In any case, the creation of the class of "mediators" must proceed very gradually. At first all nobles would be automatically selected to membership in this new class. Their younger children would become commoners, while

1 "Pervyi politicheskii traktat," p. 72, and pp. 70—72 *passim* for all the preceding.
2 *ibid.,* pp. 73, 76—77. The idea of the divisibility of property among all children might have been inspired by the sad results of Peter the Great's efforts at introducing primogeniture into the legal relations and traditions of the Russian nobility. It is questionable that primogeniture rights to status alone could have been preserved more successfully, as they too ran counter to Russian historical tradition and the interests of the majority of the nobles.
3 "Pervyi politicheskii traktat," p. 74.
4 *ibid.,* p. 78.

commoners who had risen to wealth, education, esteem, would be elevated to the status of "optimates" in the Russian Empire.

How would these "mediators" exercise their function of advising and informing the sovereign? The upper group of this new nobility would form an hereditary High Chamber, the remainder would provide the membership of a Lower Chamber (our source does not say how this was to be done). These Chambers, however, have no specified duties or functions. They do not possess any legislative power, and obviously cannot play any role in the executive. The impression created is that these Chambers, meeting at infrequent intervals, would only present their advice and opinion on specific questions the government might submit to them and would transmit to the Emperor "cahiers" describing the nation's condition and the people's wishes. [1]

Perhaps Speransky's reluctance to give his ideas an institutional form stemmed from his realization that the problem of serfdom, the most fundamental of all, had to be solved first. For as long as serfdom remained the basis of Russian society, no practical significance could be attached to the existence of fundamental laws. [2] He erroneously believed — and so did the peasantry — that serfdom was the result of a willful violation of the laws by a handful of nobles, and he felt, therefore, that the system would be necessarily short lived. [3] In any case, the Russian form of serfdom was so much against reason and nature that it could not survive for long, especially since Russia had become part and parcel of Western Europe where serfdom had been abolished. [4] Consequently, there was no need to break serfdom forcibly and hastily. At first, Speransky reasoned, the nobility would retain its right to own estates inhabited by serfs. Then the abolition of serfdom would take place in two stages. The first step would consist in clearly stating and limiting the serfs' obligations to their masters. The initial measure along this line had already been taken, though without much practical effect, by Paul I who fixed the *corvée* at a maximum of three days a week. This clear definition of the serf's obligations would result in a change in the character of the peasant's dependence. Instead of being tied to the individual serf-owner, the serf would become bound to the land only, as had been the case in the 16th and 17th centuries. The process would be furthered by transforming the

---

[1] *ibid.*, p. 79. There is a striking similarity between the functions of the Chambers proposed by Speransky and the Slavophile conception of the Zemskii Sobor.

[2] "Pervyi politicheskii traktat," p. 76.

[3] *ibid.*, p. 58. Speransky was soon to reverse his opinion completely on the historical origins of serfdom in Russia.

[4] "Pervyi politicheskii traktat," p. 80 (note), p. 76.

capitation (poll tax) into a land tax, proportional to the amount of land held and tilled (again a reversion to pre-Petrine policies). We recall that Speransky repeated this important fiscal proposal in his Financial Plan, in 1810. The second stage in the abolition of serfdom would be the return to the peasant of his right to move freely. But, Speransky warned, this last step would require lengthy and careful preparation, for otherwise it might result in the formation of a class of vagrants or "nomads." It is interesting to note that he did not propose to give the freed peasant a share in the land. The proposals, as they are cited in our source, were too general and incomplete, obviously drawn up in haste. But we definitely have the impression that Speransky was reluctant to propose anything radically new and to change the existing order fundamentally. [1]

Besides the paper just summarized, Speransky set forth his ideas concerning the crowning stone of statecraft, a code of laws. He did this in a short essay entitled "A fragment on the Commission of Codification — Introduction," written also in 1801–1802. Again we must rely on Semevskii's summary for its contents. [2] Speransky believed that a code of laws was the concrete expression of the general principles which underlie the social and political structure of a nation. Therefore, no Russian code would be truly complete until the country has obtained the fundamental laws and rules of its political existence. But the code could also play a role in preparing the nation for such a fundamental organization of the country's government. In regulating the relations between citizens, the code would set a framework and foster the civic education of the people. In their present chaotic stage, however, Russian laws — ignored even by the most responsible administrators and judges — only served to keep government on a low level of arbitrariness and lawlessness. [3]

Heretofore, Speransky continued, all attempts at codification have failed, for the task was tackled wrongly. The commissions of codification started off amidst a great deal of pomp and circumstance; high dignitaries and ministers jotted down some general ideas. But soon their interest in the project flagged, and the actual work was entrusted to under-secretaries, clerks, and even assistant-clerks who did not have the proper training or the breadth of vision necessary for such a task. Seemingly, Catherine's Commission of 1767 was an exception to this rule of procedure. But its labors, too, proved fruitless because the

---

1 *ibid.*, pp. 80–82.
2 *ibid.*, pp. 50–59. The title of the paper was: "Otryvok o komissii ulozheniia—Vvedenie."
3 "Pervyi politicheskii traktat," p. 54.

Empress' detailed prescriptions fettered the minds of the members, and also because Catherine's purpose did not meet the needs and spirit of the times. [1]

To avoid a repetition of these failures and to bring the codification to successful completion, Speransky proposed a different approach. The code is not to be a new creation, a declaration of new norms and principles, but a collection of existing laws. New laws should be introduced only if the old ones are inadequate or non-existent for specific modern needs. This approach — we have noted that Speransky did not follow it himself in 1808—1812 — also determines the procedure. The first preparatory task consists in ordering all existing legislation according to topics. At the same time, a history of Russian law should be written to help determine the proper order of classification. Speransky suggested his friend, A. Radishchev, as best qualified to write this history. [2] Then, these old laws will have to be collated and compared for textual accuracy and completeness. Finally, important foreign codes, in particular the Prussian, should be collected and translated. These preparatory labors should take approximately three years. [3] In the meantime, the guiding principles of the code can be worked out, though, in secret. The actual drafting of the code will be delegated to a specially appointed Commission which will base its labors on the preparatory work. Before their publication, the results should be submitted for comment and criticism to representatives (Speransky does not say how selected) from the various social classes of the Empire. The consultation with all representatives should not take place in common or at the same time, for at all cost Speransky wanted to avoid calling together an "assembly" for legislation or codification. [4]

---

[1] ibid., p. 51.

[2] ibid., p. 57.

[3] ibid., pp. 54, 56, 67. The study and translation of foreign codes had been suggested in the Unofficial Committee. Count Paul Stroganov noted on the session of 10 March 1802: "Le Prince Czartoryski parla ensuite de la lettre qu'il avait été chargé de rédiger pour engager les plus savants jurisconsultes de l'Europe à travailler sur le système d'un code de lois. Il dit qu'il avait un brouillon, mais qu'ensuite, en conférant là-dessus avec ses collègues, on avait paru penser qu'il serait difficile de faire dans ce moment-ci un code définitif, puisque tout ce qui était relatif à l'état civil serait soumis à de grandes mutations par la suite, mais qu'il ne fallait songer pour le moment qu'à faire un recueil de nos oukases par ordre de matière, et que dans ce moment il fallait se borner à déterminer cet ordre." Le Comte Paul Stroganov, vol. II, p. 108. Alexander I was impatient, however, to proceed to a definitive code; in any case, contacts were established with foreign jurists (cf. ibid., pp. 114—115). The correspondence with foreign jurists was carried on through the Russian embassies and the various Ministries of Foreign Affairs and was still maintained in 1809 (cf. the report of Caulaincourt to Napoleon, dated 15 Jan. 1809, cited in A. Vandal, Napoléon et Alexandre I, vol. II, p. 28).

[4] "Pervyi politicheskii traktat," p. 55, 56.

The two political "papers" we have just summarized were clearly the work of a young and politically immature person. They give the feeling that Speransky was unable to choose between two opposite conceptions. On the one hand, he had read and accepted the ideas of the prominent political writers of the 18th century, in particular Montesquieu and Blackstone. On the other hand, he did not accept the philosophical principles which lay at the basis of Western constitutionalism. He did not recognize the "self evident truths" of imprescriptible rights of man, of "no taxation without representation," the balancing of the interests of various classes and groups, the social contract which justified popular sovereignty in the American and French constitutions. His ideal was that of a *Rechtsstaat* and seemed best exemplified by Prussia where autocracy was combined with the rule of law, where traditions and the rights and privileges of estates had not been obliterated by written parchments and constitutions.

The young official's ideas — as set forth in the two *Mémoires* we have discussed — were along the lines of the various alleged imitations of English constitutionalism popular at the time. Furthermore, his practical program had a definitely conservative tinge. All this should have made Speransky a supporter of the "Senatorial party." However, Speransky sided with the opponents, the "Senatorial party" and threw in his lot with their opponents, the bureaucratic-minded members of the Unofficial Committee. For this choice, there was no doubt, first of all a personal reason. After all, Speransky himself was of very low origin and could hardly expect to be fully accepted by and allowed to play a major role among the prominent members of the aristocracy. But other reasons must surely have played a part in determining his choice. He was very much aware of the moral turpitude (due to serfdom) and political incompetence (due to the autocracy) of the majority of the Russian nobility. In the bureaucracy — of which he himself was a member — and in the group allied with the Unofficial Committee, he saw much more promise. He felt that the spiritual and material improvement of the Russian nation was more likely to be brought about by energetic, enlightened, and "modern" bureaucrats than by old-fashioned, conservative dignitaries. Finally, both his training and the bent of his intelligence made Speransky more receptive to the bureaucratic, administrative approach to government. His recent successful bureaucratic career could serve only to strengthen this attitude, and make him distrustful of the slow, "organic," and "historicist" approach of the "Senatorial party."

About a year after his first attempt at a general statement of aims and method, Speransky was asked by a member of the Unofficial Committee, possibly Count Kochubei, to write up his ideas on a reform of Russian political life, with specific suggestions for implementation. Written in 1803, this paper bears the title "Report on the establishment of judiciary and government institutions in Russia." [1] Whether it ever reached the eyes of Emperor Alexander, we do not know.

It would seem that Speransky was asked to write the *mémoire* in connection with the Emperor's study of local administration. Indeed, Speransky starts out by pointing to the close connection existing between the condition of local government and that of the central administration. Before the local institutions can be improved, he argued, order and clarity must reign at the top. However good the system of local administration, it will be neither workable nor beneficial if the central government is inadequate or bad. [2] In Russia, the first step in the right direction has been taken with the establishment of the ministries. Let us remember that young Speransky is writing only a few months after their creation, when the hopes for their success had not faded yet. It is only a beginning; the process of reorganization of the central institutions of government must continue for the improvements to bear fruit. In this connection it should be noted that throughout the period of his greatest activity, 1801 to 1812, Speransky approached all problems of political reform from the point of view of the reorganization of the central administration. Local institutions and provincial administration, if mentioned at all, were relegated by him to a subordinate plane. One has distinctly the feeling that he was rather vague and ill-informed about the local aspect of government, and he hurried past it, as if afraid of being deflected from more important matters by bothersome details. Not until much later, after years spent in direct contact with Russian provincial administration, did Speransky come to appreciate at its full value the importance of this area of government and give it its deserved place in state papers and reform projects.

The main cause for the inefficiency and poor state of Russia's political and administrative institutions, Speransky wrote in the report of 1803, is that they have been brought into existence without any system. A façade of apparent unity only serves to hide the chaos and

---

[1] "Zapiska ob ustroistve sudebnykh i pravitel'stvennykh uchrezhdenii v Rossii (1803)." Published in *Plan Gosudarstvennogo preobrazovaniia grafa M. M. Speranskogo* (Moscow 1905), pp. 121—229. Hereafter cited as *Zapiska 1803*.

[2] *Zapiska 1803*, pp. 121—122, 186.

confusion. What else can be expected from institutions which are the creations of imperial whims, sudden outbursts of anger, or impatience? The characteristic trait of Russian government is the absence of harmonious and orderly division of the functions and powers vested in the various bureaus. There is no administrative body properly speaking. There is no separate legislative organ. No attempt is made at differentiating between permanent public law and *ad hoc* administrative regulations. In the final analysis, laws, regulations, orders, and decrees are differentiated merely by the bureaucratic procedure which has brought them into being. Under such conditions, no government institution has any real power and responsibility of its own and everything depends on arbitrary decisions. Clearly, the reformer's first task is to give unity and order to this chaotic structure. Speransky suggests five principles as a guide for bringing about the desired improvement: 1. consistency with the fundamental laws of the state and of institutions, 2. unity of execution, 3. administrative acts must be accounted for both as to form and contents, 4. at each level all government functions must be uniform, 5. consideration of local conditions and regard for the means of execution available. [1]

These principles will find their application more readily if each administrative institution is organized on the basis of a hierarchical "chain of command," if, in other words, the collegial system disappears completely. In support of this position, Speransky quotes with approval the words of Bentham, "... l'unité, dis-je, est favorable puisqu'elle fait peser toute la responsabilité, soit morale soit légale sur la tête d'un seul ... son intéret est inséparable de son devoir." [2] Speransky, himself, as we know, implemented his precept in organizing the Ministry of the Interior in 1802 and gave it wider application still in the Statute on the Ministries in 1811. Unity and clarity of executive political action, as they rest in the hands of the autocratic monarch, are particularly important in a country without a "good monarchical constitution" (in Montesquieu's sense, presumably). The absence of an act embodying the fundamental laws of the realm is to be compensated — in a truly bureaucratic spirit — by the "force of clarity and orderliness in the method of administration." [3] It might be added, that unity, in Speransky's view, does not necessarily preclude allowance for differences in applying legislation in deference to special local conditions, particularly in border provinces. But this seems to have

---

1 *ibid.*, 170, 182—184.
2 *ibid.*, 156—157. On Speransky's connections with Bentham (via the latter's disciple Dumont who visited Russia), see chapter 7 *infra*.
3 *Zapiska 1803*, p. 171.

been something of an afterthought, for Speransky does not elaborate on this point — as he was to do many years later — and relegates the matter to a footnote. [1]

The *raison d'être* of social life is the security of individuals and of their property, while the primary role of government is the creation and preservation of this security. Therefore, the major functions of government are four in number: police, justice, army, diplomacy. In order to carry out the tasks set by these functions, the government needs money, and hence a fifth major division of political organization is state economy. [2] Most interesting is Speransky's analysis of the role of the police and economy in the political life of the country. He leaves out the army and diplomacy as not within his competence. As for the judiciary, we shall come back to it later.

"Law," quotes Speransky from Bentham, "is nothing but the limitation of the natural freedoms of man by certain rules."[3] If, however, this limitation is not to be weakened at any time, if the rules of law are to be enforced permanently, then exclusive reliance on judiciary procedure is impossible; indeed, he reasons not without some sophistry, if recourse to courts were the only way of enforcing these rules, there would be as many law-suits as there are individuals, or even more. Besides, the judiciary acts only intermittently, when cases are brought to its attention. The police, therefore, "are nothing more than the means chosen by the government to preserve the action of law uninterruptedly, a means for keeping the actions of men within the bounds of order and to put an end to any forcible action (*nasilie*)." [4] The police act on quite a different principle than a court of justice, for they do not examine the rights that have been violated, but merely attempt to restore things to their original state, as they were before the act of violence has been committed. Consequently, there are several categories of police which Speransky names both in Russian and in French: executive, repressive or coercitive, preservative or administrative (*police de sûreté*). [5] This is, of course, not a revolutionary or novel conception of police power, its main value lies in the theoretical limits it sets to the police function of the government and in a clear separation of the police from the judiciary. It is, however, mainly a theoretical distinction, for in practice Speransky still leaves an extremely wide range of effective action to the police. In spite of this fundamental

[1] *ibid.,* p. 172.
[2] *ibid.,* p. 125.
[3] *ibid.,* p. 127.
[4] *ibid.,* p. 130.
[5] *ibid.,* pp. 131–132.

weakness, his conception was a valuable suggestion for his time, as in 18th century Russia the lack of clear definition had led to inefficiency, disorder, and abuse in both the police and judiciary. [1]

Our previous examination of Speransky's ideas on political economy makes it unnecessary to go into much detail at this point. It is worth noting, though, that his ideas were quite clearly formulated and thought through by 1803. In the economic domain, the state's interest encompasses everything that constitutes the wealth of the country, in particular its twofold sources: natural resources and labor. Part of this wealth is taken out by the government, Speransky reasons, and applied to the needs of administration, i.e. the preservation of internal and external security. In taking out a part of the nation's wealth through taxation, the state must see to it that the future sources of wealth are safeguarded. It is the duty of the government — as he pointed out in the Report of the Ministry of the Interior at about the same time — to foster the economic development of the counry. Awareness of this duty must be the guiding principle of sound fiscal and tariff policy. [2]

As he has stated at the beginning of this report, Speransky feels that the government's attention should be focused on the reorganization of the central administration. To this end he proposes to work for the achievement of four basic goals: 1. to base the new system of administration on a true autocratic constitution (sic!) without any separation between executive and legislative powers; 2. to preserve and strengthen a public opinion which will put brakes on bureaucratic arbitrariness and tyranny by bringing the abuses to the attention of the government; 3. to make it possible to come closer to the model of a "true monarchical administration;" 4. to preserve those institutions whose slow evolution would prepare the people for a "true monarchy." [3]

Can the government start on this pedagogical task, act as a guide and leader in the evolution towards "true monarchical" (i.e. "constitutional") forms without a good code, without good laws, to regulate the relations between individuals and their property? Yes, says Speransky. A really good code cannot be written immediately, for too little is known in Russia about jurisprudence. Without a good theoretical framework all efforts at codification will be wasted, though this does not exclude minor improvements. The existence of a perfect code of laws is not an essential feature of good monarchical government, anyway. Look at Prussia and England: in both the laws are in great

---

1 *ibid.*, pp. 132—138.
2 *ibid.*, pp. 150—153. The "cameralist" tone is unmistakable.
3 *ibid.*, pp. 189—190.

disorder. And yet the defects arising out of this situation are not as noticeable there as they are in Russia, for in England and Prussia they are balanced by good administration, good monarchical government. [1] By mentioning England and Prussia in the same breath, Speransky clearly shows that he means by constitution only a clear and orderly pattern of administration based on the rule of law. In such a definition, as we have seen, Alexander I and the members of the Unofficial Committee could fully concur.

From these various considerations, Speransky concludes that the Russian state should devote its attention first to reforms which will bring immediate results, namely in the fields of police and economy. If an improvement is achieved there, the judiciary will be improved automatically, and eventually the fundamental laws of the realm themselves will follow suit. In other words, without changing the existing system basically, without seeking to establish an ideal monarchy right away, much can be done to eliminate the prevailing administrative confusion and bad conditions. A well regulated and orderly monarchical regime ("constitution" in Speransky's terminology at the time) obtains when the various organs of the state are responsible for their actions. Speransky distinguishes two forms of responsibility: as to form (external) and as to contents. The former may exist even in arbitrary, tyrannical governments, as long as certain formalities of procedure are observed. The latter, however, implies that the government and its organs harmonize their actions with the true spirit of the existing laws, whatever these laws may be. Naturally, Speransky wishes to establish the second type of responsibility, alone characteristic of a "true monarchy." Careful not to neglect any means, however inadequate, for bringing Russia closer to good government, Speransky hastens to add that even the first type of purely external, formal responsibility might prove useful. [2] The establishment of uniform executive and administrative procedures, subject to control as to their form, can be the first step towards an order based on the rule of law. "By establishing it [procedural responsibility] the autocratic ruler abandons administration without accountability and in the persons of his ministers, he subjects his own power to the law." [3] In answer to possible objections from those who might remind him that even after the creation of ministries the ministers had exercised their power without accounting for it and sometimes in disregard of the law, Speransky explains that procedural

1 *ibid.*, pp. 191—193, 195—198.
2 *ibid.*, p. 168.
3 *ibid.*, p. 169.

responsibility "assumes a law ratified by the stamp of general recognition [acceptance] and that this law is guaranteed either by government regulations affecting property or by strong and universal popular opinion. Without such a guarantee the responsibility will be purely a verbal one." [1] Speransky has correctly put the finger on the central problem: the state's accountability for its acts can be obtained and strengthened either when the government voluntarily abides by the law or when it can be forced by public opinion to do so. And he reverts again to the theme he has touched upon in his first paper. It is not written constitutions or laws that matter, but the existence of a spirit in the people which will compel the government to stay within the limits set by fundamental laws. As Speransky sees it, in Russia the main task is to bring about this spirit. [2]

In a "true monarchy," that is in a state based on the rule of law, the law is protected and guaranteed in two ways: by public opinion or by an institution that may be established especially for the purpose. For an effective existence of the first kind of guarantee, the state must give full publicity to its actions (except, of course, for military and diplomatic secrets). To this effect, the country ought to have freedom of the press and a complete knowledge of the government's doings. In turn, this will help educate a public whose spirit and opinion will, in due course, function as the guarantors of law and order, even in the absence of a written constitution or code. [3] The safeguard of a *Rechtsstaat* type involves the creation of an institution — independent of the executive — to which the executive may render account of its actions periodically. In this connection Speransky makes his most important concrete proposal in the Report of 1803. The functions of government, he writes, are to be distributed among two bodies: an Executive and a Legislative Senate. He prefers to use the term senate, rather than ministry for the executive body, because the executive functions of the state transcend the eight ministries. The Executive Senate will be subdivided into five sections, one each for the major functions of administration, as listed earlier. [4] It is to the Legislative Senate, however, that Speransky devotes most of his attention, as it would be a new institution in Russia.

It should be well understood, writes Speransky, that the functions

1 *ibid.*, p. 169 (note).
2 *ibid.*, p. 176.
3 *ibid.*, pp. 167—168.
4 *ibid.*, pp. 199—200, 201—202. In suggesting the name of Senate for this executive institution, Speransky hoped perhaps to instill greater confidence by using a familiar term, carrying with it the prestige of Peter the Great.

of the two senates are only two facets of the single absolute sovereign power (i.e. the Emperor) in which they are united and from which they both proceed. The Legislative Senate is a body of men (*soslovie*) which issues the laws. For, as is well known, laws issued by a group of individuals carry more force and prestige than those which are enacted by an individual minister or head of bureau. [1] However, this Legislative Senate is not to be an open, representative body with independent political existence. Composed of Senators appointed by the Emperor, it is in truth a constituent part of the Imperial Cabinet or Chancery. Meeting twice a week, the Senate discusses problems which come under the following major headings: drafting of a civil and criminal code, improvement of civil and criminal laws, preservation of the laws in their execution. The Senate receives complaints against ministers and inspects the reports presented by the Executive Senate. The Legislative Senate may call "Executive Senators" for consultation, but no minister may be a member of the Legislative Senate. In some very exceptional cases, such as high treason, trial of ministers, the Legislative Senate sits as a High Court. [2]

In practice, therefore, the Senates are the direct instruments of the absolute power of the Emperor. They lend it unity of purpose and secure formal responsibility, but they have no independent force of their own. Speransky is quite careful to stress that the Senates do not limit the autocratic prerogatives of the Emperor. However, by virtue of their procedure and of the publicity of their actions, the Senates will help instill greater popular confidence in the acts of the government. They will contribute to the education of the people in preparation of the establishment of a "true monarchy." And — who knows? — perhaps the Senates will become important enough to present a serious obstacle in the path of a mal-intentioned ruler. The potentialities inherent in the Senates are great, for, writes Speransky, "when, as a consequence of the spread of education and of the impact of many circumstances which depend on time, the conditions for better government will have ripened, there will be put into this same frame — almost without any changes — a new system which will rest not on an apparent order, but on a truly profound and objective basis." A few changes in nomenclature will easily complete the transformation. [3]

---

[1] *Zapiska 1803*, p. 201. On the term *soslovie*, cf. pp. 162—163 below.
[2] *Zapiska 1803*, pp. 203—206. The echoes of the American system should not be taken too literally.
[3] *ibid.*, pp. 212—213. On closer inspection, this Legislative Senate has already all the essential features of the Council of State proposed by Speransky in his plan of 1809 and established in 1810.

Speransky recommends four principal steps for the implementation of these proposals: 1. publication of the statutes for the two senates, 2. elaboration of a statute for the police functions of administration, 3. preparation of a statute for the economic functions of the state, 4. issuance of new regulations for local administration. [1] These measures can be prepared in a short time, and they will not change the prerogatives of absolute power in any way. But, warns Speransky, these measures should be worked out in secret. (Was this not in conflict with his own principle of publicity for government action?). If they are prepared in secret, the new measures can be put in effect all at once, so that criticism will have no opportunity to fasten on trivial details, but will have to consider the system in its entirety. [2] In advising this course, Speransky was following the rule of secrecy which had been decided upon by the Unofficial Committee, at the suggestion of Count Stroganov. He also was presaging his own advice of 1809 to publish all reforms at once, instead of piecemeal. [3]

In all fairness it should be said that Speransky had no illusions as to the difficulties inherent in a real transformation of Russia into a "true monarchy." "One needs only to compare the ways of monarchical government with the government existing in Russia," he commented, "to become convinced that no human power can transform the latter into the former without the aid of time and the progressive evolution of all things towards perfection" [4] This sentence illustrates his fundamental belief that a thorough and durable political change can come about only as the result of a gradual, organic transformation of the spirit of the people. It is an interesting expression of his belief in moral progress and of the role of the historic process. The people's spiritual evolution is of special import in a country where half of the population is still in slavery. Again Speransky is led to face the problem of serfdom, the most burning issue of his time, and he does it reluctantly and with hesitation. His hesitation was quite understandable, for he wished to see his program accepted by a government that still relied entirely on the services of a serfowning class. Speransky suggests, that the right of the landowners to police and administer the rural districts, as well as their own domains, should not be curtailed. "Without any doubt," he writes, "the landowners must retain wide powers within their domains; but there is nothing to prevent the basing of the exercise of their power on permanent rules and proper

[1] *Zapiska 1803*, pp. 217—218.
[2] *ibid.*, p. 219.
[3] *Le Comte Paul Stroganov*, vol. II, p. 8 (as quoted above in note 3 p. 45).
[4] *Zapiska 1803*, p. 187.

formalities." For instance, "the police in the villages must, no doubt, belong to the landowners; but their power will not suffer in any way if punishments are carried out by the township [*volost'*] administration." [1] Regularization of procedural forms, the removal of the execution of sentences from the hands of the landowner who has imposed them to the township-police (to preclude excessive cruelty on the part of individual masters), these are the only improvements in the peasant's lot Speransky feels it possible to suggest. He specifically states that the economy of the village must remain in the hands of the landowner. The suggestion is a repetition — albeit in a weakened form — of his proposals in the paper of 1802. The cautious and timorous approach of the would-be reformer when it comes to matters affecting serfdom finds further illustration in his suggestion of a rural code. The code would make uniform the rights and powers of serfowners throughout the Empire. Speransky argues that the effect of such a code would be to give the serfs the feeling that the government is not abandoning them, and it would also instill the hope that, in due time, they will be freed from the excessive hardships of serfdom. [2] We may be allowed to remain somewhat sceptical of Speransky's optimism. The peasants might also have seen in the code a legal recognition and sanction — as well as "freezing" — of their servile status and react rather strongly, for as we know, they had always considered serfdom an abuse of power by the nobility.

In spite of a clear awareness of the real problems of Russia, and in spite of an expression of a high ideal of "true monarchy," the practical bearings of the mémoire of 1803 were limited. Speransky himself expressed the value of the effort best: "Who knows how to select and plant the first root has done much, although only time and the action of the elements of nature can make it grow into a tree." [3]

In 1809 Speransky wrote his most important and comprehensive plan for a reorganization and reform of Russia's political life. This plan embodied the thought and experience of the first decade of his active career as official and administrator. No longer do we find in it the immature judgments of his first papers. Unlike the *mémoire* of 1803, the Plan of 1809 also attempted to cover all the branches of the administration with equal thoroughness.

The full text of the Plan of 1809 remained unknown to Speransky's

1 *ibid.*, pp. 226—227.
2 *ibid.*, pp. 228—229.
3 *ibid.*, p. 229.

contemporaries, and historians did not read it until almost a century after it had been written. It was published in full only in 1905. The general public learned some of the specific proposals contained in the Plan through the excerpts given by Nicholas Turgenev in his book, *La Russie et les Russes,* published in 1847 in Paris. This accounts for the many erroneous expositions and hasty conclusions which have been made by writers and scholars throughout the 19th century. We only possess the final version of the Plan, as it was presented to the Emperor and kept among the archives of Count A. Arakcheev. We do not know what the first original drafts were like, and, consequently, we cannot follow the development or changes in Speransky's mind as he was working on the plan. [1]

The Plan was written for Alexander I who was a busy man and not very familiar with political science and theory. That is why Speransky indicated the theoretical grounds of his proposals only in the most sketchy and simplified form, in terms of the current intellectual fashions and jargon, easily understood by his imperial reader. It would be quite misleading, therefore, to look for the political philosophy underlying the Plan in the vague and popular introductory statements. Rather, the State Secretary's political theory ought to be distilled from the implications contained in his practical proposals. As a mechanical summary of the Plan would not be satisfactory, we shall present his ideas and suggestions in an analytical form, not necessarily in the same order as they occur in the original.

In distinction from his earlier projects, and under the growing influence of historicist and romantic philosophies, Speransky sets his reform proposals in a broad historical framework. He seeks to justify the need for a reform of Russian political life by reference to an evolutionary and dialectical approach to historical development. The history of Europe, according to him, evidences a definite pattern of political evolution: from republic (in the classical, Roman sense) to feudalism, and again back to a form of "republic." Modern European history has been characterized by a struggle between the feudal and the "republican" principles, the latter prevailing to the extent that enlightenment spread among the people. Actually, feudalism itself went through two stages: the original feudalism of the Dark Ages and

1 For full details on the existing copies of the project, see S. M. Seredonin, "K planu vseobshchego gosudarstvennogo preobrazovaniia 1809 g", *Sbornik S. F. Platonovu* (St. Pbg. 1911), 533—544. The full text (cited as Plan 1809) has been published by *Russkaia Mysl'* in a separate volume (Moscow 1905), along with other papers of Speransky, under the title, *Plan gosudarstvennogo preobrazovaniia grafa M. M. Speranskogo.*

"absolutist feudalism" (equivalent to absolute monarchy). The latter form of feudalism in turn yielded the place to the "republic," or "true monarchy" in his terminology of 1803. All European states have followed this pattern, and Russia is no exception. At the moment, Russia is in the stage of absolutist feudalism. [1] These considerations lead Speransky to believe that each period in the life of a nation or state has its own political requirements. This form of historicism he probably has derived from his reading and study of contemporary post-Kantian philosophies. The existence of a scheme of development raises the question of the timeliness of specific political reforms and changes.

> "Wordly empires have their periods of grandeur and their periods of decline," reflects Speransky, "and for each period the character of government must be consistent with the level of the state's civic education. Every time when the ways of government lag behind or outstrip this level [of education], the government is subverted by greater or lesser convulsions." [2]

To avoid such failure as that of the reforms of Joseph II in Austria or of Anne and Catherine II in Russia, it is first essential to make sure that the time is ripe for the change, for "time is the first principle and source of all political innovations. No government which is out of harmony with the spirit of the times can withstand the powerful action of this spirit." [3]

Russia has reached the second stage of feudalism, it is in the period of absolutism and progressing towards liberty. In Russia this evolution towards "true monarchy" will be simpler and more direct than it had been in Western Europe, as Russia has no strong feudal features, primogeniture for instance. Education and enlightenment have spread at a phenomenal rate in Russia during the 18th century and as a result, politically and historically, the Russian Empire is now on a level of equality with the great monarchies of the West. This rapid and far reaching modernization has produced a cleavage between the desires of society, the needs of the time, and the system of government.

---

[1] Plan 1809, pp. 18—19, 20. Speransky defined feudalism as "absolutism tempered by material forces" (*ibid.*, p. 17) — while this definition shows Speransky's insight into at least one important aspect of the feudal system (i.e., the distinction between *dominium* and *potestas*) it also explains the seeming paradox of the phrase, "absolutist feudalism." In any case, Speransky was quite aware of the function of "estates" (*Stände*) in the political development of the West.

[2] Plan 1809, p. 15.

[3] *ibid.*, p. 16. This statement sets the Plan in a relative, historically determined framework, in contrast to the absolute ("natural") principles of the 18th century. This "historicist" position of Speransky indicates his affinity for what Mannheim has called the "conservative style of thought." K. Mannheim, "Conservative Thought," *Essays on Sociology and Social Psychology*, (London 1953), pp. 95, 113—114, 117.

"What a contradiction," exclaims Speransky, "to wish for science, commerce, and industry, and not admit their most natural consequences; to desire that reason be free and the will in bonds; to expect the passions to progress and change, while their object — the desire for liberty — remains at the same point; [we want] the people to enrich themselves and yet not enjoy the freedom which is the best fruit of the increase of their wealth! History does not know of any enlightened and commercial people that remained in slavery for long." [1] The truth of the matter is that since the reign of Catherine II, and especially since the accession of Alexander I, economic prosperity was promoted and education was spread, while changes in the political system were not allowed. The discrepancy, the "inner contradiction" in the situation are becoming more and more noticeable, and their bad effects are felt more acutely from year to year. [2]

The real strength of a political system resides not so much in the brute force of its army and police as in the moral power of the government. In Russia, alas, the moral force of the government has grown weak as a result of the basic cleavage and discrepancy just noted. The acts of the government meet with no respect and are constantly misinterpreted because the country sees no relation between the actions of the state and its own aspirations and needs. In short, "the present mental attitudes are in complete contrast to the method of government." [3] And the worst of it is that the loss in moral prestige affects most particularly the supreme power, the Emperor. The blame for it falls on the monarch and not on his ministers and councillors. This is to be expected, for under the existing system the Tsar's ministers and advisors are not publicly responsible for their actions; they can always hide behind the Emperor. From this analysis, Speransky draws his first conclusion: no partial measure of reform will prove satisfactory or materially ameliorate the situation. At this particular moment of her historical evolution, Russia is in need of a new system of administration consonant with her level of development. "The universal discontent, the predisposition to negative interpretations of the present, are nothing but a general expression of boredom and satiation with the existing state of things." [4] Though hidden and inarticulate, there is a strong urge and need for change in Russian society.

Such a situation, Speransky feels, justifies his presenting a far reaching plan of reorganization and reform, a plan that will be in

---

1 Plan 1809, pp. 19 (note), 25.
2 ibid., pp. 22–24 passim.
3 ibid., p. 28.
4 ibid., p. 29.

complete harmony with Russia's present level of development. The main purpose of his plan is to enable Russia to progress regularly and steadily on to the next "level," to prepare the people and the government for this new stage, without subverting the existing system or creating serious disruptions. The principal task is to found the absolute government, heretofore arbitrary and tyrannical in its manifestations, on stable and clearly defined laws. [1]

The primary function of sovereign power is to establish laws and execute them. But one person, that is the Emperor — who, in Speransky's mind, is identical with sovereign power — cannot supervise and unify all the institutions and laws of the realm. The difficulty can be met by dividing the actions of the sovereign power according to its three major functions. However, he hastens to add, this division is one of pure convenience. For the entire political system of the Empire forms an organic whole no part of which can be changed or destroyed without imperiling the entire structure. Certainly, Speransky is far from advocating anything that might even remotely resemble the system of checks and balances we usually associate with a division of functions and powers. Properly speaking, his plan calls only for a division of administrative functions for the sake of efficiency and greater convenience. [2] Such a result can be obtained in either of two ways. The first method would consist in giving a new legal form to the existing system, while in fact preserving arbitrary absolutism. Of course such an approach is not very desirable and could, under certain circumstances, lead to even greater confusion. But as a clever bureaucratic technician and cautious courtier, he does not rule out the solution completely. Such a mixed system could be of use during a transitional period, until people and institutions have become adjusted to the new forms and their true spirit. In the long run, however, this purely formal approach cannot provide a satisfactory permanent solution of Russia's difficulties. The other method is preferable by far. It involves the following: "1. a legislative institution must be established on such a basis that it cannot bring its legislative proposals to completion without the participation of the sovereign power, but yet have its own free opinions and express the nation's sentiment; 2. the judiciary must be organized in such a fashion that its composition depends on the free choice [of citizens] and that the government retain only the supervision of procedure and the safeguard of public security; 3. the executive power must be completely in the hands of the admin-

1 *ibid.,* pp. 30—31.
2 *ibid.,* p. 31.

istration."[1] But to prevent the executive from abusing its power and distorting the meaning of the laws, it must render account of its actions before the legislative body. Speransky believes that this method will be congenial to the slow, reflective ways of a Northern people — obviously a reminiscence from Montesquieu. It puts its main reliance on the forces of argument and conviction and eliminates appeals to passion and deceit, as had been the unfortunate practice of the French during the Revolution.[2] Under Russian conditions this was an extremely ambitious and "progressive" proposal. However, its *constitutional* character depended entirely on the composition and role given to the legislative institution. We shall see below the practical interpretation Speransky himself gave of this scheme. But first we must examine the social foundation on which he hoped to base the new system.

Russia's historical evolution has created three major social classes: the nobility, the townspeople (burgesses), and the people, i.e., the peasants and workers.[3] The nobles are the descendants of the old, best families of the "first feudal" stage who have preserved their privileged position by serving the state. The burgesses are "fragments" of the third class, in other words, individuals whom economic activities and place of residence have set apart from their original social stratum. The people, i.e., peasants, have become attached to the land and to the nobles by virtue of government acts dictated by military needs.[4] What rights and legal abilities should these classes possess under the new system? Considering that Speransky was writing at a time when serfdom and autocracy ruled Russia, his declaration of principles sounds quite liberal and reminiscent of Locke: "The rights of citizens, i.e., the security of person and property are the first and inalienable attributes of any individual entering into the social bond."[5] But then Speransky engages in a rather casuistic argument. What is the concrete content of each individual's so-called inalienable right to the possession of his person and property in full? Possession of one's own person, answers Speransky, means that a punishment can be inflicted only after a fair trial. It also means that personal services can be rendered only under conditions determined by law, and not on the basis of the arbitrary

1 *ibid.*, p. 33.
2 *ibid.*, pp. 33, 34.
3 Curiously enough, Speransky forgot the class of his own origin — the clergy. It may also be questioned whether the merchants were a full fledged class in Russia. Old Russia based class distinction on the relation to state obligations — tax-paying or service-performing (*tiaglo* or *sluzhba*).
4 Plan 1809, pp. 52—53. Here Speransky shows a more accurate conception of the origins of serfdom than he did in his first reform plan. It is a significant change, related to his growing "historical" orientation.
5 Plan 1809, p. 53.

whim of another individual.[1] This definition makes it possible to preserve serfdom, although it implies that legal and procedural forms will serve to limit its abusive consequences. As to the right to property, "everyone can dispose of his property according to his own will, within the framework of the general law; no one can be deprived of his property without trial. No one can be forced to perform services or pay dues and taxes except as established by law or agreement, to the exclusion of the whim of another individual."[2] As far as it pertains to serfdom, the last sentence implies that services and obligations can be exacted by one individual from another provided the procedures and formalities established by law are observed.

Then Speransky asks whether these rights should be given to all citizens without distinction; and he answers in the negative. The law regulating personal service cannot be the same for everyone. Equal admission to all services would bring to naught the benefits of the upper classes. Therefore, the law must be adapted according to individuals and circumstances. Only the upper class, i.e., the nobility, has the right to serve the state and the monarch, while the common people can be constrained to perform services for the nobility. Similarly, the right to property, although granted to all citizens is not the same for all. Not every Russian will possess the right to own immobile property, in particular settled real estate (i.e., lands inhabited and worked by peasants). To be allowed to own settled real estate, the individual must have some education, know something about law and government. Such a requirement, naturally, excludes the peasants from ownership of real estate and limits this right to the nobility. For, in Speransky's words, "it would be strange if a serf who has become rich by chance buys a village populated with peasants like himself and governs in accordance with the laws, while, unprepared by his education, he is unable to acquire the knowledge of the law or secure the moral respect for his power."[3] In other words, the peasant, even when successful economically, cannot be considered morally prepared to exercise the same rights as the nobleman. For Speransky, therefore, there is no such thing as social equality before the law. Each individual is equal only before the particular law of his own class or estate. And though no one can be deprived of his civil rights, the rights are not the same for everyone.

[1] *ibid.*, p. 54.
[2] *ibid.*, p. 55.
[3] *ibid.*, p. 57. It should be noted that some peasants were already beginning to buy settled lands (under cover of third persons' names) and exploit them for their own personal benefits.

After this we may expect that the citizens of the Russian Empire will not possess equal political rights either, however limited these rights might be. Speransky's plan stipulates that only those who own real estate can participate, however modestly, in the political and administrative life of the country. And, as we have just seen, the limitations put on possession of such property restrict this political right to the upper class. Adapting to the special conditions of Russian serfdom the idea of the *régime censitaire* of France, Speransky also repeats the well known argument in its defense: "... assuming the rights of individuals as equal, the greater the person's participation in the right to property, the greater his natural concern for its preservation." [1] The acquisition of property serves as evidence of reason and industriousness. A property owner is more likely to have the capacity for exercising political rights than an individual without property. However, in Speransky's opinion, mere possession of property is not quite enough, although it is the most important prerequisite. An individual's way of life, the degree of his education are equally important in enabling him to participate in the political and administrative concerns of his country. Thus, Speransky finds that the way of life of domestic servants, manual laborers, or craftsmen has not prepared them for this higher responsibility. Consequently, they should not be admitted to political rights, even if they have accumulated capital wealth. [2] From this reasoning we must conclude that only owners of settled real estate, the nobility, should be allowed the full extent of basic and inalienable rights and admitted to participate in the political affairs of the nation.

There is no question in Speransky's mind, however, of dividing the Russian people into rigid and tight castes. He conceives of the Russian people as an organic whole, an organism wherein each social class is closely and harmoniously related to the others. Social stratification ought to be flexible; there must be freedom to pass from one class to another. Perhaps this cannot be done for a single individual in his own lifetime, but at least this can be the case for a family over several generations. This principle merely restates the historical tradition of Russia which based all class distinctions on the type of service rendered to the state, permitting passage from one class to the other as reward for meritorious performance of duty or imperial favor. Speransky himself owed his rise and fortune to this flexible class structure. In the social hierarchy as conceived by Speransky, the nobility still forms the

---

1 Plan 1809, p. 60.
2 *ibid.*, pp. 60—63 *passim.*

first class of the realm. Like all other citizens, the nobleman has all civil rights, but is exempt from personal service, though he owes at least ten years of service to the state. [1] He has the right to acquire settled lands — i.e., estates with serfs — and to govern the villages they contain according to existing legislation. The owners of such property may elect and be elected to some of the new administrative and political institutions which will be established under the Plan. The nobility itself is subdivided into two categories, hereditary and personal. The hereditary nobleman obtains his status by birthright and through service. In other words, the son of an hereditary nobleman until his majority is only "personally noble" (like the English lords of courtesy), then by serving the state he can earn the full status of an hereditary noble. Personal nobility is acquired by individuals as reward for meritorious service to the state. The children of personal nobles, however, belong to the middle estate. Speransky, as we see, carefully preserved the distinction between the privileged position of the old noble families and newcomers from the bureaucracy and middle estate. At the discretion of the Emperor, but for very exceptional services only, a personal nobleman can be promoted to membership in the hereditary nobility of the realm. In any case, titles can be kept by their lawful claimants only upon condition of their continuing to serve the state. Although a nobleman does not derogate by engaging in various economic activities, such as trade or industry, he does lose his status by becoming a craftsman or worker. [2]

As to the "middle estate," it is to be composed of merchants, townspeople, odnodvortsy, [3] and free peasants owning a specified minimum quantity of land. The members of this class have the basic civil rights, but not the special ones, such as possession of settled estates, which are reserved to the nobility. Unlike the nobleman, members of the middle estate owe personal services, to be determined by special legislation, according to profession. All economic activities are open to them, and to the extent that they possess real estate, they participate in some political rights. But Speransky does no go into detail on this, for the middle estate is to be in reality what its name implies, an in-

---

[1] Speransky suggests reversion to early 18th century practice, qualified compulsory government service from which the nobility had succeeded in freeing itself under Peter III.

[2] Plan 1809, pp. 63—64. This was an innovation compared to 18th century practice, though to some extent, it was a reversion to Muscovite traditions.

[3] A category — not very numerous — of peasants originally of non-Russian ethnic origin who were free and owned their homesteads; it was found primarily among Cossacks in the South Eastern part of European Russia.

termediary and transitional class between the nobility and the people. [1]
The third class, the people, is composed of all the working people:
workers and craftsmen in the towns and peasants in the countryside.
They have no political rights whatever. Members of the third class may
gain access to the middle one by acquiring a certain amount of im-
movable property, provided they have fulfilled all the obligations of
their original status, such as personal services, payment of dues in
kind and money, etc. [2]

In Speransky's view, this hierarchy of classes guarantees the freedom
of upward vertical movement from one estate into the other, the middle
estate and the status of personal nobility acting as intermediary stages
or links. This scheme is not a very radical departure from the class
structure existing at the time. It only describes the social subdivisions
in more explicit terms and establishes clearly the principle and mechanism of social mobility. True enough, in a sense, the Plan's proposals
aim at reversing the trend which, since the middle of the 18th century,
had been freezing Russia's social structure. For this reason, Speransky
lays greater emphasis on property qualifications, while at the same time
he does not try at all to eliminate the most fundamental element of
Russian class division, state service. [3]

We have dealt at some length with the social transformations envisaged by the Plan of 1809 because they constitute the basis for
participation in the judicial and legislative bodies which Speransky
proposes to set up. These new institutions were expected to reform
the Russian administration by basing it upon the rule of law, and
by making it accountable for its actions. It is this part of the Plan
which has been most frequently described, and also most often misunderstood because it has been arbitrarily separated from the social
foundation on which it rested. We therefore must give it detailed
consideration.

Although the Plan of 1809 sets up the local administrative unit as
the first echelon of a pyramid of consultative and judicial institutions,
it does not give in great detail the suggested administrative pattern.

1 Plan 1809, p. 65.
2 ibid., pp. 66—67.
3 Compare the interesting parallel idea of vom Stein: "Durch eine Verbindung
des Adels mit den anderen Ständen wird die Nation zu einem Ganzen verkettet,
und dabei kann das Andenken an edle Handlungen, welche der Ewigkeit wert
sind, in einem höheren Grade erhalten werden." Freiherr vom Stein, "Rundschreiben
an die Mitglieder des Generaldepartments (sogenannte Politische Testament),
Koenigsberg 24 November 1808," in Freiherr vom Stein, Briefwechsel, Denkschriften
und Aufzeichnungen, vol. II, p. 585 (quoted in modernized spelling in W. Altmann,
Ausgewählte Urkunden zur Brandenburg-Preussischen Verfassungs- und Verwal-
tungsgeschichte, 2. Auflage, (Berlin 1915), II. Teil, 1. Hälfte, p. 64).

The main purpose of Speransky is to provide some means by which responsible public opinion can obtain some hearing and by which it may assist the judiciary. Every three years, each township (*volost'*) conducts elections to a Township Duma (i.e. Assembly). Active and passive voting rights depend on property qualifications, property meaning here ownership of real estate. The Township Duma elects a Township Administration (*pravlenie*), audits the accounts of taxes collected and spent by the administration for Township needs, writes petitions and reports to the higher authorities, elects deputies to the District (*uezd*) Duma. The *uezd* deputies elected by the Township Dumas meet every three years in a District Duma, in the district capital. The functions of the District Duma are similar to those of the Township Dumas, only on a higher level; but in addition, the District Dumas elect the members of the District Court. Deputies chosen by District Dumas meet every three years in a Provincial (*gubernskaia*) Duma which elects the members of the Provincial Council (*sovet*), audits the accounts of taxes collected and spent, drafts petitions to the central government on the needs of the province. We cannot stress enough that meeting only once every three years, none of the various Dumas has the right (or possibility) to legislate or issue regulations for the local administration. The Dumas act primarily as advisory bodies which keep informed of the administration's designs and present opinions and petitions to the executive heads — appointed by the central authorities — of the Township, District, or Province. The petitions and desiderata of the Dumas can be forwarded to the higher authorities only through these appointed executive officials. [1]

The pyramid of Dumas is crowned by a State Duma (Duma of the Empire — *gosudarstvennaia duma*). The State Duma meets once every year in September, without special convocation, and stays in session as long as its agenda requires it. It has equal status with the Senate and the Ministries. The session of the State Duma can be terminated by adjournment upon completion of all its business, or by order of the Sovereign power, or by the Emperor's dismissal of all members and their replacement by candidates selected from lists prepared by the Provincial Dumas. Barring a general dismissal of all members, Duma membership is for life. Deceased members (or those disqualified by court decision for some criminal act) are replaced by appointment of candidates from among those nominated by the Provincial Dumas. [2]

[1] Plan 1809, pp. 73—77.
[2] Oddly enough, Speransky did not specify by what method the members of the first Duma would be selected and called together, nor is he very clear on how a Duma will be selected if the previous one is dismissed by the Emperor.

The Chancellor of the Empire is the Duma's President *ex officio*. The Duma of the Empire receives yearly accounts of the actions of the ministers, and of the financial and legislative situation. However, the Duma is very limited in the exercise of its function of control and supervision of ministerial acts, as it can consider only those questions which the government cares to submit to it. All other affairs remain strictly outside the Duma's competence. The Duma has no legislative initiative or power at all, as these are the exclusive prerogatives of the Sovereign Power (i.e., the Emperor) acting through the central government institutions. The State Duma, like the provincial and local ones, may only present petitions and inform the government on the country's condition and needs.[1] Only in case the Duma feels that a legislative act violates the fundamental laws of the realm, or when an executive agent refuses to acknowledge responsibility for his actions, may it propose on its own initiative (after informing the monarch) legislative action leading to the impeachment of the responsible minister or official. In short, the State Duma is to be merely a consultative and deliberative body with advisory opinion only. It gives its opinion and information only on those problems which the government may desire to refer to it.[2] Speransky was not entirely unaware of the possibility that such restricted functions might render the Duma a meaningless legislative institution. Yet, he did want to keep many areas of government out of the hands of a "representative" assembly. In the final analysis, the high-sounding "legislative" body is merely an institution to which executive officers of the Crown may report on their administration and which acts as an "informant" of the country's desires and condition.

The Plan's proposals for the judiciary — the guardian of order and legality — follow pretty closely the formal organization of English justice on the county level. In each territorial subdivision — township, district, province — a court is to be established along the following lines: a group of "jurymen," elected by the respective Dumas, who deliberate on the facts of the case; the panel of "jurymen" is chaired by a Court President appointed by the Minister of Justice from among a list of twenty candidates submitted by each Duma. The President sees to it that the proper forms of legal procedure are strictly adhered to, but he does not participate in the decisions on the facts of the case. The most important benefit of the system, in Speransky's eyes, is that by

1 This too is very similar to the Slavophile conception of the functions of a Zemskii Sobor.
2 On the Duma, see Plan 1809, pp. 77—79.

breaking the bureaucracy's domination over the judiciary, it delegates judicial responsibility to citizens themselves belonging to the jurisdiction of the court. It is a qualified form of judgment by one's peers. The judicial hierarchy of the Empire is topped by the Senate which serves as the highest tribunal of the land. The Senate will be composed of two civil and two criminal departments, one of each in the two capitals of St. Petersburg and Moscow. The Senate reviews the transactions of the lower courts to check whether all procedural forms have been properly observed. In case of error — as determined by a *reketmeister* (*maître de requêtes*) — the case is referred back to the lower courts. This function of procedural review, as contrasted to the American judicial review, is patterned after the French *Conseil d'État*. The Senate also acts as the last instance of appeal — besides the Emperor, of course. The members of the Senate are appointed by the Emperor from a list of candidates drawn up by the Provincial Dumas and kept up to date by the Chancellor. The decisions of the Senate are to be announced publicly and printed for circulation to all lower courts and government agencies. [1]

In this way, Speransky's Plan aimed at separating the judicial from the administrative functions of the government, a crying need in Russia at the time. Of all the practical suggestions embodied in the Plan of 1809, those pertaining to the judiciary were most likely to contain the elements of "progressive" development. Membership, as "jury," in courts of justice was one of the best means available for raising the people to a higher level of civic and political consciousness. This in turn would then serve to secure a solid foundation for a "true monarchy." Although the proposed reorganization of the judiciary was never carried out, and we are thus left in ignorance of how it would have fared in "real life," it may not be amiss to point out one factor that might have sidetracked the reform. The local "manpower" from which the "jurymen" would be drawn was of very low calibre indeed. It lacked the training and habit of dealing with judiciary and administrative matters. Under such conditions, the representatives of the government, the Presidents of Courts and Procurators (i.e., "attorneys general"), could have easily acquired preponderant roles. That such a development was not outside the realm of possibility had been amply demonstrated by the government's experience with the assemblies and

---

[1] *ibid.*, pp. 79—86 *passim.* Speransky is not very clear as to whether the Senate takes up all cases in last resort, or only on appeal. Also, it would seem as if the decisions of the Senate could still be appealed to the Emperor, a situation which would decrease the prestige and authority of the Senate as an autonomous judicial body.

courts in equity set up by Catherine II for the nobility. Nor did the very restricted composition of the various Dumas augur well for an early triumph of a new social class with a fresh outlook and better training in these matters. As long as the serfowning nobility kept its preponderance, Speransky's improvements were more than likely to share the fate of Catherine's institutions. It was but another illustration of Speransky's undue partiality for "bureaucratic," legislative solutions which did not adequately allow for the opposition from traditional social and institutional patterns and forces.

In last place, the Plan of 1809 takes up the organization of the executive functions of government. As Speransky had occasion to stress in his previous projects and in the reforms he had succeeded in implementing, the executive must possess unity, coherence, and responsibility. The executive function is the exclusive prerogative of absolute power, i.e., of the autocratic Emperor. There can be no qualification to this principle. Unity and coherence of action in the executive are to be achieved by a proper and rational distribution of its tasks among the five functions of government (police, finance, external security, justice, economy). We need not expound the Plan's proposals in this field, for they are almost verbatim repetitions of the arguments in defense of the reform of the ministries summarized and discussed in the preceding chapter. As to the principle of responsibility, the ministers and agents of the sovereign power are not responsible politically, for they are only the executors of the Emperor's will. But they are accountable administratively. True enough, "the king can do no wrong," but should the Emperor issue orders contrary to the fundamental laws of the realm, it is the duty of the ministers to advise him against it. The Plan does not state whether the minister has to take the full responsibility and blame for the execution of the imperial will. This was a most regrettable omission. As we had occasion to note, the same idea was followed through in the ministry: the Council of the Ministry is an advisory body, each chief of a department is responsible to both the minister and the council for the actions he takes within the limits of his competence. The activities of the central executive agencies are reported yearly to the State Duma which can bring to account the individual minister. A minister who has acted in violation of the laws is tried before the Senate. [1] The modern reader will easily detect many gaps and inadequacies in the position of the minister, in particular in regard to his liability for an imperial order he has not advised but which he had to sign. Speransky's Plan provides no help

1 Plan 1809, pp. 87—98 *passim.*

ın resolving such difficulties, nor does he clarify a good many other points concerning the rights of the Duma *vis à vis* the ministers. Extreme as it may sound, we cannot forebear pointing out that the position of the imperial ministers towards the Emperor on the one hand and the Duma on the other is strongly reminiscent of the situation of the members of the Cabinet of the President of the United States. Is should be mentioned in this connection that while Speransky was acquainted with the American Constitution, there is no evidence that he consciously copied American institutions.

Unfortunately, Speransky gives little detail on the executive functions and institutions at the local level. His proposals are vague and quite inadequate for an improvement of the very seriously deteriorated provincial administration. In all probability, he was reserving for a later date a thorough examination of this aspect of Russian administration. In the Plan of 1809 he was content with indicating a few guiding ideas and principles. The central executive agencies, ministries and the like, have their equivalents or representatives on the local levels; and the sum total of these agents constitute the provincial and local administrations. On each level we find a number of bureaus to take care of each of the functions of local administration: police, public economy, treasury, postal services, state peasants, etc. The bureaus are the local agents of the respective ministries by which they are nominated. They render account to the Councils elected by the local Dumas in much the same way as the ministries do to the State Duma. The local administration, Speransky feels, should not be subdivided too much among various offices, so that the number of bureaus and officials staffing them can be kept at a minimum. Yet, the people should also have easy access to the agencies and agents governing them, and for this purpose the existing division of the country is inadequate. Indeed, the Empire is divided along geographic lines, without regard to the density of the population. To obviate this inconvenience, the Plan gives a simpler and more rational scheme. [1] The Empire is to be divided into provinces (*guberniia*), each with a population of 100 to 300 thousand souls. In turn, the provinces are subdivided into two to five districts (*okrug*), depending on the population, and the districts into several townships (*volost'*) and towns

---

[1] Areas which have some special distinct characteristics (social, economic, political) and are located on the periphery of the Empire should be given their own particular organization. Such areas, which Speransky proposes to call regions (*oblast'*), include Siberia, the Caucasus, Astrakhan, the Urals, Georgia, Orenburg, the lands of the Don Cossacks.

(*volostnoi gorod*).[1] The efficiency of this scheme — which is of course strongly reminiscent of Peter the Great's and Catherine II's territorial divisions — is open to question. Its most obvious drawback is that it does not take into consideration the historical or economic relations that have already developed between various parts of the country.

At the very top of Russia's political structure, the three main divisions of governmental power — executive, judiciary and legislative — are unified in the person of the absolute sovereign assisted by an advisory and preparatory council, the Council of State. The activities and functions of the Duma of the Empire, the Senate, and the Ministries are centralized, given unity, and legislative form in the Council of State.[2] The Council of State was actually established and took an important place in the central institutions of the Empire, and as the Statute of the Council, promulgated on January 1, 1810, was an exact copy of the proposals concerning it contained in the Plan of 1809, we need not repeat here what has been said about it in the previous chapter. The original intentions of Speransky concerning the Council of State were rapidly perverted, however, because the Council was the only institution suggested in the Plan that was given life and therefore had to survive as it were, outside its natural milieu, deprived of the support of the other members of the system.

We are struck by the truly comprehensive scope and character of Speransky's Plan of 1809. It was a blueprint for the complete over-hauling of Russia's administration as well as a declaration of the new principles which were to guide the political life of the nation in the future. The Plan endeavored to implement a set of basic concepts of government, namely, that good government required a logical and efficient division of administrative functions, orderliness and regularity of procedure, responsibility and accountability for actions taken. Furthermore, the organization of the judiciary contained features which, if they had been fully developed in conjunction with the limited degree of participation provided by the local Dumas, could have performed an extremely valuable "pedagogical" function for future generations. They could have become the training ground for a responsible citizenry and an active, nationwide "public opinion." This in turn might have raised the level of civic and political consciousness among the peasantry. No doubt this is what Speransky hoped for (and it was realized, *mutatis mutandis,* by the reforms of Alexander II). But he did not give these institutions sufficient power and strength

[1] Plan 1809, pp. 107—111, 71—72.
[2] *ibid.,* pp. 112—117.

to overcome the force of inertia inherent in a centralized, absolutist, bureaucratic state, in a nobility which, in its majority, was devoid of civic and political traditions, and in the general backwardness of Russia's social, economic, and cultural conditions. Furthermore, and perhaps most significant, he did little to pave the way for a radical change of the social structure on which the new administrative system was to depend. He could but leave intact all existing class divisions and special privileges; he did not extend these privileges to any appreciably numerous new category of people. Naturally, little success could be predicted for his project as long as serfdom remained intact in its most abusive manifestations, and as long as the serfowning, narrow-minded, callous nobleman continued to dominate Russia's public life.[1]

Despite Speransky's persistent pleas, Alexander I decided to implement the Plan's proposals piecemeal, and as a result, the reform program was never realized in full. Only the Council of State and the Ministries were established and reorganized. Contemporaries, therefore, judged the Plan on the basis of this inadequate and partial accomplishment and, as Speransky had predicted, it became easy for its detractors to undermine the incompleted structure. In the hope of salvaging something, Speransky tried to implement some of his basic concepts on a more limited scale. In 1811 he suggested the reorganization of the Senate into two, a Governing and a Judiciary one; these Senates were to take the temporary place of the State Duma and the judicial Senate conceived by the Plan. His proposals in this connection need not detain us, for they were merely re-statements — in a "watered down" form — of the principles, ideas, and arguments he had set forth in the Plan of 1809 [2]

The reader, no doubt, has noted that Speransky's plans of reform showed the influence of variegated sources. [3] Speransky was a voracious and careful reader, but the list of his library and the notes he was wont to take while reading, have not been preserved. The original

---

1 We are not forgetting the circumstances in which Speransky had to work and that it was necessary for him to abandon some of his proposals in order to get a few of his basic ideas accepted. However, it is important to point out — against his over-enthusiastic admirers — that he left much to be desired in respect to the practical implementation of even the limited proposals of his Plan of 1809. Speransky cannot be absolved for his failure to realize that hopes are meaningless in practical politics unless they are provided with a concrete institutional foundation for their development.

2 On this, see the general biographies of Speransky and *Istoriia Pravitel'stvuiushchego Senata za 200 let ego sushchestvovaniia* and the texts of the projects relative to the Governing and Judiciary Senates in Shil'der, *op. cit.*, vol. III.

3 For the details, see S. Swatikow, *Die Entwürfe der Änderung der russischen Staatsverfassung,* (Heidelberg 1904) *passim* and Georges Vernadsky, *La Charte constitutionnelle de l'Empire russe de l'an 1820* (Paris 1933), pp. 217—218.

draft of the Plan of 1809 has been lost too; and anyway, as it was not an "academic" or scholarly "paper," it would not have contained references to the sources on which Speransky had drawn for its composition. It does not seem, to our mind, a very rewarding or fruitful enterprise to attempt to track down the specific source for each statement or to find a model in Western European political practice for every concrete measure proposed by Speransky in his plans. [1] Much of what Speransky wrote belonged to the *Zeitgeist* and was common knowledge among the educated. Following the well proven practice of the *philosophes,* he took perhaps great care to dress up his ideas in the fashion of his day and to enhance their appeal by stating them in the "jargon" of the Enlightenment — a jargon which was particularly familiar to and appreciated by Alexander I. [2]

In addition to the phraseology of the Enlightenment, Speransky introduced a new note. On several occasions he stressed the peculiarities of Russian historical development — not so much qualitatively different from the Western European pattern as differing in degree and chronology. On this ground he argued for a political organization that would arise out of Russia's historical experience. He believed that all political systems were based on the specific needs of a nation's spiritual development at a given time. In this respect, Speransky followed through the ideas, developed first by Montesquieu, that later gave the foundation to "historicism" and an organic conception of national history. Even in his first suggestion (1802) concerning the method to be followed in codifying law, he manifested an attitude which Savigny would not have repudiated. Speransky's thought, therefore, contained elements of a historicist approach to politics, an approach that had been given vogue by Edmund Burke and elaborated by the German school.

From a contemporary point of view, Speransky's understanding of the historical process does not strike one as particularly profound or accurate. But when compared to that of his Russian contemporaries — and let us remember that Karamzin had not yet published the first volume of his History — and to that of the French *philosophes,* it showed perspicacity and insight. Understandably, he shared the interest for history of the late 18th century, and he had what Meinecke has called a "negative historical sense," a transitional form of the consciousness of historical development preceding and preparatory to "histor-

---

[1] Speransky quotes directly Montesquieu, Bentham, Blackstone, Sir Francis Bacon, Beccaria. Direct evidence of his use of Filangieri and J. J. Rousseau can be easily detected too.
[2] See Appendix.

icism," in the classical meaning of the term. [1] Unlike most of his colleagues in the government, Speransky was steeped in Russian history and well acquainted with the antecedents of the political and social institutions with which he had to deal. He was not, of course, a scholar or professional historian, and his analyses or conclusions have not always been confirmed by later investigation. But he had illuminating *aperçus* into the dynamics and character of the historical evolution of government policies. This permitted him to see more clearly the structural weakness of the institutions he wished to transform. For instance, Speransky was among the first influential Russian administrators to understand correctly the historical rationale of serfdom, namely, that originally it had been established gradually to meet the military and fiscal needs of the state. Therefore, if the government wished to abolish or change serfdom, it had to transform the basis on which the whole Russian state structure rested. It would be such a radical change that concrete steps towards its realization could be taken only with the utmost caution. One of the important prequisites would be the raising of the country's level of economic activity. Furthermore, as the serfs' status was not the outcome of arbitrary usurpations, any change in it must be brought about gradually, by means of cautious legal and administrative measures. The historical relativism implied in this outlook and approach shaped the political and social conservatism and cautious reformism which we have had occasion to observe in our exposition of Speransky's projects. [2]

It may be surmised — for we have no direct evidence — that Speransky's conception of the State Duma, and of its local equivalents, was inspired by the history of the *Zemskii Sobor* of Muscovy. Indeed, as our description must have shown, the Dumas contemplated by him bore little resemblance to the contemporary representative legislative assemblies in Western Europe and America. The Duma — as the *Zemskii Sobors* of another age — was rather an assembly of Estates (*Ständetag*) similar to the English Parliament and the French *États Généraux* in the Middle Ages, called to give moral support and approval to the monarch's actions. Like the medieval assemblies, the Duma was called to inform the government of the needs and wishes of the country, to give its advice, if requested, on specific problems, and to see to it that the ministers did not abuse the sovereign's confidence. This conception of a national assembly had been popular-

---

[1] F. Meinecke, *Vom Weltbürgertum zum Nationalstaat*, (2d. ed., Berlin 1911), p. 129.

[2] Mannheim, "Conservative Thought," *loc. cit.*, pp. 103, 110—111, 115.

ized by conservative thinkers after 1789 in opposition to the "atomistic" views of radicals and progressive liberals. It might be noted in passing, that Speransky's conception of a national assembly was taken up again by the Slavophiles; though the latter do not seem to have been aware of their "debt" to Alexander's State Secretary. The Duma of the Empire was supposed to be the voice of the people (*sobornyi golos,* Slavophile theologians would say later), an expression of the organic harmony of the country, in contradistinction to the representation of conflicting private interests in Western European legislative assemblies. [1]

There is no doubt that the organization of the Council, the method of selecting its members, the enumeration and classification of its functions, owe a great deal to the *Conseil d'Etat* created in France by the *Constitution de l'An VIII.* Retaining the formal aspects of the rationalistic ideals and beliefs of the 18th century, the First Consul's constitution had given virtually uncontrolled power to the executive. For this reason it appealed greatly to the absolutist monarchies of Europe and was often imitated, even after Napoleon's fall, as, for instance, in Prussia in 1817. The imitation by autocratic Russia should, therefore, not come as very surprising, and it should not be construed as implying a liberal and constitutional orientation of its government. No doubt, Speransky was familiar with the French model, for the *Constitution de l'An VIII* had circulated widely in Europe. Furthermore, the Russian Commission on Laws, as we may recall, was in regular correspondence with Portalis and other leading French jurists who could provide the full text of the Constitution with valuable comments. The ready availability of useful foreign models alone, however, is rarely sufficient reason for introducing radically new political or administrative institutions. But only the external form which Speransky gave to the State Duma and the method of selecting its membership might be said to have been imitated from French models (Napoleon's *Conseil Législatif* and Sieyès' electoral scheme). The origin, purpose, and basic character of the French institutions were so vastly different that a stress on Speransky's debt to tradition and organic and historicist theories seems to come closer to the truth and is more rewarding for an understanding of the full implications of his proposals.

[1] Compare again with the parallel argument of vom Stein: "Die Regierung vervielfältigt die Quellen ihrer Erkenntnis von den Bedürfnissen der bürgerlichen Gesellschaft und gewinnt an Stärke in den Mitteln der Ausführung." Freiherr vom Stein, "Denkschrift über die zweckmässige Bildung der obersten Behörden und der Provinzial-, Finanz- und Polizeibehörden in der preussischen Monarchie (Nassau, Juni 1807)", *Briefwechsel, Denkschriften und Aufzeichnungen* vol. II, p. 228 (cited in modernized spelling from Altmann, *Ausgewählte Urkunden,* II. p. 23).

V. G. Shcheglov's detailed and careful study of the ideological and institutional forerunners of the Council of State in Russia has conclusively shown that — contrary to Karamzin's prejudiced belief — Speransky's creation was not a radical departure from tradition and precedent. After a searching and thorough examination of much archival material, which we need not summarize or repeat here, Shcheglov has come to the conclusion that a "council," i.e., a body of men who advise the ruler and help him to prepare legislation, had been known not only in Muscovite Russia (*boiar duma*) but also throughout the 18th century (Supreme Secret Council, Imperial Cabinet, Council of the Emperor). The checkered history of the councils in the 18th century shows clearly the government's great need of a regular advisory organization to assist it in the legislative process. The practical effect of the Imperial Council instituted by Paul I, for example, was to help the monarch in the drafting of needed legislation and in dealing with important matters arising suddenly. Like its predecessors, Paul's creation was a *Regierungsbehörde*, taking direct part in the administration as well, similar to the councils of the enlightened despots in Western Europe, Maria Theresa's Austria in particular. As most of Paul's institutions, the Imperial Council was heartily disliked by the advisers and friends of Alexander I. The members of the Unofficial Committee spear-headed the opposition and advocated the abolition of Paul's council for fear that — like the Senate — it would become a rallying point for old dignitaries and disgruntled aristocrats who, eventually, might present a serious challenge to the bureaucracy. Speransky concurred in this harsh judgment of the Imperial Council and the somewhat unjustified fear of it. To obviate some of the criticisms levelled at Paul's creation, Alexander I established a new council, called the Permanent Council (*nepremennyi sovet*). [1] The function of this Council, as stated in its statute was the "consideration of important state affairs." (PSZ 19,806, March 30, 1801). Unlike the councils of the 18th century which had participated directly in the administration of the Empire (*Regierungsbehörde*), the new Council was to be strictly an advisory body. "The Council is established near Us and it has, therefore, no outside action; it does not enter into any decisions on executive matters, and has no other power in the state than the power of deliberation (*soobrazhenie*). From this it follows that the Council can issue no decrees or orders in its own name. The

[1] The original name of the body had been Council of State — see Korkunov, *Russkoe gosudarstvennoe pravo* II, pp. 63—64. The fact is alluded to in the Statute of the Council, 1 Jan. 1810, PSZ 24,064.

affairs We have entrusted to it refer only to legislative matters, executive affairs are referred to the Senate and those institutions which are subordinate to it." [1] Very soon after its establishment, however, the new Council degenerated into an organ of the judiciary, deciding civil and administrative cases on appeal from the Senate. It ceased to direct and unify the broad policies of the government. This evolution might have been the result of "sabotage" on the part of the Unofficial Committee, for the Council had been too much of a creation of the conspirators of March 11, 1801 and of the Senatorial Party to be to the liking of Alexander's youthful friends and advisers. After the establishment of the Ministries in 1802, the Council's original purpose was completely forgotten. However, the idea of a consultative council to assist the monarch in deciding on legislative needs was not abandoned.

Did foreign models and approaches play a role in orienting Speransky's search for an institutional form of an advisory and unifying council to the Emperor? The Council set up by Maria Theresa in 1760 (and also imperfectly realized in practice) had functions that were very similar to those of the Permanent Council of 1801 and its 18th-century predecessors. The similarity extends also, in some measure, to the Cabinet of Frederick II and the original design of a council of Napoleon. From all appearance, these were parallel developments, arising from similar needs, and based on a similar rationale. They all aimed at combining bureaucratic efficiency and order with absolute executive power. Perhaps Speransky was directly acquainted with Kaunitz's creation, as his references to the financial measures of Joseph II and Austrian law show that he was familiar with some Austrian legislation. But unfortunately, we have no direct proof of conscious borrowing or imitation. In any case, the Russian 18th century forerunners, Western institutions, and Speransky's own Council of State, were all responses — within the traditions of absolute monarchy and enlightened absolutism — to the necessity of "streamlining" the administration and adapting it to modern conditions, without opening the way to representative legislative assemblies. [2]

The dangers inherent in a piecemeal implementation of the proposals contained in the Plan of 1809, dangers against which Speransky had

---

[1] The Instruction (Nakaz) to the Nepremennyi Sovet, dated 5 April 1801, quoted by Korkunov, op. cit., II, p. 64.

[2] For material on the Western Councils in the 18th century and a discussion of their relation to enlightened absolutism and bureaucratic forms of administration, see: O. Hintze, "Das monarchische Prinzip und die Konstitutionelle Verfassung"

warned the Emperor, came true. Prepared in great secrecy, and published out of their "natural" context, the measures based on his Plan were misjudged and misunderstood.[1] On the whole, the Russian public reacted unfavorably to the various reforms introduced between 1809 and 1812. This negative reaction, coupled with an ignorance of the full scope of the Plan, led Speransky's contemporaries to draw wrong conclusions and inferences regarding his aims and ideals.

We may first note the interesting opinion and comment of a neutral observer whose political sophistication can hardly be doubted. John Quincy Adams, reporting to the Secretary of State, wrote:

> With this letter I have the honor to enclose a translation of the Imperial Manifesto and New Constitution of the Council of the Russian Empire, issued at the commencement of the present year. It is variously considered by different persons as a new system of government containing many features of freedom and calculated to temper the absoluteness of the Sovereign authority. As an imitation of the present organization of the French government, recommended by the energy which experience has shown to possess there — or as merely a mode of removing certain Ministers with whom, the Emperor is not altogether satisfied, but whom he does not chose to disgrace, and of concentrating power and influence in the present Chancellor of the Empire, Count Romanzof [Rumiantsov]. Upon him the appointment of President General of the Council in the absence of the Empire [sic! — Adams obviously means Emperor] has been conferred for the present year. And the office next in dignity, that of Secretary of the Empire, is at the same time bestowed upon Mr. Speransky, a person whose reputation stands very high and who has risen under the favor of Count

Staat und Verfassung (Leipzig 1941), pp. 349—379; "Der oesterreichische und der preussische Beamtenstaat im 17. und 18. Jahrhundert," ibid., pp. 311—348; "Die Entstehung der modernen Staatsministerien," ibid., pp. 265—310. It should be noted that the Austrian model was particularly relevant to Russia, for the Habsburg monarchy had similar problems arising from the fact that it was a multinational empire.

[1] The degree of secrecy surrounding the preparation of the legislation for the Council of State can be gauged from the fact that Arakcheev was shown an outline of the Council's statute only on the eve of its official publication. See V. R. Marchenko, "Avtobiograficheskie zapiski gosudarstvennogo sekretaria V. R. Marchenki (1782—1838)," Russkaia Starina, vol. 85 (1896), p. 485. Napoleon's ambassador, Caulaincourt, reporting on the new Council — on 12 Feb. 1810, wrote: "(le nouveau conseil) à l'organisation duquel ni lui [Rumiantsev] ni d'autres n'avaient été appelés, et Sa Majesté me dit qu'Elle l'avait formé seule dans son cabinet avec M. Speransky et que le comte de Romantzoff n'en avait eu connaissance que trois jours avant la publication des édits, et les autres ministres que le jour même." Grand Duc Nicolas Mikhailowitsch, Les relations diplomatiques de la Russie et de la France ... vol. IV, p. 281.

The complete Plan of Speransky was discussed only by a special committee whose members were in advance favorable to it: Kochubei, Kampengauzen, Mordvinov, Balugian'skii.

Romanzoff's particular friendship [?]. He is the reputed author of general public manifestoes and other state papers, the composition of which has excited notice in the U.S. as well as throughout Europe. [1]

Our documentation does not bear out Adams's supposition that the Council was a device for settling some court intrigues and providing an "honorable promotion" for those dignitaries who had lost the Emperor's confidence. The American Minister's opinion that the Council of State foreshadowed greater freedom, the curtailment of absolutism, and some degree of constitutionalism was shared by many contemporaries, friends and foes of constitutionalism alike. This judgment was not justified either in the light of the Plan of 1809 as a whole or in the light of the Statute for the Council of State alone. But as it was so prevalent an opinion among Speransky's contemporaries — even contributing to his eventual fall from favor — and often also maintained by subsequent "liberal" historians, it should be examined more closely. The criticism of and attack on the Council of State made by the Historiographer, Karamzin, provides a convenient basis for such an examination.

Karamzin was the most articulate and eloquent — if not the most original, logical, and best informed — spokesman for the conservative landowning nobility. The national pride of this class had been deeply wounded by Alexander's military defeats and alliance with Napoleon; its economic interests had suffered a great deal from Russia's participation in the Continental Blockade. The conservative nobility also resented the fact that its members did not participate fully in the government, for all the influential positions were occupied by bureaucrats, some of whom were mere social upstarts. In a sense, the conservative gentry complained that they had lost the social prestige and political influence they had enjoyed under Catherine II. Karamzin gave effective literary form to these somewhat diffuse sentiments of discontent. In his famous paper (privately submitted to Alexander I) *Of Old and New Russia,* he subjected to sharp criticism Speransky's plans of reform, in particular the organization of the Council of State. [2] Karamzin felt that the Council, and other measures taken or

1 *Department of State — Russia,* John Quincy Adams, dispatch to the Secretary of State, No. 11, 31 January 1810.

2 Karamzin's paper remained unknown to the public until the 1860s. An incomplete version was published in 1870, N. M. Karamzin, "O drevnei i novoi Rossii", *Russkii Arkhiv,* VIII, (1870), pp. 2225—2350. A complete edition was published by V. V. Sipovskii, *Zapiska o drevnei i novoi Rossii,* St. Pbg. 1914. Dr. Richard E. Pipes is preparing an annotated English translation (with Russian text) to appear shortly.

projected by Speransky, were mere copies of French institutions, those wicked and abhorrent creations of the French Revolution and the Usurper *Buonaparté*. There was enough truth in this accusation, if one considered only the external and formal features of the Council, to make a very effective propaganda argument. Further proof of Russia's slavish submission to France was seen by Karamzin in the fact that the changes and reforms had been introduced after Tilsit, and even more particularly after Erfurt. It was but a short step to the suggestion that Speransky had been bribed (or at best, tricked) into subverting Russia's traditions and source of strength through the introduction of alien elements. Unfortunately, continued Karamzin, the well-meaning but misguided Emperor had fallen victim to the Machiavellian scheme. Furthermore, Karamzin condemned the limitation of the absolute and autocratic power of the Russian monarch implied in the Statute of the Council of State. The Historiographer believed that such a limitation was not only contrary to Russia's historical tradition, but also harmful to the future development of the country. The limiting and restrictive intent of the Council of State was to be found, Karamzin pointed out, in the formula which had to accompany all future legislative acts: *"vniav mneniiu soveta,"* i.e., "having heard the opinion of the council." This formula, Karamzin argued, was nothing but a translation of the phrase used in all the legislative acts of Napoleonic France, *"le conseil d'état entendu..."* As France had a constitutional government — its practical non-existence under Napoleon I was conveniently disregarded by Karamzin — the formula had a constitutional meaning and aimed at limiting the power of the Emperor. Poor logic, indeed!

If the formal similarity between the Russian and French formulas is not a crucial argument, may it not be true, though, that Speransky's intention in introducing this formula, had been to limit the power of the autocratic ruler of All Russia? Most historians have answered in the affirmative and indeed have considered the use of the formula as the first breach — at least by implication and potentially — in the solid wall of Russian autocracy. The mere fact of having to hear the opinion of the Council, so the argument went, was a limitation upon absolutism. But did the Emperor not always ask and hear — not necessarily follow, of course, — the advice of his councillors and other regularly constituted administrative bodies? The autocratic, absolute character of the Russian Emperor's power found expression among others, in his prerogative of legislating without regard to the opinions and advice rendered. The use of the formula *"vniav mneniiu soveta,"* or even the mere existence of

the Council of State, in no ways restricted this prerogative. Furthermore, the Statute of the Council left to the Emperor's discretion what
problems and affairs were to be submitted to the Council for advisory
opinion. The formula, "the boiars have decided and the Tsar has
ordered," which traditionally accompanied the legislative acts of
Muscovite Russia, had even greater limitative implications, yet very
few — and at any rate, not Karamzin — have questioned the fact that
the Tsar of Moscow was an unlimited, autocratic ruler. Moreover, as
Korkunov correctly pointed out, the French formula only indicated the
advisory nature of the opinion of the *Conseil d'Etat* and did not
prevent the government from over-riding it by appropriate legislation. [1]

While the conservatives used the formula to criticize the idea of the
Council, the friends of constitutionalism seized upon another term
found in the Statute of the Council to support their joyful contention
that Speransky had taken the first step towards limiting the autocracy.
The term in question was *soslovie,* or estate, which Speransky used for
describing the Council. It was inferred that *soslovie* had a meaning
akin to that of *Etat,* as found in such expressions as *Tiers Etat, Etats
Généraux* in Ancien Régime France. The memories of 1789, still very
vivid in the minds of contemporaries, served to draw a parallel between
the Estates General which led to the *Assemblée Nationale,* and the
Council of State which in its turn might become the nucleus of a
"representative assembly." (For Speransky's contemporaries knew
nothing of his proposal for a State Duma which might have been more
logically a candidate for the role of *Assemblée Nationale*). Here again
Korkunov's incisive analysis has given convincing historical and juridical proof for the rejection of this traditional interpretation of the
meaning of *soslovie,* an interpretation which has been inherited from
the naive understanding of Speransky's defenders. Korkunov has pointed
out that in the vocabulary of Speransky, and of that of his contemporaries, *soslovie* meant a body, group of people who make up the
membership of an administrative institution. Thus, the Cabinet or
Committee of Ministers was also considered a *soslovie.* Not only does
this meaning of the word appear in the Code of 1840, which embodies
the political phraseology and administrative organization of the preceding generation, but the laws and regulations issued during the first two
decades of the 19th century contain ample illustration of a similar
usage of the term. Speransky himself used the word only in the sense

---

[1] See Korkunov, *op. cit.,* II, pp. 75—83 *passim* for an excellent statement of the
legal technicalities involved in the argument.

of an administrative organ or body, composed of several equal members, similar to the contempory idea of "board." [1]

One more point should be made in connection with the belief commonly held that the purpose of the Plan of 1809 was to inaugurate constitutional government in Russia. The doctrine of the separation of powers, i.e., checks and balances, is usually considered as a major prequisite of constitutional representative government. It had been a most important element in 18th-century political theory and propaganda, ever since Locke, and more particularly Montesquieu, had urged that the assurance of freedom resided in a separation of powers. On the surface it would appear that Speransky subscribed to this doctrine and the Plan of 1809 proposed to implement it. But our earlier description must have shown that separation of powers did not — in Speransky's view — imply anything like, let us say, the checks and balances in the American constitution. Nor did it even have the political significance given to it by Montesquieu. Speransky always insisted that in the final analysis, the legislative, executive, judicial powers rested united in the autocratic Emperor. Organically bound together, the three powers were, in his view, distinct but inseparable manifestations of the moral function of government. Therefore, separation of powers meant nothing more than a logical distribution of functions, a division of labor, as it were, for the sake of greater efficiency and justice. To this end, the three powers of government should be exercised in such a way as to preclude overlapping and interference, but within the single unitary framework provided by the autocratic sovereign.

In a very suggestive essay, Baron Boris Nolde has tried to make out a case for the proposition that Speransky's concept of separation of powers was in advance of the views held by most of his contemporaries, even in France. [2] It was Speransky's conception, Nolde maintained, which provided the basis not only for Russian administrative practice, where it received its final application after 1861, but also for the conception of administrative power held in Europe's "conservative monarchies" — Austria, Prussia, German Empire — throughout the 19th

[1] Korkunov, *op. cit.,* II, pp. 75—83. Other officials, contemporaries of Speransky who cannot be suspected of "constitutional" leanings used the term in this same sense of 'board'. For example, State Secretary Olenin referred to the Council of State as this consultative *soslovie*; see M. M. Vinaver, "K voprosu ob istochnikakh X. toma Svoda Zakonov," *Zhurnal Ministerstva Iustitsii,* vol. I, No. 10 (October 1895), p. 8. The opposite view — not quite convincing in our opinion — has been best stated by Shcheglov, *Gosudarstvennyi sovet v Rossii,* II, p. 475.

[2] B. Noldé, "L'autocratie russe et la doctrine de la séparation des pouvoirs dans la première moitié du XIXe siècle," *Revue du Droit Public et de la Science Politique en France et à l'Etranger,* 41 (Paris 1924), pp. 5—41.

century. But Nolde had to admit that in practice Speransky negated his own definition of the separation of powers by subjecting them to the complete and absolute control of the autocratic ruler. In other words, as Nolde himself implied without, however, explicitly stating it, and as amply demonstrated in Speransky's own writings, separation of powers was merely a bureaucratic device for regularizing and maximizing the efficiency of the administrative and judiciary processes. Only a complete transformation of the fundamental conception of the role and power of the Russian state — a transformation which even the reforms of Alexander II failed to bring about — could have given Speransky's definition of separation of powers a constitutional and "liberal" significance.

Neither the fears nor the hopes of Speransky's contemporaries that his proposals might usher in a constitutional period in Russian history were borne out by the practical measures he suggested or justified by the theoretical arguments he developed in his Plans. However, we are still justified in raising the question of his real ultimate intentions, the true aims which, for understandable reasons, he might have preferred to leave unsaid. He aspired at establishing a "true monarchy" in Russia. Did this not mean that he contemplated a limited, constitutional monarchy in the long run? Actually, as our exposition of his plans and measures has tried to show, he was not much interested in "constitution" in the contemporary sense. He was primarily interested in putting the relations of private citizens among themselves and in regard to the government on predictable, solid foundations, within the framework of permanent fundamental laws. [1] More specifically and narrowly, he wished to make a clear distinction between fundamental, permanent legal relations — expressive of justice and social harmony — and *ad hoc* regulations, temporary in their effect and limited to specific instances of day to day administration. The lack of such a distinction, in his opinion, had resulted in a great deal of confusion. And this confusion in turn permitted officials to act in an arbitrary fashion, in violation of the basic principles of law and justice, without fear of ever being called to account. [2] Nor must we forget that Speransky was basically conservative — "preservative" (*okhranitel'nyi*) in the phraseology of later times — concerning Russia's social structure. Social stratification had to be based on the spiritual and moral status

---

[1] Batenkov summarized it quite well by saying it was "a definition of absolutism by itself," Batenkov, "Dannye: Provest' o sobstvennoi zhizni," *Russkii Arkhiv*, (1881), No. 2, pp. 268—269.

[2] Plan 1809, pp. 3—4, 46—48.

of the various classes of society. What mattered was the spiritual and moral development of the people, not their legal and political rights. But as one important positive element in the spiritual progress of individuals and nations was their right to exercise fully the energy inherent in them, it was essential to protect and guide their economic activity. For economic activity was the most immediate and complete means of spiritual self expression and self realization.

The state, he felt, was best qualified to lead Russia in the path of national harmony, and in so doing, promote the people's moral progress. In due time, the absolute monarchical government, based on justice and law, could guide Russia to modern forms of social and political life. It alone could guard the country from class conflicts and anarchical rule, similar to those which had taken upper hand in France after the overthrow of Louis XVI. Autocracy would protect the state from the ruinous disorders which come from aristocratic and oligarchic rule, rule for the satisfaction of the narrow selfish material interests of the few. That such a rule eventually leads to national disaster, had been clearly shown by the ill-fated Polish "republic." Therefore, the state must retain some very important functions of positive leadership, and these functions are best performed by an autocratic government with the help of a good bureaucracy operating within the framework of a clear and orderly system, according to the principles of just fundamental laws. In the final analysis, "true monarchy" and "constitution" were synonymous with a *Rechtsstaat,* a state based on law and guiding the spiritual and material progress of the nation. To help the state in fulfilling this pedagogical and leadership role, Speransky suggested that it welcome the assistance of the enlightened citizens. This was the basis of his proposals for the various Dumas, courts of justice with "jury," local government councils, Council of State, and for his economic policies. But in all cases, it was the central government, through its bureaucracy of well selected and properly supervised officials, that retained the controlling and guiding roles. The similarity of this conception to the major tenets of enlightened absolutism is unmistakable. [1] And it is not at all surprising to see it come from the pen of the most able and successful bureaucrat that the Imperial administration had known so far. Speransky's program also corresponded to Emperor Alexander's predilection for orderly and hierarchical organization and catered to his desire to be the guide and educator of his people. Quite true, in the Emperor's case it was related

---

[1] Cf. the articles of Hintze in note 2 p. 158; P. Klassen, *Die Grundlagen des aufgeklärten Absolutismus* (Jena 1929).

to his militaristic inclinations, whereas in Speransky's, it was an expression of a bureaucratic and legalistic bent of mind. But essentially, the two aimed at the same thing and went at it in similar fashion. There can be no truer characterization of Speransky's and Alexander's attitudes than the remark of the great German jurist, E. I. Bekker, "a good administration is better than the best constitution." [1]

Speransky's closeness to the ideals of enlightened absolutism and to Alexander's militaristic pedagogy, brings us to a final, and quite important, observation. Although Speransky had the vision of a better and spiritually higher political and social condition for Russia, he did not devise adequate means for implementing his vision and attaining his ideal. Of course, to the extent that ideals play a role in orienting men's actions and thoughts, Speransky's statement of his ideas was a positive contribution to the meagre ideology and narrow outlook of Russian statecraft. Still Speransky's practical failure cannot be passed over in silence. His origins, early training, and career prevented him from putting much reliance in the initiative, independence, and high-mindedness of Russian society. He had been too close an observer of the demoralization prevailing among serfs and serfowners, aristocrats, merchants, and clergymen to set much faith in their capacity for regeneration without outside push and guidance. Even in regard to economic matters, an area which affects material self-interest most directly, the guiding hand of the state could not be dispensed with, at least for some time to come. His understandable lack of faith in "society," his belief in the superiority of the guiding hand of state and monarch, and his intellectual outlook combined to suggest the method for implementing his proposals. This method was that of legislation, regulation, bureaucratic administration. It was by means of rules and decrees that he hoped to educate Russian society for responsibility and self government — an approach which was essentially self defeating. [2] His analysis of the situation at hand and vision of a better future to

---

1 Quoted by K. Mannheim, *Ideology and Utopia (an introduction to the sociology of knowledge)*, (New York 1951), p. 106.
2 Contrast this to Stein's faith in society, the nobility and bourgeoisie: "Auch meine Diensterfahrung überzeugt mich innig und lebhaft von der Vortrefflichkeit zweckmässig gebildeter Stände, und ich sehe sie als ein kräftiges Mittel an, die Regierung durch die Kenntnisse und das Ansehen aller gebildeten Klassen zu verstärken, sie alle durch Überzeugung, Teilnahme und Mitwirkung bei den Nationalangelegenheiten an den Staat zu knüpfen, den Kräften der Nation eine freie Tätigkeit und eine Richtung auf das Gemeinnützige zu geben ... An die Stelle der Bürokratie muss nicht eine auf kümmerlichen und schwachen Fundamenten beruhende Herrschaft weniger Gutsbesitzer errichtet werden, sondern es kommt die Teilnahme an der Verwaltung der Provincialangelegenheiten sämtlichen Besitzern eines bedeutenden Eigentums jeder Art, damit sie alle mit gleichen Verpflichtungen

work for, was suggested by his moral sense, his belief in the harmony of national life, his understanding of the organic evolution of a people's spiritual make-up, his respect for what was conditioned by history. But in recommending a course of action to remedy the situation, he brought to bear an 18th century predilection for abstract systematization, cold reason, and bureaucratic formalism. In so doing he expressed a truly bureaucratic attitude. In Mannheim's apt characterization: "The fundamental tendency of bureaucratic thought is to turn all problems of politics into problems of administration. Bureaucratic thought does not deny the possibility of a science of politics but regards it as identical with the science of administration." [1] The milieu, the training and experience of Speransky took the upper hand over his feelings, insight, theoretical grasp of political reality, and his vision of higher spiritual social values.

### APPENDIX TO CHAPTER V

Speransky's "dressing up" of his proposals to secure a favorable reception has given rise to the question: to what extent was his an independent mind and the proposals his own? Was he not, perhaps, only the (stylistic) editor of the ideas and desires of his superiors, in particular, Alexander I? As evidence for this view, some writers have cited a passage from the letter Speransky wrote to Alexander from his exile in Perm': "In the very beginning of your reign, after the many hesitations of our government, Your Imperial Majesty set Yourself as goal the establishment of a firm administration based on law. From this single principle gradually developed all Your major reforms (*uchrezhdeniia*). All these studies, perhaps hundred talks and discussions with Your Majesty had finally to be made into an unitary whole. In essence, it [the Plan of 1809] did not contain anything new, but it gave a systematic exposition to the ideas which had occupied Your attention since 1801." ("Permskoe pis'mo," Jan. 1813, in Shil'der, *Imperator Aleksandr I,* vol. III, pp. 516—18.) The fact that these words were written at a time when Speransky experienced the greatest hardships of his banishment and were to serve as an *apologia pro vita sua,* should warn us against taking them too literally as a correct description of the origin of the Plan of 1809. But even if we do not reject them out of hand as evidence, we must take into consideration another aspect of the question. In an earlier chapter we have attempted to describe the essential characteristics of Alexander's "constitutionalism." In summa-

---

und Befugnissen an den Staat gebunden sind." Freiherr vom Stein, "Denkschrift über die zweckmässige Bildung der obersten Behörden...," *loc. cit.,* II, pp. 220, 225 (quoted per Altmann, *Ausgewählte Urkunden,* II, pp. 19, 21.). It is in respect to method that Speransky differs fundamentally from the Prussian reformer, with whom he otherwise often agrees in diagnosing the evil and in setting the ideal goal of the reforms.

[1] Mannheim, *Ideology and Utopia,* p. 105.

rizing and analyzing the plans and concrete proposals of Speransky, we have often pointed out the narrow limits of their "liberalism," their bureaucratic, almost militaristic, stress on order, hierarchial subordination, and rational organization. Quite clearly, these proposals coincided by and large with Alexander's own views and plans. Speransky's enemies and ill wishers, F. Vigel' for instance, accused him of adapting slavishly his views and ideas to the whims and caprices of the Emperor for reasons of selfish expediency and ambition. Without denying that Speransky was politically ambitious, it is only fair to point out that he sincerely believed in the beneficial effects of his proposals for Russia and in the righteousness of his basic ideas. The fact that he maintained these views so consistently in the face of bitter opposition from the influential court circles, during his exile and throughout his whole life, is more telling evidence of his basic sincerity than the malicious gossip of Vigel'. True enough, as A. Nol'de rightly points out (though he overdoes the argument for Speransky's lack of creative thought), Speransky's success was to a great extent due to his ability to give a pleasing and catching form to the inchoate ideas and vague hopes of Alexander I; and yet, one should add in the same breath, Speransky sincerely and fully shared the basic principles underlying the views of his imperial master. And we need only compare the statements of Alexander I (and other influential dignitaries and advisers, like the members of the Unofficial Committee) with Speransky's formulations, to realize how much of an original, creative element was added by the State Secretary to the common principles. By the very manner in which he stated and developed the argument in favor of the proposals, or tried to implement basic theories, Speransky set new goals and paved the way for an elaboration and development of the reforms. In short, the plans and projects expressed ideas held in common by both Alexander and Speransky, but their historic importance, their practical value and novelty for Russian administrative tradition, their potentialities, as guides for the future, were entirely the product of the Secretary's talented and fertile mind.

## SOURCES

Primary sources: V. I. Semevskii, "Pervyi politicheskii traktat Speranskogo", *Russkoe Bogatstvo*, (1907), No. 1, pp. 46—85; Speranskii, "Zapiska ob ustroistve sudebnykh i pravitel'stvennykh uchrezhdenii v Rossii" (1803), in *Plan gosudarstvennogo preobrazovaniia grafa M. M. Speranskogo* (Moscow — Russkaia Mysl' — 1905), pp. 121—229; Speranskii, "Vvedenie k ulozheniiu gosudarstvennykh zakonov," in *Plan Gosudarstvennogo preobrazovaniia grafa M. M. Speranskogo*, pp. 1—20; Speranskii, "Proekt uchrezhdeniia Pravitel'stvuiushchego Senata 1811g," in Shil'der, *Imperator Aleksandr I*, vol. III, Appendix 1, pp. 405—433; Speranskii, "Proekt uchrezhdeniia Sudebnogo Senata 1811," *ibid.*, Appendix 2, pp. 433—471; Speranskii, "Pis'mo k Aleksandru I iz Permi-ianv. 1813" in Shil'der, *op. cit.*, vol. III, pp. 515—527; Speranskii, "Otchet v delakh 1810, predstavlennyi imperatoru Aleksandru I-u M. M. Speranskim, 11 fevr. 1811," in *Sbornik IRIO*, vol. 21 (1877), pp. 447—462.

Contemporary writings: G. S. Batenkov, "Dannye: Povest' o sobstvennoi zhizni," *Russkii Arkhiv*, (1881), No. 2, pp. 251—276; N. M. Karamzin, "O drevnei i novoi Rossii," *Russkii Arkhiv*, VIII, (1870), No. 2, pp. 2225—2350; Grand Duc Nicolas

Mikhailowitch, *Les relations diplomatiques de la Russie et de la France d'après les rapports des ambassadeurs d'Alexandre et de Napoléon 1808—1812*, (St. Pbg. 1905—1914); F. F. Vigel',*Vospominaniia* (Moscow 1928).

History of government institutions: In addition to the histories of Russian public law cited earlier, see: *Gosudarstvennyi Sovet 1801—1901* (St. Pbg. 1901); *Istoriia Pravitel'stvuiushchego Senata za 200 let 1711—1911* (St. Pbg. 1911); P. Danevskii, *Istoriia obrazovaniia Gosudarstvennogo Soveta v Rossii* (St. Pbg. 1859); N. M. Korkunov, *Russkoe gosudarstvennoe pravo*, II (6th ed., St. Pbg. 1909); S. M. Seredonin, *Istoricheskii obzor deiatel'nosti Komiteta Ministrov*, vol. I (St. Pbg. 1902); V. G. Shcheglov, *Gosudarstvennyi Sovet v Rossii, v osobennosti v tsarstvovanie Aleksandra I* (Iaroslavl', 1892—1896).

Secondary studies: In addition to the general histories of the period, the following were of particular use for this chapter: N. G. Chernyshevskii, "Russkii reformator," in *Polnoe Sobranie Sochinenii N. G. Chernyshevskogo* (ed. by M. N. Chernyshevskii) vol. III (St. Pbg. 1906), pp. 292—319; M. V. Dovnar-Zapol'skii, "Politicheskie idealy M. M. Speranskogo," in *Iz istorii obshchestvennykh techenii v Rossii* (Kiev 1905), pp. 77—144; Ar. Fateev, "La Constitution russe de 1809," *Zapiski Nauchno-issledovatel'nogo ob'edineniia* (Russkii svobodnyi universitet v Prage), vol. II (1935); V. E. Iakushkin, *Gosudarstvennaia vlast' i proekty gosudarstvennoi reformy v Rossii* (St. Pbg. 1906); S. N. Iuzhakov, *Graf M. M. Speranskii — ego zhizn' i obshchestvennaia deiatel'nost'* (St. Pbg. 1891); A. Nol'de, *Biografiia Speranskogo* (Manuscript, Archives of Russian and East European History and Culture, Columbia University); A. V. Romanovich-Slaviatinskii, "Gosudarstvennaia deiatel'nost' Speranskogo," *Otechestvennye Zapiski*, (1873), No. 4, pp. 171—199; Georg Sacke, "M. M. Speranskij: Politische Ideologie und reformatorische Tätigkeit," *Jahrbücher für Geschichte Osteuropas* vol. IV (Breslau 1939), Heft 3/4, pp. 331—350; V. I. Semevskii, "Liberal'nye plany v pravitel'stvennykh sferakh v pervoi polovine tsarstvovaniia imperatora Aleksandra I," in *Otechestvennaia voina i russkoe obshchestvo*, vol. II (Moscow 1912), pp. 152—194; V. Semevskii, "Vopros o preobrazovanii gosudarstvennogo stroia v Rossii v XVIII i v pervoi chetverti XIX," *Byloe*, No. 3 (March 1906), pp. 150—200; S. M. Seredonin, "Graf M. M. Speranskii," *Russkii Biograficheskii Slovar'*, vol. 18 (St. Pbg. 1909), pp. 193—240i; S. M. Seredonin, "K planu vseobshchego gosudarstennogo preobrazovaniia 1809 g" in *Sbornik S. F. Platonovu* (St. Pbg. 1911), pp. 533—544; S. Swatikow, *Die Entwürfe der Änderung der russischen Staatsverfassung* (Heidelberg 1904); B. Syromiatnikov, "M. M. Speranskii kak gosudarstvennyi i politicheskii deiatel'," *Sovetskoe gosudarstvo i pravo*, (1940), No. 3, pp. 92—113; N. Tourguéneff, *La Russie et les russes* (Paris 1847); F. M. Umanets, *Aleksandr i Speranskii* (St. Pbg. 1910); I. I. fon Zek, "Sviatoi pamiati velikogo cheloveka (k 75-i letiiu so dnia smerti Speranskogo)", *Novyi Zhurnal dlia vsekh*, (March 1914), No. 3, pp. 37—38.

# CHAPTER VI

# DISGRACE AND EXILE

Official duties and administrative projects absorbed Speransky's attention and energy so much that he seemed quite oblivious to his social and political isolation in St. Petersburg. He felt confident that as long as he retained the trust and esteem of the Emperor, his enemies and ill-wishers could do him no real harm. Quite true, indeed, as long as Alexander I trusted him, Speransky did not need to fear the jealousies or intrigues of courtiers and dignitaries. Unfortunately, Speransky made no allowance for the peculiarities of Alexander's character, suspicious and ever-changing in his attachments. Nor did the State Secretary seem to be aware of the growing tensions and dissatisfactions in the country to which, for reasons of his own, the Emperor felt compelled to pay some attention. So that when the blow fell, it came as a complete and brutal surprise to the unsuspecting State Secretary. Yet, his fall from influence and power had been in the making for some time; in a way since Erfurt when, in the mind of Society, his name became indissolubly linked with the hated French alliance. The "campaign" against Speransky, frequently serving as a pretext to those who wished to change Alexander's orientation, proceeded slowly and deviously. It originated in Moscow from where it was taken up by some circles in St. Petersburg, and finally the Emperor himself *"se mit de la partie,"* sealing the fate of his assistant. Today it is almost impossible to unravel the intricate and confused skein of intrigue which culminated in Speransky's exile. We can no more separate and analyse the motives and roles of all participants with any degree of certainty. As a matter of fact, probably not much would be gained even if it were possible to do so. Whatever the factual details and the psychological riddles which remain hidden from us, the general course of events is clear and we can get at the main considerations that dictated the actions of the personalities involved. The story of this resounding *cause célèbre* of

Alexander's reign was, perhaps, much simpler than most contemporaries and subsequent historians have thought.

Ever since the time Peter the Great had moved the capital of the Empire to the shores of the Gulf of Finland, social and political rivalry had opposed the nobility living in Moscow to the court and bureaucracy at St. Petersburg. This rivalry developed into a most important aspect of the intellectual and social climate surrounding the Russian nobility. Moscow resented its new subaltern political role and defiantly stressed its historic and religious significance, emphasized its attachment to traditions and the "good old days." For this reason dignitaries and courtiers settled in Moscow to spend their voluntary or forced retirement in an atmosphere of reminiscence; and in turn their great number contributed to the preservation of this conservative aspect of Muscovite life. Away from the hustle and bustle of the Court, and yet not completely lost in the countryside, Moscow provided the ideal residence for the upper nobility which, at various moments in the course of the 18th century, had attempted to wrest political and social power from the weak hands of the successors of Peter the Great. The aristocracy had failed in its efforts at a political comeback, but the proceeds of past imperial favors enabled members of the high nobility to live in luxury in Moscow during the winter and on their estates in the summer. Dispossessed of their political role, but not of their wealth, the older representatives of the upper nobility in Moscow acted like potential members of a Fronde. No wonder that the Emperor viewed them with unallayed suspicion. The changes in government personnel and policy brought about by the accession of Alexander I had swollen the ranks of Moscow's sulking, retired dignitaries, while at the same time providing them with something of an active political leadership.

After *War and Peace* it would be profanation to try to describe Moscow's "society" and recreate the atmosphere of its aristocratic homes, salons, splendid soirées, and balls. What scholar dare pretend he can paint a more lively and psychologically truer tableau than Tolstoi? Nor is there any need to elaborate on Gershenzon's fine sketch of the personal joys and sorrows in the life of a prominent Muscovite family. [1] However, neither Tolstoi nor Gershenzon have described the political moods of the Old Capital. Moscow's political sentiments, though, turned out to be important in shaping Speransky's fate.

---

[1] M. Gershenzon, *Griboedovskaia Moskva*, 2d. ed., Moscow-Berlin 1922. My description of the state of Russian public opinion is based on the memoirs and correspondence cited in the bibliography to the chapter.

On the surface, Moscow's Society before 1812 appeared to live only for pleasure, in a ceaseless succession of parties, dances, receptions. It seemed as if life consisted exclusively of worm, boisterous, and extravagant display of old-fashioned hospitality. This gregariousness fostered and abetted the social lions' propensity to revel in their recollections of the past. The glories and glitter of the reign of Catherine II lived still in the memories of the aging favorites and courtiers. Naturally, idealization of the past led to a carping criticism of the present. The victories of Suvorov were contrasted to the humiliating defeats of Alexander I; the solemn, cold, military and bureaucratic atmosphere of Alexander's court — presided over by the morose Dowager Empress, Maria Fedorovna — seemed quite a come-down to the brilliant companions of the gay, clever, and extravagant "Semiramis of the North." In short, "Moscow" was dissatisfied. It resented Alexander's apparent dislike of the upper nobility, of that aristocracy which in the 18th century had elevated and dethroned Emperors and Empresses, and had even challenged autocracy. Prominent representatives of the "Senatorial Party" came to join and rejuvenate the ranks of the Moscow Fronde after they had been pushed aside by Alexander I and the Unofficial Committee. To the aristocracy and "Senatorial Party" Speransky was hateful chiefly on two counts. In the first place, he was an upstart, a priest's son. Secondly, he was considered as the most systematic, consistent, and gifted advocate of the bureaucratic principle in government. Speransky's measures and proposals were interpreted in Moscow as so many concealed moves at destroying the political and social influence of the aristocracy. [1] The State Secretary became the natural target for the criticisms of Moscow's nobles who did not dare to come out against the Emperor himself.

The Moscow Fronde, composed of elderly men whose dissatisfaction could easily be ascribed to senile jealousy, could not by itself become very dangerous. But its threat grew in the eyes of the Emperor as it became the rallying point for the concrete grievances of the numerous provincial nobility. Russia's unsuccessful wars against Napoleon had been very costly, and the burden lay heavily enough on the serf-owner. More ruinous, yet, was Russia's forced participation in Napoleon's Continental System. The landowners produced largely for the export market, and their main customer had been England. In spite of the Tariff of 1810, they feared economic ruin. Naturally, the nobility's attacks and protests were directed against the government's official

---

[1] The mildest expression of this sentiment is found in a letter of P. V. Chichagov to S. R. Vorontsov, Paris 26 March 1810, (No. 48, *Arkhiv kniazia Vorontsova*, Vol. 19, pp. 170—173).

policy of friendship with France, and more particularly against Speransky who was believed to be the most influential and convinced
francophile. It was easy for the disgruntled landowners to disguise
their selfish economic grievances behind a screen of pious phrases about
the country's welfare, for the landlord's difficulties affected the peasantry
as well. Finally, the religious and patriotic feelings of both the provincial and Muscovite nobility were deeply hurt at the sight of the
orthodox Tsar friendly with the "usurper" and tyrant of Europe, whom
the Russian Church had recently anathemized. Was the result of
Catherine's glorious reign to be a Russia humiliated by the Corsican?
The conservative nobility was convinced that Alexander's domestic
and foreign policies after Tilsit — whose duplicity and ultimate purpose
the Emperor could not reveal — was the work of a French agent, the
despised plebeian State Secretary. It was clear that Napoleon's agent
worked for the political and economic destruction of Russia's old
families.

Lastly, personal motives, too, played a role in building up Moscow's
dislike of Speransky. In this the most influential figure turned out
to be Count Rostopchin, in whom the lazy and passive nobility found
an energetic leader and an eloquent voice. A favorite of Paul I, Count
Rostopchin had been implicated in the plot of March 1801. Alexander
exiled him to his estates and forbade him to reappear in St. Petersburg.
Rostopchin then made his residence in Moscow. Despite his typically
18th century French education, and though he was to end his life in
voluntary exile in Paris, Count Rostopchin was fanatically anti-French
during the years preceding 1812. He persecuted everything that was
French, wherever he found it. Even before his appointment as Governor
General of Moscow on the eve of the French invasion of 1812, he
campaigned actively against all manifestations of francophilia in the
old capital. By means of indirect social pressure he attempted, albeit
without much success, to ban the French language, manners, and
clothes from Moscow's aristocratic homes. Paradoxically, the man who
had participated in the conspiracy against Paul I and had almost become a regicide, was an ardent defender of absolutism. Rostopchin's
great fear was that Russia might become a constitutional state, which,
in his opinion, would spell the doom of the nobility and of serfdom.
Russia's traditions and ideals were threatened by the ideas of the French
revolution. Equally great, Rostopchin believed, was the danger coming
from the new religious and ethical teachings of German-inspired
mystics, Free Masons, Martinists, Illuminates, and the like. The Free
Masons and mystics were in conspiracy to subvert the Russian soul,

Russia's religious life. If not stopped immediately, they would end by dissolving the ethical and, later, the social fabric of the nation. In Count Rostopchin's opinion, Speransky was the evil genius of Russia. "His" administrative measures and reform plans were copies of the hateful French models and aimed at transforming the Tsar's traditional absolutism and paternalism into Jacobin tyranny that would ruin the Russian people. As if this were not enough, Rostopchin also believed — not without some foundation — that Speransky was a leader among Russia's Free Masons and mystics. Gossip and rumor further exaggerated Speransky's interest in freemasonry which many thought to be dedicated to the propagation of revolutionary ideas.

Count Rostopchin was a brilliant person; he possessed a fascinating sardonic wit, good education, wide knowledge, a facile and eloquent pen. These qualities made him an excellent propagandist. Without any moral scruples, as shown by his duplicity and shady role in 1801, he did not shrink before the basest means to achieve his ends. He soon became convinced that calumny was the best weapon against the government's policy. He did not waste any time in bringing this insight into action and directed his effort at Speransky, whom he singled out as the most convenient and vulnerable target. Without any positive proof concerning Speransky's relations to freemasonry, Rostopchin took all the rumors and gossip at face value and embroidered upon them with petulant imagination. He claimed that Speransky was the unofficial high priest of the Illuminates, the *spiritus rector* and patron of all mystics and Free Masons in Russia. It did not matter to Rostopchin that mystics and Free Masons were not necessarily identical, he spoke of the two in the same breath, for both had derogatory connotations. [1] Rostopchin did not content himself with insinuations and whispering campaigns in Moscow. He resorted to open accusations and denunciations to the Emperor. To make a stronger impression on Alexander, he circulated a petition in which the "loyal nobility and subjects of the Tsar" appealed to the monarch for protection against the hardships and mistreatment they had to suffer at the hands of Speransky's policy. They implored Alexander to stop Russia from sliding into the gaping abyss. [2] This petition was sent to the Emperor on the very eve of Speransky's dismissal — it came too late to influence the sovereign. In any event, the petition proved superfluous also because in the meantime

1 Graf Rostopchin, "Zapiska o Martinistakh predstavlennaia 1811 vel. kn. Ekaterine Pavlovne," *Russkii Arkhiv* (1875), No. 3, p. 75.

2 "Pis'mo Rostopchina k Aleksandru I," 17 March 1812, *Russkaia Starina*, 122 (1905), 412–416 — also Ermolov, "Pamflet na Speranskogo," *Chteniia*, (1895), No. 3, part 2, pp. 1–24.

the Moscow group had received powerful assistance from another quarter.

The Moscow "Fronde" and Rostopchin enlisted the support of a person very near to Emperor Alexander himself, his sister, Grand Duchess Catherine Pavlovna. The closest bonds of affection tied Alexander to Catherine, the only member of his family from whom he did not feel estranged. The Emperor had a very high regard for his sister's intelligence and character; she was his intimate confidante, and his letters to her are the only documents in which he reveals himself openly and fully. The Emperor often traveled to Tver', the Grand Duchess' residence after her marriage to Duke George of Oldenburg, to hear her advice on problems that troubled him most. Grand Duchess Catherine was a woman of strong character and great will power, and was devoured by political ambition. Her great disappointment in life was that she had not become a ruling princess, and she tried to compensate for it by wielding power indirectly through her influence on her brother and her husband. For the latter she had obtained posts of importance, the Governor Generalship of Tver', Iaroslav, Novgorod, and the Direction of Transports.

Speransky's position of influence with her brother and his efforts at bringing more legality to the administrative process, seemed to Catherine so many obstacles to the fulfillment of her own ambitions. The Grand Duchess, for she kept the title even after her marriage, also had some personal grudges against the State Secretary. On occasion he had failed to give her wishes or her husband's business the exclusive and sympathetic consideration she believed was due to them. At one time, Speransky had refused one of her demands because it was against some rules. The proud Princess had not forgiven him for treating her like an ordinary mortal. Another time, Speransky had suggested his own candidate for the position of Chief of Transportations and Roads, a post Catherine wanted for her husband. Finally, the Grand Duchess deeply resented the fact that all official papers, even her husband's, had to come to Speransky before they reached the Emperor. Catherine did not conceal her feelings towards her brother's advisor and his policies. Naturally, all those who were similarly minded were attracted to her. As her residence, Tver', was close to Moscow, the conservative aristocracy of the Old Capital, with Rostopchin as their energetic and persuasive leader, joined her camp and made up her intimate entourage.

At Tver' also was found the man who wrote the principal act of indictment against Speransky. It was the well known writer and historian N. M. Karamzin. In the course of conversations with the historian at

her soirées in Tver', the Grand Duchess discovered the similarity
between Karamzin's political criticism and her own views. She asked
Karamzin to write down their common ideas in the form of a letter
or memorandum which she then would give to her brother. Karamzin
complied, and the result was the now famous tract, *Of Old and New
Russia*, which was mentioned in the previous chapter. Catherine forwarded Karamzin's screed to Alexander who, at first, was quite angry
at its independent and reproachful tone and veiled threats. But upon
re-reading and reconsidering it, Alexander found much that was true
and that coincided with his own feelings. The imminent war with
Napoleon contributed to the Emperor's *revirement*, for he felt that
he must take into full account the sentiments of the old nobility upon
whose services and devotion he would have to depend any moment
now. While *Of Old and New Russia* did not cause Alexander to
change his attitude towards Speransky, it may have helped to confirm
the Emperor's vague impressions and suspicions. In any case, it informed
the monarch of the feelings of an important segment of Russian public
opinion and society.

The value of Karamzin's piece consisted in that it expressed well and
forcefully some of the basic sentiments of the old fashioned, conservative, serf-owning nobility, whose spiritual and social center was
in Moscow. Although *Of Old and New Russia* deserves close study
and analysis as one of the significant expressions of Russian traditionalist conservatism, for our purpose — the role played by the
pamphlet in Speransky's downfall — its central message can be stated
in a few words. [1] The policies of Alexander and his State Secretary
are contributing to the decline of the nobility and to the unhappiness
of the people. If allowed to continue, this trend will ruin and destroy
the nobility which, after all, is the only source of the Emperor's (and
Russia's) strength. The establishment of a constitutional government
on foreign patterns, in disregard of the nobility and the spiritual
traditions of the country, amounts to a repudiation of Russia's past,
a past that has made her great and powerful and brought glory to her
monarchs. In the past, Russian Tsars and Emperors had had no need
for Councils of State, Committees of Ministers, and similar novelties,
and yet they had ruled with glory and benefit to the nation. If new

---

[1] The political ideas of Karamzin are a subject by themselves, which still needs
investigation. Recently, Karamzin's political views were analysed by Wolfgang
Mitter, "Die Entwicklung der politischen Anschauungen Karamzins," *Forschungen
zur Osteuropäischen Geschichte*, Bd. 2, (Berlin 1955), pp. 165—285 and Richard E.
Pipes, "Karamzin's Conception of the Monarchy" in a forthcoming volume of the
*Harvard Slavic Studies*.

laws and administrative organizations become necessary, they ought to be derived from past Russian traditions and practice, and not slavishly copied from abroad. Do not destroy the hallowed traditions and values of our country, pleads Karamzin, preserve the practices that have made Russia great and glorious. Secure the economic prosperity of the nobility by abolishing the Continental System and by checking the threats to serfdom; restore the nobility to its function of traditional servants of the Crown (by throwing out the callous and pretentious bureaucrats) and return it to its role of the first "estate" of the realm. Above all, keep autocracy intact. This is the Russian way to reform, and it is the best way, declares Karamzin. The Historiographer is not afraid to conclude on an ominous note of warning. Even the autocratic Tsar of All Russia cannot go against his people's traditions and interests, especially against those of the nobility. Paul I had attempted to do it; his son knows his fate well enough. Let Alexander listen to the voice of the people and heed the nobility's counsel, lest his father's fate befall him too.

Karamzin's tract carried weight with Alexander I as an expression of the feelings and desires of "Moscow" and "Tver'." But, however great the influence and consideration enjoyed by the aristocratic circles of the Old Capital and the Court of Catherine Pavlovna at Tver', their opinions alone would not have been of sufficient weight in determining the Emperor's course. The "Fronde," though, found support in the virulent hatred of Speransky in another section of the Russian nobility. This time it was the numerous group of petty noblemen and landowners who made up the lower ranks of the bureaucracy, both in the provinces and the capital. They hated the State Secretary for his authorship of the decree of August 6, 1809 (PSZ 23,771) on service examinations. They readily believed that he was bent upon destroying the nobility, or at least upon preventing its access to higher positions and comfortable retirement. What other reason could there possibly have been for a decree which made promotion to the 8th rank of the hierarchy dependent on the successful passage of an examination? The petty nobility, too poor to receive a proper education, had served the Emperor for many generations. The only way they could hope for promotion to the coveted rank which guaranteed an adequate retirement pay, was through seniority earned by long and faithful service. The decree of 1809 deprived many of their expected retirement benefits and wounded their pride and self-esteem. Karamzin also reflected these feelings when he remarked that it was not necessary to know Latin, chemistry, physics, history, and

have all kinds of other learning to be a loyal and good servant of the
state. Such knowledge, argued Karamzin, rather tended to undermine
the old faith, raised doubts, and gave rise to dissatisfaction with
traditional and time-tested ways. Anyway, of what use could these
various fields of human knowledge possibly be to the nobleman in the
performance of the tasks generally entrusted to him? The petty nobility's and lower officialdom's hatred of Speransky found their expression in a libelous pamphlet that circulated in the chancelries of the
administration. [1]

At this point, the movement against the influential but isolated
State Secretary received additional impetus from a regular court intrigue that was mounted against him in St. Petersburg. In an absolute
monarchy — as in a dictatorship — the struggle for power and influence
finds its expression in competition between rival factions of high
officials, courtiers, foreign residents, and diplomats. John Quincy
Adams had this in mind when he noted that an autocracy has no fewer
"parties" than a democratic constitutional regime, only the forms these
parties take are different. [2] As these rival interests could not be
organized within any institutional framework to attain their ends,
they had to gain a hearing at court and obtain the favor of the
Emperor. The changes in domestic policy after 1801 and the dramatic
diplomatic reversal of 1807 had fostered the formation of numerous
and powerful "parties" of courtiers, dignitaries, and diplomats who
competed for the Emperor's attention. These parties pursued quite
selfish aims and did not pretend that they had any general and
permanent political principles. They were only temporary alliances
of courtiers whose composition and purpose varied from one circumstance to the next. By 1811 several groups or cliques were actively
working for the downfall of Speransky and a change in Russia's
domestic and foreign policies.

First place among the "parties" at court was held by the enemies
of Alexander's alleged pro-French orientation. This group found its
main support within the Imperial family itself, in the person of the
Dowager Empress Maria Fedorovna, the Emperor's mother. [3] Alexander

1 Bychkov, "Deiateli i uchastniki padeniia Speranskogo," *Russkaia Starina* 109
(1902), pp. 469—508, *passim*. Playing up to the prevailing sentiments of Moscow,
the pamphlet was signed, "Rostopchin and Moscovites."
2 "In this country there are political parties, ambitious rivalries, and personal
animosities, perhaps not the less violent and inveterate for being much cramped
and restricted in the expression of their sentiments and purposes." *U. S. Department
of State — Russia,* John Quincy Adams to the Secretary of State, dispatch No. 86,
dated 11 June 1812.
3 See A. Vandal (ed.), "La cour de Russie en 1807—1808." *Revue d'histoire
diplomatique,* IV (1890), pp. 402—407

was the constant object of his mother's acrimonious reprimands and advice, so much so that his patience and filial respect often wore quite thin, as witness the following, written from Erfurt on August 25, 1808: "... j'avoue qu'il m'est pénible de voir que lorsque je n'ai en vue que les intérêts de la Russie, les sentiments qui sont la véritable force de ma manière d'agir puissent apparaître si peu compréhensibles..." [1] Closely connected with those Russians who, grouped around the Dowager Empress pursued purely Russian patriotic ends, were numerous foreign residents. These foreigners, who were very popular and influential in St. Petersburg high Society, worked actively at breaking up the Franco-Russian alliance. They hoped to place Alexander at the head of an anti-Napoleonic coalition for the liberation of Europe and of France. These foreign residents were a remarkable lot. Among them we find men of outstanding ability, merit, and honesty like the Freiherr vom Stein, the Duke de Richelieu, Count Joseph de Maistre, Count Langeron, and many lesser names. But there were also others, far less reputable personages. Ernst Moritz Arndt, the well known German romantic writer and friend of vom Stein, observing this motley crew noted with a tinge of sarcasm: "Petersburg ist ein rechtes Posthalt der Abenteurer, die auf Fortunas Flügel durch die Welt fliegen, ein europäisches Absteigequartier. Aus Frankreich, England, Deutschland fliegen hier alle Tage solche Vögel zusammen." [2] Among the foreign adventurers and professional intriguers we may name the Chevalier de Vernègue, Count Armfelt, the Duke of Serra-Capriola, all of whom played a part in Speransky's fall from favor. Naturally there was little in common between the ways in which the first group tried to influence the Emperor and the methods used by the adventurers and intriguers.

For a Stein or a Maistre, the personal fate of Speransky was of little concern. They were only interested in bringing about a change in Russia's foreign policy. Whereas vom Stein, who came to Russia just before the fall of Speransky, only wished to convince Alexander I that Russia's political and historic duty was to liberate Europe from Napoleon, Joseph de Maistre aimed at much more. He hoped to renovate Russian policy by giving a new direction and foundation to the political and philosophic attitudes of Russia's social and cultural élite. He wanted the Russian aristocracy to abandon the principles of 18th century Enlightenment (still very influential in Russian society), with

---

[1] Grand Duc Nicolas Mikhailowitsch, *L'Empereur Alexandre Ier* (St. Pbg. 1912), Vol. I, pp. 83—84.
[2] Ernst Moritz Arndt, *Meine Wanderungen und Wandlungen mit dem Freiherrn vom Stein* (3. Abdruck, Berlin 1869), p. 18.

its belief in reason and science. De Maistre did not tire of repeating to his Russian friends — of whom he had many — that the salvation from the destructive effects of the Enlightenment lay in a return to a strictly religious, unquestioning, non-rationalistic attitude. Men must obey their God-appointed rulers without questioning, they must renounce the pride that comes from such devilish ideas as natural rights, liberty, and man-made constitutions. Unlike France, who was justly expiating God's punishment, Russia had not progressed far on the evil path, and in her case it would be sufficient to restore religious orthodoxy and political autocracy to their traditional status. The ideas of the Sardinian ambassador became quite popular in aristocratic circles, for his remarkable intelligence, charm, brilliant wit, eloquence and erudition, coupled with long residence in St. Petersburg, had made him a leading personality in the capital. De Maistre had a wide circle of powerful admirers and acquaintances, particularly at the court of the Dowager Empress. It enabled him to make his views known directly to the Emperor himself.

De Maistre disliked Speransky not so much as a person, but as the representative proponent of the modern attitudes he hated most. In the opinion of the Sardinian Ambassador, the Russian State Secretary was the incarnation of 18th century political rationalism, whose sacrilegious purpose it was to destroy the hallowed traditional pattern of Russian autocracy. Speransky's reform proposals seemed to de Maistre to be a direct threat to the very existence of autocracy in Russia, the last best hope on earth against the spirit of he French revolution. But this was not all, de Maistre warned, Speransky's nefarious influence went much deeper. Did the State Secretary not spread the very germ of revolution? That was the significance of the questioning and even sceptical attitude towards authority and tradition which Speransky displayed when he required that every government official have some knowledge of science, history, and philosophy. With devilish cunning, Speransky had prepared the way for the spiritual corruption of Russia's future leaders by educating the best sons of the country's élite in the tenets of the 18th century at the Lycée of Tsarskoe Selo. Finally, and like Rostopchin unaware of the paradox, Count de Maistre denounced Speransky as the leading mind of the Illuminates and mystical Free Masons.[1] The accusations of the

1 "Plusieurs russes sont infectés de la philosophie allemande: un homme surtout, qui s'élève à tout et qui n'aurait pu partir de plus bas puisqu'il est fils de prêtre (popowitch), M. Speranski, est un grand partisan de Kant, comme je m'en suis aperçu dans une conversation: il influe beaucoup sur les affaires. Ces gens perdront l'Empereur comme ils en ont perdu tant d'autres." J. de Maistre, Correspondance,

Sardinian Ambassador were very similar indeed to those of the Moscow nobility. There is no certain proof that de Maistre participated directly in the intrigues which contributed to Speransky's downfall. But he was not ignorant of them, and certainly he helped provide an ideological justification for the inchoate sentiments of all those who disliked Speransky for one reason or another. Through Counts Tolstoi and Razumovskii and other influential personages at Court, de Maistre roused the suspicions and fanned the hatred of the courtiers and dignitaries close to the Emperor. [1]

The "dirty work" of the intrigue against Speransky was carried out by foreign adventurers who enlisted the help and participation of some Russian high officials. Among the main participants in this cabale was first the Chevalier de Vernègue, a French émigré, adventurer and intriguer by nature, who at the time represented the interests of the Comte de Provence (the future Louis XVIII). De Vernègue hoped that Speransky's fall would lead to a change in Russian policy towards France and towards his master, the Comte de Provence. But because of his semi-official status, and the understandable desire of hiding the participation of an émigré in a Russian affair, de Vernègue worked through others. The second leader of the cabale was Count Armfelt, whose name was associated with the administration of Finland. A Swedish nobleman by birth and a Finnish landowner, Count Armfelt had had a long, brilliant, and checkered career before he entered Russian service on the eve of the Russo-Swedish war of 1809. After having been a Swedish envoy to St. Petersburg, he played a prominent role in bringing about the annexation of the Grand Duchy of Finland to the Russian Empire. Armfelt was a typical courtier of the 18th century, *homme du monde*, roué, intriguer; he had no true political principles and chose sides only for reasons of personal convenience and interest. He was vaguely anti-French and opposed to Russia's alliance with Napoleon. This attitude he derived not so much from any deeply felt conviction or clear political principle, as from his belief that it was the best way to succeed in his new country of adoption. As to his dislike for Speransky, it had a more personal reason. As Armfelt had been instrumental in securing Finland for the Russian Crown, he hoped to play the first role in the administration

---

vol. III, p. 237 (letter of 8/20. IV. 1809 to the Chevalier de Rossi No. 282). See also *ibid.*, p. 385 (letter to King Victor Emmanuel, December 1809, No. 298).

[1] A summary of the evidence concerning de Maistre's role is to be found in the somewhat confused and fragmentary paper of Ar. Fateev, "La disgrâce d'un homme d'état," *Zapiski russkogo nauchno-issledovatel'skogo ob'edineniia v Prage*, X (Praha 1940), pp. 33—73.

of the Grand Duchy. He therefore deeply resented the fact that Speransky had become the Secretary of State for Finnish Affairs, even though Speransky had recommended him, Armfelt, to membership in the Council for Finland.

Armfelt's position in the Russian administration, Emperor Alexander's high regard for him, and his many social and political connections enabled him — without arousing the suspicion of a "foreign intrigue" — to contact Russian dignitaries and enlist their support against Speransky. As his main assistant from among the ranks of Russian officials, Armfelt chose the Minister of the Police, Count Balashev. Balashev's only concern was the promotion of his personal interest, the securing of rapid promotion and greater influence in governmental affairs. As many other high officials in St. Petersburg, Balashev saw with a jaundiced eye Speransky's ubiquitous functions. He felt that the State Secretary's participation in all and sundry areas of administration prevented the merits of others from coming to the attention of the sovereign. That this obstacle on the path to promotion and influence was due to the doings — so they thought — of an upstart, a parvenu of low birth, aroused the anger of the "well born" officials even more. Dependent on the personal favor of the Emperor, they could see with some equanimity this favor bestowed on one of their own kind, particularly if the fortunate object of the monarch's benevolence was willing to let others share in the rewards and benefits. But Speransky was too keenly aware that he had earned his high position by dint of tireless energy, work, and his own talents. He refused to employ his influence to secure benefits for people who had not done much to deserve them. The courtiers, whom he had rebuffed and who, like parasites, always lived off the imperial treasury, could not believe that Speransky was honest and free from any taint of corruption. They spread the rumor that in fact he had amassed a large fortune from bribes and dishonest manipulations of the country's finances. As evidence for their contention, they cited Speransky's close association with traders and bankers like Amburger, Perets, and Lazarev.

Judging from themselves, the Armfelts, Balashevs, and *tutti quanti* could not conceive that a man in Speransky's position would not want to extend his power and secure control of all governmental affairs. Either because they misjudged Speransky's character or as an act of deliberate provocation, the trio Vernègue-Armfelt-Balashev approached the State Secretary with the suggestion that they form a "triumvirate" of Armfelt, Balashev, and Speransky, which would in fact rule the Empire by securing a dominant influence over Alexander. Speransky indignantly refused to participate in the plot. But he made the mistake of not reporting the matter to the Emperor. The intriguers seized upon this error — particularly serious in view of Alexander's distrustful personality — and conveyed to the monarch such information on the "plot" as would imply Speransky's disloyalty. [1] Alexander's suspicion was aroused, and he did not fully believe the explanation Speransky gave of his part in the "plot." This partial success encouraged Vernègue, Armfelt, and Balashev, in continuing their "siege" of the sovereign. They were successful in obtaining bits of information which could be interpreted to the detriment of the State Secretary. Furthermore, Speransky's seemingly close connections with various mystics and masonic groups did not contribute to the alleviating of the Emperor's suspicions. Alexander's suspicions on this score were "kept warm" by the Procurator of the Holy Synod, Prince A. N. Golitsyn, the Emperor's childhood friend and active crusader against all forms of non-institutionalized religion.

Speransky's enemies were able to exploit to the full his own carelessness and indiscretion. As we recall, the secret reports sent by Count Nesselrode from Paris passed unopened through Speransky's hands. This circumstance had rendered the State Secretary desirous to know more of the Emperor's private diplomacy. Some subaltern employees of the Ministry of Foreign Affairs, the cypher clerk Beck, for instance, believing that Speransky took part in *all* government affairs, offered to show him some of the dispatches that passed through their hands. Speransky did not resist the temptation and consented to see the pieces. Unadvisedly, he sometimes kept them at his house for a few days before or after reading them. It so happened that his friend, Magnitskii, noticed them lying on the desk, and although the papers were in an envelope, Magnitskii recognized their source. Notoriously indiscreet and braggart, Magnitskii intimated to his friends that he was not ignorant of what these envelopes contained and that his powerful patron and friend, State Secretary Speransky, was fully in the know of the secrets of Russia's diplomacy. Magnitskii's boasts were picked up by secret agents of the Minister of the Police, Balashev, and duly reported to Alexander. With this information it was not difficult to give credence to the rumor that Speransky was maintaining secret, and surely treasonable, correspondence with France. It now became quite evident that his unpopular measures and reform proposals had been taken at the behest of Napoleon in order to disorganize and weaken

[1] In exile Speransky seems to have realized it had been a mistake. Grot, "K istorii ssylki Speranskogo," *Russkii Arkhiv*, (1871), pp. 2076—2077.

Russia. On the face of it, the substantial police file on the State Secretary looked quite impressive and was highly incriminating. Of course, Speransky's direct and secret correspondence with Paris had been a revelation only to Balashev and the other members of the anti-Speransky intrigue. It had long been known to the Emperor and could not impress him very much. But Alexander was painfully surprised to learn that Speransky had also been shown other secret diplomatic materials. His natural distrust of his councillors, never fully asleep, was immediately aroused. Yet, even then, the Emperor did not believe the rumor of Speransky's treason. Did he then yield to public opinion when he finally dismissed his State Secretary in March 1812?

Attacked from all quarters, Speransky stood alone. There really was no one to defend him and to intercede in behalf of his cause before the Emperor and public opinion. Speransky's tragedy was his social and political isolation. His friends were "small men" with no social prestige, men who owed their position to him and whose political role was limited to assisting the State Secretary in his manifold duties. Of those high dignitaries who had been his patrons and protectors at the beginning of his career, most had lost their former credit and influence. On the other hand, those officials whom Speransky had displaced or pushed into relative insignificance were naturally quite eager to join forces with Armfelt and Balashev. This was true of Count Gur'ev, the Minister of Finance, who had opposed Speransky's Financial Plan of 1809 and of Baron Rosenkampf who had been eased out of his chairmanship of the Commission on Laws. As for Count A. Arakcheev, at that time already one of the Emperor's closest "friends," he was somewhat jealous of Speransky's ubiquitous role, and he had not forgiven him for keeping the Plan of 1809 secret from him. However, let us add, our sources do not indicate that Arakcheev partipated in any way in the intrigue against Speransky. He remained strictly neutral. But he could not be counted upon to raise his voice in favor of the State Secretary.

Outside government and court circles, Speransky had no one who could shield him against the concerted attacks of his enemies.[1] He

1 The French Ambassador, Caulaincourt, noted Speransky's social isolation in a letter to Champagny: "M. Speransky est le faiseur de l'empereur, en quelque sorte le ministre des innovations. Il n'est lié avec personne. Son influence s'étend sur tout..." Grand Duc Nicolas Mikhailowitsch, *Les relations diplomatiques de la Russie et de la France,* V, p. 352 (letter dated 3 March 1811). Further evidence of Speransky's evasion of the limelight can be deduced from the fact that John Q. Adams does not mention once that he had met him during his stay as U.S. Minister in St. Petersburg, and Adams, as a "liberal" and highly intelligent man, could have been an interesting person to know and easy to get in touch with in diplomatic and court circles. And finally, the diary of the Court Marshal (*Kamerfur'erskii Zhurnal*)

had failed to make friends even among those who approved his political principles and the pro-French orientation of Russian diplomacy. He had scorned all offers to ally himself with the influential and rich families of Russia by bonds of marriage; his snubbing of society was perhaps even less easy to forgive than some of his ideas and policies. In spite of his literary talents and gift for "popularizing" ideas, Speransky had never attempted to "sell" his ideas and policies to public opinion. Interested only in convincing the Emperor and a few selected officials by logic and reason, he indignantly refused to resort to demagogy and emotional appeal. On his own admission, "in all my recommendations I dealt only with Your [Alexander's] intelligence, and never wanted to captivate your heart. Your reason and strict logic on my part were my only weapons; in them consisted the secret of all my labors and successes." [1] Such weapons as Speransky condescended to use against his enemies' intrigues were certainly not enough, the more so that they reached no one outside the Emperor's study. Rostopchin, Armfelt, Balashev, Karamzin, de Maistre, were all men adept at arousing and directing the prejudices and emotions of Society; to counteract them effectively, Speransky, too, would have had to make a wide appeal to public opinion, play up to the feelings and traditions of the nobility and court. But he was unable and unwilling to do so. Such a recourse would also have conflicted with his desire to prepare all reforms in secret and along strictly bureaucratic, rational lines. Thus, in the face of vicious insinuations and open attacks from all sides, Speransky remained without anyone to protect him. No one, that is, except the Emperor. Alexander's change of attitude towards his advisor and Secretary remains to be explained.

Nothing could be more erroneous than to believe that Speransky's fall from power was brought about by pressure from public opinion, a pressure which the Emperor was unable to resist. We have dealt with the legend of Alexander's weakness, lack of willpower, and pliability of character in an earlier chapter. We need not repeat the argument presented there. The Emperor did not have to bow to the clamor of his nobility in the present case, when he had disregarded it

which lists all persons invited to the court and imperial table, has relatively few entries concerning Speransky's presence at court functions and meals, although he was at the Palace almost every day for conferences with the Emperor. He apparently stayed only for the audience and was but rarely invited to join the Emperor at the table or at the evening *cercle*.

[1] Speranskii, "Permskoe pis'mo," Shil'der, *Imperator Aleksandr I*, III, p. 524 Cf. also Jacob's report on Speransky's remark: "Der Kaiser kann sich bisweilen durch das Einreden schlecht denkender Leute irre machen lassen, aber sein gesunder Verstand bringt ihn von selbst bald wieder auf den rechten Weg." *Denkwürdigkeiten*, p. 315.

so often in 1801, 1807 and was going to do it in 1815, 1820. Even when accompanied by Karamzin's dark hints about the fate of Paul I, Alexander did not need to submit to the demands of his courtiers for Speransky's dismissal after he had successfully withstood much more serious clamors in 1802 and 1807. Speransky was quite right, his influence and position depended exclusively on the personal pleasure and favor of the Emperor; as long as these lasted he could disregard Society's feelings, intrigues, and slanders. Of course, Speransky was not unaware of the sentiment against him, and he realized that in the long run it might undermine the Emperor's trust in him. To give less hold to the evil rumors and jealousies, he requested Alexander to relieve him of his manifold duties and retain him only as Chairman of the Commission on Laws, where the most important and useful work had yet to be done. [1] Alexander turned down the request; and interpreting this as an expression of the Emperor's unbounded confidence, Speransky ceased to bother about his enemies' doings. Having rejected the role of outside pressures, we must still return to the question, why did Alexander change his attitude towards Speransky so completely and suddenly?

A full analysis of the mysterious and contradictory features of Alexander's personality would certainly take us beyond the scope of the present study. But we must endeavor to explain the Emperor's motives in dismissing Speransky, his most capable and heretofore trusted councillor. In the eyes of the monarch, one of Speransky's great assets was his ability to give logical, literary, coherent, and political expression to the Emperor's love for order, clarity, and hierarchical discipline. Moreover, exceedingly jealous of his autocratic prerogative, Alexander was glad to have about him a pliable and obedient upstart, without political friends and influential connections, who was unlikely to become the leader of a "party" or clique. Speransky's social isolation and his integrity of character were well known to the Emperor, and to Alexander they seemed additional tokens of the State Secretary's dependence on him alone. That explains the Emperor's great trust in Speransky. At this point, however, we must mention another trait of Alexander's political personality. A. Kizevetter may perhaps have gone a bit too far when he argued that Alexander had an almost pathological fear of seeing his vague dreams and shapeless yearnings concretized in practical legislation and clear administrative directives. [2] However, it

---

1 Speranskii, "Otchet v delakh 1810," *Sbornik IRIO*, 21 (1877), p. 461.
2 A. A. Kizevetter, "Aleksandr I," *Istoricherskie siluety — liudi i sobytiia*, (Berlin 1931), pp. 129, 131, 133.

is true that in most instances the Emperor did not visualize in advance the implications of his wishes and dreams about constitution, liberty, the legal order, and the like. Confronted with the legislative act which concretely embodied his dream, the full meaning of the measure would suddenly become apparent to him. For the first time he would clearly perceive the possibility that the measure might be used to whittle down his absolute power. Fear that his councillors and ministers might abuse his humaneness and idealism to circumscribe his authority turned almost into an *idée fixe*. Nothing could arouse Alexander's suspicions and dislike more than the belief that his councillor's advice or recommendation might lead to a limitation of imperial prerogatives. We have tried to show that the projects which Speransky had worked out were not, in truth, a threat to Alexander's power. But no doubt, the clarifying of the basic principles of autocratic rule and the "codifying" of the relations of the absolute state to its subjects, might, conceivably in the long run, contribute to lead the country towards a more constitutional order. This was the implication which the die-hard conservatives of Moscow and St. Petersburg read into Speransky's reforms. And the same suspicion arose in the mind of the Emperor when the Plan of 1809 confronted him with a practical formulation of his original intentions. That is why Alexander refused to put into execution the complete Plan of 1809 at once and chose to temporize, implementing it piece meal. Speransky's unwise insistence to put into effect the main provisions of the Plan only contributed to heighten the Emperor's suspicions and doubts.

Relying in the goodness of heart of others — perhaps because of his own — Speransky was not a very perceptive judge of character. He did not always select his assistants very wisely from the point of view of their discretion, witness Magnitskii. Also in spite of his kindness and tact, Speransky liked to make occasional sarcastic or biting ironical comments. Colleagues of his have related that in the early years of his career he often had his fellow workers in the office "in stitches" by satirizing his superiors, picking out and turning to ridicule their foibles and eccentricities. He never completely rid himself of this habit and sometimes indulged in it at the expense of some who were not likely to appreciate this kind of humor. Unadvisedly, Speransky selected the Emperor as the object of some caustic comments, which — unfortunately — were repeated to Alexander. The mildest of these remarks was, *"il est trop faible pour régner et trop fort pour être régi."* It was quite tactless and even cruel to call the Emperor *"notre Veau Blanc"* — punning on the name of Marshal Vauban — as Speransky did after

Alexander's return from an inspection of Russian border fortresses. By themselves, of course, such remarks could not mean much. But they offended the touchy pride and dignity of the Tsar. Alexander's sensitivity to what others thought of him, his vanity, his inability to forget an insult boded ill for the uncautious State Secretary. But the element of hurt pride, although a significant factor, would have hardly led to more than a cooling of personal feeling, the replacement of the informal and almost daily contacts by a more formal and distant relationship, such as usually prevail between sovereign and minister. [1] It might perhaps have even resulted in Speransky's dismissal from some of his important functions, but it scarcely would have warranted the ignominy of a harsh exile. Explanation for the latter must be sought primarily in the political concerns which became uppermost in Alexander's mind on the eve of the war against Napoleon.

From the time of Tilsit on, and more particularly after Erfurt, the Tsar's dominant preoccupation became to prepare himself for the ultimate conflict with France. At home, he improved the administrative and military machinery of the state with the assistance of men like Speransky, Arakcheev, Barclay de Tolly. Abroad, he lay the diplomatic groundwork for an all-European coalition that was to crush Napoleon: secret understandings with Austria, peace treaties with Turkey and Sweden, negotiations with England, asylum given to vom Stein and Hardenberg, secret correspondence with Talleyrand, Nesselrode's mission to Paris. He knew well, though, that despite his preparations, the struggle with Napoleon would not be short or easy. He realized that he would need the whole-hearted support of the country. Not only did he have to be sure of the personal loyalty of his advisors, but he also wanted them to be respected and accepted by Russian society.

We have seen why the Emperor felt betrayed and hurt by his Secretary. He, therefore, had Speransky's movements and his every word watched by secret agents and reported to him. The Minister of the Police, Balashev, was ordered to keep an eye on Speransky, an assignment that must have pleased the minister immensely. Not satisfied with this precaution, the Emperor also assigned de Sanglin, the chief of the Secret Department of the Police, to spy both on Speransky and his own superior, Balashev. A curious procedure indeed, which surprised even the professional police agent de Sanglin. It alone would justify Napoleon's bitter characterization of the Tsar as *"un grec du Bas-Empire."* The reports from his agents showed Alexander to what

[1] The entries in the *Kamerfur'erskii Zhurnal* are expressive of this change in 1811—1812.

extent Speransky had become a symbol of the course pursued by the government. The State Secretary, therefore, could easily be made into a scapegoat whose sacrifice would quickly restore the country's (i.e. the nobility's) confidence in the government. Furthermore, Speransky's careless handling of the secret correspondence with Paris might have made Alexander fear that rumors of his contacts with Talleyrand, England, Prussia, and Austria might "get around." To assuage the feelings of the country, check the opposition of the nobility, and keep Napoleon from learning about the secret negotiations, it had become expedient to sacrifice Speransky. So it was that the Emperor's motives of personal jealousy and distrust conveniently combined with weighty political considerations to make Speransky's dismissal very expedient indeed. Speransky's fall from power had to rally the country around its Emperor, restore unlimited confidence in the government, and proclaim openly that — contrary to evil rumor — Russia was not a satellite of France. To achieve this political and psychological effect, Speransky's departure had to be dramatic, with an element of mystery. The State Secretary's last day in the capital was staged and enacted with these considerations in mind.

The ever-prying curiosity of the historian cannot, unfortunately, be readily satisfied. The last meeting between Speransky and the Emperor at which the former was unexpectedly notified of his dismissal and impending exile, took place behind closed doors, with no third person present. For reasons of their own, Alexander and Speransky were too discreet ever to discuss the matter, and neither of them left any comment on what must have been a rather painful moment for both. No official document registers Speransky's dismissal. As a matter of fact, the State Secretary was removed very informally, and no government correspondence or paper have recorded the matter. Speransky was never formally relieved of his duties or deprived of his rank and privileges. Only as time went by, replacements were appointed to carry on the various functions with which he had been entrusted; but in no case was the new appointment accompanied by any statement concerning the dismissal of the previous incumbent. Apart from a very brief news item in the *St. Petersburg Journal* to the effect that Speransky had left the capital, the public was kept uninformed of motives or details, which produced the desired effect of "weighty mystery." Contemporaries did not have much of a chance for exploring the unexpected event in any detail, be it only through rumor and court gossip; three months later Russia was precipitated into the most difficult of wars. Speransky's exile was quickly forgotten.

Speransky's last day in St. Petersburg is now fully known, and all events that took place during that day have been reliably established. The State Secretary had not been received in audience by the Emperor for several weeks preceding the ill-fated Sunday of March 17, 1812. Such neglect was often the harbinger of imperial displeasure, as Count Panin, for one, had found out in 1801. Alexander's avoidance of an audience seemed odd to Speransky, for during the last years he had had almost daily interviews. Repeatedly he inquired at the Palace when the Emperor could see him, for the papers which needed consideration and decision were steadily growing in number. To these requests Alexander did not reply directly, but instructed the State Secretary to submit all the papers through a messenger. Anyone else, less absorbed in his work and more attuned to the changes of atmosphere at Court would have been aroused to danger. Speransky, however, while privately deploring his inability to confer with the Emperor personally on several matters, did not seem overly concerned. [1]

On Sunday March 17, finally, a Palace messenger notified Speransky that His Majesty expected to see him that same evening. As Speransky reached the anteroom to the Emperor's study, he found several dignitaries waiting for an audience. There is some question as to who these dignitaries were, apparently the Procurator of the Holy Synod, Prince A. N. Golitsyn was one of them. Alexander called Speransky into his study ahead of the others. The audience lasted for over two hours. When it was over, the door opened, and Speransky came out looking much upset with tears in his eyes. To hide his emotion he quickly walked to a table and proceeded to put papers into his briefcase, turning his back to those present in the room. As he was about done, the door to the Emperor's study opened again, and Alexander — also very disturbed, with tears on his cheeks — stepped forward, embraced Speransky, saying, "once more, Mikhail Mikhailovich, good bye!" and turning about brusquely, retired to his apartment. Speransky left in such haste that he almost forgot to take leave from the other officials in the room. He remembered it at the door, and turning to them, in particular to Prince Golitsyn, he said "farewell" and disappeared. A few moments later, a valet announced that His Majesty was sorry but would not receive anyone else that evening.

1 Jacob, *Denkwürdigkeiten*, p. 321: "Der Feldzug gegen Bonaparte war beschlossen und der Kaiser wollte in wenigen Wochen zur Armee abgehen. Dennoch wusste Speransky noch nicht ob er den Kaiser begleiten oder zurückbleiben würde. Das Zurückbleiben hätte in den Verhältnissen, in welchen Speransky damals gegen den Kaiser stand, schon allein eine Ungnade zu sein scheinen müssen. Dennoch schien es Speransky nicht so zu nehmen. Ich war den Sonntag, wo er arrestiert und verschickt wurde, von 10 bis gegen 2 Uhr bei ihm."

From the Palace, Speransky drove to Magnitskii. He learned there that his friend had been arrested and sent away from the capital. Returning to his own house quite late — he had left the Emperor at about 11 in the evening — Speransky found Balashev and de Sanglin waiting for him with an official carriage. The two police officials notified Speransky that they had orders to seize and seal his papers and send him off to his exile without delay. Speransky did not seem very surprised, as probably the Emperor had already told him what to expect. He requested permission to go to his study alone, and Balashev assented. (In his memoirs, de Sanglin maintains that in giving this permission the Minister had exceeded his instructions.) Speransky sorted his papers, burning some of them, wrote a few notes, and finally emerging from the study, handed Balashev a sealed envelope for transmission to the Emperor. He refused to wake his daughter and mother-in-law, said good bye to his servants and, entering the police carriage that stood at the door, started on his journey into exile.

Such was the abrupt end of the most active and influential period of Speransky's career. With it went his hopes of reorganizing Russia's administration along clear, logical, orderly, and new — albeit conservative — lines. But before following the fallen dignitary to his exile and long years of forced retirement, let us note the reaction produced by his disgrace and fall from power.

Though it had been hoped and worked for by many, the sudden exile came as a great surprise and shock to most. Those near the Emperor tried to learn the circumstances and decisive reasons from the monarch himself. But Alexander either remained silent, or — in keeping with his character — gave contradictory explanations. To his childhood friend, Prince A. N. Golitsyn, who inquired on the next day after Speransky's departure for the reasons of the sovereign's sad mien, Alexander replied: "no doubt you would cry of pain and lament if one tore off your hand: last night Speransky was taken from me, and he was my right hand." [1] To some the Emperor intimated that Speransky had behaved quite suspiciously. To others still, at various times,

[1] Cited by Grand Duc Nicolas Mikhailowitsch, *Le Tsar Alexandre Ier* (Paris 1931) p. 110. See also the following reminiscences of Nesselrode: "Je veux parler de la disgrâce de M. Speransky, mon intime ami, qui, pendant sa longue faveur, avait été mon principal appui auprès de l'empereur Alexandre. Son renvoi eut lieu dans la nuit du dimanche au lundi. Le mardi, l'Empereur me fit venir, et, avec sa bonté angélique me rassura sur les conséquences que j'avais redoutées un moment, c'est à dire sur le sort de ma correspondance, que Speransky avait envoyée cachetée à l'Empereur, et qui se trouvait dans son cabinet. Je trouvais l'Empereur très ému de la nécessité dans laquelle, à tort ou à raison, il s'était cru placé de se séparer d'un homme dont il aimait le caractère et estimait le talent. Il a été évidemment la victime d'une intrigue..." *Lettres et papiers du chancelier comte de Nesselrode,* Vol. II, pp. 75—76.

Alexander said that there had been denunciations and some unreliable evidence pointing to Speransky's treason, but that on the eve of a major war he could not investigate the matter fully. He therefore decided to exile Speransky to put a halt to rumors which undermined the morale of the country.[1] The Emperor seemed to prefer this last explanation, for it corresponded best to the few facts known to the public and the frame of mind of the conservative circles in Moscow, Tver', and St. Petersburg. It also took into account Speransky's known indiscretions concerning the secret diplomatic correspondence. To counteract the bad effect which might be produced abroad by the rumor that a French agent had penetrated into the inner councils of the government, Alexander wrote to his new ally, Marshal Bernadotte, Crown Prince of Sweden: "Avant d'achever qu'elle [Son Altesse] me permette de la remercier pour l'intérêt qu'elle a pris à la découverte que j'ai faite des menées sourdes autour de moi. Cependant je dois rectifier son jugement. J'ai plus de soupçons que de données certaines; mais ils m'ont suffi pour ne pas balancer un instant dans les circonstances présentes à éloigner les individus impliqués. Des preuves auraient suspendu en moi toute clémence, et je me serais cru appelé par les devoirs de ma place à sévir contre les coupables."[2] More sincere perhaps, and indicative of the Emperor's personal reasons, was a remark made to Novosiltsev in Święciany:

"Bien moins que cela [i.e. traître] il [Speransky] n'est réellement coupable qu'envers moi seul, coupable d'avoir payé ma confiance et mon amitié par l'ingratitude la plus noire, la plus abominable . . ."
Then the Emperor went on to describe what he had told Speransky during the last audience: "En tout autre temps j'aurai employé deux années pour vérifier avec la plus scrupuleuse attention tous les renseignements qui me sont parvenus concernant votre [Speransky's] conduite et vos actions. Mais le temps, les circonstances ne me le permettent pas en ce moment; l'ennemi frappe à la porte de l'Empire et, dans la situation où vous ont placé les soupçons que vous avez attirés sur vous par votre conduite et les propos que vous vous êtes permis, il m'importe de ne pas paraître coupable aux yeux de mes sujets en cas de malheur, en continuant de vous accorder ma confiance, en vous conservant la même place que vous occupez. Votre situation est telle que je vous conseillerais de ne pas rester à Petersbourg ou dans la proximité de cette ville..."[3]

1 To this Alexander alluded in his rescript of 1816 by which he appointed Speransky as governor of Penza, and he repeated it in his rescript of 22 March 1819 appointing Speransky to the governor generalship of Siberia (see Shil'der, *Imperator Aleksandr I*, IV, pp. 148—149.)

2 Letter dated 7/19 April 1812, cited in Shil'der, *op. cit.*, III, p. 52.

3 Quoted by Shil'der, *op. cit.*, III, p. 493 — also cited in full by Grand Duc Nicolas Mikhailowitsch, *L'Empereur Alexandre Ier*, I, 90—91.

All these statements of the Emperor, adapted as they were to the person to whom they were addressed, do not provide us with any final answer. But they give a fair list of the various considerations which entered into the Emperor's decision.

As had to be expected, the news of Speransky's fall was received with great joy by the conservative aristocracy in Moscow. It even was interpreted by some as Russia's first victory over France. The only regret was that the "traitor" — and his exile was final proof of his treason — and evil genius of Russia had not been dealt with more harshly. Many would have preferred to see him hanged. The exclamation of relief of V. I. Bakunina, often quoted by historians, was quite expressive of the sentiment and bears repetition: "A great day for the Fatherland and for all of us — the 17th of March! God has shown us His favor, for He has turned towards us and our enemies have fallen . . ." [1] The lady was not alone in experiencing great elation. A. I. Bulgakov noted in his diary on March 22, 1812 (Moscow): "In St. Petersburg there has been discovered a conspiracy which aimed at betraying Russia to the French. The 'wastrel' Speransky and Magnitskii have been arrested . . . An example must be made by punishing [them], by hanging Speransky! O outcast, monster, ungrateful and base creature! You were not worthy of the name of Russian nobleman. That is why you persecuted them [nobles]. Everybody speaks only of this." [2] In St. Petersburg the moderate conservative and anglophile N. M. Longinov applauded the fall of Speransky in his letters to Count S. R. Vorontsov, the sponsor of the Charter to the Russian People of 1801. [3] As a matter of fact, not a single significant voice was raised in defense of Speransky in 1812. Among the numerous official acquaintances, colleagues, and assistants of Speransky, some of whom were high in the government and who shared most of his ideas, only Count Shuvalov showed any sign of genuine personal concern and friendship. [4] Alone Admiral Mordvinov dared to resign from the Council of State in protest. Count Kochubei, erstwhile patron of Speransky, a very cautious courtier, immediately dissociated himself from the fallen dignitary and broke off relations with him until 1816. [5]

The foreign colony, and in particular the diplomatic representatives

[1] Quoted in Shil'der, *op. cit.*, III, p. 46.
[2] A. Ia. Bulgakov, "Vyderzhki iz zapisok A. Ia. Bulgakova," *Russkii Arkhiv*, (1867), pp. 1367–1368. See also letters of same to his brother, in *Russkii Arkhiv*, (1900), No. 5, pp. 14–17.
[3] *Arkhiv kniazia Vorontsova*, Vol. 23, p. 97 (letter No. 44, 6 April 1812); pp. 144–153 *passim* (letter No. 59, 13 Nov. 1812).
[4] *Druzheskie pis'ma Masal'skomu*, p. 14.
[5] Letter of V. Kochubei, dated 4 September 1818, in *Pamiati* p. 490 (note).

accredited to the Tsar, took careful note of the event. But not all of them understood its full implication, or ascribed to it the same importance. Curiously enough, Count Lauriston, the French Ambassador, barely mentioned the event in his regular dispatch. But Napoleon, correctly discerning it as a potential harbinger of further changes in Russian policy, pressed for more details. In the meantime, Napoleon tried to obtain the desired details from the Russian Ambassador in Paris, Prince A. B. Kurakin. But the latter was quite ignorant of what had happened in St. Petersburg. [1] Eventually Lauriston was able to satisfy his master's curiosity better. The Austrian chargé d'affaires, Saint-Julien, took a serious view of Speransky's exile and accompanied his report with a lengthy analysis of Russian policy. This interesting document concerns Speransky only indirectly, and as it has been cited in full by Grand Duke Nicholas Mikhailovich, we need not repeat or summarize it. [2] John Quincy Adams, the American Minister, rather sparse in his comments on the Russian domestic scene and the members of the Russian government, tersely reported in the last paragraph of his dispatch to Washington: "The Secretary General of the Empire and the Secretary of the Imperial Council for the Department of Legislation [i.e. Magnitskii], were last evening arrested and sent into banishment. They were persons of distinguished talents and very recently in high favor. The cause of their sudden disgrace is attributed to improper communications with France, but neither is, nor probably will be, known with certainty." [3]

But soon Europe became first the spectator and then the active participant in the final act of Napoleon's career. The world's attention was deflected from the lonely and not very significant — when viewed against the dramatic events of the day — person of the former State Secretary of the Russian Empire. While Moscow burned and the

---

[1] Prince A. B. Kurakin reported to Rumiantsev from Paris on 15/27 April 1812: "(Napoleon asked Kurakin that same day) Mais dites-moi, j'ai appris que Speransky vient d'être arrête'. Pouvez vous m'apprendre les causes de cet événement? — Je [e.g. Kurakin] répondis encore qu'on ne m'avait rien appris sur la catastrophe de Speransky et que mon courrier m'avait dit seulement qu'il n'était plus en place, ni même à St. Petersbourg." "Doneseniia imperatoru Aleksandru I kniazia A. B. Kurakina i doneseniia ego zhe kantsleru Rumiantsevu za 1811 i 1812 gg," *Sbornik IRIO,* Vol. 21 (1877), p. 377. See also *ibid.,* p. 386 (report dated 20 April/2 May, 1812) in which Kurakin summarizes what the Duke of Bassano has told him about Speransky's exile on the basis of the dispatch of the French Ambassador Lauriston). Cf. also the dispatches of Lauriston (in Russian translation), *Russkii Arkhiv,* (1882), No. 1 pp. 169—176 and Grand Duc Nicolas Mikhailowitsch, *Les relations diplomatiques de la Russie et de la France,* vol. VI, pp. 253—255.

[2] Grand Duc Nicolas Mikhailowitsch, *L'Empereur Alexandre Ier,* I, pp. 92—94.

[3] *U.S. Department of State — Russia,* John Quincy Adams to the Secretary of State, dispatch No. 82, dated 31 March 1812.

*Grande Armée* wasted away on the battlefields of Europe in a last futile effort at saving Napoleon's empire, Speransky spent his days in the drab and uneventful solitude of exile in remote corners of Russia. We must follow him there.

The first destination of the exiled dignitary was Nizhnii Novgorod, the ancient and lively trading center on the Volga. According to Emperor Alexander, he had given Speransky the choice between several towns for his enforced residence, and Speransky had preferred Nizhnii Novgorod. [1] At the same time, Magnitskii had been sent to Vologda, in the North of European Russia. The disgrace of Speransky had been so unexpected that outside a very limited circle in St. Petersburg, nobody knew about it for several weeks. This resulted in the ironical situation in which the officer who escorted Speransky to the Volga had to ask his "prisoner" to use his influence to procure the horses and other necessities for their journey. The trip to Nizhnii Novgorod was completed without undue hardship, quite rapidly. As we have mentioned, Speransky had not wished to bid goodbye to his family before leaving. He left word that they should rejoin him later, with the onset of the good travel season. However, his mother-in-law, Mrs. Stephens, decided to leave St. Petersburg immediately — perhaps she was prodded by the government into taking this decision — and a few days after the State Secretary had left the capital, his daughter and mother-in-law followed him on the road to Nizhnii Novgorod.

The Civilian Governor of the Volga town, Runovskii, had been instructed by the Emperor, through Balashev, to keep the exile under close surveillance, to forward all his correspondence to the Minister of Police, and to take note of all persons who maintained contact with him. The Governor carried out these instructions strictly, and Speransky found himself cut off from his acquaintances and former colleagues in St. Petersburg. Eluding the police, though, he succeeded in maintaining some contacts with his closer friends by transmitting messages through friendly merchants who traveled between the Volga and the capital. It was also through these merchants that the slavishly devoted Masal'skii, Speransky's business agent, provided him with money.

Speransky's name had become a sort of symbol for the patriotic discontent with Russia's alliance to France. Of course such feelings were not truly "popular" feelings, they rather reflected the sentiments of the nobility and bureaucracy. But as the war against the French invader turned to Russia's disadvantage and as increasingly more Russian territory was ravaged and occupied by the *Grande Armée*,

[1] Grand Duc Nicolas Mikhailowitsch, *L'Empereur Alexandre Ier*, I, p. 91.

driving streams of refugees into the interior, the hatred for everything that was connected with France spread among the masses of the population. In the process the former State Secretary also became an object of the distrust or even hatred of the population at large. Nizhnii Novgorod was a major destination for the streams of refugees from the invaded Western provinces. The refugees, among whom could be counted many prominent noble families from Moscow, brought to the Volga rumors of Speransky's treasonable role, rumors which Count Rostopchin had done a great deal to propagate. Speransky was branded as Russia's evil genius and made the scapegoat of all the defeats and misfortunes of the country. As the conflict wore on, as Napoleon's troops progressed further East, the people and the authorities became increasingly more nervous and panicky. The routine reports of the police of Nizhnii Novgorod about Speransky's doings received a most sinister interpretation.

Police agents had observed that the exiled dignitary was often frequenting low class pubs and taverns, public markets. He seemed to be eager to strike up conversations with common folk. Accepting the factual information of these reports as correct, what were Speransky's motives for such a behavior, which — he must have realized — could arouse the suspicions of the authorities? There are no personal records preserved on this period of his life, and we have no way of knowing his reasons for seeking out the company of the lower classes. Was it because of his isolation, his bitterness toward the nobility and bureaucracy? or was it because in his period of defeat and depression he felt closer and more at ease with these simple folks who had been the companions and playmates of his childhood? Perhaps it was from a desire to take advantage of the unexpected turn of fortune and study at first hand the people's condition, opinions, beliefs, hopes, desires? One thing is certain, he had no evil intentions and did not spend his time in taverns spreading anti-governmental sentiments and pro-French propaganda, as the authorities seemed to believe. But as the proverb goes, "fear has big eyes," and in the late summer of 1812 the government was terrified at the thought of a peasant rising. The serfowners and the bureaucracy lived in the constant fear that Napoleon might issue a proclamation of emancipation (as he was urged to do by some of his advisers), reviving for Russia the original revolutionary popular slogan, "*guerre aux palais et paix aux chaumières!*" Firmly believing that while in power the State Secretary had worked for a radical change, nay a subversion, of Russia's social order, for the destruction of the nobility and the emancipation of the serfs, the authorities of

Nizhnii Novgorod viewed his contacts with the populace with more than normal suspicion.

The Governor's misgivings at Speransky's presence in the city entrusted to his care appeared to find confirmation in an incident which the police dutifully reported to him. In spite of his status, Speransky was at liberty to maintain social intercourse with prominent personalities in the city. In particular, he sought the company of the local Metropolitan, partly because of his own clerical past, and partly because of his intense preoccupation with religious questions. Speransky was a fairly regular guest at the Metropolitan's residence and table. One day, at dinner, the conversation turned to the most serious concern of the day, the invasion of Russia. The Metropolitan's guests voiced their fear over the consequences of French behavior in the occupied provinces. Speransky observed that the Church and the clergy, at least, had nothing to fear. In all the countries he had invaded or conquered so far — most recently in Germany — Napoleon had shown himself very respectful of the Church and had treated the clergy better than the rest of the population. The remark was merely a statement of fact, a piece of information gratuitously — albeit inadvisedly — contributed by Speransky to the general conversation. But under the circumstances it was given an ominous interpretation by the authorities.

The suspicions entertained by the local police received added support from a report concerning Speransky's financial dealings. It was observed that he had exchanged all the assignats in his possession for gold coins or foreign currency. In a letter to Masal'skii Speransky explained that he was doing it because the value of the ruble-assignat was falling constantly and his very limited means did not make it possible for him to take chances on a further depreciation of the currency. The police, however, interpreted this monetary operation much more crudely as speculations on the misfortune of the country.

In due course, a report of Speransky's remarks and actions was sent to St. Petersburg. The Minister of the Police ordered the Military Governor of the Province of Nizhnii Novgorod, Count Tolstoi, to verify the information. If the facts cited by the police turned out to be correct, Count Tolstoi was empowered to send Speransky further East. But Tolstoi was not in a mood to make an exhaustive investigation to check the accuracy of the reports. He had plenty of other problems, much more serious and important than the fate of a disgraced official. He was also under strong moral and psychological pressure from his friend and colleague, Count Rostopchin. Rostopchin, now Governor General of Moscow, was endeavoring to deflect from himself and the government the fear, panic, and anger of Moscow's population by resorting to the time honored practice of scapegoats. For this purpose he had used the numerous foreign residents of Moscow. Then he "discovered" alleged Russian traitors, and finally, after stirring up the populace, he had abandoned the hapless young merchant's son, Vereshchagin, to the cruel fury of the mob. To have Speransky "pay" for his alleged treason to Russia in Moscow would not only have satisfied Rostopchin's political exhaltation and vengeance, it would have been an act of great propaganda value. Under various specious and contradictory pretexts, (the need of calming the people, of preventing Speransky from carrying on harmful propaganda, of protecting the exiled dignitary from the righteous anger of the mob) Rostopchin tried to convince Count Tolstoi to have Speransky transferred to Moscow or — at the very least — arrested and tried for treason. Never scrupulous about the means he used, Rostopchin claimed that he was acting on behalf of the Emperor — which was quite false. Fortunately for Speransky, Tolstoi successfully resisted the entreaties of Rostopchin. But he was glad to seize the opportunity of ridding himself of a bothersome exile.

Without troubling to check the police reports, Tolstoi sent Speransky further east, to Perm', on the very border of Siberia. This time Speransky had to make the journey more like a criminal than a dignitary in disfavor. To the Governor of Perm', Count Tolstoi sent a very laconic message (delivered by Speransky's escort), ordering him to take charge of the "prisoner of state," Privy Councillor Speransky, censor his mail, and keep him under close surveillance until receipt of forther instructions from St. Petersburg.

This unexpected removal to the remotest corner of European Russia was a great blow to Speransky. Apart from the psychological pain, this change of residence brought also an appreciable deterioration in his material and social circumstances. In the first place, he was separated from his beloved daughter. In the second place, the Governor of Perm' — or rather his wife who was the actual ruler of the province — interpreted Tolstoi's orders in a way most unfavorable to Speransky. The exile was treated very harshly, without any respect, and placed under constant and annoying surveillance. The police chief entered his house at almost any time of the day; agents followed him wherever he went; and the Governor refused to see him or transmit any of his requests to higher authority. The Governor also made it known that the authorities would view with displeasure any manifestation of sympathy towards the exile, any attempts at befriending him. Speransky could not stay in the apartment he had first rented from a widow, because the Governor's wife forced his landlady to evict him. He found a house with great difficulty, thanks to the devoted and fearless assistance of the merchant Popov, the only person who dared to maintain close and friendly relations with the exile. For a while Speransky had to give up his daily walks, for the children pursued him with their mockeries and insults in the streets. Everywhere he went, he was received with ill-concealed fear or hatred, which grew steadily worse with Napoleon's progress into Russia. Speransky's daughter later recalled — perhaps with some exaggeration, but it was indicative of the atmosphere — that even the poor French prisoners of war were reluctant to accept alms from him. On top of all this, Speransky's pecuniary situation was extremely shaky and bad. He had never been able to take good care of his financial interests; he had no savings. Now he found himself without any income, for his salary had been his only source. For a while he had to borrow from everybody, even from his own servants. When his mother-in-law and daughter joined him after a few months, they brought some money. But it did not last very long either. Speransky had to save on everything; he deprived himself of his only and best loved "luxuries," such as French snuff and wine. The period in Perm' was the bitterest of his exile and probably the worst in his life.

Eventually Speransky succeeded in informing the Emperor of his plight, both financial and moral. (His earlier letters and appeals had not reached the Emperor, as they were mislaid or held up by subordinate officials). Alexander tersely ordered the Governor of Perm' to treat Speransky in the manner befitting a Privy Councillor. And almost overnight — Speransky was probably getting used to these sudden changes in fortune — the isolated, hated exile and "prisoner of state" became the most popular figure in town. This immediate reversal of attitude may be proof that the people never took the rumors and accusations concerning Speransky too seriously. The "hatred" for Speransky was only due to the panic and tensions generated by the invasion and the fear of displeasing the authorities. Of course, as far as Speransky was concerned, the damage had been done, and his moral sensitivity did not forget or forgive the insults and humiliations of the past. While restoring Speransky's social position in Perm', the Emperor had also taken care of his material needs by alloting him a moderate, but quite adequate, yearly stipend (6000 rubles a year). The former State Secretary could now move about freely and again take some comfort from the modest amenities of life Perm' provided. Speransky even now did not establish any close relations with the society of Perm', and he did not participate in the town's social life beyond the minimum necessary to keep up appearances. Besides the merchant Popov, the Bishop of Perm' was the only person with whom he had close contact and whose friendship he valued very highly. With the Bishop, Speransky could discuss religion and philosophy, matters always close to his heart. The Bishop also helped him in his studies of Hebrew to which Speransky applied himself with great energy and devotion.

Toward the end of 1813 Speransky sent his daughter and mother-in-law to St. Petersburg and remained alone in the small and forlorn provincial town. He took this rather painful decision, because he wanted his daughter to receive a good education and grow up in a more sophisticated environment. He also wished to use the opportunity presented by her trip to the capital to forward directly to the Emperor a long letter, the so-called Perm' letter, in the hope of receiving an opportunity to rehabilitate himself. Alexander, however, did not react to the letter at the time. But prompted by another appeal, after the conclusion of the war against Napoleon, the Emperor finally permitted Speransky to retire to his small estate, Velikopol'e, in the province of Novgorod. Accompanied by the good wishes and regrets of the Permians who had become his great admirers, Speransky left Perm' in 1814 and withdrew to his estate.

In Velikopol'e the disgraced State Secretary spent his days very quietly. There were no events important enough to be mentioned here. He shunned all unnecessary contacts with neighbors and local officials (who, incidentally, were instructed to keep him under some surveillance). Occasionally he consented to receive or visit the Vice Governor of Novgorod, Muraviev. On these occasions he met the Vice Governor's young son, the future Count Muraviev-Amurskii, Governor General of Eastern Siberia and empire builder on the Amur. The only regular absences from Velikopol'e would be to visit the neighboring monastery of Savva Vysherskii. He maintained the closest spiritual and intellectual relations with some monks and the Superior of the monastery, and in gratitude for their spiritual inspiration and guidance he contributed to the improvement of the monastery's buildings and church. From time to time some former colleague or friend would find his way to the modest house at Velikopol'e, for the village was conveniently located mid-way between Moscow and St. Petersburg. These visits kept Speransky informed of the latest political and intellectual developments in the capital. Gradually, these reminders of a more active and rewarding existence helped him in overcoming his earlier resolution to shun all social and political activities completely. Speransky's understandably keen desire to vindicate himself was another factor in his change of mind about complete withdrawal from political life. Perhaps also his wish to see his daughter properly married played a part in this change of mind. His dream now became to be appointed a Senator, a member of the Commission on Laws. The signing of the Holy Alliance was taken by Speransky as a convenient pretext for broaching the matter to the Emperor. The general principles enunciated in the Holy Alliance treaty were close to the heart of Speransky; he wrote to Alexander expressing his full approval and support. He urged the monarch to follow up the logical implications of the Alliance's principles at home too. But the Emperor did not react to this timid overture.

Speransky had to wait until 1816 before he was permitted to resume an active administrative role. Then he first had to serve as Governor in distant provinces before he was allowed to return to the capital. Even this long and roundabout way back to "favor" could be taken only after Speransky had humiliated himself by pleading with Arak-cheev, the all-powerful friend and assistant of Alexander. Perhaps it was not so much Arakcheev who had wanted to humiliate Speransky, as Alexander himself who wished to abase his former councillor and make him dependent on his new favorite. To compel the honest and able Speransky to humiliate himself before the "corporal of Gatchina" was balsam for wounds — real or fancied — the former State Secretary had inflicted on the Emperor's touchy vanity. In any case, the Emperor did not want Speransky back in St. Petersburg as the apparently innocent victim of evil tongues and of the monarch's own distrustful gullibility. Speransky could return only if he first "redeemed" himself of his past errors by humble and dutiful service in minor and remote positions. We may well believe that in this instance, Arakcheev's own feelings coincided with those of his imperial master, and in his letters he let Speransky feel them. Yet, Speransky decided to accept and suffer this humiliation. He did not even hesitate to flatter the vanity and prejudices of Arakcheev. In so doing, Speransky's moral pain may not have been as great as we think. For in an age when individual caprice rules human destinies, the humiliations inflicted by such caprice are felt not so much as insults as a natural feature of the *condition humaine*. As no one considers imperial caprice damaging to one's honor, there is no feeling of moral slight, and it is much easier to seek reinstatement to favor by any means, even if they involve some humiliation.

Speransky returned to active life in 1816, i.e. after four years of exile. For as active and energetic an individual as he, the management

of his small estate, the supervision of his daughter's education, and
occasional conversations with visitors, were hardly enough to fill the
day or to satisfy his need for constant work. Speransky kept himself
busy by developing his mind and, more particularly, by filling the
gaps in his knowledge of philosophy, theology, and languages. He also
had ample leisure and opportunity to look back with some detachment
on his earlier ideas and actions and to subject them to critical analysis.
Thereby he deepened and broadened his understanding of Russia's
political and social problems, while at the same time clarifying his
own philosophical views. From his exile, Speransky returned not only
chastened by bitter experience, but also enriched by a deeper and
more comprehensive *Weltanschauung*. An examination of this intellectual development will provide a basis for an analysis of his philosophical views and a discussion of the political philosophy which
underlay his administrative activities, not only implicitly before 1812
but also explicitly after his return to work in 1816.

## SOURCES

Both the general biographies of Speransky and Alexander I cited previously and
the general histories of the period, deal with Speransky's exile in more or less
detailed fashion.
The following lists only the major primary sources, contemporary memoirs, and
special secondary works on which the chapter is based:
    P r i m a r y   S o u r c e s :   Speranskii: "Opravdatel'naia zapiska" (in French),
*Russkii Arkhiv,* (1892), I, pp. 65—72; *Druzheskie pis'ma M. M. Speranskogo k P. G.
Masal'skomu 1798—1819* (St. Pbg. 1862); letters of Speransky to Alexander I and
Arakcheev are found in: N. Dubrovin, *Pis'ma glavnykh deiatelei v tsarstvovanie
Aleksandra I 1807—1829* (St. Pbg. 1883); important letters and other sources on
Speransky's life in exile are found in: A. F. Bychkov (ed.), *V pamiat' grafa Speranskogo*
(St. Pbg. 1872); Speranskii, "Pis'mo k Aleksandru I iz Nizhnego Novgoroda," March
1812, in Shil'der, *Imperator Aleksandr I,* III, pp. 491—493; Speranskii, "Permskoe
pis'mo k Aleksandru I," January 1813, in Shil'der, *op. cit.,* III, 515—527; Speranskii:
"Pis'mo k Aleksandru I," 9/21 July 1814 in Shil'der, *op. cit.,* III, p. 263; Speranskii,
"Pis'mo k Aleksandru I, 6. ianv. 1816 s zapiskoi po povodu manifesta 25. dek. 1815,"
*Sbornik materialov l-go otdelenia sobstvennoi E. I. V. Kantseliarii,* II (St. Pbg.
1876), pp. 36—42; Speranskii, "Pis'mo k. Aleksandru I," July 1816, in Korf: *Zhizn'
grafa Speranskogo,* II, p. 106; Speranskii, "Pis'mo k A. A. Arakcheevu" 1816, in Korf,
*op. cit.,* II, pp. 107—109.
    C o n t e m p o r a r y   m e m o i r s :   Ernst Moritz Arndt, *Meine Wanderungen und
Wandlungen mit dem Freiherrn vom Stein* (Reclam Ausgabe 1859), (3. Abdruck,
Berlin 1869); A. Ia. Bulgakov, "Pis'ma k ego bratu 1811—1812," *Russkii Arkhiv,*
(1900), No. 5; A. Ia. Bulgakov, "Vyderzhki iz zapisok Aleksandra Iakovlevicha
Bulgakova" (1811—1812), *Russkii Arkhiv,* (1867), pp. 1361—1374; E. G. "Iz zhizni
Speranskogo v Permi" *Istoricheskii Vestnik,* 48 (1892), 570—572; E. G. "Speransky
v ssylke v Permi," *Istoricheskii Vestnik,* III (1880), 637—638; V. S. Filippov,
"Arestovanie Speranskogo," *Pamiatniki Novoi Russkoi Istorii,* III (St. Pbg. 1873),
113—116; (F. Fortunatov), "Pamiatnye zametki Vologzhanina," *Russkii Arkhiv,*
(1867), 1646—1707; A. I. Golitsyn, "Rasskazy," *Russkii Arkhiv,* (1886), No. 2, pp.
52—108, 305—333; N. S. Il'inskii, "Rasskazy o Speranskom i Arakcheeve," *Russkaia*

*Starina,* V (1872), p. 470; N. S. Il'inskii, "Vospominaniia," *Russkii Arkhiv,* (1879), No. 12, pp. 377—434; L. H. Jacob, *Denkwürdigkeiten aus meinem Leben* (manuscript); F. P. Lubianovskii, "Vospominaniia F. P. Lubianovskogo," *Russkii Arkhiv,* (1872), pp. 98—185, 448—533; V. R. Marchenko, "Avtobiograficheskie zapiski gosudarstvennogo sekretaria V. R. Marchenki 1782—1838," *Russkaia Starina,* 85 (1896), 471—505, and 86 (1896), 3—20, 291—317; M. Mikhailovskii-Danilevskii, *Nekotorye vypiski iz bumag M. Danilevskogo,* (Leipzig 1875); prot. Evg. Popov, "Dvukhletnii izgnannik v Permi — Speranskii" in *Velikopermskaia i Permskaia eparkhiia* (inaccessible to me); Ia. I. de Sanglen, "Zapiski 1776—1831," *Russkaia Starina,* 37 (1883), 1—46, 375—394, 539—578; Amiral Tchitchagoff, *Mémoires de l'Amiral Tchitchagoff 1767—1849* (Leipzig 1862); F. F. Vigel', *Vospominaniia* (Moscow 1928); S. G. Volkonskii, *Zapiski S. G. Volkonskogo* (St. Pbg. 1902, 2d. ed.).

Contemporary polemical sources: G. P. Ermolov, "Pamflet na Speranskogo 16 marta 1813," *Chteniia* (1895), No. 3, part 2, pp. 1—24; N. M. Karamzin, "O drevnei i novoi Rossii," *Russkii Arkhiv,* (1870), No. 2: pp. 2225—2350. Joseph de Maistre, "Cinq lettres sur l'éducation publique en Russie, à Monsieur le Comte Rasoumovski, ministre de l'instruction publique — Juin 1810," *Oeuvres complètes, VIII* (Paris 1884), 163—232; de Maistre, "Quatre chapitres sur la Russie," *Oeuvres complètes,* VIII, 279—362; "Pis'mo grafa Rostopchina k Aleksandru I s donosom na Speranskogo 17 marta 1812," *Russkaia Starina,* 122 (1905), 412—416.

Contemporary correspondence: P. Bartenev (ed.), *Arkhiv kniazia Vorontsova* (Moscow 1870—1895); N. Dubrovin, *Pis'ma glavneishikh deiatelei v tsarstvovanie imperatora Aleksandra I (1807—1829),* (St. Pbg. 1883); (Lauriston, Blome) "Diplomaticheskie depeshi o ssylke Speranskogo," *Russkii Arkhiv,* (1882), No. 2, pp. 169—176; *Lettres et papiers du chancelier comte de Nesselrode* (Paris 1909—1912); Grand Duc Nicolas Mikhailowitsch, *Les relations diplomatiques de la Russie et de la France d'après les rapports des ambassadeurs d'Alexandre et de Napoléon* (St. Pbg. 1905—1914); Nikolai Mikhailovich, *Perepiska imperatora Aleksandra I s sestroi, velikoi kniaginei Ekaterinoi Pavlovnoi,* (St. Pbg. 1910); *Ostaf'evskii arkhiv kniazei Viazemskikh* (St. Pbg. 1899—1901); Parrot, "Lettres à Alexandre I et Nicolas I," in Shil'der, *Imperator Aleksandr I,* III, appendix No. VI, 487—491; M. Pogodin, "Otryvok pis'ma A. N. Murav'eva o Speranskom," *Russkii Arkhiv,* (1871), pp. 1945—1948; A. Vandal (ed.) "La cour de Russie en 1807—1808 — Notes sur la cour de Russie et St. Petersbourg écrites en décembre 1807 par le général Savary," *Revue d'histoire diplomatique,* IV, (1890), pp. 399—419.

Secondary works: A. Afanas'ev, "Dopolnenie k stat'e o Speranskom Longinova," *Russkii Vestnik,* 25 (1860), 26—41; T. Bakounine, *Le répertoire biographique des francs-maçons russes (XVIIIe et XIXe ss.),* (Bruxelles, n.d. — Publication de l'institut de philologie et d'histoire — Univ. de Bruxelles série slave No. 2); M. Bogdanovich, "Padenie Speranskogo" *Vestnik Evropy,* Vol. III, No. 12 (Dec. 1868), pp. 495—505. I. A. Bychkov, (ed.), "Ssylka Speranskogo v 1812 g," *Russkaia Starina,* 110 (April 1902), 5—44; *id.,* "Deiateli i uchastniki v padenii Speranskogo," *Russkaia Starina,* 109 (March 1902), pp. 469—508; *id.,* "Prebyvanie Speranskogo v Nizhnem Novgorode i v Permi," *Russkaia Starina,* 110 (May 1902), 231—249; *id.,* "Speranskii v Velikopol'e i v Penze," *Russkaia Starina,* 110 (June 1902), 467—486 and 111 (July 1902), 45—59; A. Dmitriev, "Prebyvanie M. M. Speranskogo v Permi," *Russkii Vestnik,* (1869), No. 8, 744—749; Ar. Fatéev, "La disgrâce d'un homme d'état (à l'occasion du centenaire de la mort de Spéransky en 1839)," *Zapiski russkogo nauchno-issledovatel'-skogo ob'edineniia v Prage,* tome X (old series XV), (Praha 1940), pp. 33—73 — the second part (if published) could not be located by me; Ia. Grot, "K istorii ssylki Speranskogo," *Russkii Arkhiv,* (1871), pp. 2073—2078; S. Iuzhakov, "Padenie Speranskogo," *Russkaia Mysl',* (1890), No. 11, pp. 111—131; *Karamzin i Speranskii* (Paris 1858); Robert A. Klostermann, "Speranskii's Sturz in L. H. Jakobs 'Denkwürdigkeiten'" *Archiv für Kulturgeschichte,* 23—No. 2, (1932) 217—233; P. M. Maikov, "A. A. Zherve," *Russkaia Starina,* Vol. 92 (1897), No. 10, pp. 97—120 and No. 11, pp. 393—403; E. A. Popov, *M. M. Speranskii v Permi i Sibiri* (Perm' 1879); V. I. Semevskii, "Padenie Speranskogo" in *Otechestvennaia voina i russkoe obshchestvo,* II (Moscow 1911), 221—246; A. V. Vasil'ev, "Progressivnyi podokhodnyi nalog i padenie Speranskogo," *Golos Minuvshego,* IV (July—August 1916), No. 7—8, pp. 332—340; Kenneth R. Whiting, *Aleksei Andreevich Arakcheev* (Harvard University, unpublished Ph. D. thesis, 1951).

# CHAPTER VII

# PHILOSOPHICAL VIEWS AND POLITICAL THEORY

Even though some histories of Russian philosophy mention Speransky's name, it would be wrong to pretend that he was a creative and original philosopher in any formal sense of the word. He was only a thoughtful individual with a keen analytical mind, interested in philosophy, who felt the need for understanding and explicitly clarifying to himself the metaphysical and logical bases of his thinking. Unluckily for his biographers, he had never the opportunity of formulating his philosophical ideas as consistently and as systematically as his administrative schemes. In most cases, random reflections and comments jotted down in the course of his readings, are all that has been preserved. They are fragments that have to be pieced together without the guidance of precise chronology or even certainty as to their completeness. But as a son of the 18th century, Speransky had an *"esprit systématique"* and he always tried to determine the first principles of the problems he had to face. From an attentive and close reading of all the accessible evidence, therefore, there emerges a clear and rather consistent philosophical *Weltanschauung* which may help us in better understanding his political and administrative work.

Speransky's numerous and varied writings point to two main sources of his thinking. In the first place, he possessed a profound and mystical religious faith that satisfied his deepest psychological needs and filled his emotional life almost completely (especially, after the loss of his wife). In the second place, he had a philosophy in the formal sense, consonant with his mysticism, which provided a framework for his active and intellectual life. Because of the gaps in our sources, we cannot always determine precisely to what extent and in what way these two elements interacted and interpenetrated each other. The present writer is not qualified to analyze and discuss adequately the religious and mystical components of Speransky's thought. Fortunately, this task has been exhaustively performed some time ago in two series of learned articles, with abundant illustration from original manuscript sources which were available at the time to scholars. The interested reader must be referred to them. [1] Here we shall restrict ourselves to an examination of Speransky's philosophical ideas properly speaking, as a background and foundation for an analysis of his political theory, always keeping in mind that there was a close relationship between his religious, mystical searchings and philosophical analysis and study.

It may be recalled that while a student and tutor at the Alexandro-Nevskii theological seminary, Speransky had come in contact with both science and philosophy. In those early years, he came to study and investigate nature primarily as a means for the justification and better grounding of his religious beliefs — an attitude characteristic of an earlier Christian Europe and not unexpected in someone who was preparing himself for the ministry to souls. [2] At one point he even made the naive statement that if the correct description and explanation of the physical world were given to the Moslems, it would lead to their mass conversion to Christianity. [3] Besides this purely apologetic interest, Speransky showed genuine scientific curiosity and an enthusiastic thirst for a knowledge of God's creation, a curiosity and a thirst which he retained throughout his life. [4] In this respect, he found himself quite at home in the "intellectual climate" of the Enlightenment. After he had finished his studies at the seminary, Speransky was entrusted with the teaching of two courses at the same institution, one in philosophy and one in physics; and he taught them between 1792 and 1795. A very complete set of notes on his course in physics has been preserved and published. It shows that Speransky made use of all the important classical sources of his time, but relied most heavily on the work of Winckler, which he brought up to date with remarks and speculations on the meaning of the most recent discoveries, in particular those in chemistry. [5]

[1] See El'chaninov "Mistitsizm Speranskogo" and Katetov, "Graf M. M. Speranskii kak religioznyi myslitel'" cited in the bibliography to the chapter.

[2] "The second benefit which the science of nature gives us consists in that it alone can give us a conception of the distinctive creation of the Almighty." M. Speranskii, "Fizika vybrannaia iz luchshikh avtorov, raspolozhennaia i dopolnennaia Nevskoi Seminarii filosofii i fiziki uchitelem M. M. Speranskim 1797—go g. v Sankt Peterburge," Chteniia, (Moscow 1871), kniga 3, otdel 2, p. 4. Hereafter, Speransky's course of physics will be referred to as Fizika.

[3] Fizika, p. 4.

[4] "If physics were only the science of looking at nature with pleasure, this in itself would be enough to give it the first place in our [intellectual] activities and count among the truly useful activities of man. The sight of nature is splendid, touching to the eyes of those who know, but it is dead and mute for the ignorant." Fizika, p. 1.

[5] "And thus let us leave Leibniz with his monads, in their dark and involved ways; we shall follow Newton (Principia Philosoph. Natur.) and Euler (Physical Letters), on the simple and straight road to find the true principle of the composition of bodies." Fizika, p. 8. See also, ibid., pp. 7 and v.

His course on physics follows pretty much the ordinary scheme of Newtonian physics, being primarily devoted to the study of statics, dynamics, and optics. In the later sections, he deals briefly with magnetism in which he was very much interested, electricity, and chemistry. We need not be concerned here with an analysis of the course or with its scientific merit. We may, however, note one interesting thought expressed by Speransky, something that gives a hint as to the direction in which his mind was already tending. One of the chief reasons for studying physics, he says, is to find the basic elements of things. Thus, by studying dynamics and statics we find out about the correct working of force, for it is force that provides an unitary principle of explanation for a great number of areas and phenomena of the world. And more generally, "all solutions [of physical problems] make us see at least four elements in matter, consequently matter itself is heterogeneous. But reason goes further than experience, and usually leaves us with doubt instead of a system. Who knows, are these elements not the result of a further combination of elements and don't they perhaps contain an element still simpler than themselves?" [1] Man should continue his search for a more fundamental principle than the basic elements of matter and he may eventually be able to explain all the diversity of the world on the basis of one single element. It is significant that already in the 1790's Speransky came to this idea on the basis of his study and exposition of the classical Newtonian world, and because he was dissatisfied with its adequacy. Chemistry might yield that unifying principle he was looking for, the experiments of Priestley and Lavoisier indicated the proper direction, but it was still too early to be convinced; and Speransky let the matter drop. [2]

After entering government service, Speransky kept busy with too many administrative and political affairs to have much time left for the systematic study and exposition of philosophical problems. But he did not abandon them completely and tried to keep abreast of the current literature in the field as much as his occupations permitted. Later, during and after his exile, he devoted much of his time to learning languages and concentrated his energy most particularly on the study of religious and mystical questions. Most of his philosophical statements have to be gleaned from passing remarks and fragmentary notes, usually undated, jotted down as he went along in his reading and thinking. His philosophising is determined by the needs of his religious speculations, and he treats some questions, such as the problem

1 *Fizika*, pp. 10—11.
2 *Fizika*, pp. 135—96 *passim*, in particular p. 168.

of knowledge merely as instruments and *Vorarbeiten* of theology. [1]

He remained dissatisfied with the picture of the world as constructed by classical physics. The human intellect, he felt, in its rational form cannot truly arrive at a proper knowledge of nature, for human reason has to split up, divide the material of the world to make it intelligible. In this process nature's unity and life are lost, for man "transfers the methods of his investigation, the ways of his own weakness to nature itself, and he is always cutting down nature to his own size rather than adjusting himself to nature's".[2] Descriptive and logical categories, such as time and space, which man uses to create an intelligible but synthetic order in the unity of nature are the results of the inadequacy of man's mind and reason. They should not be needed to understand the world, for the true eye comprehends nature without the help of such crutches. [3] Man must find the unifying principle, the harmony of the universe. This can be done only if he brings into play his emotional, moral, religious traits, his full confidence in the moral goodness of the universe, his direct understanding of the divinity.[4] Only the injection of "purity of soul," of "goodness" into our reason leads to the proper understanding of nature, of its principles. Thus, the eternal and all-embracing Eye does not need the categories of human reason to understand the unity of the universe:

> According to its simplest notion, *time* is the distance between the beginning and the end of *being*, but this distance is measured by our perceptions, this unit of measurement is not true and perfect, but only relative, for in truth, things are not born and do not disintegrate, but only appear and disappear from view; if, therefore, instead of our weak eye, we put the all-seeing Eye, the Eye that can follow matter in all its changes, it is obvious that for It there will be neither beginning nor end in things, and, consequently, no time. For It the universe will be a ceaselessly moving mass, passing from one system into another, but because all systems are inherent to the boundless mind, It knows neither the past nor the future. Everything is not time and not eternity. [5]

[1] El'chaninov, *op. cit.*, p. 210.

[2] Speranskii, "O poriadke," *Druzheskie pis'ma G. Masal'skomu*, p. 138 and "O prostranstve," *ibid.*, p. 137.

[3] "Only the weakness of the mind has forced men to split up bodies into parts, and we have already noted that for the all-embracing Eye there is neither time nor space nor complexity." Speranskii, "O slozhnosti," *Druzheskie pis'ma G. Masal'skomu*, p. 140.

[4] We find this idea already in a sermon given by Speransky in 1791: "Think, solve, divide, combine, penetrate in the course of your whole life; be a transformer of the systems of human knowledge; withstand all the thunders of prejudice; affirm the throne of justice among men, and call yourself its first defender; but without purity of soul your hell will always be with you, it will be in your heart, your wonderful mind will only light up the abyss over which you stand." Speranskii, "Propoved' 1791—go g.", *Russkaia Starina* 109 (Febr. 1902), p. 289.

[5] Speranskii, "O vremeni," *Druzheskie pis'ma G. Masal'skomu*, p. 136.

And quite logically, Speransky rejected entirely the perceptionist epistemology of the 18th century and substituted a moral sympathy as our
source of true knowledge of the phenomena of the world. [1] Clearly,
this analysis and this conception of nature were directly derived from
his mystical religious attitude, an attitude that he had begun to elaborate very actively in the first years of his government career, following
upon the sudden death of his wife. [2] For our purposes it is important
to note Speransky's concern with the idea of unity and uniformity in
the world.

The preceding ought to have made clear that to him the world is a
unit, a harmony of variegated elements. This harmony is also quite
permanent and stable. In a short note, probably written in the early
1820's, in which he examined the epistemologies of Kant, Fichte, and
Schelling, Speransky expressed a preference for the latter two because
they overcame the dualism inherent in Kant. He also had a marked
predilection for Schelling, because for Schelling this unity and harmony
derived from stability and immutability, whereas Fichte believed in a
permanent flux. [3] However correct and exhaustive this analysis and
interpretation of the German philosophers, they clearly illustrate
Speransky's own conception and preference.

Yet, he does not think of lifeless rigidity and stability. Speransky
realizes that the world is alive. Although its fundamental principle is
unchangeable and permanent, its manifestations come into being,
develop in time and exist in space — as defined by our human
categories of space and time. [4] Speransky has wholeheartedly accepted
the basic innovation in European epistemology of the late 18th century,
i.e., the concepts of development and becoming. He quite clearly indicates the results to which he thinks an application of these principles
will lead. "He who will prove that the essence of all creatures consists
in that they open up gradually, that the development of their abilities
demands a certain and constant time, that finally this development
cannot take place otherwise than by means of personal and often bitter
experience, will have solved all moral disputes and will have opened
an entire half of man's nature." [5] Life is one of the fundamental

1 "O slozhnosti," loc. cit., p. 140.
2 El'chaninov, op. cit., pp. 119—120. For a description of Speransky's state of
mind after the death of his wife, see his letter to Karazin in M. N. Longinov,
"Graf Speranskii," Russkii Vestnik, XXIII (Oct. 1859), pp. 353—354.
3 Speranskii, "Sistema Kanta, Fikhte, Shellinga," in Pamiati, pp. 844—845.
4 "Therefrom the uninterrupted similarity and uniformity even in that which
we call diverse." Speranskii, "Dosugi — sentiabr' 1795" Druzheskie pis'ma G. Masal'-
skomu, p. 127.
5 "Dosugi," loc. cit., p. 126. Also: "Aforizmy," Pamiati, p. 852.

qualities of the basic principle of existence. And although there is really nothing new in the world — an echo of his religious pessimism — the forms in which this world can manifest itself are extremely varied. There is always plenty to study and examine in order to know and understand the world in its fundamental unity of activity. As we shall have occasion to point out, he practiced himself what he preached. His lively curiosity about nature, people, religions, ideas never faltered. For instance, his governorship of Siberia is remembered for the stimulation and support he gave to the scientific investigation of that immense region.

But the physical world in itself, however varied and worthy of our attention, is of only secondary interest to Speransky. All man's studies and investigations to discover the unifying principle of nature have as their real purpose and goal the attainment of God. For God is the first absolute cause of phenomena. That is why wisdom and true moral knowledge are an essential part in the attainment of this knowledge of God. [1] Besides the strictly religious purpose, the study of the world is also important for another reason. Being one, the world is spiritual as well as material. [2] And man is the instrument by which this spiritualisation of the world of nature takes place. "Man is the way and door through which the physical world passes to a spiritual [form]." [3] Man is a necessary part of the universe, of its unity and harmony. Therefore, to Speransky the place, character, and features of man's individual and social life are of great importance and concern too.

In the social and moral spheres, the problems are similar to those in the physical realm. It is again a matter of transcending the seeming diversity and conflicting character of human and social forms, to give man a positive role in the world. Here too the original impulse and consideration are religious, the attainment of a proper knowledge of God. But this attainment is impossible as long as the individual is alone and isolated. True, individual prayer and mystical experience are of great help in this, and Speransky does not cease to advise his friends and acquaintances to practice them. But in traditionally Russian Orthodox fashion, he does not think this sufficient. He knows that man is a social animal and even in things spiritual he is helped by intimacy and communion with fellow men. He, therefore, advises

---

1 Speranskii, "Filosofiia," *Pamiati,* p. 773.
2 "...everywhere and in all corners of the earth there is a general movement from the material to the spiritual." Speranskii, letter to S. S. Uvarov, 18 Sept. 1819 (from Irkutsk), in *Pamiati,* p. 232.
3 Speranskii, "Vremia i prostranstvo," *Pamiati,* p. 777.

performance of the ritual of religion with other faithful, go to Church, to hear mass and partake of communion with other believers. [1] Actually, society is a means only, a stage for the achievement of a higher goal which very few individuals can attain unaided and in isolation. As Speransky explains it, "The revolt against the social order comes from the fact that men have been taught to regard this social order as an ultimate aim of being and do not see anything beyond it. Society is a stage, not the culmination of the moral order. The summit is religion." [2] These reflections lead him to an examination of the origin and character of society and of the moral aspect of men's existence.

Society is not the result of convenience and the mechanical and atomistic combination and interplay of private individual interests. Society has a high moral and unifying function in counteracting the brutishness and atomization of individuals left to themselves. Incidentally, Speransky here follows quite closely in the footsteps of Fichte and German romantic philosophy, which also developed under the influence of the religious revival of the latter part of the 18th century. Outside of society, the individual is but a savage without any moral law or order. [3] Justice too is possible only in union with others, an isolated individual cannot be just, even if he is in communion with God. [4] There is a social order when two individuals freely recognize their mutual freedom and moral rights. "As soon as two persons agree among themselves to recognize one another as moral beings ... there is formed between them a social union (le lien de la vie sociale)." [5] They arrive at this recognition in order to foster their mutual liberty and moral right and to achieve the higher goal — attainment of God.

From this follows Speransky's definition of right and liberty as an essential cause and basis of society. First of all, right and liberty are not synonymous or interchangeable. Right is truly the recognition of the liberty of the other individual and the latter's recognition of one's own. Without right we would be dealing not with individuals and persons, but with brute animal beings. [6] In the second place, liberty then, is neither an absolute nor merely the absence of restraint and freedom from something or somebody. It is the subjection of an in-

1 Cf. Speranskii's letters to P. A. Slovtsov, 6 Aug. 1813 and 3 Oct. 1829, in Pamiati, pp. 46—51 and 431, respectively; see also his letter to his daughter, 21 Nov. 1816, Russkii Arkhiv, (1868), pp. 1114—1115.

2 Speranskii, "Tsel' obshchezhitiia," Pamiati, p. 828.

3 Speranskii, "O nachale obshchestv," Pamiati, p. 793.

4 "Justice is a form of truth. One cannot be just in union with God alone or in union with oneself, one can be just only in union with others." Speranskii, "O vliianii razuma i sovesti na zhelaniia i namereniia," Pamiati, p. 838.

5 "O nachale obshchestv," loc. cit., p. 789 (sic).

6 Speranskii, "Svoboda," Pamiati, p. 788 (sic).

dividual to the dictates of reason, and, thereby, the full recognition of his moral obligations. It is "the recognition of moral necessity, the victory of moral necessity over physical necessity." [1] Basically, this implies the recognition and acceptance of an individual's obligations towards God, himself, and fellow men. "Not simple freedom is given to man, but a freedom of obligation, freedom with a debt, with limits, with obligations and these obligations are as natural to man as freedom itself." [2] The "ratification" of this recognition held mutually by all men in a group is the basis of society. Speransky rejected the strictly utilitarian and atomistic approach to society and government. He refused to accept individual rights (in our usual "liberal" meaning of the term) and their guaranty as an adequate foundation for social life and as a goal of political action. [3] He applied this attitude to his analysis and proposals concerning the social structure which underlay his Plan of 1809. His was an ideal of solidarity and interaction, the rejection of the absolute "rights" of isolated individuals and the claims of private material interests; he stressed the spiritual, moral, and religious purposes and value of society. Thus Speransky was prepared to be receptive to the political ideas of a Herder, Burke, vom Stein based on the notions of social harmony and solidarity, the organic development and unity of institutions, the creative role of history and national character. [4] We have seen some illustrations of this approach in earlier discussions of his administrative reform projects. What were the theoretical foundations of his political proposals?

Speransky's interest in political questions went far back in his life. As early as his 19th year, in one of the first sermons he delivered as a student at the theological seminary in St. Petersburg, he dealt with the problem of kingship and the role of government in society. The theme for the sermon was St. Luke, Ch. 5, 10: "Fear not; from henceforth thou shalt catch men." In quaint, semi-biblical, but powerful language Speransky set forth a basically ethical and religious approach to political rule. Government rests on laws, but these laws are only the outcome of the moral needs of men, needs brought about by man's corruption through a variety of passions, vices, appetites. Political power must be exercised with this basic situation fully in view. A glorious reign, successful wars, and efficient government are of no

---

1 *Ibid.*
2 Speranskii, "Volia," *Pamiati.* p. 780; "Svoboda," *loc. cit.*, p. 830.
3 Speranskii, "Tsel' obshchezhitiia," *Pamiati*, p. 828.
4 I have attempted to trace the sources of Speransky's thought in Part 3 of my article: "The Philosophical Views of Count M. M. Speransky," *Slavonic & East Europ. Review,* XXXI, No. 77 (June 1953) pp. 446–451 *passim.*

value if the ruler neglects his major duty which is that of spiritual
guidance and if he himself does not set an example by his own moral
behavior. It is worthwile to quote the exact words of the sermon in
spite of their length:

> Even if you be a most wise ruler, if you rest your throne on the
> firmest pillars of policy, if you use your most conspicuous talents
> for the preservation of power, if you let your intelligence radiate
> to the far ends of the world, and force glory to proclaim with
> untiring fanfares your knowledge and your high talents — the
> entire world will marvel at you; but if on the throne you are not
> a human being, if your heart does not know the duties of
> humanity, if you do not value kindness and peace, if you do not
> descend from your throne to wipe the tear of the last of your
> subjects, if your knowledge will only open the path to a will for
> domination, if you use this knowledge only to gild artfully the
> chains of slavery so that they be less conspicuous to the people,
> and if you show love of the people only from behind a curtain
> of false generosity so as to deprive [your subject] of his possessions
> for the benefit of your own passions and your favorites, if you
> maintain universal ignorance so as to erase completely the idea of
> liberty, if by most devious ways you seize all the possessions of
> your subjects, if you let them feel the weight of your hand and
> convince them through fear that you are more than an [ordinary]
> human being; then, with all your talents, all the luster, you will
> be but a fortunate criminal; the flatterers will enter your name in
> golden letters on the list of most outstanding intellects, but later
> history will add with a black brush that you were the tyrant of
> your country. [1]

Speransky does certainly not disdain completely a successful reign, in
terms of wordly power and welfare — that is where laws have their
use — and it should be worked for whenever possible. But it is not the
end; it is only a means for attaining the real goal which is spiritual.
These words could be considered as a criticism of Catherine II, for her
rule, however glorious and successful in diplomatic, military, and
economic ways, was certainly not a model of spiritual purity. Whether
Speransky really intended this as a criticism, which would have been
a rather bold thing to do in the last years of Catherine's reign, we do
not know, and it is not of decisive importance, anyway. As a matter
of fact, the argument of the sermon is by far not original with
Speransky and should not surprise us, coming as it does, from the pen
of a young student in theology, doubtlessly well read in the religious
literature and polemics of previous ages, both of his own country and
of Western Europe.

[1] "Propoved' 1791—go g.," loc. cit., p. 287.

It is, however, interesting to note that like his rhetorical models from earlier centuries, Speransky did not go beyond a statement of the moral duties and character of kingship. He drew no conclusions and gave no advice as to the possible actions the subjects should take if the ruler did not conform to this high ideal. True, it would not have been very safe to do so at the height of Catherine's persecution of all manifestations of liberalism. We should also note his strong insistence on the ethical and religious side, in particular on the idea that civil society and government are but a stage on the path towards the higher realm of God. [1] Again a natural idea for a young theologian, but significant in Speransky's case as he never repudiated it and considered his own administrative and practical activities only as means for directing Russia to the achievement of spiritual and moral ends.

Upon contact with the hard facts of Russian administration in the early years of the 19th century, Speransky's ethical and religious preoccupations receded somewhat into the background, although they never quite disappeared from his consciousness. As might have been noted, in the plans and projects of reform described previously, Speransky had no opportunity for theorizing. All his energies and attention had to be focused on the practical details of administration. His theoretical framework must be inferred indirectly from the measures he advocated and the arguments he used to support them. For this task our knowledge of the philosophical and ethical framework of his thought will be of some help. The basic moral assumptions can be detected in all of his plans and papers. Thus, for instance, in a draft proposal of a reorganization of the judiciary, in 1803, Speransky wrote of the sovereign: "... this power acting on the basis of precepts grounded only in his inner conviction, in the conscience of the sovereign is nothing but the expression or application of his personal rule [of behavior]." [2] And in a short paper he read to Emperor Alexander in 1811, analyzing the factors which make for the strength of government, he put in first place the spiritual and ethical basis of all legislation. [3]

Our previous discussion of Speransky's legislative work and projects for reform must have made clear that we can not speak of his constitutionalism and "liberalism" except with qualifications. Confusion may perhaps be avoided if we recall a distinction made by O.

---

[1] *Ibid.*, pp. 289—290.

[2] V. I. Semevskii, "Iz istorii obshchestvennykh techenii v Rossii v XVIII i pervoi polovine XIX vv.," *Istoricheskoe Obozrenie,* IX, (1897), p. 270.

[3] Speranskii, "O sile pravitel'stva (chitano imperatoru 3 dek. 1811)", *Russkaia Starina,* (Dec. 1902), pp. 495—499.

Hintze. Hintze pointed out that throughout the 19th century there were two types of constitutional monarchies in Europe. The first type was based upon truly representative institutions, as in England, France (sometimes), Belgium, Holland. The other type had no representative institutions of real significance, as for example in Prussia, Austria, and to some extent, France under both Napoleons, and the German Empire after 1870. Whereas the former was the outcome of a long organic and historical evolution of the *Stände* (estates) institutions and the *Ständestaat,* the latter was a creation of enlightened despotism through the application of *Zwangherrschaft* against the power of the estates. In the latter case, the state acted as guide and leader in bringing order to a chaotic political structure and by so doing, it secured some freedoms to the individual citizen. As Hintze correctly noted, Russia had been developing in the same direction as Austria and Prussia, although the process was not allowed to reach its logical completion. [1]

To the extent that Speransky was a constitutionalist, i.e., worked to prepare Russia for a "true monarchy," he followed the pattern set by Austria, Prussia, and Bonapartist France. But even here, we should make some qualifications. For this purpose, let us examine some of the concepts underlying his three major reform plans, of 1802, 1803 and 1809. The major theme of all three projects is the establishment of fundamental, solid laws. The daily work of the government would be directed, guided by these laws. Therefore, the first and most essential concern of Speransky is to define law and its purpose. Law, or the "constitution," defined as the *corpus* of fundamental rules of government, does *not* grant liberties or license to the individual. On the contrary, it serves to limit the individual's state of nature and to establish his obligations to other individuals. [2] As society implies a living together of individuals — and we know how essential the idea of community was to his ethical theory — it is important that society establish the limits of the freedom of action of these individuals. [3] Moreover, law also serves the related purpose of preserving the security, safety, and activity of the individual from infringement by fellow citizens and the threat of external danger. [4] The former is perhaps the more important of the two, for the threat presented by individual egoism can be countered and neutralized only by means of laws and rules governing the relations

---

[1] O. Hintze, "Monarchisches Prinzip und Konstitutionelle Verfassung," *Staat und Verfassung,* pp. 349—379 *passim.*

[2] *Plan 1809,* in *Plan gosudarstvennogo preobrazovaniia grafa Speranskogo* (Moscow 1905), pp. 46—47 (note).

[3] "Pervyi politicheskii traktat," *loc. cit. Russkoe Bogatstvo,* (1907), No. 1, p. 54.

[4] *Zapiska 1803,* in *Plan gosudarstvennogo preobrazovaniia grafa Speranskogo,* p. 124.

between individual members of society. The goal of government is to bring about a state of equilibrium between egoism and law. Fortunately, the force of virtue, tending towards general benefit, helps in maintaining this equilibrium, or harmony. [1] It follows from this that instead of giving rights and privileges to the members of the group, laws only determine their relations by defining their obligations and duties. For Speransky, rights constitute that domain of an individual's life on which his obligations towards others are based. The fundamental principle governing these obligations, the basis for all government action, is the Kantian imperative, "do not do unto others what you do not wish for yourself." [2] In any case, the private interests of individuals or groups are not of great significance in determining the positive contents of laws. For egoism, and its demands, cannot become the foundation of a durable society. [3] In the first place, individual interest and benefit are concepts both too indeterminate and vague to provide a foundation for a permanent and stable organization of the group. [4] Secondly, as we have noted, egoism is destructive of society, it must be curbed, or at least balanced by virtue, which it is the task of the government to protect. But the playing off and balancing of individual interests and egoisms, with the government acting as arbiter, alone does not make for a civilized body politic; although Speransky admits that under some circumstances it may be an important part of the state's functions.

In a sense, Speransky accepts the idea of a social contract, wherein society and government are formed in answer to the needs which arise when individuals, living together, wish to safeguard their security and mutual safety from each other's state of natural freedom. Yet, in Speransky's mind, the social bond is not a contract in the 18th century sense, implying absolute guaranty of individual interests and inalienable rights. The social bond is rather the agent by which liberty is transformed into duty, and a state of nature into moral obligations, as Fichte had it. Society is expressed in the body politic, and the purpose of the government is to change anarchical freedom into duty, i.e., into a morally determined freedom. Of course, such a purpose cannot be achieved without the will of the people, the individuals who are coming together in society. In this sense, law has a foundation in the people, although Speransky does not at all say that the law has its source in the people, a rather important distinction. Society, the state, the govern-

[1] *Zapiska 1803*, pp. 128–129.
[2] *Plan 1809*, p. 46.
[3] *Zapiska 1803*, p. 129 (note).
[4] *Plan 1809*, pp. 3, 4.

ment — Speransky does not always clearly distinguish between them, which may be significant in itself — are the expression of this general moral will of the members of society. The support of this general will gives the government its material and moral strength to restrain the manifestations of unbounded egoism. [1] There is nothing truly original or profoundly liberal in this conception, in spite of the fact that Jean-Jacques Rousseau shared it also. If Speransky perhaps found in Rousseau the idea of general will (not popular sovereignty, though), he derived the moral and theological features from an ecclesiastic, religious conception of government, and from romantic political philosophers like Fichte.

More important than the formal similarity to 18th century concepts is the fact that the ideas of Speransky imply that government has a moral purpose. Every government must have an aim, a positive goal — usually moral and theological — which guides its actions and helps determine the proper system of administration. Speransky enters directly into the stream of romantic German thought when he says that this spiritual goal, which the government must help bring about, is an expression of the ethical aspirations and moral strength of the people. [2] A similar role, as we have seen, he has reserved to the state in the economic realm, in his Financial Plan of 1810. The energies of the state should be directed to protecting and promoting the spiritual aspirations of the nation, and not to securing the happiness of individuals or the satisfaction of private interests. In rejecting the concept that the government should concern itself with the interests of individual citizens, and in having the state abandon its purely passive and negative function in society ("night watchman") in order to exercise a positive role of moral leadership, Speransky dispenses with the atomistic individualism and utilitarianism of the 18th century. The notion of a natural interplay of individual interests, which eventually leads to satisfactory compromise and balance between the various interests — with the government as friendly umpire — is quite alien to Speransky. As a matter of fact, the interest of individuals as such, is of little concern to him. He is only interested in a legal safeguard of their ethical and moral independence and freedom. The integrity of the moral individual must be secured, though this may take place even under conditions of serfdom. Once the integrity of the individual is secured, the single member of the social group does not interest Speransky anymore.

1 "Pervyi politicheskii traktat," p. 67 and *Plan 1809*, pp. 4, 5.
2 "Pervyi politicheskii traktat," pp. 53—54; *Zapiska 1803*, p. 185.

The theocratic and authoritarian implications of this approach can be avoided only if very strong institutional safeguards are provided like the estates and corporations with which the feudal medieval world opposed the extreme claims of absolutism. But Speransky does not wish to foster the development of classes or groups on the basis of interest. This, he made clear in the Plan of 1809. The "class" of intermediaries, for instance, is to have no material interests in opposition to or independently from those of the people at large. Anyway, the material or economic character of the class plays an essentially subordinate role (in spite of the property qualifications for membership). It is not so much wealth that matters for membership as the individual's spiritual and moral preparation for the tasks of his class. He must belong to the spiritual élite of the people, which alone possesses full consciousness of the nation's destiny and moral needs. As the nation is an organic unit, there can be no conflict between the interests of the élite and those of the people. The state, i.e., the élite and the government, therefore, becomes the most articulate carrier of the moral and spiritual purposes of the nation. This role of carrier finds its manifestation in the legal and administrative aspects of social life. The organic character of the body politic finds its expression in the structure of the government machinery. We have noted that all laws and political institutions and the powers and functions of the state are organically bound together; they do not keep each other in balance or check, as in liberal representative regimes. Far from protecting the interests of separate groups and individuals, the government subordinates everything to the moral and spiritual aspirations of the people, the organic harmony of the nation. But it is the government again that expresses these aspirations and plays the role of active leadership in developing them and in guiding the steps of the people towards them. And who can perform this function better than the autocratic Tsar (the leading moral personality) when he is kept informed by the spiritual élite of the nation?

Quite understandably, history, historical evolution and traditions become very important features in the political and social life of the nation. After all, history and tradition indicate and illustrate best the spiritual, ethical, and religious aspirations of the people. They are the most effective safeguards of an organic evolution. [1] As government and laws are the expression of the spiritual aims of the people, they must naturally evolve and change with the general development of the spiritual and intellectual level of the people. When a lag occurs

[1] "Pervyi politicheskii traktat," pp. 54, 56; Plan 1809, p. 16.

between laws and the spiritual needs of the nation, government becomes disorganized. Such a disorganization impedes the further development of the country's spiritual potentialities. It is then, Speransky felt, that a good and clear administrative organization will help to close the gap and restore the government to its role of effective guide and teacher of the nation. [1] This argument not only justifies change (as it did in the case of the proposals contained in the Plan of 1809), but it also sets narrow limits to desirable and possible transformations. The limits of innovation should be restricted by existing traditions and historically developed institutions. Quite logically, Speransky comes very close to Burke's "right of prescription" as established by the fact of mere historical existence. The "preservative" character of this approach found illustration in the way Speransky dealt with serfdom and Russia's social structure in his Plan of 1809. He also justified some political institutions, autocracy for instance, by means of this historicist argument. And we need only remember his admonition that new laws should be introduced only if changes in the spiritual needs of the country have made them absolutely imperative. Even then, it is preferable to adapt old laws to the new situation. For a similar reason, he did not put much stock in written constitutions, for the political values and moral needs of the nation were better preserved by the spiritual development of the people.

Any satisfactory theory of politics must take a stand on the question of how a people or group can counteract and oppose the arbitrary, tyrannical, and harmful exercise of sovereign power. Following an old ecclesiastic tradition, Speransky retained a significant silence on the practical side of this aspect in his sermon of 1791. But in his more mature political papers of subsequent years he did not say much more. He never stated specifically that there might be any institutional limitation or corrective to the power of the sovereign (or government). Sovereignty, Speransky says, does not rest in the people, as some references to Rousseau might lead us to believe, but only in the monarch. True enough, the sovereign, or his agents, should not violate the fundamental laws issued by himself, or act in disregard of the nation's basic concepts of morality, religion, and spiritual tradition. But who enacts these fundamental laws, who issues them, and who directs their application? Again the absolute monarch. Aside from the pious hope that the ruler will not violate the basic values and obligations imposed on him by nature and by God, there is nothing to prevent him from changing or abolishing existing "fundamental" laws. Prac-

1 *Plan 1809*, pp. 27—28.

tically, limitation by law is only a formal one: the state should always act according to the forms of procedure it has established itself and respect the limits it has imposed on itself. But it can always revoke or alter these formal prescriptions. Another safeguard, but equally vague and not determined by any permanent institutions, is the respect for historical tradition, the spiritual development of the nation.

The only true and effective safeguard against arbitrariness and abuse of power on the part of state and ruler, in Speransky's opinion, consists in the existence of a well developed public opinion.[1] Society's opinion alone can force the government to keep within the legal forms and fundamental rules it has established itself, and to act in accordance with the spiritual needs and ideals of the nation. But from Speransky's writings, public opinion emerges as a rather vague concept, without any clear institutional contents or form. Public opinion means the people in general, in a somewhat amorphous way, not any specific group or class. Although by implication, it probably consists only of the educated and "spiritually advanced" individuals of the moral élite of the nation. Even if such "opinion" could be brought into existence under prevailing Russian conditions, in Speransky's scheme of administration it could find expression only through the Dumas. But the Dumas did not provide any way by which public opinion could compel the government to listen to its wishes or follow its advice.

True enough, one might argue, had Speransky's system of administration been put into effect and maintained by a happy succession of good rulers for, let us say, a few generations, the Dumas (i.e., public opinion) might have become a powerful enough force to restrain the government.[2] To Speransky and many of his contemporaries, England offered a living testimonial to the success of such an evolution. But they were forgetting that not only did England have an institutional framework (corporations, classes, estates), but also that her present successful state had not come about without the help of violent revolutions. Russia had no such social institutions. As to revolutions, Speransky recoiled before them in as much horror as Burke or de Maistre. But did not Speransky's reforms justly aim at creating the conditions for the development of the social framework for a responsible public opinion? Speransky himself thought so. But it was a fundamental error of his approach and bent of mind to believe that this could be done by administrative changes alone. One might even say, that his predilection for the methods of enlightened despotism, with their emphasis on

[1] *Zapiska 1803*, pp. 175—176; "Pervyi politicheskii traktat," p. 54.
[2] "Pervyi politicheskii traktat," p. 54.

the leadership role of the absolute sovereign and the pedagogical function of state bureaucracy, prevented the realization of his own long range goals.

The dissociation of means from ends may turn out to be a very serious shortcoming in a political theory. Unfortunately Speransky did not avoid this pitfall. How can the guiding hand of despotism and bureaucracy "educate" and foster that minimum of moral independence and responsibility necessary for "public opinion" to assert itself forcefully? Nothing could be more instructive than to compare Speransky's approach with the ideas of the great Prussian reformer, Freiherr vom Stein, adumbrated in a previous chapter. The Prussian also believed in the moral and pedagogical role of the state; he too felt that for this purpose the unlimited sovereign power must be the only source of administration and government: "Sec. 1. Regierung kann nur von der höchsten Gewalt ausgehen. Nur der König sei Herr, insofern diese Benennung die Polizeigewalt bezeichnet und sein Recht übe nur der aus, dem er es jedesmal überträgt." [1] Stein also realized that for this principle to be fully effective, it was essential that the king always know exactly the needs and desires of the nation: "Sec. 4. Aber damit dieses Recht und diese unumschränkte Gewalt [des Königs] das Gute wirken kann, was in ihr liegt, schien es mir notwendig, der höchsten Gewalt ein Mittel zu geben, wodurch sie die Wünsche des Volkes kennen lernen und ihren Bestimmungen Leben geben kann." [2] Unlike Speransky, however, Stein understood that such a program must have an institutional basis which, in Prussia, was to be found in the existing "estates." These "estates," local self-governing bodies, would embody a power which could put a stop to the arbitrariness of the bureaucracy and monarch. In contrast to Speransky, Stein did not hedge on this and readily extended participation in local government to all those who possessed property, regardless of their "spiritual" preparation. [3] Of course, and herein lay the advantage of the Prussian

---

[1] Stein, "Politisches Testament," *Briefwechsel, Denkschriften und Aufzeichnungen,* II, p. 583 (cited in modernized spelling from Altmann, *Ausgewählte Urkunden,* II—I, p. 62).

[2] *Ibid.,* p. 584 (in Altmann, p. 63).

[3] "Sec. 30. Auch meine Diensterfahrung überzeugt mich innig, und lebhaft von der Vortrefflichkeit zweckmässig gebildeter Stände, und ich sehe sie als ein kräftiges Mittel an, die Regierung durch die Kenntnisse und das Ansehen aller gebildeten Klassen zu verstärken, sie alle durch Überzeugung, Teilnahme und Mitwirkung bei den Nationalanlegenheiten an den Staat zu knüpfen, den Kräften der Nation eine freie Tätigkeit und eine Richtung auf das Gemeinnützige zu geben, sie vom müssigen, sinnlichen Genuss oder von leeren Hirngespinnsten der Metaphysik oder von Verfolgung bloss eigennütziger Zwecke abzulenken, die man jetzt als Äusserungen der einzelnen Männer oder der einzelnen Gesellschaften vergeblich zu erraten bemüht ist. Sec. 38. An die Stelle der Bürokratie muss nicht eine auf kümmerlichen und

reformer over the Russian State Secretary, there already were in Prussia — specially in its Western provinces — well developed estates with a tradition of social responsibility and the necessary experience for taking care of local administration. Even the nobles (*Junker*) of East Prussia had functioned as the local authority for a long time and were experienced and strong enough to take over the job from the bureaucracy. All this was not the case in Russia. However, Speransky did not seem to be aware of the problem and proposed nothing that might have served to prepare the ground for an effective public opinion. Even his economic policy put all the burden of leadership, promotion, and guidance on the government.

In his naive and shortsighted reliance on the enlightened despotism of an absolute Emperor assisted by efficient reliable servants, Speransky displayed a traditional form of Russian political psychology which saw in an autocratic Tsar the best defense against the tyranny of nobles and the abuse of private individuals. It did not come as altogether unexpected in the son of a village priest. Perhaps his rise along the bureaucratic ladder had only confirmed him in this attitude, an attitude he shared with the common people of Russia. Distrusting the nobility, and well aware of the weakness and inadequacy of the "bourgeoisie," he argued for the maintenance of autocracy as best defense against chaotic tyranny. He only wished to give the autocratic government orderly and clear forms of procedure. "The sovereign power in Russia is the autocratic Monarch, who combines in his person the legislative and executive powers and who disposes without limits of all the forces of the state. This principle has no material limitations. But it has some mental limits, established by opinion, habit, and long practice, namely that its power is brought into play only in a uniform way and according to well established forms..." [1] In truly "bureaucratic"

---

schwachen Fundamenten beruhende Herrschaft weniger Gutsbesitzer errichtet werden, sondern es kommt die Teilnahme an der Verwaltung der Provinzialangelegenheiten sämtlichen Besitzern eines bedeutenden Eigentums jeder Art damit sie alle mit gleichen Verpflichtungen und Befugnissen an den Staat gebunden sind.
Sec. 46. Die Regierung vervielfältigt die Quellen ihrer Erkenntnis von den Bedürfnissen der bürgerlichen Gesellschaft und gewinnt an Stärke in den Mitteln der Ausführung. Alle Kräfte der Nation werden in Anspruch genommen, und sinken die höheren Klassen derselben durch Weichlichkeit und Gewinnsucht, so treten die folgenden mit der verjüngten Kraft auf, erringen sich Einfluss, Ansehen, und Vermögen und erhalten das ehrwürdige Gebäude einer freien, selbständigen, unabhängigen Verfassung." Freiherr vom Stein, "Denkschrift über die zweckmässige Bildung der obersten Behörden und der Provinzial-, Finanz- und Polizei-behörden in der Preussischen Monarchie (Nassau, Juni 1807)," *Briefwechsel, Denkschriften und Aufzeichnungen*, II, pp. 219—228 *passim* (cited in modernized spelling in Altmann, *Ausgewählte Urkunden*, II—1, pp. 19—23 *passim*).
[1] *Zapiska 1803*, pp. 84—85. Also quoted in *Istoriia Pravitel'stvuiushchego Senata*, III (St. Pbg. 1911), p. 64. It is interesting to note that Speransky's description of

fashion, he turned "problems of politics into problems of administration." [1]

Speransky soon experienced himself dramatically the danger of
relying entirely on the personal qualities of the sovereign. His sudden
dismissal and exile were a telling reminder that to live under an autocracy meant to be at the mercy of the monarch. During his long exile
and retirement, he had ample opportunity to reflect on this lesson. His
return to active life gave him an opportunity to broaden his political
and administrative knowledge in an area he had slighted until then —
local administration. He came to appreciate better the importance of
local government, and he related his political analyses more closely to
the state of Russia at the time. This newly gained awareness found
expression in a series of fragmentary notes which he wrote down
between the years 1812 and 1826.

In becoming better acquainted with German romantic philosophies
during his exile, he was fascinated by their view of the organic character of the world and of nature's development. He felt that these cosmol-
ogical ideas could be applied to political societies as well. Societies and
nations go through different stages of development; like living beings,
they have a childhood, mature age, and an old age. It is essential not to
confuse these ages; "the legislator cannot and should not change this
age, but he should know it exactly and govern each according to its
own character." [2] One cannot expect a child to perform the actions of
an adult, nor should one be surprised if an old man refuses to be
treated like a child. "Each age has its advantages and its weaknesses.
One can forestall an age by means of laws, but this is highly unreason-
able, unless there are some very strong arguments for it in external
circumstances." [3] This is true of political bodies as well. And though
it may be perhaps best to preserve a society at a given "age level," it is
well nigh impossible, for everybody is part of a larger organism. This

Napoleon's "constitution" could be applied almost literally to his own: "Les prin-
cipaux traits de cette organisation sont les suivants: 1. constituer un corps dépositaire
en apparence d'un pouvoir legislatif indépendant, mais qui dans le fait soit sous
l'influence et entière dépendance du Pouvoir absolu. 2. Régler le pouvoir exécutif
sur la base d'une loi dont la lettre le rende responsable, tandis que par l'esprit de
cette même loi il se trouverait réellement indépendant. 3. Laisser au pouvoir
judiciaire toutes les prérogatives d'une liberté apparente, mais le lier par des
institutions qui le mettent à la disposition du Pouvoir absolu." (Speransky's statement
to Alexander I in 1809 — manuscript in *Repinskoe sobranie*) quoted by S. Prutchenko, *Sibirskie okrainy: oblastnye ustanovleniia, sviazannye s Sibirskim Uchrezhdeniem 1822 g. v stroe upravleniia russkogo gosudarstva*, vol. I, (St Pbg. 1899),
p. 176 (note 1).

[1] K. Mannheim, *Ideology and Utopia*, (N. Y. 1951), p. 105.
[2] Speranskii, "O vozraste obshchestv i o soobrazhenii s nim mer zakonodatel'nykh,"
*Pamiati*, p. 800.
[3] *Ibid.*

situation is further complicated by the fact that a given society, though an organic unit, may include groups of different age levels. This, of course, was especially true of Russia — as Speransky had observed in the provinces. In Russia the nobility had reached the "maturity" of Western Europe, while the peasantry was still in the "youthful stage" of a more primitive civilization. One of the aims of education and of government action is to help equalize these levels. [1] But the process of development, whether of separate social groups or of society as a whole, cannot be speeded up artificially by mechanical means. It cannot be forced upon an unprepared and unwilling population. Agreeing with the romantic thinkers of his time, Speransky believed only in a gradual transformation. The social organism should not be forced into ready-made molds. Only slow and careful efforts aiming at a spread of education and, more particularly, at a spiritual transformation of the people, can secure permanent amelioration and progress in government. [2] As in gardening, the growth of the body politic can be guided, but only on the condition that no violence is done to the natural predisposition of the "plants." Actually, government is an auxiliary in the spiritual development and education (in the broadest sense) of the people. Thus, for Russia, the question is: can the necessary moral forces be developed? [3] Speransky was certain that government and kingship should never be founded on considerations of the private interests of individuals or groups. Because "everything which we call interest (*intérêt*) is but a relative good, and all relative good is nothing else but benefit, a means towards an end, a goal." [4] He developed this idea in a letter from Tobol'sk, dated August 15, 1820: "The predominance of the nobility is harmful, the predominance of the merchants more harmful, and the predominance of the people a real tragedy," and to prevent it, one must have the rule of one man. [5] But this one ruler, the autocrat, can and should be above all private interests, for if he were to ally himself with any single interest, it would lead to its complete dominance at the expense of the people's welfare. In Speransky's view, such a misuse of the divine and

---

[1] *Ibid.*, p. 801.

[2] In Burkian manner, Speransky said: "The former [government measures] are easy but not durable, for they do not have guarantees [of prescription]. The latter [legislation] are difficult but enduring, for they are founded not on the letter [of the law] but on the living, active moral force." "Nuzhdy i zhelaniia," *Pamiati*, p. 814.

[3] "O sile pravitel'stva," *loc. cit.*, p. 496.

[4] Speranskii, "Poniatie dobra i pol'zy," *Pravoslavnyi Sobesednik*, (1889), part III, p. 564.

[5] "The confusion of sovereign right with lower rights (i.e., that of individuals and groups) is actually called despotism. It is not a special form of right but a confusion of rights, a blending of the divine with the human (*miscet divina humanae*) of the sovereign and of the subject," "Pravo verkhovnoe," *Pamiati* p. 802 — see also, *Pamiati* p. 819.

absolute character of supreme sovereignty can only lead to a disintegration of civil order. The government and the laws it administers should
have a common purpose and unity of approach. Basically this unity is
ethical: justice on the one hand, the preparation of the Russian
people for the higher goals of being on the other. "And as justice itself
is unlimited, so the power which rests on it is unlimited, otherwise it
would not be a sovereign power. It cannot be the outcome of any contract ..." [1] Laws must be over and above personal interest, never their
instrument. In a well organized state, therefore, a clear and good code
of laws is the best method for attaining the higher spiritual goal of
government.

A primary condition for Speransky's analysis was that the political
system be founded on the true historical traditions of Russia. This did
not mean that he believed in a static conservatism. Like all adherents
of the organic view, he believed in movement, in development and
progress towards a higher goal, beyond this earthly existence. He felt
that Russia's present could not serve as absolute and rigid norm or
standard. However, in seeking the correct path of development, one
should not rely on reason and intellect exclusively. Paralleling the evolution of his epistemology, Speransky came to believe that the rationalism
and atomism of the 18th century were not adequate. They were too
utilitarian and superficially mechanistic. Interests, at best, should be
used only to progress from lower relative interests to absolute higher
ones. [2] Since the guiding principle should be the unity of life and of
the universe, the standard was to be set by the living being. [3] By
separating, analysing, and dissecting, our minds are killing that which
is alive, and if we were to base our society on the product of the
deadening minds, we should have but dead things. And quite naturally,
Speransky rejects the idea of manufacturing laws. First of all, he is
quite sceptical of the abilities of a group of people to legislate for an
entire country. At best, they will legislate for their exclusive interests.
That was one of the theoretical reasons why he gave no real legislative
power to the Dumas. New legislation should not be resorted to, except
in case of absolute necessity. In particular, inventions in legislation
should not occupy the first, but the fourth place; "In the first place are
existing laws of other countries [presumably tested and hallowed by
experience and history]. One should turn to invention of new laws if
one has first proven 1. that there is no appropriate law or that it is

---

[1] "Pravo verkhovnoe," *Pamiati* p. 802, also Semevskii, "Iz istorii obshchestvennykh
techenii ...," *loc. cit.*, p. 270.
[2] "Poniatie dobra i pol'zy," *loc. cit.*, p. 565.
[3] Speranskii, "Mysli, zhelaniia, strasti, deianiia," *Pamiati,* p. 831.

inadequate, 2. that there is no custom or that it is perverted, 3. that foreign laws cannot be applied." [1] How such an approach could lead to conservatism has been seen in Speransky's treatment of serfdom. [2] And even in the case of necessary innovation, law should not be merely the artificial creation *ex nihilo* of human reason alone. It should rather be the expression of the higher norm inherent in the moral and religious character of sovereign power. "Sovereign right is distinguished from civil rights in that 1. its goal is not in itself but outside itself; it is the power established for the defense of another power [i.e., the divine], 2. that it disposes of moral forces which are not inherent in it but are given to it . . ." [3] For this reason too, Speransky, like Burke, wanted very much to preserve the concept of unlimited sovereignty, wherever it might be vested, sovereign right in a nation is the only acceptable source of new legislation if there be any need for it, because sovereign power acts in accordance with the moral foundations and spiritual aims of the people. This, a combination of group interests is incapable of doing. For Russia it means that the Tsar must be the source of all legislation. But to be effective, legislation cannot be backed by naked force alone; it must be backed by moral strength as well. Speransky was quite aware that fear is only a temporary force with which to back government measures. [4] Social life has very narrow temporal and spatial limits. It can only be a stage in preparation of a higher goal which is indicated by religion, in the same sense as man's moral life is but a "gateway" to God. For this reason, political life and governmental action should be based on the clear moral tenets of Christianity. Ultimately, then, the power of the rulers rests on the proper performance of this last mentioned moral function. We recognize again the theme of Speransky's first sermon of 1791.

We should not be surprised to find that the Holy Alliance of European sovereigns, concluded after the defeat of Napoleon, appeared to Speransky as the practical realization of his conception of the spiritual function of kingship. [5] From Velikopol'e he wrote to his friends in praise of the alliance and hailed it as the fulfillment of a long cherished

---

[1] Speranskii, "Kogda nadlezhit pristupat' k vydumkam v zakonakh," *Pamiati*, p. 805.

[2] For a later view on serfdom, cf. Speranskii, "Istoricheskoe obozrenie izmenenii v prave pozemel'noi sobstvennosti i v sostoianii krest'ian," *Sbornik IRIO*, XXX, (1881), pp. 450—460.

[3] "Pravo gosudarstvennoe," *Pamiati*, p. 855.

[4] See letter of Speransky to Count Kochubei, 20 May 1820, *Pamiati*, p. 313 and letter to A. Stolypin, 4 Dec. 1817, *Russkii Arkhiv*, (1870), pp. 1147—1148.

[5] As Meinecke has shown, a similar feeling, though for different reasons, was shared by the important political thinkers and leaders in Germany, as, for example, Stein, W. von Humboldt, Fichte. *Weltbürgertum und Nationalstaat*, pp. 164—205 *passim*.

hope. [1] To the Emperor he wrote that, as stated in the Holy Alliance, "1. the true aim of human societies is to lead men to the union in Christ, 2. Christ must be the head of Christian states"; and that the Alliance will endure if "the sovereigns will pray, read the Scriptures, be true Christians..." [2]

In the final analysis, for him — as for some Slavophile thinkers later — the primary role of government was the preservation of the ethical and spiritual values of the nation's and individual's personality. To this end he advocated rule by clearly defined laws and regulations, expressive of the natural moral law, and an organic order of political harmony firmly rooted in the country's historical traditions, under a spiritually pure Tsar, assisted by a good bureaucracy. Though in form and style, as well as in his practical suggestions for implementing his ideas, Speransky proved himself a genuine son of the Enlightenment and enlightened absolutism; his philosophic premises were clearly those of a "19th century figure." His closeness and debt to the romantic and conservative spirit of the early 19th century were unmistakable. His epistemology and metaphysics were strongly influenced by Schelling's *Naturphilosophie* and *Identitätslehre;* his ethical and social concepts bore the impress of Fichte, and in his respect for national traditions and historical evolution he stood close to Herder and Savigny. Nor did Speransky escape the religious and mystical features of "romanticism", and he treated this world merely as a stage in man's progress to the ultimate union with the divine. In his views on political economy, he adopted a physiocratic version of Adam Smith and the latter's followers, a method which had the merit of emphasising the dignity and worthiness of individual achievement as a school for

[1] "Enfin un grand trait de lumière m'éclaire et décide toutes mes incertitudes: c'est le manifeste du 25 décembre. Je puis donc me livrer à tout l'entraînement de mes idées, j'ose dire de mon inspiration, et entretenir l'Empereur sur le seul sujet digne de son attention. Malheur à moi si je me tais maintenant... Je me propose d'envoyer à l'Empereur un livre qui contient une prophétie complète du manifeste, avec des maximes étendues sur ce qu'on doit faire en vertu de cette union. Oh, union sacrée! Que toutes les bénédictions du Ciel descendent et s'attachent à toi. Longtemps ce livre (traduit en 1784 de l'allemand, un appel aux souverains de régner chrétiennement) a fait le fond de mes rêveries sur la perfectibilité des gouvernements et sur l'application de la doctrine de Notre Seigneur aux affaires publiques. Je conviens cependant, que je croyais l'époque de cette application bien éloignée... A la lecture de ce Manifeste, toutes ces idées se retracèrent dans mon esprit... je courus vite consulter mon visionnaire et le trouvant encore plus précis que je ne pensais, je me crus dès lors obligé d'en faire l'usage que j'en fis [i.e., send it to the Emperor]." Letters to F. Zeier, 31 Dec. 1815 and 11 Jan. 1816 in M. A. Korf, "Iz bumag o grafe Speranskom v dopolnenii k ego *Zhizni* izdannoi v 1861 g." *Russkii Arkhiv*, V (1867), pp. 444–453 and 453–454, respectively.

[2] Letter to Alexander I, 6 Jan. 1816, in *Sbornik materialov 1-go otdeleniia E. I. V. Kantseliarii*, II (St. Pbg. 1876), pp. 38–39.

moral education, without challenging the bureaucratic and autocratic political system.

Speransky did not become aware of the discrepancy between the ends he hoped for and the means he proposed for their realization. He was firmly convinced that enlightened despotic and bureaucratic measures could bring about the "organic" and harmonious development of a public opinion capable of restraining tyranny and promoting the nation's spiritual progress. But his merit in Russian administrative history was that he had shown the benefit which could be derived even from formal reforms and improvements in the administration. It was a lesson that future generations of administrators and statesmen did not forget; but in learning it, they also absorbed the weakness of Speransky's practical approach.

## SOURCES

Relevant primary sources are cited in the footnotes. There are almost no secondary studies on this aspect of Speransky's life and thought. What there is, is not very satisfactory, and I list it only for the sake of bibliographical completeness.

N. G. Chernyshevskii, "Russkii reformator," *Polnoe sobranie sochinenii*, VIII (St. Pbg. 1906), 292—319; M. V. Dovnar-Zapol'skii, "Politicheskie idealy M. M. Speranskogo," *Iz istorii obshchestvennykh techenii v Rossii* (Kiev 1905), 77—144; A. El'chaninov, "Mistitsizm M. M. Speranskogo," *Bogoslovskii Vestnik*, (Jan. 1906) 90—123 and (Feb. 1906) 208—245; I. V. Katetov, "Graf M. M. Speranskii kak religioznyi myslitel'," *Pravoslavnyi Sobesednik*, (1889), Part II, pp. 82—96, 264—318, 428—444, 572—625 and Part III pp. 122—152, 209—261, 412—439, 531—567. The last two mentioned articles give an exhaustive picture of Speransky's theological and religious views. N. M. Korkunov, "Politicheskie vozzreniia Speranskogo do ego znakomstva s imperatorom Aleksandrom I," *Vestnik Prava*, XXIX (Oct. 1899), 1—40; N. Poletaev, "Nekotorye dopolneniia k issledovaniiu g. Katetova o religioznoi myslitel'nosti grafa Speranskogo," *Pravoslavnyi Sobesednik*, (March 1890), No. 1, pp. 415—418; Georg Sacke, "M. M. Speranskij: Politische Ideologie und reformatorische Tätigkeit," *Jahrbücher für Geschichte Osteuropas*, IV (Breslau 1939), Heft 3/4, pp. 331—350; B. Syromiatnikov, "M. M. Speranskii kak gosudarstvennyi i politicheskii deiatel'," *Sovetskoe Gosudarstvo i Pravo*, (1940), No. 3, pp. 92—113. I have dealt at greater length with the intellectual influences on Speransky in two articles: "The Philosophical Views of Count M. M. Speransky," *The Slavonic and East European Review*, vol. XXXI, No. 77 (June 1953), pp. 437—51; "The Political Philosophy of Speranskij," *The American Slavic and East European Review*, vol. XII, No. 1, (February 1953), pp. 1—21.

# CHAPTER VIII

# GOVERNING RUSSIA'S PROVINCES

## 1. PENZA

The exile of the former State Secretary ended in late 1816 with his appointment to the governorship of Penza, one of the eastern provinces of central Russia. Speransky wished to return to active public life in order to clear himself of the accusations leveled at him before his disgrace. His new appointment appeared at first as a step in this direction. "Whatever the opinions in St. Petersburg," he wrote to his friend Masal'skii, "I am sincerely happy and completely satisfied. For the first step this is more than I had ever expected." [1] But the manner of his appointment and the refusal to grant him permission to pass through the capital on his way to Penza, strongly undermined his selfconfident optimism. He vented his feelings to Count Kochubei: "...neither vindicated nor accused, they have sent me to vindicate myself and at the same time to govern the just." [2] In truth, however, very few still believed in Speransky's guilt in 1816. His reappointment to office was therefore viewed as an indication of the Emperor's desire to deal seriously with the domestic problems that had lain neglected since the invasion of Napoleon. Many thought that Speransky was being sent first to Penza in order to obtain first-hand information on local needs and conditions.

In any case, the appointment opened up a new field of activity to Speransky. Until this time, his knowledge of and familiarity with provincial life and conditions had been most superficial. As a boy, he had known the Russian village quite well, an experience the ordinary official or governor usually lacked completely. But in his mature and

---

[1] Letter to Masal'skii, 6 Sept. 1816, in *Druzheskie pis'ma k Masal'skomu*, p. 87.
[2] Letter to Count V. Kochubei, 21 September 1818, *Russkaia Starina*, 111 (1902), p. 52.

active years his contacts with local administration had been indirect, only through the official papers that came to the Chancery of the Senate or to the Ministry of the Interior. As State Secretary, his concern with provincial matters had been purely theoretical and strictly from the point of view of the central administration. And during his exile, as we have noted, he had lived in relative isolation without entering into the life of the provinces where he resided.

Provincial life, however, was a world apart from that of either St. Petersburg or Moscow. The conditions and way of life of the serfs, the most numerous class of the population, are known well enough from the descriptions of numerous contemporary writers and publicists. The daily routine of the small landlord has been admirably sketched by S. Aksakov, Gogol, and Turgenev. But the political conditions under which the governor and local administration had to work have not inspired the descriptive powers of *littérateurs,* and therefore need some explanation.

While intellectual, artistic, social, and even political interests dominated life in St. Petersburg and Moscow, the countryside continued in its century-old sleep. Compared to the brilliance and elegance of the two capitals, the provinces seemed bleak and dismal indeed. On the local level, Peter the Great's revolutionary reign had brought about a double cleavage: culturally between the peasantry and the nobility, politically between the noble landlords and the bureaucracy (in spite of the common origin of these two groups). Peter's reforms were not welcomed with any enthusiasm by the provincial nobility. The average nobleman was very reluctant to go to St. Petersburg to serve in the modern armies, navies, and administration of the Reformer. After the death of Peter, the provincial nobility strove to liberate itself from the duties and obligations he had imposed. The majority of the provincial nobles looked upon military and state service, and in particular on the educational requirements for it, as a burdensome duty to be avoided.[1] Their striving found additional stimulus in the rule of foreigners and personal favorites under Empresses Anne and Elizabeth. In these reigns, state service was fraught with danger and insecurity while its rewards were often quite small, as everything tended to go to only a few favorites. Throughout the 18th century the nobles fought

---

[1] I wish to emphasize that I am speaking only of the nobility who lived on their estates in the provinces. The description is not at all applicable to the nobility that lived and served in the capitals. When a nobleman left for the capital to take up service, he usually broke with his former group and became a part of the city bureaucracy and military aristocracy.

for their "liberties," i.e. freedom from compulsory state service. They succeeded in 1762, and Catherine II had to ratify this "emancipation" by the Charter to the Nobility of 1785. As a result, the Russian provincial nobility was reluctant to assume administrative duties on behalf of the government. Beyond the preservation of its freedom from compulsory service and unquestioned mastery over the peasants, the nobility had no social or political interests. The nobles were quite satisfied with the *status quo* and did not wish to exert themselves further for the benefit of either state or province.

The central government thus gained the impression that the local nobility could not be counted upon in the performance of administrative tasks. It therefore preferred to deal with all problems through the regular bureaucracy or special agents. The small number of officials, though, stood in the way of the creation of an effective bureaucratic machinery for provincial government. And so the paradoxical situation arose that the provincial nobility did not develop the habit of taking care of local affairs, while the central administration could not provide the countryside with an adequate corps of officials. In these circumstances the government took action only when the need had become crying; it acted by fits and starts, with little sense of continuity and responsibility. In "normal times" the disadvantages of the system were not felt too keenly, as important problems were pretty rare, and things went their routine way. But they became tragically obvious during the Pugachev Revolt. The rebellion threw the fear of doom into the hearts of the Russian serf-owner and brought home to Catherine II the need of transforming the local administration to prevent a similar recurrence.

The government's efforts in this direction culminated in the Statute on the Provinces (*guberniia*) of 1775. This law aimed at putting the management of local affairs into the hands of the local nobility, under the general supervision — but not direct interference — of the personal representative of the monarch. The Province (*guberniia*) was headed by a governor (or in some cases, a lieutenant of the sovereign or a governor general) representing the monarch, who supervised and controlled the proper functioning of the judiciary, fiscal, and police aspects of administration. The governor was responsible to and in direct communication with the Senate, whose decisions and orders he transmitted and supervised. The actual management of local affairs rested in the hands of various officers elected by the body of noble landowners. It was Catherine's hope and intention that the system would increase the nobility's participation in the administration of the

Empire as well as develop a greater sense of responsibility and purposeful activity in those nobles who resided permanently on their estates. The central authorities would then be relieved of many details and strictly local problems. The noblemen elected to local offices might also exert a stimulating and progressive influence on the life of the countryside (as the *zemstvos* did eventually).

The expectations raised by the Act of 1775 foundered on two reefs: the indolence and distrustful apathy of the lower nobility and the highhanded, tyrannical habits of the appointed officials. It had been somewhat naive and rash on Catherine's part to assume that the nobility which had fought government service for almost a century, would change its outlook overnight. But even had there been more willing cooperation on the part of local serf-owners, they lacked the education, training, and traditions for the performance of the tasks set them by the statute of 1775. Perhaps cooperation and competence could have been developed slowly over several generations, but what was to be done in the meantime? The Governor (and other high officials appointed by the Crown) was usually either a career bureaucrat, who had risen in the ranks of the central administration, or a military figure. Both types were accustomed to seeing precise orders issued and blindly obeyed throughout the Empire. They were not used to take into account the desires and suggestions of outsiders. Moreover, the Governor came invested with the personal confidence of the monarch; corresponding directly with the sovereign, he by-passed the Senate and — after 1802 — the ministries. Under such conditions, the Governor's power naturally became much greater than had been intended. Faced by the apathy, lack of tradition and experience, and the personal rivalries of the nobles, the representative of the autocratic monarch brushed aside the "local elements" and imposed his own will; in fact governed according to his own notions.

Even in those cases when the nobility mustered enough courage, found a leader (usually some retired dignitary or magnate), and opposed the Governor, it had little chance of winning the contest for power. The Russian monarchs were rarely sympathetic to the noblemen in the provinces. They scorned the cultural backwardness of the average landowner, while preserving a lingering distrust of his political and social views. As a rule, the provincial nobility had no direct access to the ear of the Emperor, as did the governors. The latter could always bring the matter to the monarch's attention in such a manner as would justify his position and prejudice the sovereign against his *administrés*.

At the beginning of the 19th century, therefore, provincial life was culturally drab, socially backward, and politically passive, quite at the mercy of the misrule and despotism of the local bureaucracy. We have no evidence pertaining directly to the province of Penza which Speransky was called to administer for almost two years. But the picture there was undoubtedly not essentially different from that in any other province of the European part of the Empire. [1]

The nobility of the central provinces of Russia was composed of two groups. First there were the very wealthy estate owners, usually former high court dignitaries, retired government officials, or military commanders who spent their last years in the country on their estates. Some of these "magnates" lived in truly regal manner: their mansions were small palaces, servants, and hangers-on numbered into the hundreds; frequently they had a private theater or opera company (staffed by serfs and directed by a foreigner); numerous visitors came and went throughout the year, some of the guests staying for weeks, months, or even years; lavish receptions, balls, hunting parties attracted the nobility from the entire district or province. Even though in most cases these magnates neglected to participate in local affairs, they wielded a great deal of influence in the provincial assembly of the nobility. Elected marshal of the nobility, such a magnate could at times even challenge the local governor, mainly on the strength of his former connections at court. Such an instance was, therefore, rather a conflict between court parties than a struggle between the forces of local self-government and the central authorities. In the remote province of Penza, however, there were no magnates, as they preferred to live near Moscow where they could spend the winter months.

The second group, on the other hand, was well represented in Penza. It consisted of the descendants of the old rank and file service nobility, the local "squires" who had reluctantly accepted the reforms of Peter the Great, but then had striven for their "freedom." Their political and social outlook was limited to the maintenance of their unchallenged mastery over the serfs. Their wealth was relatively modest, all of it in land, of course; and their prosperity and comfort depended entirely on the yields of serf labor. [2] These nobles lived on their

---

[1] For a good picture of Russian provincial life at the beginning of the 19th century see N. F. Dubrovin, "Russkaia zhizn' v nachale XIX v.," *Russkaia Starina*, vols. 96—99, (Dec. 1898—Aug. 1899) *passim*.

[2] Although Penza bordered on the Urals, the local nobility did not engage or participate in state-sponsored industrial and commercial enterprises like the Demidovs and Stroganovs farther East. Nor were there any owners of large estates, run along capitalist lines, with their own factories, such as were beginning to appear in the Ukraine.

estates and left their district as rarely as possible. If forced to take up service, they usually went into the army, and, retiring at the first opportunity, they returned to their estates. European education and enlightenment had not penetrated very far into their midst, and at times had by-passed them almost completely. Whatever education or knowledge they possessed, they had learned from the local priest or some poor devil of a private tutor — the latter more often than not a lowly uneducated foreigner whom fate had thrown into Russia and who took to tutoring for want of a better profession. Interest in education, wherever it existed, was very limited and entirely pragmatic. Noblemen only cared to know the minimum required for a commission in the army. They whiled away the long winter evenings by reading the Almanach and cheap sentimental novels. In many houses, the reading matter consisted only of a few old religious books and chance copies of journals several decades old. Although the nobles' social and economic security depended on agriculture, they made little effort to apply themselves towards an improvement of their economic knowledge or managerial skills. They rarely put to use the new developments in agriculture which were reported in the serious journals and books of the period (and which men like A. Samborskii had popularized among the nobility of the capital). They were not particularly interested in political events, quite satisfied when they knew the names of the ruling emperor and present governor. Of course, Napoleon's invasion of Russia had shaken them from their lethargy for a while; but no sooner had Napoleon been expelled from Mother Russia, than they fell back into their apathetic half-slumber, to the great disgust and indignation of the young officers who had participated in the campaigns of Germany and France. Returning to live on their family estates, these young officers — some of whom later joined various secret societies — tried to shake their neighbors from their lethargy, but with little success.

The limited education and simple psychology of the average nobleman in remote provinces like Penza rarely put complicated schemes or complex ideas into his head. He did not try to overcome his own indolence or his peasant's passive resistance to any change. As a result, his interests and activities centered almost entirely on comfortable (though by no means very luxurious) living, as defined in terms of gargantuan meals, long naps, hunting, visiting, and entertaining. Of course some "squires" had to participate in local affairs, in the assemblies of the nobility, at the elections of the marshals and Land Captains (*ispravnik*). One might have expected that in the exercise of these functions, the nobleman would shake off his usual passivity, for these were matters that affected his own personal and class interests. This was what Catherine II had expected. It would have been a significant contribution to the development of a self-reliant, active, educated and experienced nobility whose services would be of use in the capital of the Empire as well as in the provinces. But, as pointed out, these hopes did not materialize. Many local nobles were so poorly educated as to be ineligible for any office. Many others were too poor to afford the expenses connected with active participation in provincial assemblies and public affairs. Their very poverty put them at the mercy of rich magnates whose clients they became. Personal jealousies, petty rivalries for prestige, and lack of political experience rent the yearly provincial assemblies of the nobility. Magnates formed factions, and their clients deepened and perpetuated the discord. Sometimes petty squabbles ended in open fights, so that the governor had to intervene to secure a proper election of candidates to office. Naturally, such interventions — either at his own initiative or at the request of the nobility itself — enhanced the governor's power. As the governor could also refuse his approval to the assembly's choice of a marshal, his influence outweighed by far that of the nobility's.

The governor's importance grew still more in the reign of Alexander I who usually appointed his personal friends, and who recalled them to the capital after a relatively short period. Expectation of the governor's future influence in St. Petersburg tended to make him still stronger, more powerful, and "autocratic" during his stay in the province. Experience also soon taught that in case of conflict between the governor and the provincial marshal of the nobility, Alexander I invariably supported the governor as more trustworthy. In addition the bureaucratic machinery was entirely under the governor's control. Little wonder that he was well nigh an unlimited ruler; and in some cases, alas not too infrequent, the governor tyrannized the province for a long time without being called to account.

The assembly of the nobility, the marshal, the Land Captains, and the local judges were reduced to the role of mere executors of the orders and regulations issued by St. Petersburg or the governor. Such a subordinate and "menial" role was particularly characteristic of the office of the *ispravnik* (Land Captain), the local police and executive officer. As early as 1803 Speransky had asked: "In what way can a *zemskii ispravnik* [chosen] among the poor nobles, for a piece of bread — and with assistance of men like himself — bring about respect of and compliance with the law in an area of five or six hundred miles?" [1] On the shoulders of this unsuitable individual rested many different matters and the responsibility for the entire district, sometimes a very large one at that. The temptation to use this position for personal advantage was very great indeed, and all too often the *ispravnik* did not resist it. On the other hand, his responsibilities put him at the mercy of the caprices and demands of the governor and other superior officials. And while the position of marshal of the nobility might have some attraction as a source of social prestige, the duties of an *ispravnik* or of a local judge were merely burdensome impositions. They did not attract anyone but the least qualified and worst elements of the local nobility. Doing more harm than good, the *ispravniks* could not provide the necessary firm foundation for an efficient and orderly administration. Speransky recognized this clearly and set it as the first task for the reformer of local administration.

For an honest man who sincerely desired to establish an efficient and beneficient administration, the task of provincial governor was a very arduous one indeed. He could not count on the help and support of local society — i.e. the nobility. But, if the "elected" officials were woefully incompetent and inadequate, the situation was not much better in regard to the regular bureaucracy which staffed the numerous offices of the provincial and district capitals. The governor himself had but a handful of responsible officials to assist him in his daily work; even to these he could not delegate much authority or rely on their initiative. The majority of the officials were ignorant, timorous clerks without either the power or the ability to take decisions. The circumstances of these clerks on whose honesty, efficiency, and energy depended the good running of the administration were simply appalling. The salaries were so low that the poor devils had barely enough to eat and could not afford adequate clothing; on days of bad weather, only half of an office staff might show up for work, as there was but one pair of boots for every two clerks. Unmarried copyists slept in the rooms in wich they worked, for they could not afford regular lodgings. Drunkenness was the most common remedy for drowning the humiliations of such an existence. Under such conditions, the clerks were only too willing to accept bribes and gifts. Venality started at the lowest rung where it weighed most heavily on those who needed the protection of the government most. These vices, in addition to their inadequate education and training, made it impossible to entrust to the ordinary

[1] Quoted in A. Fateev, "Speranskii — gubernator Sibiri," *Zapiski Russkogo Nauchno-Issledovatel'nogo ob'edineniia v Prage*, vol. XI, No. 82, (Prague 1942), p. 120. See also the almost identical words in Speranskii, "Zamechaniia o gubernskikh uchrezhdeniiakh," *Arkhiv istor. i statist. svedenii*, (1859), No. 4, pp. 100–101.

officials, important or responsible tasks. They could only copy papers and file reports. As a result, the governor had to do almost everything himself, while at the same time he himself was weighted down with a welter of useless paper work.

There was very little a well-intentioned governor could hope to accomplish in improving these conditions appreciably. At most, he could try to get things to run smoothly, to clear up the backlog of matters submitted for his decision or pending in lower courts. He could see to it that his subordinates committed no flagrant abuses. Lastly, if allowed to stay in the province long enough, he might inspire confidence and sympathy to the local nobility and thereby obtain their willing cooperation. Speransky decided to devote himself to this limited program of "small deeds" after he had taken stock of the situation.

Sending his daughter to St. Petersburg to complete her education unter the supervision of his old friend, Mrs. Weickardt (Mrs. Stephens, his mother-in-law, having died not long before), Speransky set out alone to his new post. Though most of them proved superfluous, friendly suggestions were not slow in reaching the new governor from former colleagues and acquaintances. Remembering that his disgrace in 1812 had — at least in part — been due to the nobility's opposition to some of his measures, his friends impressed upon him the necessity of gaining the favorable disposition of the local nobility. But Speransky himself was well aware of this; he intended to do everything in his power to make his administration a complete success. Not only did he wish to confer the benefits of good government on the province entrusted to his care, he also wanted to create a good impression in St. Petersburg. After all, his major goal was still to obtain permission to return to the capital.

Once again his tact and ability to get along with people stood him in good stead. At first, the local authorities and nobility received him rather coldly and without hiding their distrust. The nobles in particular were afraid that he might favor the peasantry at their expense. But Speransky was tactful, cautious, patient, and took great pains to avoid head-on clashes with any group or individual. Fortunately, he found valuable help and alliance in the influential Stolypin family, the father and brothers of his old-time friend, Senator A. A. Stolypin. Very soon after his arrival Speransky had the opportunity to prove that he was not unmindful of the interests of the nobles and that he would not suffer violence or lawlessness, whatever their reasons or source. In imitation of serfs in a neighboring province, peasants of an outlying district of Penza had rebelled against their lords. Speransky did not hesitate to use military force to quell the uprising and to punish the offenders according to all the rigors of the law. To the local land-owners it was evident proof that the new governor would preserve their property rights secure and safe. A short time later, Speransky himself became a local land and serf owner by acquiring an estate. From that time on, his solidarity with the landowning nobility became a matter of personal interest, as he himself admitted in a letter to Stolypin "... for to tell the truth I defend no less daringly than others my Khanenevka [his newly acquired estate], that is 30,000 rubles of revenue, everything I have and shall be able to have." [1]

But this did not mean that he was going to tolerate abuses on the part of the nobility either. In all cases where the landlords exceeded their authority or rights, he took energetic action. This strict justice, this dispassionate adherence to the law, made him very popular, and he became the best liked and most respected governor the province of Penza ever had had. In the words of a contemporary, "Ce qu'il a fait dans ce gouvernement doit être marqué au coin de la justice et de la prudence, vu la manière dont il a capté l'opinion générale de toutes les classes. C'est la première fois que je vois produire cet effet par un homme en place... Monsieur Speransky a été un des premiers à agir de rigueur et par là il s'est fait adorer de la noblesse." [2]

His tenure of office in Penza was not marked by any dramatic events or important changes. He fulfilled the routine obligations of his posi-tion quietly, honestly, and efficiently. This was the only outstanding and somewhat unusual feature of his governorship. From the point of view of his personal career and the development of his political think-ing, the period in Penza is interesting only in that it was his first direct contact with the problems of administration on the local level. This experience did not significantly modify his basic conceptions, but it mitigated the exclusively centralistic and somewhat doctrinaire orien-tation of his earlier thinking.

The governor's principal accomplishment was to restore order to the chaotic state of current affairs. Speransky endeavored, and with success, to wipe out the arrears in the financial obligations of the province and to clear away the backlog in the calendar of the courts. At the time of his arrival, the province owed 1.5 million rubles in tax arrears to the Treasury. Within a short time, the figure was brought

---

1 Letter to Stolypin, 2 May 1818, *Russkii Arkhiv* (1869), p. 1698.
2 Quoted by Fateev, "Speranskii — gubernator Sibiri," *loc. cit.*, p. 129 (the letter is from 1817).

down to 200,000, and when Speransky left Penza, the books had been balanced. This he accomplished without any changes in the fiscal system or in the methods of collection. His authority did not go that far. He merely streamlined the fiscal administration, held all officials to strict account, and he supervised carefully and constantly the tax collectors' performance of their duties. The courts were in still worse state, perhaps. The number of prescriptions of the Senate that were left unfulfilled, the number of cases pending in the courts was staggering. Speransky applied all his energy, his capacity for long sustained work, and his ability to organize the work of others to break this logjam. He made repeated inspection tours; and in each town or city he stayed as long as was necessary for all cases to be settled and all regulations put into application. Spurred on by the personal presence of the governor, and helped by his experience and opinions in more difficult cases, the judges brought their task to a speedy conclusion. Only then did Speransky move to the next town.

His greatest difficulty — a difficulty that lay at the bottom of most abuses and mismanagement — was the absence of adequately trained and honest officials. Speransky soon became convinced that no matter how good the laws or the administrative system, nothing would come of them as long as the bureaucratic personnel remained unsatisfactory. This applied both to the regular functionaries and to the elected officials. In Speransky's opinion, the importance of the officials elected by the local nobles was directly proportional to the honesty and efficiency of the governor and the other officials appointed from St. Petersburg. Under an honest and efficient governor, the marshal of the nobility stuck to his duties and was prevented from using his position for illicit purposes; the land captains were supervised effectively and held to account for their actions. But in the absence of good governors and officials, the elected officers were left to their own devices; and as the majority was neither well educated nor very conscientious, the administration deteriorated and led to abuses.

The first task, Speransky felt, was to educate the nobility to a proper awareness of its social and political duties. This in turn would contribute to the development of a "public opinion" which in due course of time might provide a firm guarantee of legality and orderly administration. As we see, Speransky's ideas had not changed since the time he wrote his projects of reform; only now he was more cautious and, wisened by his direct experience with provincial society, he paid more attention to the human side of things. The difficulty of local administration, he wrote to Count Kochubei, still is that "it is difficult to convince [men] that institutions, even the best, can run by themselves; on the contrary, everything is expected from men and the distrust of the new institutions is nothing else than fear for the manner of their execution." Many years would pass, Speransky added, until Russia's provincial society would be educated enough to give spiritual welfare the same due it gave today to physical comfort. [1]

To develop a responsible and enlightened public opinion had been Speransky's wish ever since he had begun to think and write on the subject of government. He was convinced of its importance and need now more than ever. But the very same experience which confirmed him in his basic belief also showed that there was little hope for its realization in the near future. Consequently he grew still more distrustful of any representative body endowed with legislative powers, even for purely local needs. This conclusion explains his reaction to the Emperor's famous Warsaw speech of 1818 in which Alexander I vaguely hinted at his desire to see in Russia a *Sejm* like that of Poland. The Emperor's words were generally interpreted to mean that Russia would soon receive a real constitution; the rumor spread throughout the country, arousing fear and panic among serf-owners (who viewed it as a prelude to emancipation) and hope in the hearts of the "liberal" officers, aristocrats, and intelligentsia of the capitals. In a long and very interesting letter to his old friend, A. Stolypin, Speransky reported on the rumors and then commented on his own reaction. First of all, he wrote, the rumor of a constitution had spread a dangerous mood of panic in the countryside. If the educated and informed nobleman has interpreted Alexander's words as a promise of emancipation, it is easy to imagine the effect they must have had on the illiterate and dull serfs. A false hope, quickly dispelled by the facts, might lead easily to dangerous consequences, e.g. rebellions. To counteract the panic, the government should establish a committee (the eternal bureaucrat!) to study the problem and formulate recommendations. To demonstrate that the country's true conditions would not be left out of sight, several provincial governors (including himself?) should be appointed to the committee in an advisory capacity. Later still, invitations might also be extended to a few marshals of the nobility. In any case, the first task was to improve the administration by bureaucratic means. Once this was done, one could think of constitutional laws and even of civic liberty, i.e. emancipation. As Speransky put it, "Who sweeps the staircase from below? Épurez la partie administrative. Venez ensuite à établir les lois constitutionnelles, c'est à dire la *liberté politique* et puis

[1] Letter to Kochubei, 1 October 1818 from Penza, in *Pamiati*, pp. 491–492.

ensuite et graduellement vous viendrez à la question de la *liberté civile,* c'est à dire la liberté des paysans. Voilà le véritable ordre des choses." Such a program would take at least 10 to 20 years. [1]

In the meantime, in the absence of a responsible public opinion, the best course was to recruit as many honest and competent officials as possible. But where and how? The best men from among the nobility did not stay in the provinces but went to the capitals where their chances for promotion and success were so much better. Only the misfits, or the incompetent, condemned to remain minor clerks for all their life, stayed in the provinces. A partial solution might be to bring into the administration members of other classes. The so-called middle class, the merchants, was too small and its members were extremely reluctant to enter government service. Many merchants, especially among local traders, were Old Believers and therefore labored under some legal limitations. The prosperous merchant was the most conservative individual in Russia at the time and felt (as had his forebears in Muscovy) that it was not his God-ordained function to participate in the governing of men. As for the small merchant or craftsman, his status was almost that of the peasant; he could not afford to give his children an adequate education, so that they could never expect to rise very high in the bureaucratic hierarchy.

Speransky therefore cast his eyes in another direction, to the class from which he himself had come, the sons of the clergy. As governor, he took a lively interest in the theological seminary of Penza and supported the most promising students in whatever way he could. The following episode reported by one of the students at the Penza seminary, illustrates Speransky's concern. Along with a few other youngsters, the narrator was sent to Penza to finish his training at the local seminary. They arrived at the provincial capital (from their home villages) rather late in the evening. After registering with the local police, they decided to stay overnight at an inn, for they did not want to rouse the seminary authorities so late. The next morning, upon waking, they were told that a constable was waiting to take them to the Governor's residence. The young lads were quite frightened, but had no other choice than to obey the summons. The constable could not tell why they were being summoned to the Governor and treated them — out of habit — like individuals suspected of a crime. Trembling with fear and full of apprehension, they reached the Governor's office. They were greatly surprised, indeed, when the Governor received them most cordially,

---

[1] Letter to Stolypin, 2 May 1818, *Russkii Arkhiv,* (1869), pp. 1697–1703 (French sentences in the original).

inquired about their past studies, their families, their interests, needs, and desires. After a pleasant and very friendly conversation, Speransky gave them some expense money and had them driven to the seminary in his own carriage. As long as they remained at the seminary, Speransky regularly inquired about their progress and welfare; occasionally he invited them to his house, and eventually offered them entry to government service. Some of them, including the narrator of the story, accepted the offer and stayed as Speransky's loyal assistants. [1]

As might have been expected, Speransky was on friendly and close terms with the Bishop of Penza, Aaron. In the Bishop, the Governor found an intelligent and educated prelate with whom he could discuss the theological and philosophical problems which, as we know, interested him deeply. After he had completed the initial task of putting the provincial administration into good working order, philosophical and theological studies and dissussions took the uppermost place in Speransky's daily occupations. They helped to break the dreary routine of public life and to avoid unnecessary social functions. Apart from the personal and intellectual reasons, Speransky was in close contact with the Bishop also because of his concern for the local ecclesiastical institutions, like the seminary, the cathedral church, and the like. As governor, Speransky took the lead in organizing local branches of the Bible Society, an activity which had the enthusiastic support of the Emperor and of the Minister for Religious and School Affairs, Prince A. N. Golitsyn. Many contemporaries and subsequent historians have condemned Speransky's participation in a movement which became, it is true, closely connected with political reaction and cultural obscurantism. [2] Speransky was accused of hypocrisy and flattery, for his work on behalf of the Bible Society was viewed merely as a device for winning the good graces of Alexander. Such an opinion, however, does injustice to Speransky, for it ignores completely the sincerity and intensity of his own religious preoccupations along similar lines. We know that all aspects of religious experience and striving for a deeper and purer Christian way of life were always present in his mind. They constituted, so to speak, the permanent substratum of his spiritual and intellectual make-up. His own religious outlook stressed the importance of close familiarity with the Scriptures. The stated purpose of the Bible Society was to spread knowledge of the Scriptures; it therefore

1 Troitskii, "Speranskii v Penze," *Russkaia Starina*, 112 (1902), pp. 342—344.
2 Letter of Prince P. A. Viazemskii to Alexander Turgenev, 4 April 1819 from Warsaw: "...but this interlude in Penza and Bible circles have dragged into the crowd this man [i.e. Speranskii] whom I would have liked to see as giant." *Ostaf'evskii Arkhiv kniazei Viazemskikh*, I (St. Pbg. 1899), p. 212.

coincided with Speransky's own feelings. Of course, there is no denying that in many instances unscrupulous careerists used the establishment of branches of the Bible Society as means for gaining imperial favor. And the zealots of the Society did often work for the supression of science, learning, and philosophy, as witness the notorious activities of Runich and Magnitskii. But this was certainly not the case of Speransky in Penza.

The practical problems Speransky had to solve every day led him to reflect on the ways and means of improving the provincial administration and for resolving the most vital social question, serfdom. Traces of his thinking about these questions are found in his letters to Kochubei. Especially revealing are the letters he wrote à propos Balashev's scheme of Lieutenancies in 1818. In principle Speransky approved of Balashev's plan, but only as a starting point which might eventually lead to a general reorganization of the government. His newly gained insight into local conditions led Speransky to advocate that reorganization should be started on the level of provincial administration, and not at the top. But he still did not abandon his trust in the advantage of working though well trained officials, bureaucratic committees, rather than elective representative assemblies. To Kochubei he repeated his opposition to a representative assembly or council that would have to work out a new system of administration. Appealing to the authority of Montesquieu, he warned that representative assemblies are good only for consultation, to find out the opinions and wishes of the people. This was the role he had proposed in his Plan of 1809 for the various Dumas. But to be truly constructive, a reform should be prepared in secret, by the highest central authorities with the assistance of expert provincial administrators. [1] For the time being, Speransky limited himself to criticizing Balashev's plan and did not recommend his own solution. Not until he had gained additional experience in Siberia, did Speransky develop fully his proposals for a reform of the local government of the Empire. Let us therefore postpone until then a fuller discussion of the ideas and suggestions contained in his letters to Count Kochubei.

Speransky's duties as governor of a pre-eminently agrarian province, and his personal concern as a landowner, served to revive his interest in agriculture. We find him exchanging ideas and information with his old correspondent and adviser on agricultural questions, Poltoratskii. "I too," he writes, "preach here the idea of crop rotation

---

[1] Letter to Kochubei, 21 September 1818, *Russkii Arkhiv*, 111 (1902), pp. 51—54. Also quoted in Fateev, "Speranskii — gubernator Sibiri," *loc. cit.*, pp. 137—138.

and even think of introducing it next summer in my own village, which has no woods but is blessed with fertile fields."[1] Nor did he neglect his intellectual development, for as must have become apparent, Speransky was an eternal student, always learning, seeking new information, broadening his knowledge and deepening his understanding of the first principles of things. In his spare time at Penza, he completed the translation of St. Thomas à Kempis' *Imitatio Christi* and had it published with the help of government subsidy. To understand German idealistic philosophy better and to help his daugther in her own literary studies, he decided to learn German. In the process of learning the language he became well acquainted with its literature and quite fond of some of its writers, especially of Schiller, his preferred poet. To achieve fluency in the language more rapidly, Speransky withdrew to his study literally for several weeks, refused to have any contact with people except for the absolute minimum necessary in his official capacity. When he left Penza, Speransky could read fluently the most abstruse German authors and by the time he returned to St. Petersburg, he possessed a speaking knowledge of the language as well. Nor were his old favorites, the ancient classics, forgotten by him. For instance, when his appointment to the Governor Generalship of Siberia reached him, he was engrossed in his beloved pastime, reading Homer in Greek. [2]

In spite of what might appear to have been a rewarding period, Speransky came to feel that he had exhausted his usefulness to the province of Penza. His task had been to restore efficiency and orderliness in the routine of administrative business. He had accomplished this task and yearned to return to more active participation in the central government. In particular, he wished to resume his previous work at giving stable and clear laws as a foundation of a thorough reorganization of the political life of the Empire. He was still ambitious for an appointment to the Senate as a member of the Commission on Laws. As his petitions and requests for this appointment, transmitted by friends and wellwishers in St. Petersburg, did not produce any results, Speransky applied for a leave to attend to his personal affairs in the capital. He hoped to accomplish his purpose by pushing the matter in person. Should this fail too, he wrote to his daughter, he would resign from government service altogether and retire to his estate in the Penza province. Whether or not this was an empty threat

[1] Letter to D. M. Poltoratskii, 12 March 1818 from Penza, *Russkaia Starina*, 111 (1902), pp. 50—51.
[2] On this, see the remarks scattered in his letters to his daughter (*Russkii Arkhiv* 1869 and in *Pamiati*).

which he did not intend to carry out, we do not know for sure. There is strong indication that this was the case. Anyway, he had no opportunity of putting his threat to the test.

Alexander I, for reasons known only to himself, was as yet not willing to see Speransky back at court. A convenient pretext offered itself to keep the governor of Penza a while longer away from the capital. Siberia was in a dreadful state of disorganization and someone with energy and ability was needed to put things in order. It had become quite clear that only a thoroughgoing reorganization of Siberia's administration could put an end to the perennial difficulties and problems of that vast territory. But first a survey of Siberia's needs had to be made; a concrete and detailed plan of reform could then be drawn up on the basis of the findings. Speransky was a natural choice for such an important and complex task. Without answering Speransky's request for a leave, the Emperor appointed him Governor General of Siberia in March 1819. Speransky submitted grudgingly to what, he felt, was a new mark of imperial disfavor and a prolongation of his exile. He was also quite saddened at the thought that he would not see his beloved daughter for a few more years.

In quite a despondent mood he set out on his journey eastward, accompanied by the regrets and good wishes of the inhabitants of Penza whom he had governed so well for almost two years.

## 2. SIBERIA BEFORE THE COMING OF SPERANSKY

For a century and a half after the beginning of Russian penetration and settlement, Siberia had remained a peripheral and quite neglected area of the Empire. At first, the central authorities had seen in it only a source of valuable furs and later, as a convenient place of exile for obstreperous peasants and officials. Little was known of the vast subcontinent and even less was cared about it by either the government or the people. As a result, there was no clear or consistent policy toward it and the local administration was left to shift for itself, without much guidance or much interference from Moscow or St. Petersburg. As long as the local governors managed to send an adequate quantity of furs, they were left alone by the central authorities. Endowed with wide powers, not easily controlled at such distance, without any clear instructions and rules of procedure, the Siberian governors were truly satraps. Only the government's practice of replacing them at frequent intervals prevented them from becoming quasi-independent rulers. Every announcement of a new governor's appointment was joyfully greeted by the Siberian population in the expectation of a better administration. But it did not take long ere the new governor followed in the footsteps of his predecessors. It was the path of least resistance, and it was advised by the subordinate officials on the spot. The desire to get rich quickly was an added reason. To secure as good a treatment as possible and to carry on their own activities undisturbed, the Russian settlers bribed the newly appointed governor and put him in a false position from the very start. Not long after his arrival, the new governor behaved no better than his predecessors, and the Siberians were again wistfully yearning for the next change in administration. Bribery, corruption, arbitrary rule, and ruthless exploitation of the people were the endemic traits of all those who held authority in Siberia.

From time to time, St. Petersburg made half-hearted efforts at improving the situation and at rectifying abuses. But nothing came of it, for, as Speransky correctly noted, distance and difficult communications gave the Governor security from direct supervision, control, and immediate prosecution. At the same time, the absence of clearly defined laws, norms and institutional safeguards, left to his discretion not only a wide range of concerns but also the manner of implementing the policy the government or himself had decided upon. Considering Siberia part and parcel of Russia, Catherine II extended the law of 1775 on provinces to the subcontinent. The region's conditions and needs were quite different from those of European Russia, however, and a mechanical application of the statute was not likely to yield good results. The need for effective supervisory control was not satisfied and no stable and clear rules of procedure were established. Nor could the local gentry act as a brake on the Governor, for Siberia had no nobility and no other social class could take its place readily.

While the character of Siberia's administration remained pretty constant throughout the entire 18th century, deepening the disorder, gradual transformations were taking shape in the economic and social realms. And more important still, both the government and the people were beginning to see Siberia's role and potentialities in a different light. It was becoming increasingly evident that Siberia could offer more than a few valuable pelts, and that it could be more than the forced residence of criminals or undesirable individuals. [1]

The scientific explorations of geographers, ethnographers, and mission-

---

[1] Incidentally, Siberia as *the* land of exile dates only from the middle and second half of the 19th century. But even then the total number of individuals exiled to Siberia was much smaller by far than the yearly migration — legal or extra legal — of peasants, artisans, merchants, etc.

aries on the one hand, and the physiocratic belief in the primary value of agriculture and trade, on the other, combined to produce a more positive evaluation of the region's economic possibilities. As furs were no more of major economic importance, Siberia began to be thought of as a mining center, a granary, and a cattle ranch. From the reign of Catherine II, the Russian government took various steps to promote trade and agriculture. Agricultural migration and settlement were planned, but the projects failed because of the incompetence of the officials and the defects of the administration. The authorities in Siberia were not ready for the task the central government wished to set them. The territory was not surveyed; agicultural techniques were poorly known, and local administrators used the money and implements sent from Europe to line their own pockets instead of helping the establishment of prosperous farmers. Trade, however, was successfully promoted by the abolition of various internal customs dues, the bettering of relations with China, as well as a general relaxation of guild restrictions.

Parallel to these changes, Siberia's native populations were also undergoing a transformation in their way of life. The transformation was perhaps less profound at first sight, but in the final analysis, it was of great importance to the future of Siberia.

At first, in the 17th century, the Russian government had tried to force its agents to leave the natives alone, provided tribute in form of pelts was delivered regularly. The local officials, however, desirous to make their own fortunes, collected the tribute (iasak) quite ruthlessly, and oppressed the natives. As a result, many of the smaller tribes of trappers had moved away to less easily accessible districts in the North and Northeast. The more advanced populations, however, were slowly being drawn into the orbit of Russian administrative requirements and civilization. Since the reign of Peter I, the natives had been more and more frequently employed for various government services, such as providing postal relays or doing guard duty on the border. These services were sometimes quite onerous and destructive of the original ways of life of the natives, and also led to a change in their outlook. Some of the tribes, the Buriats for instance, were becoming more and more interested in agriculture. The reasons for this change were principally that: they had less land than before for extensive cattle raising, and at the same time there was a greater need for foodstuffs, both for themselves (to feed those engaged in government service) and for sale to the numerous Russian soldiers, officials and merchants. The Buriats were among the first to engage in agriculture successfully, and some other tribes followed suit.

As a result, some of the smaller and more backward tribes, isolated and subjected to disease and periodic famines, were dying out, or at any rate, rapidly decreasing in numbers. This decline made for administrative and fiscal difficulties, as their tribute had to be reassessed and measures taken for their protection. The more advanced tribes, on the other hand, seemed to prosper economically, but their traditional way of life was changing. Their old customs, legal norms, and traditions did not correspond any more to the new emerging reality. And as both the tribal and Russian administrations were still operating on the basis of the old ways, there resulted a discrepancy which made for difficulties and confusion. The new activities of the natives required greater consideration and regard for their interests. To insure success in their novel ways, they had to be protected against the rapacity, exactions, and arbitrary rule of the local administration.

The change in the natives' way of life was leading to a social transformation, particularly noticeable and fraught with important consequences among those natives who had settled and taken up agriculture. This social transformation consisted primarily in the breakdown of the old clan system and the development of a class differentiation on the basis of economic activity and wealth. The old customs determining property and family relations were breaking down. The more successful settled native, working his land and selling his own surplus, did not want to be tied to his poorer or nomadic fellow clansmen; he also wished to be able to transmit the fruits of his labors to his own children. Changes in the economic and social position of a tribe's members led to a transformation of their outlook and brought them closer to Russian values, interests, and culture. They aspired — at least within their tribe — to the privileges, status, and security enjoyed by the better among the Russians (officials and merchants). As frequently these successful native individuals belonged to the upper class of the clan, to the "aristocracy" (and some had acquired titles and wealth in the service of the Russian administration), they demanded a corresponding say in the management of tribal affairs. In the hope of drawing the natives into the mainstream of Siberian life and of promoting uniformity, the Russian administration was not unwilling to support their demands. But naturally, it raised new problems and provoked the resistance and discontent of the other members of the clan. Not much could be expected in the way of a satisfactory readjustment to these new conditions until the Siberian administration itself was reorganized.

By 1800, it had become imperative to adjust the pattern of Siberian administration to the changed conditions, in regard to both the Russian and native populations.

A serious effort at solving these accumulated problems was made in the first decade of the 19th century. In 1805, Ivan Borisovich Pestel (father of the Decembrist leader) was appointed Governor General of Siberia and his devoted assistant, N. I. Treskin, Civil Governor at Irkutsk. For the next 14 years the two were almost unchallenged masters of Siberia. Working closely together, Treskin on the spot and Pestel in St. Petersburg, they tried to reshape Siberia according to their own views and lights. Their names have become almost bywords for arbitrary rule, inhuman cruelty, and ruthless exploitation; and it is difficult to obtain a balanced picture of their activity. But there was much more to it than the persecutions and cruelties invariably mentioned in connection with Pestel's and Treskin's names. Our records do not give a full characterization and motivation of their policy with absolute confidence and completeness. But a few important basic features do emerge from the documents. They are an essential background for a proper understanding of the aims and actions of Speransky. [1]

Pestel and Treskin, quite able and energetic in their own ways, followed in the traditions of the 18th century police state. Without much imagination, they had absorbed the intellectual and political fashions prevailing in their younger days. It was a blending of physiocratic economic theories with ruthlessly strict militaristic despotic methods. The necessity of developing agriculture occupied first place among their social policies. Treskin, a native of Siberia, was absolutely convinced that the future of the region lay in the expansion of its agricultural potential. He applied all his administrative ability and great energy to the promotion of this end. By various means, both direct and indirect, he fostered and protected farming and spread it to areas where it had not been practiced before. Following up attempts made before his time, he settled Russian peasants along Lake Baikal. Through generous awards of titles, rewards and decorations, he encouraged the Buriats to take up farming as a basic occupation. He followed up his encouragement by loaning them money and implements, giving them technical advice, and easing their tax burden.

To stimulate the peasant's incentive, Treskin took measures to give a greater return to the farmer on his crop: he had the state stores buy up the grain offered by the peasants at advantageous prices; to this

---

[1] The names of Pestel and Treskin can be used undifferentiatedly, as both stood for the same policies. Pestel pushed them and protected Treskin from St. Petersburg, whereas Treskin suggested and implemented them on the spot.

same end he used his right to license direct export of grain to China and to contract grain purchases for military uses and distribution to needy nomads across the border. To assist in the development of agriculture, Pestel and Treskin built roads, protected the highways, improved navigation on the rivers, and re-zoned the trading areas of the major towns. Treskin's tireless and constant supervision, which sometimes went to extremes (for instance his personal inspections of private shops, stalls, and taverns in Irkutsk), helped to bring some law, order, and security to Siberia.

The growing of grain and other agricultural produce was only one side of Siberia's economic development, though. The farmer's products had to be marketed; they had to be distributed over a large area, for not all parts of Siberia were equally suited to agriculture. Siberia also served for the transit of merchandise to and from China and Inner Asia (Mongolia, Thibet), and the peasant's products were of value both as an exchange commodity and for the upkeep of the merchants. Finally, the comparatively large number of soldiers, officials and officers who resided in remote areas unsuitable for farming and far from the main economic centers, had to be fed and supplied. Thus the marketing and distribution functions had to be developed also. Naturally, this function had been performed by the traders. But even more so than the merchant in European Russia, the Siberian trader was - economically speaking - highly conservative, nay reactionary, and extremely inefficient. He was afraid of competition and operated primarily on the basis of specially granted privileges which made it possible for him to establish his monopolistic control over the buying and selling markets. He had no regard for the need of the region and cared little for developing the local economy. As he was the only means by which any producer, be he Russian or native, could market his output and purchase the necessary manufactured goods, the merchant in fact "owned" the local inhabitant. But more nefarious yet, the Siberian merchant stifled the growth of the region's economic potential because of his extortionist practices and his conservative methods of operation.

Pestel and Treskin decided not to put up with this state of affairs any longer, and aimed at a transformation of Siberia's economic structure. They followed two approaches which to them seemed complementary, though they appear mutually exclusive to us. On the one hand, they promoted free trade and active competition, so as to break the monopolistic hold of old-established merchants. To this end, internal tariffs and customs were abolished throughout Siberia; special or exclusive privileges were refused to the prominent merchants; grain trade with

China was liberalized by lowering export requirements. But free competition could not be effectively secured in Siberia right away, because there was a great dearth of capital, and no group could readily be found to challenge the older merchants. No one, that is, except the state. So that, on the other hand, the two governors used the administration to break the merchant monopolies. The government entered into the trade of agricultural products directly through the state granaries. State stores and state granaries had been established long before Pestel and Treskin; they supplied the troops and officials. But at the end of the 18th century the stores were usually kept filled by levying taxes in kind on the population and — most important — by sub-contracting grain deliveries with merchants. Pestel and Treskin reduced the private contracts and favored direct purchase from the peasants by government agents. To hit the merchant monopolies more effectively, these direct purchases were made on generous terms, the government paying directly in cash (whereas the merchant often paid by lending money or giving goods in exchange). A similar policy was adopted to supply the state distilleries. It was not always cheapest for the government, but Treskin thought that the state ought to shoulder the extra cost for the sake of fostering freer trade and more competition.

Without entering into the question whether this policy was desirable from the point of view of economic theory, it can be argued that it had some merit and did recommend itself under Siberian conditions of the time. Sooner or later, the state would have had to take a hand in breaking the monopolies, as the *Ancien Régime* had done in France and on the Continent. The major difficulty with Treskin's and Pestel's course was their method. Not only did they believe in state participation and guidance of economic activity, they also implemented their belief in the worst traditions of despotism and bureaucratic tyranny. In a sense, Pestel and Treskin were disciples of Paul I; they had some good intentions, but negated them by their absolute disregard of the means by which they could be achieved. We have referred to Treskin's minute supervision of the details of town trade. Another example is provided by his decision to rebuild Irkutsk and some other towns. The towns were truly in need of improvement, but Treskin proceeded by evicting inhabitants at short notice, by razing buildings and erecting new structures with impressed labor from the local population, and covered the cost of the work by levying extra taxes. Obviously, these methods created much resentment. Adding insult to injury, Treskin ferociously repressed any sign of discontent by an effective police terror. His subordinates followed his example with equal severity and ruthlessness. But as they were open to bribery and corruption (which Treskin himself apparently was not), the administration's ordinances became a source of further oppression and exploitation of the population without the benefit of the policy ever manifesting itself. Those who could not buy themselves off, had to face persecution, expulsion, banishment, etc. Paternalistic police control was the order of the day; only the accidents of personalities determined the extent of its tyranny and hardship.

While the smaller people, the peasants and natives, often welcomed the new regime as it meant relief from the pressure of the merchants, the latter protested. They correctly saw in Treskin's policy a threat to their economic position and a challenge to their growing social and civic importance. But they were not, as yet, in a position to oppose Pestel and Treskin effectively. The governors were able to prevent their forming a united front by playing off one monopoly interest against the other, enlisting the help of the less prosperous against the big tycoons. The latter were isolated as a group. Some individuals tried to raise their voices in protest. But Treskin's counter-attack was swift and ruthlessly effective. Some of the most prominent merchants were arbitrarily exiled to remote parts of Siberia where they ended their days. Others were ruined by long and costly law suits, numerous fines, and onerous services which the administration imposed on them. The ruthless arbitrariness of these persecutions was in the "best" Siberian traditions. This time, however, it was not taken with the same fatalistic submission as in the past. Eventually, some merchants worked up enough courage and delegated someone to present their grievances to Alexander I. The envoy reached St. Petersburg (by a circuitous route to elude Treskin's agents) and through him the central government learned something of the extent of the abuses, exactions, and terror visited by Pestel and Treskin on Siberia.

Alexander I and his ministers were ready to act favorably on the complaints of the merchants and "crack down" on Treskin and Pestel, because by this time opposition to the Siberian administration had found powerful support in the Ministry of Finance. Indeed, while they welcomed Pestel's and Treskin's aim of fostering free trade and free competition, the agents of the Ministry of Finance could not approve of the administration's purchases of grain and supplies at prices higher than it had paid in the past or that prevailed in the open market. Furthermore, the fiscal authorities, who followed Adam Smith rather than the physiocrats, felt that the government should abstain as much as possible from directing the economy. The Ministry of Finance was convinced that left alone, the merchants would develop more competition once the old-time privileges were withdrawn. The agents of the Ministry had the impression, not entirely incorrect as we have seen, that the governors were replacing the monopolies of some merchants with the monopoly of the state in alliance with some other traders. In any case, the policies of the Siberian administration were not benefiting the treasury and their advantage to the population was felt to be questionable, to say the least. The Ministry's misgivings, though it had been kept from the Emperor for a long time, could not be hidden any longer; and coming into the open after 1815, contributed to the government's withdrawing its support from Pestel and Treskin.

The accumulation of complaints and growing dissatisfaction in Siberia, along with the questioning of the premises of Pestel's policies led the government to a close examination of Siberian affairs in preparation of a thorough reform. Such an examination, though, could not be conducted from a distance, without direct acquaintance with the actual circumstances prevailing in Siberia. For this reason Alexander I decided to send a reliable and expert administrator to Siberia and chose Speransky for the task. He knew that the latter would not only untangle the existing disorder, but also make valuable suggestions for a complete overhauling of the system by which Siberia had been governed for at least a century.

### 3. SPERANSKY IN SIBERIA

The task of Speransky was not an easy one. The Emperor defined it in the following words:

> I have already had repeated evidence that short term inspections rarely attain their aim; in particular, one is even less justified in expecting their success in such a remote and vast region. This is why I consider it most useful to give you the title of Governor General and to entrust you, as the chief of the region, with all the rights and powers pertaining to this position, and with a survey of the province's condition. On the basis of these powers, you will correct everything that can be corrected, you will uncover the persons who are given to abuses, you will put on trial whomever necessary. But your most important occupation should be to determine on the spot the most useful principles for the organization and administration of this remote region. After you have put on paper a plan for such a reorganization, you will bring it to me personally, to St. Petersburg, so that I have the means

of learning from you orally the true condition of this important region and of basing on solid foundations its wellbeing for future times. [1]

This assignment, in the Emperor's opinion, an opinion based on his acquaintance with Speransky's speed and efficiency, should not take more than one to two years.

Speransky, as we know, was not very happy about this new assignment. He therefore was in haste to finish his survey of Siberia, untangle the administrative confusion, correct the abuses, and punish the guilty. As soon as he decently could, he reported the termination of his mission and impatiently waited for the Imperial command to return to St. Petersburg. One has the feeling that his activity in Siberia was marked by a sort of febrility, by an unwillingness to get at the bottom of each particular situation. But to satisfy his own scientific curiosity and as if to make up for his lack of thoroughness, Speransky was determined to see as much as possible with his own eyes. He spent most of his time inspecting Siberia, traveling to the remotest corners of the territory, to places where no previous governor had ever set foot.

Well aware that Pestel's and Treskin's misrule had been possible only because of the cooperation and complicity of the local authorities, Speransky selected his own private chancery. It included some of his old time assistants like Zeier; others, like Troitskii, he took along from Penza and also had young men who were taking their first steps in government service under his careful direction (Wil'de, Weickardt). Finally, he persuaded a few young officials whom he met during his travels through Siberia to join his personal staff. Among these was Captain of Engineers Batenkov, the future Decembrist, who by virtue of his ability, energy, and first-hand knowledge of Siberia, became Speransky's right-hand man.

The fear instilled by a decade of Pestel's and Treskin's arbitrary and cruel rule made the Siberian population wonder whether they could rely on Speransky as a protector and true righter of wrongs. At first, people were afraid to present their petitions and complaints publicly in the towns. Speransky related that petitioners stopped his carriage in the middle of forests, where they had hidden to await his passage, and presented their complaints in secret from local authorities. In some cases fear of the local official equalled or even exceeded that of the dreaded Emperor, Paul I. The story is told that when Speransky publicly demoted and arrested one of the worst local officials, Loskutov, an old

[1] Alexander I to Speranskii, letter dated 22 March 1819, cited in N. K. Shil'der, *Imperator Aleksandr Pervyi*, IV, p. 149.

man could not refrain from shouting to Speransky: *"Batiushka,* what are you doing? Don't you know that this is Loskutov?"

The first and most urgent task was to dismiss and turn over to the courts the officials who had abused their power, plundered the treasury, and persecuted the population. As he had done in Penza, Speransky traveled from one administrative and judiciary center to another, staying in each until all officials had been investigated, the guilty ones removed, and the backlog of the court's calendar cleared up. Speransky had the power to bring to account the lesser officials directly. He also could suspend vice-governors, as he did in the case of the vice-governor of Tomsk. But the top officials, those most responsible for Siberia's condition, like Pestel and Treskin themselves, could be tried only by the Senate. There their cases remained under consideration for a long time, way beyond the period of Speransky's stay in Siberia. And at the end, the defendants obtained the mitigation of the accusation and suffered but the slightest punishment. The computation made by Vagin — the chronicler of Speransky's activities in Siberia — gives an idea of the limits of the governor general's action and shows that more than one good administrator was needed to reform the territory. In all, 681 were charged with various misdeeds; of these only 43 received various degrees of severe punishments, while 375 were vindicated, and the balance got off with slight disciplinary action.

The great difficulty was that while practically every official in Siberia was guilty in some way or other according to the letter of the law, Speransky could do little about it, for there was no one to replace him. Thus the smaller fry went scot free. The lack of adequately trained and honest officials was even more glaring than in European Russia, while at the same time the remedy was more difficult to find. Siberia had no gentry that could — potentially at least — be tapped to replenish the ranks of government service. While "public opinion" was weak in European Russia, it was completely absent in Siberia. There was not even a potential source for it, as education was as sadly lacking as orderly administration. [1] But what about the other classes, could they not provide candidates for both government service and "public opinion"? Unfortunately not, Speransky felt. The peasants, though free, were out of question for fear of the repercussion their participation in public life might have in Russia proper. Furthermore, the peasants were scattered over vast territories and were highly uneducated. The clergy was very

---

[1] "In Siberia there has not been, and there is not now a public opinion; and for a long time yet there will not be any because of the lack of a nobility." Speranskii, *Obozrenie glavnykh osnovanii mestnogo upravleniia Sibiri* (St. Pbg. 1841), p. 13.

small and even less influential than in Europe. There remained
the merchant class, the so-called middle class. But Speransky, as most
observers of his time, was unfavorably impressed by the Siberian merchant group (with some individual exceptions, of course). Their backward economic and social attitudes and the unsavory character of their
business practices had not — for the time being at least, Speransky
thought — qualified them for leadership or even membership among the
spiritual élite of the population.

The second problem was the need for more education and enlightenment in Siberia; it was an absolutely essential prerequisite for building
up local leadership. Speransky turned his attention to the intellectual
and spiritual needs of the province. As in Penza, he established branches
of the Bible Society to which he invited representatives of other local
religions, in particular the Buddhist lamas. He seems to have had hopes
of bringing all the creeds together and of making them play an active
part in the moral and spiritual education of the people. He therefore
viewed favorably the selfless efforts of the English missionaries who
had settled among the Mongols beyond Lake Baikal. [1] Speransky also
devoted much time and thought to the education of the Russian settlers. As the need for schools was extremely great and the facilities quite
limited, he established many Lancaster schools of mutual instruction
right away without waiting for the full development of a regular school
system. In this domain he had the devoted assistance of P. Slovtsov, a
former classmate of his at Alexandro-Nevskii seminary, and now inspec-
tor of schools at Irkutsk. Slovtsov, one of the early Siberian regionalists
(oblastnik), helped Speransky to put Siberia's education on a firm basis.

Speransky was one of the first governors of Siberia to take an active
interest in furthering the scientific knowledge of the region. He seriously endeavored to obtain correct statistical data on which to base his
administrative regulations and fiscal policy. The diary he kept during
his journeys through Siberia reflects his personal interests in this respect.
It is curiously barren of all political matters, but there are daily entries
on the climate, atmospheric pressure and vegetation. He was the first
governor who went to Nerchinsk and inspected the local mines (noting
the appalling conditions which prevailed there, he recommended that
the mines be transferred to the jurisdiction of the civilian authorities).

[1] On the activities of the English missionaries see in particular Vagin, *Istoricheskie
svedeniia o deiatel'nosti grafa M. M. Speranskogo v Sibiri s 1819 po 1822 g.* (St.
Pbg. 1872) I, pp. 280—284, 721—726; Bogdanov, *Ocherk istorii buriat-mongol'skogo
naroda* (Verkhneudinsk 1926), pp. 162 ff; B. Laufer, *Ocherk mongol'skoi literatury*
(Leningrad 1927), pp. 78, 90—91; for a contemporary description and appreciation
see A. Martos, *Pis'mo o Vostochnoi Sibiri 1823—1824* (Moscow 1827), pp. 67—71.

He aided expeditions to explore the region by all the means at his disposal. In reward for his efforts on behalf of science, the Academy of Sciences elected him to honorary membership. [1] Assisted by Batenkov, Speransky initiated the proper surveying and exploring of the Iakutsk province, which until his time had been a neglected part of Siberia.

For reasons of intellectual and scientific curiosity, as well as political and administrative grounds, Speransky was very much interested in the natives. He studied — from the material available to him — their social, political, and religious customs. He also was much concerned to establish good personal relations with their chieftains. He invited them to his receptions on an equal basis with the Russians and visited their encampments and festivities. His interest and concern for them earned him a good name among the natives. It also permitted him to secure some immediate benefits to the Empire, as he was able to persuade some Kirghiz tribes on the border to recognize the overlordship of Russia during the interval between the death and election of their khans. In this manner, at no financial or military cost to Russia, he spread the Tsar's influence over a very appreciable territory which later became a springboard for further Russian expansion into Central Asia.

The studies, explorations, and observations he made of Siberia, convinced Speransky that the real wealth of the territory had been barely touched and was still largely unknown. He suspected that the eastern sections of the country were harboring great mineral and agricultural resources which only awaited exploitation. He tried to stimulate and channel the spirit of enterprise of the Siberian merchants in this direction, but met with little response. He helped to organize a trading company for Iakutiia (with the help of his friend and admirer, the merchant Basnin). But except for a couple of trips, nothing came of the venture. Speransky's and Basnin's enthusiasm was not shared by others and Iakutiia had to wait for the discovery of gold within its borders before it became of interest to the Russians. Speransky wanted also to give more variety to Siberia's limited trade with neighboring areas. He believed that Russia's desiny was to open up the Chinese market. At the time, Russian trade with China was conducted only at the border post of Kiakhta and was quite limited and one-sided. The Russians were mainly interested in Chinese tea (and a few costly silk textiles). The Chinese in turn, were taking very few Russian goods, as they cared mostly for manufactured products which the Russian could not supply. Therefore, with the exception of the tea trade, Kiakhta held importance

---

[1] Letter to Count S. S. Uvarov, 17 September 1819 from Irkutsk, *Russkaia Starina* 113 (March 1903), p. 444.

only for Siberia proper. Speransky thought that even before Russia had developed her own industries she could play the role of middleman between Western manufacturers and China. He therefore suggested that the import duties on tea be refunded when the tea was re-exported to Western markets. This would permit Russian merchants to invest the proceeds of tea sales abroad in purchases of Western machinery for export to China. He was impressed by the fact that China had 200 million people with whom Russia could trade directly across a single border. [1]

Along the same lines he showed great interest in the Russian possessions on the Pacific Ocean. He envisaged a great future for them and believed that they could play a very important part in Siberian life. Siberia was still deficient in foodstuffs; agriculture was very primitive and its yield quite unreliable because of the harsh climate and lack of proper techniques. Transportation difficulties made for exorbitantly high prices on all goods brought from European Russia. Access to the interior of Siberia was much easier from the Pacific by way of the river system. Speransky therefore wanted to make the coastal area into a center for the distribution of foodstuffs and other articles to the interior regions of Siberia. He thought that the Russian colonies in America, especially California, would become the source for foodstuffs and other products to be consumed in Siberia. He pointed out these facts and possibilities to Zavalishin —the future Decembrist — as the latter took leave from him in Irkutsk on his journey to California for the Russia-American Company. Hoping to include Russian America into the economic domain of Siberia, Speransky actively supported the Russian-American Company. In drafting the regulations for the administration of the coastal areas, he suggested that the Company be given a say in the nomination and supervision of the local officials. In this connection it might be of interest to note that Speransky was quite wary of the Americans, especially of the whalers and traders in the Northern Pacific. He feared that their energy, spirit of enterprise, and better commercial and organizational talents would create unfair competition for the Russians. He did not object to Americans carrying on trade on the high seas between Manila and Okhotsk, for instance. But he feared that if American whalers were permitted to establish stations on the coast or islands of the Sea of Okhotsk, they would eventually settle permanently, extend their influence, and threaten Russian control over Eastern Siberia. Speransky gives the impression that his distrust and fear of America was motivated by the feeling that Russian institutions

[1] Letter to Count Gur'ev, May 1820, in *Pamiati*, pp. 321—323.

and organization were no match for the Americans. In a more limited way, he displayed the same attitude toward English traders. [1]

A distinguishing trait of Speransky's administration of Siberia was its humanity and mildness. It was such a contrast to the traditional pattern that it left a greater impression on the administrative practices than might have been supposed. Speransky mainly acted on the consciences of his subordinates and of the people. His mild treatment of the guilty and particularly his willingness to accept at its face value any change of heart might be ascribed to his meek and soft personality. But in fact — whether by design or not — his method had quite a lasting effect. His tactful and considerate treatment of the people entrusted to his administrative care gave the more prominent citizens of Siberia the courage and even the habit of coming to him for advice and of supplying the Governor General with much needed and interesting information. Contrasted to the rigid aloofness of former governors and to the fear inspired by Treskin, Speransky's manner was a revolution in itself. No more did the Siberians fear being asked to the Governor's residence. This attitude permitted the administration to obtain valuable data directly; the governor no longer needed to rely exclusively on the spotty and dry reports of unreliable and easily bribed subordinate officials.

Speransky also endeavored to bring the administration and the population closer together by increasing their social contacts. He believed that this was especially important in Siberia where, in the absence of a nobility, other social classes should be given a chance of becoming a leadership group by establishing closer intellectual and social contact with the administration. The administration might use this opportunity to impress upon the leading inhabitants the desirability of more education and more civic consciousness. To bring about this kind of rapprochement between the authorities and society, Speransky organized and encouraged social gatherings at his residence. Although himself a retiring person who shunned social occasions, in Siberia he abandoned his usual reserve somewhat. He was effectively helped by his assistants, for the most part younger, gay, and outgoing persons who could make a success of any party and gathering. And as some of his aides, like Batenkov for instance, were themselves of Siberian origin, they had a good understanding of the local population. The winters Speransky spent in Irkutsk were later remembered for their particularly exciting, novel and lively social life. The example set by Speransky and his sub-

[1] See Speranskii's letters to Count Kochubei, 29 September 1820, from Tobol'sk, *Pamiati,* p. 501 and to Count Gur'ev, 2 October 1820, *ibid.,* p. 485.

ordinates was not forgotten. In a sense, though on a much smaller scale, Speransky's role in forming a Siberian society can be compared to Peter the Great's a century earlier in European Russia.

As a result of his travels across the width and breadth of Siberia, his close contacts with the inhabitants, Speransky came to change his opinion about the region very radically. He had come to Siberia with the stereotype picture of a backward, cold, dreary, and unpromising country, fit to be only a penal colony, deprived of any serious economic and social value to Russia. The first impressions confirmed the stereotype image, Siberia was a colony, and not a very rich or nice one at that. In his first letters from Siberia he complained of the drabness and unfriendliness of the region. He detected no natural beauties and no human values. But travelling extensively, Speransky was struck by Siberia's variety in respect to the natural, climatic, economic, and human environment. In the South, it was almost Persian; in the Southeast it was not far from being completely Chinese. And while the North and Northeast remained unfriendly, cold, and not very inviting, the Central districts held out great promise of becoming rich agricultural centers. The people too were not as hopeless as he had thought at first. True, they were not as yet ready to play even a limited role in the government of the territory. But they were a hard-working, patient, and resolute people, with great potentialities. It was not true that Siberia was populated only with convicts and former convicts. As a matter of fact, Speransky found that the convicts and their descendents were but a tiny fraction of the population. Not more than 2000 persons a year came to Siberia on penal servitude. If Siberia would only be opened up to the good elements of the Russian peasantry, if the local inhabitants would be taken care of by an honest and efficient administration, the future of Siberia could look very bright and promising. Far from being a colony, an appendage of Russia, Siberia would become part and parcel — and not the least useful or the poorest at that — of the Russian Empire.

To bring this about, a proper political, administrative, legal, and social framework had to be created first. This was his most important task. He reflected on it all the time he was in Siberia, and upon his return to St. Petersburg in 1822, he was ready with specific recommendations of reform. These recommendations were discussed and adopted without major opposition or qualifications by the Committee on Siberian Affairs and by Emperor Alexander I. Speransky's suggestions received legislative implementation in the statutes of 1822. They were the most important and durable contribution of his short governorship.

They justified Count Uvarov's saying that the history of Siberia could be divided into two periods, before and after Speransky.

### 4. REORGANIZING SIBERIA

The reformed administration which was set up in 1822 remained — without many appreciable changes — the basis of Siberia's political, social, and economic life down to the end of the Imperial regime in 1917. The reform was spelled out in ten statutes which Speransky and his assistants drafted in 1821-1822. The statutes (PSZ Nos. 29,124 — 29,134) comprising a total of 3,027 paragraphs, filling pp. 342 to 565 of Volume 38 of the *Complete Collection of the Laws of the Russian Empire,* concerned themselves with a great variety of topics and many details of Siberian administration. It would therefore be quite impossible, and not very rewarding, to summarize them fully. As our task is the political and intellectual biography of their main author, it will be sufficient to discuss briefly the main features of the new administration, mention the statutes' chief contributions to the economic development of the region, and finally analyze the principal traits of the administrative status of the natives.

In Speransky's own opinion, his first and most pressing task was to set up the administration of Siberia in such a way that in the future it would not fall easy prey to a governor's abusive or capricious exercise of power. A contemporary characterized the main intent of the reorganization quite correctly, despite a touch of sentimental rhetoric: "To eliminate arbitrariness, to establish the rule of law, to improve the judiciary, insure the safety of everyone, to develop trade and agriculture. In a word, make Siberia completely happy." [1] In the opinion of Speransky and of his assistants, the role of the administration was to foster the economic and political conditions which were necessary for the social and moral maturation of the people. This was a much more pressing need in remote and backward Siberia than in European Russia.

The administrative reform of 1822 was based on the following general principles: 1. to transform the personal power of officials into a power vested in institutions; 2. to strengthen the task of supervision of local officials by vesting it into one central organization, and to compensate for the remoteness of Siberia from St. Petersburg and for the absence of a mature public opinion; 3. to bring order into the

[1] I. Kalashnikov, "Zapiski irkutskogo zhitelia," *Russkaia Starina*, 123 (September 1905), p. 248.

confused relations between various administrative bodies; 4 to give the local institutions an organic unity and latitude for autonomous action without constant reference to central authorities; 5. to adapt the administration more closely to local circumstances and conditions; 6. to simplify and clarify the mode of operation of this machinery. [1] They illustrate an important advance made by Speransky over his own past policies and attitudes. They showed his awareness of the need of seriously taking local conditions into consideration: a legislation devised for one type of society cannot be applied mechanically to another. Speransky's historical and philosophical studies no doubt contributed in helping him to gain this awareness.

Inspired perhaps by Balashev's scheme of Lieutenancies (1818), and desirous to combine unity of policy with some independence of action from far away St. Petersburg, Speransky divided Siberia into two Governor-Generalships, Western and Eastern Siberia. These in turn were subdivided into smaller units (provinces — *guberniia*) which, though by-and-large patterned on the regular provincial administration of European Russia, were left enough freedom and flexibility to take care of special conditions of geography and social composition. To insure that local conditions would be taken into account, the governors general were permitted to set up four different types of district administrations, depending on individual local needs. [2] Some areas, for the time being at least, were to have a simplified pattern of administration. It was expected that in due course of time, as their settled population grew and their economic and social pattern became more complex, these special administrative units would receive regular provincial status. [3]

On the first level of Siberian administration — in greatest need of reorganization — was the office of Governor General, which had been the source of so much abuse and arbitrary rule over the last century. Here the major problem was to combine a reasonable latitude of gubernatorial action with effective supervision. As we recall, lack of supervisory control had been the major feature of Siberia's administration in the 18th century and the rule of Pestel was a reminder that it still could take place in the more enlightened and efficient 19th. Speransky

[1] "To transform the personal power into [the power of] an institution; and having reconciled the unity of its action with its public character, preserve this power by legal means against arbitrariness and abuses ... To establish the action of this power in such a manner that it be neither personal nor 'domestic,' but public and official." *Obozrenie glavnykh osnovanii mestnogo upravleniia Sibiri*, pp. 50—52 and PSZ 29,125, par. 474.

[2] PSZ 29,125 pars. 54, 62.

[3] PSZ 29,125, pars. 573, 574.

decided on a solution which had the merit of being relatively simple and of having some historical precedent. The Governor General, according to the law of 1822, was to be assisted by a Council. Both together, governor and council, composed the Main Administration (glavnoe upravlenie) with a wide power of executive decision. The Main Administration supervised the proper functioning of local administration in its territory, and could take special emergency action without referring first to St. Petersburg. [1]

A central problem was the staffing of the Governor General's Council. In 1819 the Minister of the Interior, O. Kozodavlev, had urged upon Speransky the creation of elective advisers to the Governor, to be chosen among the wealthier and more prominent citizens. Not much impressed by the spiritual and moral quality of the human material he had found in Siberia, and also possibly because of his own bureaucratic predilections, Speransky decided against an elective Council. While not rejecting out of hand the establishment of a representative body in the far future, Speransky provided the Governor with a council of local high officials, some appointed by St. Petersburg, and some selected by the Governor General (and confirmed by the central government). [2]

The Council of the Main Administration is appointed by Imperial decree. It has general supervision of current administration, examines the yearly reports of the provincial governors, considers private complaints against officials and government institutions, and decides jurisdictional disputes between courts. It reviews all contested matters pertaining to taxation, contractual obligations, state supplies, recruitment of soldiers, etc. [3] But the Main Administration has only the right to prescribe the manner in which decrees received from St. Petersburg will be implemented in its territory. [4] Except in those cases for which his powers are specifically enumerated, the Governor General can act only after submitting the matter to the Council. [5] But the Council has only an advisory opinion; the Governor is not bound by its advice and

[1] PSZ 29,125, par. 511.

[2] The Governor General, stipulated the statute of 1822, represents the monarch, he is the head of the Main Administration. In some cases he acts alone, entirely on his own; in others, he first seeks the advice of the Council. His major function is to supervise the proper and rapid execution of administrative measures; he also inspects the region regularly. He makes recommendations for promotions and honors; he has a qualified right to appoint and dismiss officials. In emergencies he may issue temporary executive orders, subject to eventual confirmation by St. Petersburg. (PSZ 29,125, pars. 18, 19).

[3] PSZ 29,125, pars. 14, 15, 16, 20.

[4] PSZ 29,125, par. 522.

[5] PSZ 29,125, pars. 543, 544.

the Council has no means of implementing its decisions. [1] Though the autonomy of the Main Administration's executive action is preserved, the range of its initiative is quite limited. In no case can the Main Administration cancel or limit existing regulations, it may not introduce any new rules (this was a restriction compared to the power held by governors in the past), it cannot establish new expenditures or demand from subordinate agencies any sums not regularly provided for by ordinances from St. Petersburg. [2] In the final analysis, the independent role of this Council of subordinate officials was very limited indeed, and in practice almost nil. Eventually it deteriorated to the extent of becoming merely a body dealing with a few specific matters. It lost almost completely its original function of supervising and advising the Governor General on questions of general policy (it was eventually abolished by Alexander III in 1887). [3] As on previous occasions, Speransky had failed to see clearly the practical difficulties which his new bureaucratic creations might face and did not provide adequate institutional safeguards to assure their proper development.

Following the pattern he had set in his previous administrative plans and reform projects, and in harmony with a basic trait of Russian political organization since Paul I's time, Speransky set up the Siberian administration along hierarchical lines. It was a pyramid, formally under the Senate, in fact under the Emperor and various ministries. All lower authorities were strictly subordinated to the higher ones. While any deviation from the regular procedure by a subordinate body had first to be sanctioned by superior authorities, the higher institutions could cancel decisions taken by the lower agencies on the flimsiest of pretexts. [4]

The Main Administration sets the pattern for all subordinate bodies. Each Governor Generalship is to be subdivided into several provinces (guberniia), each with its provincial administration (gubernskoe upravlenie) consisting of a Civil governor and a provincial council (gubernskii sovet). This council's functions and its relationship to the Civilian Governor parallel those of the Main Administration and Governor General. The Provincial Council, however, is composed exclusively of the province's chief administrative, judicial, and fiscal officials. [5]

---

[1] PSZ 29,125, pars. 545, 546.
[2] PSZ 29,125, pars. 537, 538.
[3] V. V. Ivanovskii, "Administrativnoe ustroistvo nashikh okrain," *Uchenye Zapiski Kazanskogo Universiteta*, vol. 58, No. 6, (Nov.—Dec. 1891) p. 38.
[4] PSZ 29,125, pars. 480, 500.
[5] The Council is composed of: Presidents of the Provincial Board (*gubernskoe pravlenie* — the general police and administrative office), of the Chamber of the Treasury (*kazennaia palata*), and of the Provincial Court (*gubernskii sud*), of the

Speransky, as we have noted, was very much aware of the special conditions of Siberia and of the need for greater administrative flexibility than in Europe. Some areas were too sparsely settled and too remote for regular and easy communications. It would be quite cumbersome and disproportionate to their needs if the complex administrative system were extended to them in full. They were therefore set up as separate regions (*oblast'*) directly under the Governor General, on the same level as the provinces. There were three such regions in Eastern Siberia and one in Western Siberia. [1] They had a much simpler administrative organization, and usually the chief official in the area combined military (or naval) and civilian functions. It was considered to be a temporary arrangement, and the regions would eventually make place for a regular provincial setup once they had been adequately settled (somewhat along the idea of the territorial stage in the United States).

The provincial pattern was repeated on the district (*okrug*) level. Provision, however, was made for local differences. There were to be three types of districts, depending on the density and character of the population. The district chief (*nachal'nik okruga*) was assisted by a council of six members, all of them major local officials. [2] The district chief was appointed by the governor and the other officials by their respective functional superiors. The police of the district was taken care of by the Land Court (*zemskii sud*) consisting of the Land Police (*zemskaia politsiia*) with a Land Captain (*zemskii ispravnik*) assisted by several deputies, depending on the size of the district. The deputies were assigned along geographical, not functional, lines. The functions of police were construed in the widest possible sense, and the Land Court supervised the fiscal administration, kept account of the harvest and grain reserves, checked on tax evasions, and executed the sentences of the courts. It had therefore numerous occasions of intervening in

Provincial Procurator (*gubernskii prokuror*), and the three Chiefs of the Police, Economy and Justice departments of the Council (PSZ 29,125, pars. 21—35).

The three major functions of provincial government — police, economy, and justice — are taken care of by three separate special agencies. The police and the administration, in the wider sense, are handled by the Provincial Board (*gubernskoe pravlenie*), consisting of several functional departments (PSZ 29,125, pars. 39—44). The Provincial Chamber of the Treasury (*gubernskaia kazennaia palata*) takes care of all matters pertaining to public economy (*ibid.*, pars. 45—53); and the judiciary is in the hands of the Provincial Court (*gubernskii sud*) (*ibid.*, pars. 54—56).

1 Iakutsk, Maritime Region, and Troitsko-Savsk in Eastern Siberia; Omsk in Western Siberia. PSZ 29,125, pars. 321—472.

2 The District Council included: the District Chief, the Police Chief (*gorodnichi*) of the District capital, the District Judge (*okruzhnoi sud'ia*), the Land Captain (*zemskii ispravnik*), the District Treasurer, the Clerk, and the elected town 'mayor' (*gorodskoi golova*) of the district capital, if there was one. PSZ 29,125, pars. 64—69.

local affairs. [1] A District Treasury Administration and a District Court completed the picture. In the more remote, socially less complex districts, all functions were exercised by a Land Deputy *(zemskii zasedatel')* so that the burden of a numerous and complicated bureaucracy would not weigh too heavily on the inhabitants. Completely underpopulated districts were managed by a Land Captain, directly responsible to the District Council, and who worked usually in close relation with the tribal administrations of the local natives. [2] The district was only a bureaucratic link between the province and the lowest administrative unit, the township. None of the district bodies had any autonomy or initiative of action.

The township *(volost')* was the lowest administrative unit with which Speransky concerned himself. As in his later plans of local government for European Russia, he did not make any provisions for the village. This was a curious omission, for after all the village was the basic social unit of the Russian peasant.

The township administration consisted of a township head ("mayor," *volostnoi golova)*, one elder *(starosta)*, and one clerk *(pisar')*, elected by indirect suffrage by property owning household heads (one elector for every 100 souls). The elections had to be confirmed by the Governor. [3] The functions and responsibilities of the township administration were generally left as they had been before. There was no township assembly, and the functions of the organization were more limited than those which Speransky later suggested for European Russia. It again showed that he was by far not convinced that the Siberian peasantry had reached nearly as high a spiritual level as the European peasant. The Siberian township administration was exclusively an executive one. It had general police; it administered the repartition of dues, cared for the village supply stores, and executed sentences of the courts as they applied to its villages. It had autonomy only in respect to the trial of a few petty and insignificant misdemeanors (rowdiness, drunkenness). [4] It therefore possessed only subordinate functions and was nothing but the passive and obedient tool of the higher bureaucratic authorities.

Speransky and his assistants tried to keep the three major functions of government — executive, economy, justice — separate. But not with complete success. They did not carry out their intention — if such it was — very consistently and effectively. In particular, the judiciary was not freed from pressure by the executive, for the procedural aspects of jus-

[1] PSZ 29,125, pars. 75—79.
[2] PSZ 29,125, pars. 99—102, also *infra*.
[3] PSZ 29,125, pars. 135—141.
[4] PSZ 29,125, par. 142.

tice remained under the control of the Governor General and his aides. [1]

The distinctive feature of the system, as noted by both contemporary and succeeding generations, and often adduced to condemn Speransky, was its bureaucratic character. Almost all functions of the administrative, economic, and even social life of Siberia rested in the hands of officials. Local "society" participated in an extremely limited way, and only in matters affecting the towns and townships. The reasons for Speransky's course were twofold: on the one hand was the old bureaucratic and paternalistic tradition of Russian government; on the other was Speransky's skepticism of the ability of a crude and in many ways backward Siberian society to be of positive help to the administration. There was no local nobility, and it was not expected that it would develop there because of the prohibition to extend serfdom into Siberia. There was no enlightened or even formally educated class, except the bureaucracy itself. Of course, the bureaucracy was not very good either, but it at least could be improved under a proper system; and it indeed did show some improvement in the decades following the application of the statute of 1822. [2] Until the population at large had matured sufficiently to participate in the administration, the bureaucracy had to be entrusted with the task of control and leadership. Speransky's conception of the role of the Siberian bureaucracy corresponded to his fundamental political belief that the prime function of the state was to be the guide in the nation's progress towards moral improvement. He hoped that, as this progress took place, the role of the bureaucracy would be restricted. Then the membership of the councils set up with each executive head (Governor General and provincial governor) would include not only bureaucrats, but also delegates or representatives of the local population. In this flexibility, in this ability to become the framework for a "representative" as well as a bureaucratic system, Speransky saw the great merit of his work. Unfortunately, he had counted without the timorous caution of the government, without its almost pathological fear of the participation of "public opinion" in administration; a fear which made for even greater rigidity and bureaucratic control in later decades. Yet, the fact remains that in spite of all these drawbacks, the Statute of 1822 introduced to Siberia for the first time in its history something which we can call the rule of law,

---

1 Prutchenko, *Sibirskie okrainy: oblastnye ustanovleniia, sviazannye s Sibirskim Uchrezhdeniem 1822 g. v stroe upravleniia russkogo gosudarstva* (St. Pbg. 1899), vol. I, p. 279.

2 As one contemporary put it: "the bureaucracy could bring forth a man of Speransky's caliber, whereas the merchant class produced only Baranov, 'a vicious and drunken muzhik'."

a *Rechtsstaat*. The basis for clear and orderly governmental procedure had at last been established, and even though the practice continued to fall short of the aim, progress was being made in the right direction. This was a necessary condition for attracting free settlers and developing to the full the economic potential of the region. In this sense too, Speransky could find some justification for his boast that "I have discovered the true political problem of Siberia. Only Ermak can compete with me in this respect." [1]

The new system of administration helped to promote and secure economic and social changes fostered by some of the other statutes of 1822. They aimed at resolving the difficulties that had arisen at the end of the 18th century. Pestel's and Treskin's methods had failed and had aroused violent distaste and opposition. A new approach was in order, and Speransky provided it.

First, Speransky turned his attention to the promotion and creation of a healthier economy. He had a twofold task, to break the old established monopolies of merchants (something Treskin had attempted to do in his harsh and tyrannical way) and to abolish all unnecessary bureaucratic controls (which Pestel and Treskin had fostered). The executive orders which Speransky issued during his residence in Siberia and various provisions of the statutes, abolished most of the detailed regulations heretofore imposed on trade. [2] The law of 1822 enjoined the Governors General, the Civilian Governors, and the District Chiefs to exercise their power of supervision for the benefit and preservation of free economic activity. Specifically, at each level of the administrative hierarchy, the chief executive official was to safeguard freedom of trade. [3] Although it was realized that under Siberia's special conditions, the government had to play an active supervisory role to maintain state granaries in the remoter regions for emergencies, the law of 1822 did bring about a gradual liberalization of the grain trade. [4] As a

[1] Letter to his daughter, 1 February 1820, from Irkutsk, No. 37, *Russkii Arkhiv*, (1868), No. 11, p. 1735.

[2] Vagin, *op. cit.*, I, pp. 178, 352.

[3] "The Main Administration (*glavnoe upravlenie*) protects with all its power and through its ordinances the freedom of enterprise and trade, the freest exchange of the necessities of life throughout all of Siberia without any distinction between districts and provinces." PSZ 29,125, par. 523. See also pars. 561, 397, 95.

To promote and secure free trade, the following provision was included in the statutes; it speaks for itself: "It is forbidden to all officials serving in the Provinces to enter into debt relations with peasants and natives, in their own name or under the cover of the name of a third person. All debt obligations contracted in this manner, with written proof or without it, private or communal, are invalid, there can be no judicial action on them and their collection cannot be enforced." PSZ 29,134, par. 53.

[4] "The first and principal means for supplying the people with bread [i.e. grain] is private enterprise and trade. The second means, serving as aid and complement

result, not much time passed ere several new markets and fairs opened up in Siberia and developed into most active trading centers. [1]

In the hands of Treskin, the state granaries had become perhaps the most important pretext for state interference in the economy and for the administration's abuse of power. A reform of their organization was a most pressing need. The state granaries could not be abolished outright, for quite a few peasants and natives, especially in the remote areas of the Northeast where harvests were very precarious, depended on them to help them over lean periods. Speransky recognized this function of the granaries, but he made it quite clear that in no case should their essentially humanitarian and social function be perverted for the benefit of the Treasury or of a few officials. [2] To this end, the grain stores were put under the direct supervision of the president of the Provincial Administration, i.e. the Civilian Governor and his representatives in the district. In this way, it was hoped, the stores would be used for the general interest of the entire population and and not only for narrow local and selfish purposes. [3] Faithful to his fundamental belief in the state's role of moral and spiritual leadership, Speransky also emphasized the pedagogical aspect of the grain stores. They could play a leading part in the promotion of agriculture in areas where it was not practiced as yet. By their example, and with their help, agriculture would be stimulated among the nomadic natives and other backward groups. [4] In spite of defects in their implementation, the rules of 1822 did put an end to direct bureaucratic interference in state stores, and their new organization did offer more incentive for the peasantry's efforts and labor.

Naturally, the stability and prosperity of Siberia's economy, and more particularly of its agriculture, depended on the increase of its land-tilling population. Earlier in the century, Treskin and others had endeavored to promote agricultural settlement and colonization. Speran-

---

to the first, in years of crop failure, is the network of village stores in the countryside and communal stores in the towns. But because in Siberia, due to the character of its population, communal supplies cannot be established in every town, there must be added a third means to the former two, state supplies." PSZ 29,133, par. 26.

[1] I. D. Zavalishin, *Opisanie Zapadnoi Sibiri* (Moscow 1862) I, p. 68; S. M. Seredonin, *Istoricheskii obzor deiatel'nosti Komiteta Ministrov* (St. Pbg. 1902), vol. II, part 2, pp. 228—229.

[2] "...2. not to prevent, but by all means foster private grain trade; 3. that state grain stores serve only as aid in case of necessity, but not as a means of introducing exclusive grain trade by the Treasury." PSZ 29,133, par. 7.

[3] PSZ 29,133, pars. 9, 10.

[4] The need of enlightening examples to stimulate agriculture was also felt by Speransky's old schoolfriend and Siberia "expert," P. A. Slovtsov. See P. A. Slovtsov, *Pis'ma iz Sibiri* (Moscow 1828), p. 92. Also, PSZ 29,127, pars. 163. 164.

sky wholeheartedly approved of these efforts. Large-scale migration of Russian peasants from Europe, however, could not be expected until the state either resettled its own peasants or allowed freedom of movement to the serfs. The former occurred in a limited way as a result of the reforms of Count P. Kiselev; the latter had to wait until after the Emancipation. In the meantime, Speransky decided to take all possible advantage of the one permanent source of Siberia's population: the exile system. Although he realized that it was a very poor substitute for large scale free migration, he believed that greater benefit would come to the state and the exiles themselves if better rules were provided for the latter's settlement on the land. One of the statutes of 1822 (PSZ 29,128) dealt with this question.

A few highlights of this law are worth noting. The children of exiles, for example, automatically became state peasants and inherited none of their parents' legal disabilities. [1] Individuals whose punishment was limited to ordinary exile and criminals who had been released from forced labor without right to return to European Russia, had to join an existing village community of settled peasants. [2] The absorption of exiles into the settled population was made easier by a series of provisions such as tax exemptions. [3] Unfortunately, the results were not too good, for Speransky had based his rules on the number of exiles entering Siberia in the early 1820's, i.e. about 2000 persons a year. Soon, however, their number grew enormously as a result of the new policy of sending to Siberia petty criminals, chronic vagrants, and the old soldiers of fortress garrisons. These new categories swelled the number of exiles into the tens of thousands, and their gradual and normal assimilation into the local population became impossible.

Similar economic considerations led to a new and better organization for the Cossacks. The Cossacks acted as a border guard and police force; they usually were part-time soldiers and part-time peasants. The law of 1822 attempted to pave the way for their gradual transformation into full time husbandmen or regular peasants. Except for a minority to be garrisoned in or near the larger towns and engaged almost exclusively in police work, the Cossacks were freed from most of their military obligations. They were thus given an opportunity of devoting all their time and effort to agriculture (PSZ 29,131). Eventually, the administration of these settled Cossacks was to be assimilated to that of the regular peasantry.

[1] PSZ 29,128, par. 262.
[2] PSZ 29,128, par. 401.
[3] PSZ 29,128, pars. 345, 346, 347, 350—393.

Speransky also hoped to bind to Siberia the officials who worked in the administration by allotting them land. It would not only increase their income, but also give them a greater stake in the future of the region. A similar provision was made for soldiers serving in Siberian garrisons (PSZ 29,124). The plan did not work out too well, because the officials longed to get back to Europe. Anyway, the absence of cheap — or unfree — labor precluded the formation of regular estates on the model of the gentry holdings in Russia proper. The idea, though, is interesting as it illustrates again Speransky's search for an élite and "public opinion."

Finally, to improve Siberia's economy and give its population more mobility and security, Speransky did what he could to promote a money economy. He wished Siberia to outgrow its prevailing natural and barter economy that made possible the monopolistic domination of a few merchants. To this end, he proposed that the services and dues in kind which the Siberian peasant furnished to the government (and which were particularly onerous) be replaced by money payments. It would free the peasant's labor completely and make him master of his own time and energy. The peasant could then be assured that nothing and nobody would tear him from his task or upset his routine. This in turn would raise his productivity and give him some incentive to produce a surplus which he could sell to pay his taxes and dues. The statute on local dues and services (PSZ 29,132) implemented these considerations; it set an example which was eventually also imitated in European Russia. As for the services that heretofore had been performed by reluctant and unskilled peasants, they were to be taken over by a special corps of trained personnel to be paid for through taxation.

The intent of all these measures was quite clear: to raise Siberia to the economic, social, and cultural level of European Russia. The law's success would enhance the region's value for the Empire; at the same time it would secure an orderly administration for good. The government would serve as guide towards this goal. The aim was certainly laudable, the task set for the new administrative system a challenging one. And while it is true that in many cases the officials did not live up to the situation and that several decades were to pass before his plans bore full fruition, it must be said in all fairness that Speransky had planted a seed that could not be cast out. He had helped Siberia onto an entirely new path of development.

Naturally, before progress could be made along this new road, the Siberian natives had to be given a proper administration too. It was an essential part of Speransky's reform, and it was accomplished by the statute on the natives, PSZ 29,126, also issued in 1822.

As we have noted, since about the accession of Catherine II, there had been a decisive change in the economic, social, and political conditions of the natives. On the one hand there was a serious deterioration among the primitive trappers and hunters of the far North and Northeast. On the other, an important, more positive transformation was taking place among the advanced, socially better organized peoples of Central and South-eastern Siberia. But as these changes had as yet not been integrated into either the native or the Russian patterns, there was a great deal of disorganization and confusion. Speransky undertook to clarify the situation and to bring order into the social and administrative relations of the natives as part of his reorganization of Siberia.

He followed in the wake of Catherine's humanitarian protectionism of the native customs and way of life. But at the same time he favored a synthesis between the cultural values, the economy, and social ways of both the native and Russian populations. As point of departure he took the fact that Siberia was already a *Staatsgemeinschaft*, and now he wanted to help it on the way to a true *Kulturgemeinschaft*. With such a goal in mind he devoted most attention to those natives who could be easily integrated into the social community of Siberia, the more advanced and economically differentiated peoples (e.g. the Buriats).

As he had done with the Russian population, Speransky cultivated social contacts with the natives so as to bring them closer to the administration. He showed a keen interest in Buddhism and the Buriat traditions and philosophies. He aided and promoted the study of oriental languages at Irkutsk (and later St. Petersburg). Finally, he took steps which led to a more active and positive approach to the education for the natives, in particular among the Buriats. [1]

In regard to the administration, Speransky believed that it was mainly a question of adapting the existing agencies to the actual needs of the situation. He based his approach on five principles: 1. divide the natives into three categories — settled, nomads, and vagrants — according to their way of life and basic economic character; 2. the administration of the nomads and vagrants should be based on their old customs, but these had to be better defined and organized; 3. local authorities should have only general supervisory police functions, and the internal autonomy of the tribes should be left untouched; 4. the freedom

[1] N. M. Iadrintsev, *Sibirskie inorodtsy, ikh byt i sovremennoe polozhenie* (St. Pbg. 1891), pp. 230—240 *passim*; Bogdanov, *Ocherk istorii buriat-mongol'skogo naroda*, p. 164; F. A. Kudriavtsev, *Istoriia buriat-mongol'skogo naroda ot XVIII v. do 60kh godov XIX v.* (Moscow-Leningrad 1940) p. 219.

of trade and industry should be protected; 5. taxes and tribute should
be proportional to the abilities of each tribe and assessed at regular
intervals (to prevent cases where the same tribute was levied over
several generations, though the composition and way of life of the
tribe had changed). [1]

The settled natives were classified as state peasants. Wherever their
number was large enough, the natives could use their language for
official purposes in separate townships. Administratively, they were
identified with the Russian peasantry. [2] This was all the statute said
about the settled natives (a relatively small minority in Speransky's time)
and it very clearly implied the ultimate goal of making their administrative and social pattern uniform with that of the Russian peasantry.
For all practical purposes the law concerned itself with the nomads and
vagrants.

The basic assumption was that the government should not interfere
any more than necessary into native life. It was particularly important
for the judicial cases. The natives should have all means to settle their
affairs and disputes on the basis of their own local customs. Except
for five specified types of major crimes (rebellion, premeditated murder,
pillage, counterfeiting, theft of government property) the natives were
to be tried in accordance with their customs and by their own chiefs. [3]

The administrative system for the natives was relatively simple. That
of the nomads served as model. Each encampment *(ulus)* of 15 families
or more forms a Clan Administration *(rodovaia uprava)*, consisting of
one elder, either elective or hereditary, depending on the custom of
the tribe, and one or two elected assistants. The elected officials must
be chosen among the "better" and most honored members of the clan.
Within the clan, the elder may keep the traditional native title, but in
his dealings with the provincial administration, he is only an elder.
The Clan Administration conducts its business orally; therefore it
cannot be very complex. Several encampments constitute a Native
Administration *(inorodnaia uprava)*, consisting of one head *(golova)*,
two elected elders, and if possible, one clerk. The Clan Administration
is subordinate in every respect to this *inorodnaia uprava*. In a sense, the
relation is similar to that between the township and village administrations for the Russian populations. The Native Administration is in
direct contact with the Russian authorities (Land Police), either orally
or in writing. [4] The setup for the vagrants is quite similar, except that

[1] *Obozrenie glavnykh osnovanii . . .*, pp. 60—61.
[2] PSZ 29,126, pars. 12, 13, 17—23, 88—92.
[3] PSZ 29,126, pars. 25, 68, 70, 72.
[4] PSZ 29,126, pars. 94—110.

it is much simpler and comprises only a clan administration with one elder.

The Clan Administration performs the functions of general police in the clan; it executes the orders and regulations from higher authorities, collects taxes from the entire clan, distributes the tax burden among its members, gives permission to clan members to absent themselves for short periods, and keeps a record of all events and changes in the clan. The Native Administration supervises and inspects regularly the clan administrations under its jurisdiction. It is the executor of instructions from the central administration; it must protect the rights of the natives against interference and abuse of local officials, outsiders, and merchants. But it has no initiative of action, except in some rare emergency situations. [1]

These two bodies of native self-government are under the jurisdiction of the Land Police (zemskaia politsiia) which, as we know, is a part of the regular Russian administrative hierarchy. Its main function is to link the natives with the Russian authorities. It transmits all regulations from the central offices and it can issue limited executive orders of its own. [2]

In spite of its use of the term clan, the system was not truly based on clan and family groupings. Changed conditions had, by the end of the 18th century, broken down the unity and significance of clan organization in many instances. The clan had become more of a territorial and administrative unit rather than a kinship group. The process of disintegration of the clan had gone so far that artificial "clans" were set up to take care of natives that had lost their membership in well defined kinship groups (especially in and near towns).

Several clans combined are to have their Duma of the Steppe (stepnaia duma) which replaces the kontora of the 18th and the zemskaia izba of the 17th centuries. The Duma is composed of a principal clan chief (glavnyi rodovoi nachal'nik), deputies elected among the native nobility or prominent individuals, and its own clerk. It is primarily a fiscal and economic institution, keeping a permanent census of the tribes and accounting for the monies and property held in common. It should help to promote agriculture, and supervise the proper supplying of the natives with foodstuffs. It deals only with the head and elder of the clans, not with individual members of the tribes. [3]

[1] PSZ 29,126, pars. 187—201.

[2] The Land Police can try to settle disputes between clans, reconcile natives after their own courts have failed to reach a settlement, and if it fails too, forward the matter to a regular Russian court. PSZ 29,126, pars. 214—222.

[3] PSZ 29,126, pars. 114—121, 202—222.

The judicial organization runs parallel to the administrative. First, cases and suits can be brought to the local native authorities, elders, clan and native administration, where they are decided orally and according to tribal custom. In the second place, suits are brought to the Land Police; and, if the parties wish it, or if the case warrants it, the Land Police can refer the suit to the regular hierarchy of Russian courts. In other words, on the lower level, the judiciary is not separated from the administration (as was also the case for the Russian villages). It was hoped though, that all intra-tribal affairs would be dealt with adequately on the basis of local customs and by the lower native institutions. [1]

The elders and chiefs, whether elected or hereditary, receive no salary (which limits membership to the well-to-do); the clerks, however, can be hired and paid by the clan or tribe. The native officials are confirmed in their office by the civilian governor, whereas the principal clan chief is confirmed by the Governor General. Denial of confirmation or removal from office can only be for cause in specifically enumerated instances. Only the collegiate body of the district administration can deal with the natives. [2] This was one of the notable accomplishments of the statute. The natives were protected against the direct and constant interference of individual officials. In this respect the natives had more internal autonomy than the Russian villages and townships.

Various rules safeguarded the economic interest and time of the natives, as for instance the limits put on the obligation to furnish postal relays or to appear as witnesses far away from their encampments. Preventive imprisonment also was abolished. [3] For the convenience of the natives and to stimulate their economy, yearly fairs were to be established by the governor. Finally, the native was protected against the traditional hardships accompanying the collection of taxes by the provision that no collector was to go to the clan in person, except if the clan had defaulted for more than two years. The clan elders themselves should bring the tax payments to the nearest Treasury Administration or to the fairs. As with the Russian peasants, dues in kind and services were to be replaced by money payments wherever possible. [4] All these measures aimed at limiting the officials' opportunities for interfering in native affairs.

---

[1] PSZ 29,126, pars. 122—132, 223—235.
[2] PSZ 29,126, pars. 157—162.
[3] PSZ 29,126, pars. 246—251, 254.
[4] PSZ 29,126, pars. 133—141, 296—339.

Some provisions aimed at safeguarding the economic productivity of the natives, especially in the case of backward tribes of trappers and fishermen. The state would sell them those articles which were absolutely essential to their economy (gunshot, powder, salt, grain). This would keep the price on articles of prime necessity low. The principle was similar to that concerning the state granaries, and the basic rules applied in both instances. [1] Native land possessions were guaranteed by the state. The legal form of this guarantee was that the state owned the land and granted it to he natives in permanent possession. (By implication, of course, this meant that the state could revoke the right of the natives.) This provision was designed to control Russian peasant encroachments on the land of the natives. [2] But it did not prove very effective once the tidal wave of peasant migration swept into Siberia at the end of the 19th century. '

The statute also dealt with the social aspects of the natives' rapprochement with Russian society and culture. Freedom of religion was guaranteed to the natives. They were allowed to establish, at their expense, schools in their own language. But native children could, if they wished, be admitted to the Russian schools on equal terms with the Russians. It was hoped that this provision would promote the natives' russification, gradually and without resistance. The missionary zeal of the Russian church was curbed and its disciplinary power over new converts checked. Titled personages among the natives might preserve their titles and status within the tribe. But their status and titles were recognized outside the tribe only for services to the state. Native noblemen were not considered members of the nobility of the empire, though they could be promoted to it. [3]

Speransky also took steps to collect and systematize a complete code of the customary laws of the Siberian natives. It would serve as a guide to both the Russian and native officials in administering justice. Materials for the code were collected in the years immediately following his governorship. In some instances clan or tribal assemblies were called together to draw up the text of their customs; in others, prominent and presumably knowledgeable persons were interviewed. The materials so gathered were forwarded to St. Petersburg; using them as a basis, a Code of the Laws of the Steppes *(Svod stepnykh zakonov)* was drafted in 1841. Unfortunately the Code never received formal legislative sanction. Yet a few copies reached Siberia; they were copied and

---

1 PSZ 29,126, pars. 270—285.
2 PSZ 29,126, pars. 28, 30, 31, 45, 52, 300.
3 PSZ 29,126, pars. 53, 55, 56, 57, 58, 59, 63—67, 286—292.

served as the basis for the legal relations of the natives down to 1917. [1]

The provisions of the statute of 1822 for the natives remained the basis for the natives' administration until the end of the century, and even beyond. Upon examination, the principal feature of the reform was that it clearly and effectively restricted the Russian administration's interference in native judicial matters. The foremost student of Siberian native customary law, V. Riazanovskii, has summarized the effects of the statute in the following words: "It established clearer limits to the jurisdiction of native courts, it set up a system of judiciary instances, of firm terms for appeals, it introduced a few general principles of judiciary procedures, and a few other things. But the system of the statute was not devoid of serious defects: the union of justice and administration, a great number of institutions, lack of acquaintance of higher authorities with the customary law of the natives, absence of detailed procedural rules and of a code of the material customary law, etc." [2]

In strictly administrative matters, the Russians maintained their dominant role, and for all practical purposes the natives had wide autonomy only in applying the policy set by Russian officials. The statute did not protect the natives fully against the collegiate bodies of the administration, though it did shield them from abuses by individual officials. Another characteristic feature of the law was the dominant role assigned by it to the "better" among the natives. In so doing, Speransky was not only bowing to existing conditions — as they had developed in the second half of the 18th century — but he was also implementing the basic principles of his own political philosophy. Only the "better" people, economically, and what was more important yet, spiritually, could be given positions of responsibility. But it is also significant to note that the better among the natives were also more russified, or at least tended to become it. Through its new administrative functions, the native aristocracy was in a position to play the leading role in a progressive and organic russification of the natives. [3]

[1] V. A. Riazanovskii, *Mongol'skoe pravo — preimushchestvenno obychnoe* (Kharbin 1931), p. 153; V. A. Riasanovsky, *Fundamental Principles of Mongol Law* (Tientsin 1937), p. 76.

Besides Riazanovskii, materials for the native code were published in Russian by D. I. Samokvasov (ed.) *Sbornik obychnogo prava sibirskikh inorodtsev* (Warsaw 1876).

The history of the codification work on this Code of the Laws of the Steppe is summarized by A. Nol'de, "K istorii sostavleniia proekta 'Svoda Stepnykh zakonov kochevykh inorodtsev Vostochnoi Sibiri'," *Sbornik S. F. Platonovu, ucheniki, druz'ia i pochitateli* (St. Pbg. 1911), pp. 502—521.

[2] Riazanovskii, *Mongol'skoe pravo*, p. 232.

[3] Bogdanov, *op. cit.*, p. 101; V. G. Kartsov, *Ocherk istorii narodov severozapadnoi Sibiri* (Moscow 1937), pp. 78—79; I. I. Mainov, "Russkie krest'iane i osedlye inorodtsy

To relate in detail the difficulties encountered in applying the statutes of 1822 and the resulting perversions would take us beyond our
subject, Speransky's life and work. By and large, the law was perverted
either because Speransky had tried to implant principles for which
"objective" conditions were not fully ripe, or because he failed to
provide the proper institutional safeguards for the correct realization
of his design. The former deficiency was well illustrated in the statute
on the natives; much of its value lay in that it facilitated and fostered
the shift from one kind of way of life to another (from nomadic to
settled, for example). But this process took much longer and was
fraught with much greater difficulties than Speransky had imagined.
The second weakness — inadequate institutional safeguards — found
expression in Speransky's insistence on the role of the state in fostering
the desired changes. It opened the door to abuses and arbitrary interference by officials who were not prepared for or aware of their high
responsibilities.

Speransky's work in Siberia illustrated very clearly his major political principle of the government's benevolent guidance of people and
country to a higher level of economic and spiritual development. This
guidance is to be the task of well meaning and adequately trained
officials whose actions and power are carefully defined and circumscribed by various rules of procedure. The success of the statutes rested
on the benevolence of the bureaucracy and the smooth working of
basic procedural rules. The people, of course, could not supervise and
control and administrate. It was to be self-controlling, self-restraining
by virtue of a proper operation of its rules and the collegiate advice
and guidance of the colleagues and subordinates of the chief executive
officials. As to the participation and influence of *"public opinion,"* it
was out of the question as long as the population was not mature
enough and without an élite leadership.

Speransky gave much thought and attention to the formation of a
leadership group. He tried to stimulate it by his own example and
by the new spirit he instilled into the social and cultural life of
Siberia. In this respect he was fortunate. Unforeseen circumstances
brought to Siberia individuals who carried on his work. The exiled
Decembrists acted as a leavening ferment and became the nucleus of
a Siberian intelligentsia and professional class. Wealthy merchants,
and especially their sons, caught Speransky's interest in cultural betterment; and they continued to support and promote intellectual and

Iakutskoi oblasti," *Zapiski Imperat. Russk. geograficheskogo obshchestva po otdelu*
*statistiki,* vol. XII, (St. Pbg. 1912) pp. 93—94.

artistic activities after his departure. Speransky labored hard to lift the spiritual level of Siberia by expanding and modernizing its economy. A principal instrument for achieving this purpose were his rules for freeing trade and preventing monopolies and bureaucratic interference. Speransky's merit lay in the fact that he had seen Siberia's possibilities most clearly, had called the attention of the government to them, and had indicated the way in which their development could be best supported and promoted. For this reason alone, his governorship and reform opened a new period in Siberian history.

Finally, he did much to link Siberia more closely to European Russia, economically, culturally, socially, and administratively. His long range goal was to have Siberia become part and parcel of Russia, in no way different except for its size, wealth, and productivity. Then Siberia would be able to play a more active part in Russia's trade and cultural contacts with China and Mongolia; it would pave the way for a more intensive and rewarding exploitation of the Empire's position on the Pacific. It might be added that Speransky also envisaged further Russian agricultural expansion into the relatively empty steppe lands of the Kazakhs. [1] Siberia's new position in Asia would also enhance the role of Russia as a world power. It would become the link, economically and culturally, between Europe and Asia.

The experience Speransky gained as governor of Penza and as Governor General of Siberia proved of great significance both for Siberia and his own political career and development. He returned to St. Petersburg with a first-hand acquaintance of Russian local conditions and needs. Not surprisingly therefore, Alexander I and Nicholas I used his talents and counsel in the area of provincial administration.

### SOURCES

Primary sources: *Speranskii: Obozrenie glavnykh osnovanii mestnogo upravleniia Sibiri (po bumagam Speranskogo i Sibirskogo Komiteta)*, St. Pbg. 1841; "Raport Speranskogo Gosudariu Imperatoru, 1 iunia 1820," *Russkii Arkhiv*, (1870), pp. 598—599; "Pis'ma M. M. Speranskogo k ego docheri iz Penzy i s dorogi v Sibir', 22 okt. 1816—18 mai 1819," *Russkii Arkhiv*, (1868), Nos. 7 & 8, pp. 1103—1212; "Pis'ma Speranskogo k ego docheri iz Sibiri, 30 maia 1819—17 marta 1821," *Russkii Arkhiv*, (1868), No. 11, pp. 1682—1811; "Pis'ma k V. P. Kochubeiu," *Russkaia Starina*, 111 (July 1902), pp. 51—54; "Pis'ma k A. A. Stolypinu s 23.II.1813 do 18.IX.1819," *Russkii Arkhiv*, (1869), Nos. 10 and 11, pp. 1682—1708 and 1966—1984;

---

[1] Cf. PSZ 29, 127, the statute on the Kirghiz, as an instrument for preparing the penetration of Russia into the Kirghiz (Kazakh) steppes.

V. Kochubei, "Pis'ma k. Speranskomu," *Russkaia Starina,* 112 (Nov. 1902), pp. 301—322.

Contemporary memoirs on Speransky's stay in Penza and Siberia: P. T. Basnin, "Iz proshlogo Sibiri," *Istoricheskii Vestnik,* 90, (1902), pp. 532—574; I. A. Bychkov (ed.), "Speranskii v Velikopol'e i v Penze," *Russkaia Starina,* 110 (June, 1902), 467—486 and 111 (July, 1902), 45—59; "Graf M. M. Speranskii v Tiumeni," *Russkaia Starina,* 87 (Aug. 1896), p. 294; Protoierei Evgenii Popov, *M. M. Speranskii v Permi i v Sibiri,* Perm' 1879; Troitskii, "M. M. Speranskii v Penze," *Russkaia Starina,* 112 (1902), pp. 341—345.

Major secondary works on Speransky's governorship of Siberia: I. A. Bychkov, "M. M. Speranskii general gubernator Sibiri i vozvrashchenie ego v Sankt Peterburg," *Russkaia Starina* 112 (1902), pp. 35—56; A. N. Fateev, "Speranskii general gubernator Sibiri," *Zapiski Russkogo nauchnoissledovatel'nogo ob'edineniia v Prage,* vol. XI, Nos. 82 and 88, (Prague 1942), pp. 111—151 and 323—362; N. M. Iadrintsev, "Chuvstva Speranskogo k Sibiri," *Sbornik gazety Sibir',* I, pp. 397—408; N. M. Iadrintsev, "Speranskii i ego reformy v Sibiri," *Vestnik Evropy,* (1876), No. 5, pp. 93—116; S. Prutchenko, *Sibirskie okrainy: oblastnye ustanovleniia, sviazannye s Sibirskim Uchrezhdeniem 1822 g v stroe upravleniia russkogo gosudarstva,* 2 vols., St. Pbg., 1899; V. I. Vagin, *Istoricheskie svedeniia o deiatel'nosti grafa M. M. Speranskogo v Sibiri s 1819 po 1822 g.,* 2 vols., St. Pbg., 1872.

*The Statutes of 1822 on Siberia:* PSZ, vol. XXXVIII (1822—1823), pp. 342—565. The list of the individual laws is as follows: Nos. 29,124 — General Introduction; 29,125 — General Administrative Statute; 29,126 — Statute on the Natives; 29,127 — Statute on the Kirghiz; 29,128 — Statute on the Exiles; 29,129 — Convoys and Transportation of Exiles; 29,130 — Statute on Land Transportation; 29,131 — Statute on Siberian Cossacks; 29,132 — Local dues (*zemskie povinnosti*); 29,133 — State granaries; 29,134 — Statute on Loans and Debts.

I have dealt in greater detail with the background and the character of the transformation of Siberia before Speransky, as well as with the reform measures, in a monograph: *Siberia and the Reforms of 1822,* University of Washington Press (Seattle 1956). See there also for a more complete bibliography on Siberia.

# CHAPTER IX

## PROJECTS FOR REFORMING
## THE PROVINCIAL ADMINISTRATION

With the return of Speransky to St. Petersburg from Siberia in 1821, a new period began in his political career. It would be an exaggeration to maintain, as some historians have done, that exile and service in remote provinces of the Empire had broken him morally and had transformed him into a spineless courtier, willing to undertake any assignment, however unpleasant. It is nonetheless true that Speransky returned to the capital a somewhat changed man. He never had been a very willful personality; his origins and early seminary schooling had developed in him a timid flexibility which could easily be taken for spinelessness. Also, by 1822 Speransky had lost most of his earlier energetic enthusiasm and self-confident faith in his work. After a decade of humiliation, loneliness, and wandering, he returned to the court a more humble, cautious, and "plodding" high bureaucrat.

In contrast to the years before his exile, he displayed a full awareness of the limitations, and perhaps even uselessness, of general and "fundamental" solutions. He had lost faith in the support of the monarch who alone, in his opinion, might lead in a general transformation of the country. Speransky had observed the lack of understanding and suspicion with which the population greeted the government's innovations and experiments. He foreswore any effort at sweeping, basic reforms based on the most modern theoretical considerations. This new mood of his fitted well with his position at court after 1821. He had lost the favor and confidence of Alexander I and never regained anything like the influence he had enjoyed before his exile. To Alexander's mind, he now was merely the capable bureaucrat who could be entrusted with a variety of tasks, but always in a strictly technical capacity. As for Nicholas I, who succeeded his brother Alexander in 1825, he was notoriously suspicious of theories and general principles in politics, a suspicion that had been fostered by his technological military training and confirmed by his interpretation of the testimonies of the Decembrists. During his reign, there was no more question of sweeping political reforms. Nicholas avoided any fundamentally new approaches to Russian political and social needs. He only permitted the tackling of concrete and practical issues as they arose; he preferred to seek the help of *ad hoc* secret committees set up to deal with specific problems requiring immediate solution. These personal and political circumstances limited Speransky's role to that of a foremost administrative technician in a strictly bureaucratic and "conservative" government.

After 1821, and more particularly after 1825, we find Speransky devoting all his energies and talents to the elaboration of many projects and proposals for the numerous secret *ad hoc* committees established by Nicholas I. These plans and projects have a distinctly "bureaucratic" character. They were primarily concerned with the details of office practice, rules of law, the technicalities and narrow objectives of re-medial administrative measures. And on these, he was much more ready to compromise, to accept the changes suggested by his colleagues in the committees or demanded by the monarch. For after all, there was no purpose in insisting stubbornly on matters which did not involve fundamental theoretical issues; the relative merits of various procedures and concrete suggestions for solving practical problems could best be tested pragmatically. Even Speransky's most important accomplishment in the last period of his life, the codification of Russian laws, was largely intended as a technical aid for the smooth and orderly running of the machine of government.

But even in its new, narrow way, Speransky's work continued to play an important role in shaping the practice and thinking of the imperial administration. His thorough examination of every problem's historical and institutional roots and his logical and clear formulation of possible solutions helped later generations of officials to see the situation more clearly in its proper perspective. Some of his observations and conclusions, based on wide and deep experience, brought their fruits in the reign of Alexander II.

From his exile and governorships, Speransky returned with a five-year long direct acquaintance of Russian provincial conditions and administration, an acquaintance which high dignitaries — even himself before 1812 — had always lacked woefully. Working over his observations, he was prepared to give a comprehensive picture of the situation and to make specific practical recommendations for the elimination of abuses and defects. As we noted, in all the proposals and plans he had submitted before his exile, he had always kept in mind an ultimate goal, a moral aim for the development of the nation. Although he by no means abandoned such a long range purpose, it was no longer the immediate basis of his proposals after 1821. It is not so much a change in direction or final aim, as a shift to practical and immediate solutions of concrete, specific ills. His experience as governor had convinced him of the importance for the Empire of a proper organization of the executive authority in the provinces and of the improvement in the quality of the local administrative personnel. All his efforts at improvement and reform were now to be directed to these two points. If a general transformation of the political system of the Empire was ever to be brought about, he felt, it could be successful only in the measure that a solid basis had been laid for good local administration. Speransky stated the problem quite well in a letter to Count Kochubei written in 1818:

> If one were to ask now what institutions are most needed for the internal organization of Russia, one could answer with certainty and without loosing oneself in airy clouds: an organization or statute for the governing of the provinces is needed most. The present organization is not adequate to the times, the range of affairs, the population and the intelligence of those administered. A revision and reformulation of the organization is the first need of the provinces. As long as it remains in its present sick state, the spirit of the people and the general moral education not only will not progress, but will fall back from year to year. The idea of a better provincial statute will by itself lead to other institutions which are necessary for internal civic order. [It will lead to] institutions which, in any case, will have to precede political changes if one wishes that the latter come about eventually solidly and profitably, without upheavals. In one word: a good [local] administration is the first step; and in administration, rules and institutions occupy the first place, the selection of executives and instructions to them, the second place. Consequently, to begin with the latter is to begin the business from its end. [1]

"What was wrong with the provincial administration?", asked Speransky. And he answered, "Almost everything." From the top down, pervading the whole structure, an absence of accountability was combined in most harmful ways with a maximum of personal discretion. In the first place, the powers of the governor, (and particularly those of the governor-general wherever he existed) were extremely wide because

[1] Letter to Count V. Kochubei, dated 21 Sept. 1818, *Russkaia Starina*, vol. 111 (July 1902), pp. 53—54 (also cited in Fateev: "Speranskii, General Gubernator Sibiri," I, *loc. cit.*, p. 138).

these officials acted as the direct personal representatives of the monarch. At the same time, these wide powers were not clearly defined; and since the time of Paul I, at least, the governor was not even subject to the control and supervision of the central colleges (or ministries after 1802) and the Senate. In principle, the governor carried out the orders of the ministers, but in practice he was not responsible to the minister, whom he could by-pass by addressing himself to the Emperor directly. The Statute on the Provinces of 1775 had adjoined to the governor a Council whose members were directly subordinate to the Senate. Some matters had always to be submitted for the Council's advice before action could be taken. The Council was seen as a consultative college to the governor and a brake on his personal despotism. In practice, however, the Council's power and influence were negligible. In the first place, the prestige of a governor as the personal representative of the Autocrat exercised an overwhelming fascination on the Council. And with the decline of the political and administrative role of the Senate under Alexander I, the position of the governor grew stronger still. Secondly, by virtue of the Law of 1775, the councillors could not prevent the execution of the governor's decision; they merely registered their dissent and reported it to the Senate. This was a "right", Speransky noted, which was held by even the lowliest of government clerks to protect him from the consequences of his superior's illegal actions. [1] Furthermore, there was no effective appeal from the governor's decisions. Appeal from a decision, whose execution could not be stayed anyway without the governor's consent, involved a very long and cumbersome procedure. The outcome of an appeal was always very much in doubt, and its procedural complexities ruled it out for the class that needed it most, i.e. the peasantry. To add to the governor's actual power, the entire bureaucratic apparatus of the provincial administration was in his hands. He could hire and fire most of his subordinates, and often he came with his personal chancery (Speransky himself had done so as Governor-General of Siberia). In short, the most serious defect of the local administration was the governor's extensive power; power that was almost without limit or control. As Speransky phrased it, "an inadequacy of legal power under conditions of excessive personal arbitrariness." [2]

The wide powers of the governor might have been a blessing in disguise, had they been conducive to an orderly and speedy flow of

---

[1] Speranskii, "Zamechaniia o gubernskikh uchrezhdeniiakh" *Arkhiv istoricheskikh i prakticheskikh svedenii*, (1859), No. 4, pp. 95—96.
[2] *Ibid.*, p. 97.

business. But the governor was burdened with such a welter of duties that he could not properly exercise his supervision and control. He had to decide so many questions, important as well as trivial ones, attend so many committee meetings, that it was physically impossible for him to give each case the attention it deserved. The amount of routine work which burdened the governor and prevented him from giving thought and consideration to important things, is graphically illustrated by the following figures: in the 1840's (and the picture was not significantly different in the 1820's) a governor had to sign up to 270 papers a day (i.e. about 100,000 a year!). This task alone would take him 4½ hours a day if he spent only one minute on each paper. Then the governor had to attend 17 meetings of committees and bureaus daily; in addition, all criminal cases in the province (both big and small) were submitted for his "review".[1] As noted in a previous chapter, the governor did not even have the help of a reliable and competent staff which could prepare and digest the material coming up for his decision. The number of educated policy-making assistants was extremely small, and they too were overburdened with work. As for the run of the mill clerical staff, they were, in Speransky's words, "a mob of 'office boys', semi-literate and poor as beggars."[2] No constructive help could possibly be expected from them.

This all-powerful and much harassed governor was not provided with any clear and systematic rules to guide his actions. The instructions he received were always extremely broad and vague. The governor had to decide individual cases without the benefit of a general directive; or else, he had to apply for a specific ruling to St. Petersburg, a ruling which was of little use in other cases. The absence of clear directives, the labyrinthian maze of *ad hoc* decisions, the frequent exemptions from common rules by imperial or ministerial decree, gave the governor a wide range for exercising his own discretion. Little wonder if this latitude was frequently abused for selfish personal ends and if governors sometimes tyrannized their provinces for years without being detected. A glaring recent illustration had been the administration of Pestel and Treskin in Siberia.

Therefore, the first concern of Speransky was to devise some means for supervising and controlling effectively the power and actions of the provincial governor. In an introduction to a project written in 1821, which remained incompleted, he pointed out that the main lack of Russia's provincial administration was some means for supervising

---

1 I. Blinov, *Gubernatory — istoriko-iurdicheskii ocherk* (St. Pbg., 1905), p. 161.
2 "Zamechaniia o gubernskikh uchrezhdeniiakh," *loc. cit.*, p. 96.

the governor. He therefore suggested the establishment of a lieutenant (of the sovereign) or a governor general over several provinces whose exclusive task it would be to control the actions of the individual governors under him. [1]

What was the situation on the lower rungs of the local administration? In European Russia the most important institution was the Land Police (*Zemskaia politsiia*) which combined judicial with executive functions on the local level. The head of this institution in each province was the *ispravnik*, Land Captain, elected by the local nobility and confirmed by the local governor. In a preceding chapter we had occasion to cite Speransky's description and opinion of these Land Captains. A poorly educated, inexperienced official, the Land Captain was the meek and obedient executor of the governor's decrees and wishes. The *ispravnik* was also overburdened with many variegated duties. He had to take care of fields as widely diverse as sanitation, collection of tax arrears, transportation of criminals and government officials, road repairs, general police of the district. In addition, all judiciary cases — both civil and criminal — had to pass through his hands first, and he had to implement and execute decisions of the courts as they affected his district or its inhabitants. As Speransky noted

---

[1] "Vvedenie k namestnicheskomu (oblastnomu) uchrezhdeniiu," *Materialy ... komissii o preobrazovanii gubernskikh i uezdnykh uchrezhdenii, I* (1870), the discussion of the point is on pp. 75—78, the concrete proposals pp. 81—82, 83—84, in particular paragraphs 1—3, 5—6, 10, 11, 13: "I. Besides the *general* supervision entrusted to the Governing Senate, there is established a *local* main supervision over the provincial administration (with the name of Regional Administration).

II. To this end the provinces are combined into regions (*oblast'* or *okrug*).

III. The main local supervision in each Region is entrusted to a Lieutenant (Governor General) and a Council.

V. The Regional Administration (Lieutenancy) belongs to the order of state administration and is, in essence, the Ministry acting on the spot.

VI. The Lieutenant (Governor General), *ex officio* is member of the Governing Senate, 1st Department, and of the Committee of Ministers.

X. The power of supervision covers: 1. the flow of business, 2. the procedure of business.

XI. The power of administration, of decision, is of two kinds: 1. *general* — it consists in that all matters requiring authorization from higher authorities are forwarded through the Regional Administration, 2. *particular* — which consists in the following: a) inform the Senate of local difficulties in case new regulations are being implemented, and in the meantime, stop the application of these regulations, b) in criminal cases, decide without appeal any divergence of opinion between the Civilian Governor and the Criminal Court, c) to order guardianships over those who engage in too wanton a display of luxury or cruelty, d) to take decisive measures in case of popular disasters, when such measures cannot be delayed, e) to dismiss, remove, officials according to the rules established for these contingencies, f) assign to positions and nominate for rewards.

XIII. The power of supervision and correction is entrusted to the Regional Administration, it also extends to those areas which are not part of the provincial administration, such as postal service, customs, etc. From this the military administration is excluded ..."

with some sarcasm, the Land Captain had to catch murderers as well as petty thieves, collect a fine of a few pennies as well as 100,000 rubles in tax arrears. [1] And when we recall the background, education, and experience of this *factotum*, we shall be surprised not so much by the abuses and defects of his administration as by the fact that he could administer at all.

Writing to his friend, Senator Stolypin, about the difficulties he had in finding replacements for local officials he had to dismiss in Penza, Speransky characterized the essential weakness of the provincial administration in the following terms: "Not a single honest, even mediocre individual wants to serve in the subordinate, debased, and poverty-stricken Land Police; noblemen flee from the elections, and soon they will have to be coralled by gendarmes to force them to make use of those valuable rights which, for intelligent and natural reasons, have been given to them so generously." [2] Observations like this, served to strengthen Speransky's reliance on centralization and bureaucracy.

Speransky pinned little hope on the nobility — or any other social class for that matter — to help the overwrought *ispravniks* in the supervision of the regular flow of justice and administration. Nor could the basic change of local administration be entrusted to an elective representative assembly, he felt. Even if suitable men could be found to fill such an assembly — and this was highly doubtful — they would be of little help and only an expensive and useless luxury. The accomplishments of an elected assembly depended on the preparation its members might have for participating in the work of a representative assembly. But what was the Russian situation in this respect? The nobles formed the most educated social class, but if one were to exclude the officials (who could not be made to participate in an elected representative assembly, of course), the ranks of the nobility would be reduced to the lazy and uneducated "old timers" residing on their estates. Such men were quite unprepared for the job, either theoretically or practically; and anyway, they were not numerous enough. The same, even with more justification, could be said of the merchants and townspeople. The conditions of Russian commerce, on the retail level, were not conducive to wide information or experience with matters social and political. Furthermore, the number of merchants was so small that they could not be distracted from their usual occupations without upsetting the economic life of the nation. As to the

---

[1] "Zamechaniia o gubernskikh uchrezhdeniiakh," *loc. cit.*, p. 100.
[2] Letter to Senator Stolypin, dated 19 November 1818, *Russkii Arkhiv*, (1869), p. 1977.

clergy and peasantry, Speransky concluded, they were not "classes" in the real sense of estates, the former because it was too poor, the latter because it had no property. [1] Under the circumstances, Speransky felt justified in his scepticism of the feasibility and success of a representative assembly, be it only for local matters.

Of course, as Speransky well understood, it would be rather senseless to regulate all minutiae of local government from St. Petersburg. It would take too much time and add a load of papers to the already excessive amount processed in the provincial chanceries. He therefore argued for a greater degree of latitude for the provincial institutions dealing with fiscal and judiciary matters. This greater freedom of action, however, must not be allowed to increase the vast powers of the governor and lead to his uncontrolled despotism. In order to prevent such an undesirable result, the collegiate features of the governor's chancery should be strengthened. This idea became the core of Speransky's proposals for the reform of the provincial administration; and, as we have seen, he managed to introduce it to some extent in Siberia in 1822.

As model for the collegiate organization of the governor's chancery he used the organization of the ministries suggested by him in 1811. The governor's office is like the Ministry of the Interior on the local level. The Council of the governor must participate in the discussion of all matters in which the governor does not act as the personal representative of the Emperor (e.g., review of sentences). Except in great emergencies, the governor should never act without the advice and consent of the Council, although the latter's opinions need not be binding on him in some instances. Similar to the Council of a ministry, the governor's council is not to be merely a group of individuals more or less closely connected with the government, but the collegiate body of the chiefs of the several departments of the administration. While each Council member may take independent action on routine matters in his own department, the Council as a body is to act whenever a question pertains to several departments or involves general policies. By strengthening thus the role of the Council, Speransky believed that it would become both a tool for more efficient administration and a brake on the personal despotism of the governor. [2] He advocated a similar arrangement for the district administration. It could be achieved by appointing a number of Deputy Land Captains along lines of

---

[1] Speranskii, "Nuzhdy i zhelaniia," in *Pamiati*, pp. 816—817.
[2] "Zamechaniia o gubernskikh uchrezhdeniiakh," *loc. cit.*, pp. 98—99.

functional specialization. [1] Thereby, the prestige of lower local administrative bodies would be raised and equal — within the limits of the district — that of the provincial government.

The principle of a division of functions had already been introduced at the level of the local administration in 1775. But as a functional division had not been carried out adequately or systematically, Speransky wanted to bring the process to completion. He realized, however, that the ideal of a complete separation between police powers, fiscal duties, and judicial functions at all levels, could not be achieved in Russia at the time. First of all, it would require a greater number of trained officials, and for these the Empire had neither the manpower nor the money. At any rate, on the district level, the basic functions of administration could be separated more clearly and effectively. The independence of the judiciary from the governor, for one, could be strengthened by giving the Provincial Court a status equal to that of the Provincial (governor's) Council. This could be easily achieved: the combined civil and criminal courts of the province would become the highest instance of the judiciary from which — in specified cases — appeal could be made directly to the Senate, by-passing the office of the governor. Furthermore, supervision of the judiciary process as to form and speed, should rest in the hands of an official (Procurator) nominated by the Minister of Justice and with a status equal to that of the governor. Speransky had offered these ideas in embryonic form in his Plan of 1809, but now they were stated precisely and their scope was specified. [2]

The lowest levels of local government should be the township or canton (*volost'*) and the village. Speransky believed that the occasions for abuse of power by the local police officials could be limited by having them deal only with groups, instead of with isolated and weak individuals. The traditional role of city and village "communities" (*obshchestvo* — i.e., "society") had been to stand between the individual and the administration. Consequently, the village commune should be strengthened and given more latitude in carrying out its specific function. Such a strengthening would also have another very important and beneficial consequence. It would be a first step in the training of the peasant for self-administration; it would raise the peasant's confidence and self-respect, and thus provide a training ground for future leaders of the nation's "public opinion". As we see, Speransky never left out of sight the pedagogical and "spiritual" benefits of

1 *Ibid.*, p. 101.
2 *Ibid.*, p. 99.

administrative schemes. It should be added, however, that when speaking of peasants, Speransky had in mind only the state peasants which, of course, limited the *portée* of his proposals to a minority. But the reasoning was applicable to the other classes of society as well: strengthen the "society" of the nobility by giving a greater role to their assemblies and marshals, extend the range of self-administration of the merchants and artisans in the cities. [1]

The preceding considerations provided the basis for concrete suggestions of reform made by Speransky on several occasions in the 1820's. The first instance was the reorganization of Siberia which we have examined earlier in its own context. Then he started — but did not complete — the drafting of a statute for the establishment of Lieutenancies. It followed very closely the provisions of the statute of 1822 on the administrative organization of Siberia. In truth, Speransky seems to have only made a superficial adaptation of the Siberian reforms to European Russia. Several paragraphs of the project were literally copied from the statute on Siberia. In it Speransky was mainly concerned with the establishment of some machinery by which to supervise (and restrain) the overly extended and arbitrary powers of the provincial governor. To establish such a machinery in every province of European Russia, would be too cumbersome; it would make the administrative apparatus more top-heavy than it already was. The solution was to organize the supervision on a higher level than the provinces, and still not concentrate it in the capital, for St. Petersburg was far away and the ministries overburdened with too much detail as it was. [2]

As in Siberia, and in imitation of Balashev's and Novosiltsev's earlier plans of a federalistic character, Speransky recommended that several provinces be grouped together in one region (*oblast' or okrug*) under a Lieutenant or a Governor General. The Lieutenant or Governor General — a member of the Governing Senate and of the Committee of Ministers — would not concern himself with the routine matters of provincial administration. These would remain in the hands of the local governors. The Lieutenant's function would be to supervise and control the governors under his jurisdiction, under instructions from the Governing Senate. In the performance of his duties, the Lieutenant or Governor General was to be assisted by a Council and together they form the Regional Administration (*oblastnoe or namestnicheskoe upravlenie*). The Regional Administration would act as the Committee

---

1 *Ibid.*, p. 102.
2 "Proekt uchrezhdeniia oblastnogo upravleniia," *Materialy... komissii o pre-obrazovanii gubernskikh i uezdnykh uchrezhdenii*, I (1870), pp. 86—87.

of Ministers on the local level. The organization and operating procedures of the Lieutenant's council were similar to those of the council of a ministry. The Council's composition would be as follows: the Governor General (or lieutenant) as president, the regional commander of the internal police, the regional chief of transportation, and a Councillor from the Regional Administration. The civil governors, the provincial marshals of the nobility, the vice governors, the presidents of the courts, the provincial procurator, the director of the postal office, and the director of schools might be invited to participate in the deliberation of questions under their respective jurisdictions. The Council was to have a purely advisory function. No decision taken by it had any force unless confirmed by the Governor General. The functions of this regional administration were to be purely supervisory, except in emergencies. It had no authority to issue new rules, edicts, laws, or to halt the execution of existing legislation. It could only recommend such courses of action to St. Petersburg as it deemed useful. [1] The similarity to the Main Administrations in Western and Eastern Siberia was unmistakable, except that in Siberia the Governor Generals received greater executive authority, and quite understandably so, in view of the region's remoteness from the capital.

Finally Speransky drafted a general statute on the administration of provinces for the Committee of December 6th, 1826, which discussed it at length in 1829 and 1830. His draft was adopted by the Committee — with only very minor modifications — but, like all the labors of that body, it never received legislative sanction. Some of Speransky's basic ideas, however, were incorporated in the Instruction (*Nakaz*) to the Governors of 1837 (which, as far as we know, Speransky did not help to write). This Instruction, defining more carefully the rights and obligations of the governors, remained the guiding directive throughout the 19th century. This alone is reason enough for a brief summary and analysis of Speransky's draft.

The major functions of local government, at whatever level, writes Speransky, are three in number: general police, economy, and justice. Like the Emperor at the center, the governor — personally representing the monarch — supervises the accurate flow of business in all three branches of the provincial administration. To exercise this function effectively, the Governor has the assistance of a Provincial Administration (*pravlenie*), composed of one president, two councillors for the police and four for the treasury, assessors, and the chiefs of departments who may be called for consultation on matters affecting their

[1] *Ibid.*, pp. 94—95.

departments. [1] The major concerns of the Provincial Administration are the safeguarding of the security of persons and property, the execution of judicial decisions, the implementing of economic and fiscal measures. To meet his own criticism of inadequate functional division, business is apportioned among various bureaus on the model of the organization of the ministries. [2]

To overcome the inadequacy and small number of trained administrative personnel, Speransky made an interesting and valuable proposal which was put into effect only many years after his time. It consisted in giving the Provincial Administration the right to employ a few supernumerary assessors, to be selected among young men with a university diploma. [3] Thereby, a young university graduate would have a chance to get acquainted with the practical side of government on the provincial level while awaiting a permanent appointment in the central administration. Such an apprenticeship should then give preference for later promotion. It would give an incentive to university graduates for entering government service; and this in turn would help to attract more students to the universities. To educate and enlighten local public opinion on government policies, Speransky advised the establishment of a weekly paper in each province, to be called the *Vedomosti* (news) of such or such a province. The paper would publish all government decrees and measures, give statistical data on the state of the province, and carry information of general interest or benefit to the public. This suggestion, modeled on the *St. Petersburg Journal,* which Speransky had helped to establish in 1804, was readily taken up and became a general practice by the middle of the century in even as remote a province as Eastern Siberia. [4]

Leaving the existing economic and fiscal administrations untouched, except for some minor details into which we need not enter, Speransky suggested some fundamental changes in the judiciary. As before 1812, the main purpose of these suggestions was to dissociate the judicial from the police functions of local government, and to raise the prestige and efficiency of the courts by giving them a status equal to that of the Provincial Administration. Speransky recommended the establish-

[1] "Proekt uchrezhdeniia dlia upravleniia gubernii," *Sbornik IRIO,* vol. 90, pp. 275—276 (pars. 8—9, 12).

[2] *Ibid.,* pp. 280—285, Pars. 38—41.

[3] *Ibid.,* pp. 275—276, Par. 10. A similar idea on the eventual membership of a delegate of the nobility in the chancery of the Regional Administration (*oblastnoe pravlenie*) is set forth in "Proekt uchrezhdeniia oblastnogo upravleniia," *loc. cit.,* p. 93, Par. 21.

[4] "Proekt uchrezhdeniia dlia upravleniia gubernii," *loc. cit.,* p. 293, Par. 108 and p. 294, Par. 110.

ment of four judiciary bodies on the provincial level: a Civil Chamber (*grazhdanskaia palata*) composed of 1 president, 2 councillors, 4 "jurymen" (2 nobles and 2 burgesses); a Criminal Chamber (*ugolovnaia palata*) staffed in the same way as the Civil one; a Court in Equity (*sovestnyi sud*) based on the provisions of the Law of 1775 and the Charter to the Nobility of 1785; and a Commercial Court (*torgovyi sud*). The latter was an innovation which Speransky had advocated before 1812 as a means of fostering and protecting economic activity. The proposal on the judiciary aimed at implementing Speransky's basic idea of a limited advisory participation of "public opinion" in local judicial matters as a means for developing civic consciousness. At the same time, the proposal introduced an embryonic jury system in the guise of four "public members" selected among the nobility and towns-people in each Civil and Criminal court. To safeguard the independence of the judiciary and to prevent long delays, Speransky suggested the formation of a General Provincial Judiciary Assembly (*obshchee sudebnoe gubernskoe prisutstvie*) to supervise the administration of the courts. For greater effectiveness and independence, the Commercial Court was to have its own executive officers (*pristavy* — sergeants at arms) to supervise the execution of its sentences and decisions. Like the Provincial Administration, and for similar reasons, the courts might employ young graduates of law schools of Russian universities in the capacity of supernumerary assessors. This last provision, Speransky hoped, would serve to increase the number of legally trained and experienced men in the courts of the country. [1]

Turning to the lower levels of local administration, Speransky recommended that the subdivision of the provinces into several districts (*uezd*) be preserved. But as it might be impractical to maintain a strict separation of the three major functions of local government at this level, police and economy were combined into one institution. The judiciary was to remain separate and independent. There were to be two types of district administration, for the country-district and for the larger towns. The latter had some special features, into which we need not enter, arising from the fact that, on the basis of the Charter to the Towns of 1785, the "societies" of burgesses possessed certain rights of self-administration in fiscal matters and cases in equity. According to Speransky's project, the regular country-district administration was to consist of one Chief of the district (*pravitel' uezda*) assisted by a collegiate council composed of the land captain, town police chief, the

---

[1] For the organization of the judiciary, see *ibid.*, pp. 295—310, pars. 112—198 *passim*.

district treasurer, and the "mayor" (*gorodskoi golova*) of the district capital. [1] The district chief was to have one assistant for every ten townships of state peasants. [2] But Speransky did not establish true collegiate control over the appointed executive district chief. The latter may take a decision and order its execution even when opposed by the majority of the Council of the District Administration, although in such a case, he acts on his own personal responsibility. [3] In some cases at least, Speransky suggested, the district chief could be the same person as the district marshal of the nobility. This might help to raise the civic consciousness of the provincial nobility. In so doing, Speransky was also implementing Catherine II's original intention of making the nobility the active element of the country's public life and the leader of the nation. Far from proving that Speransky was now bowing to the necessities of the moment and to the conservative prejudices of his colleagues on the Committee of December 6, 1826, the suggestion shows that he was still thinking in terms of his old idea of building up an "organic" leadership group to guide Russia's spiritual and political progress.

The judiciary on the district level, is the district court, consisting of 1 president, 2 deputies elected by the nobility, and 1 elected by the townships of state peasants. But the deputies from the peasant townships have no voice in cases involving members of the nobility. The president of the court may add one assessor selected among law school graduates to the court staff. The court hears both civil and criminal cases in first instance. Cities have similar courts, with the notable feature that all their members are to be elected by the city council, as they hear only civil cases involving townspeople. [4]

Following the pattern in existence, Speransky envisaged the township (*volost'*) as the lowest division of regular administration. There were two parts to the *volost's* administration: the township proper and the village. The *volost'* administration proper, in Speransky's plan, was to consist of one *volost'* headman, two elders, six village judges, the *volost'* assembly, and the *volost'* secretary. The latter was to be nomiated by the district administration and confirmed by the provincial

1 *Ibid.*, p. 317, pars. 245, 248, 249.

2 The following subjects were specifically reserved for the jurisdiction of the District Administration: "1. state peasants, 2. supervision of guardians appointed over noblemen's estates, 3. deeds and loans on security of serfs, 4. census of sales of real estate, 5. the disciplining of officials, reporting on local needs to higher authorities, control of the routine administration, accounting of treasury monies, preparation of yearly reports." (*Ibid.*, pp. 321—25, par. 261).

3 *Ibid.*, p. 332, Par. 314.

4 *Ibid.*, pp. 332—335, pars. 320—335 *passim*.

authorities. In view of the role played by the secretary, among a largely illiterate peasantry, it is easy to see that in his person, the bureaucracy had a powerful agent and informant. The other members of the administration would be selected directly by the *volost'* assembly. All elections were subject to confirmation by the district and provincial authorities. Membership in the township assembly was to be limited to the chiefs of households only, a very important restriction. [1]

Although the basic unit in an agrarian country is the village, it did not receive much attention in Speransky's project. Perhaps it was because his plan affected only the villages of state peasants — villages of private serfs being under the absolute control of the landlord. As the state peasants formed only a minority of the rural population of Russia and had their own customs and traditions, Speransky preferred to keep away from this last remnant of peasant autonomy. For the village administration of every twenty-five households of state peasants, Speransky suggested a system which paralleled the township setup closely. A village elder, village judges, and a village assembly were to perform functions similar to those of their *volost'* equivalents. To execute the decisions of the village administration and serve as liaison with the township authorities, the village assembly was to elect a few "ten-men" (*desiatnik*), proportionately to the population of the village. [2]

In making his proposals for the village and township administrations, Speransky aimed at keeping the regular bureaucracy and the officials elected by the nobility from executive functions among the peasantry. The major task of the village and *volost'* administrations was to execute the decisions and orders of district and provincial authorities. The peasant "officials" retained some small degree of power and initiative only in matters affecting the village's public order and fiscal obligations. It would therefore be exaggerated to speak of Speransky's proposal as introducing self-government or autonomy for the state peasantry. But, no doubt, an unqualified application of its provisions might have served as the point of departure for a gradual development in this direction.

---

[1] The *volost'* performs the following tasks: keeps a permanent and correct census of the population, acts as the general police for the township or its members, apportions the tax burden among the inhabitants, takes care of petty civil cases and minor misdemeanors. The township administration can impose light sentences, as, for instance, a fine not to exceed ten rubles, temporary indentured labor (for debts), moderate corporal punishment, advance recruiting into the army (a most important right, even though every case had to be confirmed by the district administration). (*Ibid.*, pp. 345—54, pars. 342, 397—468).

[2] *Ibid.*, pp. 336—344, pars. 343—396 *passim*.

Speransky did not intend to introduce (or maintain wherever they may have existed) equalitarian and democratic principles, even on the village level. Indeed, the right to participate in the village and township assemblies — as of old — was exclusively reserved to the heads of households possessing a "homestead". The junior member of the peasant household, the landless peasants, the so-called *bobyl'*, and the artisans, were specifically excluded from these rights and privileges. One is tempted to speak of Speransky as the first Russian statesman to have "wagered on the strong peasant". In fact, he was not so much "wagering on the strong" as he was implementing his own notions of the role the élite — economical and spiritual — played in guiding the mass of the people towards a higher level of moral, social, political, and material life.

We might perhaps summarize Speransky's position and approach towards provincial government as follows: first, he wished to replace the irresponsible and despotic rule of the provincial governor by subjecting him to collegiate control and by clearly separating the judiciary from the administration and the police. In the second place, he aimed at fostering the political and cultural development of the leading social elements in such a manner as to pave their way to a more active and responsible participation in the business of local government. And let us not forget that this new administrative scheme was to find support in a strengthened economic individualism and initiative. His proposals would also contribute to the government's being better informed about the conditions and needs of the people in the provinces. Yet, at no time, did Speransky intend to surrender the principle of the state's role of leadership and to place real political initiative and self-government in the hands of the local population.

Speransky's projects on local administration we have considered up to now, had only been concerned with the free men of the Russian Empire — the nobility, the burgesses, and the state peasants. The latter, of course, were not free in the narrow sense of the term, but they were under the direct jurisdiction of the state and not that of other individuals. Speransky insisted on this distinction: "Serfdom is distinguished from the power held by the sovereign, 1. in that it implies only the power over labor (*praestationis*) [sic!], 2. and though the latter [sovereign power] also demands labor, it is not for a private benefit, but for the public welfare, also its power over labor is exercised only for a specified time and is equal for all on the basis of a public law; that is why such labor is called service." [1]

1 Speranskii, "Krepostnaia vlast'," *Pamiati*, p. 852.

In his schemes for local administration Speransky had not yet taken into account the millions of personal serfs, for he did not expect their early emancipation. And, as we know, in his view only free individuals could be allowed to participate in public life, for they alone had the spiritual and moral qualities prerequisite for the task. He felt that the emancipation would be the last stage, the crowning stone of the reconstruction of Russian political life. It could not be hoped for in less than a generation or two. [1]

Anyone studying Speransky's views on Russia's social structure and his suggestions for transforming it, has the feeling that he shied from dealing with the problem except in a narrow and formal way. [2] Was it because he still felt uneasy about his own lowly social origin and hesitated to show his true attachments? Or was it because he realized the inadequacy of bureaucratic palliative measures in this field and the need for a fundamental change in attitude towards serfdom which he was too cautious and timid to advocate overtly? We do not know which of these was paramount: perhaps they both played their part. But still, his reluctance to deal more fully with serfdom in his major political papers and in the projects devoted to local government, does come as a surprise. The abolition of serfdom, by whatever method, was certainly well in keeping with Speransky's philosophical premises and political ideal of developing the potentialities of the individual, of educating and guiding the nation towards a higher moral and spiritual goal. Obviously, as long as the majority of the Russian people was in a state of serfdom, his ultimate aims had no chance of being ever achieved. Even his very valuable proposals for improving the local administration, if they meant more than a bureaucratic scheme for state peasants and nobility alone, were closely bound up with emancipation.

But, besides this apparent avoidance of the subject, an unwillingness to tackle its complexities, Speransky's views present another difficulty to his biographer. Whatever he wrote on this subject has remained extremely fragmentary, a reflection perhaps of his reluctance to deal with the subject thoroughly. In his writings, he conceived of serfdom in narrow historical and legal terms, taking little account of the actual social realities. Besides, even these unsatisfactory fragments have not been published in full and remain inaccessible in their original form. Speransky wrote at least one lengthy memorandum on the subject of

1 Letter to V. Kochubei, 21 Sept. 1818, *loc. cit.*, and letter to Stolypin, 2 May 1818, *Russkii Arkhiv*, (1869), p. 1703.
2 Cf. V. Semevskii, *Krest'ianskii vopros*, I, p. 348 (note).

serfdom for Count Kochubei's subcommittee in the Committee of December 6, 1826. In spite of its great historical importance, the paper has never been published in full. Kalachev printed a shortened and somewhat inaccurate text in his *Arkhiv istoricheskikh i prakticheskikh svedenii*. A more accurate version was given in Bartenev's compilation, *Deviatnadtsatyi vek;* but it is only a very good and intelligent summary made by Nicholas Miliutin, one of the leading figures of the Emancipation of 1861. Incidentally, Miliutin's summary shows that the leaders of the reforms in the reign of Alexander II were familiar with Speransky's ideas and probably made good use of them in their own work. There are a few more scattered items written by Speransky on serfdom and on the peasantry, but their value is very limited. [1] We are mentioning these details not only to describe the state of our records, but also to warn that the discussion to follow is not as full a description of Speransky's views and plans as we might wish. But as these fragments show a striking consonance with his political philosophy, we are entitled to infer that they are an accurate reflection of his basic views on the peasant problem.

One of the first Russian statesmen to do so, Speransky approached the problem of serfdom from a historical and legal point of view, an approach promising to lead to the formulation of concrete measures of reform. It was quite a change from his previous dogmatic and theoretical approach, a change brought about by his own observations in the provinces and by the philosophic attitude he had elaborated since 1812. True enough, his information on the origins of Russian serfdom, especially on the historical evolution of land tenure, was inadequate, as was natural, for these thorny historical questions have come closer to solution only thanks to the labors of more recent scholars.

Speransky started with the erroneous belief that the peasant had originally settled on land which did not belong to him but to his future owners. This conception might have contained a grain of important truth if Speransky had been of the opinion that the original landowner had been the state. But from his remarks, it does not appear that he had this in mind, for he spoke specifically only of *dvorians* and

---

[1] Emperor Nicholas I perhaps ordered the destruction of those items found among Speransky's papers which might have seemed too radical, dangerous, or undesirable. It was a regular practice of Nicholas to subject to selective sifting the literary remains of all his ministers and officials. Cf. Letter of Nicholas I to General Vasil'chikov on hearing the news of Speransky's death, 11 February 1839: "A l'instant même je viens d'apprendre la fin de notre respectable Speransky... Je crois nécessaire de Vous engager à envoyer de suite Korff mettre les scellés sur les papiers. A demain le reste..." "Iz zapisok barona M. A. Korfa," *Russkaia Starina*, Vol. 99, (July 1899), p. 7.

*pomeshchiks.* [1] By stating this idea in rather extreme form, he disregarded the important social and psychological fact that the peasants believed that the land was theirs (or perhaps God's and the state's); that it was theirs by virtue of the labor they had put into it to make and keep it productive. This erroneous perspective prevented Speransky from reaching the conclusion that, as a matter of right, the peasant must be freed with all the land he is working. It is true, before 1812, Speransky had advocated the freeing of the serf with land and had argued against sale and emancipation without land. But even then he had been satisfied in giving the peasant only a portion of the land he worked. In any case, he did not concede to the peasant a legal or moral right to the land but rather viewed the land grant as a favor or gift given by the nobility.

On the other hand, Speransky correctly understood the process which had resulted in the intensification of serf relations from the 16th century onwards. This process had taken place in two stages: first, the peasant had been tied to the land, had become inseparable from it. In the second place, he had lost his personal freedom; he had become an "object" which could be disposed of independently from the land on which he was settled and which he worked. [2] This evolution had largely been the result of policies dictated to the state by its fiscal and military needs, especially in the reigns of Peter the Great and of his successors. For this reason, from the outset, the state could not take steps which might stop or alleviate the harmful effects of this historical development. [3] All of Speransky's descriptions and arguments concerning serfdom pertain only to the second stage. One has the distinct impression that the first stage, i.e., the tying of the peasant to the land, did not meet with his disapproval in principle. As a matter of fact, his concrete proposals pointed to the reestablishment of the peasant to his earlier status of *glebae adscriptus,* perhaps as a transitional phase.

In his historical and legal analysis, Speransky emphasized that serfdom was a perfectly legal and regular form of social relationships. He explicitly denied that serfdom — even in its undesirable consequence of personal slavery — was the outcome of abuses and illegal acts. What-

---

1 Speranskii, "Opredelenie i ustroistvo krepostnogo sostoianiia," *Pamiati,* p. 846; "Zapiska o krepostnom prave...," in P. Bartenev (ed), *Deviatnadtsatyi vek,* II (1872), p. 160; cf. also "Istoricheskoe obozrenie izmenenii v prave pozemel'noi sobstvennosti...," in "O zakonakh — Besedy grafa M. M. Speranskogo...," *Sbornik IRIO,* XXX (1881), pp. 450ff.

2 "Istoricheskoe obozrenie izmenenii v prave pozemel'noi sobstvennosti...," *loc. cit.,* p. 464.

3 "Zapiska o krepostnom prave..." *loc. cit.,* p. 160. Also, "Opredelenie i ustroistvo krepostnogo sostoianiia," *loc. cit.,* p. 847.

ever our moral attitude and whatever its present economic and social disadvantages, Speransky argued, serfdom was a legitimate (in the sense made popular by Talleyrand) form of human relations. [1] Indeed, the fundamental fact about serfdom is that the labor of the serfs benefits not only individual owners, but the entire state and society. Serf labor enables other Russian subjects to serve the military and political needs of the state. At one point, Speransky even went so far as to say that the basic serf relationship, i.e., the *potestas dominationis* in the form of *praestationis* (right to labor) was something immutable, that it could be altered or surrendered by neither of the two parties, and that the obligation of labor could not even be changed into monetary payments. [2] Admittedly, this was quite a strong statement, and Speransky did not attempt to follow it up with practical suggestions. Nevertheless, it was indicative of his conviction that serfdom had been established for the good of the state and of society at large. It was not a private contract, but an act of public law. And on strictly legal grounds his position was unassailable.

Although serf relations were not based on a contract, i.e., an agreement made between two independent individuals for their private benefit; they were still relations of mutual obligations. But the obligations involved in serfdom were to society, as personified by the state. Therefore they derived from and were determined by laws which only sovereign power could change, and which involved a basic change in the ways of satisfying society's needs. Since 1797, in theory at least, this legal relationship specified that the peasant give $\frac{1}{2}$ of his labor to the landlord, and in return the landlord must give the serf enough land to insure not only the peasant's survival, but also the education and livelihood of his children. The justification for the peasant's giving his labor was twofold: first, to free the nobleman for service to the state; secondly — and which is of greater concern to a modern government — to put into cultivation the arable land belonging to the nobleman.

Although in theory and in law the obligations of the serf were determined by the needs of the state, in practice the distinction between these needs and the wishes of the landlord could not be easily maintained. As the landowner was nearer to the serf than the state, the peasant depended more on his lord's will than on the policies of the state. And so the serf had become an object, chattel, which the

---

[1] "Istoricheskoe obozrenie izmenenii . . .," *loc. cit.*, p. 464; "Opredelenie i ustroistvo krepostnogo sostoianiia," *loc. cit.*, p. 846.
[2] "Krepostnaia vlast'," *Pamiati*, p. 851.

landlord could buy and sell at will, and the idea of mutual obligations for the general benefit to society, had been lost. It was this evolution, Speransky believed, which lay at the root of all the evils and abuses to which the serfs were subject in his time. Neglect of serfdom's historical and legal foundation had resulted in the practical loss of the peasant's rights. Not even the state could now protect him effectively against the cruelties of his master.

Speransky reflected, however, that processes were taking place which served to show clearly the drawbacks of serfdom, even from the point of view of the landowners. As serf relations had been dissociated from land tillage, the number of domestic serfs had grown to unmanageable proportions. At first, the numerous domestics had satisfied the vanity and craving for luxury of their owners. But by now they had become a costly and inefficient labor force. Their upkeep was growing to be more and more of a burden to the average nobleman, and their usefulness was very limited at best. Economic unproductivity had resulted in the demoralization of both serfs and owners. At the same time, the last decades had witnessed an increase in education, a raising of the level of enlightenment, and a growing awareness of the destructive effects of serfdom. Since the second half of the 18th century, there had taken place among the best men of Russian society — no doubt Speransky had in mind his friend Radishchev and the latter's teacher, Novikov — a moral revulsion against the conditions of serfdom. In other words, both interest and moral sentiment were turning the educated Russians against serfdom. An ever growing number of individuals was recognizing the desirability and even necessity of emancipation.

While the actual economic condition of the personal (private) serfs was deteriorating, their tastes, desires, and needs were developing and growing. This was one result of the spread of enlightenment, of the example set by their masters, and of the success attained by some serfs in trade. The serfs found it more and more difficult to accept their condition. Their propensity to rebellion was awakening anew and the danger to public peace was waxing more threatening. Furthermore, serfdom prevented the full development of trade and industry in the cities. Serf labor was not encouraged and stimulated by competition; it was not eager to increase its productivity, for it could not dispose of its fruits in full. Speransky's basic economic ideas, discussed earlier, had made him keenly aware of the economic consequences of serfdom. But we also note that the major ground for his criticism of the institution was not so much the economic disadvantages by themselves, as the moral consequences. The unproductive and demoralizing character of serf labor contributed to the depopulation of towns, the deterioration and disappearance of handicrafts. The legal fetters imposed on the peasants in general, and on the serfs in particular, limited greatly their participation in trade. Not being able to dispose of the product of their labor in complete freedom, the incentive for producing more and more efficiently was killed at the very outset. Improvements in agricultural techniques were stymied, for the Russian peasant suffered not so much from a lack of land as from a lack of capital. But capital for improvements could be obtained only through the sale of surplus products. Hence the absolute necessity for eliminating the legal disabilities which handicapped the serf and peasant in the market. [1]

Speransky noted, however, that the situation was not too serious yet. For the time being at least, the desires and demands of the peasants were determined by specific local and temporary grievances and by the indifference shown by local authorities to the decrees and prescriptions of the government. This passive and as yet inchoate discontent, though, could become more intense and then the danger of a revolt and of a second *Pugachevshchina* would be great indeed. Interest and duty demanded that the government stop this dangerous deterioration and that it take the necessary measures right now. These measures could and should be very gradual; there was no need for ill-considered haste. [2]

Unlike some other publicists of his time, Speransky put no faith in the actions of individual serf-owners (the failure of the Law on Free Agriculturists of 1803 had been a lesson that could not be easily dismissed). He relied entirely on government action, an attitude which was consonant with his own basic political thinking and also a reflection of the traditional outlook of the lower classes from which he had sprung. As he had occasion to observe, the nobility, and even more so the merchants, had woefully lagged behind the state in leading the country to a higher level of cultural and moral development. It was natural to assume that in the peasant question, too, success was more likely to come from the leadership and guidance of the state.

The gradual process of solving the vital problem should begin by an equalization of the legal and material conditions of private and state peasants. For if the material circumstances of privately owned serfs were at times much better than those of state peasants, the latter en-

---

[1] "Zapiska o krepostnom prave...," *loc. cit.*, pp. 160—162; "Nuzhdy i zhelaniia," *Pamiati*, p. 813.
[2] "Nuzhdy i zhelaniia," *loc. cit.*, p. 813.

joyed a more advantageous legal status and had more real freedom. By giving the private serfs the same status as the state peasant, serf relations would revert to their original basis; they would again be based on obligations to society (i.e. the state) and not to particular individuals. Speransky believed that such a program met with the approval of the peasants themselves, for he had noted that the desire of every privately owned serf was to become a state peasant. [1] Acceptance of this approach would be an important step forward in the final solution of the vexing problem. Indeed, it implied that, on the one hand, the government was willing to take the place of the individual serf owner in the relations of mutual obligation; and, on the other, it proclaimed the state's decision to consider the emancipation as its own responsibility. No longer would the government put faith in the personal sentiments of individual owners as a sufficient stimulus to emancipation. The Soviet historian, Druzhinin, correctly noted that from the acceptance of Speransky's approach dates the government's "progressive" attitude towards the solution of the peasant question. [2]

What were the concrete measures the government should take to this effect? Speransky suggested two sets of actions. In the first place, steps must be taken immediately to return to the original serf status, i.e. fixation to the land. Secondly, after the completion of the first task, long range policies could be initiated which, in due course of time would lead to the full emancipation of the Russian peasantry. [3] For the first part of the program, Speransky proposed six measures of which only three pertained to the serfs themselves: 1. prohibition to sell serfs or to offer serfs as security without land (but preserving the validity of deeds disposing of land and peasants); 2. permission to resettle peasants within the domain, but prohibition to sell them for resettlement elsewhere; 3. prohibition of all sales which tend to decrease the land holdings of the peasants. [4] As for the long range measures, their first purpose would be to introduce definite contractual relations between peasants and landowners, so that the obligations and duties of each party are stated clearly and specifically (though this still would not make of serfdom a matter of private contract in the narrow technical

1 *Ibid.*, p. 811.
2 Druzhinin, *Gosudarstvennye krest'iane i reforma P. D. Kiseleva*, I. p. 172.
3 Before these steps are taken, Speransky lectured to the heir presumptive, Grand Duke Alexander, one should first clarify and state explicitly the various obligations a serf has to his lord. Much of the abuse is due to the absence of such clear rules, and if they are introduced, they will not only protect the peasant but also help develop a more responsible and "civilized" attitude towards the peasant on the part of the nobility and the officials. "Istoricheskoe obozrenie izmenenii...," *loc. cit.*, p. 466.
4 "Zapiska o krepostnom prave..." *loc. cit.*, pp. 162—163.

sense). In turn, this would make it possible for the officials to enforce the obligations undertaken by both parties and to prosecute violations on the ground of specific, precise, and publicly stated rules. The most important long term measures envisioned by Speransky were four: 1. reform of the status and conditions of the state peasants (an idea taken up by Count Kiselev in the 1840's); 2. transfer of privately owned serfs to the same status as the state peasants, i.e. the relations between landowner and serf would be the same as those between the Treasury and the state peasants; 3. reorganization of the district and township administration; 4. improvement of the rules governing the serfs' right to work in towns and the abolition of all restrictions on peasant movement for this purpose. [1]

All the acts just mentioned would take care only of the legal aspects and the administration of the peasantry. Speransky expected that, along with changed legal and administrative relations, there would also come a transformation in the way of life in the villages. The expected transformation was Speransky's clearest statement of what social change he considered best for Russia. It was perhaps the most influential heritage he bequeathed to subsequent generations of Russian officials, more particularly to the reformers in the reign of Alexander II.

An important peasant institution whose fate had to be considered most carefully, in the first place, was the village commune (*obshchina*). By Speransky's time, it had already become the subject of interesting and lively controversies. In the early part of the 19th century, most influential Russian writers on political economy were followers of the physiocrats and of Adam Smith, J-B. Say, and the like. Naturally, they looked at the commune with some disfavor as a survival of more primitive conditions and as a handicap to Russia's economic progress. This opinion was held by outstanding and influential economists like Admiral Mordvinov, Nicholas Turgenev, and the plethora of German political economists at Russian universities and in government offices. Speransky, however, in spite of his doctrinaire economic liberalism and modernism, took a more realistic point of view and refused to be dogmatic on the question of the role and future of the commune. On the basis of his first-hand observations of conditions in the village, he felt that the commune was such an important and old institution,

---

[1] *Ibid.*, pp. 164—165 — It might be added that individual ideas of Speransky's, we have just described, had been proposed by various officials previously, for example Jakob, Storch, Kankrin. But none of these foreign authors had systematized them in a way that was directly applicable to Russian circumstances. The most complete exposition of these other suggestions is still V. I. Semevskii's *Krest'ianskii vopros v Rossii.*

possessing great psychological and moral significance, that it would be both dangerous and unprofitable to destroy it merely for the sake of some economic doctrine. If the commune could still play a useful role in the peasant's relations to the state and the landowner, and if the peasant himself wished to preserve it, the commune should be kept. But the commune should not be preserved by force of law against the will of the peasants. Moreover, to develop individual self reliance and initiative, only such measures should be taken as would bring about the commune's gradual, "organic", disappearance. [1] For once, Speransky approached a vital aspect of Russian life from the point of view of its social reality. He could do it in this instance the more easily as it performed a desirable spiritual function.

Speransky therefore envisaged the eventual disappearance of the commune and its replacement by individual "strong" peasants. His position should not come as a surprise to us. We have seen that as early as 1809 he had relied on the property owner for the success of his plan of reorganization. Similarly, in his draft statute for the provincial administration submitted to the Committee of December 6, 1826, he had clearly specified that only the heads of households, i.e., the actual owners of houses and land, would be allowed to participate in the volost' and village administrations.

Speransky never ceased to stress the desirability of developing a class of active and energetic peasants who themselves might become rich landowners and traders. He therefore suggested that the forcible periodical redistribution of lands in the village communes be stopped. The surplus population for which land could not be found in the old settled districts should be resettled in areas where free land was plentiful, Siberia for instance. (This idea was taken up and partly implemented by Kiselev in the 1840's and 1850's as far as the state peasants were concerned). Such a resettlement was naturally possible only if the raison d'être for periodic redistribution, the capitation (poll) tax (podushnaia podat'), were eliminated and replaced by a general proportional land tax. [2] This was an idea that was taken up by the reformers of the 1860's, but was not realized until the end of the century.

Holding out as his ideal an harmonious and organic nation, Speransky wished to see the rise of a class that would serve as "transition"

---

[1] Druzhinin, op. cit., I, p. 183.

[2] Speranskii, "Mery k ustroistvu gorodskikh i kazennykh sel'skikh obyvatelei," Pamiati, p. 817. Though Speransky mentions specifically only state peasants, the suggestion would apply to all peasants once they have attained equality of status with the state peasants as envisaged in the first part of the program.

between the common peasantry and the upper classes. He therefore advocated — as he had before 1812 — that individual family households be transmitted untouched from generation to generation, and that their owners be allowed to dispose of them freely like any other kind of privately owned real estate. It would put an end to the constant splitting up of peasant holdings. Of course, keeping the households intact might lead to an increase in the number of landless agricultural laborers, but Speransky was not very afraid of such a consequence. The surplus of peasant labor would be drained off into the cities, once the legal disabilities and restrictions on their movement and residence had been lifted. As for inequality of condition and well being, "it is quite natural; it exists everywhere, even under present conditions..., and [among] private and state peasants it depends on their industry or their luck in agriculture. This very same inequality which will develop mutual benefits and needs will also be the main bond between landowners and hired hands." [1]

It is true that such a solution would lead to "class differentiation" in the villages, the great bugbear of the populists at the end of the century. Speransky knew it and favored it. He believed that the peasant should be given a chance to get rich, to acquire wealth, and even to move into another social class. Not everybody would be able to do so, but Russia was large and wealthy, so that even the unsuccessful individuals would find a livelihood if they were at all willing to work. To underline the social status of the property-owning peasant, Speransky thought it desirable to make a legal distinction between the head of a household (the "farmer" in the American sense) and the hired hands. [2] Quite a similar approach was taken by Stolypin over 75 years later, though the historical parallel should not be overdone, as conditions were so radically different. Anyway, it is doubtful that Stolypin was well acquainted with Speransky's views on the peasantry.

Speransky definitely wanted to give the peasant the opportunity to expand his economy, produce a saleable surplus, acquire more machinery, reinvest the capital earned in this manner, improve his standard of life, and become a small capitalist. To this end, the peasants should be permitted not only to trade freely, but also be relieved of the discriminatory taxes and duties they paid at the present time. For as long as there were only few rich commercial and industrial entrepreneurs from the peasantry, they could not become the leaders of their class or show the way and spur on their fellow villagers by their

[1] Quoted by Druzhinin, *op. cit.*, I, p. 182.
[2] "Mery k ustroistvu gorodskikh i kazennykh sel'skikh obyvatelei," *loc. cit.* p. 814.

example. Rather they would become the object of envy and discontent, and upset the social harmony in the village. [1] Through the growth of peasant capital, the peasants, merchants, and industrial entrepreneurs would be brought closer together. The passage from one group into the other would become easier, with benefit to the country at large. Speransky was perhaps not consciously planning the growth of a Russian middle class (bourgeoisie in the Western sense); but he obviously did sense that the 19th century was destined to see the rise of a new aristocracy, the aristocracy of commercial, industrial, and landed wealth. [2] It would be to Russia's advantage — both economic and political — not to hamper this process, so that the Empire of the Tsars keep in step with the other countries of Europe.

After 1821, as before his exile in 1812, Speransky exhibited a somewhat dualistic, contradictory approach towards the basic social and economic problem of his time. Politically, he clearly was a conservative and a firm believer in the state's active role in directing the progress of the nation. In the economic realm he wished to promote the untrammeled activity and free enterprise of individuals. To attain this double goal the most effective way, he thought, was to respect and make use of the institutions and traditions of Russia's social and economic life which had grown over the centuries. In the villages, for instance, the commune should be preserved to help maintain stability and peace, to alleviate the hardships of dislocation during the period of transition. It also explains his extremely cautious — over-cautious from our point of view — approach to serfdom.

Speransky's ambivalent attitude was dominant among the Slavophile reformers in the 1860's, the ("legal") liberals in the 1870's, and even the "progressive reactionaries" à la Katkov. Economic and social laisser-faire liberalism was to be established by bureaucratic methods combined with a political conservatism which stressed the pedagogical function of the bureaucratic state. It was a strange kind of mixture, full of contradictions and vagueness — and these provided one of the dominant themes in Russian political thought throughout the 19th century and into the 20th. The ordinary meanings of liberalism and conservatism hardly characterized adequately this type of attitude, not even an ideology. Speransky was one of the influential originators of this mode of thought which intermittently, and not too consistently, helped shape the policies of the Imperial Government.

---

1 *Ibid.*, p. 818 and "Nuzhdy i zhelaniia," *loc. cit.*, p. 814.
2 "Narodnye smiateniia," *Pamiati*, pp. 822–823.

## SOURCES

General material: Bychkov (ed.), *V Pamiat' grafa Speranskogo* has several short papers and letters by Speransky on the peasant question; Speranskii: "Zapiska o krepostnom prave v komitet 6go dekabria 1826 g.," (N. A. Miliutin ed.) in P. Bartenev, *Deviatnadtsatyi vek — istoricheskii sbornik*, vol. II (Moscow 1872) pp. 159—165; the same under the title "Zapiska o krepostnykh" in *Arkhiv istoricheskikh i prakticheskikh svedenii* (1859), vol. III, section 1, pp. 1—15 (it is an abbreviated form of Speransky's paper more fully summarized by Miliutin); "Istoricheskoe obozrenie izmenenii v prave pozemel'noi sobstvennosti i v sostoianii krest'ian," Appendix VII to "O zakonakh — Besedy grafa M. M. Speranskogo s E. I. Vysochestvom Gosudarem Naslednikom..." in *Sbornik IRIO*, XXX, (St. Pbg. 1881) pp. 450—466; "Vvedenie k namestnicheskomu (oblastnomu) uchrezhdeniiu (1821)," in *Materialy... komissii o preobrazovanii gubernskikh i uezdnykh uchrezhdenii*, I (1870) pp. 68—85; "Proekt uchrezhdeniia oblastnogo upravleniia (1822)," *ibid.*, I, pp. 86—112; "Proekt uchrezhdeniia upravleniia gubernii," *Sbornik IRIO*, vol. 90 (St. Pbg. 1894), pp. 274—358; "Zamechaniia o gubernskikh uchrezdeniiakh," *Arkhiv istoricheskikh i prakticheskikh svedenii*, (1859), No. 4, pp. 92—104. Further material is found in various letters of Speransky's to Count Kochubei in *Russkaia Starina* vol. 111 (July 1902), pp. 51—59 and to Senator A. Stolypin in *Russkii Arkhiv*, (1869), pp. 1682—1708, 1966—1984, and (1870), pp. 1125—1156.

On the peasant problem see: N. M. Druzhinin, *Gosudarstvennye krest'iane i reforma P. D. Kiseleva*, vol. I (Moscow-Leningrad 1946); V. I. Semevskii, *Krest'ianskii vopros v Rossii v XVIII i pervoi polovine XIX veka*, 2 vols., St. Pbg. 1888. The titles on the history of Russian economic thought and conditions cited in Chapter 4 are relevant and often quite useful in this connection.

On Russian local administration, see: I. Blinov, *Gubernatory — istoriko-iuridicheskii ocherk*, St. Pbg. 1905; I. I. Ditiatin, *Ustroistvo i upravlenie gorodov Rossii*, St. Pbg. 1875; A. D. Gradovskii, "Istoricheskii ocherk uchrezhdeniia general-gubernatorov v Rossii," *Russkii Vestnik*, (Nov.-Dec. 1869), pp. 5—31 and 396—413; V. V. Ivanovskii, "Administrativnoe ustroistvo nashikh okrain," *Uchenye Zapiski Kazanskogo Universiteta*, vol. 58, No. 6 (Nov.-Dec. 1891), pp. 27—70.

On the reign of Nicholas I, see: M. Polievktov, *Nikolai I — biografiia i obzor tsarstvovaniia*, (Moscow 1918); A. E. Presniakov, *Apogei samoderzhaviia — Nikolai I*, (Leningrad 1925); Th. Schiemann, *Geschichte Russlands unter Kaiser Nikolaus I.* 4 vols., (Berlin 1908—1913); N. Shil'der, *Imperator Nikolai I*, 2 vols., (St. Pbg. 1903); C. de Grunwald, *La vie de Nicolas Ier*, (Paris 1946).

# CHAPTER X

AN UNPLEASANT INTERLUDE
SPERANSKY AND THE DECEMBRISTS

Speransky's exclusive preoccupation with his work on the administrative reform of the provinces did not prevent his being affected by the dramatic events which took place in December 1825 on the occasion of the death of Alexander I and the ensuing interregnum. Much against his will, he was at first himself implicated in the Decembrist movement, and later given an important part in the trial of the conspirators of December 14. This involvement affected his relations to the new sovereign, Nicholas I, and his position in the new reign. It deserves therefore some consideration in a political biography.

The unexpected death of Emperor Alexander I in far-away Taganrog, and the ensuing confusion over the succession, brought into the open the secret societies that had been organized in the course of the preceding decade. While Grand Dukes Constantine and Nicholas were debating as to who should occupy the throne, the members of the secret societies (Northern and Southern branches) staged their ill-fated and unsuccessful uprising on December 14, in the Senate Square in St. Petersburg (and in some mutinies in Southern Russia a month later). The details of the revolt are known well enough and need no repetition here. In itself the affair was not greatly significant; it never developed into a serious threat to the imperial regime. But its social and historic consequences were far-reaching. It split the educated class in two irreconcilable camps: those who broke the revolt, tried, and punished the Decembrists, (in a word, the government and its bureaucracy) and the friends, followers, and future disciples of the Decembrists, the progressive intelligentsia. The Decembrists' multiple and close connections with the court, the army, the government, and "society" meant that their uprising affected all and every member of the social and cultural élite directly or indirectly. Speransky was no exception to this.

After dispersing the mutinous regiments by artillery fire on the

Senate Square, the government proceeded to arrest and interrogate the leaders, and their suspected accomplices. It did not prove difficult for Nicholas I and his assistants (Generals Benkendorf, Chernyshev, and Levashev) to obtain extensive confessions from the accused and draw up a list of all participants and their sympathizers. The result, as noted by Emperor Nicholas, was that "among the testimonies incriminatory of individuals, but without adequate evidence to start interrogation, there were such as to involve N. S. Mordvinov, Senator Sumarokov, and even M. M. Speransky. Such testimonies gave rise to doubts and distrust which for a long time could not be dispelled completely." [1]

Naturally, Nicholas lost no time in ordering a thorough investigation of the relations Speransky (and the other prominent officials) had or might have had with the Decembrists. This investigation was conducted in utmost secrecy, unknown to (if perhaps not entirely unsuspected by) its objects. The documents and papers pertaining to it were kept separate from the general file on the Decembrist affair. The chief secretary of the committee of investigation, Borovkov, recalled in his memoirs: "The investigation of the connection between these persons and the criminal society [of the Decembrists] was conducted in such secrecy that even the officials of the committee [of investigation] knew nothing about it. I myself wrote the protocols and kept them separately and did not merge them into the general file." [2]

Speransky's name came up when several of the leaders testified that he — along with Admiral Mordvinov, Senator Stolypin, General Ermolov — had been considered as a prospective candidate for a provisional administration or Duma which they would set up. [3] According to some sources his name was put forward to reconcile the programs and plans of action of the Southern and Northern societies of the Decembrists. [4] In replying to his interrogator, the leader of the Northern Society and

---

[1] B. E. Syroechkovskii, *Mezhdutsarstvie 1825 g. i vosstanie dekabristov...* (Moscow-Leningrad 1926), p. 30.

[2] N. A. Borovkov, "Avtobiograficheskie zapiski," *Russkaia Starina,* 95 (Nov. 1898) p. 348.

[3] Iakushkin, *Zapiski,* p. 146 and M. Murav'ev, "Ideia vremennogo pravitel'stva u dekabristov i ikh kandidaty," *Tainye obshchestva v Rossii v nachale XIX v.,* (Moscow 1926), pp. 68—88 *passim.*

[4] Ryleev recalled: "In the course of the conversation on the formation of a Great Assembly (*sobor*), we also talked about a Provisional administration. This was, it seems, at the house of Mit'kov. M. Murav'ev-Apostol proposed to nominate to it the directors of Pestel's Society, one more from the Southern Directorate, and N. Turgenev or Trubetskoi. To this the latter objected that the Provisional administration should include people already known to all of Russia and proposed Mordvinov and Speranskii. To this all agreed. I also was in agreement, and from then on, to the very 14 December, this idea remained unchanged in the Northern Society," *Vosstanie dekabristov,* vol. I, p. 176, quoted by Nechkina, *Vosstanie 14 Dekabria 1825 g.* p. 28. Also Semevskii, *Politicheskie i obshchestvennye idei dekabristov,* p. 492.

its would-be "dictator", Prince Trubetskoi, declared: "One would have
had to force the Senate to appoint a Provisional Governing Duma and
see that among its members be included persons respected in Russia,
for example Mordvinov or Speransky." But, as the Prince hastened to
add, "I did not say that Mordvinov or Speransky belonged secretly to
any society. I truthfully do not know anything about it and do not
think that such was the case." [1] The very fact that Speransky was
considered a candidate for a provisional revolutionary government was
sufficient evidence to lead the Emperor to suspect much closer and active
ties between Privy Councillor Speransky and the Decembrists. This
point Nicholas had to clarify fully before he would call Speransky to
active government work. [2]

It was natural for Speransky to have known many members of the
Northern Society, in some cases even quite intimately. After all, most
of the leading conspirators had been prominent in St. Petersburg
society as members of the military and civil services. Nicholas A.
Bestuzhev was acquainted with Speransky socially, visited his house, and
took part in the *soirées* organized by Speransky's daughter. [3] The fiery
revolutionary poet, K. Ryleev, was employed by the Russian-American
Trading Company. Speransky made his acquaintance while participating
in the discussions of the new statute for the company. [4] Other casual
meetings with Decembrists could be mentioned, and many probably
took place without leaving a record.

But the most important direct link between the Decembrists and
Speransky was Lieutenant Colonel Batenkov, who had been Speransky's
chief assistant in Siberia. Speransky took Batenkov back with him to
St. Petersburg to make use of his talents and knowledge in drafting
the Siberian statutes. After completion of this task, Batenkov was
transferred to the Military Colonies Administration under Arakcheev
to whom Speransky had strongly recommended him. But even after
joining Arakcheev's staff, Batenkov continued to live in Speransky's
house. Batenkov played a prominent role in the Northern Society.
Through Batenkov the Decembrists hoped to reach Speransky and to
enroll his support and even collaboration. The importance the Decembrists attached to Batenkov's connection with Speransky can be inferred
from the statement Kakhovskoi sent from prison to General Benkendorf
(dated May 14, 1826). Kakhovskoi — himself a leading member and one

[1] *Vosstanie dekabristov*, I, p. 159.
[2] S. Trubetskoi, *Zapiski* (St. Pbg. 1906), pp. 57 ff.
[3] "Zapiski M. A. Bestuzheva," *Russkaia Starina*, vol. 32 (1881), p. 610.
[4] Murav'ev, "Ideia vremennogo pravitel'stva," *loc. cit.* p. 77.

of the five to be hanged for his active role — wrote that in the course of one of his conversations with Ryleev he expressed the fear that they might not find support among influential leaders and government officials. To this Ryleev answered: "Do not worry, we have people in the Senate and in the Council of State. I shall tell you, but ask you to keep it quiet and not to tell it to anyone, Ermolov and Speransky are ours." When some time later Kakhovskoi checked again with Ryleev whether it was true that Speransky was "ours", Ryleev said: "Oh, he surely will be ours, we are working on him through Batenkov." [1]

As appears from Ryleev's statement, Speransky's participation and collaboration after a successful revolt was only hypothetical. Actually, none of the conspirators had approached Speransky directly or enlisted his support. [2] Even Batenkov, who was supposed to have sounded him out, maintained that Speransky would not go along. He insisted that one could not count on Speransky, for the simple reason that it was too difficult to find out what "our old man really thought." [3] The special investigation concluded that the evidence did not indicate that Speransky was ever approached by the Decembrist leaders or even knew that he had been considered for membership in a provisional revolutionary government. All the sources available to this day support this conclusion of the Committee. As the accused Decembrists eventually told everything quite truthfully, there is no particular reason to doubt the testimony of Batenkov himself who was in the best position to know. And Batenkov stated very clearly that he felt: "...there is no need of Speransky," and did not divulge to him the plans the Decembrists had for him. [4]

The question arises why was Speransky's name mentioned for the provisional administration to be established by the Decembrists? Our analysis of his political plans, philosophy, and ideology has shown that he could hardly have been called a revolutionary or even a radical reformer. Even Muraviev's moderate "constitution" for the Northern Society would have been too extreme and uncongenial to Speransky. In the years following his exile, he had become if anything more cautious

---

[1] *Vosstanie dekabristov*, I, p. 374.

[2] Semevskii, *Politicheskie i obshchestvennye idei dekabristov*, p. 493. On the basis of the documents published so far, it does not seem that all Decembrists were enthusiastic about Speransky's participation in the movement or even in their provisional administration. There was much distrust of him, perhaps a lingering carry-over from the pre-1812 feelings against him.

[3] *Ibid.*, p. 495.

[4] "Prilozhenie k dokladu sledstvennoi kommissii...," *Russkii Arkhiv* (1875), No. 3, p. 435; also, Oreus, "G. P. Batenkov — istoriko biograficheskii ocherk," *Russkaia Starina*, (1889), p. 314.

than before. He maintained the closest relations with Arakcheev and other "reactionary" favorites of the day. Mindful of the disadvantages of his social isolation before 1812, Speransky now endeavored to gain admittance to the high society of St. Petersburg. He wanted to see his daughter well settled by making an advantageous marriage. These social and political interests of his did not make of Speransky a likely sympathizer with the Decembrists. And yet his name was put forward with some insistence by the conspirators. The fact that he was the best known and most talented official whose name would lend respectability and prestige to the new regime could have contributed to the choice, but would perhaps not have been decisive.

Actually, the Decembrists thought of Speransky's candidature because, as Prince Trubetskoi put it, "he was not considered to be an enemy of innovation." [1] At first glance this does not seem a very strong argument. What Trubetskoi meant was that Speransky was known to have been the Emperor's assistant in working out plans and measures of reform during the first "liberal" decade of Alexander's reign. The Decembrists believed that before his exile Speransky had been engaged on a thorough reorganization of Russian political life along modern, liberal, constitutional lines. Though this characterization is questionable, as we have tried to show, one still must ask how the members of the secret societies knew about Speransky's intentions and proposals. His major reform project, the Plan of 1809, had remained secret and was known in its entirety only to a very select few. Speransky's silence on his activities before 1812 also makes it unlikely that even his close assistants, like Batenkov, knew very much about the specific contents of the Plan of 1809. But the discussions and various constitutional reform proposals of the Decembrists show that they were acquainted — albeit superficially and in a somewhat biased way — with the ideas of Speransky.

The answer to the question lies in the disposition made of the papers which were seized at Speransky's house on the night of his exile. [2] Three trunks containing all his political plans and projects were deposited under seal in the State Chancery. In 1813 they were opened and examined by Senator Koshelev and State Secretary Molchanov, and

---

[1] "Prilozhenie k dokladu sledstvennoi kommissii," *loc cit.*, p. 435.

[2] The following exposition is based on Fateev, "Bumagi Speranskogo," *Zapiski Russkogo Istoricheskogo Obshchestva v Prage*, I (1927), pp. 105—111 *passim*. After the manuscript had gone to press, there appeared a circumstantial and more up to date account of the fate of Speransky's papers and of their present state in S. N. Valk, "Zakonodatel'nye proekty M. M. Speranskogo v pechati i v rukopisiakh", *Istoricheskie Zapiski*, 54 (1955), pp. 464—472.

a part filed in various offices; the remainder was returned to the State Chancery. In 1816 Speransky requested that his translation of St. Thomas à Kempis' *Imitation of Christ,* which was kept in one of the trunks together with his political papers, be returned to him. Alexander I granted the request. Alexander Turgenev was ordered to search the papers, to take out the translation, and to send it to Speransky. Therefore, in 1816 already, Alexander Turgenev — whose brother Nicholas was close to the Decembrists — had had a glimpse into the political papers of Speransky. In 1820 A. Turgenev made a more searching examination of these papers when he was directed to extract all those which might be of value to the Commission on Codification. Alexander Turgenev gave some of the papers (for instance, a copy of Speransky's 1802 *mémoire*) to his brother Nicholas. Nicholas copied or extracted the contents of these projects and, in all probability, circulated them among his Decembrist friends. But either accidentally or by design, N. Turgenev communicated only excerpts, thereby creating the impression that they were quite liberal. That this was indeed the case is confirmed by the wording of the extracts of the Plan of 1809, published in Paris in 1847 by N. Turgenev in his book *La Russie et les Russes.* It is not very material for our purpose whether N. Turgenev consciously slanted Speransky's ideas by his own selection of the passages he circulated or whether he himself possessed only inaccurate and incomplete versions. The result was that the Decembrists were acquainted with a liberal interpretation and form of Speransky's ideas. This proved enough for them to believe that, if successful, they could count on his support and assistance.

But they never went beyond this vague hope. As Borovkov testified in his autobiographical notes: "The most searching investigation revealed that this hope [of enlisting Speransky] was pure invention and loose talk to win over the gullible." [1] In the final analysis, as the investigating committee concluded: "The leaders of the Northern Society, planning the formation of a provisional government, selected for it members of the Council of State, namely — as they said — Admiral Mordvinov and Privy Councillor Speransky. But only because the former, Admiral Mordvinov, often expressed in the Council of State opinions in opposition to the proposals of the ministers, and because the latter, Privy Councillor Speransky (in the words of Prince Trubetskoi), *'was not considered by them to be an enemy of innovations'."* [2] The Emperor's suspicions were allayed, and he resolved to use Speransky's talents (and

---

[1] Borovkov, "A. D. Borovkov i ego avtobiograficheskie zapiski," *loc. cit.,* p. 348.
[2] "Prilozhenie k dokladu sledstvennoi kommissii...," *loc. cit.,* p. 435.

at the same time test his loyalty) by calling him to participate in the trial of the conspirators.

The role played by Speransky in the trial proceedings has been described, on the basis of archival materials, by Prince Golitsyn in an article published in 1916. As Golitsyn's findings quite adequately cover Speransky's participation in the trial — and as no other important sources on this episode are available — we shall merely summarize them. [1] The imperial decree setting up the High Criminal Court to try the Decembrists was issued on June 1, 1826. But a couple of months before that, in April, Speransky had begun working on the preparation of the trial and of the instructions by which the Court was to be guided. He became the closest collaborator and assistant to the Emperor on all matters pertaining to this important business.

The Court was composed of 72 members drawn from the three major government bodies (soslovie), i.e., 18 from the Council of State, 3 from the Holy Synod, 36 from the Senate, and 15 special appointees. The President of the Council of State, Prince Lopukhin, was appointed President of the Court. Speransky copied many rules of procedure for the Court from past extraordinary political trials, especially those of Mirovich and Pugachev in the reign of Catherine II. But he added some special rules for the needs of the present court. Thus, he was responsible for the Court's asking only three questions of each accused: whether he acknowledged his signature beneath the testimony, whether he had given the testimony of his free will, and whether he had been confronted with other witnesses. Such a procedure eliminated, for all intents and purposes, a personal examination of the accused in Court and based the Court's ultimate verdict exclusively on the written records of the pretrial investigation and interrogations. Speransky also suggested (and the suggestion was adopted) that a special committee of members of the Court make a search for all legal precedents pertinent to the case and then classify the defendants into various categories for easier and more equitable assignment of punishments. Following the intention of Emperor Nicholas, Speransky envisaged death sentences (even before the trial had been held!). This is shown by his opposition to the appointment to the Court of too many members from the clergy, for clerics could not vote capital punishment.

The documents and papers found and examined by Golitsyn show clearly that "Speransky, while remaining officially in the shadow, and a rank and file member of the High Court, was at the same time the

[1] Golitsyn, "Speranskii v verkhovnom sude nad dekabristami," *Russkii Istoricheskii Zhurnal*, Nos. 1—2 (1917), pp. 61—102 *passim*.

mainspring of its work, the hidden driving wheel which moved the complicated mechanism of this extraordinary judiciary." [1] The manuscript papers of Speransky show that he did all of the important work himself. The main task was to distribute the condemned into categories, for which purpose a special committee was elected by the Court. It consisted of Speransky (who received 47 voices, the highest number), P. A. Tolstoi, I. V. Vasil'chikov, E. F. Komarovskii, G. A. Stroganov, S. S. Kushnikov, F. I. Engel', D. O. Baranov, P. I. Kutaisov, and Zhuravlev as main secretary. [2] Speransky also drew up the scheme of the various categories of guilt according to which the defendants were classified. Although it suffered from an excess of schematization and a neglect of subjective factors which might enter into the picture in individual cases, the classification was an excellent piece of work. Without this guide the Court, composed of individuals who had no legal competence and who were not all too clear and just in their thinking, would have been unable to do its job. Finally, Speransky outlined the schedule for the Court's labors, planning each session to be held between June 28 and July 9, 1826. All of this Speransky worked out in close consultation with the Emperor, who set the tone and indicated the expected outcome of the trial in not too uncertain terms.

True enough, eventually the Court disregarded some of Speransky's suggestions and thereby introduced some confusion in the classification of the categories of guilt. The Court also decided on harsher punishments than those which had been suggested by Speransky, proceeding probably on the assumption (which proved correct) that the Emperor would scale down all sentences. There were, in the final analysis, 11 categories of guilt; an additional five leaders (Ryleev, Muraviev, Kakhovskoi, Bestuzhev, Pestel) were placed beyond all categories because of the gravity of their guilt. This group of five complicated matters somewhat. After deliberation, the Court decided (on the basis of Article 19 of the Military Statute of 1716, "incitement and participation in mutiny") to sentence them to be quartered. Even Speransky voted for the application of this law, knowing full well its horrible implications. In all, there were 63 voices for this sentence, 5 for various milder forms of death, 3 abstentions (the clergy), and only one — that of Admiral Mordvinov — against any kind of death sentence. Nicholas refused to confirm the Court's verdict as it stood, but he did not directly suggest any changes (as he had for the other categories of sentences), and returned it for further deliberation and revision. At the same time,

[1] Ibid,. p. 74.
[2] Komarovskii, "Zapiski grafa Komarovskogo," Istoricheskii Vestnik (1897), p. 455.

however, he had his trusted aide, General Dibich, write on July 10, 1826, to the President of the Court, Prince Lopukhin, to the effect that the Emperor was opposed not only to the cruelty of quartering, but also to the firing squad, or to any kind of death that would involve the shedding of blood (e.g. beheading). [1] The only other form of death — and it was obvious that the five would be sentenced to die — was hanging. And so it was that the five chief leaders were sentenced to the gallows and executed on July 13. It is interesting to note, though, that the first draft of General Dibich's letter to Lopukhin was found to have been in Speransky's hand. So that in this grisly detail too, Speransky was the interpreter of Nicholas' will to the Court.

The last action of the drama in which Speransky had to participate, was the writing of the manifesto, made public on July 13, 1826, which announced that the sentence of the Court had been carried out. With it, the Decembrist affair was closed officially. The Emperor could be well satisfied with Speransky's services. It had also given him ample opportunity to observe at close quarter the special abilities of Speransky; Nicholas I did not forget them.

Like many another loyal official, but with much greater talent and efficiency, Speransky took an active part in the liquidation of what, in his eyes, was an open rebellion against the traditional legal authority in the Russian state. The overwhelming majority of the officials who sat in judgment over the Decembrists were quite mediocre men, without much moral strength. Their duty as judges do not seem to have given rise to any particularly significant conflicts of conscience, not even to the members of the clergy. The only one who dared to speak out his mind and raise his voice in defense of mercy and moral justice was Admiral Mordvinov. Speransky remained silent. We shall probably never know his inner feelings, his mental and spiritual attitude toward this role of judge over his own friends and assistants. The only evidence on the way he might have felt is indirect and comes from long after the events. One defendant, Basargin, recollected that when he was called in to answer the three questions put by the Court, he stood near Speransky at whose house he had been a visitor and who was well acquainted with his father. Speransky looked at him sadly, and a tear rolled down his cheek. [2] Speransky's daughter also remembered that during the entire duration of the trial, her father often cried and spent

---

[1] The full text of the letter was first published by Shchegolev, "P. G. Kakhovskoi" in *Byloe* (Jan. 1906) and then in *Dekabristy*, p. 227. Also Golitsyn, "Speranskii v verkhovnom sude...," *loc. cit.*, p. 84.

[2] Golitsyn, "Speranskii v verkhovnom sude...," *loc. cit.*, p. 96.

many sleepless nights. [1] Of course, such evidence is by no means conclusive, yet there is no particular reason to discard it. Speransky was kind-hearted and somewhat sentimental. He surely was very conscious of the moral position in which he found himself. We can only surmise that this was indeed a very painful episode in his life. Quite possibly, as Golitsyn suggests, Speransky thought that the best and most effective way in which he could help the defendants was to see to it that the trial was conducted in as correct, orderly, and equitable manner as possible. It would be quite in keeping with his conviction that good administrative procedure is the best way to solve most difficulties.

Of more immediate interest to us is how Speransky's role in the trial affected his relations to Emperor Nicholas. In the very first days of his reign — or more precisely during the short interregnum that lasted from the death of Alexander I to December 14 — Nicholas called in Speransky to help in the drafting of the manifesto of accession after Karamzin had failed to produce a satisfactory text. For three days, between December 10 and 13, the Emperor saw Speransky every day to discuss the text of the manifesto. [2] It is significant, though, that Speransky was only a second choice and that he was called only after Karamzin had proven unsatisfactory. Nicholas harbored some suspicion towards Speransky, a suspicion which seems to have been based on Alexander's treatment of Speransky in 1812. Deservedly or not, and in our opinion, it was undeserved, Speransky had the reputation of being somewhat of a liberal. And Nicholas I loathed anything that was even faintly connected with liberalism and constitutionalism. The young Emperor's suspicions and distrust appeared to be further confirmed by the revelations of the Decembrists.

The zeal and ability displayed by Speransky as a member of the High Court, helped him to regain the full confidence of Nicholas. It has been suggested that the efficiency, enthusiasm, and devotion he displayed in the performance of his task at the trial was motivated by his desire to dissociate himself clearly from the Decembrists and demonstrate his absolute loyalty. Perhaps such considerations played a role in shaping Speransky's attitude, but we have no evidence to support it. It seems equally convincing, both psychologically and on the evidence of his entire career, that Speransky had always made it a point to perform the task assigned in as perfect and expert a manner as he could. Further, the performance was always carried out so as to satisfy the desire — expressed or implied — of his superiors. It was a technique

[1] Korf, *Zhizn' grafa Speranskogo*, II.
[2] Syroechkovskii, *Mezhdutsarstvie*, pp. 77—79.

that he had learned in the seminary, and which he had applied from the very start of his public life, as we recall from his relations with Prince Kurakin and Procurator General Obolianinov. It was his way of courting and gaining favor, of achieving his ends.

In 1825—1826 his immediate goal was — and could not have been anything else — to gain the confidence and respect of the new master, Nicholas I. In this he succeeded completely. After 1826 he was one of the most prominent and respected high officials in the bureaucracy, though he never came as close to Nicholas as he had been at one point to Alexander I. His prominent position in the new reign is shown in his participation and active role in the Committee of December 6th, 1826 and other secret *ad hoc* committees — the favorite instrument of Nicholas' government. Speransky's greatest assignment was to come in 1826, when he was put in charge of the codification of Russian law.

### SOURCES

The literature on the Decembrist movement and revolt is immense, and still constantly growing thanks to the numerous contributions and archival publications in Soviet Russia. It is impossible to survey it here. For a complete guide of the literature up to 1926 consult N. Chentsov, *Vosstanie Dekabristov — Bibliografiia,* Tsentrarkhiv, Moscow-Leningrad 1929. There is a summary account in English of the principal events, Anatole G. Mazour, *The First Russian Revolution 1825 — the Decembrist Movement, Its Origins, Development, and Significance* (Berkeley, Calif. 1937). The most recent summary is M. V. Nechkina, *Dvizhenie Dekabristov,* (Moscow 1955).

For our present limited purpose the most important sources are: Tsentrarkhiv, *Vosstanie Dekabristov — Materialy,* vols. I & II, Moscow 1925—1926; N. A. Borovkov (ed.), "Aleksandr Dmitrievich Borovkov i ego avtobiograficheskie zapiski," *Russkaia Starina,* Vol. 95 (Sept. 1898) pp. 533—564, vol. 96 (Oct. 1898), pp. 41—63, (Nov. 1898) pp. 331—362, (Dec. 1898) pp. 591—616; "Donesenie Sledstvennoi Kommissii, 30 maia 1826 g.," in *Tainoe obshchestvo i 14go dekabria 1825 g v Rossii,* (2d ed., Leipzig, n d), pp. 99—204; M. V. Dovnar-Zapol'skii, *Memuary Dekabristov* (Kiev 1906); I. D. Iakushkin, *Zapiski, stat'i, pis'ma dekabrista I. D. Iakushkina,* (Moscow 1951); graf E. F. Komarovskii, "Zapiski grafa E. F. Komarovskogo," Chapter XI, *Istoricheskii Vestnik,* LXX (1897), pp. 443—458; B. L. Modzalevskii and Iu. Oksman (eds), *Dekabristy — neizdannye materialy i stat'i,* (Leningrad 1925); "Prilozhenie k dokladu sledstvennoi kommissii o tainykh obshchestvakh, otkrytykh v 1825 g.," *Russkii Arkhiv,* (1875), No. 3, pp. 434—438; B. E. Syroechkovskii (ed.), *Mezhdutsarstvie 1825 g. i vosstanie dekabristov v perepiske i memuarakh chlenov tsarskoi sem'i* (Tsentrarkhiv, Moscow-Leningrad 1926); "Verkhovnyi Ugolovnyi Sud nad zloumyshlennikami uchrezhdennyi po Vysochaishemu Manifestu lgo iunia 1826 g." in *Tainoe obshchestvo i 14go dekabria 1825 g. v Rossii,* pp. 235—286; D. I. Zavalishin, *Zapiski Dekabrista* (Munich 1904).

Secondary studies particularly relevant to our theme: M. A. Aldanov, "Speransky et les Décembristes," *Le Monde Slave,* (Décembre 1926), pp. 432—448 (also appeared in Russian, "Speranskii i Dekabristy," *Sovremennye Zapiski,* vol. 26, 1925); A. Fateev, "Bumagi Speranskogo (kak mogli popast' v ruki Dekabristov preobrazovatel'nye plany Speranskogo)," *Zapiski Russkogo Istoricheskogo Obshchestva v Prage,* Bk. 1 (Prague 1927), pp. 103—113; B. B. Glinskii, *Bor'ba za konstitutsiiu 1612—1861,* St. Pbg. 1908; Prince N. V. Golitsyn, "M. M. Speranskii v verkhovnom sude nad dekabristami," *Russkii Istoricheskii Zhurnal,* Nos. 1—2 (1917), pp. 61—102;

I. O. (ed.), "Graf N. S. Mordvinov, A. A. Zakrevskii, P. D. Kiselev, kniaz' A. N. Golitsyn, Balashov i A. P. Ermolov v donose na nikh v 1826 g.," *Russkaia Starina,* (1881), pp. 187—190; M. Murav'ev, "Ideia vremennogo pravitel'stva u dekabristov i ikh kandidaty," in *Tainye obshchestva v Rossii v nachale XIX v. (Sbornik materialov, statei, vospominanii — 100 letie vosstaniia dekabristov)* (Moscow 1926), pp. 68—88; N. Murav'ev and S. Lunin, "Razbor doneseniia Tainoi Sledstvennoi Kommissii Gosudariu Imperatoru 1826 g." in *Tainoe obshchestvo 14go dekabria 1825 g. v Rossii,* pp. 204—235; M. V. Nechkina, *Vosstanie 14. dekabria 1825 g.* (Moscow 1951); I. I. Oreus (ed.), "Gavril Stepanovich Batenkov — istoriko-biograficheskii ocherk," *Russkaia Starina,* (1889), No. 8, pp. 301—362; V. I. Semevskii, *Politicheskie i obshchestvennye idei dekabristov,* St. Pbg. 1909; P. E. Shchegolev, "Imperator Nikolai I i M. M. Speranskii v verkhovnom sude nad dekabristami," in P. Shchegolev (ed.), *Dekabristy* (Moscow-Leningrad 1926), pp. 277—293 (also under title, "Nikolai I i dekabristy, ocherki," izd. *Byloe,* 1919, pp. 16—35); P. E. Shchegolev, "P. G. Kakhovskoi — istoriko-psikhologicheskii etiud," *Byloe* (Jan. 1906), pp. 129—166 (also in *Dekabristy,* pp. 154—228).

# CHAPTER XI

# CODIFYING RUSSIAN LAW

The investigation of the Decembrist movement brought home to Nicholas I with full force the glaring disorders, inadequacies, and injustice of Russia's administration. One of the most serious deficiencies was the absence of clear laws and a general lack of knowledge of the pertinent legislation even by those who had to apply it. The relations between individuals and the procedures of the courts were regulated in a haphazard way instead of being the object of firm and clear laws. Alexander I had turned his attention to the problem early in his reign, but nothing concrete had been accomplished. Now Nicholas I took it up again, even before the completion of the trial of the Decembrists. To this purpose, on 31 January 1826, the Emperor added a special section to his private chancery, the so-called Second Section of His Imperial Majesty's Own Chancery (*Vtoroe otdelenie sobstvennoi Ego Imperatorskogo Velichestva Kantseliarii*) and set it the task of completing the codification of Russian law. The official chairman was M. Balugianskii, but its chief *rapporteur* was Speransky. In fact, the latter became the main driving wheel and directing genius of the enterprise. It was the eleventh commission organized to codify Russian law and the first — in over a century — to bring its labors to successful conclusion.

An exhaustive analysis of the work accomplished by the Second Section — culminating in the Complete Collection of the Laws of the Russian Empire (*Polnoe Sobranie Zakonov Rossiiskoi Imperii,* abbreviated as PSZ) and the Digest of Laws (*Svod Zakonov*) — is beyond the scope of the present biography. It is a task for the jurist or historian of law, and the present writer cannot claim any competence as either. Complex technical problems of law are involved in a proper and exhaustive assessment of the juridical worth of these compilations. Unfortunately, such a complete analysis has not yet been done; it had barely begun when the Revolution interrupted it, and since then the problem has lain neglected and forgotten. A definitive judgment and evaluation of Speransky's work as codifier of Russian law is therefore still impossible. Our aim has perforce been quite limited. We only intend to describe the work done by Speransky in the Second Section and give an appraisal in terms of his political concepts and administrative practices. We shall first examine how Speransky proceeded in compiling the codes, then give a tentative appraisal of some of the results, and finally, try to see what significance the work of codification may have for an understanding of his attitudes. Although we have examined all of Speransky's pertinent writings that have been accessible to us, our treatment is based to a large degree on the research and studies of historians of Russian law at the start of the present century.

The distressing situation of Russian law, noted in a previous chapter, had not changed or materially improved since the ill-fated attempt at codification undertaken by Speransky in 1809–1812. The defects of his early codification consisted in his uncritical readiness to imitate (if not to copy outright) foreign legislation which had no direct relevance or meaning for Russia and in his belief that new legal norms, not rooted in tradition and past practice, could be introduced by *fiat*. Fortunately, his draft for a Civil Code did not receive practical implementation.

After Speransky's departure for exile, the Commission on Laws again fell under the influence of Baron Rosenkampf who had been a proponent of the historical-practical approach. Under his guidance, the Commission took steps to lay the ground for a more complete and scientific acquaintance with Russian jurisprudence and the history of Russian law. It published a *Zhurnal Zakonodatel'stva* (Journal of Legislation) in 1817 and in 1819 planned the publication of a *Kriticheskii zhurnal rossiiskogo zakonodatel'stva* (Critical journal of Russian legislation). [1] Baron Rosenkampf was also the first to take concrete steps to search the archives for legal monuments. He ordered a survey of archival holdings in the capital and prepared a preliminary register (30,000 titles) of past legislation that would have to be included in a code. On the basis of this work, the Baron edited a "Systematic survey of active laws of the Russian Empire with the foundations of law derived from them" (*Sistematicheskii svod sushchestvuiushchikh zakonov Rossiiskoi Imperii s osnovaniiami prava iz onykh izvlechennymi*). It consisted of 15 volumes and was published between 1815 and 1822. In it he also attempted to formulate the basic norms and principles of

[1] P. M. Maikov, "Kommissiia sostavleniia zakonov pri imperatorakh Pavle I i Aleksandre I," *Zhurnal Ministerstva Iustitsii*, (Nov. 1905), p. 279.

Russian legislation and to order them clearly and systematically.[1] In so doing, Baron Rosenkampf took an important step which paved the way for the Digest compiled later by the Second Section. In spite of these significant, but limited, technical contributions, the work of the Commission on Laws between 1815 and 1825 was rather desultory. Alexander I did not show much interest in it, and it was allowed to stagnate.

During his exile Speransky had come to realize (in spite of his more or less disingenuous self-justification) that in 1809 he had taken the wrong course for codifying Russian law. The Benthamite idea of working out a completely new set of legal norms was not well suited to Russia at the time; neither could Roman law and the *Code Napoléon* be applied directly, as there was no tradition of a well worked out civil law. In connection with his studies of German romantic literature and thought, Speransky had also become acquainted with the historical school of jurisprudence and the writings of its main proponent, Savigny. As a result, he had become aware — even if he did not fully realize all the implications of the position — of the value of laws formed and determined by the historic evolution of a nation.[2] Taught by bitter experience of his own lack of professional training in law, he actively pursued the study of history and jurisprudence. He now understood more clearly than before that ere a code could be drawn up, much work would have to be done first to find and order the necessary documents and sources of Russian legislation.

This preparatory task was immense. Until very late in the 18th century many decrees and laws were issued without being printed; before that time they had been circulated in manuscript copies only to those agencies that might need them. Furthermore, there was no single source of legislation; laws were issued by many various government offices (until the establishment of the Council of State in 1810 there was no single authority or uniform procedure for processing the legislation). Some decrees had not even been published, especially when they pertained to private cases, though they might contain and develop important general concepts of civil law. A further difficulty, which Speransky only suspected (but which is quite obvious to us today)

---

[1] P. Maikov, "Kommissiia sostavleniia zakonov pri imperatorakh Pavle I i Aleksandre I," *loc. cit.*, (Dec. 1905), pp. 206—207; L. A. Kasso, "K istorii svoda zakonov grazhdanskikh," *Zhurnal Ministerstva Iustitsii*, (March 1904), p. 74.

[2] P. M. Maikov, "Speranskii i studenty zakonovedeniia," *Russkii Vestnik*, vol. 263, No. 1, (1899), p. 247; cf. also N. M. Korkunov, "Teoreticheskie vozzreniia Speranskogo na pravo," in *Sbornik statei N. M. Korkunova 1877—1897* (St. Pbg. 1898), p. 99 for a critical view of the influence of Savigny on Speransky.

stood in the path of the would-be codifier. Muscovite law had developed quite "organically", with each piece of legislation or each judicial decision taking its place within the general pattern of legal concepts developed by tradition. But during the 18th century many new norms, new outlooks, new approaches, and many foreign borrowings were introduced into the body of Russian legislation. Law was created by the arbitrary and capricious decisions of the sovereign and of various government bodies for specific individual cases, without regard to general concepts, legal tradition, and precedent. As a result, the body of law which had accumulated since the code of 1649 presented quite an incoherent and shapeless aspect. [1] The codifier had first to become acquainted with and digest the mass of variegated and disparate legal material of the 18th century, and only then could he try to distill the basic norms from it.

These historical circumstances of Russia's legal development precluded, on the part of the codifier, a blank acceptance of all the legislation and juridical norms that had been created since 1649. Uncritical acceptance of the existing body of legislation would only have meant a perpetuation of the confusion and conflicts among contradictory concepts and principles of various origin. Respect for history and tradition did not imply, in Speransky's opinion, the complete rejection of the 18th century belief in natural law. To his mind, the two attitudes were not so much opposed to each other as they were complementary. He never abandoned a desire to create a new and better, i.e., more harmonious and clear, system of fundamental legal concepts that would guide the political and social relationships in Russia. [2] Unlike his 18th century and Benthamite predecessors, however, and in contrast to his own approach of 1809, Speransky now felt that the best *way* to reach this goal of clarity and harmony was to build on the nation's history and tradition. The bringing together of all the legislation issued since 1649 had to be capped by a clear and systematic formulation of the principles of law.

In January 1826, Speransky presented to Nicholas I his conception of the task of the Second Section. As first goal he set the collection and publication of all legislation issued since 1649 (including the code of Tsar Alexis). In the second place, using this collection as a basis, the Second Section would compose a compendium, or Digest (*Svod*) of all

---

[1] A. N. Filippov, *Uchebnik istorii russkogo prava,* (5th ed., Iur'ev 1914), vol. I, p. 563.

[2] Korkunov, "Teoreticheskie vozzreniia Speranskogo na pravo," *loc. cit., passim* who exaggerates the limit of Savigny's influence.

the legislation still in force, eliminating all the laws which had been revoked or amended. The Digest would provide a bird's-eye view of the legal norms and institutions currently in force. The third and final task would be the composition of a new code (*ulozhenie*), using the Digest as a guide. Such a new code would harmonize all useful and desirable legal traditions with new concepts and norms that were required under modern conditions. It is interesting to note that Speransky had advocated a similar sequence of codificatory procedure in his first political paper, written in 1802. Almost the same approach was also recommended by the Commission on Laws in 1812, after the defects of Speransky's civil code of 1809 had become apparent. [1] In his paper of January 1826, Speransky expressed a rather optimistic view as to the time such a triple task would take. He thought that a couple of years would be sufficient for the first part, then a few months for the compilation of the Digest, and finally another year for working out a new code. In fact, the first two tasks alone took seven years. [2]

His suggestions, though, met with the Emperor's objections. Nicholas I accepted readily enough the first two goals, as they corresponded to his fundamentally pragmatic and empirical way of thinking. But he rejected the third, the drafting of a new code. The Emperor felt that a new code smacked too much of theory and of an ideological dogmatism that was alien to him, and which he distrusted profoundly for its connection with the *philosophes* and revolutionaries of 18th-century France. Nicholas was narrowly conservative and afraid of bringing any radically new elements into Russia's political organization. His aim was quite modest and limited: he wanted to preserve all that was good and useful in the existing system, making only minor, "mechanical" improvements and adjustments where they were needed for the good functioning of the machinery of government. The compilation of existing legislation to clarify legal relations and procedures for the guidance of subordinate officials was such an improvement. It was as far as he was willing to go; such a clarification would be sufficient in bringing to the imperial administration consistency, uniformity, and order — the supreme virtues

---

1 Cf. Semevskii, "Pervyi politicheskii traktat Speranskogo," *Russkoe Bogatstvo* (1907), No. 1, pp. 54, 55, 56, 57, 67; cf. also, S. V. Pakhman, *Istoriia kodifikatsii grazhdanskogo prava, I* (St. Pbg. 1876), pp. 434—436 on the thinking of the Commission on Laws in 1812.

2 Speranskii, "Predpolozheniia okkonchatel'nomu sostavleniiu zakonov," *Russkaia Starina*, XV, (1876), pp. 434—441 *passim;* Speranskii, *Obozrenie istoricheskikh svedenii o svode zakonov* (St. Pbg. 1833), *passim;* A. F. Bychkov, (ed.), "K L-ti letiiu IIgo otdeleniia Sobstvennoi E. I. V. Kantseliarii," *Russkaia Starina*, XV, (1876), p. 431.

to the military and technological mind of Nicholas I. [1] Speransky was therefore given the green light to compile a full collection of laws issued since 1649 and a digest of the laws in force.

Efficiently set up by Speransky, a past master at bureaucratic organization, the Second Section embarked upon its task with great energy and speed. Several subsections were established, new officials appointed, including some jurists and young men with legal training. [2] First, all the legislation since 1649 had to be gathered, its textual accuracy established, the laws arranged chronologically, and the documents prepared for publication. All laws up to 1825 (the cut-off date was the day of the death of Alexander I) were to be included in a first series of the Complete Collection. Legislation issued since December 1825 was to be the subject of a second series. With the help of the *répertoire* prepared by Rosenkampf and of the labors of previous Commissions and jurists, work proceeded quite rapidly, considering the amount of material that had to be sifted. The first volume of the *Complete Collection of the Laws of the Russian Empire* (PSZ) was ready for printing in 1828; and with the presses of the Imperial Typography working at full speed, by 1830 the first series had been completed. It consisted of 45 volumes, plus several volumes of appendices. While this first job was still in its last stages, Speransky set the Second Section to compiling the Digest (*Svod*). [3] This took another two years, and the final text of the Digest was based on all the laws in force as of January 1, 1832. The Digest was submitted for comment and review to various government bodies to make sure that it was clear and complete. On January 1, 1833 this task too had been accomplished, and the 15 volumes compiled were presented to the Emperor. The Digest came into force on January 1, 1835 as the sole authoritative source of Russian law.

The truly huge job had been accomplished only thanks to Speransky's organizational talent and driving energy. He did not spare his own time, or labor, but neither was he sparing of that of others. As was his

---

[1] Among others, see A. Filippov, "Imperator Nikolai I i Speranskii," *Imperatorskii iur'evskii universitet (Tartu Ulikool), Uchenye Zapiski*, (1897), No. 2, section I, pp. 7—8.

[2] V. Bil'basov, "Speranskii i dva Nikitina," *Russkaia Starina*, 87 (1896), p. 446; cf. also Maikov, "Speranskii i studenty zakonovedeniia," *loc. cit., passim* and the interesting article by A. Fateev, "K istorii iuridicheskoi obrazovannosti v Rossii," *Uchenye zapiski osnovannye Russkoi Uchebnoi Kollegiei v Prage*, vol. I, fasc. III (Prague 1924), pp. 218—255 on juridical education in Russia in the first half of the 19th century.

[3] The Svod was a compilation of all laws that were in application at the time of its publication. The closest term in English would be *Digest*, in its Justinian meaning. See Speranskii, "O sushchestve svoda" (1828), *Russkaia Starina* XV (1876), pp. 586—592 *passim*.

wont, Speransky supervised all the phases and details of the work personally. He set the schedule and made the plans, and at every stage, the entire material was presented to him; he went over every sheet prepared for publication, pencil in hand. His direct participation was particularly noticeable and important in the compilation of the Digest. His method to a large extent determined the character of the results. [1]

Before proceeding to a more detailed examination of the end product of the Second Section's labors, let us first mention some of the by-products of its activity. Not only are they of significance for the history of Russian jurisprudence; they also illustrate characteristic traits of Speransky's approach.

Copies of the laws of the Russian Empire were scattered among many archives, libraries, and government institutions. As a first step, therefore, they had to be gathered (or copied) so that they could be included in the Complete Collection. It had to be decided with what date the Collection should start. 1649 was an obvious enough date, as the last code had been issued in that year by Tsar Alexis. But should the Code of 1649 itself be included? Previous codifiers (and Alexander I) had tended to answer in the negative. Speransky on the other hand, rightly felt that all the succeeding laws had some connection with the Code of 1649 and to exclude it would deprive Russian legislation of its basis. It was not true, as he himself had thought at one time, that later legislation had completely eliminated the usefulness of the Code of 1649. [2] To this end, he sent for the original copies of the Code of Tsar Alexis so as to collate the various versions. Search for copies of the code led to the realization that other legislation was to be found, forgotten in various archival depositories. Speransky therefore became interested in the work of P. Stroev who was then just beginning his explorations and surveys of archives and old libraries. He encouraged this kind of activity by all the means at his disposal. [3] The results of these searches showed that if the Collection were going to be complete, the Second Section could not rely exclusively on the materials available in the files of the former Commission on Laws. Other depositories had to be combed as well. And while at the beginning the Second Section

---

[1] Nicholas I followed the progress of the Second Section's labors very closely, too. Cf. G. Tel'berg, "Uchastie imperatora Nikolaia I v kodifikationnoi rabote ego tsarstvovaniia," *Zhurnal Ministerstva Iustitsii*, XXII, No. 1, (Jan. 1916), pp. 233—244 *passim.*

[2] A. Filippov, "K voprosu o sostave pervogo Polnogo Sobraniia Zakonov Rossiiskoi Imperii," *Otchet Imperatorskogo Moskovskogo Universiteta za 1915 g.* (Moscow 1916), part I, pp. 78—79 (separate offprint used).

[3] Cf. N. Barsukov, *Zhizn' i trudy P. M. Stroeva* (St. Pbg. 1878), pp. 133, 134, 157, 213—215.

only looked into the archives of the Senate (for which a register had been compiled earlier), it later also undertook to search for relevant documents in various other archives of St. Petersburg and Moscow; but not energetically enough perhaps. [1]

These forays into the historical archives gave Speransky the idea that it would be of advantage to have a repertory of all the ancient laws of Russia — i.e., those issued before 1649, beginning with Kievan times. He was quite aware of the fact that some existing institutions and laws could not be properly understood without a good knowledge of their historical background, which at times went back quite a bit. He therefore proposed that the Second Section sponsor two subsidiary publications: a collection of the ancient laws and a complete history of Russian law from earliest times. [2] For some reason, which has remained unknown, the Second Section did not complete the task. But Speransky's suggestion was not forgotten, and it was eventually carried out privately by former members of the Second Section, the first Russian jurists and historians of law (Nevolin, Kunitsin, and their students). [3]

The work of codification also brought into sharp focus the need for more and better trained Russian jurists. As we recall, a school of law attached to the Senate had been established in 1806; but it did not prove very successful and was closed in 1809. Balugianskii, himself trained in Germany, made the suggestion, which Speransky endorsed and supported before the Emperor in 1828, that a few promising young men be selected every year to study law abroad for two years. Upon their return, and the satisfactory passing of an examination, they would continue to study for a higher degree at a Russian university while working for the Second Section. These studies and practical apprenticeship would prepare them either to teach jurisprudence or to take up a responsible legal post in the Second Section. As the better schools were restricted to young nobles who were interested only in higher policy-making positions in the bureaucracy, the prospective candidates were to be found mostly in theological seminaries. The sons of the clergy therefore provided the main contingent of students under this program. On the recommendation of Alexander von Humboldt, Speransky asked Savigny to supervise the study program of the Russian students who were sent to the University of Berlin. Savigny accepted, and though he did not take his supervisory role too seriously, the students received

---

1 Filippov, "K voprosu o sostave pervogo PSZ," *loc. cit.*, pp. 87—88.
2 Speransky had advocated the writing of a history of Russian law in his first political paper and recommended A. Radishchev for the job. See Ch. V *supra*.
3 A. Filippov, "Dva istoriko-kriticheskikh izdaniia," *Istoricheskie Izvestiia* (1916), pp. 26—42.

their training from Savigny's assistant and pupils. It meant, of course, that the first Russian jurists — Nevolin, Redkin, Blagoveshchenskii, Kunitsin — were trained in the spirit of the historical school. In this manner the codification led to the establishment of jurisprudence and the history of law as academic disciplines in Russia. [1]

Another important by-product was the codification of local customary law. Speransky and his assistants learned soon that several provinces of the Empire (even if Poland and Finland were excluded) had legal traditions quite different from the Russian. In some cases, as in Moldavia, Bessarabia, the Western Provinces (formerly part of the Grand Duchy of Lithuania), local law was based on ancient statutes — e.g., the Lithuanian statute and the Magdeburg law in the towns of the Western Ukraine. In other instances, local legal norms were based on customs and oral tradition, for example in the Caucasus and in Siberia. The Second Section established special commissions to deal with the problem. But except for the Baltic Code, none of the compilations of local law received legislative sanction. Nonetheless, they did play some role in the political and legal history of the provinces. The character of these codifications of local law and their implications for Speransky's approach to the multinational aspect of the Empire appear better when viewed against the pattern of codification of Russian law. Therefore, let us turn first to an examination of the accomplishments of the Second Section in respect to Russian law.

The compilation of a Complete Collection of the laws issued between 1649 and 1825 presented some serious difficulties and, contrary to the impression created, the collection published in 1830 was far from complete. To begin with, what was to be considered law? It was by no means an easy thing to decide, for throughout the 18th century, there had been many methods for issuing laws, and many different bodies and institutions had had a hand in the legislation at one time or another. To include only the legislative acts that dealt with broad issues and set general precepts of law would exclude a host of casuistic decrees and prescriptions that dealt with individual petitions and specific cases. Legislation issued to take care of a specific case, however, often acquired a much wider significance and sometimes set a precedent for a whole series of decisions. Equally unsatisfactory was a selection according to the source of the legislation, the government body or organ that had enacted the law. The Emperor and his private chancery had

---

[1] Maikov, "Speranskii i studenty zakonovedeniia," *loc. cit., passim* and Ia. Barshev, *Istoricheskaia zapiska o sodeistvii vtorogo otdeleniia sobstvennoi E. I. V. kantseliarii razvitiiu iuridicheskikh nauk v Rossii* (St. Pbg. 1876).

not been alone in drafting and issuing laws (especially before Catherine II). Though up to the reign of Alexander I the Senate had been the major source of imperial legislation, a great number of other bodies and *ad hoc* institutions, for example the Supreme Secret Council or the Cabinet of Empress Anne, also had made laws for the Empire. Speransky was quite right in saying that only a thorough and reliable history of Russian law could provide the codifier with an adequate standard for selection. But such a history had not been written yet, and there was no time to wait until one had been completed. As a result, almost arbitrarily, Speransky included in the Collection of Laws only the acts issued by the Supreme Sovereign Power, i.e. the Emperor, or in its name, whether they dealt with general issues or specific cases. His excuse for the inclusion of decrees bearing on individual special cases was that they illustrated the conditions of the past. But in fact, his arbitrary standard of selection led to a disregard of the juridical rank of the documents he included in the Collection. In short, the set of criteria that guided the editors in their selection of the laws for inclusion was not a satisfactory one in the light of the legislative practices of the 18th century. [1]

We have mentioned the fact that it was difficult to locate accurate copies of the laws and have pointed out that not all archives were searched with equal thoroughness. Speransky did request various depositories of official documents, for instance the Moscow archives of the Ministry for External Affairs, the archives of the Holy Synod, and the Ministry of Justice, to submit registers of their holdings. On the basis of these registers, the Second Section selected the documents it wished to see. This procedure put the Second Section at the mercy of the archives and ministries. The registers sent to the Section, if sent at all, were neither complete nor did they give a satisfactory description of the documents. The Second Section obviously could not undertake a thorough verification of the registers to determine which of the documents listed were of relevance to its task. As a matter of fact, it merely looked at the information that was sent to it and disregarded all those materials that seemed to present too many complexities. It did not go out of its way to search for material; it was largely satisfied with what it found in the archives of the Commission on Laws, the Senate, and whatever was sent to it. In all fairness, though, Speransky and his collaborators cannot be blamed entirely; at the time historical

1 Filippov, "K voprosu o sostave pervogo PSZ," *loc. cit.*, pp. 25, 30, 118; A. Filippov, "Speranskii kak kodifikator russkogo prava," *Russkaia Mysl'*, 101 (1892), pp. 215—216.

science and archival investigation were still in their infancy in Russia. Little was known of the documentary wealth contained in even the most important and accessible archival depositories. Some of these holdings were not touched by scholars until the 1870's; and only then did a host of new laws, edicts, and decrees come to light. These discoveries, of course, shed much light on the development and character of Russian legal norms and administrative practice. Though through no fault of Speransky's, and of the Second Section, the omission of so much source material was a significant drawback in a compilation that pretended to be complete. [1]

Of equal importance in limiting the fullness of the PSZ was the fact that many acts had not been made public. Some of them were still considered secret and kept behind lock and key. Oddly enough, this secret legislation included not only some international treaties and decrees concerning the Imperial Family, but also several imperial decisions in private civil law suits. In some cases, the latter decisions were not made public only because they had been decided by a secret government body, the Supreme Secret Council or the Secret Expedition, for instance. The archives where this "secret" legislation was kept could not turn over their material to the Second Section without a direct order from the Emperor in every case. Nicholas I gave his permission only after being told the exact contents and nature of the documents, and he made his decision not on the basis of any juridical consideration, but of what he felt was desirable politically. In this respect, the acts issued by the Supreme Secret Council and the Secret Expedition presented the greatest problem, because of their large number and importance. The Emperor was reluctant to have them published, and only a few were included in the Complete Collection. Nicholas I also vetoed the publication of any legislation dating from the interregnum regency of the Duke of Courland and Princess Anne of Brunswick-Lueneburg (1740—1741). As a result of these restrictions and omissions — conscious or accidental — an appreciable amount of important leg-

---

1 Filippov, "K voprosu o sostave pervogo PSZ," *loc. cit.*, pp. 44, 48, 64, 72—73, 87—88; A. Fateev, "K istorii i teorii kodifikatsii — stoletie Polnogo Sobraniia Zakonov," *Russkii Narodnyi universitet v Prage — Nauchnye Trudy* IV (1931), pp. 11—12. Filippov cites the following examples (pp. 105—108, 112—113): Only 38 decrees of the known 2,089 from the Supreme Secret Council (1726—1730) are to be found in PSZ, only 313 items from the 3,895 of the Cabinet of Empress Anne; almost no trace in PSZ of registers 7—12 of the archives of the Senate in St. Petersburg and consequently of the 30,000 items for the years 1711—1762, only 17,500 found their way into the PSZ. Of the known imperial decrees for the 18th century, the PSZ has only 1/3 for the years 1707—1725, 1/5 for the period 1725—1740, and 1/8 only for the years 1740—1762. The reign of Catherine II is covered fairly well and that of Alexander I is almost complete.

islative material was left out of the compilation of the laws of the Russian Empire. [1]

The Complete Collection is also defective from the point of view of its strict textual accuracy and as a scientific edition of historical sources. Although Speransky claimed that when several versions of an act were available, they had all been compared and the copies carefully collated with the original text, wherever available, the practice of the Second Section and the results themselves belie the claim. We know that the Section did not always wait until the original had been obtained from Moscow or elsewhere and prepared their text from a copy. Even when versions were compared and texts collated, the sources used were not indicated, nor were the varied readings reproduced, so that the final text is based on a version that has been selected by the editor arbitrarily and cannot be verified. It was not a very significant defect in regard to those laws which had been printed earlier and were easily available. But in the case of many acts that were in circulation only in a few manuscript copies the textual *varia* might be of great significance for a proper understanding and interpretation of the legislation. For instance, we know of several versions of the Code of 1649, but the text printed in the Complete Collection of 1830 is not an absolutely faithful copy of any of the known versions; it is rather a composite of several. As Russian law before its codification had been casuistic rather than dogmatic and systematic, these differences mattered a great deal for a correct appreciation of the norms involved. Speransky's superficial approach was fraught with serious consequences when relied upon in the preparation of the Digest. [2]

The incompleteness of the Complete Collection was by no means balanced by the inclusion of various expletive acts, projects, tables of organization, which had little legal value. Nor was the external form of the Collection overly satisfactory. The acts were arranged mechanically, chronologically, without adequate headings. There was no index to each volume, only a general index for the entire compilation, and the tables of contents did not specify clearly the subject matter of each act listed. At first glance, it would seem that the Complete Collection had only historical value, as a selective record of old legislation. This was the opinion held by Nicholas I. [3]

[1] Filippov, "K voprosu o sostave pervogo PSZ," *loc. cit.*, pp. 98—99 and 100—101.
[2] Filippov, *Uchebnik istorii russkogo prava*, I, p. 588; Filippov, "K voprosu o sostave pervogo PSZ," *loc. cit.*, p. 78.
[3] Nicholas I wrote to Balugianskii on the latter's proposal to furnish a set of the PSZ to all district courts: "I do not see any need for it, for the PSZ is now a purely historical book, for which district courts have no use," quoted by Filippov, "K voprosu o sostave pervogo PSZ," *loc. cit.*, p. 130.

Yet, in spite of these drawbacks, some of which were determined by
the historical circumstances of Speransky's time, the level of legal and
historical scholarship, and the peculiarities of the Emperor's views, the
accomplishment was an important one. Speransky's work should be
judged in terms of the 1830's and not in terms of the 1900's as too
many historians have done. For the first time in Russian history all
major legislative monuments were gathered in one place and made
easily accessible to those who might need them. Jurisprudence, the
study and history of law became possible. Judges and administrators
were provided with a relatively reliable source book, and their interpretations and decisions could be checked by reviewing authorities
(something that had been almost impossible in the past, as every court
and office had a different and incomplete set of legal sources). The
historian, too, might well be grateful to Speransky and the Second
Section, for much material is now easy to find in the Collection (and
it is virtually complete for the reign of Alexander I). In any case, the
Collection itself and the preparatory work involved in compiling it,
set a precedent and blazed the trail for later — and more accurate and
successful — searches in archives, publications of documents, and the
like. The Collection now only needed to be supplemented; the basic
foundation had been laid.

To the minds of Nicholas I, Speransky, and their assistants, the Complete Collection of Laws was only the first step, the preparation for a
more important task, the compilation of a Digest of the laws in force.
In a sense, the first series of the PSZ was only a "complete" historical
reference to the Digest. [1] In drawing up the Digest, Speransky's intention was to present in a compact, systematic and clear form, a handy
reference book to all those legislative acts that were still in force. It was
to provide a basis for judicial decisions and administrative practice.
To keep the Digest up to date, a yearly supplement would be published,
and at periodic intervals a new edition would eliminate all the acts
that had been superseded in the meantime. (Actually, however, only
three editions of the Digest were published during the 19th century
and the supplements appeared at irregular intervals).

The material included in the Digest was to be arranged in logical
fashion, according to some convenient scheme to facilitate its ready use
for reference purposes. To this end, of course, legislative acts might
have to be rearranged or even rephrased (if redundant or in obsolete
language). Laws or decrees enacted to take care of specific situations
were to be put together with the general laws and principles which they

1 Filippov, "K voprosu o sostave pervogo PSZ," *loc. cit.*, p. 137.

illustrated or explained. When several laws dealt with the same problem, or when two or several such laws were conflicting, the act issued last was alone to be taken into the Digest; for presumably it best expressed the most recent intention of the legislator. Arranged logically and pointing up fundamental legal principles, concepts, and norms, the material in the Digest had to be coherent. Wherever the legislation did not provide this coherence, transitional and connecting paragraphs had to be added. In some cases, a summary of several acts could be made to ensure the balance, clarity, and logic which might be lost if all the pertinent original legislation were quoted in full. In other instances expletive paragraphs might have to be added also. The text of the Digest, though, had to be based on actual legislation to which reference was made in notes.

The procedure followed in compiling the Digest was stated by Balugianskii, speaking for Speransky, in a report to the Minister of Justice, Prince Dashkov, March 23, 1832:

1. ... laws dealing with whole subjects of legislation are reproduced textually from the legislative act itself; no changes are made in such legislation, except for changes in the plan and organization of the subject matter: when [found] scattered among several statutes, acts, or laws, [legislation] has been combined by the Second Section, but the contents of the articles have always been reproduced textually ... 2. In the case of laws which do not deal with complete subjects of legislation, the Digest ... reproduces the more recent version textually, with the omission of words which are self evident; where earlier laws are only explained or complemented, the Second Section has reproduced only the very words that complement and explain, while preserving the earlier [laws] that contained the essence of the act. 3. Finally, in the case ... of private acts with general force, or of only several articles of the major legislation, or [in the case] where the meaning of the laws is obscure or imprecise, the Second Section has been forced to compose a new article from these old ones; [but in so doing] it has preserved the meaning of the original on the basis of the decrees of July 29, 1821 and October 21, 1823. The first [of the two decrees] says that 'senators, when deciding cases state their opinions freely, not hampered by anything and base their opinion exclusively on the essence of the case and the direct meaning of the law'; the second [of the decrees states], 'when, as a result of the multiplicity of legislation and decrees, difficulty is encountered in selecting and applying the law to which the case pertains, in those cases, and if it is found impossible to adjust the literal meaning of one law to the literal meaning of another, necessity itself prescribes ... to follow the general spirit of those laws which most nearly correspond to the spirit of the legislation'." [1]

1 Quoted in G. E. Blosfel'dt, *"Zakonnaia" sila Svoda Zakonov v svete arkhivnykh*

Such a method obviously involved extremely delicate operations. The authors of the Digest had to have a perfect command of the meaning and intention of the legislation they included in the Digest. Moreover, the available legislation had to be complete enough to cover all the general categories and principles of law without the authors of the compilation being forced to compose additional material. Neither of the two conditions was really present in Russia. The Complete Collection itself, as we have pointed out, was not an adequate foundation; moreover, as Speransky found out (or knew), Russian legislation was quite deficient in some very important areas of civil law, as for instance in regard to the concepts and rules for legal personal status, contracts and deeds. [1]

As a matter of fact, Speransky planned the Digest on the basis of his own definitions of a legal bond. According to him, there are two kinds of bonds of legal nature: the political (state) bond and the civil bond. Each necessitates laws defining and laws preserving it. Hence, four major categories of laws: 1. defining and preserving the political bond, 2. defining and preserving the civil bond. The first include fundamental laws, government institutions, laws on state power, laws on personal legal status. The second group consists of police laws (*ustavy blagochiniia*) and criminal law. The civil bond is defined by the laws on the family, general property laws, and special laws of property. The civil bond is preserved by law in equity, procedural law, and civil law. [2] On the basis of these definitions, the Digest was arranged into eight books and fifteen volumes as follows: Book I, vol. 1 Fundamental laws, central political institutions; vol. 2, provincial institutions; vol. 3, statutes on service and pensions. Book II, vol. 4, statutes on state obligations (recruits, taxes). Book III, vols. 5—8, statutes on Treasury administration. Book IV, vol. 9, personal legal status (*état civil*). Book V, vol. 10, civil law. Book VI, vols. 11—12, statutes on state welfare (credit, fire, transportation, roads); Book VII, vols. 13—14, police statute; Book VIII, vol. 15, criminal law.

The creative influence of the codifier could manifest itself most strongly in rephrasing old laws or in providing logical connections. Speransky was convinced — and quite rightly so — that Russian legislation was hopelessly confused, that its civil law lacked many fundamental concepts and norms. He therefore sought the help of

*dannykh* (Petrograd 1917), pp. 26—27. A similar formulation is to be found in Speransky's *Précis des notions historiques sur la formation du Corps des lois russes* (St. Pbg. 1833).

[1] Speranskii, "O sushchestve svoda," *Russkaia Starina*, XV (1876), pp. 592—97.

[2] Speranskii, *Précis des notions historiques*, pp. 116—119 *passim*.

French, Austrian, and Prussian models. [1] He needed to define legal concepts and principles which he believed were used in the legislation, but never clearly defined there. Here again he drew on foreign models. But these were not the only novelties he introduced. By citing out of context, by running together several acts, summarizing them, and providing connecting paragraphs, Speransky actually interpreted the laws and sometimes even created new norms and concepts.

Jurists and historians of Russian law have as yet not made an exhaustive analysis of the Digest. Only a few scattered sections have been subjected to close scrutiny by scholars at the beginning of this century (their work was interrupted by the Revolution and never resumed). Attention has been paid particularly to the 10th volume which contains the civil law properly speaking (the reason for this concentration on the 10th volume was that Russian civil law was due for drastic renovation and new codification on the eve of the Revolution). Scholars have shown that in some sections of the 10th volume (and many sections have not yet been analysed in full), Speransky introduced a number of new definitions and concepts which had not existed in Russia previously and which he obviously had taken over from Prussian, French and Austrian codes. These borrowings are strictly technical in character, and they do not seem to have direct bearing on Speransky's political attitude. He merely felt — and not without justification — that Russian law lacked these modern concepts. On examination of the studies made of this aspect of the Digest, it would appear that Speransky was mostly interested in modernizing Russian law on contracts and property, presumably as a contribution to the promotion of a modern, "capitalistic" economy (which he had been working to develop since the beginning of his government career). Indirect evidence of this may be provided by the fact that in the years 1826—1832, i.e., during the preparation of the Digest, the government — at Speransky's urging — issued a series of statutes dealing with such questions as wills, government contracts, inventory of property, custom dues. [2]

[1] On the influence of Prussian law and the contributions of Rosenkampf and the earlier Commission on Laws in this respect, see: L. Kasso, "K istorii svoda zakonov grazhdanskikh," *Zhurnal Ministerstva Iustitsii*, (March 1904), pp. 71, 81—84 and the suggestive comments in connection with a specific issue by B. E. Nol'de, "Zakony osnovnye v russkom prave," *Pravo* (1913), Nos. 8—9, pp. 447—461 and 524—541.

[2] The discussion is based primarily on M. M. Vinaver, "K voprosu ob istochnikakh X toma Svoda Zakonov," *Zhurnal Ministerstva Iustitsii*, (Oct. 1895), pp. 1—68 and (June 1897), pp. 87—102. But I disagree with the conclusions drawn by Vinaver concerning the political implications of Speransky's method; my disagreement derives from my understanding of the political ideology of Speransky as basically not a "liberal" one.

The method used for compiling the Digest led not only to innovations and creations of norms and concepts, it also brought about the simplification or destruction of existing legal relationships. The most interesting instance (and apparently the only one to have been examined by jurists so far), involved the definition of personal legal status or membership in a legally recognized estate. Starting from the premise — historically quite correct — that in Russia the legal status of a person was a function of the nature of his service to the state, the Digest recognized four estates: nobility, clergy, inhabitants of towns, and inhabitants of the countryside. The nobility had been an estate since Muscovite times, and very much like a corporation (in the Western medieval sense) since the 18th century. The clergy and the townspeople had become corporations (also in the *Ancien Régime* sense) in the 18th century. As far as these three classes were concerned, the Digest only fixed and elaborated the legal implications of their status. The great innovation, however, concerned the rural population, the overwhelming majority of the Russian people. In Speransky's time, the rural settlers were not an uniform and homogeneous group, class, or even estate. The Digest disregarded this situation completely. It failed to distinguish between serfs and nonserfs (probably a reflection of the belief or hope that it would be only a temporary distinction). More important still, Speransky and his assistants overlooked completely the great social and legal complexity of the peasantry, a complexity which was the result of an important and interesting historical development. The peasants in Russia enjoyed a great diversity of status and rights, a diversity that might be useful in bringing about a fundamental reform of the peasant class (along the lines of equalization of status contemplated by Speransky in his projects for the local administration). As in the case of the other classes, peasant status, too, was determined by service to the state. By 1830 the peasantry comprised not only the original tillers of the soil, but also various types of servicemen. There were personally free peasants whose status and livelihood depended entirely on services they rendered to the state (for example, the maintenance of postal relays). In border regions, there were groups of free peasants, often of non-Russian ethnic origin, who possessed their land in return for military frontier service or the payment of a special tribute (not a tax). In the Western provinces, there existed also some individuals who lived on the land, paid taxes like ordinary peasants, but enjoyed personal freedom and special legal privileges, as they were descendants of the local service nobility.

Speransky's Digest made a clean sweep of this variety. The historical

rights and privileges that might have served as an entering wedge for
a gradual emancipation with land, were eliminated. The final step in
this process of levelling the peasants' legal status was taken quite
easily in 1861. It is of course possible to argue that the bringing about
of such a uniformity in the peasant status had beneficial results for the
future development of the country. But in any case, it was in flagrant
violation of the Digest's avowed purpose of being only an accurate
reflection of existing conditions.

Speransky's disregard for a complex reality was much more than mere
lack of respect for tradition or historically determined conditions, quite
surprising in a follower of Savigny and German historicism. It involved
and illustrated a basic attitude which was shared by both Speransky
and the government of Nicholas I. [1] Theirs was essentially a mechanical
bureaucratic approach, and they obviously aimed at uniformity and
simplicity of legal relationships and categories. In spite of their willingness to take into consideration — up to a point — the creations of the
past, they did aim at re-directing the evolution of Russia by bureaucratic means. Minor exceptions and special cases had to be eliminated
to bring about uniformity and a streamlining of legal relations that
would pave the way for bureaucratic orderliness and military efficiency.

The state, by means of statutes, codes, and digests worked out by
the bureaucracy defined the legal status of the people, assigned and
ordered their rank, role, and function. By redefining legal concepts,
contractual practice, and civil relations, the government smoothed the
way for a different economic and social order. This is not to say that
Speransky's solution or goal were necessarily bad. But it does illustrate
his rather high-handed, mechanistic manner of dealing with the social
and economic problems of Russia. In final analysis it resulted in a
narrowing of the area and a limiting of the ways of gradual, autonomous, and organic change. It smacked of an "enlightened" absolutism
that simplified social complexities and introduced new social values
and principles by bureaucratic police action. Despite his respect for the
customs and traditions of people who were completely different from
the Russians (as shown in Siberia), Speransky did not like to admit of
variety and great differences within one group. Aiming at uniformity
of law and administration, he used the Digest as a means for achieving
it in Russia.

Speransky was not unaware of the fact that he was introducing legal

---

1 The foregoing discussion is based on: B. E. Nol'de, "Svod Zakonov o sostoianii
liudei v gosudarstve," *Sbornik statei posviashchennykh P. B. Struve ko dniu 35 letiia
ego nauchnopublitsisticheskoi deiatel'nosti 1890—30.I.1925* (Prague 1925), pp. 313—323.

novelties and creating new norms. This is evidenced by the manner in which he introduced them — furtively, illegally, as it were. As the Digest was only a summary and extract of existing laws, its paragraphs should have been based on actual legislative acts to which the official or judge could refer to check the accuracy and full meaning of the statement. But how could Speransky have footnoted and underpinned with references some of his novelties and innovations? And how do it for linking statements? Speransky resorted to two methods to get around this difficulty, methods which show that he was not quite disingenuous. First of all, he gave references only to whole sections of the Digest, and not to individual paragraphs. These citations were so numerous and referred to such a welter of laws that they could not possibly be checked. He also used the system of multiple and vague references, so that it was quite difficult to find the relevant text and specific context on which a given statement in the Digest might be based. Upon close examination of some paragraphs and the citations to them, students have found that none of the references really support the statements in the Digest. The second method was more devious yet. Speransky used some concepts and definitions from his own code of 1809, pretending that it could now be considered as actual Russian legislation because it had been adopted in the Council of State. But as if aware of the "fraud" he tried to perpetrate he did not give any direct references to the code itself. [1]

The reason for introducing legal novelties in this indirect way was probably not so much that Speransky wanted to deceive Nicholas I, as that he knew Nicholas would not permit the writing of a new code where these innovations might be brought in openly and coherently. Yet, Speransky felt that Russia was in need of the innovations in order to have a solid foundation for a modern and progressive social and economic development. This being the case, he naturally expected that the Digest would be recognized as the authoritative source of Russian law on which judicial decisions would be based. He did not care to have judges and officials go back to the antiquated laws and concepts of the original acts (which would negate his work of modernization and innovation *en sourdine*).

Theoretically, however, the Digest was supposed to be only a convenient reference compendium, at most a summary, of existing laws — an

---

[1] On the preceding, see the articles of Vinaver cited earlier, and Kasso, "K istorii Svoda Zakonov grazhdanskikh," *loc. cit.*, who — while disagreeing as to the political implications pointed out by Vinaver and the sources of Speransky's inspiration — confirms the picture of the method used in the composition of the Digest.

incorporation, rather than a codification in the technical sense. [1] In doubtful cases, therefore, when the Digest seemed unclear or incomplete, should the judges (or government officials) not go back to the Complete Collection of Laws for the original text of the statute on which the relevant paragraphs of the Digest were based? To this Nicholas I answered in the negative, for he believed that the Complete Collection had only historical value. Speransky also — for the reasons just mentioned — wanted the Digest to stand as the final authority. But he felt that it might prove useful to have the Digest first checked and tested by experience. He therefore suggested that for a few years the Digest's authority should be qualified by reference to the original acts; but once all the necessary amendments had been made in the light of experience, the Digest should stand as the only authoritative text. It was to be then, as it became in fact, the official interpretation of Russian law.

The matter was discussed at a session of the Council of State in 1832. The Minister of Justice, Prince Dashkov, argued for the exclusive authority of the Digest, Speransky for a transitional testing period, while some others felt that the old law texts should be preserved as the final authority in cases of doubt. The vote was nineteen to thirteen in favor of the compromise, trial period solution; and Nicholas I concurred with the majority. The Emperor, however, worded his final decision in such a way as to leave no doubt that from January 1, 1835, the Digest alone would have the force of final authority in all cases. As a result, the status of the Complete Collection became that of a handy compilation that might be kept on the shelves of historical libraries. [2] And it also meant that the Digest played the role of the full code that Speransky had suggested, but which Nicholas I had not wanted.

This decision raised some complex legal technical problems into which we cannot enter here. The problems obviously arose because of the basic features of the Digest: its legal innovations, the careless presentation of some concepts and laws, and the difficulty of checking back to the original sources. Some jurists, like Pobedonostsev, went so far as to maintain that a conscientious judge, to arrive at an equitable decision in line with the spirit of Russian law, would have to do the entire work of codification himself in every important and complex

[1] Korkunov, "Znachenie Svoda Zakonov," *Sbornik statei N. M. Korkunova 1877–1897* (St. Pbg. 1898), p. 77.

[2] Blosfel'dt, "Zakonnaia" *sila Svoda Zakonov*, pp. 33, 34, 51–53, 54–57. The text of the Imperial manifesto, 31 January 1833 (2d PSZ, No. 5947), is cited by Blosfel'dt on pp. 67–68. For a scholarly juridical discussion of the implications of the problem, see Korkunov, "Znachenie Svoda Zakonov," *loc. cit.*

case. Most jurists, however, have felt that the Digest was the "authentic interpretation of the law". At any rate, the acceptance as final authority of an inadequate and somewhat confusing Digest handicapped greatly the Russian legal profession in the exercise of its functions in the interest of equitable justice.

The Digest had to be accepted as the only final authority for one additional reason. After the draft of the fifteen volumes had been completed, they were sent to various government offices for comment and check. The offices were instructed to add all the necessary rules and legislation on which they operated and which had not been included in the Digest. In this way, many ministerial decisions and regulations were included (in particular for the parts dealing with commercial and customs law). As a result, the Digest admitted of a further confusion, namely that of law (as issued by the legislator) and bureaucratic regulation and prescription. To deny the Digest full and exclusive force of law would have meant that ministerial regulations could be easily disregarded and voided, as they were not supported by true legislative acts.

Parallel to the collecting and digesting of Russian law, the Second Section was also busy with the codification of the local laws of various provinces of the Empire. Wherever written law existed, as in the case of the Magdeburg law and the Lithuanian Statute, the procedure was very similar to that of Russian codification. The monuments of law were collected, collated, translated into Russian, and edited. They were then reviewed for completeness and accuracy by selected individuals called to St. Petersburg for that purpose (or found in the capital). In the case of the law of the Western provinces the task was entrusted to a very highly qualified scholar, Danilovich (a pupil of the Polish historian, Lelewel) who acquitted himself very creditably. In many other instances, however, the choice was not so fortunate. The Second Section was not allowed to submit the codes for review to representatives of the provinces concerned (except in the Baltic lands) or to send them to practicing judges, lawyers, and scholars.

Except for the Baltic provinces, none of the local codes received legislative sanction or application. Nor were they really ever intended to. From the very beginning, Speransky conceived of the local laws only as an addition to Russian law, to take care of special social conditions or exceptional cases for which the Imperial code made no provision. Two observations should be made in connection with the codification of local law. One deals with the text of the codes themselves, and the other with their implementation.

By asking that the non-Russian customs and laws be collected, Speransky was acknowledging the peculiarity and special role of local tradition and conditions. Also by accepting the idea (even though with qualifications) that the local codes be checked by someone familiar with the history and tradition of the region, he was also acknowledging the difference and bowing to empirical method. It was obvious that Speransky was recognizing and respecting the multinational character of the Russian Empire and the diversity of its peoples' historical experience. In another sense, though, he was only making the best of a situation that he had not helped to bring about and which he had to accept. He was not at all desirous to ratify without qualifications the existing local diversities and traditions. The government, it is true, had to know the local laws so as to be better aware of local conditions and differences. The administration ought to be familiar with the ways of its non-Russian subjects, but not necessarily bow to them. After all, by virtue of their conquest or annexation, these provinces and peoples had become part of the Empire, and Russian imperial law should apply to them too, except in a few limited and well-defined instances (for example, with respect to a nomadic way of life or a non-Christian religion). Wherever the situation could be dealt with according to Russian law, the latter had to prevail regardless of the traditions and peculiarities of the region. Such an attitude gave the local codes a very weak basis and restricted their practical value from the very outset.

But the process of codification itself had effects on local law which tended to undermine its position, authority, and vitality. Indeed, the codification was carried out with the same hastiness and technical superficiality as the collection and digesting of the Russian laws. By using an uniform vocabulary in translating the local norms into Russian and by disregarding the finer distinctions arising out of the interpretation and application of customary concepts, new legal principles and values were introduced into the old laws. More frequently than not, these innovations were derived from Russian law, for the work of compilation and editing was done by Russian (or Russian trained) officials. Furthermore, especially in the case of the more backward alien minorities (e.g., the nomads of Siberia) the natives wanted to please the authorities and used words and approaches which they thought were familiar and acceptable to the Russians. Lastly, as in the case of any codification of customary law, the setting down in writing of laws and norms heretofore known only orally, tended to fixate, stabilize living and evolving customs and interpretations. It withdrew from circulation the entire realm of court-made laws and the effects of the laws' organic evolution. It bureaucratized what had been living and constantly changing legal relations. With the modernization of the native ways of life, it was perhaps an inevitable process anyway, but it was still a pity that it had to be speeded up and congealed by a fundamentally bureaucratic procedure. [1]

The local codes, with the exception of the Baltic, were never implemented, even within the narrow limits of Speransky's conception of their role. Nicholas I was very reluctant to give even limited authority to laws whose historical and social traditions were different from those of Russia. He delayed the application of the codes and looked for the first convenient pretext to abrogate local law altogether. In the case of the Western provinces, this pretext was offered by the events of Poland and the revolutions of 1848. Desirous of obliterating Polish influence, he forbade the application of the Lithuanian Statute; the same happened in the Ukraine. As to the Siberian laws of the steppe, though applied in fact, they were never given legislative sanction and administrative recognition. Only the influence at court and better organization of the Baltic nobility secured the application of the "Ostsee" codes. [2]

In the final analysis, the codification of local law had no positive practical results. But to the extent that it led to a change in legal norms and administrative practices, it illustrated and furthered Speransky's basic aim: organic Russification by means of the gradual and voluntary assimilation of the peculiarities of non-Russian peoples. It led to the superimposing of a centralized, standardized, and systematic bureaucratic pattern upon the variety and complexity of an historically conditioned reality. But it was to be done gradually, indirectly, by bending rather than by breaking the local pattern. In this sense, codification was only another means for creating a *Kulturgemeinschaft* in the existing *Staatsgemeinschaft* of the Empire. Again it showed Speransky's belief that far going social and economic processes can be introduced and helped along by administrative measures.

---

[1] In the case of oral customary law (as that of Siberian nomadic natives), the material was gathered by means of interviews and decisions of the leaders of the tribe. As we had occasion to mention, this was the procedure followed in Siberia. The history of the codification of local law is most fully and ably told by A. E. Nol'de, *Ocherki po istorii kcdifikatsii mestnykh grazhdanskikh zakonov pri grafe Speranskom*, 2 vols. (St. Pbg. 1906—1914); an interesting picture on the codification of the law of the Baltic provinces is given by A. Ch(umikov), "Speranskii i Balug'-ianskii-Uchastie ikh v sostavlenii svoda uzakonenii dlia Pribaltiiskikh gubernii (iz zapisok ochevidtsa: F. Grinval'dt)," *Russkaia Starina*, XXXV (July 1882), pp. 41—58; for the codification of the customary law of the Siberian natives, see note 1, p. 276.

[2] Nol'de, *Ocherki po istorii kodifikatsii mestnykh grazhdanskikh zakonov*, I, pp. 230—247, 255—282 *passim*.

The picture we have given of the codification work of Speransky has perhaps not been a very favorable one. Early 20th century scholarship has put an end to the uncritical praise showered on his accomplishments during the 19th century. Much of what seemed at first so impressive turned out to have feet of clay. But this is not to deny the great historical role played by the codification. It marked a period in Russian administration and jurisprudence. The existence of a Collection of Laws and more particularly the existence of a Digest (however inadequate from a technical point of view) did provide the government and the courts with a rigid and stable framework on which to base their actions and decisions. For better or for worse, it proved useful and solid enough to survive to the very end of the Empire. It could be changed and improved upon, no doubt. But by making laws accessible and stable it had given that basis of legality and permanence of legal relationships which Russia had sadly lacked until then. The great role played by the jury-courts and by the legal profession in the defense and development of the rule of law in Russia after 1864 would not have been possible without this first foundation. From 1835 on, there is more of an *esprit de suite* in Russian legal life; civil and political relationships were based firmly on known rules and stable procedures. Viewed in retrospect, it was much for 1830, though quite inadequate for the situation as it developed after 1861. As so many things done in the reigns of Alexander I and Nicholas I by narrowly bureaucratic and despotic methods, the codification could not cope with the problems created by the reforms of Alexander II.

On the debit side, the inadequacies of the Digest we have mentioned saddled Russian jurisprudence with many problems which might have been avoided. They perpetuated the difficulties arising out of the discrepancy between traditional Russian norms (and their institutional manifestations) and the dogmatic innovations introduced by Speransky. At times, the Digest acted like a dead weight which prevented an easy adaptation to newly arising circumstances. The worst feature of all, due less to the Digest itself perhaps than to the rigid attitude of the government, was that it precluded the elaboration of court-made law, which is such an important element in a living body of law. [1] It was an especially serious shortcoming in a country that was undergoing rapid and far reaching social and economic changes.

Several features of the codification throw interesting light on Speransky's political attitude. We note first his blend of a historical and

[1] Although it is only fair to note that the decisions and "clarifications" of the Senate played the role of "court-made" law.

a doctrinaire approach. He himself put it rightly when, quoting Montesquieu, he said that he had history illuminate the present and the present illuminate history. [1] He was willing to recognize the role of history in creating the present, but rather as a negative factor, i.e., as a limit on his ability to change and transform the present radically. But history, he felt, had not said its last word, nor was it absolute and infallible. A properly enlightened state, with the help of an able bureaucracy, could do a great deal to channel the further evolution of the people in the proper direction by codification. Laws are the norms and basic concepts which help to shape the spiritual moral and economic development of a people. A proper set of laws, therefore, can influence the future, provided it is not in direct opposition to the past evolution of the nation. It is in this last qualification that Speransky differed from the enlightened absolutist and doctrinaire radical of the 18th century. This attitude of his was no doubt his justification for introducing new legal norms and concepts into areas where they were lacking and where he thought they would do most good.

Another feature of the codification we have already had occasion to point out. It was the desire to bring greater uniformity and system into legal relations. In simplifying the process of government, legal uniformity made it possible for the bureaucracy to operate more effectively. Why preserve all the complexities of the peasants' status if one category was adequate for proper administration? Speransky was not aware, or did not care, that perhaps some important rights or psychological attitudes might be destroyed in the process. But perhaps this simplification helped to set the stage for the more radical transformation in 1861 and after.

In a sense then, the codification is a culmination and the highest expression of Speransky's basic political tenets: systematic clarification of the laws provides the administration with clear-cut and stable rules. The government must be able to act on the basis of law, and the subjects must feel that these laws are permanent. At the same time, these rules and laws permit the government to influence positively the evolution of the people, direct its path toward higher levels of spiritual and economic existence.

---

[1] Speranskii, "O sushchestve svoda," loc. cit., p. 588.

SOURCES

The present chapter is based primarily on secondary works, as an exhaustive analysis of the primary sources is beyond the comptence of the present writer (it is the task of a jurist and specialist in the history of law). For this reason, the bibliography has no claim to exhaustive completeness. It cites only those works that were of major help in the compilation of the present chapter.

S p e r a n s k i i : "Obshchee vvedenie k iz'iasneniiam na proekt grazhdanskogo ulozheniia" (1821) in M. Vinaver, "K voprosu ob istochnikakh X toma Svoda Zakonov," *Zhurnal Ministerstva Iustitsii*, (June 1897), pp. 88—89; "Kratkoe istoricheskoe obozrenie komissii sostavleniia zakonov," *Russkaia Starina*, XV (1876) pp. 433—434; "Predpolozheniia k okonchatel'nomu sostavleniiu zakonov," *Russkaia Starina*, XV (1876) pp. 434—441; "O zakonakh rimskikh i razlichii ikh ot zakonov rossiiskikh," *Russkaia Starina* XV (1876), pp. 592—597; "O sushchestve svoda" (1828), *Russkaia Starina* XV (1876), pp. 586—592; "Ob'iasnitel'naia zapiska soderzhaniia i raspolozheniia svoda zakonov grazhdanskikh," *Arkhiv istoricheskikh i prakticheskikh svedenii*, II (1859); "O svode i sobranii zakonov," *Arkhiv istoricheskikh i prakticheskikh svedenii*, VI (1861), 1—8; "Plan ob izdanii drevnikh uzakonenii rossiiskogo gosudarstva," in Fateev, "K istorii i teorii kodifikatsii," *Nauchnye trudy Russkogo Narodnogo Universiteta v Prage*, IV (1931), pp. 20—22; *Obozrenie istoricheskikh svedenii o Svode Zakonov* (St. Pbg. 1833), also in French, *Précis des notions historiques sur la formation du Corps des lois russes* (St. Pbg. 1833). P. M. Maikov, *Vtoroe otdelenie sobstvennoi E. I. V. Kantseliarii 1826—1882* (St. Pbg. 1906) contains also important sources on the progress of the codification work.

C o n t e m p o r a r y   o p i n i o n s :   A. Ch(umikov), ed., "Speranskii i Balugianskii-uchastie ikh v sostavlenii svoda uzakonenii dlia Pribaltiiskikh gubernii (iz zapisok ochevidtsa: F. Grunval'dt)," *Russkaia Starina*, XXXV (July 1882), pp. 41—58; N. P. Druzhinin, "Pamiati M. M. Speranskogo," *Istoricheskii Vestnik, 35* (January 1889), pp. 141—164.

S e c o n d a r y   w o r k s   o n   t h e   c o d i f i c a t i o n   o f   R u s s i a n   L a w :   A. Babichev, "O redaktsii ispravleniia Svoda Zakonov," *Chteniia* 55 (1865), No. 4, pp. 222—241; Ia. Barshev, *Istoricheskaia zapiska o sodeistvii vtorogo otdeleniia sobstvennoi E. I. V. kantseliarii razvitiiu iuridicheskikh nauk v Rossii* (St. Pbg. 1876), S. Berezkin, *Speranskii kak kodifikator* (Odessa 1889) has remained inaccessible to me; G. E. Blosfel'dt, *"Zakonnaia" sila Svoda Zakonov v svete arkhivnykh dannykh* (Petrograd 1917); A. N. Fateev, "K istorii i teorii kodifikatsii — stoletie Polnogo Sobraniia Zakonov," *Russkii narodnyi universitet v Prage, Nauchnye trudy*, IV (1931), pp. 3—22; A. N. Filippov, "Dva istoriko-kriticheskikh izdaniia, zadumannye M. M. Speranskim pri Nikolae I," *Istoricheskie Izvestiia pri istoricheskom obshchestve Moskovskogo universiteta*, (1916), No. 1, pp. 26—42; A. Filippov, "K voprosu o sostave pervogo Polnogo Sobraniia Zakonov Rossiiskoi Imperii," *Otchet Imperatorskogo Moskovskogo Universiteta za 1915 g.* (Moscow 1916 — also separate offprint); A. Filippov, "Speranskii kak kodifikator russkogo prava," *Russkaia Mysl'* (1892), No. 10, pp. 195—221; A. Filippov, "Znachenie Speranskogo v istorii russkogo zakonodatel'stva," *Russkaia Mysl'*, (1889) No. 4, pp. 1—21; L. A. Kasso, "K istorii svoda zakonov grazhdanskikh," *Zhurnal Ministerstva Iustitsii*, (March 1904), pp. 53—89; N. M. Korkunov, "Teoreticheskie vozzreniia Speranskogo na pravo," *Sbornik statei N. M. Korkunova (1877—1897)*, (St. Pbg. 1898), pp. 97—102; same, "Znachenie Svoda Zakonov," *ibid.*, pp. 77—96; M. A. Lozin-Lozinskii, "Kodifikatsiia zakonov po russkomu gosudarstvennomu pravu," *Zhurnal Ministerstva Iustitsii*, (April—May 1897), pp. 143—186 and 107—173, respectively; P. M. Maikov, "Kommissiia sostavleniia zakonov pri imperatorakh Pavle I i Aleksandre I," *Zhurnal Ministerstva Iustitsii*, (Sept. 1905), pp. 256—291, (Nov. 1905), pp. 236—282, (Dec. 1905), pp. 189—214; P. M. Maikov, "Speranskii i studenty zakonovedeniia," *Russkii Vestnik*, Vol. 262, No. 2 (1899), pp. 609—626, vol. 263, Nos. 1 & 2 (1899), pp. 239—257, 673—683; A. N. Makarov, "K istorii kodifikatsii osnovnykh zakonov," *Zhurnal Ministerstva Iustitsii*, XVIII, No. 10 (Dec. 1912), pp. 222—278; A. N. Makarov, "Svod Zakonov 1833—1933 — zum hundertjährigen Jubiläum der Kodifikation des russischen Rechts," *Zeitschrift für Osteuropäische Geschichte*, VII (1933), Heft 1, pp. 39—55; A. E. Nol'de, *Ocherki istorii kodifikatsii mestnykh grazhdanskikh zakonov pri grafe Speranskom*, 2 vols.,

St. Pbg. 1906—1914; A. E. Nol'de, "Retsenziia na trudy P. M. Maikova," *Zhurnal Ministerstva Narodnogo Prosveshcheniia*, XV (May 1908), No. 5, pp. 168—191; B. Nol'de, "Svod zakonov o sostoianii liudei v gosudarstve," *Sbornik statei posviashchennykh P. B. Struve ko dniu 35 letiia ego nauchno-publitsisticheskoi deiatel'nosti 1890 — 30.I.1925* (Prague 1925), pp. 313—323; B. E. Nol'de, "Zakony osnovnye v russkom prave," *Pravo*, (1913), Nos. 8—9, pp. 447—461 and 524—541; S. V. Pakhman, *Istoriia kodifikatsii grazhdanskogo prava*, 2 vols., St. Pbg. 1876; E. Pontovich, "Osnovnye zakony i kodifikatsiia,"*Russkaia Mysl'*, (1910), No. 7, pp. 165—190; G. Tel'berg, "Uchastie imperatora Nikolaia I v kodifikatsionnoi rabote ego tsarstvovaniia," *Zhurnal Ministerstva Iustitsii*, XXII, (Jan. 1916), pp. 233—244; M. M. Vinaver, "K voprosu ob istochnikakh X toma Svoda Zakonov," *Zhurnal Ministerstva Iustitsii* (June 1897), pp. 87—102 and the same, same title, *ibid.*, October 1895, pp. 1—68; M. Winavert (Vinaver), "L'influence française sur la codification russe sous Nicolas Ier," *Annales Internationales d'Histoire — Congrès de Paris 1900*, 2e section, *Histoire comparée des institutions et du droit* (Paris 1902), pp. 155—172.

General histories and textbooks of Russian law: I. D. Beliaev, *Lektsii po istorii russkogo zakonodatel'stva*, Moscow 1879; A. N. Filippov, *Uchebnik istorii russkogo prava (posobie k lektsiiam)*, 5th ed., Iur'ev, 1914; A. A. Kizevetter, *Osnovnye zakonodatel'nye akty, kasaiushchikhsia grazhdanskikh uchrezhdenii XVIII i pervoi chetverti XIX st.*, Moscow 1909; N. M. Korkunov, *Russkoe gosudarstvennoe pravo*, 2 vols., 6—7th eds., St. Pbg. 1909; V. N. Latkin, *Uchebnik istorii russkogo prava perioda imperii, XVIII i XIX st.*, 2d ed., St. Pbg. 1909; V. N. Latkin, *Zakonodatel'nye komissii v Rossii (istoriko-iuridicheskoe issledovanie)*, St. Pbg. 1887; N. I. Lazarevskii, *Lektsii po russkomu gosudarstvennomu pravu*, 2d ed., St. Pbg. 1910; N. I. Lazarevskii, *Russkoe gosudarstvennoe pravo — I. Konstitutsionnoe pravo*, 3d ed., St. Pbg. 1913; D. I. Meier, *Russkoe grazhdanskoe pravo*, 10th ed. (edited by A. Kh. Gol'msten), Petrograd 1915; B. E. Nol'de, *Ocherki russkogo gosudarstvennogo prava*, St. Pbg. 1911; N. K. Rennenkampf, *Iuridicheskaia Entsiklopediia*, 3d ed., Kiev—St. Pbg., 1907; A. Romanovich-Slavatinskii, *Posobie dlia izucheniia russkogo gosudarstvennogo prava po metodu istoriko dogmaticheskomu*, Kiev 1872; G. F. Shershenevich, *Uchebnik russkogo grazhdanskogo prava*, 2 vols. 11th ed., Moscow 1914; G. V. Vernadskii, *Ocherk istorii prava russkogo gosudarstva XVIII—XIX vv (period imperii)*, Prague 1924; M. F. Vladimirskii-Budanov, *Obzor istorii russkogo prava*, 6th ed. St. Pbg.—Kiev, 1909; N. P. Zagoskin, *Nauka istorii russkogo prava*, Kazan' 1891; N. P. Zagoskin, *Istoriia prava russkogo naroda*, vol. I, Kazan' 1899.

For the customary law of Siberian natives and its codification, see note 1, p. 276 and bibliography in my monograph, *Siberia and the Reforms of 1822*.

# CHAPTER XII

## LAST YEARS – CONCLUSION

By bringing to a successful conclusion the task of codifying and digesting Russian law, Speransky had accomplished the major goal and purpose of his administrative work. It was the fulfillment and crowning glory of his career. When in January 1833, at the Council of State, Nicholas I bestowed his own star and sash of the Order of St. Andrew, 1st class, upon Privy Councillor Speransky in reward for his labors on the code, the son of the priest of Cherkutino village could well feel that he had attained the pinnacle of bureaucratic success. From then on, until his death in 1839, Speransky continued as an active member of the government, a high ranking and respected official, but he contributed no fresh ideas or methods. He participated in practically all important government discussions and administrative reorganizations, but played no leading role; and his voice was not a decisive one.

He was an elder statesman, though it might be more accurate to call him an "elder bureaucrat" — as during the reign of Nicholas I statecraft had been replaced by plodding committee work and limited, piecemeal administrative ameliorations. Even more than his advice and opinion, it was his pen that was in demand; after all, Speransky was Russia's most skillful *rédacteur*. In that capacity he drafted the manifesto on the war with Turkey in 1828 and the proclamation on the majority of Grand Duke Alexander, the heir presumptive. Speransky's recent success at codification gave him the aura of legal expert. He was selected to give lectures on law to the heir presumptive. The lectures have been preserved and published. They illustrate Speransky's fundamental political attitudes with great clarity and full force. Though some of his statements seem somewhat colored by a consideration for his imperial pupil, they are a truthful picture of his views. He starts with a definition of laws that is very close to that of natural law, but tempers it with the historical approach (especially when he comes to discuss serfdom and the political organization of Russia). We need not go into Speransky's arguments, for — oddly perhaps, but not unexpectedly — they are not essentially different from those he had elaborated during his exile and which we have described and analyzed in Chapter Seven. In lecturing to the Grand Duke he again expressed his reliance on the enlightened autocrat who, ruling on the basis of clear and just laws, prepares and guides his people towards the achievement of higher spiritual and moral goals. [1] Did Grand Duke Alexander remember Speransky's words and apply them after he had become Emperor Alexander II? There is no direct evidence for it in the existing biographies (which stress the moral and humanitarian influence of the poet Zhukovskii), but a more searching examination of the sources might perhaps show some traces of it.

After 1833, Speransky spent most of his working time in various committees, in the discussion and elaboration of a great number and wide range of problems and measures. We cannot follow his participation in detail, nor do we really need to, because — as noted previously — Speransky played a secondary role, being at best only a part-time member. As usual, he wrote numerous papers and opinions, drafted acts and proposals of legislation; but almost none of them were implemented in the form he had suggested. They were collaborative efforts from which originality and creative innovation were banned by the necessity of reaching some compromise solution that would be acceptable to the conservative Emperor. Speransky could no longer feel, as he had before his exile, that he was able to *"tailler dans le vif"*. [2]

We might mention a few of the matters in which Speransky's participation has been recorded. Of anecdotal rather than real significance was his voice in favor of railroad building in Russia, which the Minister of Finance, Count Kankrin, bitterly opposed. Of greater positive value was his role in the discussions on education. Speransky helped to write the statute of the Vladimir University at Kiev. He managed to include provisions for a limited form of academic autonomy, though he had to bow to the Emperor's wish to put the university under the supervision of the bureaucracy. In any case, considering the period at which it was established, the Vladimir University was very well treated indeed, and enjoyed greater freedom than the other Russian universities of the time.

[1] A more complete analysis of Speransky's lectures to the Grand Duke is to be found in my article, "The Political Philosophy of Speranskij," *The American Slavic and East European Review*, vol. XII, No. 1 (February 1953), pp. 14—18.

[2] F. P. Lubianovskii, "Vospominaniia F. P. Lubianovskogo," *Russkii Arkhiv*, (1872), p. 486.

A subject that occupied the minds of many officials was the better organization of primary and secondary education. At stake was the opening of the schools to children of serfs and of peasants. Oddly enough for someone who himself had come from the village, but not too surprising in view of his general political orientation, Speransky was opposed to the admission of serf and peasant children to secondary schools. He felt that primary education on the village level was adequate enough for them; and if the children of peasants were to go higher, they would encounter serious psychological and social problems, for they would not be able to adjust their superior intellectual condition to their lowly social status and legal disabilities. It was quite a reasonable position which had something to commend it. But it was a position that had been always argued by those who wanted to prevent the spread of education among the people and the lifting of the peasantry from its lowly and ignorant state. Speransky probably did not intend it in this way. He recognized that the sons of those peasants who had acquired wealth, freedom, and some education could be admitted to secondary schools. In other words, let the state first give primary education to all peasants and the opportunity of bettering their economic lot. Only then will the question of admission to secondary education become a practical issue. By that time, perhaps, it will be possible to grant equal admission to the peasants without risking major social or psychological difficulties. Speransky's position on this problem provides but another illustration of his gradualism and dilatory bureaucratic approach.

In connection with the peasantry it might also be mentioned that Speransky participated in the committee that eventually worked out the basis of Count Kiselev's program for the state peasants. His participation was to be expected, for he had probably been the first influential official to recommend that the solution of serfdom, i.e., emancipation, be tackled first with regard to the state peasants. He had suggested that they be the first to return to their previous status of being tied to the land and carry very strictly defined obligations only, and that this serve as a model for the reform of the position of private serfs. Speransky had also been the first to point out that the state peasants in European Russia might soon be faced with a shortage of land. In that event they must be allowed to resettle elsewhere, preferably in Siberia where there were splendid opportunities and many more agricultural laborers were needed. Though his ideas did not receive legislative implementation at the time, they were not forgotten by later officials who tackled the peasant question. They no doubt influenced the slow shift in thinking about the serf problem that can be detected in the committees of the second half of Nicholas' reign.

Speransky actively participated in the discussions concerning the improvement of the legal status of the domestic (household) serfs. It had been a long standing preoccupation of his, and he aimed at abolishing that category of serfs, the most unfortunate one in Russia. He felt that the very complicated and fundamental problem of serfdom in general could be given a good start toward solution if its worst manifestation could be abolished first. Speransky also took a prominent part in the long and drawn out discussions that led to the currency reform of 1839—1840. But his views did not prevail against those of Finance Minister Count Kankrin.

In all these, and some other matters, Speransky was called in as an expert, even when his grasp of the subject was not very firm. What was asked of him was to solve a problem "bureaucratically", by drafting the right kind of balanced and well written committee report or legislation. His facile pen, clear and analytical mind, tactful manner, and great capacity for work were ideal for achieving success in a government like that of Nicholas I. Not that Speransky was influential in suggesting policies, in directing the Emperor's political attitudes and decisions — as he had with Alexander I, for a while at least — but Nicholas listened readily and with respect to all his technical suggestions. His ubiquitous activities left traces in all government committees and agencies. In this respect he was the model and the teacher for an entire generation of government officials, at least in the techniques of bureaucratic work. Some of these younger officials took over his function as technical advisers in drafting reports and legislation — among these were Nadezhdin and Baron Korf, his future biographer. Some others developed Speransky's political ideas and attitudes further and tried to implement them in the reign of Nicholas' successor. In this group we find the names of men like Nicholas Miliutin, Iurii Samarin, K. Kavelin to mention but the more prominent ones. The similarity between some of the political attitudes of Speransky and the "Slavophile reformers" of the 1860's makes one wonder whether Speransky exercised any direct influence on them. Unfortunately, no definitive answer can be given. There is some indirect evidence that men like N. Miliutin, I. Samarin, A. Koshelev might have been directly acquainted with Speransky's plans, projects, and proposals. There is also some indication that a few of the "older Slavophiles" might have had personal contacts with Speransky in the first years of their mature life (the 1820's). However, until new archival material is found and published or the views of the Slavophile reformers analyzed very carefully and completely, the connection must remain a mere suggestion and hypothesis. It is of course quite plausible that Speransky's goal and the approach of the Slavophile liberal reformers were similar because both had the same philosophical and religious roots: the social and political traditions of the Russian church on the one hand, and of German romantic metaphysical and ethical systems, on the other. Yet, it is not easy to escape the impression that the similarity between K. Aksakov's "Zemskii Sobor" and Speransky's Dumas is too great to be accounted for by a common metaphysical, ethical, and religious source of thought alone. We should hasten to add, though, that in one important particular the difference between the Slavophiles and Speransky was immense: Speransky's reliance on the bureaucracy, however enlightened, could not be to the taste of the Slavophiles. [1]

Speransky's relation to the Slavophiles brings us to the question of his relations with Russian society in general. The last time we dealt with this aspect in some detail had been to point out his complete isolation from society at court and in the capital just before his exile. At that time, he had lived absorbed completely in his work and had relied only on the company of people much inferior to himself intellectually and socially. Apparently, the harsh experience of disgrace and exile taught Speransky the lesson of the danger of social isolation for a person in his position. As provincial governor he also had to recognize the value of social contacts from an administrative and political point of view. And when he returned to St. Petersburg in 1821 he decided that he would not repeat the same mistake again.

Conditions were favorable, as "society" was elated by the news of his return to the capital. People believed that it was proof of Alexander's return to his earlier liberal policies and preoccupation with internal reform (after so many years of war and absorption with foreign affairs). The rumor of Speransky's treason had either been forgotten or was dismissed as an expression of war hysteria. Francophilia did not have any more the derogatory political implications it had had in 1812. And the more ardent enemies of Speransky, Rostopchin, Armfelt, Balashev, and others were either dead or removed from influence. Whatever the reasons, the return of Speransky was welcomed by most. Rumor assigned him a bewildering variety of posts: various ministries, the chairmanship of the Council of State, or the chairmanship of a

---

[1] For instance, A. Khomiakov's disparaging opinion of Speransky, as cited from a letter of his to I. S. Aksakov (1859) by N. P. Barsukov, *Zhizn' i trudy M. P. Pogodina*, XVI, p. 397.

new comission on laws. The more "liberal" intelligentsia saw in Speransky's return the solution of all Russia's ills, as witness the emotional outburst of the director of the Lycée at Tsarskoe Selo, Engel'gardt, who wrote: "Please be to God! This [the State Secretaryship] is the most important post in the entire mechanism of state administration; it has been created by him [Speransky] and there is no other man in the state who could occupy it. He, and only he, has all the qualities requisite for the post: intelligence, goodness of heart, firmness, knowledge of affairs, clarity of concepts, and the ability to carry out business easily, rapidly, and well. May it please God that he be with us, may it please God that at the throne of our father Tsar there be three or four men like Mikhail Mikhailovich, who would inform him of the truth without fear; we would have an earthly paradise!" [1] And we have seen that the Decembrist conspirators were toying with the idea of securing his participation in their revolutionary government.

With "society" welcoming him back — as if shamefacedly making up for its treatment of him in 1812 — and Speransky's awareness of the danger of social isolation, it would seem that nothing stood in the way of his social success. Speransky bought a relatively big house, where his daughter could be hostess to a large gathering. He himself frequented soirées, balls, receptions, and in turn had his regular "days". To these days there came not only young men interested in obtaining the hand of Miss Elizabeth Speransky, but also the Privy Councillor's colleagues, members of the higher ranks of the bureaucracy, courtiers. The American Minister — Henry Middleton — and his family were also frequent visitors. Apparently, these receptions were quite successful affairs, for Speransky could be a charming host when he chose to. [2]

But his decision to lead a social life seems to have been due so much to rational considerations that it failed to carry the warmth and softness of sincere emotion and personal feeling. Speransky had realized the political error of social isolation, but he still did not feel the need of the company of others, of the friendship and devotion of his

---

[1] N. Gastfreind, *Tovarishchi Pushkina po Imperatorskomu Tsarskosel'skomu Litseiu*, Vol. II, p. 39 (Letter to F. Matiushkin, 25 June 1821).

[2] Thus Count Kankrin, the Minister of Finance, was telling a younger official who had been invited to Speransky's house: "I would advise you to follow suit to the request of Mikhail Mikhailovich. You know it, my dear, that this is our most intelligent and interesting person, and you will be perfectly satisfied with his charming conversation. I shall also tell you that he is a clever man, and also a good-hearted one, and this is a rare combination." I. A. Bychkov (ed.), "Dopolnitel'nye zametki i materialy dlia 'Zhizni M. M. Speranskogo'," *Russkaia Starina*, 115 (Sept. 1903), p. 515.

equals and colleagues. Psychologically, he remained lonely and an *Einzelgänger*. As a result, he created the impression — and not entirely without some foundation — that there was a touch of exaggeration and insincerity in his desire to make friends and penetrate into the highest circles. Speransky was too obviously craving social and psychological recognition, even though his manners and outward behavior were quite reserved and correct.

The evidence on Speransky's contacts and connections with the intellectual élite of the period is very fragmentary. We may list a few details, though. In recognition of his interest in and contributions to letters (in particular, his translation of *Imitatio Christi* of Thomas à Kempis), he was elected to membership in the group called "Lovers of the Russian Word" (*Liubiteli rossiiskogo slova*), alongside other prominent littérateurs and dignitaries. Since the time he had been elected to the Academy in reward for his efforts at promoting the scientific exploration of Siberia, Speransky was also in contact with Count S. S. Uvarov, the President of the Academy of Sciences and perhaps the most learned and best educated man in Russia.

Speransky was also close to the younger generation through his daughter's circle, and more particularly through his assistant, Batenkov, the future Decembrist. Also, some of the students of the Tsarskosel'skii Litsei, the sons of his old colleagues, would come to see him. Sharing many philosophical and metaphysical interests with this young intellectual generation, Speransky found himself close to the future leaders of Russia's intellectual and artistic life.

But this close relationship with Russia's intelligentsia ended rather bruskly as a result of the events of December 1825. In part, the change is to be explained by the fact that the rigorous regime of Nicholas did not encourage its officials to keep up the easy informality of social and intellectual contacts which had been the rule during Alexander's reign. The militaristic, narrow-minded, and "practical" outlook of Nicholas put a damper on St. Petersburg society. But of greater influence on the social and intellectual climate than the personal and political character of Nicholas' regime, was the impact of the Decembrist revolt. At first, the revolt spread anxiety and fear among St. Petersburg high society, for few were the families or circles that did not have someone who belonged to the Decembrist societies. Even after the conclusion of the investigation and trial, social life never returned to its previous easy going pattern.

The Decembrist revolt split Russian society, e.g. the upper educated classes, in two. On the one side were the Decembrists, and their spiritual and intellectual successors: making up the intelligentsia properly speaking, they never forgave the government for suppressing and convicting the Decembrists. From this time on, Russia's literary and intellectual élite was to be found among the opposition to the government. Even when members of the intelligentsia entered government service, they always did it with mental reservations. Either they felt that under Russian conditions they had no alternative and tried to resign as soon as they could (Khomiakov, Aksakov, for example), or else they entered government service with the express purpose of being of some use in a specific situation (Iu. Samarin, Koshelev, Cherkasskii), but they never identified themselves with the bureaucracy at large, remaining outside the regular career hierarchy. On the other side stood the government. It too included men of great intelligence, men with lively intellectual and artistic interests, and frequently not devoid of unselfish civic consciousness. But they were solidary with the government; they rejected the path taken by the Decembrists and approved of the Emperor's punishment of the rebels. And consequently, to the intelligentsia, they were the obedient servants of an abhorred despotism and the objects of social and cultural ostracism. There could be no common language, after 1825, between an Orlov, Chernyshev, Benkendorf, Korf, Bludov, or Uvarov and the intelligentsia. For a while yet, a few outstanding personalities of Russia's intellectual élite did not identify themselves exclusively with either group. Among these were Pushkin, Prince Viazemskii, Zhukovskii. But they were a small and dwindling group, and their influence vanished after the middle of the 1830's.

This fateful split of Russian society changed the social position of men like Speransky, who in a previous generation might have been perfectly at home in both groups. It ended for all times the close relationship and intellectually fruitful collaboration of intellectuals (in the narrow sense) and officials. While tracing the intellectual make-up of Speransky, we could point to his connections with writers, teachers, scholars, religious personalities, and philosophers. After 1825 such a tie between the bureaucratic and intellectual élites becomes more and more rare and difficult (at least until the 20th century). As, not unexpectedly, Speransky cast in his lot with the government, he cut his ties with the intelligentsia.

And so it was that the generation of intellectuals who came to maturity and prominence in the 1830's had no contact or connections with him. It was not, incidentally, due to a discrepancy in age, for Speransky remained intellectually alive and vigorous to his very end. Writers like Pushkin and Zhukovskii might still be seen at Speransky's house after 1825 (and Speransky was a regular visitor to Zhukovskii's weekly receptions); but they no longer represented the thoughts and opinions that were slowly coming to dominate the intellectual scene of Russia. Thus in his last years, Speransky was isolated from the mainstream of Russian artistic and literary life.

The events of 1825 also had their repercussion on Speransky's relations to society and the court. Speransky's active efforts at gaining full recognition by court society either misfired or were stopped short by the changed atmosphere following the Decembrist revolt. For the period after 1825, we have no evidence to indicate that Speransky led an active social life. He continued to receive some friends (at one of such Sundays, Pushkin talked to him about Pugachev [1]), but otherwise does not seem to have been very much in the limelight. His many duties left him little time, and with advancing age, he grew too weary to make extra efforts. And so it was that for the last years of his life he went back to pretty much the same social isolation as at the beginning of his career. There was of course a difference; he now was a respected and esteemed official. But perhaps his isolation was even greater than at the start of his government service. His old friends and acquaintances from the lower social classes, classmates from the seminary, the merchants, doctors, and professional people whom he had met at Samborskii's house, were all gone now — either dead or living in retirement. His family life too had become more restricted, since his daughter was married and had a family of her own.

The only new activity he took up in the 1830's was traveling abroad. In 1830 he went abroad for the first time in his life (if we except the short official trip to Erfurt). He visited foreign countries pretty regularly thereafter, to undergo treatment at watering places, or simply to rest. He went to Germany, Paris, and Prague. He expressed keen interest in the revival of the Western Slavs. Curiously enough, though, his travel notes and letters from abroad are remarkably uninteresting and empty. They reveal a very naive artistic taste and an astonishing lack of sophistication in observing and judging life and conditions abroad. In any case, this direct acquaintance with Western Europe came too late to change or influence in a new way his work and thought.

We have noted that after the brief period of distrust during the investigation of the Decembrist movement, Speransky's relations with the Emperor became very good. But the relationship remained always

---

[1] I. A. Bychkov (ed.), "Neskol'ko dannykh k istorii knigi barona M. A. Korfa, 'Zhizn' grafa Speranskogo' — iz bumag akad. A. F. Bychkova," *Russkaia Starina*, 109 (1902), p. 150.

formal and distant: Nicholas was not a person to whom one could be close; and the great discrepancy in age between the Emperor and his Privy Councilor could not be easily bridged either. But Nicholas respected Speransky and even came to like him in his own formal and rigid way. The Emperor showed his esteem and appreciation of Speransky's services to the state by elevating him — the son of a village priest — to the rank of Count of the Russian Empire, in December 1838. When Speransky fell ill, the Emperor visited him at his sickbed, a rare distinction, and was genuinely grieved by his death, which came in February 1839.

But for all the sympathy and respect with which he was surrounded in his last days, Speransky died as he had lived — lonely and isolated from the mainstream of Russian society.

The news of the death of Speransky created no great stir in Russia. The public at large and the intellectual élite took almost no notice of the event. Besides the official eulogies, we have the reactions of only those who had known him personally as a colleague or superior in the administration. Let us first cite two contemporary comments. The first is by a man who had known Speransky since 1808, but had never fully liked him and who, at the time of this comment was living in Paris. The second reaction was based on an acquaintance made during the last decade of Speransky's life.

Alexander Turgenev wrote from Paris to his friend A. Ia. Bulgakov:

"It is a pity about Speransky! He did much that was useful for Russia! But with a more independent and more elevated soul, he would have accomplished more yet. The Lvovs, Magnitskiis, Zhuravlevs [subaltern bureaucrats in Speransky's entourage] who surrounded him, would not refreshen the moral climate in which he smothered himself. In spite of this, posterity — more than ourselves — will be grateful to him, not so much for the difficult and multi-volumed accomplishment of the Digest of Laws, as for the Council [of State], for the supervisory control . . . and for the idea of the responsibility of ministers which is hidden in the general statute on the ministries. He loved work and never bragged about it. In him there was the seed of a better future, but the fear of the Jews and Pharisees of our times did not allow it to grow . . . [sic!]. He did not understand his role, either before or after his exile, nor did he understand Alexander who, after the Siberian and Penza experiences, was offering himself completely to him, and he sought out Arakcheev who embraced him and smothered him in his military colonies . . . Peace be to his remains! I have forgiven him long ago his faintheartedness in a situation that was important for me. He knew the innocence of my brother, and even demonstrated it to me himself, and yet kept silent, he kept silent when silence was a crime. Well, anyway, who did not keep silent, except Zhukovskii? . . . Speransky labored, and in his work he found nourishment and glory. His collaborators were mediocrities and more of a handicap than of any help to him . . ." [1]

The second comment is to be found in the autobiographical notes of Senator K. Lebedev:

"Count M. M. Speransky died, after having been for more than forty years a government official and for some time the first man in the Empire. He left after himself the renown of a reformer of institutions, an experienced legislator and the compiler of the Digest of Laws. He did not manage to complete his task: the revision of the laws remains in its first stage. Speransky belonged to the small number of those extraordinary upstarts who can appear only under conditions of an uneven education of the nation and which now are becoming more and more rare. He had an extraordinary native intelligence, which lacked theoretical knowledge and strict logic. He adapted everything and adapted himself to everything. If his education had been in diplomacy, he would have been the Talleyrand of Eastern Europe. But he could not be a Metternich, and still less a Lord Chatham. Secretive and evasive, he acted decisively only when he was convinced of the support of the authorities and not because of his conviction in the truth [of what he was doing]. Aiming at honors, he was always wary of expressing his opinion fully and awaited confused situations to open his mouth; he worked in the dark and ambiguously, so as not to offend any party and to prepare further ground for his indispensability in the future. But because of his experience, his sure touch, he belongs to those national giants who concentrate upon themselves general popular attention, and for this reason — whether rightly or wrongly — he received as his share both glory and infamy for the innovations and improvements. Like all seekers, divested of any definitive character, but endowed with great cleverness and long experience, he had many persecutors and men who envied him. He was respected by all, but loved by none. Whatever the case may be, even with this dark side of his life, he left a great memory." [2]

In spite of their divergencies, the two comments show some interesting agreement. Though neither can of course be accepted as a definitive

[1] A. I. Turgenev, *Pis'ma A. Turgeneva Bulgakovym* (M. 1939), pp. 224—225, letter from Paris, dated 14 March (2 March) 1839 to A. Ia. Bulgakov.
[2] K. N. Lebedev, "Iz zapisok senatora K. N. Lebedeva," *Russkii Arkhiv,* (1910), No. 7, pp. 394—395.

judgment on Speransky's life and work, both point out some of the factors which render it difficult to pass a final judgment. We are struck by the absence of any definite or sharply delineated features in Speransky's character. He obviously must have had some personality trait which made everybody attribute this absence of definiteness to a lack of honesty and frankness or to a lack of moral courage. What little we know of his relations to society and individuals and of his psychological reaction to situations, confirms the impression. Probably to a large extent, it was a by-product of his early seminary training.

The two comments we have cited also indicate that it was difficult to characterize Speransky as a person. Indeed, as the preceding pages have illustrated, there is almost no record of a person called Speransky. We know some things of the student, the young government employee, the dignitary in favor and the dignitary in disgrace, the prominent official and the codificator of laws, but we have almost no picture of the individual behind these labels.

The personality of Speransky was grey; there is no doubt about it. He had a number of positive traits; he was intelligent, good hearted, honest, hard working, tactful, and well mannered. We also have some fleeting glimpses of him as a family man, a loving husband and a devoted father. But such traits do not add up to anything very striking. Perhaps it was his most notable quality that his was not at all a striking personality. His lowly origin and seminary education which aimed at the bending of strong individuality, may have been a factor in bringing about this result. Surely though, Speransky himself must have had also a predisposition for it. Several contemporaries have noted that he was the most disconcerting person to talk to. He listened attentively and politely, and seemed to agree with everything one said. But he never expressed his opinion definitely; he never gave the impression that he had a mind and will of his own. One never quite knew what he thought or felt at the moment; his poise and apparent equanimity were marvelous. But was it genuine tact and self control, or was it coldness, apathy, or something else again? There is no denying, in the final analysis, that he was what the vernacular calls a "cold fish", without a clearly delineated individual character. Let us admit it, his personality eludes us. But this does not seem to be of major importance in assessing either his career or his accomplishments. Only in a few instances (his fall from favor in 1812, his relations to society, for example) do we note the intrusion of his personality, but even here it was not a major factor. Such an indefinite personality, however, when coupled with genuine technical ability, may be the best factor for success in a big bureaucratic organization, where striking and strong personalities are distrusted and kept down.

As a successful and prominent official in the large bureaucratic machine of the Russian government, Speransky was involved in many things and dealt with most facets of Russian public life. And yet, his creative imprint is not easily discernible at first glance. Was it due to his own indeterminate character or to the self-effacing devotion of the public servant? Probably a little of each. But a further and more important reason was that he was never allowed to bring any of his own ideas and plans to successful and complete implementation. He was not permitted even to carry through his last major assignment, the codification, as he wished, for Nicholas I opposed what should have been its crowning piece, a new code. As a result, all of Speransky's work is fragmentary and touches upon widely divergent areas. As though aware of his special position and of his helplessness in securing adequate implementation of his ideas, Speransky made his projects and proposals pretty general, and even at times vague. They allowed of several interpretations and of several methods of implementation. To a large extent, these features of his work were the result of his omnivorous and syncretic mind and of his talent for combining and ordering logically and coherently disparate elements by means of a clear style and effective presentation. Paradoxically, therefore, in the light of his long and variegated government service, in the final analysis, Speransky left little direct imprint on the political and social institutions of Russia. His indirect influence, on the other hand, proved great and lasting.

The areas in which Speransky has left concrete traces of his own work are not many. The organization of the Ministries, the Council of State, and of the Siberian administration were in large measure due to his planning (though he built on an existing situation and the empirical experience accumulated in the past). In the case of the codification of laws, his contribution was mainly that of method and procedure. Its results were not, truly speaking, consciously planned or foreseen by Speransky. When we examine all these accomplishments of his closely, we find that he only put the key stone, the last touch, to an edifice that was in process of construction and had been gotten well under way by his predecessors. It demonstrates that he knew how to set up and complete in orderly fashion a far-going reorganization of the Empire's administration. Whether in so doing he introduced new concepts and gave a new direction to the future development of the institutions he reorganized, we shall try to see later. For the moment let us note that in essence, Speransky introduced little that had not been known before, but he streamlined the procedure and clarified the aims and task. For example, the idea of well-run and controlable ministries had been in the air since the days of Catherine II. A concrete start had been made under Paul; later the decrees of 1802 contained many good suggestions. On these preparatory efforts Speransky built his organization of the Ministry of the Interior in 1803, which in turn served as model for the statute of 1811. His Council of State — often considered as his most original contribution to Russian central government institutions — was a direct lineal descendant of the earlier advisory councils of the sovereign; and even some of its concrete and specific features had been adumbrated in the Council set up in 1801, and in the discussions of the Unofficial Committee. In Siberia, too, Speransky in large measure carried on the policies of Pestel and Treskin, though by much better methods. Finally, Speransky's approach to codification showed that he had repudiated his first false start and had returned to some of the conceptions and methods advocated and initiated by his predecessors and by his rival, Baron Rosenkampf.

All this in itself was by no means a small achievement. At the time, perhaps, no one else could have brought these various tasks to a successful conclusion. But why did this upstart, the son of a village priest, without connections and party at court, alone succeed where other dignitaries had failed? The answer, it would seem, lies not so much in his superior intellectual abilities (though they were no mean factor), as in his superb mastery of bureaucratic technique. He was a virtuoso of bureaucratic operation, unsurpassed in Russia either before or after.

The elegance of his style and the facile clarity of his exposition, which we have pointed out earlier, were a significant factor in his personal success as *rédacteur,* but they are only one side of the picture. [1] Had his influence been only one of style, its impact would probably have been limited to giving welcome relief to the historian working through the official records of the period. While his style was imitated and perpetuated by succeeding generations of Russian officials, it alone would not have made his great fame. His way of thinking, on the other hand, was an important factor in his success. To begin with, unlike his less logical and less acute colleagues, he saw the problem clearly right away in terms of its practical, organizational, and administrative implications. Seeing the problem in this fashion was already half the battle

---

[1] Speransky's stylistic talent as an explanation of his successful career is, in our opinion, greatly exaggerated by A. E. Nol'de in his (manuscript) biography of Speransky.

of finding a solution for it in institutional terms. The solution in turn, broken down analytically and presented logically by outlining the procedure step by step, imposed itself with compelling force in its proper administrative and bureaucratic framework. Like any good administrator, Speransky knew that in a complex bureaucratic machine a goal had to be approached gradually, step by step, through a succession of intermediate stages — but always keeping the final aim and complete picture well in mind — so as to give every official a chance to participate in it, thereby sharing both praise and blame for it. Speransky presented his analysis and proposed his solution of a problem in terms the sovereign and his bureaucracy could understand, appreciate, accept, and implement.

In order to do this kind of thing effectively, the bureaucratic machine had to be well set up and operate smoothly. For this good organization was essential. Each government office and institution had its specific area of competence, its well defined duties, and its officials trained to perform them. Hierarchical subordination assured discipline, *esprit de suite,* and supervision of the component parts of the system. But organization had to be given directives; these were to be embodied in stable, clear, well known, and easily understood rules and laws. Only on the basis of such rules would the machine of government operate smoothly (it was very much the application of the 18th century idea of the laws of nature, and hence came very close to the political ideal of the enlightened despots). Therefore, Speransky's second important contribution to Russian administration was its clear functional organization and the guidance of its actions by stable, clear, and uniform rules and laws.

The imperial administration of Russia in the 19th century had many defects; it sinned against many a thing that men of the time held dear and important. But compared to the 18th century, it was a model of organization and regularity of procedure and stability of goals. This was to a large degree the consequence of Speransky's work, supported by Alexander and Nicholas. To this outlook and approach, the codification was the crowning stone. Speransky removed Russian bureaucratic administration from the domain of personal caprice and irregular organization and, putting it on a par with the governments of contemporary monarchical Europe, based it solidly on functional principles and stable rules. It remained — generally speaking — in that state to the end of the Empire, except to the extent that it was perverted by the personal policies of the autocratic Tsar.

Speransky's work had a double significance. As we have suggested, it was first of all a technical improvement. But it also set new goals to national political life. Indeed, by specifying that the administration had to be based on solid and stable laws and rules, and had to act in a consistent fashion, the state implied that there was a goal for the actions of the government. In the past, before Speransky's time, the Russian state had set goals for itself; but these goals were limited to the finding of means for solving mainly military and diplomatic problems. It did not have a clear conception of an over-all domestic policy or of a long range purpose for its actions. Hence the great vacillations, contradictory policies, and personal caprices which were characteristic of Russian political life in the 18th century. This was not changed overnight, of course, by Speransky. But he introduced the Russian government to an awareness of the need for a national policy goal. Following in his footsteps, the more progressive and "liberal" officials began to formulate concrete goals for government. Besides its obvious role of internal and external protection, the government and the state, in Speransky's view, should lead the nation unto the path of higher spiritual and moral progress and of greater economic prosperity. The reforms of Alexander II were predicated on that very same idea, and so were the desiderata put forth by the liberal and *zemstvo* leaders in the early 20th century. Even the "reactionary" Katkov and right-wing Slavophiles shared this attitude. In developing this outlook on the function of government, Speransky played a seminal and leading part. For better or for worse, it helped Russia to avoid the extremes of absolute *laisser faire* and maximum restriction of the area of government action (as Karamzin had advocated) for the duration of the entire 19th century.

With most of his contemporaries (and many liberal officials of later generations), Speransky saw in the preservation of autocracy the best guarantee for the proper performance of the function of the state just mentioned. For the autocratic ruler, he felt, assisted by an enlightened bureaucracy, could disregard all particular and narrow selfish interests and work exclusively for the transcendant good of the nation. Moral and economic betterment of the nation fostered by the actions of the state (i.e., autocratic sovereign) by means of a well ordered government and clear and stable laws administered by an enlightened bureaucracy, this was Speransky's political program and that of many reformers after him. In respect to the Russian administration, it laid the foundation of a tradition of service to the true interests of the people, a tradition that had not existed earlier, and that found its best representatives in the *zemstvo*, health, school and judicial officials of a later period. Speransky was convinced (as were the reformers of the 1860's and 1870's) that with the people's economic, spiritual, and moral progress, the number of "mediators" — representing the people and capable of helping the government in its task — would increase vastly. Such a development would supply the nucleus, not exactly of a representative constitutional system, but of an efficient, benevolent, and paternalistic regime acting in full accord with the needs and desires of its peoples.

Speransky's stress was on spiritual and moral progress. He was not overly concerned with institutional safeguards, for his romantic notion of organic unity precluded an appreciation of the value that resides in expressing and reconciling separate interests by compromise. It tended to bring out the fundamentally conservative political implications of his proposals, which was very welcome indeed both to his imperial masters and his colleagues in the administration. The "liberal" implications of his proposals were remote and Speransky left them quite vague on purpose. For the time being, his aim was to help bring about (within the limits of Russian autocracy) a *Rechtsstaat,* so as to limit to a minimum the abuses by the bureaucracy. Such a goal was directly in the tradition of enlightened absolutism and of German idealistic philosophy (especially of Fichte), and might even have met with the tacit approval of Edmund Burke.

In his suggestions for implementing his projects, however, Speransky tended to be much more rigid and bound by his own experience and environment than later reformers. He was strictly the bureaucrat; he firmly believed that his reform plans would be best implemented by an enlightened bureaucratic absolutism, operating under law. That such a course might defeat his final goals, did not seem to have occurred to him. [1] As a man of practical political action, Speransky was rooted in the tradition of the 18th century, while as a man of thought, he was a romantic idealist. This same dualism is reflected in his attitude towards history. On the one hand, he was respectful of historical precedent and of conditions created by the past. But unlike the romantic conservatives (though more like Burke), he did not accept the present as necessary or "rational" in the sense of final. He used the past only as a limiting factor on his ability to transform and change the direction of the country's development. He felt that something stable and good could come only from a slow organic evolution. Paradoxically though, like the 18th century enlightened despots, he believed that moral, spiritual

[1] The Slavophiles, however, realized it, and shied away from bureaucratic government as much as possible. Speransky's reliance on a bureaucracy in part explains why he was rather acidly criticized by the liberals in the late 19th and early 20th centuries.

and economic progress could be guided in a specific direction by the state.

His negative historicism and his belief in administrative guidance were particularly strong in the first period of his life, and they often led him to disregard the particularities of the social and economic millieu in which he had to operate. In later years, he qualified his position somewhat, but he never completely renounced his conviction of the malleability of social conditions under the impact of administrative means. This conviction has plagued Russia's administration throughout the imperial regime, as frequently the bureaucracy ordered measures which could not be profitably applied to Russian circumstances and conditions.

In a yet more indirect way, Speransky exercised an appreciable influence on the minds and thoughts of later generations. His ideal of a *Rechtsstaat* was interpreted as an advocacy of a truly liberal representative constitution as in Western Europe. We have seen that this was a misunderstanding, but a natural one, for his words left room for some doubt (especially as his proposals were only partially known); and his complicated blend of romantic evolutionary conservatism and 18th century rationalistic dogmatism was not easy to disentangle. Interestingly enough, though, the liberal intelligentsia saw in Speransky the victim of autocracy. Thus arose the legend of the theoretical, doctrinaire liberal official who advocated constitutional forms but proved to be too much in advance of his own times. His fate was one more proof that no reform could be accomplished through the government. The liberal intellectuals rejected Speransky's method of bureaucratic implementation completely and in so doing, unwillingly turned from his program. The liberals, therefore, completely misunderstood him. His fault, if any, lay exactly in his too great timidity in suggesting methods of application, and in his fundamental respect for Russia's autocratic tradition and for its social system. It did not lie, as the liberals erroneously thought, in his actual inability to implement his program. Often men prove to be influential less by what they actually thought or did than by what others believed their opinions and acts to have been. This was the case of Speransky's influence and fame among the intelligentsia. His name became the symbol of a tradition of moderate liberalism, and of a constitutional development.

It is probably fair to say that Speransky personified the Russian imperial bureaucratic regime that was to last until 1905, and with some qualifications until 1917. He represented what was best in this bureaucracy, but also its inherent weakness and inadequacy. He set it a high standard of honesty, devotion to the good of state and country, and concern for the national welfare (it remained an accepted and respected ideal, even if not always attained in fact by some officials). He helped to inculcate a belief in orderly and just administration on the basis of clearly defined rules. He tried to establish an effective supervisory control over all authorities to prevent arbitrary bureaucratic despotism. He set for the government a high goal of spiritual progress towards which it could guide the nation. And he revived the traditional belief that as long as a ruler was absolute, he had the obligation of ruling according to the tenets of Christian justice and morality (something Peter the Great's successors had been prone to forget).

By extending the government's concern from mere efficient administration to the fields of social welfare and the people's economic prosperity, Speransky gave a new direction to the administration's thinking on economic matters. The idea of having the government play a guiding role had some merit for a country that was quite backward and where no class had developed qualities of social leadership. Yet the drawbacks of such a course were equally significant and in historical perspective, tended to cancel the positive value. But complete reliance on the autocratic monarch hurt not only Speransky personally in 1812, but proved to be a handicap for Russia's development as well. Speransky's belief that the bureaucracy could always provide leadership and inspiration and act as the guiding hand, was uncritically accepted later by less insightful, less devoted, and less high minded officials who perverted his goal. But most fatal to the success of the approach proved to be his basic conservatism in social and institutional matters. He was radical only in the bureaucratic, organizational sense, but not in the social or political. All important problems ultimately became for him — and Russian bureaucracy — technical problems of administration. Such problems could be solved by some appropriate decree or change in the organization of a government body without touching upon the fundamental political or social regime of the country.

Speransky's influence consisted mainly in the attitude and frame of mind he brought to his task and its challenges. [1] He was a man of

---

[1] The French historian, Léonce Pingaud, put it rather neatly: "quant à lui [Speransky], il se présente à nous comme un Turgot moscovite, plus remarquable par ce qu'il a souhaité que par ce qu'il a réalisé. Il eût désiré l'abolition du servage et du tchine, c'est à dire le droit du peuple à la propriété, de la noblesse à l'indépendance." Léonce Pingaud, *Les Français en Russie et les Russes en France* (*L'Ancien Régime — l'émigration — les Invasions*), Paris 1886, p. 261.

his own times and very much determined by them; in this sense, he was much less of a creative personality than many statesmen. On the other hand, he carried the calling of his times furthest and exemplified it best. The setting of a high standard and of a goal to the imperial administration was an important contribution, and a lasting one. Probably without his contributions to the administrative machinery of the Empire, the reforms of Alexander II would not have been possible or, at any rate, as readily implemented.

In another sense, Speransky illustrates the inner split of the Russian enlightened official. On the one hand, he had a clear intellectual awareness and understanding of the country's problems and an idea of what had to be done. On the other, he was beset by an inability to carry it out in institutional terms. One of the reasons for this weakness was that he often took his ideals out of the blue, from foreign models, and on the basis of theories which had no immediate social relevance. As he refused to transform radically the social fabric of Russia, his views could not be implemented without being corrupted by the conditions to which they were applied. And when — after his exile and governorships — Speransky came to understand and know intimately the true conditions of Russia, he was frightened by their complexity and difficulty and fell back on limited bureaucratic solutions. In spite of the inadequacies, though, Speransky helped to bring about a fundamental break with the past. The 18th century in Russia had been a period of administrative confusion, disorganization, and aimlessness. The merit of Alexander I, building on the accomplishments of his grandmother Catherine II, and of Speransky, was to bring some order, *esprit de suite,* lawfulness, and stability into the governmental machinery.

During the 18th century a relatively close bond had tied the officials to the educated classes of society (though a serious break between the latter and the people had occurred at the time of Peter the Great). There was only one educated society in Russia. But at the end of the 18th century, the coming into prominence of people like Speransky, who had no social ties with the upper classes, breached this unity. The government of Alexander I deepened this rift by favoring the bureaucratic administrative organization and rejecting the aristocratic, estate approach suggested by the Senatorial party. The Decembrist uprising only completed the break. From that time on, the bureaucracy was isolated from both the people and the educated upper classes, the intelligentsia. Speransky had not consciously contributed to this development, but his own career was an interesting illustration of it. The change in atmosphere which occurred during his own lifetime is shown by the fact that his social isolation contributed to his downfall in 1812, but did not affect his position in the reign of Nicholas I. The creation of a bureaucratic machine that had to be operated by skilled technicians, only continued and sharpened this situation. As one of the most important figures in the creation of such a bureaucratic machine, Speransky contributed to the growing isolation of the administration from the intellectual and spiritual élite of the nation. Again one of the paradoxical, contradictory results of his ways of working.

An evaluation of the role and significance of Speransky's life and work leads directly to a characterization and assessment of the bureaucratic regime of Imperial Russia. This can still be only tentative, for much more detailed study has to be done before a satisfactory synthesis can be achieved. But any careful investigation finds traces of Speransky's work and influence at the origin of most administrative institutions and policies of 19th century Russia. His ideological eclecticism, his cautious progressive conservatism, his timidity in the face of fundamental social problems, and his reliance on the benevolent action of the autocratic sovereign to promote economic, spiritual, and moral progress, make of Speransky not only the best representative of his own times, but also the *Wegweiser* for later generations of imperial officials. In this sense, he was the most influential "statesman" of modern Imperial Russia.

### SOURCES

An account of the main events in Speransky's life after 1 8 2 6 is to be found primarily in M. A. Korf *Zhizn' grafa M. M. Speranskogo,* Vol. II. For Speransky's plans and proposals during his last years the reader is referred to the bibliography of Speransky's writings at the end of the volume.
Additional information can be gleaned from:
"Iz zapisok barona M. A. Korfa," *Russkaia Starina,* 99 (July 1899), pp. 3—30; K. N. Lebedev, "Iz zapisok senatora K. N. Lebedeva," *Russkii Arkhiv,* (1910), No. 7, pp. 333—408; No. 8, pp. 465—524; No. 10, pp. 183—253; No. 11, pp. 353—376; No. 12, pp. 542—582; F. P. Lubianovskii, "Vospominaniia F. P. Lubianovskogo," *Russkii Arkhiv,* (1872), pp. 98—185 and 448—533; A. S. Pushkin, "Dnevniki," in Vol. 8 of *Polnoe Sobranie Sochinenii,* (Moscow-Leningrad 1949); A. I. Turgenev, *Pis'ma A. Turgeneva Bulgakovym,* Moscow 1939; N. P. Barsukov, *Zhizn' i trudy M. P. Pogodina.* 13 vols., St. Pbg. 1888—1899; N. Gastfreind, *Tovarishchi Pushkina po imperatorskomu Tsarskosel'skomu Litseiu,* 3 vols., St. Pbg., 1912—1913; M. A. Korf, "Iz bumag o grafe Speranskom v dopolnenii k ego 'zhizni' izdannoi v 1861 g.," *Russkii Arkhiv,* V (1867), pp. 432—455; M. A. Korf, "Smert' grafa Speranskogo," *Russkaia Starina,* (1893), No. 11, p. 317. M. Aronson and S. Reiser, *Literaturnye kruzhki i salony* (Leningrad 1929) and N. L. Brodskii (ed.), *Literaturnye salony i kruzhki — pervaia polovina XIX v.,* (Moscow, 1930) are only two of a very large list of titles relating to the history of the intellectual élite in Russia *ca* 1820—1839; they proved most helpful in tracing specific social contacts of Speransky in that period.

# BIBLIOGRAPHY

The sources, primary and secondary, used in this study are cited at the end of each relevant chapter.

It was felt desirable, however, to list together in one place all the primary materials. The following, therefore, is an attempt at a comprehensive bibliography of all writings (public and private) of M. M. Speransky published so far. For convenience's sake, a list of the most important articles and books dealing directly with some facet of Speransky's career has also been appended.

Not all the items listed have been accessible to the writer, so that complete page references could not always be provided.

The bibliography is arranged in the following manner:

A. Writings by M. M. Speransky
   1. Religion and philosophy
   2. Political and administrative writings
   3. Codification
   4. Letters

B. Sources concerning M. M. Speransky
   1. Letters to Speransky
   2. Memoirs and reminiscences

C. Selected secondary studies.

### A. WRITINGS BY M. M. SPERANSKY

A. F. Bychkov (ed.), *V pamiat' grafa M. M. Speranskogo,* St. Petersburg 1872 — a collection of letters, notes, and short essays by Speransky. Covers material trom all periods of his life.

#### 1. Religious and philosophical writings

"Propoved' 1791 g," *Russkaia Starina* 109 (Febr. 1902), pp. 283—291; "Dosugi — sentiabr' 1795," in *Druzheskie pis'ma k Masal'skomu* (see under 4, below), pp. 126—136; "Dnevnik za 1795 g," *Syn Otechestva* (1844), Nos. 1—2; "Propovedi v bytnost' studentom v seminarii," *Iaroslavskie Eparkhial'nye Vedomosti,* (1862), Nos. 6, 13, 25 and (1893), Nos. 4, 20 [three sermons, with the following titles: "Slovo v nedeliu miasopustnuiu: 'Egda zhe pridet Syn chelovecheskii v slave svoei ... i soberutsia pred nim vse iazytsy, (Matth. XXV—31)'" "Slovo na den' Usoknoveniia sv. Ioanna Predtechi: 'Irod bo boiashesia Ioanna' (Mark, VI, 20)"; "Slovo na den' sv. Ioanna Zlatousta 'Az es'm' dver'; mnoiu ashche kto vnidet, spasetsia ...' (John X, 9)."]

"Fizika vybrannaia iz luchshikh avtorov, raspolozhennaia i dopolnennaia Nevskoi Seminarii filosofii i fiziki uchitelem M. M. Speranskim, 1797 g. v Sankt Peterburge," *Chteniia,* (1871), bk. 3, section 2, pp. 1—56 and (1872), bk. 1, section 2, pp. 57—248; *Pravila vysshego krasnorechiia* (St. Pbg. 1844).

The following short religious essays are reprinted in appendix to article by I. Katetov, "Graf M. M. Speranskii kak religioznyi myslitel'," *Pravoslavnyi Sobesednik,* (Dec. 1889), part III, pp. 531—567: "O liturgii," (Perm' 6.ix.1813), 531—549; "Smysl iskhoda," (4.x.1818), 550—553; " 'Byst' pervyi chelovek Adam v dushu zhivu; — poslednii Adam v dukhe zhivotvoriashch," 553—555; "Drevo poznaniia dobra i zla," 555—556; "Pervyi i poslednii Adam," 557—558; "Molitva, tserkov'," 559—560; " 'Imamy khodataia k Bogu, izhe est' chelovek' " (25.xii.1831), 560—563; "Poniatii dobra i pol'zy," 564—567, (also in *Sbornik IRIO,* XXX, pp. 435—438).

["O martinizme," "Millenium" have not been published].
"O sile, osnove, i estestve," *Moskvitianin*, (1842), No. 1; *"Filosofskie otryvki,"*
*Russkaia Starina*, (1872), No. 5, pp. 68—81; "O vremeni, o prostranstve, o poriadke,
o slozhnosti," in *Druzheskie pis'ma k Masal'skomu*, pp. 136—141; "Kratkii ocherk
sviashchennoi istorii i ucheniia khristianskoi very," appendix to *Druzheskie pis'ma
k Masal'skomu*, no pagination.

2. *Political and administrative writings*
(in chronological order)

V. I. Semevskii, "Pervyi politicheskii traktat Speranskogo" *Russkoe Bogatstvo*,
(1907), No. 1, pp. 46—85 (the only published form of Speransky's first political paper).
"Iumoristicheskoe opisanie odnogo zasedanii Gosudarstvennogo Soveta (23.vi.1802),"
*Russk. Star.*, 109 (Febr. 1902), pp. 298—300; (authorship in dispute) "Tretii proekt
manifesta o pravakh i preimushchestvakh Senata, Vysochaishe Utverzhdennyi,
8.ix.1802," *Sbornik Arkheologicheskogo Instituta*, vol. I, No. 2 (1878), pp. 119—123
and 168; "Otchet Ministerstva Vnutrennikh Del za 1803 g" *Zhurnaly Komiteta
Ministrov*, I (1801—1810), (St. Pbg. 1888), pp. 54—79; "Zapiska ob ustroistve sudebnykh
i pravitel'stvennykh uchrezhdenii Rossii, 1803," *Istoricheskoe Obozrenie*, XI, (1899),
pp. 1—53 also reprinted in *Plan Gosudarstvennogo Preobrazovaniia grafa Speranskogo*
(Moscow 1905), pp. 121—229; "Dve zapiski M. M. Speranskogo" comprise: 'Predvaritel'-
nye rassuzhdeniia o prosveshchenii v Rossii voobshche' and 'Ob usovershenii obsh-
chego narodnogo vospitaniia (chitano 11.xii.1808)' in S. V. Rozhdestvenskii, "Materialy
dlia istorii uchebnykh reform v Rossii v XVIII—XIX vv.," *Zapiski istorichesko-
filologicheskogo fakul'teta Imperatorskogo Sankt Peterburgskogo Universiteta* vol. 96,
fasc. 1 (1910), pp. 372—374 and pp. 374—379, respectively; the second paper also in
*Russkaia Starina*, 132 (1907), pp. 729—735; "Zapiska ob osobennom litsee (1808),"
*Litseiskii zhurnal*, IV (1906—1907), No. 3, pp. 132—134.
N. Dubrovin (ed), "Dokumenty otnosiashchiesia do voiny s Shvetsiei i do
prisoedineniia Finliandii 1809—1815," *Sbornik istoricheskikh materialov izvlechennykh
iz arkhiva S. E. I. V. Kantseliarii* fasc. III (St. Pbg. 1890), Nos. 355—390, pp. 247—328;
"O soedinenii Staroi i Novoi Finliandii pod odno namenovanie i odin obraz prav-
leniia," *Arkhiv Gosudarstvennogo Soveta, Dela Gos. Sov. Komiteta predsedatelei v 1810,
1811 gg.* (St. Pbg. 1908), No. 35;
"Plan Finansov M. M. Speranskogo (1809 g)," *Sbornik IRIO*, XLV (St. Pbg. 1885),
pp. 1—73; "Ob uchrezhdeniiakh, otnosiashchikhsia do ekonomii gosudarstvennoi i
pravitel'stvennoi," *Arkhiv istor. i prakticheskikh svedenii*, (1859), No. 6, pp. 13—21;
"Zamechaniia na proekt Lobysevicha (15.i.1809) o preobrazovanii narodochisleniia,"
*Arkhiv grafov Mordvinovykh*, III, pp. 641—643;
*Plan gosudarstvennogo preobrazovaniia grafa M. M. Speranskogo (1809)* (Russkaia
Mysl', Moscow 1905) contains a number of papers and letters (the Perm' letter, for
instance) some of which are also published (complete or abbreviated) elsewhere:
"O krepostnykh liudiakh (also in *Arkhiv istor. i praktich. svedenii*, 1859—II);
"Permskoe pis'mo"; "O gosudarstvennykh ustanovleniiakh" (also in *Arkhiv istor.
i prakt. sved.* 1859—III); "Zapiska ob ustroistve sudebnykh i pravitel'stvennykh
uchrezhdenii v Rossii" (1803) (also in *Istoricheskoe obozrenie*, XI, 1899, pp. 1—53);
"Vvedenie k ulozheniiu gosudarstvennykh zakonov" (the Plan of 1809 properly
speaking, also *Istoricheskoe obozrenie* X, 1898, pp. 1—62);
"O neobkhodimosti uchrezhdeniia soveta (1809)" in Korkunov, *Gosudarstvennoe
Pravo*, II, pp. 70—72; "Otchet v delakh 1810, predstavlennyi imperatoru Aleksandru
I—u M. M. Speranskim, 11.ii.1811", *Sbornik IRIO*, XXI (1877), pp. 447—462; "O
sile pravitel'stva, chitano imperatoru 3.xii.1811", *Russk. Starina*, (Dec. 1902), pp.
495—499;
"O skorosti monetnogo dvizheniia — zamechanie M. M. Speranskogo ot 4.xi.1811,"
*Arkhiv grafov Mordvinovykh*, IX, pp. 588—590;
"Dve zapiski M. M. Speranskogo po politicheskim delam," includes: 'O vidakh
Frantsii po brachnomu soiuzu s Avstriei 1810' and 'O vidakh frantsuzskogo pravitel'stva na Pol'shu, avg. 1810', *Russk. Starina*, 104 (1900), pp. 429—436 (the second
paper is translated in Th. Schiemann, *Geschichte Russlands unter Nikolaus I*, Bd. I,
(1904), Anhang, pp. 518—526);

"Proekt uchrezhdeniia Pravitel'stvuiushchego Senata 1811g" in Shil'der, *Imperator Aleksandr I*, vol. III, appendix, pp. 405—433; "Vvedenie k proektu uchrezhdeniia Sudebnogo Senata," *Sbornik IRIO*, vol. 90 (1894), pp. 176—181 (same in Shil'der, *Imperator Aleksandr I*, III, pp. 433—471); "O preimushchestvakh i dolzhnosti Senata" (authorship in doubt), *Sbornik Arkheologicheskogo Instituta*, vol. I, Sect. 2, (1878), pp. 128—134 (includes, pp. 130—134, "O prichinakh unizheniia Senata"); "Zapiska o pravakh Senata" *Sbornik Arkheolog. Instituta*, vol. I, sect. 2, (1878), pp. 125—128;

"Istoricheskoe obozrenie gosudarstvennykh ustanovlenii v Rossii s 1710g," *Sbornik IRIO*, 74 (1891), pp. 45, 46, 53 (full text unavailable — written in 1811? used in 1826);

"Vsepodanneishaia zapiska M. M. Speranskogo, 11.vi.1811, po delam Finliandskim i Pol'skim," *Sbornik materialov lgo otdeleniia S.E.I.V. Kantseliarii*, III (1876), pp. 214—217; "Opravdatel'naia zapiska" (1812), *Russkii Arkhiv*, (1892), No. 1, pp. 65—72.

"Proekt prosheniia vladel'tsev permskikh solianykh promyslov k Ministru Finansov, sostavlennyi grafom Speranskim," in *Pis'ma M. M. Speranskogo k Lazarevu* (see infra), appendix IV, pp. 84—88; "Ob uspekhe vvedeniia obezpechennykh bessrochnykh dolgov" (in *Pamiati*, pp. 466—469);

"Bumagi otsosiashchiesia k sluzhebnoi dciatel'nosti M. M. Speranskogo v 1818 i 1819 gg," *Sbornik materialov lgo otdeleniia S. E. I. V. Kantseliarii*, II (1876), pp. 375—389;

"Proekty prosheniia k Gosudariu Imperatoru Aleksandru I ot osnovatelia Lazarevskogo Instituta, Ioakima Lazarevicha Lazareva" in *Pis'ma M. M. Speranskogo k Lazarevu*, appendix I, pp. 77—80 and 82—84;

"Proekt prosheniia k Gosudariu Imperatoru Aleksandru I ot Patriarkha vsekh armian Efremiia, sostavlennoe grafom Speranskim," in *Pis'ma M. M. Speranskogo k Lazarevu*, appendix II, pp. 80—82;

"Puteshestvie v Sibir' (Dnevnik) s 31.iii.1819 po 18.ii.1821", (in *Pamiati*, pp. 3—102); "Raport Speranskogo Gosudariu Imperatoru lgo iuniia 1820g," *Russkii Arkhiv*, (1870), pp. 598—601;

"Vsepodanneishie doklady tainogo sovetnika M. M. Speranskogo s rezoliutsiami Aleksandra I" includes: 'O korabliakh prishedshikh v Kamchatku (1821)' and 'O narochnom iz Irkutska (1822)',*Russkii Arkhiv*, (1915), No. 2, pp. 147—152; "Otchet tainogo sovetnika Speranskogo v obozrenii Sibiri, s predvaritel'nymi svedeniiami i osnovaniiami k obrazovaniiu ee upravleniia," in Prutchenko, *Sibirskie okrainy*, vol. II, (St. Pbg. 1899), appendix 1, pp. 1—96, (includes: "Stepeni upravleniia," pp. 75—95; "Obshchie svedeniia o granitsakh i razdelenii Sibiri," pp. 67—71; "Osnovaniia k obrazovaniiu upravleniia Sibiri," pp. 71—75; "Predvaritel'nye svedeniia k obrazovaniiu upravleniia Sibiri," pp. 29—65; "Ob uchrezhdenii komisarstv," pp. 65—67); *Obozrenie glavnykh osnovanii mestnogo upravleniia Sibiri po bumagam Speranskogo i Sibirskogo Komiteta 1821—1822*, St. Pbg. 1841;

"Vvedenie k namestnicheskomu (oblastnomu) uchrezhdeniiu (1821)" and "Proekt uchrezhdeniia oblastnogo upravleniia (1822)" in *Materialy sobrannye dlia Vysochaishe uchrezhdennoi Kommissii o preobrazovanii gubernskikh i uezdnykh uchrezhdenii, otdel administratsii*, part I: *Materialy istoricheskie i zakonodatel'nye*, sections 1 and 2 (St. Pbg. 1870), pp. 68—85 and 86—112, respectively; "O voennykh poseleniiakh," *Russkii Vestnik* (1890), No. 4, pp. 108—116;

"Kratkaia sobstvennoruchnaia zapiska Speranskogo o sobytiiakh 27.xi.1825," in Shil'der, *Imperator Nikolai I*, I (St. Pbg. 1903), appendix XXVIII, p. 616;

"Zapiska o krepostnom prave v Komitete 6.xii.1826" in P. Bartenev, *Deviatnadtsatyi vek — istoricheskii sbornik*, II (Moscow 1872), pp. 159—165; "Zapiska o krepostnykh," *Arkhiv istor. i prakticheskikh svedenii*, (1859), No. III, section I, pp. 1—15 (shorter summary of preceding); "Zamechaniia o gubernskikh uchrezhdeniiakh (1827)," *Arkhiv istor. i prakt. svedenii*, (1859) No. 4, pp. 92—104 and No. 5, sect. I, pp. 71—72 (also in *Materialy Kommissii po preobrazovaniiu gubernskikh i uezdnykh uchrezhdenii*, I, sect. 1, pp. 1—13 and 14—56); "Proekt uchrezdeniia dlia upravleniia gubernii," *Sbornik IRIO*, 90 (1894), pp. 274—358;

"O edinoglasii i raznoglasiiakh v resheniiakh, 20.iv.1827," *Arkhiv istor. i praktich. svedenii*, (1859), No. III, sect. 1, pp. 1—7; "O poriadke ispravleniia okonchatel'nykh sudebnykh reshenii v Senate, 20.iv.1827," *Sbornik IRIO*, 90 (1894), pp. 181—194; "Istoriia poshlin v Rossii," *Russkaia Starina*, XV (1876), p. 597 (also in *Sbornik IRIO, XXX*, 1881, p. 472); "Istoriia poshlin v Anglii," *Russkaia Starina*, XV (1876), pp. 597—598 (also *Sbornik IRIO*, XXX, 1881, pp. 472—473); "Zamechaniia, mart 1830, po povodu proekta zakona o sostoianiiakh," *Sbornik IRIO*, 90 (1894), p. 569; "Mysli o novykh biletakh kaznacheistva, 27.v.1831 — pis'ma Kankrinu," *Russkaia Starina*, (1873), No. 8, p. 585; "Istoriia assignatsii," *Sbornik IRIO*, XXX, (1881), pp. 466—471; "Kratkoe istoricheskoe obozrenie trekh glavnykh gosudarstvennykh ustanovlenii: Sovet, Senat i Ministerstva," *Sbornik IRIO*, XXX, 1881, pp. 440—450; "O zakonakh — besedy grafa M. M. Speranskogo s E. I. Vysochestvom Gosudarem Naslednikom Tsesarevichem Velikim Kniazem Aleksandrom Nikolaevichem s 12.x.1835 po 10.iv.1837," *Sbornik IRIO*, XXX (1881), pp. 323—491; "Imperatorskoe uchilishche pravovedeniia, 24.i.1835," *Russkaia Starina*, 48 (Dec. 1885), pp. i—iv; "Zhurnal Komiteta 1837 g o stepeni obucheniia krepostnykh liudei, 30.iv.1837," in *Sbornik S. F. Platonovu* (St. Pbg. 1911), pp. 267—273; "Istoricheskoe obozrenie izmenenii v prave pozemel'noi sobstvennosti i v sostoianii krest'ian, 1836," *Arkhiv istor. i prakt. svedenii*, II, (1859), pp. 27—51, (also in *Sbornik IRIO*, XXX, pp. 450—466); "O monetnom obrashchenii," *Chteniia*, (1872); "Zapiska gr. Speranskogo o monetnom obrashchenii, 1839," *Materialy po voprosu ob ustroistve denezhnoi sistemy*, (1896), pp. 134—176, (answers of Kankrin are on pp. 176—190).

### 3. Papers on codification

"Plan vseobshchego gosudarstvennogo obrazovaniia: Proekt grazhdanskogo ulozheniia," *Arkhiv Gosudarstvennogo Soveta*, IV (St. Pbg. 1874); "Zapiska o grazhdanskom i ugolovnom ulozheniiakh" (1821), in M. M. Vinaver, *Iz oblasti tsivilistiki* (St. Pbg. 1908), pp. 80—93 and in M. M. Vinaver, "K voprosu ob istochnikakh X. toma Svoda Zakonov," *Zhurnal Ministerstva Iustitsii*, III—6, (June 1897), pp. 88—99; "Obshchee vvedenie k iz'iasneniiam na proekt grazhdanskogo ulozheniia" (1821), in Vinaver: "K voprosu ob istochnikakh X. toma Svoda Zakonov," *loc. cit.*; "Nastavlenie II-u otdeleniiu o poriadke ego trudov," in P. M. Maikov, *2e Otdelenie sobstv. E. I. V. Kantseliarii 1826—1882* (St. Pbg. 1906), Appendix, pp. 1—4; "Zamechaniia i vzgliady Speranskogo na reviziiu Svoda," *ibid.* pp. 12—13; "Predpolozheniia k okonchatel'nomu sostavleniiu zakonov" (1826?), *Russkaia Starina*, XV, (1876), pp. 434—441; "Kratkoe istoricheskoe obozrenie komissii sostavleniia zakonov" (Jan. 1826?), *Russkaia Starina*, XV, (1876), pp. 433—434; "O zakonakh zemskikh," (1827?), *Arkhiv istor. i prakticheskikh svedenii*, (1859), No. 6, pp. 8—12; "O zakonakh rimskikh i razlichii ikh ot zakonov rossiiskikh," (1828), *Russkaia Starina*, XV, (1876), pp. 592—597; "O sushchestve svoda," (14.1.1828),*Russkaia Starina*, XV, (1876), pp. 586—592; "Ob'iasnitel'naia zapiska soderzhaniia i raspolozheniia svoda zakonov grazhdanskikh," *Arkhiv istoricheskikh i prakticheskikh svedenii*, II, (1859); "O svode i sobranii zakonov," *Arkhiv istor. i prakticheskikh svedenii*, VI, (1861), pp. 1—8; "Plan ob izdanii drevnikh uzakonenii Rossiiskogo Gosudarstva," in A. Fateev, "K istorii i teorii kodifikatsii," *Nauchnye Trudy Russkogo Narodnogo Universiteta v Prage*, IV, (1931), pp. 20—22; "Zapiska Mordvinovu, 15.1.1833, s peredachei ekzempliara Svoda Zakonov," *Arkhiv grafov Mordvinovykh*, VII, p. 9; "Predislovie k Polnomu Sobraniiu Zakonov," *PSZ*, I (1833); *Obozrenie istoricheskikh svedenii o Svode Zakonov* (St. Pbg. 1833), 2d ed. 1837; *Précis des notions historiques sur la formation du Corps des lois russes,* (St. Pbg. 1833); *Rukovodstvo k poznaniiu zakonov* (St. Pbg. 1845) [the same as "O zakonakh — besedy grafa M. M. Speranskogo s E. I. Vysochestvom Gosudarem Naslednikom ...," *Sbornik IRIO*, XXX, (1881), pp. 323—491].

### 4. Letters

K. Masal'skii (ed), *Druzheskie pis'ma grafa M. M. Speranskogo k P. G. Masal'skomu, pisannye s 1798 po 1819 god, s istoricheskimi poiasneniiami*, St. Pbg. 1862; *Pis'ma grafa M. M. Speranskogo k Kh. I. Lazarevu*, St. Pbg. 1864; to A. Samborskii, 16.VI.1788, Vladimir, *Russkii Arkhiv*, (1871), p. 1944; to N. Karazin, in Longinov, "Graf Speranskii," *Russkii Vestnik*, 23, (1859), pp. 353—354 and *Moskvitianin*, (1842), VI, p. 339; to Veikardt, 27.X.1799, *Moskvitianin*, (1842), VI, p. 339; to Admiral N. Mordvinov, 25.XII.1809, *Arkhiv grafov Mordvinovykh*, III, pp. 44—45; varia in connection with the annexation of Finland, in Ordin,

*Pokorenie Finliandii*, II (St. Pbg. 1889), Appendix, pp. 78—115; to A. A. Stolypin, Nos. I—XVII (9.VIII.1809 to 5.II.1817) and Nos. I—XXV (20.II.1817 to 2.IV.1818), *Russkii Arkhiv*, (1870), pp. 880—893 and 1125—1156; to A. A. Stolypin, (23.II.1813 to 18.IX.1819), *Russkii Arkhiv*, (1869), Nos. X—XI, pp. 1682—1708 and 1966—1984; varia in connection with the Fessler affair, 1809—1810, *Sbornik istoricheskikh materialov iz sobstvennoi E. I. V. Kantseliarii*, vyp. 12 (St. Pbg. 1903), pp. 441—444; to A. Balashev, 16.II.1810, *Russkaia Starina*, 115 (1903), p. 85; to G. P. Derzhavin, 17.III.1811, in *Sochineniia Derzhavina* (Ia. Grot ed.) VI (St. Pbg. 1871), No. 1017; to Alexander I, March 1812, Nizhnii Novgorod, in Shil'der, *Imperator Aleksandr I*, III (St. Pbg. 1897), pp. 491—493.

to F. I. Tseier, Nos. 1—9 (1812? to 9.VII.1818), *Russkii Arkhiv*, (1870), pp. 174—199; to Alexander I, Jan. 1813, Perm', in: *Plan Gosudarstvennogo Preobrazovaniia gr. M. M. Speranskogo* (1905), pp. 326—359, *Russkii Arkhiv*, (1892), pp. 51—65, *Druzheskie pis'ma k P. Masal'skomu* (1862), pp. 32—52, N. Shil'der, *Imperator Aleksandr I*, III, Appendix, pp. 515—527, incomplete summaries appeared in several other places;

to A. Arakcheev and Alexander I (1812—1825) in N. Dubrovin, *Pis'ma glavneishikh deiatelei v tsarstvovanii Aleksandra I* (St. Pbg. 1883); to Alexander I, (9/21.VII.1814), in Shil'der, *Imperator Aleksandr I*, III, p. 263; to Alexander I, 6.I.1816 (with memorandum concerning the manifesto of 25.XII.1815), in *Sbornik materialov lgo otdeleniia sobstv. E.I.V. Kantseliarii*, II (St. Pbg. 1876), pp. 36—42; to P. A. Slovtsov, 6.VIII.1813, Perm', *Moskvitianin*, (1845), No. 3, pp. 41—51; to A. Arakcheev, 1816, Velikopol'e, in Korf, *Zhizn' grafa Speranskogo*, II, pp. 107—109; to Alexander I, July 1816, Velikopol'e, *ibid.*, p. 106; "Pis'ma M. M. Speranskogo k ego docheri iz Penzy i s dorogi v Sibir'," Nos. 1—65, (22.X.1816 to 18.V.1819), *Russkii Arkhiv*, VI (1868), pp. 1103—1212; to A. N. Golitsyn (and prince Golitsyn's answers), 11.XII.1816 to 3.XII.1818, *Russkaia Starina*, 110 (June 1902), pp. 479—486 and 111 (July 1902), pp. 45—48; to D. M. Poltoratskii, 16.I.1817 and 12.III.1818, *Russkaia Starina*, 111 (July 1902), pp. 49—51; to O. P. Kozodavlev, 8.III.1817, *Russkaia Starina* 109 (Febr. 1902), pp. 300—303; to Alexander I (1.I.1817 and 20.II.1817, Penza) and A. Golitsyn, 20.II.1817, Penza, *Russkaia Starina*, 115 (July 1903), pp. 85—88; to Alexander I, 1.VIII.1818, *Sbornik materialov l-go otdeleniia...*, II, pp. 378—379; to Governor General Viazmitinov, 1.VIII.1818, *ibid.*, 376—378; to V. P. Kochubei, 21.IX.1818, *Russkaia Starina*, 111 (July 1902), pp. 51—54; (Kochubei's answer, *ibid.*, pp. 54—59); to Alexander I, 4.II.1819, in *Sbornik materialov l-go otdeleniia...*, II, p. 385; to Viazmitinov, 4.II.1819, *ibid.*, p. 384; to his daughter from Siberia, Nos. 1—94, (30.V. 1819 to 17.III.1821), *Russkii Arkhiv*, VI (1868), pp. 1682—1811; to S. S. Uvarov, 17.IX.1819, Irkutsk, *Russkaia Starina*, 113 (March 1903), p. 444;

to P. A. Slovtsov, 24.VII.1820, *Sbornik Starinnykh bumag Shchukinskogo muzeia*, VI (Moscow 1900), p. 399; to Metropolitan Filaret (and answers), 1822, *Russkaia Starina*, 113 (Febr. 1903), pp. 359—360; to A. Arakcheev, 22.XI.1822, (excerpt) in Shil'der, *Imperator Aleksandr I*, IV, p. 477; to A. O. Imberg (1828), Prince Vorontsov (1837), Count M. S. Vorontsov (1838), in *Arkhiv kniaz'ia Vorontsova*, XXXVI (1890), pp. 457—459; to V. P. Nikitin, 2.VII.1831, in Bil'basov, "Speranskii i dva Nikitina," *Russkaia Starina*, 87 (1896), p. 446; to I. V. Lopukhin (undated), *Russkii Arkhiv*, (1870), pp. 623—626; to S. M. Bronevskii (undated), *Russkii Arkhiv*, (1870), pp. 199—202.

B.  SOURCES CONCERNING M. M. SPERANSKY

*1. Letters to Speransky from:*

I. V. Lopukhin, 22.IX.1804 to 19.VI.1806, *Russkii Arkhiv*, (1870), pp. 609—622; P. Slovtsov (1796?), *Russkaia Starina*, V (1872), pp. 469—470; Count D. Gur'ev, 7.III. 1818, *Russkaia Starina*, 112 (Oct. 1902), p. 164; V. P. Kochubei, 18.X.1818, *Russkaia Starina*, 111 (July 1902), pp. 54—59; S. S. Uvarov, 1.XII.1819, *Russkaia Starina*, 112 (Nov. 1902), p. 242; A. N. Olenin, 30.X.1821, *Russkaia Starina*, 114 (June 1903), pp. 714—716; Count M. S. Vorontsov, 28.V.1823, *Russkaia Starina*, 114 (May 1903), p. 350; V. P. Kochubei, 9 letters, 1823—1825, *Russkaia Starina*, 112 (Nov. 1902), pp. 301—322; Prince A. B. Golitsyn, (1812?), *Russkaia Starina*, 96 (1898), pp. 517—518; Alexander I, 22.III.1819, in Shil'der, *Imperator Aleksandr I*, IV, pp. 148—150.

## 2. Memoirs on Speransky

Anonym., "Vospominaniia o grafe Speranskom," *Syn Otechestva* (1844), Nos. 1 and 2; G. Aleksandrov, "Moi vospominaniia o grafe Speranskom," *Sovremennaia Letopis'*, (1865), No. 18; P. T. Basnin, "Iz proshlogo Sibiri," *Istoricheskii Vestnik*, 90 (1902), pp. 532—574; P. P. Basnin, "Vospominaniia o Speranskom," *Istoricheskii Vestnik*, 91 (Jan. 1903), pp. 152—173; G. S. Batenkov, "Dannye: Povest' o sobstvennoi zhizni," *Russkii Arkhiv*, II—2, (1881), pp. 251—276; G. S. Batenkov, "Graf Speranskii i Arakcheev (po vospominaniiam, 31.III.1826)," *Russkaia Starina*, 92 (1897), pp. 83—92; V. P. Burnashev, "Predstavlenie M. M. Speranskomu v 1828 g," *Russkii Mir*, (1872), No. 183. I. I. Dmitriev, "Vzgliad na moiu zhizn'," in *Sochineniia Iv. Iv. Dmitrieva* (A. Floridov ed.), II (St.Pbg. 1895), pp. 1—151; V. S. Filimonov, "Arestovanie Speranskogo," *Pamiatniki Novoi Russkoi Istorii*, III (St. Pbg. 1873), pp. 113—116; E. G. "Speranskii v ssylke v Permi," *Istoricheskii Vestnik*, III (1880), pp. 637—638; E. G. "Iz zhizni Speranskogo v Permi," *Istoricheskii Vestnik*, 48 (1892), pp. 570—572; fon Gauenshil'd, "M. M. Speranskii," *Russkaia Starina*, 110 (May 1902), pp. 251—262; N. S. Il'inskii, "Vospominaniia," *Russkii Arkhiv*, (1879), pp. 377—434; N. S. Il'inskii, "Rasskazy o Speranskom i Arakcheeve," *Russkaia Starina*, V (1872), p. 470; L. H. Jacob, *Denkwürdigkeiten aus meinem Leben für meine Familie und für vertraute Freunde in den Jahren 1802 bis 1820*, Calligraphische Abschrift, Bibliothek, Halle; I. Kalashnikov, "Zapiski irkutskogo zhitelia," *Russkaia Starina*, 123 (July 1905), pp. 187—251, (aug. 1905), pp. 384—409, (sept. 1905), pp. 609—646; M. A. Korf, "Iz bumag o grafe Speranskom," *Russkii Arkhiv*, (1867), pp. 432—455; "Iz zapisok barona, (vposledstvii grafa) M. A. Korfa," *Russkaia Starina*, 99 (July 1899), pp. 3—30; Magnitskii, "Duma pri grobe Speranskogo," in *Pis'ma grafa M. M. Speranskogo k Kh. I. Lazarevu* (1864), pp. 90—100; I. I. Martynov, "Zapiski," *Pamiatniki Novoi Russkoi Istorii*, II (1872), pp. 68—182 (also in *Sovremennik*, (1856), IV); A. Nikitenko, "Vospominaniia o M. M. Speranskom," (Rech' v godichnom sobranii Akademii Nauk 29.XII.1872), *Zapiski Imper. Akademii Nauk*, XX, No. 2 (1872), pp. 258—271; (F. Fortunatov) "Pamiatnye zametki Vologzhanina," *Russkii Arkhiv*, (1867), pp. 1646—1707; Ia. I. de Sanglen, "Zapiski 1776—1831," *Russkaia Starina*, 37 (1883), pp. 1—46, 375—394, 539—578; Troitskii, "M. M. Speranskii v Penze" *Russkaia Starina*, 112 (1902), pp. 341—345; P. S. Usov, "Sluchai iz zhizni grafa M. Speranskogo," *Istoricheskii Vestnik*, X (1882), pp. 721—722; "Autobiographie eines Russen (Notice sur Mr. de Speranskij), *Zeitgenossen*, Neue Reihe, Bd. IV, No. 2, (1824), Ss. 167—178. (an alleged autobiography of Speransky).

### C. SELECTED SECONDARY STUDIES

A. Afanas'ev, "Dopolnenie k stat'e o Speranskom Longinova," *Russkii Vestnik*, 25 (1860), pp. 26—41; A. A. Bestuzhev (Marlinskii), "Neskol'ko slov po povodu stat'i barona Korfa o Speranskom," *Moskvitianin*, (1848), No. 8—9; V. A. Bil'basov, "M. M. Speranskii," *Russkaia Starina*, 110 (May 1902), pp. 251—262; V. Bil'basov, "Speranskii i dva Nikitina," *Russkaia Starina*, 87 (1896), pp. 445—447; M. I. Bogdanovich, "Padenie Speranskogo," *Vestnik Evropy*, III (Dec. 1868), pp. 495—505; I. A. Bychkov, "Deiateli i uchastniki v padenii Speranskogo," *Russkaia Starina*, 109 (March 1902), pp. 469—508; I. A. Bychkov (ed), "Dopolnitel'nye zametki i materialy dlia 'zhizni M. M. Speranskogo'," *Russkaia Starina*, 115 (Sept. 1903), pp. 497—518; I. A. Bychkov (ed), "Neskol'ko dannykh k istorii knigi barona M. A. Korfa 'Zhizn' grafa Speranskogo'," *Russkaia Starina*, 109 (Jan. 1902), pp. 141—174; I. A. Bychkov (ed), "Prebyvanie Speranskogo v Nizhnem Novgorode i v Permi," *Russkaia Starina*, 110 (May 1902), pp. 231—249; I. A. Bychkov (ed), "Speranskii v 1808—1811g," *Russkaia Starina*, 114 (April 1903), pp. 29—40; I. A. Bychkov (ed), "Speranskii v Velikopol'e i v Penze," *Russkaia Starina*, 110 (June 1902), pp. 467—486 and 111 (July 1902), pp. 45—59; I. A. Bychkov, "M. M. Speranskii general-gubernator Sibiri i vozvrashchenie ego v Sankt Peterburg," *Russkaia Starina*, 112 (Oct. 1902), pp. 35—56; I. A. Bychkov (ed), "Ssylka Speranskogo v 1812 g," *Russkaia Starina*, 110 (Apr. 1902), pp. 5—44; I. A. Bychkov (ed), "Zametki barona M. A. Korfa k biografii grafa M. M. Speranskogo," *Russkaia Starina*, 109 (Febr. 1902), pp. 283—306; A. F. Bychkov, "Speranskii v 1826 g," *Russkaia Starina*, 15 (1876), pp. 430—441; N. G. Chernyshevskii,

"Russkii reformator," *Polnoe Sobranie Sochinenii N. G. Chernyshevskogo* (M. N. Chernyshevskaia ed.) VIII (St. Pbg. 1906), pp. 292—319 (also in *Sovremennik*, 1861); I. Chistovich, "V pamiat' grafa M. M. Speranskogo," *Khristianskoe Chtenie*, (1871), No. 12; F. M. Dmitriev, "Speranskii v ego gosudarstvennoi deiatel'nosti s obshchim ocherkom istorii vnutrennogo upravleniia v XVIII v.," *Russkii Arkhiv*, VI (1868), pp. 1527—1656; A. Dmitriev, "Prebyvanie M. M. Speranskogo v Permi," *Russkii Vestnik*, (1869), pp. 744—749; M. V. Dovnar-Zapol'skii, "Politicheskie idealy M. M. Speranskogo," *Iz istorii obshchestvennykh techenii v Rossii* (Kiev 1905), pp. 77—144; Duret, *Un portrait russe. Spéranski* (Leipzig 1867); A. El'chaninov, "Mistitsizm M. M. Speranskogo," *Bogoslovskii Vestnik*, (Jan. 1906), pp. 90—123 and (Febr. 1906), pp. 208—245; G. P. Ermolov, "Pamflet na Speranskogo," *Chteniia*, (1895), No. 3, part 2, pp. 1—24; A. N. Fateev, *M. M. Speranskii 1809—1909 — Biograficheskii ocherk*, Khar'kov 1910; A. N. Fateev, "M. M. Speranskii — vlianie sredy na sostavitelia Svoda Zakonov v pervyi period ego zhizni," *Iuridicheskii Vestnik*, X, (1915), pp. 133—155 (same in separate offprint, Moscow 1915); Ar. Fatéev, "La Constitution russe de 1809," *Zapiski nauchno-issledovatel'skogo ob'edineniia*, Russkii Svobodnyi Universitet v Prage, vol. II, (old series VII), Prague 1935; Ar. N. Fateev, "Speranskii — general gubernator Sibiri," *Zapiski russkogo nauchno-issledovatel'skogo ob'edineniia*, vol. XI (old series XVI), Nos. 82 and 88, (Prague 1942), pp. 111—151 and 323—362; Ar. Fatéev, "La disgrâce d'un homme d'état (A l'occasion du centenaire de la mort de Spéransky en 1839)," *Zapiski nauchno-issledovatel'skogo ob'edineniia v Prage*, vol. X (old series XV), No. 72, Russkii svobodnyi universitet v Prage, (Praha 1940), pp. 33—73 (the second installment does not seem to have been published). A. N. Fateev, "K assignatsionnoi reforme 1839 g.," *Zapiski russkogo nauchno-issledovatel'skogo ob'edineniia*, vol. XI (old series XVI), No. 78, (Prague 1941), pp. 13—24; A. Fateev, "Bumagi Speranskogo," *Zapiski russkogo istoricheskogo obshchestva v Prage* No. 1, (Prague 1927), pp. 103—113; N. V. Golitsyn (ed), *Opis' bumag M. M. Speranskogo 1812 g*, Petrograd 1916; N. V. Golitsyn, "M. M. Speranskii v Verkhovnom sude nad dekabristami," *Russkii Istoricheskii Zhurnal*, Nos. 1—2, (1917), pp. 61—102; "Graf M. M. Speranskii v Tiumeni," *Russkaia Starina*, 87 (aug. 1896), p. 294; Ia. Grot, "Eshche o Speranskom i Voeikove," *Russkii Arkhiv*, (1871), pp. 2121—2124; Ia. Grot, "K istorii ssylki Speranskogo," *Russkii Arkhiv*, (1871), pp. 2073—2078; Hephel, "Les deux Spéranski," *Revue Britannique*, (Juillet 1875); N. M. Iadrintsev, "Chuvstva Speranskogo k Sibiri," *Sbornik gazety 'Sibir'*, I (St. Pbg. 1876), pp. 397—408; N. M. Iadrintsev, "Speranskii i ego reforma v Sibiri," *Vestnik Evropy*, (1876), No. 5, pp. 93—116; V. Iakushkin, *Speranskii i Arakcheev*, St. Pbg. 1905; S. N. Iuzhakov, *Graf M. M. Speranskii — ego zhizn' i obshchestvennaia deiatel'nost'*, St. Pbg. 1891—92; S. Iuzhakov, "Padenie Speranskogo," *Russkaia Mysl'*, (1890), No. 11, pp. 111—131; Kalachev, "O zaslugakh grafa Speranskogo v finansovom otnoshenii," *Iuridicheskii Vestnik*, *(date?)*, pp. 3—16 seen in undated offprint; I. V. Katetov, "Graf M. M. Speranskii kak religioznyi myslitel'," *Pravoslavnyi Sobesednik*, (May—Dec. 1889), part II, pp. 82—96, 264—318, 428—444, 572—625 and part III, pp. 122—152, 209—261, 412—439, 531—567; Robert A. Klostermann, "Speranskij's Sturz in L. H. Jakobs 'Denkwürdigkeiten'," *Archiv für Kulturgeschichte*, 23, No. 2 (1932), pp. 217—233; A. A. Kochubinskii, "Graf Speranskii i universitetskii ustav 1835 g," *Vestnik Evropy*, (Apr. 1894), pp. 655—683 and (May 1894), pp. 5—43; N. M. Korkunov, "Politicheskie vozzreniia Speranskogo do ego znakomstva s imperatorom Aleksandrom I," *Vestnik Prava*, XXIX (Oct. 1899), pp. 1—40; M. A. Korf, *Zhizn' grafa Speranskogo*, 2 vols. St. Pbg. 1861; M. A. Korf (I. A. Bychkov ed), "Deiateli i uchastniki v padenii Speranskogo," *Russkaia Starina*, 109, (March 1902), pp. 469—508; M. A. Korf (ed), "Dostopamiatnaia cherta v chastnoi zhizni Speranskogo," *Russkii Arkhiv*, (1884), No. III, pp. 55—57; M. A. Korf, "Iz bumag o grafe Speranskom v dopolnenie k ego 'Zhizni' izdannoi v 1861 g," *Russkii Arkhiv*, V, (1867), pp. 432—455; M. A. Korf, "Smert' grafa Speranskogo," *Russkaia Starina*, (1893), No. 11, p. 317; M. N. Longinov, "Graf Speranskii," *Russkii Vestnik*, XXIII (1859), pp. 337—358 and 527—576; A. E. Nol'de, *Spranskii — biografiia* (Manuscript, Columbia University); M. P. Pogodin, "Speranskii (kritiko-istoricheskoe issledovanie — pokazaniia de Sanglena)," *Russkii Arkhiv*, (1871), pp. 1097—1252; N. Poletaev, "Nekotorye dopolneniia k issledovaniiu g. Katetova o religioznoi myslitel'nosti grafa Speranskogo," *Pravoslavnyi Sobesednik*, (March 1890), I, pp. 415—418; Protoierei Evgenii Popov, *M. M. Speranskii v Permi i v Sibiri*, Perm' 1879; Dm. Protopopov, "Neskol'ko slov o Speranskom," *Russkii*

*Arkhiv*, (1876), No. 2, pp. 225—230; S. Prutchenko, *Sibirskie okrainy: oblastnye ustanovleniia sviazannye s Sibirskim Uchrezhdeniem 1822 g. v stroe upravleniia russkogo gosudarstva*, St. Pbg. 1899; M. Raeff, "The Philosophical Views of Count M. M. Speransky," *The Slavonic and East European Review*, vol. XXXI, No. 77 (June 1953), pp. 437—51; M. Raeff, "The Political Philosophy of Speranskij," *The American Slavic and East European Review*, vol. XII, No. 1, (February 1953), pp. 1—21; M. Raeff, *Siberia and the Reforms of 1822*, Seattle 1956; A. V. Romanovich-Slavatinskii, "Gosudarstvennaia deiatel'nost' Speranskogo," *Universitetskie Izvestiia*, Kiev, (Febr. 1873) and *Otechestvennye Zapiski*, (1873), No. 4, pp. 171—199; S. V. Rozhdestvenskii, "M. M. Speranskii i Komitet 1837 g o stepeni obucheniia krepostnykh liudei," *Sbornik S. F. Platonovu* (1911), pp. 254—279; "Karamzin i Speranskii" in *Russkii Zagranichnyi Sbornik*, VI Berlin-Paris-London, 1858; Georg Sacke, "M. M. Speranskij. Politische Ideologie und reformatorische Tätigkeit," *Jahrbücher für Geschichte Osteuropas*, IV, (Breslau 1939), Heft 3/4, pp. 331—350; Saint-René Taillandier, "Le comte Spéranski," *Revue des Deux Mondes*, (1856), No. 5, pp. 802—835; V. Semevskii, "M. M. Speranskii," *Entsiklopedicheskii Slovar' Brokgauza-Efron* XXXI, (1900), pp. 188—192; V. I. Semevskii, "Padenie Speranskogo," *Otechestvennaia voina i russkoe obshchestvo*, II (Moscow 1911), pp. 221—246; S. M. Seredonin, *Graf M. M. Speranskii (Ocherk gosudarstvennoi deiatel'nosti)*, St. Pbg. 1909; S. M. Seredonin, "Graf M. M. Speranskii," *Russkii Biograficheskii Slovar'*, XVIII (St. Pbg. 1909), pp. 193—240i; S. M. Seredonin, "K planu vseobshchego gosudarstvennogo obrazovaniia 1809 g," *Sbornik S. F. Platonovu* (1911), pp. 533—544; D. N. Seslavin, *M. M. Speranskii*, Kiev ("Vsia Rossiia" — entsiklopedicheskaia biblioteka) 1899; L. I. Svetlichnaia, *Preobrazovatel'nye plany i administrativnaia deiatel'nost' M. M. Speranskogo v Sibiri 1819—1822*, (unpubl. dissertation, Moskovskii Gosudarstvennyi Pedagogicheskii Institut imeni Lenina, 1953?); B. Syromiatnikov, "M. M. Speranskii kak gosudarstvennyi i politicheskii deiatel'," *Sovetskoe gosudarstvo i pravo*, (1940), No. 3, pp. 92—113; I. I. fon Zek, "Svetloi pamiati velikogo cheloveka," *Novyi zhurnal dlia vsekh* (March 1914), No. 3, pp. 37—38; F. M. Umanets, *Aleksandr i Speranskii*, St. Pbg. 1910; V. I. Vagin, *Istoricheskie svedeniia o deiatel'nosti grafa M. M. Speranskogo v Sibiri s 1819 po 1822 g*, 2 vols, St. Pbg. 1872; A. V. Vasil'ev, "Progressivnyi i podokhodnyi nalog i padenie Speranskogo," *Golos Minuvshego*, IV (July-Aug. 1916), Nos. 7—8, pp. 332—340; A. P. Velichko, "Neskol'ko slov po povodu knigi 'Zhizn' grafa Speranskogo'," *Sankt-Peterburzhskie Vedomosti*, No. 24 (31.I.1861) and No. 25 (1.II.1861);

M. A. Aldanov, "Speranskii i dekabristy," *Sovremennye Zapiski* 26, (Paris 1925) — the same: "Spéranskij et les Décembristes," *Le Monde Slave*, (Déc. 1926), pp. 432—448.

Studies relating to Speransky's work on codification are listed at the end of Chapter XI.

## INDEX OF PERSONAL NAMES

# INDEX OF GEOGRAPHICAL NAMES

# SELECTIVE SUBJECT INDEX

(Broad categories and discussions of theoretical problems mentioned throughout the book have not been listed)